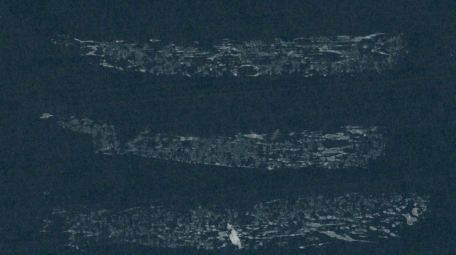

Manual of

PERSONNEL

POLICIES, PROCEDURES, and OPERATIONS

Second Edition

Manual of
PERSONNEL
POLICIES, PROCEDURES, and OPERATIONS

Second Edition

Joseph D. Levesque

PRENTICE HALL
Englewood Cliffs, New Jersey 07632

Prentice-Hall International, Inc., *London*
Prentice-Hall of Australia, Pty. Ltd., *Sydney*
Prentice-Hall Canada, Inc., *Toronto*
Prentice-Hall of India Private Ltd., *New Delhi*
Prentice-Hall of Japan, Inc., *Tokyo*
Prentice-Hall of Southeast Asia Pte. Ltd., *Singapore*
Editora Prentice-Hall do Brasil Ltda., *Rio de Janeiro*
Prentice-Hall Hispanoamericana, S.A., *Mexico*

© 1993 by
PRENTICE-HALL, INC.
Englewood Cliffs, N.J.

10 9 8 7 6 5 4 3 2 1

"This publication is designed to provide accurate and
authoritative information in regard to the subject
matter covered. It is sold with the understanding that
the publisher is not engaged in rendering legal, accounting, or other professional service. If legal advice
or other expert assistance is required, the services of
a competent professional person should be sought."
—*From the Declaration of Principles jointly adopted by
a Committee of the American Bar Association and a
Committee of Publishers and Associations.*

Library of Congress Cataloging-in-Publication Data

Levesque, Joseph D.
    Manual of personnel policies, procedures, and operations / Joseph D.
Levesque.—2nd ed.
        p.   cm.
    Includes index.
    ISBN 0-13-020231-2
    1. Personnel management—Handbooks, manuals, etc.   I. Title.
HF5549.L4627 1993
658.3—dc20   93-9305
                                                              CIP

ISBN 0-13-020231-2

PRENTICE HALL
Career and Personal Development
Englewood Cliffs, NJ 07632

Simon & Schuster, A Paramount Communications Company

PRINTED IN THE UNITED STATES OF AMERICA

This book is dedicated to my mother, Ellen R. Levesque,
an author in her own right,
without whose inspiration to pursue new challenges over the years
this book would not be.

ABOUT THE AUTHOR

Joseph D. Levesque (B.A., M.A., M.P.A.) is the founder and managing director of HR & Management Systems Consultants, a human resource and organizational management consulting firm located in Cameron Park, California. He is the author of such nationally sold books on human resource management as:

The Complete Hiring Manual: Policies, Procedures, and Practices
(Prentice-Hall, 1991)
People in Organizations: A Guide to Solving Critical Human Resource Problems
(American Chamber of Commerce Publishers, 1989)
A Model Guide for Development of Assessment Center Selection Processes
(Personnel Systems Books, 1991)
The Human Resource Problem-Solver's Handbook (McGraw-Hill, 1992)

He has authored numerous published articles on employment law, managing human resources, and organizational development.

Prior to entering private practice in 1983, Mr. Levesque worked as a personnel director and management practitioner for eleven years where he was responsible for the development and operations of comprehensive human resource departments, including recruitment, selection testing, policy and program design, compensation and benefits administration, information systems, performance programs, training, organizational analysis, forecasting, and labor relations. As a visiting lecturer, Mr. Levesque has also designed and taught courses and workshops at the Universities of California (Davis), Nevada (Reno), and Hawaii. As a frequently sought trainer and speaker, he has conducted numerous workshops for the California Chamber of Commerce, national business associations, in-company training programs, and the Society for Human Resource Management.

Mr. Levesque is an accredited Senior Professional in Human Resources (SPHR) by the Society for Human Resource Management, Certified Management Consultant (CMC) by the Institute of Management Consultants, 1990 President of the Sacramento Human Resource Management Association, and 1987–1992 member of the California State Human Resource Management Council.

The author offers a unique blend of experience in a wide range of human resource management operations based on his work as a personnel director, professional consultant, university instructor, employer trainer, and author. This blend of experience has resulted in books that are practical, thorough, and most of all, usable tools to guide employers toward more effective human resource management practices.

WHAT THIS MANUAL WILL DO FOR YOU

Manual of Personnel Policies, Procedures, and Operations is a comprehensive, concise, and ready-to-use *Manual* that provides virtually everything needed for a thorough personnel program. By using this *Manual* as a model, kit, and frequent decision-making reference, you can devise a personnel program uniquely tailored to your organization and avoid many common employment-related problems such as turnover, absenteeism, and low morale.

This *Manual* provides all the tools to set up a complete personnel program in easy-to-understand language by providing:

- A comprehensive and up-to-date model of customary, optional, and suggested personnel policies and practices keyed to advisory and reference notes;

- Sample forms and letters for setting up an easy-to-use records system, including legally required and recommended forms;

- Detailed explanations of significant employment laws and influential legal decisions;

- Step-by-step checklists for following personnel procedures;

- *At-will* employment policies and practices that will reduce the likelihood of a weak defense in wrongful discharge litigation;

- Equal employment opportunity recommendations, including sexual harassment policies and practices that aid employers in dealing with potential workplace discrimination;

- Progressive discipline and grievance procedures that demonstrate fair and reasonable treatment of employees and improve morale by using objective management practices;

- Classification and compensation policies and practices that develop the necessary relationship between work and pay; and

- Instructions showing how to prepare job descriptions . . . interview applicants . . . develop a pay plan . . . acquire group medical insurance . . . evaluate employee performance . . . and control workplace conduct.

Those using this *Manual* to develop their own personnel policies and practices handbook should bear in mind that policies are partly a reflection of current employment law and partly the result of the unique philosophy, structure, and culture of each organization. Where the opportunity presented itself to write the policies in this *Manual* in a particular style and tone, a moderately democratic approach was taken. This approach seems to be most acceptable to those subject to its provisions—and to outsiders looking for insights into the way the employer treats its employees.

To clarify the basis of particular policy provisions, over 120 advisory and reference notes are provided throughout Chapters 2 and 3. The notes give the background, reasoning, and guidance needed to understand fully the implications of policy provisions. The model policies include:

- No gender references;
- Concise equal employment opportunity policy;
- Reinforcement of *at-will* employment;
- A workable internal grievance system (dispute resolution);
- Use of the concept of progressive discipline with disclaimer and defining causes of discipline with latitude for the employer;
- Performance evaluation with meaning and relevance;
- Special employment condition policies; and
- Alternative policies to provide the reader with choices.

Manual of Personnel Policies, Procedures, and Operations also provides you with a number of ready-to-use sample forms, letters, and job descriptions. The forms provided in this *Manual* are the result of considerable research, and they are designed to minimize the number of forms while assuring the capture of crucial records. You need only reproduce these forms, letters, and job descriptions with your business's name or logo to give them a customized appearance that will attest to the professionalism of your personnel operations. You must not overlook the importance of sufficient and proper documentation in today's legalistic employment environment, and it is essential for employers, managers, and supervisors to practice what the organization has subscribed to in writing!

If you believe that employees are an organization's most important resource in determining its success or failure, this book will be a most beneficial investment. It can save you thousands upon thousands of dollars in turnover, loss of productivity, attorney and consultant fees, and lawsuits.

HOW TO USE THIS MANUAL

Manual of Personnel Policies, Procedures, and Operations is a reference that can be used entirely or in part as needed. It should be kept within arm's reach to guide the organization toward sound decision making in employment and personnel matters. This *Manual* takes a comprehensive *program* approach to establishing an entire personnel operation, and it does so by providing you with all the necessary ingredients, including background information and ready-to-use documents.

Related procedures and forms have been grouped together in four major parts:

Part I: Developing Personnel Policy Manuals

Part II: Setting Up a Complete Personnel Records System

Part III: Keeping Up with Employment Laws and Court Decisions

Part IV: How to Develop Key Support Systems

Those readers who want to use this book to set up an entire personnel program can develop some basic background information in the principles of key personnel issues by first reviewing Parts III and IV. Armed with this legal and managerial orientation, you are in a much better position to begin drafting a personnel policies and practices manual using the model provided, and the advisory notes will take on more meaning. You need merely select those policies from Chapters 2 and 3 that suit your organization's needs and then insert the proper business's name and those of appropriate officers, with their titles. When you are finished, you'll have a thorough manual for employees and a solid policy guide for supervisors. Those who wish merely to update their existing personnel policy manual will want to compare these model policies with their own, paying particular attention to advisory notes and determining the proper sequence of topics, format, clarity of content, consistency, tone, and integration with associated policy provisions.

Next, you will want to read the introduction to Part II, Setting Up a Complete Personnel Records System, order serviceable file folders, and begin thinking about the types of forms needed to process employment information in the most efficient manner. The ready-to-use forms and letters in Chapters 5 and 6 should be considered before money is wasted on stock forms bought through stationery suppliers, because the forms provided are based on years of experience and research into the kind of information that should be recorded, or must be documented. Each of the ready-to-use forms in this manual is preceded by an explanatory note to better inform the reader as to its use.

While working on the organization's personnel records system you will want to begin establishing other key functional components of the personnel program, consisting of job descriptions, a pay plan, insurance benefits, and the performance evaluation system. Job descriptions produce a more accurate system for classifying different aspects of work, clarify distinctions between jobs, and serve as the primary catalyst for decisions related to recruiting, testing, pay, training, performance evaluation, promotion, work flow, and organizational structure. For these reasons, you are given easy-to-understand "how-to" information about analyzing jobs to develop job descriptions and provided with sample formats and a number of ready-to-use job descriptions from various occupations.

Once job descriptions have been prepared, you will be in a better position to conduct a prevailing wage survey based on *comparable* positions among comparable employers within the same labor market region as fully explained, step by step, in Chapter 26. Examining external and internal pay considerations will result in a more competitive, fair, and systematic pay plan for the organization—thereby reducing or eliminating low morale because of pay inequities.

For many employees, pay is also integrally linked to performance; the "merit" of one's performance is a determinant of his or her pay raise. Hence, we refer to a pay-for-performance system as a *merit pay plan* wherein employees can advance by varying amounts within their designated pay range, based on their demonstrated level of performance during the preceding year. Once the organization's pay plan is established, you will next want to set up a performance evaluation system by reviewing Chapter 28, the ready-to-use evaluation form in Chapter 5 (or any other form suitable for meaningful measurement) and the personnel policies—to assure program consistency. You will also want to train those who will be conducting evaluations.

So there you have it—a complete personnel program consisting of all the essential ingredients:

- A personnel policies and practices manual
- Thorough and useful job descriptions
- A records system with all necessary forms and letters
- A competitive and fair pay plan
- A performance evaluation and control system
- All the background and operations advice needed to handle most situations, based on today's demands of a personnel program

Use it thoroughly and frequently, and prosper from the results!

CONTENTS

PREFACE TO SECOND EDITION

Indeed, much has changed in the field of human resource management since the original publication of this book in 1986. With over 25,000 copies in use, the time has come to revise, update, and otherwise ensure that this book remains a vital and current source of information for those seeking to operate meaningful personnel programs. Human resource management has clearly become one of the most crucial functions of business today, whether the business is small or large, and affecting virtually any type of enterprise. Simply stated, without the right people (our employees) performing work as needed, business fails. So it follows that every successful employer must place considerable emphasis on developing thorough and efficient human resource programs that achieve three goals: (1) to attract and retain quality employees, (2) to gain maximum benefit of payroll expenditures, and (3) to avert costly and damaging legal violations, of which there are many.

Since the original publication of this book, there have emerged several federal laws and significant court decisions affecting both personnel policies and practices. Likewise, there have been many more personnel- and employment-related laws enacted, and court cases decided, in every state. Naturally, it is beyond the scope of this book to attempt any meaningful presentation of how each state deals with various labor law matters, other than to illustrate the trends in legal thinking on some issues. Therefore, the more practical "federalized" orientation has been taken, with notes to the user, on which of the policies in Part I should conform with state laws. You should consult a qualified labor attorney for advice concerning state laws.

The most prominent laws affecting personnel policies and practices since 1986, and included in this revised edition, are:

- Consolidated Omnibus Budget Reconciliation Act (COBRA) of 1985 with updated compliance standards and instructions;
- Immigration Reform and Control Act (IRCA) of 1986, including common violations and the 1990 revised I-9 Form and Employer's Instruction Booklet;
- Americans with Disabilities Act (ADA) of 1990, including definitions, compliance standards, suggested practices to avoid violations.

- Civil Rights Act of 1991, which applies new standards and definitions to the earlier Civil Rights Act of 1964, Title VII.

In addition to these changes, other features have been added to provide you with new tools to carry out a more complete personnel program. Some of these additions include:

- A new human resources information systems (HRIS) software guide;
- A new list of drug testing laboratories certified by the National Institute on Drug Abuse;
- A checklist on nondiscriminatory personnel practices;
- A new illustration of discriminatory interview questions;
- At-will employment policy samples;
- New policies on such topics as employment references, affirmative action, employment rehires, and personnel records access and disclosure;
- Basic and advanced interviewing question guidelines and techniques; and
- A revised Employment Application form and the addition of other new forms.

It is believed, and hoped, that these additions, revisions, and other changes made in this edition will continue to provide you with everything you'll need to operate an effective human resources management program.

Joseph D. Levesque

Manual of

PERSONNEL

POLICIES, PROCEDURES, and OPERATIONS

Second Edition

Part One

DEVELOPING PERSONNEL POLICY MANUALS

Chapter 1

WHY PERSONNEL POLICY MANUALS AND HANDBOOKS ARE IMPORTANT TO SOUND BUSINESS OPERATIONS

One of the first things most owners and managers of smaller businesses learn about doing business is that many new employment laws are conceived by both federal and state legislatures, courts, or compliance agencies. These laws and regulations often represent stringent compliance requirements for nearly all employers throughout the United States. For this reason, there have been differing reactions between overzealous labor attorneys—some of whom take an overreactive approach in advising their employer clients—and business owners and practitioners who are most mindful of their need to operate a business in a profitable manner and make corresponding decisions about those they employ. Some attorneys have even induced many employers to refrain from preparing written personnel policies and practices handbooks or manuals by suggesting there are too many "trip wires" in the proverbial mine field of employment laws for employers. They tend to use scare tactics, and, when working with personnel policies, they may recommend the use of legal jargon or unending disclaimers to the extent that neither the employer nor their employees understand what the policies mean. Conversely, the overcautious labor attorney may jeopardize an employer's business operations by suggesting that the employer "bend" too far in the framing or application of personnel policies.

What is paramount for smaller companies is that their business operates as efficiently and economically as possible while still complying with the vast array of labor laws that frame employment practices. To do so, it is imperative for businesses of all sizes to tackle some basic "administrative" measures aimed at supporting the businesses' goals and helping to ensure their success and profitability. Small businesses in particular (because they have to compete with larger businesses and other competing small-business operators) should acquire such administrative support as accounting, marketing, employment, and business planning services. As the business grows, some and perhaps all of these administrative services can be performed by internal, full-time employees. Until then, the smaller business may want to handle these tasks by using external consultants, attorneys, and accountants as the most economical way of acquiring business support services. *It is a major error of smaller businesses to avoid attending to administrative support services until the business reaches a certain growth level!* Such thinking has caused numerous small businesses to collapse merely because they underestimated the effect of an erroneous decision, and in most states a wrong personnel decision can cost even small employers upwards of $20,000.

HOW A WELL-WRITTEN PERSONNEL POLICY AND PRACTICE MANUAL CAN HELP YOU ELIMINATE COSTLY DECISION ERRORS

Quite simply, a personnel policy manual or handbook is an operational guide for employers, including their managerial and supervisory staff. For employees, the handbook serves as an important communications device in terms of gaining a better understanding of how the business works, what the employee can expect under varying circumstances, and a host of other vital interest information to employees concerning employment programs. For the employer, the handbook accomplishes two very important objectives: it establishes *consistency* of operational decisions relative to employment and personnel matters, and it enhances the *integrity* and *credibility* of the business because everyone knows the "rules of the game" so to speak. When these elements exist in a personnel handbook, along with legally sound practices, the likelihood of demoralizing and litigious misunderstandings between employees and their employer are dramatically reduced and often eliminated entirely.

Assisting Supervisors and Improving Employee Productivity

Supervisors are often "promoted from within" and given oversight responsibility for a small group of subordinate employees. What usually distinguishes supervisors from "line" employees is that supervisors are legally considered official agents of the business and they have decision-making authority over those employees assigned to them. Yet most supervisors in American businesses are typically not trained well in the requisite management skills and knowledge that should accompany these types of responsibilities, so frequent errors in their actions and decisions occur. To overcome this problem *at the level where most employment decision errors occur*, the use of a thoroughly written personnel handbook provides exactly the type of guidance supervisors need when a vast array of employment conditions arise (consider how some of your supervisors would handle such issues as employment interviews, tardiness, overtime, sick leaves, abused privileges, discipline, problem employees, performance appraisals, and terminations).

When supervisors are provided with decision-making "guide books," such as a personnel manual or handbook and standard operating procedures (SOPs), and given at least some training to better acquaint them with the reasons and skills necessary to carry out their responsibilities, errors are reduced significantly. Reduced supervisory errors mean that employees gain higher confidence, understand the boundaries of their work performance, and the resultant effect is higher and more consistent productivity within the work unit. This is not conjecture, it's a proven fact. Consider the cost and disruptive effect of employee absenteeism and turnover due to an unstructured work environment or low morale—usually related to the employee-supervisor relationship.

Saving Management Time and Costly Lawsuits

Too often, owners and managers of a small business must get directly involved in adverse employment matters and, regrettably, they learn about problems after the "die has been cast." Owners and managers of small business should not be expected to be experts on employment and personnel matters, yet they represent the last resort of internal decision making on these concerns—or the only resort if they make the error of not delegating such decisions to supervisors. Smaller businesses must focus the time and attention of its owners and managers on the organization itself—planning and preparing their products or services for delivery to customers, acquisition of new business, negotiating leases and contracts, and the like. If employment and personnel matters are not well defined and understood by employees and supervisors alike, there is the *high* probability that someone will make an illegal decision, or commit an illegal act, under either federal or state law, resulting sooner or later in an employee taking their concern to a compliance agency or an attorney.

Whether complaints of illegal employment practices are filed by employees with a federal or state compliance agency or an attorney, you can be certain that the owner or managers of a small business *must* become directly involved in defending the action. Doing so takes a considerable amount of time, energy, and *unnecessary* expense away from the primary business of the employer. To reduce, or perhaps eliminate, the prospect of this major liability, it is clearly worthy of the less imposing time and effort to prepare a well-conceived personnel handbook, provide your supervisors with adequate training on the application of policies, give new employees a thorough orientation on your policies, and ensure that all employees receive a (verified) copy of the handbook including subsequent revisions.

HOW TO DEVELOP A PERSONNEL MANUAL WHEN YOUR BUSINESS IS UNIONIZED

In a unionized employment setting, whether only a portion or all of your employees, excluding management, are represented by one or more unions, the development and administration of personnel policies can become a bit more complex. First, unions tend to want more liberal pay, benefits, and policies provisions in their labor contracts than the employer is likely to implement without this type of third-party intervention. Consequently, unionized employers end up with companywide personnel policies and, sometimes duplicative or conflicting, labor contract provisions. As a rule-of-thumb, labor contract language is generally considered more controlling than a company's personnel policies because, from a legal view, labor contracts are conditions and agreements arrived at by bilateral agreements between the employer and the organization representing employee interests, as opposed to unilaterally imposed terms and conditions of employment prescribed by the employer in the personnel handbook.

Second, there is nothing preventing an employer from preparing or revising, then implementing, company personnel policies. However, unionized employers are generally required to negotiate such policies with any recognized labor unions or employee associations prior to implementation. For this reason, employers may wish to add an employers' rights policy in either the personnel handbook or as a negotiated labor contract provision.

Finally, when you have both labor contracts and personnel policies, it is highly advisable for supervisors and managers to consult both documents before rendering employment decisions or taking personnel actions with unionized employees to ensure proper handling the first time. Remember, violations of labor contracts are often decided through binding arbitration or the courts, and violations by an employer of their own personnel policies can be subject to scrutiny by the courts. The best prevention of an employer's wrongdoing is to (1) ensure that all facts are known about any given employee situation, (2) have practical policies in place, (3) train supervisors to prepare and check applicable documents so that their actions are proper, and (4) consult with qualified advisors on all adverse actions against an employee.

CHECKLIST: DEVELOPING AND IMPLEMENTING A PERSONNEL POLICY MANUAL

Development of Policy Manual

Research Legal Issues: Federal and State Laws

- [ ] Workers' compensation
- [ ] Unemployment insurance
- [ ] Mandatory health care plans and employer contributions
- [ ] Disability insurance
- [ ] Privacy rights (personnel files, documents, intrusive testing, etc.)
- [ ] Wage and hour laws (definitions of exempt employees, overtime, record keeping, payroll payments, etc.)
- [ ] Fair employment practices laws
- [ ] Health, safety, and smoking laws/ordinances

Determine Existing Practices or Desired Changes in Practices Concerning

- ☐ Vacations, holidays, sick leave, family leave, and jury duty leave
- ☐ Overtime, pay for work in a higher class, compensatory time off
- ☐ Employer's contribution to employee insurance benefits
- ☐ Employer's establishment/contribution toward employee retirement program
- ☐ Method and practices of dealing with performance appraisals/incentive compensation
- ☐ Causes for discipline and progressive discipline procedure
- ☐ Determine legality/compliance of existing policies/practices with current law

Method of Preparing Written Draft/Revision of Personnel Policy Manual

- ☐ Assignment to a singular experienced staff member
- ☐ Organized committee of internal (cross section) employees—for review and advice of existing, draft, and final document
- ☐ Use human resource department section heads
- ☐ Engage external consultant with expertise in policy manual development

Review of First and Subsequent Drafts of New/Revised Personnel Policy Manual

- ☐ Qualified labor attorney and/or expert consultant (initiate revisions for second draft)
- ☐ Review by department heads and unit supervisors
- ☐ Review by executive managers
- ☐ Review by cross section of employees and/or union stewards
- ☐ Finalize draft copy (all changes, final format, print camera-ready copy, etc.)

Implementation of Policy Manual

Training and Distribution

- ☐ Prepare a full-day training program for executives, department heads, and supervisors on basics of personnel law and interpretation of new/revised personnel policy manual
- ☐ Prepare a half-day orientation program for all employees on new/revised personnel policy manual
- ☐ Schedule both training programs to coincide with receipt of the manual from the printer
- ☐ Develop distribution list and number each copy to be provided to individual employees
- ☐ Provide manual to managers and supervisors one week prior to training and at the orientation session for employees
- ☐ Amend new employee orientation form to include giving them a copy of personnel policy manual

☐ Amend exit interview/separation form to include recovery of personnel policy manual

☐ Provide copy to labor counsel and other applicable external advisors

Maintenance of Policy Manual

☐ Keep a log of changes that need to be made based on operational experience

☐ Review manual every six months with department heads and supervisors

☐ Consult with labor counsel and keep abreast of changing legal issues (make notes of needed changes in log)

☐ Make necessary revisions annually and distribute to all copy holders with explanatory memo indicating reasons for changes and what pages to replace

☐ Add and delete policies as they become apparent in need

Chapter 2

CUSTOMARY AND LEGALLY ORIENTED PERSONNEL POLICIES AND PRACTICES WITH ADVISORY FOOTNOTES

This chapter consists of major policy and practice categories dealing with the most prevalent, standard policy issues found among most employers. Throughout, the model alternative policies are provided to show different approaches to creating a policy. Examine these alternatives to see which policy fits your organization's personnel requirements. Advisory and reference notes found in each policy section elucidate specific points of the policies.

Writing personnel policies and procedures for any business concern is no small task. One must not only understand the functions, practices, and laws relating to personnel operations, but also have the ability to be analytical about a wide range of conditions that can influence one another when just one decision is rendered in a particular case. In the personnel field, this is often referred to as the "domino effect"—make a wrong decision with one employee and, sooner or later, several others will be adversely affected.

It would be an understatement to say that personnel operations, and associated organizational responsibilities, have undergone considerable change from the days when its functions were entirely service oriented and merely dealt with receiving applications, passing out benefit booklets, keeping records, and arranging the annual picnic.

With the onslaught of legal requirements during the last three decades, personnel has had to include *control* measures in its operations to protect the interests of the organization (employees and those who manage), while maintaining some semblance of *service* to the separate departments and the organization as a whole. Without organizationwide understanding and support of the two, often opposing, service/control forces within personnel, they may mix about as well as oil and water. These control measures have necessitated a somewhat legalistic tone and bureaucratic process orientation to policy and procedure manuals, as well as to the day-to-day relations between employees and their supervisors. In an attempt to compensate for the harshness and formality of control-oriented language, a more casual or explanatory tone has been used to express policy *intent*.

The policies in this chapter and the one following are generic rather than customized, and conform to federal laws. It is beyond the scope of this manual to specify the vast array of differences and nuances of separate state labor laws. Prospective differences between federal and state laws have been cited in the reference notes, and employers would be well advised to have a competent labor attorney or consultant review their policies to ensure compliance with state laws. By assembling the initial draft of a personnel policies and procedures manual, then merely having it reviewed for legal compliance with state laws, the business employer can save a substantial sum of money.

Clearly, the integrity of personnel policies—and of those in the organization that must use them to guide critical employee decisions—relies heavily upon the wisdom for the existence of such policies, and the consistency with which they are practiced. An organization's consciousness of this goal should be a persistent one.

The major categories in this chapter, and those you should consider as the basis of a practical, legal, and well-rounded employee manual, are:

- A Welcome to New Employees;
- General Administration of the Personnel System;
- Selection, Orientation, and Initial Employment;
- Position Classification and Allocation;
- Hours, Meals, and Rest Periods;
- Compensation and Payroll Practices;
- Benefits, Holidays, and Leaves;
- Performance Evaluation and Promotion;
- Training, Safety, and Health;
- Employment Conduct, Discipline, Dispute Resolution, and Suggestions; and
- Employment Separation.

SAMPLE OUTLINES OF TOPICS FOR EMPLOYEE HANDBOOKS

Here are four sample outlines of topics to consider if you are contemplating the preparation of an employee handbook apart from the more detailed policies and procedure manual, typically given only to supervisors and managers. If a separate employee handbook is developed, topics selected should be of interest to employees, or necessary for the organization to communicate to every employee. Handbooks should be written in a positive, easily understood style rather than the more complex and regulatory style of policy manuals.

Samples A and B are brief topic formats (usually fewer than forty pages) while samples C and D are expanded formats typical of handbooks exceeding forty pages, and used as a combination employee handbook and policy manual. Topics listed are illustrative only.

Sample A	**Sample B**
Introduction	Introduction
Employment	Affirmative Action Program
Sample Ad Formats	Group Medical, Dental, and Vision
Definition of an Employee	Benefit Plans
Probationary—Performance Review	Retirement Plans
New Employee Orientation	Long-Term Disability Insurance
Training	State Disability Insurance
Attendance—Absenteeism	State Unemployment Insurance
Hours and Days of Work	Workers' Compensation
Seniority	Salary Administration
Wage and Salary Administration	Sick Pay
Performance Evaluation	Vacation Pay
Benefits—Vacation	Leaves of Absence
Benefits—Holidays	Employee Time Records
Benefits—Jury Duty	Probation—New Employees
Benefits—Leave of Absence	—Promotional Employees
Benefits—Group Health Insurance	—Rehired Employees
Benefits—Education Reimbursement	Job Postings
Benefits—Shop Purchases	Transfers
Benefits—Company Equipment	Employee Education Policy
Benefits—Retirement Plan	Dress Policy
Benefits—Refrigerator	Union Policy
Benefits—Death of an Employee	
Company Rules	
Safety	
OSHA Inspection	
Maintenance and Housekeeping	
Suggestions and Complaints	
Termination	

Sample C

I. *Introduction*

    A. Introduction
    B. The Growth of (business name)
    C. Our Product: SERVICE
    D. Employee Relations
    E. Equal Employment Opportunity Commitment

II. *Orientation*

    A. Orientation
    B. Duties of Employee

C. Identification Cards
D. Fingerprinting
E. Driver's License

III. The Employment Relationship

A. The Employment Relationship
B. Categories of Employment
    1. New-Hire or New Employment Period
    2. Regular Full-Time Employee
    3. Regular Part-Time Employee
    4. Part-Time Employee
    5. Temporary Employee
    6. Rehired Employee
    7. Exempt and Nonexempt Employees
C. Employee Change of Status
D. Transfers
E. Promotions

IV. You and the Public

A. Dress and Grooming Standards
B. Smoking, Eating, Chewing Gum
C. Telephone Etiquette

V. Employer Standards and Guidelines

A. Employer Proprietary Interests
B. Conflicts of Interest
C. Outside Interests
D. Nondiscrimination Policy
E. Alcohol and Drugs
F. Distribution of Literature
G. Solicitation for Organizations/Selling Products
H. Long-Distance Telephone Calls
I. Personal Telephone Calls
J. Disciplinary Action
K. Communicating with Management
L. Administrative Reviews

VI. Work Hours, Attendance, Pay, and Performance Reviews

A. Public Hours
B. Employee Wages and Hours
C. Attendance
D. Tardiness
E. Absences
F. Meal and Rest Periods
G. Overtime Meals
H. Payroll Time Records

Sample D

I. *Introductory and General Information Policies*

  A. Introductory Statements
  B. Equal Employment Opportunity Commitments
  C. Employee Relations Policies

II. *Employment Classifications*

  A. Probationary Periods
  B. General Employment Categories
  C. Temporary Employees
  D. Commissioned Employees
  E. Rehired Employees

III. *Orientation, Transfer, and Promotion Policies*

  A. Orientation Policies
  B. Physical Examinations
  C. New-Hire Policies
  D. Transfer and Promotion Policies

IV. *Payroll, Scheduling, and Overtime Practices*

  A. Hours of Operation and Work Schedules
  B. Meal and Rest Periods
  C. Time Card Procedures
  D. Overtime Policies
  E. Exchanging Shifts
  F. Callback Pay
  G. Wage Reviews and Adjustments
  H. Uniforms
  I. Paydays
  J. Advances
  K. Wage Garnishment Policy
  L. Payroll Deductions

V. *Benefits*

  A. Introductory Statement
  B. Discretionary Benefits
    1. Sick Leave Benefits
    2. Vacation Benefits
    3. Holiday Benefits
    4. Paid Time Off (PTO) Benefits
    5. Severance Pay
    6. Miscellaneous
  C. Legislated Benefits
    1. Workers' Compensation Benefits
    2. State Disability Insurance
    3. Unemployment Insurance
    4. Social Security

VI. *Leaves of Absence Policies*

A. Medical Leaves
B. Other Leaves
   1. Bereavement Leaves
   2. Jury Duty
   3. Witness Duty
   4. Voting Time

VII. *Performance, Discipline, and Grievances*

A. Standards of Performance and Conduct
B. Work Rules
   1. Sexual Harassment Policy
   2. Dress and Grooming Standards
   3. No-Solicitation Rule
   4. Employment of Relatives
   5. Telephone Use
   6. Safety Rules
   7. Other Rules
C. Tardiness and Absenteeism
D. Performance Appraisals and Progressive Discipline
E. Exit Interviews and Final Pay
   1. Resignations
   2. Exit Interviews
   3. Pay in Lieu of Notice
   4. Final Pay
F. Grievance Procedures

VIII. *Layoff Policies*

FIFTEEN WAYS TO COMMUNICATE YOUR POLICIES AND PRACTICES[1]

In addition to distributing manuals or handbooks to your employees, it is vital to communicate with them in other ways.

If policies and procedures are not communicated frequently, in a manner that your current work force will accept, they will not be followed or used properly. In addition, any communication program must stay current with the times and with changing business conditions.

Following are fifteen ways to communicate with employees:

1. Conduct one-on-one communication between supervisor and employee at least once a month, quarterly, and at the yearly performance review.

---

[1]   Adapted from Mary F. Cook, *Human Resource Director's Handbook*, (Englewood Cliffs, N.J.: Prentice Hall, 1984).

2. Publish employee newsletters, articles, and stories about employees who are actively supporting the company and its business plans.

3. Use the media. Show films and slides on topics of current interest. Use video to train employees and for special programs.

4. Have programs during the lunch period, where speakers come in to speak on a variety of subjects pertinent to your business and industry. The company may want to donate thirty minutes' extra if the program helps employees on their jobs.

5. Some organizations have started monthly discussion group programs, aimed at managers and professionals. This is used as a management development tool. A particular book is chosen, all participants read the book, and a vice president leads a discussion group on the merits of the principles set out in the book.

6. Sometimes, when companies are going through a particularly difficult time, a question box or telephone hotline will encourage dialogue. The employee does not have to give a name. Guarantee a response to all reasonable questions within a few days. You can reply through a special newsletter to all employees. If you do have a question box or hotline, it is important to reply in timely fashion, and you and your top management must agree to be open and honest if these avenues are to work well.

7. Create a communications task force to identify communication problems and suggest solutions. The task force should include people from a variety of functions and all levels in the company. People feel they have more ownership in programs they or their peers help create.

8. To communicate policies and procedures in your own department, route the policy book throughout the department and ask each employee to read it.

9. Put an extra copy of the policy manual in your library or in the personnel office, where employees can refer to it.

10. Implement an orientation program for families so they understand the company, its products, its policies, and the office or plant facilities.

11. Publish an annual report to employees and their families, updating them not only on employee benefit statements, but also on the company's business plans and accomplishments.

12. Use athletic activities and health programs as avenues for employee communication.

13. Start an employee speakers' bureau. Give employees training in public speaking, and select topics that would be of benefit to the company as well as employee's topics.

14. If you have extra space that can be used occasionally, have an employee crafts fair where employees can sell their crafts.

15. Set up closed-circuit TV/VHF programs to inform employees about important management meetings, and pass on specific information for employees to read.

A WELCOME TO OUR NEW EMPLOYEES

It is with pleasure that I welcome you to the staff of *(Company)*. Your appointment to your new position with the *(Company)* is one of which you can be proud. The *(Company's)* primary commodity is service to our *(customers, clients, patients, etc.)*, and they come first—which is our way of ensuring that we maintain their trust and continued desire to do business with us.

To our *(customers, clients, patients)* and others in the community with whom you will have contact as an employee, YOU are the *(Company)*. The extent to which the *(Company)* is considered friendly, knowledgeable, efficient, reliable, and trustworthy will be measured by how others see these qualities in you. We hope that you will use your talents in a way that stimulates *(customer, client, patient)* relations, and thereby contributes to the growth of our business and further employment opportunities. If, during the course of your employment, you find ways to improve the company's operations or services, or to save the company unnecessary costs, I and other company officers welcome your written ideas. If you need help in the presentation of your ideas, don't hesitate to seek the advice or assistance of your supervisor.

The personnel *(manual, handbook)* that follows has been prepared to guide you and other employees in better understanding our policies, procedures, and practices concerning employment matters. You should familiarize yourself with its contents at your earliest opportunity and keep it handy as a periodic reference source. As changes are made to this *(manual, handbook)*, we'll endeavor to see that you get replacement pages so that your copy can be kept current.

As you start employment with the *(Company)*, you will find that your associates are ready to assist you, and you will receive on-the-job guidance to acquaint you with your new duties and responsibilities. Therefore, your success is largely up to you. Again, welcome to our team of hard-working and talented staff, and please accept my wishes for success in your new position. I look forward to meeting you in the near future.

(Name, Title, and Signature)

GENERAL ADMINISTRATION OF THE PERSONNEL SYSTEM

Purpose and Principles of the Personnel Policies and Procedures Manual

It is the purpose of this manual to establish and maintain a uniform system for managing personnel matters; to comply with applicable employment laws; and to provide for the standards, terms, and conditions of employment with *(Company)* in a clear and comprehensive fashion to maximize the efficiency and orderliness of operations. It is further intended, by adoption and periodic amendment of these policies and procedures, that they serve as a guide for employees of the *(Company)* in their routine work activities and relationships to the extent that the objectives of both *(Company)* and individual employees can be achieved. *(Company)* believes that the success of a business is largely due to the quality of its employees, the development of each employee's full potential, and the *(Company's)* ability to provide timely and satisfying rewards. The *(Company)* also recognizes that employees differ in their skills, goals, perceptions, and values and that it is basic to human nature that conditions may arise that are either insufficiently addressed in these policies and procedures, or that result in conflicts. In such cases, the *(Company)* will endeavor to make personnel decisions that are fair and equitable, while at all times assuring that the best interests of *(Company)* are served. *(Company)* hereby asserts that it has the right to employ the best qualified persons available; that the continuation of employment is based on the need for work to be performed, availability of revenues, faithful and effective performance, proper personal conduct, and continuing fitness of employees; and that all employees are terminable at will unless otherwise specified in writing as a prescribed employment term. Conversely, employees deserve to be fully informed of their duties and responsibilities; to be provided with adequate administrative and supervisory direction; to be informed of their performance levels; to be compensated based on the value of their contributions; to be considered for promotional opportunities; and to be treated with dignity and respect at all times.

Therefore, the policies and procedures set forth in this manual prescribe the terms, conditions, and standards of personnel operations for *(Company)*, the content of which is neither contractually binding upon the *(Company)* nor restrictive in terms of amendment or interpretation by the *(Company)*. Employees are expected to acquaint themselves fully with the content of this manual to establish an employment relationship based on a complete understanding of *(Company)* personnel requirements, expectations, and methods of conducting personnel matters. Since it is the policy of the *(Company)* to encourage employee participation in all matters that affect their work, employees are encouraged to offer suggestions for improvement to these policies, employment practices, or working conditions.

Administration of Personnel System

These personnel policies and procedures shall be interpreted, applied, and enforced by supervisory and managerial employees of *(Company)*. *(Company)* believes that the most rewarding employment relationship results from the open, fair, and consistent interaction directly between staff and those who supervise or manage operations. While no business is free from day-to-day problems, or unusual employment situations not covered by existing policy, it is the desire of the *(Company)* to foster effective policy dealings at all levels. To ensure fairness and consistency in these personnel matters, the *(Company)* has designated the *(Human Resources Manager)* to be responsible for centralized personnel operations.[2]

Ultimate authority for interpretation, application, and enforcement rests with the *(Human Resources Manager)* or designee, who will be responsible for impartially resolving matters where questions or issues arise. The *(Human Resources Manager)* or designee will additionally be responsible for such personnel matters as:

1. Initiation of amendments and revisions to these policies and procedures at times determined by the *(Company)* to be necessary or warranted;

2. Initiation or revisions to job descriptions, wage and salary schedules, benefit plans and programs, and performance evaluation systems;

3. Recruitment, selection evaluation, equal employment opportunity, and personnel records;

4. Enforcement of all applicable state and federal employment laws and their resultant effect upon personnel policies, procedures, and practices; and

5. Performance of other duties that may be necessary to carry out the practices and provisions of a contemporary personnel system.

Application, Amendment, and Deviation of Personnel Policies

Application of these policies and procedures is effective for all employees of the *(Company)* except _____ whose employment conditions shall be determined by the *(President)*. Persons hired under emergency or contract or for periods of fewer than _____ months shall likewise be excluded from the provisions of these policies and procedures unless otherwise stated.[3]

Amendments to these personnel policies, procedures, and practices are subject to change at the *(Company's)* discretion to maintain their legal compliance, operational effectiveness, and the general scope of desired workplace conditions. Upon amendment of any

---

[2]   The designation of a particular position title of an individual in the organization who will act as the principal personnel decision maker is imperative to establish and maintain continuity of decisions, and greater objectivity over matters that may arise as a result of line supervisor's interpretation of varying conditions. This "differential treatment" by virtue of differing supervisory management styles, perception of situations, and interpretation of personnel policy is undoubtedly one of the most frequently cited complaints of employees in their workplace treatment as well as the cause of discrimination law suits.

[3]   Some companies may want to exclude certain persons in the organization such as members of the board of directors, the president/chief executive officer, owner(s), and perhaps even senior level managers, whose employment conditions may be either covered by individual contracts or completely altered in an instant! Including such positions by making "all employees" subject to these rules and procedures can turn out to be too restrictive on operational or particular personnel decisions.

part of this manual, the company will endeavor to use normal communication channels to apprise employees, in a timely fashion, of such changes and their effect, if any.

Each employee covered or affected by this manual is responsible for knowledge of and compliance with all provisions contained herein. Violations of these policies and procedures will be corrected on a case-by-case basis depending on individual merit and circumstance. Only as a last resort, or under repeated or serious infractions, will the *(Company)* initiate disciplinary measures as a means of correcting violations, as the *(Company)* is fully committed to the success of every employee and the belief that all people must be willing to assume responsibility for their own actions.

Unit Operating Rules

Each separate and identifiable department, division, or work unit of the *(Company)* may develop, implement, and revise as necessary such policies, procedures, and rules pertaining to unique operational requirements and their effect upon unit employees as are needed for efficient and effective performance of the unit. Such policies, procedures, and rules should not conflict with these policies and procedures, or amendments thereto, and must therefore be approved by the *(Human Resources Manager)* prior to implementation. Where conflicts may arise, the policies and procedures contained in this manual will prevail.

Reports and Records

The *(Human Resources Manager)* or designee will be responsible for providing the forms and maintaining records required to sustain a complete personnel system for the *(Company)* and will furnish or prepare such forms and records as are appropriate.

Roster Card   A roster card or form for each regular and active employee will be maintained bearing the name, title of position(s) held, the assigned work unit(s), assigned salary and salary changes, employment status changes, and such other information as may be deemed pertinent.

Change of Status Report   Every new hire, transfer, promotion, demotion, change in significant duties or salary rate, employment separation, or any other temporary or other change in employment status must be reported to, and in a manner prescribed by, the *(Human Resources Manager)*. Such notification should be made no later than _____ working days before the end of the pay period affected by the change; otherwise, the change may not be made until the next pay period.

Review of Personnel File   Employees wishing to obtain specific information, or for any other good reason, may, upon reasonable advance notice, inspect their own personnel files at any reasonable time during normal office hours. However, such records may not be reproduced, removed, or altered without the consent of *(Human Resources Manager)*. [4]

---

[4]   It is advisable for every employer to designate a particular position title as the person in charge of personnel records for legal custodial purposes. With increasing frequency, such records

All personnel records are considered confidential and the property of the *[Company]*. Personnel records and files will therefore be available or disclosed only to those persons who are authorized by the *[Company]* to have access to them on a need-to-know basis, or such other persons authorized by the *[Company]* under legal rights to review or obtain applicable parts of such records.

Records Access and Disclosure[5]

Personnel files are kept on all employees. They contain the employees' employment application, salary and employment histories, performance appraisals, emergency contact data, signed acknowledgment forms, orientation form, and other documents as required by law or regarded as necessary by the *[Company]* *(if permitted by state law)*, secondary files are kept on employees that contain medical history, employment reference, and investigative information, the contents of which are not subject to access or review by the employee. However, employees wishing to review their primary personnel file may do so during normal business hours, at convenient times, and with advance notice to the *[Human Resources Manager]*. Such records may not be reproduced, removed, or altered without the consent of the *[Human Resources Manager]*.

To ensure employees' rights to privacy, personnel files are considered confidential. The *[Company]* limits information disclosed to third parties to only lawful access and disclosure, unless an employee signs a release authorizing the *[Company]* to provide file information. Reference information on employees, including letters of employment reference, will be provided when appropriate only by the *[Human Resources Manager]*.

It is each employee's responsibility to keep information, such as address, marital status, birth of children, emergency notification and other important personal information current in their file by notifying the *[Human Resources Office]* promptly when these events occur. Many status changes affect benefit and insurance plans, so it is essential that employees let the *[Company]* know when these changes occur.

---

4 *continued*   and documents as personnel files, application forms, preemployment tests, job descriptions, performance evaluations, and disciplinary notices are being scrutinized very closely by attorneys, judges, and administrative compliance agencies. It is also recommended that employers know what should and should not be included in personnel files and how long documents should be retained. This information is included in Part Two. As a recent example of this legal trend, courts seem to be suggesting that it is not proper for employers to retain a minor disciplinary notice in an employee's file indefinitely, it could serve to jeopardize a future promotion or job recommendation. Employers have been encouraged to establish recall and review dates upon entering disciplinary notices into an employee's file.

To preserve the integrity of personnel files, employers are encouraged to restrict internal access to a "need-to-know" basis to avoid the situation experienced by one employer, in which a management employee—for his personal use only—acquired marital, medical, and home phone information about a female employee not within his supervisory jurisdiction, but whom he was interested in wooing. She won a sizable settlement in a Privacy Act violation suit!

5   From Joseph D. Levesque, *The Complete Hiring Manual* (Englewood Cliffs, N.J.: Prentice Hall, 1991), pp. 62–63.

Alternative Policy: Personnel File Access and Disclosure

General Policy   The *(Company)* keeps certain records on each employee in a personnel file kept in the Human Resources Department.

The Personnel File   The *(Company's)* policy is to keep only the most essential documents such as applications, payroll information, performance reviews, and disciplinary records in the personnel file. The *(Human Resources Department)* has ultimate discretion to determine what documents should go in each employee's personnel file.

Employee Inspection of File   An employee may inspect his or her personnel file and copy documents in it. To do so, the employee must make an appointment with the *(Director of Human Resources)* or designee to inspect the file at a time that is both convenient for the *(Human Resources Department)* and outside of the employee's normal working hours.

Information Employees Are to Provide Human Resources   Employees are expected to notify *(Human Resources)* of any changes in name, address, phone number, marital status, names or number of dependents, and persons to be notified in case of an emergency.

Requests for Information About Employees   All requests for information about current or former employees are to be forwarded to the *(Director of Human Resources)*. No information will be released in response to oral requests. The *(Director of Human Resources)* will normally release only the dates of employment, last position held, and final salary.

Equal Employment Opportunity

It is the *(Company's)* policy to employ, retain, promote, terminate, and otherwise treat any and all employees and job applicants on the basis of merit, qualifications, and competence. This policy shall be applied without regard to any individual's sex, race, religion, national origin, pregnancy, age, marital status, or physical handicap.[6]

In establishing this policy, the *(Company)* recognizes the need to initiate and maintain affirmative personnel measures to ensure the achievement of equal employment opportunities in all aspects of our workplace settings, conditions, and decisions. It shall be the responsibility of all employees to abide by and carry out the letter, spirit, and intent of the *(Company's)* equal employment commitment. It is prohibited for any employee of the *(Company)* to refuse to hire, train, promote, or provide equitable

---

[6]   Although briefly stated, this basic policy statement covers most major and significant state and federal antidiscrimination laws as well as the intent of prevailing court decisions across the country. In adopting such a policy statement, employers express their intent to abide by nondiscriminatory personnel practices and alert all employees to the fact that any employment-related decision made on behalf of the organization will not be made solely on the basis of these protected characteristics. With the adoption of a policy statement of this type, employers are in a better position to take corrective or even disciplinary action against any employees found to exhibit discriminatory intent in their decisions.

employment conditions to any employee or applicant, or to discipline or dismiss an employee solely on the basis of such person's race, national origin, age (over 40 years), sex, marital status, religious beliefs, or physical handicap; except where the doctrine of business necessity or a bona fide occupational qualification can reasonably be established.

It shall further be prohibited for any employee, contractor, or other agent of the (Company) to engage in the following types of discriminatory conduct:

1. *Race, National Origin, and Religion:* Making statements or jokes, or committing acts regarding a particular race, ancestry, or religion that are regarded as derogatory, offensive, prejudicial, or harassing.

2. *Sex/Sexual Harassment/Marital Status:* Intimidating or interfering with an employee's work or work environment, through unwelcome, offensive, or harassing sexual comments, questions, or acts (implicitly or explicitly), including prejudicial statements or acts regarding pregnancy or marital status.

   Any employees who believe they have been harassed by a coworker, supervisor, or agent of the employer should promptly report the facts of the incident or incidents and the names of the individuals involved to their supervisor or, in the alternative, to the (Human Resources Manager). Supervisors should immediately report any incidents of sexual harassment to the Personnel Department. The (Human Resources Manager) will investigate all such claims and take appropriate corrective action. If you have any questions concerning this policy, please feel free to contact the (Human Resources Manager) at your convenience.

3. *Employment of Relatives:* Nothing in the (Company's) equal employment opportunity policy is intended to be interpreted as preventing the (Company) from reasonably regulating nepotism for reasons of supervision, safety, security, or morale.

   Generally, employee's relatives will be eligible for employment with the (Company) as long as no conflicts in supervision, safety, security, or morale, or potential conflicts of interest exist. Relatives include an employee's parent, child, spouse, brother, sister, in-laws, and step relationships.

   If two employees marry or become related, and a conflict arises, only one of the employees will be permitted to stay with the (Company) unless reasonable accommodations can be made to eliminate the potential problems. The decision as to which relative will remain with the (Company) must be made either by the two employees within _____ calendar days, or by the (Company) on the basis of service value.

Alternative Policy: Equal Employment Opportunity

It is the policy of (Company) to create a favorable work environment in which all employees, regardless of race, color, national origin, sex, age (over 40), physical handicap, or religious affiliation, can enjoy equal opportunities in their employment relationship with the (Company). In an effort to maintain equal employment opportunities, the (Company) has recognized the need to adopt, implement, and periodically evaluate its affirmative action program consisting of specific measures to be taken, and its goals statements.

(Company) policy concerning equal employment opportunity requires that:

1. In establishing qualifications for employment, no provision or requirement will be adopted that would be discriminatory on the basis of such protected characteristics as race, color, national origin, age (over 40), sex, handicap, or religious affiliation, except where a bona fide occupational qualification exists.

2. No questions in any examination, application form, or other personnel proceeding, will be so framed as to attempt to elicit information concerning protected characteristics from an applicant, eligible candidate, or employee.

3. No appointment to or removal from a position will be affected in any manner solely by the person's protected characteristics and further that it will be the responsibility of all employees to abide by and carry out the provisions of the *(Company's)* affirmative action program.

Any employee or job applicant who feels that he or she has been subjected to discrimination by employees, officers, or agents of the *(Company)* are requested to report the incident or complaint directly to the *(Human Resources Manager)* who will investigate and attempt to resolve the matter.

Alternative Policy: Harassment/Sexual Harassment

The *(Company)* has established a strict policy prohibiting unlawful harassment of employees, including implied or expressed forms of sexual harassment. As used here, sexual harassment means any verbal, written, visual, or physical acts that are offensive in nature, intimidating, unwelcomed, or that could reasonably be taken as objectionable.

Any employee who feels that he or she has been legitimately subjected to harassment of any type, whether by a coworker, supervisor, officer, or agent of the *(Company)*, should promptly report the incident to the supervisor or the *(Human Resources Manager)*. The supervisor or the *(Human Resources Manager)* will take appropriate measures to resolve or correct the situation in an expeditious manner.

Employees having any questions concerning this policy circumstance should contact the *(Human Resources Manager)* for a confidential and frank discussion, and employees are assured that the utmost discretion will be used in the handling of such matters.

Alternative Policy: Sexual Harassment

Title VII of the Civil Rights Act of 1964 provides that it shall be an unlawful discriminatory practice for any employer, because of the sex of any person, to discharge, refuse to hire, or otherwise discriminate against that person with respect to any matter directly or indirectly related to employment. Harassment of an employee on the basis of sex violates this federal law.

To help clarify unlawful sexual harassment, the Federal Equal Employment Opportunity Commission has recently issued guidelines on the subject. Those guidelines state that unwelcome sexual advances, requests for sexual favors, and other verbal or physical conduct of a sexual nature will constitute unlawful sexual harassment when:

1. Submission to sexual conduct is an explicit or implied term or condition of an individual's employment;

2. The submission to or rejection of sexual conduct by an individual is the basis for any employment decision affecting that individual; or

3. Sexual advances, requests for sexual favors, or other verbal or physical conduct of a sexual nature have the purpose or effect of unreasonably interfering with an individual's work performance or create an intimidating, hostile, or offensive working environment.

THE *(Company)* STRONGLY DISAPPROVES OF ANY FORM OF SEXUAL HARASSMENT AT THE WORKPLACE, INCLUDING ACTS OF NONEMPLOYEES. DISCIPLINARY ACTION WILL BE TAKEN PROMPTLY AGAINST ANY EMPLOYEE, SUPERVISORY OR OTHERWISE, ENGAGING IN UNLAWFUL SEXUAL HARASSMENT.

Complaint Procedure

1. Any employee who feels that he or she has been the victim of sexual harassment should contact the *(Human Resources Manager)* within *(fifteen (15))* days of the incident. This report can be oral or written, but a written and signed statement of the complaint must be submitted by the complaining employee within *(three (3))* days of the initial report before an investigation can proceed.

2. Upon receipt of the written complaint, the *(Human Resources Manager)* will contact the person who allegedly initiated the sexual harassment, and inform that person of the basis of the complaint and the opportunity to respond within *(seven (7))* days to the complaint in writing.

3. Upon receipt of the written response, the *(Human Resources Manager)*, after conducting a thorough investigation, will submit in writing a confidential summary of the complaint, the response, and the facts of the investigation to the *(General Manager)*. The *(General Manager)*, after conducting a thorough review of the facts of the investigation, including possible interviews with all parties involved, will determine whether sexual harassment has occurred. Both parties will be notified of the *(General Manager's)* decision.

4. If it is determined that sexual harassment has occurred, appropriate disciplinary action up to and including discharge will be taken. The severity of the discipline will be determined by the severity and frequency of the offense or other conditions surrounding the incident.

5. An employee's failure to report the occurrence of sexual harassment within *(fifteen (15))* days may be deemed a waiver of any *(Company)* action. Failure to file a written complaint within *(three (3))* days of the verbal report will be considered a withdrawal of that report. If the person against whom the complaint of sexual harassment is filed fails to respond to the complaint within *(seven (7))* days of notification, the complaint will be taken as true, and the appropriate disciplinary measure will be taken if circumstances warrant.

Alternative Policy: Employment of Relatives

Employment of Spouse

It is the policy of the *(Company)* not to discriminate in its employment and personnel actions with respect to its employees, prospective employees, and applicants on the basis of marital status. No employee, prospective employee, or applicant will be denied employment or benefits of employment solely on the basis of marital status. This policy applies to the selection of persons for a training program leading to employment.

Notwithstanding the above provisions, the *(Company)* retains the right:

1. To refuse to place one spouse under the direct supervision of the other spouse where such has the potential for creating an adverse effect on supervision, safety, security, or morale.
2. To refuse to place both spouses in the same department, division, or facility where such has the potential for creating an adverse effect on supervision, safety, security, or morale, or involves potential conflicts of interest.

Employment of Other Relatives

1. Relatives within the third degree of kinship by blood or marriage of the *(Company's)* *(senior management/administrative)* employees, or any person exercising hiring, promotion, and termination authority, may not be hired into *(Company)* service without written approval of the *(President/General Manager)*.
2. Relatives within the third degree of kinship by blood or marriage of any *(Company)* employee, regardless of status, will not be hired in the same department, division, or facility where such has the potential for creating an adverse effect on supervision, safety, security, or morale, or involves potential conflicts of interest, without the written approval of the *(President/General Manager)*.

At-Will Employment Policy[7]

All employees who do not have a written individual employment contract, signed by the *(President)* of the *(Company)*, for a specific, fixed term of employment are "at-will" employees. This means that these employees may resign at any time, and the *(Company)* may terminate their employment at any time with or without notice for any or no reason. This policy may be modified only in a written document signed by the *(President)* of the *(Company)*. This manual *(handbook)* does not constitute, and should not be read to create, any promise by the *(Company)* that the policies set forth will be followed in every case. Nothing in this manual *(handbook)* alters an employee's at-will status.

Alternative Policy 1: At-Will Employment Policy, Large Company

Employment at *(Company)* is for no definite period and may, regardless of the time and manner of payment of wages and salary, be terminated at any time by the *(Company)* or by an employee, with or without cause, and without any previous notice.

Further, no organization manager or representative of *(Company)*, other than the *(President)* and *(Chief Executive Officer)* or the *(Executive Vice President)* of *(Human Resources)*, has the authority to enter into an agreement for employment for any specified period of time or to make any agreement contrary to the foregoing. This lack of guarantee or employ contract also applies to other benefits, working conditions, and privileges of employment at *(Company)*.

Alternative Policy 2: At-Will Employment Policy, Small Company

This handbook does not represent an employment contract between *(Company)* and its employees. The guidelines herein are for information purposes only and may be changed by the

---

7   Levesque, *The Complete Hiring Manual,* p. 48.

(Company) at its sole discretion. The *(Company)* is also not bound by any oral promises concerning an employee's length of employment. The policies and procedures set forth in this handbook, then, are for the purpose of providing employees general information about *(Company)* operating policies and guidelines concerning employment matters.

Employees and the *(Company)* are engaged in an "at-will" employment relationship, meaning that either are free to terminate the relationship at any time, with or without reason, and with or without notice. Employment contracts, on the other hand, are only authorized in writing by the *(President)* of the *(Company)*.

SELECTION, ORIENTATION, AND INITIAL EMPLOYMENT

Employee Selection Examinations

The selection techniques used in the examination of prospective new or promotional employees shall be impartial and of a practical nature; they shall relate to the job content in a way that fairly and accurately measures the applicants' capability to perform those duties of the position under consideration.[8] Examinations may include, but are not limited to, performance and achievement, aptitude tests, other written tests, personal interviews, work samples, medical or other examinations, or any combination of these or other requirements for the job, provided that such tests shall not be intentionally discriminatory.

The *(Human Resources Manager)* shall determine the selection method of employee examinations, including the use of such alternative techniques as certified promotional examinations based on the achievements and capacities of a singular employee, consistent with promotional requirements of the *(Company)* to promote the most suitable and capable persons.

Conduct of Examinations

The *(Human Resources Manager)* will determine the manner and methods of employment examinations, and will arrange the use of necessary facilities and equipment related to the conduct of examinations. No person taking a selection examination will be treated in any preferential way to any other person participating in the same examination process to the extent that such difference in treatment would compromise the impartiality of the examination process. Persons participating in the examination process who are found to cheat, falsify information, or be disruptive to others shall be immediately disqualified from further consideration and, if such persons are current employees, may be subject to termination.

---

[8]   Employers should be extremely cautious of preemployment selection examinations including oral interviews. Such examinations have been the subject of nationwide legislation and Supreme Court decisions concerning the validity of employment examinations dating back to 1969 in the *Griggs v. Duke Power Company* decision. Employers are advised to take necessary steps to ensure that each and every question or process used in preemployment examinations is *directly* related to the specific duties, responsibilities, and requirements of the position in which an applicant is being tested, and that there is consistency in the application of such tests.

Supplemental Examinations

When examinations have been completed and it is subsequently determined by the *(Human Resources Manager)* either that there is an insufficient number of qualified candidates available or that the hiring department has reasonably determined that available candidates do not meet the specific needs of the position, the *(Human Resources Manager)* may authorize the conducting of a supplemental examination. Candidates placed on an eligible list from a supplemental examination shall have their scores merged with other existing eligible applicants.

Applicant Limitations

Examinations may periodically result in an unusually large number of applicants who meet the prescribed minimum qualifications. When such circumstances arise, the *(Human Resources Manager)* may limit the number of applicants or candidates to advance through the examination process based on such considerations as the following:

1. Length, type, and level of work experience related to the position;
2. Applicability of past work experience to the *(Company's)* facilities, special needs, and problems; and
3. Type, degree, and recency of job preparation for prescribed responsibilities, to include certificates, technical training or course work, and educational achievements.

Medical Examinations

It is the policy of *(Company)* to employ persons who have physical and mental health consistent with the bona fide requirements of the positions to be filled and to assure that all employees have a standard of health that will contribute to safe, healthy, and efficient performance of work. It is likewise the policy of the *(Company)* not to discriminate against applicants because of physical handicaps where such handicaps can be reasonably accommodated.[9] To achieve these goals, the *(Company)* will provide physical examinations pursuant to the following.

Appointment to an initial employment position may be subject to certification of physical qualifications for employment provided by a physician of the *(Company's)* choice and expense. If certification of medical suitability is issued by the physician to the

---

[9]   This is the most recent target of the Equal Employment Opportunity Commission (EEOC). EEO administrative staff nationwide have been vigorously challenging employers on the standards used to accept and reject applicants with specific emphasis on blood pressure, back disorders, and various elements of the preemployment physical where there appears to be a dubious correlation between the medical test and job duties; for example, cervical examinations. Employers should also keep in mind that, under provisions of the Americans with Disabilities Act (ADA), preemployment medical exams cannot be administered to new hires until a tentative or conditional offer of employment has been made. Then, if the prospective new hire fails the exam due to a disability, but can perform essential duties of the job by reasonable accommodation of the employer, the employer is obligated to hire the individual unless doing so would move to be an undue hardship for the employer.

(Human Resources Manager), the applicant may be hired any time thereafter. If a certificate of employment suitability is not issued by the physician, or is issued conditionally, the applicant may not be hired until and unless the physician:

- Issues a revised certificate;
- Revises conditions of the certificate such that the condition does not present undue complications or hardships to the *(Company);* or
- Advises that a remedial program has been initiated that will permit employment consistent with *(Company)* needs.

The *(Human Resources Manager)* will be responsible for arranging medical examinations and coordinating results thereof with the person supervising the position under consideration. Failure on the part of an applicant to appear for a scheduled medical examination may result in disqualification from employment consideration.

Alternative Policy: Medical Examinations

For those positions in *(Company)* service that require particular physical conditions to carry out properly or withstand the prescribed tasks of the position, it may be necessary for job applicants to pass a medical evaluation by a *(Company)*-selected and -paid physician prior to an employment offer. Such medical examinations will be based on bona fide occupation standards that are reasonably related to the position in question, with consideration given by the *(Company)* to accommodating physical handicaps and limitations. Job applicants who fail to appear for *(Company)*-arranged medical examinations without good cause will be automatically disqualified for further employment consideration.

Examination Results and Records

The *(Company)* takes the position that employment consideration reflects upon the reputation of *(Company)* in the business community, as well as the quality of our employees, supervisors, and managers. It is therefore the desire of the *(Company)* to make fair and impartial judgments of prospective employees, to leave a positive impression of the *(Company)*, and to be thorough in its selection determinations. To facilitate communications between *(Company)* representatives and interested job applicants, the *(Human Resources Manager)* will be responsible for the timely notification of job opportunity and examination results information to interested persons.[10]

Records pertaining to any employment-related examination are, however, considered confidential and private documents of the *(Company)* and may not be divulged to any person who does not possess the legal or operational right to know. Access to such records shall be determined by the *(Human Resources Manager)*.

---

[10]   This is undoubtedly one of the biggest failings of many employers who choose not to notify interested job applicants of the organization's hiring decision. Even if employers choose not to put this into a policy statement, it is strongly recommended that they adopt it as an ongoing practice. It is a courtesy to inform people who show an interest in employment with your organization whether they have been accepted for further consideration or another decision has been made.

Employment References[11]

In keeping with the *(Company's)* policy on taking reasonable measures to determine the overall suitability of new hires, and to provide the *(Company)* with greater assurance of a new employee's successful adaptation to employment conditions, the *(Company)* reserves the right to investigate and obtain prior employment, educational, credit, character, and other pertinent information about any prospective applicant under consideration for hire. While most reference investigations are conducted at the time of hire, the *(Company)* may additionally determine the propriety of gathering similar information on existing employees when doing so is deemed suitable and in the best interests of the *(Company)*.

Reference information may be obtained by (designated management personnel or the *Human Resources Officer*), however all such information shall be treated in strictest confidence and kept on file in the *(Human Resources Office)*. Conversely, reference information may be given to inquiring and verified employers *only* by the *(Human Resources Officer, President,* and/or *Department Heads)*, including letters of reference, only when a written request and authorization has been obtained by the respective employee.

Employment Status Categories

It is the policy of *(Company)* to categorize the status of employees to make distinctions in benefits and conditions of employment among employees, and to aid in a better understanding of employment relationships with the *(Company)*.

Initial/Introductory employees   New, rehired, or promoted employees who serve a prescribed period of close supervision and evaluation to assess their ability and adaptation. Probationary employment may be terminated at the will and discretion of the *(Company)* without advance notice, or by the employee.

Regular full-time employees   Employees who regularly work a minimum of *(forty, (40))* hours per week on a continuous basis following satisfactory completion of a probationary period.

Regular part-time employees   Employees who complete a satisfactory probationary period and regularly work more than *(twenty (20))* but fewer than *(forty (40))* hours per week on a continuous basis.

Temporary employees   Employees holding jobs of limited or specified duration arising out of special projects, position vacancy pending appointment, the absence of a position incumbent, abnormal work loads, emergencies, or other reasons established by the *(Company)*. Temporary employees may work either full- or part-time work schedules, but will not be eligible to receive *(Company)*-sponsored benefits, accrue any form of service credit, or use the Administrative Review Procedure to file formal grievances except in matters pertaining to alleged discrimination.

Nonexempt employees   Employees covered by overtime pay and other distinctive provisions of the Fair Labor Standards Act or applicable state laws. Such employees are

---

[11]   Levesque, *The Complete Hiring Manual,* p. 59.

entitled to overtime pay for work required to be performed by the *(Company)* over *(forty (40))* hours per workweek.

Exempt employees   Employees classified by the *(Company)* as exempt are ineligible for overtime pay and other employment conditions as provided for in the Fair Labor Standards Act and applicable state laws. Generally, such employees are those occupying executive, administrative, professional, or outside sales positions.

AS ALL EMPLOYEES ARE HIRED CONDITIONALLY ON THE BASIS OF CONTINUING FITNESS OR NEED, THESE STATUS CATEGORIES OR ANYTHING CONTAINED IN THESE POLICIES AND PROCEDURES DO NOT GUARANTEE EMPLOYMENT FOR ANY SPECIFIED LENGTH OF TIME. RATHER, EMPLOYMENT IS AT THE MUTUAL CONSENT OF THE EMPLOYEE AND *(COMPANY)*, AND CAN BE TERMINATED AT WILL BY THE EMPLOYEE OR *(COMPANY)*.[12]

Employment Offers[13]

Neither supervisors nor department heads have the authority to offer employment to any applicant; only the *(Human Resources Department/President)* does. All offers of employment are conditional, subject to satisfactory results of a background investigation, reference check, preemployment alcohol and drug tests, and production of documents sufficient to demonstrate identity and authorization to work in the United States, as required by the Immigration Reform and Control Act.

Alternative Policy: Employment Offers

It is the *(Company's)* policy to confirm all offers and acceptance of offers of employment in writing. Upon notice from the hiring authority to the *(Human Resources Officer)*, a letter will be prepared by the *(Human Resources Office)* to the selected applicant making an offer of employment and providing such information as the new employee's start date, time, job title, rate of pay, employment orientation instructions, and that acceptance of the employment offer must be made in writing by a specified date. Only the *(President, General Manager, Human Resources Officer)* will be authorized to sign employment offer letters.

Employment offers may not be made until the selected applicant has satisfactorily demonstrated that he or she possess suitable job abilities, background, physical condition, and legal requirements that are a customary part of the hiring process. When this process is completed, and results are satisfactory, the *(Human Resources Officer)* shall promptly notify the hiring authority who may then request that an employment offer letter be presented to the applicant. Upon acceptance of the offer by the applicant, the *(Human Resources Officer)* shall notify the hiring authority of the applicant's report date and request that preparations be made to orient the new employee.

---

[12]   This clause, together with similar references throughout this manual, such as the last paragraph under the Purpose and Principles of the policy manual, are meant to reinforce the employer's *at-will* employment condition.

[13]   Levesque, *The Complete Hiring Manual*, p. 60.

Employee Orientation and Integration

(Company) believes that a smooth and thorough orientation of new employees results in a positive integration into the company's operations, and will lead to a more productive and satisfying employment relationship. For this reason, new employees are to be scheduled for a thorough orientation promptly following their report date; they receive information about the company's employment benefits and complete related documents. The employee's supervisor is to provide each new employee with such information as background about the *(Company)*, its personnel policies, each department's organization and functions, the employee's role in helping to achieve *(Company)* goals, the employee's job content and performance evaluation standards, job safety, promotional opportunities, and any other information deemed pertinent to establish employee comfort.

New employees should also be introduced to their coworkers, and other supervisors and managers with whom they will be working.

The topics covered by a supervisor in a new employee orientation shall be documented on a form prescribed by the *(Human Resources Manager)*, who will receive completed orientation forms, including the employee's signature, for placement in the employee's personnel file.

Following initial orientation, supervisors and managers should regularly check with employees concerning questions they may have, their working conditions, any problems or difficulties they may have encountered, and feedback concerning their performance or job progress.

Alternative Policy: Employee Orientation

During each new employee's first workweek, the designated supervisor or *(Department Head)* will conduct a thorough orientation of the employee on such matters as the *(Company's)* and *(Department's)* organization and functions; the employee's role in helping to achieve *(Company/Department)* objectives; the employee's job content and scope; training, performance and evaluation standards, and promotional opportunities; job safety; and any other matter of *(Departmental)* importance. Departmental orientations are to be recorded on the prescribed orientation form, signed and dated by both the new employee and person administering the orientation, and placed in the employee's personnel file as a permanent record.

Within the new employee's first _____ days of employment, *(Personnel Office Staff)* will provide an additional orientation consisting of the completion of employment forms and records, an explanation of the *(Company's)* compensation and benefit program and personnel policies, and any other information as determined appropriate to the employee's orientation and integration into *(Company)* service.

Purpose of Initial/Introductory Employment Period

The introductory period is an intrinsic part and extension of the employee selection process during which the employee will be considered in training and under careful observation and evaluation by supervisory personnel. Generally, this period will be utilized to train and evaluate the employee's effective adjustment to work tasks, conduct, observance of rules, attendance, and job responsibilities, and to provide for the release of any introductory employee whose performance does not meet required standards of job progress or adaptation.

Length of Initial/Introductory Employment Period

The *(Human Resources Manager)* shall establish introductory periods for each separate occupation in *(Company)* service on the basis of such factors as the complexity of job tasks, unique or difficult nature of work operations, the importance of work activities and decisions, and the time involved to reasonably accomplish an evaluation of full job adaptation. Generally, nonexempt employees will serve a *(ninety-day or six-month (90-day or 6-month))* introductory period, during which time their job progress will be formally evaluated by the standards established for their areas of job responsibility. Part-time employees will serve introductory periods commensurate to the number of hours served in probation by full-time employees.

Alternative Policy: Length of Initial/Introductory Employment Period

All nonexempt employees, whether new, rehired, or promoted, are required to serve a *(ninety-day or six-month (90-day or 6-month))* introductory period. New and rehired employees will not be eligible to accrue or use paid sick leave, vacation, or any other form of paid absence, excluding designated holidays. Additionally, introductory employees will be limited to filing complaints or grievances on matters related only to discrimination and harassment.

Introductory periods may be extended by the *(Company)* for a limited additional period where it is determined that such an extension is necessary to thoroughly evaluate the employee's ability to perform the full scope of assigned duties. In these cases, the employee will be advised of the extended duration of the introductory period prior to the conclusion of the initial introductory period.

Notwithstanding the provisions of the *(Company's)* introductory period policies, the *(Company)* reserves the right to terminate the employment relationship with any probationary employee at will and without advance notice.

During the Initial/Introductory Employment Period

Introductory employees are not eligible for some benefits paid for or sponsored by the *(Company)*. However, upon successful completion of the introductory period, employees are considered regular employees of the *(Company)* and become eligible for the benefits described herein provided they satisfy the terms and conditions of the various benefit programs.

The introductory period may be extended for a limited period only by approval of the *(Human Resources Manager)*, and only where it is deemed necessary and appropriate for *(Company)* interests or due to circumstances beyond the *(Company's)* or employee's control such as absence due to unforeseen events.[14] In all cases of requests to extend

---

[14] The trend of various court decisions has been against employers' extending predetermined introductory (probationary) periods, particularly for what appears to the courts to be arbitrary,

an employee's introductory period, the supervisor or manager must submit a statement of the employee's current performance levels in assigned areas of responsibility, the justification for extension, and the amount of time such extension is needed. No request for extensions will be approved if submitted after the date of the normal conclusion of the employee's introductory period.

Confirmation to Regular Status

If, at the conclusion of the employee's introductory period, the employee's performance and employment conditions have been satisfactory in all respects in the opinion of supervising personnel, and advancement to regular status is deemed mutually advantageous to the *[Company]* and the employee, such a retention recommendation is to be made to the *[President/General Manager]* at least *[ten [10]]* calendar days prior to expiration of the employee's introductory period.

Such a recommendation will be accompanied by a completed, final introductory performance evaluation. Upon approval of the *[President/General Manager]*, the employee shall then be advanced to regular employment status and thereby deemed eligible for those *[Company]* benefits provided to regular employees.

Release of New Employee

Employment may be terminated at the will and discretion of the *[Company]* at any time should such termination be regarded as necessary and appropriate by either the employee of the *[Company]* with or without notice or stated cause.

Should the introductory employee not be formally recommended for advancement to regular status as prescribed, the employee shall be considered unacceptable and released from *[Company]* service not later than the last day of the introductory period.

Release of Promoted Employee During Introductory Period

A regular employee under a promotional introductory period whose performance or other employment conditions are determined to be unsatisfactory may be reinstated to the former position or a comparable position, or released from *[Company]* service, the determination of which shall be at the sole discretion of the *[Company]*.

Employment Rehires Policy[15]

Former employees may be considered for rehire by the *[Company]* without taking competitive tests, provided the rehire is being made to a position in which the former employee

---

[14] *continued*   indecisive, or capricious reasons. On the other hand, the courts have generally been willing to support employers in these circumstances where there is valid reason to extend these periods for a reasonable length of time, and such justifiable reasons might include an employee's unforeseen absence resulting from a workers' compensation injury or other similar circumstance.

[15]   Levesque, *The Complete Hiring Manual*, p. 55.

held regular status with the *[Company]* in the same or substantially similar position as determined by the *[Human Resources Manager]* in accordance with the following.

REEMPLOYMENT

Employees who resign from the *[Company]* in good standing may be eligible for reemployment consideration within *[twelve (12)]* months of the date of their employment separation. To determine eligibility, the former employee must file an employment application form with the *[Human Resources Office]* and await notice as to the existence of an available position within this time period.

If a former employee is reemployed under these conditions, no credit will be given for former service with respect to benefit accruals or other forms of longevity entitlements that are normally associated with an employee's continuous service. Each reemployment will be assigned a new probationary period and accrue benefits as would any other new employee, except that reemployments may be assigned a pay rate commensurate with the rate received at the time of their separation.

REINSTATEMENT

Employees who are laid off from their jobs with the *[Company]*, and who had at least a rating of satisfactory in each performance category on their last formal appraisal, may be eligible for rehire within *[twenty-four (24)]* months from the date of their employment separation. To determine eligibility, the former employee must file an employment application form with the *[Human Resources Office]* and await notice as to the existence of an available position within this time period. Since employment application forms are kept active for a period of *[twelve (12)]* months, those who file for reinstatement may have to renew their application to keep it active.

If a former employee is reinstated under these conditions, credit will be given for former service with respect to (vacation and other longevity related) accruals that would have occurred had the employee not had a break in service. Additionally, each reinstatement will be assigned a pay rate commensurate with the rate received at the time of their separation, however a new anniversary date will be established on the basis of the date of reinstatement even though a probationary period of employment will not be required.

POSITION CLASSIFICATION AND ALLOCATION

Position Classification

To develop and maintain a clear structure of job responsibility and work activity relationships within the *(Company)*, and to keep meaningful the relatedness of an employee's job and associated pay, performance standards, and other employment conditions, the *(Company)* has adopted a policy to maintain job descriptions on each separate class of employment, to allocate individual employee positions into job classes, and to classify or reclassify positions as is necessary based on the best interests of the *(Company)*. While it is the intent of this policy to describe and classify jobs in specific ways as a means of benefiting the organization's employment structure, this policy should not be misconstrued to restrict or confine job responsibility assigned to employees where flexibility in assigning employees new but related job activities is tantamount to the success of business operations. In so doing, *(Company)* officers shall remain mindful of the provisions set forth in this section.

The *(Human Resources Manager)* will be responsible for preparing and maintaining thorough job descriptions on all separate classes of employment with the aid and assistance of supervisors and employees. Such job descriptions should contain the designation as to whether position(s) covered by the job description are categorized as exempt or nonexempt, in addition to duty and qualification specifications.[16] All job descriptions should be reviewed periodically to determine their continued accuracy, completeness, compliance with applicable standards of state and federal laws, and relevance to the *(Company's)* pay and performance evaluation systems. Each employee will be allocated to a position approved by the *(Human Resources Manager)* and position vacancies will be filled on the basis of job description standards after notification of the (pending) vacancy to the *(Human Resources Manager)* and approval to fill by the *(President/General Manager)*.

Revision of Job Descriptions and Position Allocation

Job descriptions and the allocation of employees to positions may be revised or altered from time to time at the sole discretion of the *(Company)* as a means of operational efficiency and the changing nature of conducting business. When and where it is deemed appropriate, the *(Company)* will endeavor to advise affected employees of changes in job description details or their allocation to a specific position, including the determination to abolish positions, in which case employees may be offered other positions for which they are qualified.[17]

---

[16]   The development of thorough job descriptions is an important managerial tool to establish organization structure, work flow relationships, selection and promotional standards, performance evaluation criteria, and pay plans. It is also useful in defending against claims made by employees or administrative compliance agencies such as the Workers' Compensation Appeals Board, state labor commissioner's office, or state and federal fair employment commissions. If written properly, a job description need not be a restrictive document upon the operation of any business.
[17]   In recent years, the courts have taken a dim view of employers' hiring an employee with a prescribed set of duties and responsibilities, and in the ensuing years substantially modifying or

New Positions

New positions are those in which there is an identified, justified, and approved list of job tasks and qualification standards sufficiently different from existing position descriptions, or the position is in addition to positions of the existing work force. In either case, new position requests must be approved by the *[President/General Manager]*. Upon approval, and if required, a thorough job description will be prepared and a pay rate established for the position prior to filling such position.

Position Reclassification

Positions whose duties and responsibilities have changed to depart significantly from an assigned job description, or positions that have been structurally effected by organizational changes may be authorized by the *[President/General Manager]* for reclassification consideration. Reclassification requests may be initiated by individual employees or supervisory personnel, and all such requests must be substantiated in writing with specific detail given to those duties and responsibilities being performed continuously that are different in scope from those contained in the applicable job description. The presence of job performance attributes greater than those required is not, in itself, sufficient justification for reclassification.

Upon approval of a reclassification request, the person assigned to evaluate the position may consult with the affected employee(s) and supervisory personnel, and gather any other information pertinent to the issue(s) under consideration. A report of the evaluation findings and recommendations will be submitted to the *[President/General Manager]*, who may also consult with applicable supervisory personnel to determine a proper course of action. Should a reclassification evaluation involve the creation of a new job description, the *[President/General Manager]* may approve the reclassification pending final approval of the new job description and pay rate recommendation.

Upon reclassification of a position to a class having a higher pay rate, the *[Human Resources Manager]* will determine whether the incumbent employee meets the qualification requirements of the new position. If so, the employee may be allocated to the new position. If not, the *[Human Resources Manager]* will determine the proper disposition of the employee and the method and means of filling the new position. Reclassification of a position shall not be intentionally used for the purpose of prejudicial or disciplinary promotions or demotions. Employees who feel that the initiation or results of a reclassification were based on these factors should present their cases to the *[Human Resources Manager]*.

---

17 *continued*   increasing those duties and responsibilities without a commensurate increase in compensation. For this reason, employers are encouraged to maintain a policy similar to this one, expressing a good-faith commitment to reevaluate assigned duties and responsibilities periodically by means of job description revisions and to communicate in some manner with employees about modifications to their job assignments. The issue of a corresponding adjustment or evaluation of compensation for changed job duties is not discussed in this particular policy. However, employers would be well advised to take that under consideration at the time of major revision to job descriptions or to job assignments.

HOURS, MEALS, AND REST PERIODS

General Hours of Work

The *(Human Resources Manager)*, upon consultation with supervisory personnel and with approval of the *(President)*, will determine operational days and hours of work or the modification thereof. Unless otherwise assigned, the normal days and hours of work for employees will be as follows:

1. *Workday:* For full-time positions shall be *(eight (8))* hours, excepting unpaid meal periods, between the hours of *(8:00 A.M. and 5:00 P.M.)*.[18]

2. *Workweek:* For full-time positions will consist of *(forty (40))* hours between *(12:01 A.M., Monday)* and *(12:00 midnight, Sunday)*.

3. *Work Schedules:* Will be established for each employee by supervisory personnel who may change such schedules based on the needs and requirements of work unit operations. Supervisory personnel may also require an employee to work an unscheduled day in place of a scheduled day within the same workweek, in which case the unscheduled day worked shall be treated as a modified work schedule and not subject to overtime compensation on the basis of a changed workday.

Alternative Policy: General Hours of Work

For full-time nonexempt employees, the regular workweek will consist of eight hours per day, five days per week. Most employees will be assigned to a work schedule of 8:00 A.M. to 5:00 P.M., Monday through Friday, excluding the nonpaid lunch period. However, the *(Company)* can assign employees to other days and hours within the workweek that begins at 12:01 A.M. *(Monday)* and ends at 12:00 midnight of the following *(Sunday)*.

Other work shifts, days, hours, and periods can be established and modified by the *(Company)* within the limits prescribed by law, based on operating conditions and requirements of the *(Company)*. With approval of the *(Department Head)* and *(President/Human Resources Manager)*, supervisors may grant employees the opportunity to work flexible work schedules so long as such a schedule does not diminish operational effectiveness or create an overtime liability that would not otherwise occur.

---

[18] The workday time period *should not* be confused with normal office hour times. Using normal office hours as a definition of the workday can have a detrimental effect on employer defenses of certain types of wage claims (overtime) made by employees.

Employers should also note that split workdays or workshifts within a twenty-four-hour period can have additional compensation requirements under many state laws. For example, if the employer schedules or otherwise requires an employee to work for a period of time, and then take an unpaid break of two or more hours before returning to work to complete the work shift, many state laws will require that the employer pay a minimum of one to two hours of straight-time compensation for the split time. Therefore, employers are advised, where split shift schedules are utilized, to check with qualified counsel to determine the applicability of state labor laws.

Attendance

Consistent attendance and punctuality are considered imperative ingredients in the *(Company's)* business operations, and therefore an integral part of each employee's performance standards based on objective measurements. Poor, uncertain, or irregular attendance produces disruptive results for *(Company)* operations, lowers overall productivity and continuity of work, and often is burdensome to other employees.

Employees are expected and required to report to their designated work locations at the prescribed time and manner work activity is to commence. Tardiness, unexcused absence, or failure to report as required may result in disciplinary action. In the event an employee cannot report to work as scheduled, the employee must so notify supervisory personnel at least *(one (1))* hour prior to scheduled reporting time or be prepared to provide evidence of extenuating circumstances. In all cases of an employee's absence or tardiness, the employee shall provide supervisory personnel with a truthful reason for the absence and, if applicable, the probable duration of absence. If circumstances render the absence duration speculative or unknown, the absent employee will be required to call supervisory personnel daily to report the status of the absence.[19]

Excessive absenteeism, regardless of reason(s), that renders an employee insufficiently available for work will be evaluated on a case-by-case basis to determine the merits of correctional retention or termination.[20]

Alternative Policy: Attendance

Employees are expected and required to be in attendance, prepared to commence work activities, at designated work locations, days, and hours. Employees are also expected to remain at work for the entire work period excluding rest and meal periods. Late arrival, early departure, and other personal absences are disruptive and should be avoided. Where employees are found to abuse absence time from scheduled work, the *(Company)*

---

[19]   The absence of a policy statement of this type often places employers in a precarious position to take corrective measures, including disciplinary action. While many employers assume that they have such an authority, such may not be the case if the employer is unable to site rules or policies to that effect upon taking action against an employee who has violated this situation. In most such cases, the employer must be in a position to show that the employee had knowledge of the rule or working condition.

[20]   This particular clause is important for employers who have found themselves in the legally weak situation of desiring to terminate an employee on the basis of absence due to medical conditions. In reviewing terminations based on medical condition of the employee, many state and federal courts have found that the employer violated, intentionally or unintentionally, either fair employment laws, which prohibit discrimination on the basis of physical handicap, or the 1991 Americans with Disabilities Act, which requires employers to accommodate certain physical disabilities or medical limitations of employees. It therefore becomes important for employers to scrutinize the factual circumstances of cases that may arise with employees and to seek professional counsel. Generally, if the employer can show that an employee's absence from work, regardless of the nature or circumstances surrounding such absences, is disruptive or significantly affecting operations or the job for which the employee was hired, the employer is far more likely to prevail in the event of litigation, presuming there is no overriding evidence of discrimination.

may find it necessary to attempt correction of the situation by counseling, disciplinary measures, or termination. Any employee on an unauthorized absence for more than *[three (3)]* scheduled work *[days/shifts]* without acceptable notification to the *[Company]* will be deemed to have abandoned the position and will be automatically terminated. In such cases, the *[Department Head]* is to so notify the *[Human Resources Manager]*, who will handle related personnel processing.

Unauthorized Absences

An employee who is absent from his or her assigned work location or schedule without official leave approval from supervisory personnel for *[three (3)]* or more days shall be considered absent without authorized leave. In such cases, the *[Company]* shall regard the job as abandoned and the employee automatically terminated, unless the employee can provide the *[Company]* with acceptable and verifiable evidence of extenuating circumstances.

Employees who are absent without notice or authorization for less than *[three (3)]* days, and who subsequently report to work, shall provide a detailed written reason for such absence and, regardless of stated reasons, may be subject to disciplinary action including termination.

Unauthorized leave or unexcused absence will not be compensated in any form by the *[Company]*, including *[Company]*-sponsored employment benefits.

Overtime, Callback, and Emergency Work Hours

As business or specific operational needs of the *[Company]* dictate, it may become periodically necessary for employees to be available for work beyond their daily or weekly work schedule, or to return to work after departing the *[Company]* premises, following completion of their normal work schedule. Either an extension of the workday or a returned resumption of work activity prior to the next scheduled workday may be treated as overtime for the purpose of nonexempt employee pay calculations, depending on the number of actual hours worked during the applicable workweek.

Should an emergency occur, the nature of which affects business operations, employees may be required to work unusual or reduced schedules, or they may be laid off indefinitely because of business disruption. For reasons of potential emergency situations, all employees must keep the *[Company]* advised of a current address, phone number, message phone number, and person to contact in case of personal emergency.

Work Schedule Exchanges

The exchanging of workdays is generally discouraged because of its inherent disruptive effect on record keeping and the continuity of work progress. However, under circumstances where an employee can demonstrate a legitimate reason for exchanging a work schedule with another agreeable employee, and where affected supervisory personnel approve of the exchange, such exchanges may be authorized on a limited basis. Under no circumstances will exchange work schedules be authorized if the exchange is likely to result in a disruption or interference of the work unit operations, or in either employee's working overtime.

Employees wishing to have a work schedule exchange considered by supervisory personnel should submit a written request restating the dates and times of the exchange, the exchange employees involved, the reason(s) for the exchange, and the date and signature of both employees. Such a written request must be submitted to affected supervisory personnel not later than _____ working days before the requested exchange, whereupon supervisory personnel will respond with approval or disapproval in a timely manner. Should the request be disapproved, supervisors should note their reason(s) on the employee's written request, and retain a file copy.

Modified Duty Schedule

To encourage and accommodate employees who are recovering from a work-related disability to resume partial work duties when the nature of their disability so allows, the *(Company)* has established the following policy and provisions.

1. Any employee who is receiving benefits under the *(Company's)* workers' compensation plan for a work-related disability, and whose recovery is determined by a physician to be satisfactory to resume at least partial duties and/or hours of work, may be allowed by the *(Company)* to return to work on a modified duty schedule. Such a work schedule and/or the nature of work to be performed by the returning employee shall be at the *(Company's)* sole discretion based on case-by-case circumstances; however, the *(Company)* shall endeavor to provide reasonable accommodation for each such case. Modified duty assignments may end at the time the disabled employee is determined to be "permanent and stationary" by the *(Company's)* workers' compensation insurer or certified as able to resume normal work activities and schedules by a physician.[21]

2. Nonexempt employees who are placed on a modified duty schedule shall be compensated at their normal hourly rate for hours worked and may continue for a period to be entitled to reduced payments for temporary disability by the *(Company's)* workers' compensation insurer. Exempt employee shall receive full

---

[21]   This policy is in response to the legal relationship between the Americans with Disabilities Act and workers' compensation provisions as provided by most state laws. As the two laws relate to each other, the ADA requires employers to provide "reasonable accommodation" to disabled workers whose recovery from an industrial injury has progressed to the extent that the worker can perform one or more essential duties of their job. Employers may, of course, establish more liberal policies which allow such employees to return to work, at their normal rate of pay, to perform a less demanding job until such time as the employee is able to resume normal duties. What remains vague and ambiguous under the ADA in light of work-related disabilities is the guidelines employers should use to determine clear distinctions between essential and nonessential duties for each job. It is also unclear as to what extent the employer must go to prove a good-faith attempt in providing reasonable accommodation without suffering an undue hardship. For these reasons, employers should consult with qualified advisors whenever these circumstances arise, or as they begin to progress.

pay, less any payments for temporary disability benefits, provided such employees work at least *[twenty (20)]* hours per week. Both nonexempt and exempt employees shall be entitled to normal employment benefits, including contributions to health care plans, during modified duty assignments up to a period of *[four (4)]* months.

There are two ways a modified duty schedule can be activated: (1) employees so disabled can submit a written request to the *[President, Human Resources Manager]* accompanied by a physician's statement of physical abilities, limitations, and nature of physical accommodations needed to perform partial work—if any, or (2) the *[Company]* can require a partially disabled employee to return to work on a modified duty schedule where, in the *[Company's]* opinion based on available medical findings, the disabled employee is sufficiently able to perform partial work activities.

Meal and Rest Periods

In accordance with applicable law, nonexempt employees are entitled and encouraged to take meal and rest periods at times and under conditions prescribed by supervisory personnel. It is the intent of this policy to provide opportunities for employees to meet their dietary and health needs, as well as to rest and relax periodically from assigned work tasks.

Noncompensable meal periods of at least *[thirty (30)]* minutes are provided for all full-time nonexempt employees and should be taken not more than *[five (5)]* hours after the start of the employee's workday. Employees are encouraged not to consume food at their work stations, except under special conditions approved by their supervisors, and will therefore be relieved of duty entirely during the meal period to leave the *[Company's]* premises if so desired. However, under certain circumstances where it is in the best interest of the *[Company]*, employees may be required to consume a meal while actively engaged at work at their duty station, whereupon the employees shall be paid for the *[thirty (30)]*-minute meal period. Employees are responsible for recording or reporting the beginning and end of each meal period, and should be prepared to resume work promptly after the conclusion of the meal period.[22]

Nonexempt employees will also be provided *[fifteen (15)]*-minute rest periods during each continuous *[four (4)]*-hour work period. Full-time employees may take two such rest periods; one during the first half of their work schedule and the other during the second half of their work schedule. Part-time employees working a schedule of *[three and one-half (3½)]* hours or less per day are not required by law to be provided with a rest period. Rest periods may not be combined with or added to an employee's meal period unless special conditions warrant the supervisor's approval.

---

[22]   Meal period provisions are covered both in the Fair Labor Standards Act (FLSA) and under state labor laws as noncompensable time. The employee must be relieved of duty and allowed to leave the premises or at least free to go to another location within the business (employee lounge) to consume a meal. However, employees who are either required or strongly encouraged by employers to consume their meals at their workstations, or to perform work while eating, can generally hold their employer liable for compensation during that period of time.

Alternative Policy: Meal and Rest Periods

Nonexempt employees will have at least a *(thirty (30))*-minute unpaid meal period and two *(fifteen (15))*-minute paid rest periods assigned by supervisory personnel. During meal and rest periods, employees are to be relieved of their job duties and permitted to leave their work locations.

Meal periods are not to be taken more than five hours after the beginning of the work *(day/shift)*. One rest period may be taken during the first *(four (4))* hours of work, with the second rest period taken during the last *(four (4))* hours of work. Part-time employees who work *(six (6))* hours or less per day may not take the second rest period.

Rest periods cannot be used in conjunction with meal periods, nor may rest periods be taken during the employee's first or last scheduled hour of work.

COMPENSATION AND PAYROLL PRACTICES

Compensation Policy

It is the policy of the *(Company)* to pay and provide other compensatory incentives to its employees in a competitive and equitable manner to attract and retain the most capable employees, who will contribute to their own success by their contributions to the *(Company)*. To accomplish the basic intent of this policy, the *(Company)* has established the following plan, provisions, and standards for employee compensation. Additionally, the types of compensation provided in this manual shall be regarded as payment in full for all employee services rendered to the *(Company)*, and no employee may accept any other compensation for services performed in behalf of the *(Company)*.

Salary/Wage Plan

The *(Human Resources Manager)* or person/agency retained for this purpose shall prepare a Salary/Wage Plan for all classes of positions in exempt and nonexempt company service, except the *(list position(s))* whose compensation shall be determined by the *(President/Board of Directors)*. The plan will consist of a base salary, salary range, or hourly wage rate for each separate class of employment. In arriving at such compensation rates, consideration will be given to such factors as:

- Prevailing rates of pay for comparable work in similar employments, including conditions of work.
- Regional cost-of-living indexes.
- Internal consistency of relationships between pay and the collective worth of each class of work.[23]
- The equitability of pay between classes of work having the same or substantially similar duties, responsibilities, requirements, and conditions of work.[24]
- The organization's economic condition.
- The available supply of persons meeting the organization's particular needs and requirements.

Thereafter, further studies, evaluations, and recommendations for the modification of the *(Company's)* compensation plan shall be made on a regular basis, and submitted to the *(President)* for consideration.

Job classes assigned to salary or wage ranges will have at least a minimum, midpoint, and maximum rate of pay. Pay range midpoints establish the rate a fully qualified

---

[23]   This simply means that the organization will keep an eye toward the consistency of pay relationships both vertically and horizontally throughout the organization based on both tangible and intangible factors of job worth, or contribution to the organization, when it comes to job pricing.

[24]   This language accounts for the employer's intent not to violate the principles, provisions, and standards set forth in the Equal Pay Act.

employee receives after sustained demonstration of satisfactory performance according to occupational and *(Company)* standards. Pay levels above the midpoint are carefully reserved for employees who demonstrate consistent and enduring performance at varying levels of excellence.[25]

Hiring Rate   All new employees should be advised at the time of hire as to their starting rate of pay and their exempt or nonexempt classification status for purposes of compensation treatment, particularly overtime eligibility.

New nonexempt employees will be hired at a pay rate equal to the minimum rate assigned to the position, and shall remain at their established pay rate for at least the period of probationary employment.[26] Where warranted by unusual conditions, new employees may be hired at a pay rate greater than the minimum in consideration of such factors as advanced or specialized education or training, level of experience, possession of highly developed technical skills, demonstrated achievements, or labor market competitiveness. New hire rates above the minimum must receive advance approval of the *(President/General Manager)* who may also authorize individual pay rate adjustments at any time where inequitable conditions are found as a result of the administration of the *(Company's)* compensation plan.

Reemployment/Reinstatement Rates   Employees who are reemployed within *(six (6) months/one (1) year)* from their date of resignation will be assigned a pay rate in the same manner as a new hire, will be required to establish a new anniversary date, and will not be eligible for bridged service credit.[27]

---

[25]   There are, of course, many variations of establishing pay and pay rates for different positions in an organization. Employers are encouraged to establish consistency and particular rationale associated with the type of pay plan adopted by the organization. The practice of establishing pay ranges, regardless of whether the pay is an hourly or salary rate, is probably one of the most common methods because it provides latitude for the employer to recognize special achievement or skills performance of employees, and to extend an economic incentive to employees viewing their jobs with a long-term employment relationship in mind. Conversely, single-rate pay plans have proven a disincentive for employees over a period of time, as pay increases are generally unclear and uncertain beyond their initial hire-in rate.

[26]   Court decisions concerning compensation rates for new employees seem to disfavor employers who use the employee's immediate past salary as a predominant determinant in establishing the hire-in rate, particularly in cases where the new hire is a female and the hiring pay rate is less than that of a male employee doing the same (or substantially the same) work, under similar working conditions, skills, effort, and other qualifications for the position. Given this and similar trends in legal thinking, it is not difficult to speculate that the courts will be broadening this theory of discriminatory effect when past wages are used to set new hire rates. For this reason, employers are encouraged to avoid using an employee's past pay rate as a major consideration in setting the employee's hire-in rate. The remainder of this policy section will, however, give the employer the latitude to establish some differential pay within the pay range established for a position based on specific criteria that will differentiate one person from another.

[27]   See definition of terms for "bridged service." Bridged service credit can be used in decisions concerning pay increases, promotion, and the like, where the employee's longevity may be a factor the employer will want to take into consideration regarding pay matters.

Employees who are reinstated within *(six (6) months/one (1) year)* from their date of layoff by the *(Company)* will receive a pay rate of not more than the current rate for their position at the time of layoff, provided reinstatement is to the same or substantially similar position as the former position. If not, the employee may be treated under the provisions of reemployment. Reinstated employees will be assigned a new employment anniversary date and bridged service.

Pay Limits   Employees will receive compensation that is established for each pay grade rate, including revisions, or within range limits of their position. If an employee's base compensation falls below that established or revised for the position, the employee's pay shall be increased to a level of the rate or within the applicable range. Conversely, nonexempt employees may not have their base compensation exceed the established rate or range limit.

Alternative Policy: Salary/Wage Plan

(Company) has established a Salary/Wage Plan that assigns each job to a particular pay scale representative of prevailing rates in the community, the nature and scope of each job, and the relationship of job responsibility among all categories of positions in *(Company)* service. Because of the *(Company's)* commitment to the doctrine of equal pay for equal work, no employee will be assigned to a job and paid a rate less than that established for the position as long as performing the full scope of duties of the position.

To assure that the *(Company's)* Salary/Wage Plan remains competitive and fair, a periodic review of pay rates will be conducted. Based on the results of these reviews, some positions might be eligible for a pay rate increase. Individual pay rate increases may be granted based on each employee's annual performance evaluation where meritorious work has been demonstrated during the preceding year.

Exempt/Nonexempt Classifications

Job classifications in the executive, administrative, professional, or sales structure of the *(Company)*, and which fall within the definition of applicable state and federal law, shall be designated exempt employees.[28] As provided for by law, exempt employees shall receive a monthly salary representative of payment in full of services rendered inclusive of required or voluntary extra hours worked. Those administrative or professional positions not meeting statutory eligibility for exempt status may also be salaried for reasons of internal consistency, but will be classified as nonexempt and thereby

---

[28]   Improper classification of employees into exempt status can expose employers to significant unpaid overtime liabilities. Additionally, such improper classifications can raise issues of the employer's failure to apply the proper policies and benefits due misclassified employees. Employers should, therefore, familiarize themselves with the FLSA and state law concerning the definition of exempt versus nonexempt employees or seek professional counsel to assure that such classifications are consistent with prevailing law. Employers would also be well advised to seek professional counsel concerning the consistency of exempt status job descriptions with the definitions of exempt employees; job titles alone are *not* sufficient!

eligible for overtime compensation as well as pay withholding for hours not worked. For purposes of payroll accounting, salaried/exempt employees will be calculated on the basis of a flat monthly salary, while salaried/nonexempt employees may be calculated on an hourly rate basis, or on an hourly rate equivalent to their monthly salary.

In either case, nonexempt employees will be compensated for actual hours worked and hourly credits earned such as paid time off, and will be eligible for overtime pay. Nonexempt employees will not be paid for time not worked unless such time off work is based on the use of such other compensatory employment benefits as vacation, holiday, or sick leave as described in this manual.

Salary and Wage Adjustments/Merit Increases

In addition to the *(Company's)* periodic revision of pay rates or ranges resulting from pre-vailing wage studies and other influential considerations, the *(Company)* is committed to the principle of compensatory recognition of employees who demonstrate meritorious performance. These merit increases in base compensation will be determined directly in conjunction with, and at prescribed times of, each regular employee's performance evaluation based on predetermined performance standards levels. An overall performance evaluation rating of *(satisfactory/average)* does not qualify for merit increase consideration. While such a rating is acceptable for retention of an employee's services, it is not meritorious in the sense of compensatory advancement in recognition of "consistent and enduring performance at varying degrees of excellence."[29]

To be eligible for merit increases up to and including the pay rate or range midpoint, employees must minimally have an overall performance rating above *(satisfactory)*, with at least one categorical rating of *(excellent/outstanding)*, and no categories rated below *(satisfactory)*.[30] Merit increase eligibility above the established pay rate or range mid-point will minimally require an overall rating of *(above satisfactory/exceeds standards)*, with at least three categorical ratings of *(excellent/outstanding)*, and no categories rated below *(satisfactory)*.

---

[29]   Employers should exercise caution in giving "satisfactory" or "above-average" ratings to an employee for merit pay purposes unless they are *clearly* demonstrated through the employee's *consistent* and *enduring* performance. The most essential reason for this is that the employer may subsequently find it necessary to take disciplinary action against an employee for reasons of performance deficiencies or infractions of the personnel policies that are performance related. In litigated cases where an employee has been terminated for any performance-related condition, the employer's defense becomes seriously compromised when the employee's attorney submits into evidence copies of past performance evaluations in which the employee was rated satisfactory or above. It therefore becomes important for employers to distinguish between the uses of performance evaluations in cases of pay-versus-retention decisions.

[30]   While it is true that performance evaluation systems remain an artform, it is imperative for employers to establish some clear standards (preferably written definition) of *performance levels* in establishing a relationship of one's performance to that of potential merit pay increases.

Alternative Policy: Merit Increases

In recognition of exemplary or above-average job performance demonstrated by employees during the year preceding their annual performance evaluation, the *(Company)* has established a pay incentive program that rewards commendable performance by granting merit pay increases. Supervisors who determine in the course of preparing the performance evaluation that an employee has demonstrated consistent and enduring superior performance, or has achieved an eligible rating for a merit increase, are to provide a specific written recommendation concerning the proposed amount of merit increase and its justification.

Final approval of the proposed merit increase will be subject to review by the *(Human Resources Manager/Personnel Committee)* to assure conformance with *(Company)* practices and uniformity of its compensation decisions. Approved merit increases will generally be effective for a minimum of one year, subject to a continuation of the employee's satisfactory performance, attendance, and conduct.

Part-Time and Temporary Employees

Regular part-time employees will receive base compensation in the hourly equivalent of the rate or monthly salary established for the same full-time classification or position to which they are assigned.[31] Such employees may be eligible for merit increase consideration in the same manner as full-time employees, provided that the part-time employee has worked the full-time equivalent number of hours in the present pay rate or range rate. Regular part-time employees working in a classification different from that of full-time employees shall have their base compensation rate determined by the *(Human Resources Manager)* prior to employment and internally consistent with the *(Company's)* existing salary/wage plan.

Temporary employees, whether full- or part-time will receive only a base compensation hourly rate equivalent to the established full-time rate for their assigned position, or a rate determined by the *(Human Resources Manager)* where the class or position is without precedence within the *(Company's)* structure.

Compensation upon Promotion or Demotion

Regular employees who are promoted to a classification or position with a higher rate or range may be placed in the new higher rate or range which is at least equal to a pay advancement of *(amount/percentage/or one range step)* over that held in their former

---

[31]   Here again, employers are vulnerable to Equal Pay Act violations where regular part-time employees are paid a different pay grade for work that is performed by similar full-time employees or part-time employees working under the same job description as full-time employees. Conversely, regular part-time employees may be treated differently in their pay considerations than is necessary for temporary part-time employees, but employers should be cautious of the duration and conditions under which they hire *temporary* employees whether full-time or part-time based on state law standards.

position.[32] Upon the effective date of promotion, the employee will be assigned a new anniversary date.

An employee who is promoted to a higher-paid position effective within *(thirty/ sixty/ninety (30/60/90))* calendar days of a merit increase anticipated by the *(Company)* due to the employee's performance in the lower position, may have the anticipated merit increase taken into consideration at the time of promotional recommendation for purposes of determining an equitable compensation rate in the higher position.[33]

Any regular employee who is demoted to a position with a lower pay rate or range will be reduced to the rate or range rate in the lower position as follows:

- Nondisciplinary demotions will be assigned to that pay rate the employee would have achieved in the lower position if the employee's service had been continuous in the lower position based on his or her original hire date, which will be retained.[34]

- Disciplinary demotions may be assigned any pay rate in the lower position that is at least one pay rate less than that received by the employee in the position from which demoted. The employee will also be given a new anniversary date effective upon the demotion date.

Compensation upon Position Transfer or Reclassification

Regular employees transferred from one position or classification to another position having the same or substantially similar duties and pay rate will be compensated at an unchanged rate and with an unchanged anniversary date. Transfers of employees to other positions having a lower or higher established base compensation rate or range must be treated in accordance with the promotion or demotion provisions in this manual.

The compensation of an employee in a position that is reclassified shall be determined as follows:

---

[32]   The employer may also want to state that pay must be "at least equal to that for the former position." In some cases, the promotional position can lead to benefit levels of higher maximum pay such as promotion from a nonexempt to an exempt position, but the employer may not want to increase the promoted employee's pay immediately because of the initial need by the employer to train the employee in the higher-level responsibilities.

[33]   Promoting an employee to a higher-paid position under the condition described here can demoralize a promotional employee who may be paid no more in the higher position than in the lower one if they had stayed in the lower position and received their next merit increase, if it would have been warranted.

[34]   Nondisciplinary demotions include a variety of situations where the employer or employee find that the performance or other circumstances in a particular position are not working out very well, yet the employee possesses attributes for successful performance in a lower-level position. For example, some employees promoted to a supervisory position may find that the responsibility or certain job conditions are not suitable to them, or this may be ascertained by the employer. In either case, it may be seen as mutually beneficial to allow the employee to transfer back or voluntarily demote, to their former position.

- If the position is reclassified to a class having the same pay rate or range as the previous class, and if the employee meets the requirements of the reclassified position, the employee's pay rate and anniversary date shall not change.

- If the position is reclassified to a class with a higher pay rate or range than the previous class, and if the employee meets the requirements of the reclassified position, then the employee's pay rate shall be unchanged or set at the rate nearest the former rate, and the employee will be given a new anniversary date.

- If the position is reclassified to a lower pay rate or range class, and if the employee is retained to occupy the reclassified position, the employee's pay rate shall be unchanged or set at the rate nearest the former rate, and the employee will be given a new anniversary date. If the employee's pay rate in the former position is greater than the maximum rate established for the lower position, the employee's pay rate will be frozen until such time as the rate or range of the reclassified position reaches the employee's frozen rate.[35] The employee's anniversary date will remain unchanged.

Compensation for Work in a Higher Position

It is the policy of *(Company)* to compensate employees for performing work in a higher position, to establish a system by which employees may receive pay comparable to the job factors that determine pay differentiation for each class of work in the *(Company)*.[36] The principle for temporary additional compensation for performing higher-level job responsibilities *due to operational necessity* is based on such considerations as:[37]

- The employee's ability and qualifications to perform the higher-level job responsibilities.

- Whether the employee would be required to perform routine work (ineligible) or a significant range of the higher job responsibilities.

- Whether the higher-level job responsibilities are in direct line and job scope of the lower position.

- The length of time necessary for an employee to perform at the higher job level.

---

[35]   This is called "Y-rating" an employee's salary, the effect of which is to freeze the employee's salary under this condition until the salary established for the new classification reaches or exceeds the employee's frozen salary.

[36]   This is also referred to as "interim assignment pay" or a temporary promotion. Employers should guard against the liability of potential Equal Pay Act violations by assigning employees significant higher-level duties and responsibilities for any substantial period of time without a commensurate increase in compensation, particularly in cases where the employee is assigned additional responsibilities wherein the whole job may now be viewed as similar to another position that has an established higher compensation rate.

[37]   Employers should make sure that all supervisory personnel know what "operational necessity" means. Examples might include vacancies due to pregnancy-related leave, time needed to refill a vacant position, covering peak work load periods, critical job assignments, and the like.

Authorization for an assignment to work in a higher position must be given in writing by supervisory personnel and approved in advance by the *(Human Resources Manager)*. The following shall prevail as the conditions of compensation for work in a higher position:

- Compensation in excess of an employee's base rate will not be authorized unless the employee is in all respects qualified to perform in the higher position and required to perform at least a substantial range of the more essential tasks of the higher position. Eligible employees shall receive additional compensation for the actual number of hours worked in the higher position.[38] However, if an employee is temporarily assigned to perform in a higher position, but such assigned duties are generally within the scope of his or her regular position, additional compensation will be considered unwarranted.

- Higher-position work assignments shall not have any application toward time-in-position considerations such as merit increases, promotion, layoff, or the like.

Overtime Compensation

It is the policy of the *(Company)* to require any employee to work overtime hours in order to meet special or unusual business operation needs beneficial to the *(Company)*.[39] However, exempt employees are ineligible for compensation resulting from these overtime work provisions. Further, it is the intent of this policy to specify the terms and conditions by which overtime compensation will be paid to applicable employees, and under what conditions overtime compensation is not payable. The basis for making such determinations will be the actual number of hours a nonexempt employee is required to work rather than payroll hours. Therefore, time off for any reason, even if the time off is paid for such absences as vacation, holiday, and personal leave, will not be counted in determining overtime compensation as these hours do not represent hours worked. In calculating overtime compensation, the employee's "regular" hourly rate of pay will be used rather than the employee's "base" hourly rate which may include add-on forms of pay such as bonuses, commissions, or special assignment compensation.[40]

---

[38] Some employers may want to require additionally that an employee work, say, five days, in the higher position before becoming eligible for additional pay. The theory here is that the initial five-day period is used for training the employee and for the employee's adjustment to the higher-level responsibilities.

[39] Most employers *assume* that all employees will understand the employer's authority to require overtime as necessary whether such a policy is written or not. In the absence of any specific written policy, employers are always subject to challenge regarding their authority or the conditions under which employees can be required to work.

[40] The distinction here is that often for payroll purposes, an employee may be shown as having either compensable hours on a particular day, but in actuality the employee may have perhaps worked only two or three hours. For example, an employee takes a vacation day and is shown on the payroll as having eight paid hours. The employee was also called in to work two hours after the employee's usual work schedule hours. Because nonworked compensable hours do not have to be

Incidental overtime, defined here as a less than fifteen-minutes nonrecurrent extension of the work schedule is not compensable. All other overtime as provided herein will be compensable in completed time increments of fifteen minutes.

All overtime must be requested or required in advance by supervisory personnel who shall attempt to provide affected employees as much notice time as possible, and who will schedule or assign overtime work as fairly and consistently as possible given the nature of work to be performed and employee capacities.[41]

Record Keeping   Eligible employees are required to record and report all incidents of overtime hours worked at the time such additional hours are worked. Supervisory personnel will review and record approved overtime hours at the conclusion of each pay period on the employee's time card or payroll time sheet.[42]

Overtime Rate   The regular rate of overtime pay is one and one-half times the employee's regular hourly rate. Eligible employees will be paid the regular overtime rate for all hours worked in excess of forty hours worked each workweek, provided that the employee actually worked the specified number of hours prior to working overtime hours.[43]

Time not worked, but incidental to overtime work such as travel to and from the work location or meal breaks, will not be compensable except as otherwise agreed to in writing.[44]

[40 continued]   figured into the calculation of overtime, the two hours the employee actually worked would be at the employee's straight-time hourly rate.

Also, the distinction of "regular" hourly rates and "base" hourly rates is an important one for employers calculating payrolls. If the employer uses base hourly rate as defined to derive an employee's overtime hourly rate, it will lead to an exaggeration or inflation of the employee's overtime rate over what it would be if the regular hourly rate were used. See "Hours Worked" and "Regular Pay Rate" checklists at the end of Chapter 12.

[41]   Labor commissions tend to view this circumstance as a matter within the control of the employer; that is, if an employer knew, or "should have known," the employee was working overtime without official permission, the employer typically is held liable for compensating the employee. It therefore becomes important for supervisors to ensure that employees do not work unauthorized overtime, and to authorize all necessary overtime in writing. While an employee may be subject to disciplinary action by the employer for disobeying the overtime work authorization rule, the employer must still pay for overtime hours worked by the employee.

[42]   Time entries on payroll sheets should be written in ink and it is advisable, though not required, to have individual employees sign end-of-pay-period time reports. Errors on completed and submitted payrolls can be corrected in the subsequent pay-period report.

[43]   The Fair Labor Standards Act requires overtime to be paid in excess of forty hours worked per week, while many states have additional requirements where employees must be compensated for over eight hours in a workday. If your state does not have the "over-eight" provision, it is not advisable to include it in your policy unless you wish to make it a voluntary provision. Having to satisfy only the FLSA requirement provides the employer with more flexibility in scheduling employees on a daily basis that may result in forty cumulative hours for the workweek and yet avoid the daily overtime liability.

[44]   A collective bargaining agreement or the employer's common past practice will supersede this exclusion, which is intended to clarify the overtime treatment of an employee's callback to work, an extension of scheduled hours, or work on unscheduled days. On the other hand, employers

Weekend Work   Employees who work on a Saturday or Sunday are not automatically eligible for overtime compensation. Work assigned on a Saturday and/or Sunday may be part of an employee's normal work schedule, thereby compensable only at the employee's basic pay rate.[45] Hours worked on weekend days will therefore qualify for regular or premium overtime compensation only if the hours worked on such days meet the standards cited.

Holiday Work   (Company)-recognized holidays as prescribed in this manual are days in which normal business operations will generally not be performed, will be considered time not worked but compensable at the employee's basic hourly pay rate commensurate with the employee's normal work schedule, and will generally be compensable for eligible employees who work on designated holidays at the overtime rate provided the employee has actually worked a minimum (two-thirds, three-fourths, etc.) of his or her scheduled hours in the workweek in which the holiday falls.[46]

Where a designated holiday occurs on an employee's regularly scheduled day off, and the employee works the holiday, the employee will be compensated for holiday hours worked at the overtime rate provided the holiday work hours are in excess of forty hours worked in the workweek in which the holiday falls. Alternatively, the employee may be scheduled a different day off during the workweek in which a holiday falls, whereby the employee would receive only the basic hourly rate for actual hours worked on the holiday unless such hours exceed forty hours worked for the workweek.[47]

Alternative Policy: Overtime Compensation

All nonexempt employees are eligible to receive overtime compensation at the rate of (one and one-half (1½)) times their regular rate of pay for hours worked in excess of (forty (40)) hours each workweek in accordance with federal law. Employees classified as executive, administrative, professional, or outside sales, based on legal definitions, are exempt from overtime pay, and therefore not covered by this policy.

All overtime worked by nonexempt employees must be approved in advance by the employee's supervisor. Overtime hours worked without supervisory approval may be regarded as a violation of (Company) policy and therefore subject to disciplinary measures.

---

[44] *continued*   should be aware that under most state workers' compensation laws, an employer is held liable for injuries sustained in connection with travel to and from work locations in connection with callbacks, work schedule extensions, and work on unscheduled days. This is commonly referred to as the "portal-to-portal" rule.

[45]   Barring a collective bargaining agreement or an employer's past practice to the contrary, there is no provision in the Fair Labor Standards Act that requires an employer to pay overtime compensation rates for work performed on weekends or holidays unless such work meets the standard definition of regular or premium overtime.

[46]   This policy is slightly more liberal than that required by the Fair Labor Standards Act but reflects the most common practice of employers in recognizing that some monetary reward should be extended to employees who work on holidays in addition to their regular work schedule of hours. Where an employer pays straight time for holidays, it would be foolish for employees to work for virtually nothing above what they would have received if they didn't work.

[47]   Rescheduling regular days off when they fall on a paid holiday is both legal and advisable for employers who wish to avoid costly overtime payments.

Employees who work approved overtime will record such hours on their *(time sheet or time card)* rounded to the nearest quarter of an hour. Overtime pay will be calculated on the basis of actual hours worked over *(forty (40))* in a workweek; therefore, paid time off such as vacation, sick leave, and holidays do not count as hours worked for the purpose of determining overtime pay eligibility.

Compensatory Time Off/Alternative Work Schedule (Optional)

Nonexempt employees may take compensatory time off in lieu of overtime hours worked under the following conditions:[48]

- The determination as to whether an employee will receive pay or paid time off shall be made by the employee based on supervisory approval.

- Compensatory time off (CTO) will be earned on the basis of one and one-half hour off for each overtime hour worked, up to a maximum of *(four/eight/sixteen or twenty-four (4/8/16 or 24))* CTO hours, beyond which the overtime will be treated as regular overtime pay.

- Accrued CTO hours must be taken by the employee, with approval of supervisory personnel, in the same payroll period it is earned. End of payroll period balances of CTO hours will be converted to regular overtime pay.

- Earned overtime hours to be taken as CTO must be reported by the employee to supervisory personnel, and supervisors must record the use of CTO hours on the employee's time sheet for payroll purposes.

- In calculating an employee's overtime pay, CTO will be treated as paid time not worked.

Compensation During Temporary Work Disability (Optional)

For compensation purposes, there are two types of temporary work disability: personal and work related.

Temporary work disability resulting from personal circumstances of injury, illness, maternity, or other disabling conditions creating an employee's absence are compensable based on the terms, conditions, and provisions of the *(Company's)* or employee's disability plan.[49] However, eligible employees may be allowed to liquidate part or all of any accrued forms of paid time off prior to, or upon exhaustion of, compensation benefits made available through the disability plan, upon written request to supervisory personnel.

---

[48]   Although it is generally inadvisable for employers to adopt CTO policies due to complex limitations by the FLSA and state laws, this policy is offered for those wishing to use it in states where it is a lawful practice and who so desire. You'll note a deliberate absence of a reference to exempt employees. If they were included, it could cast doubt on the very definition of exempt status. Exempt employees should therefore be dealt with informally on an individual basis for paid time off in the cases of unusual hours worked. As you may correctly surmise from reading the policy, CTO record keeping can become nightmarish.

[49]   Delete this section if the employer does not sponsor or provide a temporary disability plan based on personal disability (not to be confused with workers' compensation disability benefits, which are legally required by all states).

Temporary disabilities that arise out of, and in the course of, employment with the *[Company]* are compensable through the *[Company's]* workers' compensation insurance carrier based on specific amounts and provisions of state law. Employees so disabled must immediately report the details of such injury/illness to their supervisors, including their medical progress and the anticipated duration of disability. On a case-by-case basis where an employee reaches a point of physical recovery in which a partial resumption of work has been medically approved, the *[Company]* may allow an employee to return to work on a reduced workday schedule or to perform modified work activities.

Employees may not be allowed to return to work after a disability absence of more than _____ workdays, or where any absence is caused by a contagious condition of a threatening nature to others, without the written medical release of a qualified physician. The *[Company]* reserves the right to have such employees examined by a *[Company]* paid physician.

Employees who are found to abuse, or fraudulently use, these temporary disability provisions may be subject to disciplinary action, including termination.

Compensation During Attendance at Seminars, Outside Meetings, and Travel (Optional/Advisable)

Periodically, it may be necessary, desirable, or appropriate to the benefit of the *[Company]* and/or individual employees to attend or participate in activities outside the normal work location.[50] Such activities may include attendance at lectures, meetings, training programs, conferences, or specialized courses of instruction. Attending or participating in these activities may be either at the request of an employee or required by the *[Company]*, but in no case will it be regarded as an officially authorized activity until advance written approval has been granted by the *[Department Head]*. Employees seeking approval must submit a written request detailing relevant information upon which a decision can be rendered such as the date, hours, location, costs and expenses, nature and purpose of activity, and justification for attending.

This policy is not applicable to an employee's voluntary attendance in a course of formal educational instruction, or instruction that may generally lead to improved or upgraded job skills. Although the *[Company]* encourages all employees to self-initiate various methods and means of enhancing their job performance, particular skills, and promotional qualifications, such outside involvements will not qualify for hours-worked compensation unless the *[Company]* requests or directs the nonexempt employee's attendance.

Educational/Meeting Activities   Employee attendance at *[Company]*-approved seminars, lectures, conferences, business-related meetings, and training programs will be considered hours worked for nonexempt employees and compensable in accordance with the payment provisions contained in this manual for all employees.

---

[50]   In the absence of a policy/procedure concerning these compensable conditions, the employer may experience considerable confusion and irregular decisions in these circumstances and later find itself at the mercy of state labor commissioner interpretations.

Where the employee's attendance constitutes an expense to the *(Company)*, the employee will provide an advance itemization of known or estimated costs in connection with attendance, whereby the *(Company)* may pay in advance or reimburse the employee upon submission of receipts in reasonable form and amount. Customary expenses may include, but not necessarily be limited to, registration fees, materials, meals, transportation, and parking.

If an employee is advanced *(Company)* funds to cover expenses, the employee will be required to submit receipts and an accurate accounting of expenses within *(five (5))* working days after the employee's return to work. Company overpayments will be refundable by the employee, and underpayments will be reimbursable to the employee.

Travel/Travel Time   Travel costs in connection with approved and bona fide business activities will be paid by the *(Company)* where use of private or commercial transportation is necessary, and such payment will be on the basis of the least cost mode of transportation where there is a choice. The mode of transportation must be known to, and approved by, the *(Company)* by advance written notice.[51]

Where travel has been approved for use of an employee's personal vehicle, the employee shall incur necessary expenses to assure that the vehicle is in sound and safe operating condition and may be required to prove that the vehicle is properly indemnified.[52] In cases of an employee's business-related travel by personal vehicle, the employee will be reimbursed by the *(Company)* on the basis of a predetermined amount per mile, excluding customary mileage to and from the employee's residence and work location.

Travel time in connection with *(Company)* approved travel will be considered compensable hours worked for nonexempt employees as follows:

---

[51]   Nothing in this policy will or could limit the employer's liability for workers' compensation resulting from an injury/illness sustained in connection with job-related travel—even if such occurred when the employee was not directly engaged in business activities. The typical workers' compensation theory is that if an employee is injured in *any* connection with business that benefits the employer, or if the employee would not have been injured had the employee not been sent, the employer is held liable for providing workers' compensation benefits.

[52]   Many states have what is commonly called "joint and several" liability laws wherein a third party who sustains damage or injury as a result of an employee's action or negligence (e.g., running a red light) can bring a tort suit against both the employee and employer. Once damages have been established in behalf of the third party by the court, the third party is then free to seek relief by either or both parties, or the party who has the greatest ability to pay. In states where the joint and several liability law exists, it is not an uncommon practice for the third-party attorney to investigate the amount of insurance coverage held by the employee at fault as well as the employee's employer, the policy amounts of which are used to determine the amount of damages that will be sought by the third party's attorney. Consequently, it is prudent for employers who allow or require employees to use their own vehicles in connection with business travel to, in some way, assure that the employee's vehicle is in proper operating condition and insured in adequate amounts and types of coverage. Similarly, third-party attorneys may also file for damages under the theory of "negligent hiring/retention" by the employer. In defending such claims, it is important for the employer to be able to demonstrate "reasonable care" with regard to testing and background checking all new hires.

- One-day travel out of town or as part of the day's work activities will be counted as hours worked, excluding the employee's usual meal period and normal travel time to and from the employee's residence and work location where the day's travel starts and/or ends at the employee's residence.

- Overnight travel out of town will be counted as hours worked only for those hours in which the employee is engaged in direct travel to the destination, and the hours during which actual business is transacted for the purpose for which the employee was sent.

Payroll Periods and Records

The *(Company's)* payroll periods are from the *(first (1st))* to the *(fifteenth (15th)* and the *(sixteenth (16th))* to the *(last day)* of each month. Payroll periods are separate and distinct from the workday or workweek, which are time periods used to determine overtime compensation calculations to be entered on payroll records for each payroll period in which overtime is earned.[53]

Payroll records are to be prepared and promptly submitted by the *(Controller/Finance Manager or Department Head)* to supervisory personnel, or by persons authorized to do so by the *(President/General Manager)*. Such records will minimally contain the following entries in ink:

- The employees name and identifying number
- Payroll-period date
- Dates and hours worked at basic pay rate
- Dates and hours worked at overtime pay rate
- Dates and hours of leaves and absences
- Total payroll-period hours at basic pay rate
- Total payroll-period hours at overtime pay rate
- Date, title, and signature of person completing payroll record
- Date and signature of applicable employee(s)[54]

Payroll record errors found after submission by the person completing the record will be adjusted on the next payroll record with proper notations to explain the error and

---

[53] Employers should verify whether these time periods meet with state law provisions by obtaining qualified legal advice or contacting the nearest state labor commissioner's office. Employers may also want to change the payroll period to weekly rather than the provided semimonthly, although the semimonthly is the most common and less costly of the two.

[54] It is the absence or uncertainty of one or more of these payroll record entries that results in insufficient documentation of employer records in labor commissioner hearings on back pay or overtime claims. Employers would be well advised to keep clean, accurate, and easily read records on *every* employee—in ink!

adjustment. Under unusual circumstances of payroll record errors, exceptions to this policy may be authorized by the *[Human Resources Manager]*.

Alternative Policy: Payroll Time Reports

All nonexempt employees are required to complete payroll time *[sheets/cards]* provided by their supervisor, and supervisors will check the accuracy of entries on a weekly basis prior to signing approval. Entries on the time *[sheet/card]* should include

- The time the employee begins and concludes the work *[day/shift]*. Employees are cautioned not to commence work more than seven minutes prior to the designated starting time unless otherwise instructed by their supervisor.
- Regular hours worked excluding meal periods. Supervisors may additionally enter such payroll timekeeping information as overtime hours worked, absences, vacations, holidays, and other paid and unpaid status hours.

A nonsupervisory employee is expressly forbidden by the *[Company]* to enter any information or another employee's time *[sheet/card]*, or to falsify information on his or her own time *[sheet/card]*. Employees found to violate this policy will be terminated. Any errors discovered in an employee's time *[sheet/card]* are to be reported immediately to the supervisor, who will determine the manner and method of correcting legitimate errors.

Paydays and Place/Manner of Payment

Paydays will be on the *[seventh (7th)]* and *[twenty-first (21st)]* of each month following the close of the preceding payroll period.[55] All employees will be paid by the *[Company's]* bank draft, which will normally be made available to employees by *[11:00 A.M.]* on paydays at the employee's customary work location, or mailed to the employee's last known mailing address upon written request of the employee. If at any time an employee wishes to authorize any other person to receive his or her paycheck, the employee must submit such a written authorization to supervisory personnel.[56] Only in unusual or emergency circumstances will paychecks be authorized by *[Human Resources Manager]* for advance release to employees, and such circumstances will be few and narrowly interpreted to avoid specialized payroll processing.

Payroll Deductions and Attachments

Deductions from each employee's gross pay period earnings are of two types: mandatory and voluntary. Mandatory deductions are those required to be made by the *[Company]* by law, court order, or other legally compelling influence on payroll. Such deductions include state and federal income tax withholding, social security, and wage garnishments. Voluntary deductions are those requested by employees to be made on

---

[55]   In the case of weekly pay periods, the customary payday is the following Friday to allow time for proper recording, record keeping, and payroll processing.

[56]   It is inadvisable for employers to release payroll checks to anyone but the employee, even if it is another employee well known to the organization or the payee.

their behalf and may include such items as the employee's contributions to health care, optional pension or retirement plans, credit union or savings accounts, and charitable organizations.[57]

Mandatory deductions in accordance with applicable legal requirements will be made automatically by the *(Company)*. However, such mandatory deductions as *(state and/or)* federal income tax where the *(Company)* must rely on information provided by an employee, will be the sole responsibility of the employee to provide accurate information within legal limitations.[58]

Voluntary deductions will not be made without the employee's written request or authorization, and advance approval by the *(Human Resources Manager)*. Attachments made to employee paychecks by legal authority of wage garnishment, regardless of cause, will be regarded as a mandatory deduction in the amount, and for the time, specified in the order. Employees are discouraged from placing their personal financial matters into their employment relationship with the *(Company)*. Where such attachments become administratively burdensome to the *(Company)*, the affected employee may be subject to reimbursing the *(Company)* an amount commensurate to actual processing costs.[59]

The *(Company)* recognizes its obligations both to employees and laws that prohibit discrimination solely on the basis of wage attachments.[60] However, in cases where wage garnishments directly and detrimentally reflect upon the employee's job duties and responsibilities, or reflect upon the *(Company)* in a way that adversely affects its reputation or general business welfare, the employee may be subject to termination. Cases of this type will be reviewed by the *(Human Resources Manager)* to seek corrective measures prior to a termination decision and to ensure that all termination decisions are free of discriminatory reasoning.

Compensation upon Employment Separation

It is the policy of *(Company)* to provide final compensation to employees in a timely and accurate manner. Employees receiving final compensation who feel some error has been

---

[57]   Employers should seek the advice of qualified legal counsel on any further or more specific policy language concerning deductions, as the laws affecting taxes, other deductions, and wage and hour laws are complex and can vary widely from state to state.

[58]   This is intended to alert employees that if they wish to claim an unusual number of deductions on the W-4 forms, they personally will be liable for tax consequences—although in some cases employers have been ordered by the Internal Revenue Service to substantiate an employee's deductions (exemptions) or declarations or to modify them.

[59]   Most state laws allow the employer to recover administrative processing costs in connection with garnishments or where garnishments become repetitive and thereby costly to the employer. Check with your legal counsel or labor commissioner to determine treatment of this in your state.

[60]   Employers should exercise caution here. The federal Consumer Credit Protection Act, and many state discrimination laws, prohibit employers from terminating employees for single wage garnishments. However, the courts have generally recognized an employer's need to legitimately protect its business interests, including the termination of employees whose jobs require judgment on financial matters. This policy should provide documented evidence that the employer does not intend to use discriminatory judgment, but wants to establish a policy statement to alert employees to possible consequences of this situation.

made should immediately contact the *(Human Resources Manager)* to resolve the matter as expeditiously as possible.

Final compensation shall be inclusive, up to the hour and date of separation, and all hours worked, all forms of accrued but unused time off deemed compensable in this manual, and deductions made against such compensation including legally authorized setoffs against pay, which will be regarded as a voluntary deduction in consideration of the employee's knowledge and participation in such setoffs.

1. Discharged employees will receive their final paychecks within the time period, and in the manner, prescribed by law.[61]
2. Resigning employees who give a minimum of *(seventy-two (72))* hours' advance written notice will receive their final paychecks by mail to the last known address on the next regular payday, or in person if the employees so request.

In the event employment separation is the result of an employee's death, the employee's beneficiary as shown on *(Company)* personnel records shall be entitled to receive the employee's final paycheck, except where the beneficiary is a minor, in which case the *(Company)* may hold the employee's final paycheck until a legally proper recipient can be identified by the *(Company)*.

Alternative Policy: Compensation upon Employment Separation

Employees leaving *(Company)* service will receive their final paycheck within the period prescribed by law. Final pay will consist of all hours worked from the last pay period to the employee's last day and hour of work, and any form of accrued hours deemed compensable in this manual. The final paycheck may also be reduced by the amount or value of any setoffs allowable by law and normal deductions required.

Any property issued to the employee by the *(Company)* must be returned prior to or at the time the final paycheck is provided. Unless the employee asks to pick up the final paycheck in person, it will be mailed automatically to the employee's last known address on record. Returned paychecks will be held by the *(Company)* for a maximum period of *(thirty (30))* calendar days.

BENEFITS, LEAVES, AND HOLIDAYS

General Provisions and Applications

(Company) strives to provide the best, most equitable, and cost-effective benefits for employees in recognition of the influence employment benefits have on the economic and

---

[61] Here again, employers should check with legal counsel or labor commissioner to determine specific restrictions on final payment of wages, particularly as violations can, and often do, result in the employer's payment of penalties.

personal welfare of each employee.[62] Employees should likewise recognize that the total cost to provide the benefit program described herein is a significant supplement to each employee's pay and should therefore be viewed as additional compensation, paid in various benefit forms, in behalf of each employee.

Policies, provisions, and procedures that govern the *(Company's)* benefit program will apply to all regular full-time and part-time employees, whether exempt or nonexempt status, unless otherwise provided in a particular benefit plan. While some benefits may earn credit during an employee's probationary period, eligibility in many cases will not occur until employees obtain regular status, or other conditions of employment specified herein or contained in the benefit policy/plan booklets.

Proration and Cost Sharing of Benefits

Where employees work a regularly scheduled workweek of less than full-time, some benefits will be determined on a prorated amount of hours based on the employee's accrual rate.[63] For example, regular part-time employees will be credited with vacation and personal leave, but at a smaller accrual rate than that for full-time employees. Similarly, should an employee terminate employment prior to completing the next full year of employment based on the applicable anniversary date, the employee may be entitled to a prorated amount of pay in lieu of accrued vacation.[64]

Benefit costs have risen sharply over the years, particularly in the area of insurance plans. These include such mandatory insurance benefit plans as workers' compensation,

---

[62]   Employers should be aware that there are surprisingly few employment-related benefits that are lawfully required; however, as there are three very important such employment benefits set out in this section under the heading of Mandated Benefits. Beyond those, employment benefits predominately become a discretionary matter for employers, wherein the design, eligibility, entitlement, provisions, and employer contribution are a matter of employer discretion. As a consequence, these discretionary benefits tend to be varied and highly diversified in type. The contents of this section, then, sets forth the more common types of benefit plans and provisions found among the majority of smaller employers. Perhaps regrettably, recent studies on the matter of employment benefits have concluded that smaller employers are not immune to the role that a well-rounded benefits program plays for employees. Clearly, the availability of competitive health care and leave programs can be well worth the cost to the smaller employer in terms of avoiding costly turnover, absenteeism, and related problems.

[63]   This allows the employer to calculate any equivalency of benefits for those regular employees who work less than a forty-hour workweek. Although the employer does not have to provide equivalent benefits for part-time employees, it is becoming a more common practice for regular employees who work less than full time. Where applicable, this allows the employer to prorate the amount of the employer's contribution or employee's entitlement eligibility.

[64]   Again, the employer's willingness to compensate employees on a prorated basis when they separate employment, based on partial accrual of benefit credits rather than eligibility upon the completion of a full year of service, is a discretionary matter at this point in nearly all states. Here the wording of personnel policies and employee handbooks becomes critical, since the courts have recently reviewed a number of cases in which it was not clear as to the employer's intent on allowing prorated or total accrual (by year) of employment benefits when an employee terminates. This language takes the more liberal form which is likely to be the future thinking of the courts (i.e., if employees get paid for hours worked, then it follows that they should accrue benefits on the same basis).

Social Security, and unemployment insurance whose rates are controlled by law rather than competitive insurance providers. Discretionary benefits are those selected and controlled by the *(Company)* based on such considerations as cost, work force composition, operational efficiency, and desirability of benefit provisions. Where costs of discretionary insurance benefit plans exceed the *(Company's)* interest, ability, or willingness to pay the full premium rate to maintain a previous benefit level, employees may be required to share in the cost to continue such insurance plan coverage.[65] Additionally, should a sufficient number of employees desire a particular insurance benefit plan without contributions from the *(Company)*, such a benefit plan may be adopted at the sole discretion of the *(Company)* and participating employees will be required to pay the entire amount of the benefit premium through payroll deduction.[66]

Design and Modification of Benefits

The *(Company)* reserves the right to design provisions and to add, eliminate, or in other ways modify any discretionary benefits described herein where and when it is deemed in the *(Company's)* best interest to do so. Under most circumstances, there will be ample opportunity to provide employees with advance notice of such modifications, and to consider the effect of the decision.

Mandated Benefits

SOCIAL SECURITY

Employees and the *(Company)* are required to contribute toward federal Social Security benefits from the first day of employment. The amount deducted from an employee's wages is considered a social security tax used, together with the *(Company's)* contribution, to fund benefits. Employees need not apply for this benefit or payroll deduction—it is taken automatically by the *(Company)*. Both the employee's and the *(Company's)* contribution rates are established by law and represent a percentage of earnings. Social Security provides four basic benefit provisions consisting of retirement income, disability,

---

[65]   This clause introduces the prospect that it may become necessary for the employer to share costs of employment benefits, particularly health care–related programs with the employee, should such costs continue to rise at their former unprecedented rates, or should such costs merely exceed the ability/willingness of the employer to pay.

[66]   Because of the rather high costs of insurance benefits, many employers feel financially overextended in terms of their contributory involvement in such programs. However, some employers may find that a significant number of employees desire a particular insurance program, and are willing to pay for the entire cost of the plan, knowing that the employer can obtain such a plan at a lower cost through group coverage than the employees could individually. In these cases, it may be a prudent measure of good management to adopt such a plan and make it available for employees, contingent upon employee's paying the full cost. While there may be future repercussions on the employer for not playing a contributory role, as has been the trend in the past, it is nevertheless worth the employer's serious consideration to add such no-cost benefits. Should the employer's involvement in these no-cost programs become controversial in future years, it may be worthwhile for the employer to examine the prospect of moving benefits to a cafeteria plan as discussed in Chapter 27.

death, and retirement health care. Eligibility varies among the benefits, and entitlements are subject to individual circumstances too detailed for explanation here. Booklets explaining these details are available at your nearest Social Security office.

WORKERS' COMPENSATION

The *(Company)* pays the entire amount of the workers' compensation insurance premium that provides benefits to employees who experience injury or illness in connection with *(Company)* employment.[67] Eligibility automatically begins on the first day of employment. Benefit entitlements are governed by state law, and if employees have questions concerning their rights or benefit amounts, they should contact the *(Human Resources Manager or insurance representative)*, or the Public Information Officer at the state Workers' Compensation Appeals Board. Benefits available to employees injured on the job consist of the following provisions:

- Replacement income
  - Temporary disability
  - Permanent partial disability
  - Permanent total disability
- Medical expenses including doctor's visitation, treatment, surgery, drugs, and hospitalization.

Compensation entitlement begins on the first full day of hospitalization, or after the third day of absence due to the injury if an employee is not hospitalized, during which employees *(may/may not)* use accrued sick leave.

The timeliness of payments to injured employees is dependent upon the *(Company's)* ability to expedite injury reports through our insurance claims representative. Therefore, when an employee is injured, the employee and supervisor must complete an injury report form at the earliest possible time, and submit the form to the *(Human Resources Manager)*, regardless of how minor the injury may be.

UNEMPLOYMENT INSURANCE

Employees may be eligible for unemployment benefits upon termination of service with the *(Company)*, depending on state law and circumstances connected with termination. After leaving *(Company)* employment, the terminating employee can file an unemployment claim with the state employment office, which will explain the rights,

---

[67] Smaller employers may be interested to note that some states are "monopolistic" worker compensation states. That is, there is only one source of obtaining workers' compensation insurance as opposed to reviewing the rates and claims administration abilities of several different insurance carriers. Although workers' compensation insurance is generally calculated on fixed tables pertaining to the number of employees and the nature of their work, there are a number of other variables that go into the calculation of an employer's premium, such as the cost of past claims experience, estimated costs of administering claims, including the potential of litigated cases. For this reason, employers with, say, twenty-five or more employees may do well to examine these cost issues among various carriers in nonmonopolistic states.

benefits, and eligibility determination process provided by state law. This benefit is paid entirely by the *(Company)*.

Discretionary Benefits: Insurances[68]

GROUP HEALTH CARE PLAN

The *(Company)* makes available a health care plan for *(all/full-time/etc.)* employees and their dependents and contributes an amount equal to the cost of *(employee only, employee and X dependent(s))*. Benefits of this plan consist of routine medical care, hospitalization *(drugs, major medical expenses, dental, and a $X life insurance policy)*. Specific types of coverage and benefit payment schedules are described in the *(Company's)* health care plan booklet available to all eligible employees through the *(Human Resources Manager)*.[69]

To be eligible, regular employees must complete *(thirty/sixty/ninety (30/60/90))* days of continuous employment. Upon eligibility, employees may complete enrollment forms available through the *(Human Resources Manager)*. If an employee does not wish to enroll at the time of eligibility, and later decides to request enrollment, a verification-of-insurability form may be required from the employee's physician, and it is subject to possible rejection by the health care plan insurance carrier.

Health care benefit coverage under the *(Company's)* plan terminates the day after an employee leaves employment.[70] Conversion privileges to an individual plan may be

---

[68] One of the most complex laws pertaining to employment benefits is the Employment Retirement Income Security Act of 1974 (ERISA). The law is too complex for discussion here; however, employers should be aware that ERISA regulates fiduciary and disclosure responsibilities of the employer concerning any employment-related benefit. What this means in terms of policy manuals and employee handbooks is that employers should confine the language to eligibility and general entitlements as opposed to specific language that relates to precise benefits, particularly concerning insurance programs. That information should be contained in separate handbooks provided by the insurance carrier. Even then, these general insurance benefit provisions are subject to a rather wide range of plan design features, so the language that has been provided here is intended to express basic and optional plan provisions.

If an employer does make available a health care program for its employees, employers may want to take note of the existence of a federal law that requires employers with twenty-five or more employees to provide what is called a health maintenance organization (HMO) in those geographic regions where they are available. Simply stated, HMOs are prepaid health care programs whose services and facilities are governed by federal standards of health care, including emergency services, critical care facilities, and preventive health care services. If an HMO health care facility is not within a reasonable distance of an employer's business location, the employer is relieved of the responsibility to provide an HMO health program.

[69] Most health care policies acquired by smaller employers are "broad form" policies, wherein the carrier provides a package set of insurance benefits including medical, major medical, drugs, dental, life insurance, and sometimes long-term disability or vision care within the same insurance policy. Employers who intend to adopt a benefit program that includes these various elements may wish to examine the comparative cost of establishing separate benefits under separate policies from different insurance carriers.

[70] The common practice among insurance policies is to allow a thirty (30)-day grace period for a terminating employee to convert the policy to an individual plan. However, the language provided is intended to make it clear that the employer's contribution toward the terminating employee's benefits terminates the day after they separate employment.

extended to a terminating employee by the insurance carrier upon application directly to the carrier within a specified period following termination of employment. Some employees and/or their dependents may also be eligible for health plan extensions under the *(Company's)* group policy. Details of conversion and extension privileges are available through the *(Human Resources Manager)*.

Alternative Policy: Group Health Care Plan

Full-time regular employees are eligible to enroll in the *(Company's)* health care plan. Part-time regular employees may also enroll, but they will be eligible only for a proportionate amount of contribution by the *(Company)* to the premium rates. Premium rates are established by the insurance carrier and are subject to change—usually based on increased costs to provide medical services and the amount of services required by employees.

Eligible employees wishing to enroll or reenroll in the plan can obtain premium rate, benefit, and enrollment information from the *(Human Resources Manager/Personnel Department)*. Employees leaving employment who have been enrolled in the *(Company)* health care plan should contact the *(Personnel Department)* concerning possible opportunities to convert the plan to an individual policy or extend their existing plan.

HEALTH CARE PLAN EXTENSIONS

In compliance with federal law, eligible employees may have their health plan either extended during active employment periods in the event of their prolonged absence or made available to a separated, divorced, or widowed spouse and dependents in accordance with the following conditions, both of which require advance written notice to the *(Company)*.[71]

1. Any eligible employee who is terminated, except for gross misconduct, or who is reduced in their work hours having the effect of eliminating their eligibility for health plan benefits may apply to the *(Company)* for up to an 18-month extension of their health plan enrollment; or

2. Upon the death or divorce of an eligible employees, the employee's current spouse may apply to the *(Company)* for up to a *(three (3))*-year extension of coverage under the *(Company's)* plan. In the case of divorce, eligible employees are required to notify the *(Company)* *(sixty (60))*-days in advance so that the eligible spouse can be notified.

Where these allowances are made available to an employee, or to a divorced/widowed spouse and/or dependents, the policyholder will be required to pay the entire premium amount in a timely manner for the duration of entitlement and shall be required to inform the *(Company)* whenever conditions change, such as eligibility for other health plans under a new employer's benefit entitlements, that might effect eligibility to continue in the company's plan.

---

[71]   These are legally mandated conditions on all employers as a result of the Consolidated Omnibus Budget Reconciliation Act (COBRA). California employers must therefore allow employees and their dependents to remain on the company's group health plan under the conditions and provisions specified here.

STATE DISABILITY PLAN

The state offers a program for insuring the temporary disability of employees who are so disabled primarily because of nonwork-related injury.[72] State disability benefits provide qualified employees with partial income replacement for a prescribed maximum period of disability, and this benefit is funded by *(employees/employer/joint)* contributions through payroll deduction.[73]

All regular employees are eligible from their first day of employment, and continue so long as they remain in active service. Benefits begin from the *(first (1st))* day an employee is hospitalized, or after the *(seventh (7th))* day of the disabling injury if the employee is not hospitalized.[74] Descriptive brochures of the plan and benefit provisions are available through the *(Human Resources Manager)*.

Discretionary Benefits: Leaves

HOLIDAYS

The following holidays are observed by the *(Company)*, and all regular employees normally scheduled to work on these days will be given the day off *(with/without pay)*.[75]

Holiday	Date Observed
New Year's Day	January 1
Washington's Birthday	Third Monday in February
Memorial Day	Last Monday in May
Independence Day	July 4
Labor Day	First Monday in September
Veteran's Day	November 11
Thanksgiving Day	Fourth Thursday in November
Day after Thanksgiving	Fourth Friday in November
Christmas Day	December 25

---

[72]   Some states may not provide state-sponsored disability insurance plans, while many other states do, and they are often at a lower cost than private insurance plans. Those states that do provide disability plans often require that it be fully paid by employees rather than by the employer and that a majority of the employees voluntarily enroll in such a plan to initiate or terminate the plan. For that reason, it has been listed under Discretionary Benefits; however, it could as well be listed under Mandated Benefits. Employers would be well advised to seek competitive bids from both state and private insurance carriers if their interest is in adopting nonwork-related disability plans.

[73]   State disability plans typically require employees to pay for the entire plan; however, private insurance plans can require employer, employee, or joint contribution to the plan. Employers should therefore refer to the insurance policy or the insurance representative to determine who pays.

[74]   Benefit provisions can vary, however, this is the most common eligibility requirement.

[75]   The observance of, and payment for, holidays is completely discretionary on the part of the employer. Nothing in the Fair Labor Standards Act requires employers to observe a holiday, close for business, or pay employees on any specified holiday. However, employers would do well to seek advice on state laws that may minimally require observance of particular holidays for certain employers. Holidays observed or paid by employers who choose to adopt such a benefit are at the employer's discretion. Those listed are considered the most common holidays observed by employers large and small.

Holidays that occur on a Saturday will be observed on the preceding Friday, and Sunday holidays will be observed on the following Monday. Should a holiday occur during an employee's scheduled vacation, the employee may either receive a paid holiday absence for the day or extend the vacation period by the number of holidays occurring during the scheduled vacation period.

To be eligible for holiday pay, an employee must work the last regularly scheduled workday preceding the holiday and the first regularly scheduled workday following the holiday, unless the absence is approved by the supervisor, or the employee is on a paid-time-off status.

Nonexempt employees required to work on a scheduled holiday will be paid *(one and a half (1½))* times their regular rate for hours worked in addition to their regular holiday pay. A paid holiday not worked will not be credited as a regular workday for computation of overtime.

Alternative Policy: Holidays

(Company) recognized holidays will be posted at the beginning of each year. Regular employees will receive full pay for normally scheduled work hours on designated holidays, so long as the holiday occurs on a normally scheduled workday. Probationary employees are not eligible for holiday pay unless they receive supervisory approval to work on the holiday, whereupon they will be paid their normal rate of pay for hours worked.

Employees who would otherwise be eligible, but who are on a leave of absence, workers' compensation leave, or disciplinary suspension will not be entitled to pay for a recognized holiday. Eligible employees who are on vacation during the occurrence of a recognized holiday will have the day treated as a paid holiday and may extend their vacation by one day, unless the holiday occurred on a normally unscheduled workday.

ANNUAL VACATION LEAVE

The *(Company)* believes that employees and the *(Company)* alike benefit from scheduled time for each regular employee to enjoy relaxation and recreation, and to return to work in a revitalized condition. To provide for such absence without concern for pay continuation, the *(Company)* has adopted the following paid annual vacation leave plan.[76]

Eligibility   An employee's eligibility to use accrued vacation is based on the employee's anniversary date. Introductory employees are not eligible to take vacation, but will be given credit for accrued vacation hours once regular employment status is achieved retroactively to their date of employment.[77]

---

[76]   Vacation leave is not a legally required benefit to be given or paid by employers. However, it is a well-established and customary practice, and employees expect to have some reasonable amount of paid vacation time. Employers without such a program may have considerable difficulty in acquiring or retaining employees because of the prevalence of this benefit among employers today.

[77]   The most common practice for time-off benefits for introductory (both new and promotional) employees is to disallow their eligibility to use such benefits during the introductory period as a means of encouraging their presence during the period in which they are being evaluated for suitability to the position in which employed. Conversely, it is also common that these employees be allowed to accrue credit during their introductory employment that becomes retroactively available to them once they achieve regular status.

Accrual Eligible employees accrue vacation credit for each full month *(thirty (30) continuous calendar days)* of service in which the employee is actively in *(Company)* employment and in a paid status. Vacation credit will not be earned for any month in which the employee is on a leave of absence of disciplinary suspension, regardless of the number of workdays absent for these reasons.

Full-time employees, defined here as working a regularly scheduled workweek of *(thirty-five to forty (35–40))* hours, will accrue paid vacation credit as follows:[78]

Service Length	Monthly Credit Hours	Annual Vacation Days
New employee—end of year 4	6.67	10
Start of year 5—end of year 9	8.00	12
Start of year 10—end of year 14	10.00	15
Start of year 15	12.00	18

Regular part-time employees must normally work *(twenty to twenty-seven (20–27))* hours per week to be eligible for vacation credit equivalent to one-half the full-time rate, and part-time employees working a *(twenty-eight to thirty-four (28–34))*-hour scheduled workweek will accrue vacation credit at the rate of three-fourths the full-time rate.

Use Vacation may be taken in a single continuous period, in separate weeks, or in days. Under unusual, necessary, infrequent, or emergency circumstances, vacation time may be granted by the employee's supervisor in a minimum of *one*-hour increments. In keeping with the intent of the *(Company's)* annual vacation leave plan, employees will be required to use a minimum of five accrued and consecutive vacation days per accrual year.

Selection of vacation dates is subject to approval of the employee's supervisor with preference given to longer-service employees.[79] Vacation requests must be submitted to the supervisor in writing at least *(ten (10))* working days prior to the vacation start date unless otherwise approved by the supervisor. The supervisor will confirm or disapprove each vacation request, and will post the hours of vacation use on the employee's time sheet accordingly. Approved vacation requests and time sheets reflecting vacation use must be submitted to the *(Human Resources Manager or Payroll Department)* in a timely manner.

---

[78] Design of vacation accrual schedules is a matter of employer preference. The schedule provided here is common in recognition of approximate five-year progressions of employment service, including the concept that longer-term employees deserve greater benefits of employment. Another common variation of the vacation accrual schedule is to provide ten days of vacation during the first two to three years and increase by two to three days every three to five years thereafter.

[79] Some businesses, particularly manufacturing companies, close their entire facility for a one-to two-week period each year, whereby employees who have longer vacation time coming, take it on an as-requested basis at other times during the year. Other employers use an annual vacation schedule whereby employees must sign up for their vacations when the vacation schedule is issued at the same time each year. In such cases, appropriate language should be substituted for that provided.

Alternative Policy: Annual Vacation Leave

Regular employees accrue and are eligible to use paid vacation based on the scheduled service length established below. Probationary employees do not accrue vacation credit until they achieve regular status, then the credit is applied retroactive to the hire date. New employees may not use paid vacation leave until they have completed at least *(six (6))* months of continuous service.

Length of Service

First through end of year 4	10 days
Fifth through end of year 9	13 days
Tenth through end of year 11	18 days
Twelfth and additional years	21 days

A minimum of *(five (5))* vacation days must be taken consecutively. All additional vacation days must be taken in minimum increments of a whole day. Only scheduled vacation time that has been canceled by the *(Company)* can be carried over into the next year, if there is no opportunity to reschedule it in the same year.

Upon leaving *(Company)* service, employees will be paid at their prevailing rate for accrued but unused vacation time, provided they give *(two (2))* weeks' written notice or are not being terminated for misconduct. Conversely, vacation time used but not yet accrued will be deducted from the employee's final pay.

PERSONAL LEAVE

In establishing this policy, the *(Company)* has intended to provide a method of furthering the health and general welfare of regular employees, as well as establishing standards to ensure maximum and reasonable job attendance.[80] Therefore, *(Company)*-provided personal leave should not be viewed as a right to be used at an employee's discretion nor as a permissive level of absence. Rather, it is a privilege of paid time away from work duties where such absence is necessary in the following circumstances:

1. *Sick Leave—Self:* An employee's disabling injury, illness, or contagious condition threatening to other employees, that occurred away from the job setting, except when in connection with off-duty employment.[81]

2. *Sick Leave—Immediate Family Member:* The required or necessary medical care or doctor's visitation of the employee's immediate family defined as the employee's

---

[80]   This personal leave policy accounts for a variety of conditions that have in the past been the subject of separate policy provisions, including sick leave, emergency leave, personal disability leave, funeral and bereavement leave, and maternity leave. Recent trends have been toward taking this profusion of separate paid leaves from work and including them in one policy that deals with all forms of individual circumstances that can, and often do, arise in an employee's life during the course of employment.

[81]   Attention is drawn toward the exclusion of an employee's disability that resulted from off-duty employment, which is a condition that is frequently overlooked in policy language. If an employer is particularly concerned about the conditions that surround an employee's off-duty employment, it is suggested that the employer may wish to examine the off-duty employment policy included in Part 1.3.

spouse, child, parent, grandparent, or other dependent relative residing in the employee's household.[82]

3. *Funeral Leave:* To attend a funeral or deal with matters related to death, or critical illness/injury where death appears imminent, of a member of the employee's immediate family.

4. *Maternity Leave:* A female employee's pregnancy, childbirth, or pregnancy-related condition.[83]

In any case where the *(Company)* determines an employee's misuse or abuse of personal leave, the employee may be subject to discipline, including termination.

Eligibility Employees begin to accrue personal leave credit on the first of the month following their hire date. Introductory employees are not eligible to use personal leave, but will be given credit for accrued personal leave hours once regular employment status is achieved retroactively to the month in which credit began to accrue. Introductory employee absence due to illness or nonwork-related injury may have their pay adjusted to reflect an unpaid absence.

Accrual Personal leave accrues monthly for eligible employees.[84] On the first day of each successive month following completion of a month of continuous service, full-time employees will accrue personal leave credit as follows:

---

[82] Here again, the employer's willingness to define liberally the use of paid absence from work due to health-related problems of the employee and/or certain family members should be given careful consideration. Given the composition of today's work force, it may be reasonable for an employer to include the family members specified here; it is what most employees would regard as fair and reasonable, but employers should be very careful in defining immediate family members too vaguely, causing confusion and differences of interpretation.

[83] This provision should bring an employer's policy into compliance with federal antidiscrimination law pertaining to pregnancy, which essentially requires employers to treat pregnancy and pregnancy-related conditions like any other temporary personal disability of an employee. While employers are not required by law to have temporary disability benefits available to employees, if the employer does provide such a benefit by virtue of either allowable absence or paid time off, the employer must treat pregnancy like any other form of disability. When employers adopt separate maternity leave policy provisions in their personnel manuals, others reviewing the manual may suspect that pregnancy and related conditions may be treated in a different fashion from any other disability. Employers are reminded that the treating, or the *apparent* treating of one employee differently from other employees, is considered *prima facie* evidence of discrimination. Therefore, if an employer intends to adopt a personal disability policy relating to the availability of paid or unpaid time away from work, it would be wise to include pregnancy as a temporary disability condition in the same policy.

[84] Most sick leave policies provide accrual for all employees regardless of their length of service. However, the accrual rate provided here is being recommended not only to conform to the vacation accrual schedule based on service length, but also because of the combining of different personal leave conditions in this policy, and the simple fact that an accrual system based on length of service makes more sense in terms of employee motivation and morale concerning employment benefits.

Service Length	Monthly Credit Hours	Annual Personal Leave Days	Maximum Accumulation Days
New employee—end of year 4	5.33	8	16
Start of year 5—end of year 9	6.67	10	20
Start of year 10—end of year 14	8.00	12	24
Start of year 15	10.00	15	30

Part-time employees working a *(twenty to twenty-seven (20–27))*-hour workweek schedule will accrue at one-half the full-time rate, and employees working a *(twenty-eight to thirty-four (28–34))*-hour scheduled workweek will accrue at three-fourths the full-time rate.

The accrual of personal leave credit can be, and is encouraged to be, accumulated up to the established maximum number of days in the event of serious disability. Upon separation from *(Company)* service, accrued personal leave will not be paid in any manner.

Use   Eligible employees are to notify their supervisors promptly whenever the use of personal leave becomes necessary. Employees are expected to:

* Advise their supervisors of the specific reason for taking personal leave;
* Advise their supervisors of the probable duration of absence;
* Seek their supervisors' verbal or written approval to use personal leave; and
* Keep their supervisors informed of conditions during a personal leave absence, including requested medical verifications.

Personal leave may be granted in minimum units of *(one (1))* hour provided such time has been earned at the time of use. The use of any personal leave taken must be so noted on the employee's time sheet by the supervisor for each pay period in which time is taken.

At the *(Company's)* sole discretion, an employee using personal leave may be required to produce evidence (attending physician's statement, death certificate, employee's affidavit, etc.) to substantiate the reason for or length of personal leave. Where personal leave is taken due to health reasons, the *(Company)* reserves the right to require that the employee be examined by a *(Company)*-paid physician prior to returning to work to assure fitness for a resumption of duties, and the welfare of other employees.

If a legitimately absent employee exhausts his or her accrued personal leave, the employee will be required to use accrued vacation leave. Thereafter, the employee will be subject to a leave-of-absence request.

Should an employee receive disability insurance payments during a personal leave, the employee may only use that number of personal hours that, together with such insurance payments, would not represent more than full normal pay.[85]

---

[85]   The reasoning behind this policy statement is to discourage the opportunity for employees to earn more income during a period of disability than they normally would if they were working. The fact that an employer is willing to "supplement" any compensation made available through a disability insurance program should serve to relieve any anxieties the employee may have about serious loss of income during an unforeseen disability.

Alternative Policy: Sick Leave

All employees who are unable to report to work due to personal or other sick leave conditions are required to notify their supervisor at the earliest opportunity, but no later than *[one (1)]* hour after their scheduled starting time. Employees who must leave work due to illness or sick leave condition should likewise advise their supervisor. It is the responsibility of every employee to report the circumstances of the sick leave, recovery progress, and probable duration. Supervisors are responsible for verification, reporting, and record keeping of sick leave.

Regular employees are eligible to receive paid sick leave based on the case-by-case circumstances where such absence becomes necessary. Sick leave may be used for conditions related to the employee's personal (nonwork-related) injury or illness, the necessary medical care of an immediate family member, pregnancy-related medical needs, and required medical treatments.

Maximum paid sick leave entitlement will be *[six (6)]* days per calendar year, which may be accumulated to a maximum of *[twenty-four (24)]* days. Sick leave days earned in excess of *[twenty-four (24)]* but not used will be paid at one-half the employee's base hourly rate at the end of each year.

Sick leave benefits begin *[the first hour/on the second day]* of absence. Employees who exhaust their sick leave entitlement may continue their necessary absence by use of accrued vacation, and thereafter only by request for a leave of absence. Employees will not be compensated for accrued but unused sick leave upon separation from *[Company]* service.

In all cases of an employee's use of paid or unpaid leave for reasons of a threatening contagious condition, the employee will be required to submit a medical certification of fitness to resume work activities from a physician. Similarly, an employee on sick leave for *[three (3)]* or more days may be required to submit a physician's certification to resume work.

Employees found to abuse or fraudulently use sick leave will be subject to disciplinary action including termination. Failure of employees to follow these procedures may be treated minimally as an unexcused absence.

Alternative Policy: Funeral/Bereavement Leave

The death or imminent death of an employee's spouse, child, parent, or grandparent may warrant special consideration of paid absence from work on a case-by-case basis. Generally, the determination of whether an employee will be granted paid *[funeral/bereavement]* leave rather than other types of absence will be based on such factors as the employee's service length, performance history, and apparent hardship conditions.

Employees who wish to be considered for paid *[funeral/bereavement]* leave should complete a leave request form, providing ample details of the situation and number of days required, available from their supervisor. The supervisor, in consultation with the *[Department Head]*, will make a recommendation for paid leave, unpaid leave, or accrued vacation leave to the *[Human Resources Manager/General Manager]*. The type of absence approval will be entered on the employee's time *[sheet/card]* by the supervisor.

FAMILY LEAVE

Regular-status employees may be entitled to take an unpaid family leave for up to *[four (4)]* months in any *[twenty-four (24)]*-month period during their active and continuous employment with the *[Company]*.

Exclusions

1. Regular employees who are *(in the highest 10 percent of gross salary, the five highest-paid employees—whichever is greater)*.
2. Any employee occupying a position whose prolonged absence would cause an undue hardship to *(Company)* operations.
3. Where the request is to attend to the employee's child and that child's other parent is on a similar leave or unemployed.

Limitations

1. Family leave is limited to such conditions as the birth, adoption, or serious illness of the employee's child or to provide necessary care for the employee's spouse or parent who has a serious health condition.
2. Eligible employees must have at least one year of continuous service with the *(Company)* and be eligible under *(Company)* policies for other employment benefits.

The length of family leave granted shall depend on the nature and extent of the employee's family member situation based on a case-by-case assessment of each leave request and supporting facts. Should a leave of less than *(four (4))* months be granted, the employee may request additional leave time under this provision, so long as such total leave does not exceed four months in any *(twenty-four (24))*-month period, and that such additional requests otherwise meet the standards of this policy.

Eligible employees requiring such a leave should submit a written request to their immediate supervisor as far in advance as possible. Such leaves shall not be considered authorized until the requesting.

JURY DUTY

Employees are to notify their supervisors promptly upon receipt of a jury summons and subsequent notice of selection to serve as a juror. Employees so required to provide this community service will receive their regular rate of pay for normal hours worked, up to a maximum of *(thirty (30))* workdays for this occasion of absence, provided the employee submits evidence of the summons and selection notice.[86] Paid absences for jury duty must be so noted on the employee's time sheet by the supervisor for each pay period in which this form of absence occurs. Employees will be allowed to retain any mileage and other compensation paid by the respective court jurisdiction.

MILITARY LEAVE

An employee who enters active military duty in a branch of the U.S. Armed Forces will be granted an unpaid military leave for that period of time in which reemployment is

---

[86]   Employers are typically required by state law to release an employee without prejudice to serve on jury duty. Federal and most state laws do not require an employer to provide normal compensation while employees are serving on jury duty, yet it remains the most common practice among employers, including smaller employers, particularly where jury duty is for a short period of time.

protected by law.[87] Such employee will be eligible for reemployment to the same or equivalent position held prior to the leave, provided the employee applies to the *[Company]* for reemployment into the former position within *[ninety (90)]* days from the date of military release, and unless it would present an unreasonable burden for the *[Company]* to do so.

If reemployed to a former position held, returning employees will be entitled to the same seniority, status, and pay they would have received had they not entered military service. Additionally, employees returning from military service may be terminated from reemployment only for just cause during their first year of reemployment.

LEAVE OF ABSENCE

Regular employees may request, subject to the sole discretionary approval of the *[Company]*, a leave of absence without pay[88] or employment benefits for a period not to exceed *[three (3)]* months. Requests for a leave of absence should be submitted in writing to the supervisor as far in advance of the anticipated leave date as possible. The leave request must be dated, signed by the employee, and state the reasons, circumstances, duration, and location of the employee during leave. The supervisor will submit his or her recommendation to the *[Department Head or Human Resources Manager]*, who will approve or disapprove the leave, and so notify the employee through the supervisor. Extensions of an initial leave of absence must be requested in the same manner, but will additionally require the approval of the *[President/General Manager]*.

During a leave of absence, employees will be responsible for either maintaining or discontinuing any employment-related discretionary insurance benefits.

Upon expiration of a leave of absence, the employee may be reinstated in the position held, or an equivalent one, at the time leave was granted if such a position is available. An employee who fails to report promptly for work at the expiration of a leave of absence, or who applies for and receives unemployment insurance while on leave, will be considered to have voluntarily resigned.

Upon returning from a leave of absence for *[thirty (30)]* days or more, the employee's normal *[anniversary]* date for performance and pay review will be advanced by the number of days absent.

---

[87]   Federal law requires an employer's compliance with the provisions specified in this policy, whether or not an employer adopts it as a policy matter. Employers should consider adopting such a policy provision in their basic policies manual to avoid confusion should the situation ever arise.

[88]   Here again, employers are not required to adopt nonpaid leave of absence policies, but in its absence, employers may encounter more than one situation in which an employee does not have available paid time away from work, yet has a condition requiring an absence from work longer than available paid leave, and wishes to be considered entitled to resume their employment after such an absence. While some employers may not be too fond of this policy, particularly concerning a marginal performing employee as opposed to the employer's congeniality to accommodate good performers, either case requires policy guidance. Furthermore, the decision-making process that goes into authorizing leave of absence should focus primarily on those conditions specified in the language given (i.e., whether or not the organization's business operations can accommodate the waiting of the return of this particular employee) rather than the particular performance level of the requesting employee.

PERFORMANCE EVALUATION AND PROMOTION

Performance Policy and Standards

It is the policy of the *(Company)* that regular reports be made as to the competence, efficiency, adaptation, conduct, merit, and other job-related performance conditions of its employees. To accomplish a meaningful performance evaluation system upon which the *(Company)* can continuously monitor the effectiveness of its operations, it will be the responsibility of the *(Human Resources Manager)* to determine performance standards, methods, and procedures and to assume overall responsibility for a performance evaluation system. It is also the responsibility of all supervisory and management personnel to provide reasonable training of employees; to assign, direct, control, and review the work of subordinate employees; to make efforts to assist employees in correcting deficiencies; and to evaluate employees objectively for their performance during the evaluation period.[89]

The preparation and use of employee performance evaluations are intended for the mutual benefit of the *(Company)* and its employees in terms of decisions related to such employment conditions as training, merit pay increases, job assignments, employee development, promotion, and retention. Therefore, performance evaluation reports should be used primarily to identify specific levels of appropriate standards being performed, to acknowledge the merit of above-standard performance, and to prescribe the means and methods of correcting deficiencies to a required level of performance.

Initial/Introductory Employment Evaluations

Each employee will receive a formal performance evaluation at least *(three (3))* times during their initial/introductory employment period as a means of determining such job characteristics as adjustment to employment conditions, integration into the *(Company)* work force, job learning progress, attendance, and any other feature of the individual's job that is significant to retention decision making and the prospects of job success. During this period of employment, each employee is to receive close supervision, instruction, review of work, training, and any other guidance that is supportive of the employee's opportunity for success on the job.[90]

The final introductory period evaluation should be completed and submitted to the *(Department Head)* at least *(five (5))* working days prior to the conclusion of the employee's introductory period. Upon the signed authorization of the *(Department Head)*, the applicable employee will be given a copy of the final evaluation report as confirmation

---

[89]   Too often, employers overlook stating the purpose or intent of conducting annual or other performance evaluations. No doubt there are many other reasons for conducting performance evaluations, but this statement at least suggests to employees that the employer has an interest in the effectiveness with which work is done, be it cost, time, method, or other typical measures of performance.

[90]   Let's not forget that the reason we hire and promote employees is to contribute to the success of the organization. It is therefore reasonable for employers to initiate certain measures during the employees' trial period to ensure maximum opportunity for their success.

of the *(Company's)* intent to continue his or her at-will employment as a regular employee rather than as a selection decision. Following completion of the employee's introductory period, formal performance evaluations are to be completed upon the employee's anniversary date each year, or at other discretionary times when formal evaluations become important for the recording of performance information.[91]

Annual Performance Evaluations

Annual reports of each employee's performance during the preceding year are to be completed by supervisory personnel and discussed with the *(Department Head)* prior to presentation to the employee. The approximate date for completing and submission of the annual evaluation will be based on each employee's anniversary date. The rating supervisor will provide the employee with a copy of the evaluation report at the time of discussion with the employee. A completed, signed, and dated copy will then be submitted to the *(Human Resources Manager)* for placement in the employee's personnel file.

Where rating supervisors have identified characteristics of an employee's performance needing improvement, the supervisor should be as specific as possible in describing the deficiency, and the ways and means of improving to an acceptable level. Supervisors are therefore entitled to retain a copy of each of their employee's evaluation report for the purpose of follow-up to any actions required, or for reference in general.

Alternative Policy: Performance Evaluation

(Company) maintains a policy of evaluating the job performance of its employees as a means of measuring efficiency and effectiveness of our operations, providing employees with meaningful information about their work, and aiding the *(Company)* in making personnel decisions related to such areas as training, compensation, promotion, job assignments, retention, and long-range planning of our operations. Evaluation of employees is intended to be participatory in nature, involving the employee's input as much as that of the rating supervisor, thereby helping employees to contribute to the betterment of the *(Company)*.

During the initial year of employment, employees will be evaluated at least twice: once within the *(90-day/6-month)* probationary period and at the conclusion of their first year. Thereafter, evaluations will be conducted annually or more frequently, as deemed appropriate by supervisory personnel.

Among the factors evaluated during formal performance reviews are the employee's quality and quantity of work, work habits, interpersonal relations, and adaptability to job conditions. Each employee is to be given an opportunity to meet with the evaluating supervisor to discuss openly and candidly the evaluation before it is finalized, whereupon the employee will be given a copy of the completed form.

Where an employee has received deficiency ratings in any category or aspect of work that represents a significant area of job responsibility, the evaluating supervisor may recommend specific corrective action to the *(Department Head)* and notify the employee accordingly.

---

[91] This language reinforces the concept that the introductory period is intended as a final selection tool, as opposed to regular employment, which remains "at will" thereafter, and further serves as a reinforcement of the employer's at-will employment policy.

Discretionary Performance Evaluations

When, in the opinion of supervisory or management personnel, there arises a marked change in the performance of an employee that is not disciplinary in nature, an unscheduled performance evaluation can be completed in the same manner as an annual report. Typically, discretionary performance reports are completed, reviewed with the employee, and placed in the personnel file as a means of formally recognizing the need to correct significant declines in an employee's performance.[92]

Review with Employee

Each formal performance evaluation will be thoroughly discussed with the applicable employee to point out both areas of successful performance and areas that need improvement, or that are unacceptable. Employees are to be encouraged to comment about their work performance, in writing or verbally, and to discuss working conditions and offer suggestions for improving business operations.[93]

The employee should sign the performance report to acknowledge awareness of its contents and discussion with the rating supervisor. The employee's signature does not necessarily mean that the employee fully agrees with the contents of the report, and the employee may so state on the form before signing.

Effects of Substandard Rating

A substandard rating, as applied to performance evaluations, means any rating below the rating level of *(satisfactory/average/standard)*. Employees receiving a substandard rating or ratings may have their employment conditions modified in the following manner:

---

[92]   It is very important that employers specify in their policies that they retain the right to do performance evaluations at other than regularly scheduled times. This provides an opportunity for employers to document notable deviations in performance levels or characteristics early as a means of documenting specific performance deficiencies in the ways and means to correct them. Further, should the particular performance deficiency not be corrected, or correctable, within acceptable limits, the discretionary evaluation can serve as important documentation when it comes time to terminate the services of such an employee. The intent, however, is primarily that of bringing to the employee's attention a performance decline and the ways and means to correct it. It is hoped that the problem will be resolved in this way and that disciplinary measures, including termination, will not have to be considered.

[93]   Too often, employers fail to sit down with an employee and go over the performance evaluation in some detail. This can be a mistake of monumental proportions, if in fact the employer truly expects its employees to believe in the credibility and usefulness of evaluations. In the absence of such an opportunity for the employee to participate in a discussion of the particular performance measures, it is likely that the employee will regard performance evaluations as suspect, if not completely invalid.

- Ineligibility for promotional consideration until the deficiency is corrected
- Withholding of a merit or performance-based salary increase for which the employee may have been eligible, until the deficiency is corrected[94]
- Transfer to a comparable position or demotion of an indefinite duration
- Termination

Specific action that may occur as the result of a substandard rating(s) will depend on, but not be limited to, such considerations as the weight or significance of the evaluation category compared to the importance of other aspects of job performance, and the length of time pertinent job factors have been observed by the rating supervisor.

Employees receiving substandard ratings will be reevaluated within *[three (3)]* months to document the particulars of progress in deficient categories unless the rating has resulted in transfer, demotion, or termination. If the employee's performance in the deficient categories has improved to at least a *[satisfactory/average/standard]* rating, while maintaining acceptable performance in other performance categories, the *[Department Head]* may recommend the implementation of any merit or performance pay increase otherwise due and/or restoration of promotional considerations.

Promotion Policy

It is the policy of the *[Company]* to promote employees to vacant or new higher-level positions when qualified employees are available or deemed suitable in all respects, and where it is determined to be in the best interests of the *[Company]* to do so. In such cases, the promoted employee will be assigned a new anniversary date effective upon assumption of the higher position responsibilities and will be required to serve a probationary period of employment in the higher position.

Promotional Evaluations

Employees promoted to higher positions will receive at least *[one (1)]* formal performance evaluation during the course of their promotional introductory period. The evaluation will

---

[94]   The annual performance evaluation characteristically serves as the catalyst for the granting of pay increases. Conversely, employers should give consideration to the consequence of an evaluation where there are substandard measures of performance. Again, the intent is not to discipline but rather to identify and correct deficient performance of employees. Some attention does need to be given to what happens if an employee is evaluated in one or more rating factors as substandard. The language provided here should give employers some ideas about ways in which low performance ratings can be dealt with when they are based on differing conditions of substandard performance. For example, if an employee receives a substandard rating and a rating factor that is present but not significant to the employee's overall job, the employer may not want to initiate any of the conditions cited here, but rather focus on improving the performance in that category. However, where the performance deficiency is significantly weighted to the employee's overall job, the employer may want to withdraw temporarily certain privileges or benefits otherwise enjoyed by employees who perform well until the deficiency is corrected through specific means.

carefully consider the nature, scope, and detail of the promotional position, and in what manner and circumstance the employees are adapting to all conditions of the position.

As it is the intent of the *(Company)* that employees be successful in all their work-related endeavors, promotional employees should receive the support, guidance, encouragement, training, and direction of senior personnel in the most effective way of contributing to the employee's adaptation to the promotional assignment.

Retreat to Former Position

The *(Company)* recognizes that the responsibilities and requirements of higher-level positions may not prove suitable to a particular employee so promoted or to the *(Company)* as determined by the performance results of the promoted employee. In the event a promotional assignment is found unsuitable by either the employee or the *(Company)*, consideration will be given to allowing the promoted employee to retreat to a former or comparable position for which the employee possesses demonstrated skill, knowledge, ability, and interest.[95] If no such retreat position is available, the promoted employee may be subject to termination with the opportunity to be rehired at a later time.

---

[95]   This policy gives promotional employees peace of mind by assuring them that they can move back into a former position should either the employee or employer decide that performance in the higher position during an introductory period is not to either's expectation. The absence of a retreat policy under conditions of promotion serves to discourage employees from seeking such opportunities as it ultimately places them at risk when they accept such a position. On the other hand, employers must give consideration to how they will deal with the employee hired to fill the vacancy of the promoted employee. Under such circumstances, the employer may do well to inform employees who are hired to fill positions previously occupied by a promoted employee that their continued employment may depend on the promoted employee's successful completion of an introductory period and his or her acceptance to regular status in the higher position.

TRAINING, SAFETY, AND HEALTH

Employee Training Policy

It is the belief of *(Company)* that training is an integral part of the success and efficiency of the *(Company's)* operation and instrumental to employee development within their jobs and in preparation for career advancement.[96] Training is therefore viewed as a shared responsibility of management and employees to accomplish the mutual benefit of an increasingly skilled and efficient work force.

Responsibility for the development of employee training programs is assigned to the *(Human Resources Manager, President/General Manager)*, who will be reviewing training needs at regular intervals to assure that effective training is accomplished within the *(Company's)* financial resources and training priorities. Such training programs may include lectures, demonstrations, reading assignments, or such other methods as may be instrumental in broadening the skill and knowledge of employees in the performance of their respective duties.

Responsibility for vocational training and observance of safe work practices is shared equally by each employee. In this regard, employees are responsible for attending, learning, and applying the information provided by in-service training and will be responsible for self-initiation of that training outside the work environment that could reasonably lead to, or be required by, the standards for promotional employment opportunities.[97]

Payment for Training

Training programs authorized or required by the *(Company)* shall be paid by the *(Company)* unless otherwise specified by the *(Human Resources Manager or Department Head)* prior to an employee's participation in such training. Payment for these training programs is separate and distinct from the compensation paid to employees in the form of salary or wages.

Employees may be authorized to attend training programs during scheduled working hours subject to the approval of their *(Supervisor or Department Head)*. When the needs of the *(Company)* so require, the employee may be directed to attend training programs, meetings, or conferences as part of the vocational training required of the position. In such cases, attendance may be mandatory, and reasonable *(Company)* payment for meals, lodging, travel, and associated expenses may be authorized.

---

[96] The existence of an effective training program is instrumental to a business's keeping pace with competitive businesses, as well as with other employers who vie for the organization's more talented work force. Also, the presence of an employer's training program tends to give employees a sense of employer interest and involvement in their careers and produces a more interested work force.

[97] It is important for employees to understand that employer-paid training that provides new knowledge should be applied to the job. In this regard, some employers make it a practice to have employees complete a brief summary of their learning experience at training seminars and conferences and to show how this information can enhance their jobs.

Employee Health and Safety Policy

It is the policy of the *(Company)* to provide for the continuous development, implementation, and maintenance of an ongoing program that assures a healthy and safe work environment for all employees. Employees will be held responsible at all times to observe and practice the highest possible standards of health and safety in carrying out assigned duties.

It will be the responsibility of the *(Human Resources Manager)* to manage the *(Company's)* safety program, including record keeping and processing of injury reports, safety records, and safety training. Such responsibility may be conducted independently or through cooperative efforts of others.[98]

Supervisory personnel will:

- Be responsible for the enforcement of safety rules among employees under their supervision.

- Be responsible for familiarizing employees with the hazards of the job to which they are assigned and instruct their personnel in the safe methods of performing the job.

- Periodically review the work practices of subordinate employees who work under their charge to ascertain that they continue to work in a safe manner, and in accordance with the safe practices covering specific work.

- At the end of each workday, inspect work areas for proper housekeeping, for fire or other hazards, and for safe condition.

- Report all injuries promptly to the *(Human Resources Manager)*.

Alternative Policy: Employee Health and Safety

The health and safety of employees and others on *(Company)* property are of the utmost concern. It is therefore the policy of the *(Company)* to strive constantly for the highest possible level of safety in all activities and operations, and to carry out our commitment of compliance with all health and safety laws applicable to our business by enlisting the help of all employees to ensure that public and work areas are free of hazardous conditions.

The *(Company)* will make every effort to provide working conditions that are as healthy and safe as feasible, and employees are expected to be equally conscientious about workplace safety, including proper work methods, reporting potential hazards, and abating known hazards. Unsafe work conditions in any work area that might result in an accident should be reported immediately to a supervisor. The *(Company's)* safety policy or practices will be strictly enforced, including possible termination of employees found to be willfully negligent in the safe performance of their jobs.

If an employee is injured in connection with employment, *regardless of severity of the injury*, the employee must immediately notify the supervisor, who will see to necessary medical attention and complete required reports. In any case of serious injury, employees are to receive prompt and qualified medical attention followed by the filing of necessary

---

[98]   Under the federal Occupational Safety and Health Act (OSHA) and most state OSHA laws, supervisors now possess a legal responsibility to oversee and ensure the safety of the work environment, methods used, and the establishment and enforcement of specific safety rules.

reports. Should an injury prevent an employee from returning to work for more than *(two (2))* days, the *(Human Resources Manager/workers' compensation carrier)* will notify the employee of employment benefits under this condition.

Smoking[99]

The *(Company's)* interest in establishing this policy is not based on moral judgments, nor with the specific intent to deny one group of employees their rights over other employees. In workplace conditions, however, the *(Company)* claims a greater right, and that is to establish such controls and safeguards as deemed in the best interests of the *(Company)*.

The *(Company's)* interest in this matter is governed by three operational considerations:

1. Fire insurance premiums and costs related to fire damage including the potential for layoffs and business disruption
2. The health and safety of employees including health-related absences
3. The comfort and convenience of others visiting the *(Company)*, and the image of the *(Company)* created by an appealing environment

The following, then, is to be observed by all employees concerning smoking and nonsmoking locations on *(Company)* premises:

- *General No-Smoking Areas:* The lobby/reception area, any location visible to the public, elevators and stairways, corridors, and meeting rooms, except where there is unanimous consensus to permit smoking.

- *Posted No-Smoking Areas:* Designated areas in the employee lounge, the computer room, locations where there exists the real or potential hazard for fire or explosion, and private offices at the occupant's discretion.

- *Smoking-Permitted Areas:* Private offices not within public view, designated areas in the employee lounge, rest rooms, and meeting rooms where there is no objection.

Failure on the part of employees to comply with these standards may result in disciplinary action.

---

[99]   Policies governing smoking in the workplace are more frequently being included in those controversial issues requiring employers to regulate a heretofore-considered self-regulating condition of employment. Employers, and many counties where regulatory smoking laws are being enacted, can no longer sidestep the issue of the employer's obligation to control and maintain the health and safety of the workplace. The language provided here is an attempt to establish reasonable control measures, yet preserve the "rights" of smoking and nonsmoking employees. Central to a policy on smoking in the workplace is the need for the employer to eliminate controversy before it arises. If it does arise, the employer will ultimately have to step in and construct resolutions on a case-by-case basis. At present it is not unlawful for an employer to establish an entirely smoke-free workplace and work force; however, it may be in the employer's best interest to notify employees and prospective employees if this course is chosen.

General Safety Rules

The following general safety rules will apply in all *(Company)* workplaces. Each work unit may prepare separate safety rules applicable to the specific nature of work in their area but not in conflict with these rules.

1. No employee will be assigned to work under unsafe conditions or with unsafe tools or equipment. In the event that such a condition develops, it will be immediately reported to the supervisor, who will determine and initiate corrective action if necessary.[100]

2. Employees should pay strict attention to their work. Practical joking and horseplay will not be tolerated.

3. Warning signs and signals posted to point out dangerous conditions are to be obeyed by employees.

4. Employees will not take shortcuts in, or over, dangerous places.

5. Extreme caution should be exercised by employees operating any type of power equipment.

6. Employees should not jump from truck beds, platforms, fences, or other elevated places unless absolutely necessary to the performance of duty.

7. Because of the hazard inherent in running, employees should refrain from running unless it is absolutely necessary to the performance of duty.

8. Employees will use safety equipment appropriate to the job, such as safety glasses, gloves, toe guards, and hard hats, if required or appropriate to the work performed.

9. Employees will avoid wearing loose clothing and jewelry while working on or near equipment and machines.

10. All accidents, regardless of severity, personal or vehicular, are to be reported immediately to the supervisor.

11. Operators and passengers in a business-use vehicle equipped with seat belts must wear them when the vehicle is in operation, and all employees operating vehicles will observe all local traffic laws.

12. In all work situations, safeguards as required by state and federal safety orders will be provided.

General Safety Precautions

The following are some common accidents and their causes. Each employee, supervisor, or other involved person should survey the work area and work procedures frequently to eliminate these and any other unsafe condition.

---

[100] If any of the safety rules listed are not applicable to a particular business, they should be eliminated or substituted for similar rules that are more appropriate to the industry type. In either case, for purposes of general information, as well as future enforcement of safety rules, it is advisable for employers to include a section similar to this in their personnel policies.

1. *Falls:* slippery surfaces, uneven walkways, broken or missing railing on steps or landings.

2. *Strains:* improper lifting techniques.

3. *Falling or Moving Objects:* improper storage of equipment.

4. *Striking Against Dangerous Objects:* drawers left open and improper disposal or storage of equipment.

5. *Electrical Shock:* worn-out equipment, plugs, cords, or ungrounded equipment.

6. *Vehicles:* seat belts not used, excess speed, backing, brakes, signals, and so on.

7. *Chemical Injury:* improper knowledge of safety procedures or personal protective equipment not used.

Reporting Work Injuries

Employees who are injured on the job, or whose injuries are directly related to the performance of job duties, should report all injuries to their supervisors immediately, regardless of how minor the injury may be. If medical care is needed immediately, supervisors should assist their employees in getting the necessary medical attention promptly, after which the full details of the injury are to be reported to the *(Human Resources Manager)* so that payment of medical and other benefits provided by law can be initiated in a timely fashion if circumstances warrant.[101]

Should an employee experience a disabling work injury, the nature of which necessitates an absence from work, the *(Human Resources Manager)* or the *(Company's)* workers' compensation representative should provide the injured employee with information concerning his or her lawful benefits. Employees having questions concerning the payment of workers' compensation benefits are encouraged to contact either of these individuals.

---

[101] Employers can avoid the penalties often associated with workers' compensation late payments by ensuring that injury reports are promptly recorded on required forms to the organization's workers' compensation insurance carrier. Lateness of payments to employees by workers' compensation carriers is one of the most frequent causes of claims being appealed to the Workers' Compensation Appeals Board.

EMPLOYEE CONDUCT, DISCIPLINE, DISPUTE RESOLUTION, AND SUGGESTIONS

Honest and Loyal Service

An obligation rests with every employee of the *(Company)* to render honest, efficient, and courteous performance of duties. Employees will therefore be responsible and held accountable for adhering to all *(Company)* policies, rules, directives, and procedures prescribed by the *(Company)* through supervisory or management personnel.[102]

1. All employees have a duty to report, verbally or in writing, promptly and confidentially, any evidence of any improper practice of which they are aware. As used here, the term "improper practice" means any illegal, fraudulent, dishonest, negligent, or otherwise unethical action arising in connection with *(Company)* operations or activities.

2. Reports of improper practice should be submitted through the line of administrative supervision except when the alleged impropriety appears to involve a management employee. In such cases, reports should be referred to the next higher level management employee, who will advise the *(President/General Manager)* of the situation.

Security and Confidentiality

It is the policy of the *(Company)* to maintain strict control over entrance to the premises, access to work locations and records, computer information, and cash or other items of monetary value. Employees who are assigned keys, given special access, or assigned job responsibilities in connection with the safety, security, or confidentiality of such records, material, equipment, or items of monetary or business value will be required to use sound judgment and discretion in carrying out their duties, and will be held accountable for any wrongdoing or acts of indiscretion.

Information about *(Company)*, its *(customers, clients, suppliers)*, or employees should not be divulged to anyone other than persons who have a right to know, or are authorized to receive such information. When in doubt as to whether certain information is or is not confidential, prudence dictates that no disclosure be provided without first clearly establishing that such disclosure has been authorized by appropriate supervisory or management personnel. This basic policy of caution and discretion in handling of confidential information extends to both external and internal disclosure.

Confidential information obtained as a result of employment with *(Company)* is not to be used by an employee for the purpose of furthering any private interest, or as a means of making personal gains. Use or disclosure of such information can result in civil or criminal penalties, both for the individuals involved and for the *(Company)*.

---

[102]   Employers may want to add a section dealing with business conduct such as that provided in Chapter 3. The policy as stated here constitutes the essence of a "whistle blowing" provision. Under federal and many state laws, employees are entitled to disclose improper/illegal practices, so why not encourage internal reporting and correction first?

Personal Appearance Standards

(Company) has taken the position that the success of our business is determined in part by establishing and maintaining a proper business atmosphere, which is determined by the image employees project as well as business conduct. Employees are therefore expected to dress in a manner consistent with the nature of work performed. If there are questions as to what constitutes proper attire, employees should consult with supervisory personnel. Employees who are inappropriately dressed, in the opinion of supervisory personnel, may be sent home and required to return to work in acceptable attire. Under this circumstance, employees will not be paid for the time away for work.[103]

Employees are also expected to observe good habits of grooming and personal hygiene at all times, and to avoid any personal practices or preferences that may prove offensive to others.

Alternative Policy: Personal Appearance Standards

Employees will be expected to present themselves during working hours in attire that is appropriate to their position and the nature of work performed. Employees having personal contact with our *(customers, clients, vendors, the public)* should be particularly conscious of maintaining dress, grooming, and hygiene standards that present the business image desired by the *(Company)*.

Employees who are in doubt, or have questions about the specific personal appearance standards in their work unit, should consult with their supervisor. Any employee who appears for work in a manner that does not conform to *(Company)* standards may be required to return home to correct the situation, and the period of absence will be treated as unpaid leave.

Financial Affairs

Employees are cautioned that the *(Company)* does not condone, nor assume any liability for, the practice of lending or borrowing money, or anything of monetary or personal value, between employees. Employees who voluntarily participate in such activity, or create these obligations, do so at their own risk.

Unauthorized Visitors

Employees must recognize that the *(Company)* may have an insurance liability for persons visiting any *(Company)* business locations. Therefore, it becomes necessary for the *(Company)* to establish this policy, the intent of which restricts business hours and work

---

[103]   This is sometimes a delicate area; however, the language provided is both general and specific enough to get the point across to employees regarding the importance of dress and grooming standards as an important issue to the employer. The key here is that dress must be appropriate to the nature of the job being performed, including contact with customers or clients, as well as the customary practice of the business itself. Enforcement can include requiring an employee to discontinue wearing sexually provocative apparel as a result of an employer's legal obligation to control potential sources of sexual harassment.

location visitation, excluding suppliers, vendors, applicants, business associates, and *(customers, clients, etc.)*.

Friends, relatives, or other unauthorized persons will not be permitted to visit an employee during working hours or at work locations without the express permission of supervisory personnel. Should such advance notice not be practical or possible, employees will be expected to exercise good judgment in their handling of an unforeseen visit, and should inform the visitor of the *(Company's)* policy. If warranted by the nature of an unforeseen visit, the employee may request taking an authorized unscheduled break from work away from *(Company)* property, the time of which may be considered noncompensable.

This restriction includes conducting personal business by telephone during business hours, but does not restrict necessary delivery of meals or messages to employees. Visits for the purpose of touring the *(Company's)* facilities, the employee's work location, or other reasons not specified must be approved by supervisory personnel.

Off-Duty Conduct and Employment

Generally, *(Company)* regards the off-duty activities of employees to be their own personal matter rather than that of the *(Company)*. However, certain types of off-duty activities by employees represent the potential of a material business concern to the *(Company)*, and for that reason the following is established with the intent to specify conditions and guide employees.[104]

1. Employees who engage in, or are associated with illegal, immoral, or inimical conduct, the nature of which adversely affects *(Company)*, or their own ability or credibility to carry out their employment responsibilities, may be subject to disciplinary action including termination.

2. Employees may engage in off-duty employment, provided that:

    a. Written approval is granted in advance by the employee's supervisor and the *(Human Resources Manager)*.

    b. The employment does not conflict with the employee's work schedules, duties, and responsibilities.

    c. The employment does not create a conflict of interest or incompatibility with *(Company)* employment.

    d. The employment does not create a detrimental effect upon the employee's work performance with the *(Company)*.

    e. The employment does not involve conducting business during hours of employment with the *(Company)*.

---

[104]   As mentioned previously, an employer's ability to regulate employee conditions outside duty hours is extremely limited, but because an employee's conduct or particular life-style outside employment can, and sometimes does, reflect upon the employer, or the employee's job performance or credibility, it is not prohibited for employers to establish reasonable policies concerning the effect of certain types of behavior. Employers should be guided in these cases by considering the influence of unusual employee behavior upon the employer's reputation, the welfare of other employees and the employee's ability to perform in a certain capacity, and the necessary credibility of an employee who does something notably unacceptable while off duty.

Self-employment is considered off-duty employment and falls under the same conditions as other off-duty employment, with the addition of the restriction that employment does not involve ownership of a private business that is incompatible with an employee's *(Company)* position.

3. Employees wishing to engage in off-duty employment are required to submit a written request explaining pertinent details to their supervisor. If approved by the supervisor and the *(Human Resources Manager)*, copies of the request will be given to the employee and the supervisor, and entered into the employee's personnel file.[105]

    Upon any subsequent change in off-duty employment, including the employer, type of work performed, modification of work schedule, or work location, the employee will be required to submit a new or revised written request for off-duty employment and it will be processed as described earlier.

4. An employee who sustains an injury or illness in connection with off-duty employment will:

    a. Not be entitled to receive workers' compensation benefits provided by the *(Company)*.

    b. Not be entitled to receive paid sick leave. If sick leave is paid in error, the *(Company)* will be entitled to recover such wages from the employee.

    c. Not accrue credit for vacation, sick leave, or any other discretionary employment benefits during a period of absence resulting from such injury or illness.

    d. Not be entitled to the normal contribution by the *(Company)* toward health care benefit premiums during a period of absence resulting from such injury/illness.

    In those cases where an off-duty, employment-related, injury or illness results in an employee's temporary disability, the employee must either request and obtain a leave of absence without pay, request and use accrued paid time off whereby items c and d would not apply, or be subject to termination by the *(Company)* due to lack of availability for work.

5. An employee's authorization to engage in off-duty employment may be revoked at any time, and at the sole discretion of the *(Company)* where it is determined that it is in the best interest of the *(Company)* to do so. Such revocations will generally be based upon a finding that the conditions set forth herein have not been met.

Conflicts of Interest

Employees will not be allowed to solicit, obtain, accept, or retain any personal benefit from any supplier, vendor, *(customer, client, etc.)*, or any individual or organization doing or seeking business with the *(Company)*. As used here, personal benefit means a gift, gratuity, favor, service, compensation in any form, discount, special treatment, or anything of monetary value. The following may serve as exceptions, but employees should consult with supervisory personnel when circumstances are difficult or doubtful as to the propriety.[106]

---

[105]   See "Request to Engage in Off-Duty Employment" form in Chapter 10.

[106]   Employers may want to substitute or add the less formal policy on gifts and gratuities in Chapter 3.

- The purchase of business meeting meals
- Consumable gifts offered to an entire work group during the holiday season where rejection would damage the spirit in which the gifts were offered

Alternative Policy: Conflicts of Interest[107]

As a means of ensuring that the impartiality and integrity of the *(Company)* remains constant, and to prevent employees from placing themselves in positions of potential or actual conflict of interests, the *(Company)* will require that employees avoid engaging in the following types of activities:

1. Disclosing private or confidential information about the *(Company)*, its employees or customers, operational plans and activities, methods of operation, pricing, trade secrets, or any other information to persons outside the *(Company)*
2. Engaging in outside employment that conflicts with the nature of the *(Company's)* business, is a competitor of the *(Company)*, conducts business with the *(Company)*, or otherwise interferes with an employee's work performance with the *(Company)*
3. Soliciting or accepting any favors, gifts, or special consideration from persons or businesses who have, or seek to have, business interests with the *(Company)*
4. Soliciting or representing any private or personal interest unrelated to the *(Company's)* business interests or the employee's job responsibilities
5. Using the *(Company's)* name, likeness, facilities, assets, or resources, or representing the authority of one's position with the *(Company)*, for personal gain or private interests

Employees who violate the *(Company's)* conflict of interests policy, or who create equally detrimental impact on the *(Company)*, may be subject to disciplinary action including termination for first offenses.

Drug and Alcohol Program[108]

GENERAL POLICY

The *(Company)* is committed to maintaining a safe and healthy work environment free from the influence of alcohol and drugs. To that end, the *(Company)* has adopted a drug and alcohol abuse policy. Compliance with the *(Company's)* drug policy is a condition of employment. The *(Company)* intends to take severe disciplinary action, up to and including termination, against an employee who violates the *(Company's)* drug and alcohol abuse policy.

PREVENTION AND TREATMENT

The Human Resources Department has developed a Drug-Free Awareness Program to educate employees and their families about the dangers of drug and alcohol abuse and the *(Company's)* drug and alcohol abuse policy.

---

[107] Levesque, *The Complete Hiring Manual,* p. 64.
[108] Ibid., p. 58.

The *(Company)* encourages any employee with a drug or alcohol abuse problem to voluntarily seek treatment. The *(Company)* had established an employee assistance program to provide counseling and referral services for employees with drug or alcohol abuse problems who voluntarily seek help.

PROHIBITED ACTIVITY

The *(Company)* strictly prohibits unauthorized use, possession (including storage in a desk, locker, car, or other repository), manufacture, distribution, dispensation or sale of illegal drugs, drug paraphernalia, controlled substances, or alcohol on *(Company)* premises or *(Company)* business, in *(Company)* supplied vehicles or during working hours; any activity that compromises the integrity or accuracy of the *(Company's)* drug and alcohol testing program; any failure or refusal to abide by the *(Company's)* alcohol and drug abuse policy; and conviction under any criminal drug statute.

TESTING

The *(Company)* may require employees and applicants to be tested for drugs or alcohol upon hiring *(all offers of employment are conditional on passing a drug or alcohol test)*; when the *(Company)* suspects that the employee's work performance or on-the-job behavior may have been affected in any way by drugs or alcohol; when *(Company)* policy requires an employee to undergo a physical examination; or when the *(Company)* determines that an employee may have contributed to an accident involving fatality, serious bodily injury, or substantial damage to property. Any positive drug or alcohol test is a violation of the *(Company's)* drug and alcohol abuse policy.

Supervisors are trained to identify job performance and on-the-job behavior that may reflect drug or alcohol abuse. When a supervisor concludes that declining job performance or erratic on-the-job behavior may be the product of personal problems, the supervisor will refer the employee to the *(Medical Department)* for a breath, saliva, urine, and/or blood test for alcohol or drug abuse.

Any test for drug or alcohol abuse will be conducted using reasonable procedural safeguards.

SEARCHES

Where the employee's performance or on-the-job behavior may have been affected in any way by drugs or alcohol, the *(Company)* may search:

1. The employee;
2. A locker, desk, or other *(Company)* property under the employee's control; and
3. The employee's personal effects or automobile on *(Company)* property.

Alternative Policy: Drug-Free Workplace Act Policy[109]

Illegal drugs in the workplace are a danger to us all. They impair safety and health, promote crime, lower productivity and quality, and undermine public confidence in the work we do.

---

[109]   Levesque, *The Complete Hiring Manual*, pp. 58–59.

We will not tolerate the use of illegal drugs here—and now, by law, we cannot. Under the federal Drug-Free Workplace Act, for this *(Company)* to be considered a "responsible source" for the award of federal contracts, we have developed the following policy.

Effective immediately, any location at which *(Company)* business is conducted, whether at this or any other site, is declared to be a drug-free workplace. This means:

1. All employees are absolutely prohibited from unlawfully manufacturing, distributing, dispensing, possessing, or using controlled substances in the workplace. Any employee violating the policy is subject to discipline, up to and including termination, for the first offense.

2. Employees have the right to know the dangers of drug abuse in the workplace, the *(Company's)* policy about them, and what help is available to combat drug problems. We will institute an education program for all employees on the dangers of drug abuse in the workplace. To assist employees in overcoming drug abuse problems, the *(Company)* may offer the following rehabilitative help:

   • Medical benefits for substance-abuse treatment

   • Information about community resources for assessment and treatment

   • Counseling program

   • Employee assistance program

   In addition, the *(Company)* will provide supervisory training to assist in identifying and addressing illegal drug use by employees.

3. Any employee convicted of violating a criminal drug statute in this workplace must inform the *(Company)* of such conviction (including pleas of guilty and nolo contendre) within *(five (5))* days of the conviction occurring. Failure to so inform the *(Company)* subjects the employee to disciplinary action, up to and including termination for the first offense. By law, the *(Company)* will notify the federal contracting officer within *(ten (10))* days of receiving such notice from an employee or otherwise receiving notice of such a conviction.

4. The *(Company)* reserves the right to offer employees convicted of violating a criminal drug statute in the workplace participation in an approved rehabilitation or drug abuse assistance program as an alternative to discipline. If such a program is offered, and accepted by the employee, then the employee must satisfactorily participate in the program as a condition of continued employment.

ALL EMPLOYEES ARE ASKED TO ACKNOWLEDGE THAT THEY HAVE READ THE ABOVE POLICY AND AGREE TO ABIDE BY IT IN ALL RESPECTS. BY LAW, THIS ACKNOWLEDGMENT AND AGREEMENT ARE REQUIRED OF YOU AS A CONDITION OF CONTINUED EMPLOYMENT.

Please refer any questions on the foregoing policy to your supervisor or the *(Personnel Department)*.

The following information is included here for your benefit. It is only a partial listing.[110]

---

[110]   Levesque, *The Complete Hiring Manual,* p. 186.

Partial List of Drug Testing Laboratories Certified by the National Institute on Drug Abuse

To be certified by the National Institute on Drug Abuse, a laboratory must succeed in each of the three rounds of performance testing and an on-site inspection. To maintain certification, a laboratory must participate in a performance testing program every other month and allow periodic on-site inspections. The following are some of the laboratories to receive the Institute's original certification.

American BioTest Laboratories, Inc.
3350 Scott Blvd., Bldg. 15
Santa Clara, CA 95054
(408) 727-5525

American Medical Laboratories
11091 Main St.
P.O. Box 188
Fairfax, VA 22030
(703) 691-9100

ARUP
500 Chipeta Way
Salt Lake City, UT 84104
(800) 242-2787

Center for Human Toxicology
417 Wakara Way, Rm. 290
University Research Park
Salt Lake City, UT 84108
(801) 581-5117

Chem-Bio Corporation
140 E. Ryan Rd.
Oak Creek, WI 53154
(800) 365-3840

CompuChem Laboratories, Inc.
600 W. North Market Blvd.
Sacramento, CA 95834
(916) 923-0840

CompuChem Laboratories, Inc.
3308 Chapel Hill/Nelson Hwy.
P.O. Box 12652
Research Triangle Park, NC 27709
(919) 549-8263

Doctors and Physicians Laboratory
801 E. Dixie Ave.
Leesburg, FL 32748
(904) 787-9006

Med Arts/South Community Hospital
1001 S.W. 44th St.
Oklahoma City, OK 73109
(405) 636-7041

MetPath, Inc.
1355 Mittle Blvd.
WoodDale, IL 60191
(312) 595-3888

MetPath, Inc.
One Malcolm Ave.
Teterboro, NJ 07608
(201) 393-5000

MedTox Laboratories, Inc.
402 West County Rd., D
St. Paul, MN 44112
(612) 636-7466

National Center for Forensic Science
Maryland Medical Laboratory, Inc.
1901 Sulphur Spring Rd.
Baltimore, MD 21227
(301) 247-9100

Nichols Institute
7323 Engineer Rd.
San Diego, CA 92111
(619) 278-5900

Northwest Toxicology, Inc.
1141 East 2900 South
Salt Lake City, UT 84124
(800) 322-3361

Poisonlab, Inc.
7272 Clairemont Mesa Rd.
San Diego, CA 92111
(619) 279-2600

Roche Biomedical Laboratories
6370 Wilcox Road
Dublin, OH 43017
(614) 889-1061

SmithKline Bio-Science Laboratories
2201 W. Campbell Pk. Dr.
Chicago, IL 60612
(312) 885-2010

SmithKline Bio-Science Laboratories
8000 Sovereign Row
Dallas, TX 75247
(214) 638-1301

South Bend Medical Foundation
530 N. Lafayette Blvd.
South Bend, IN 46601
(219) 234-4176

Southgate Medical Laboratory
21100 Southgate Park Blvd.
Cleveland, OH 44137
(800) 338-0166

Discipline Policy

The intent of this policy is to openly communicate the *(Company)* standards of conduct, particularly conduct considered undesirable, to all employees as a means of avoiding their occurrence. The *(Company)* also believes that such policies and procedures are necessary for the orderly operation of our business and for the protection and fair treatment of all employees. Employees are therefore urged to use reasonable judgment at all times, and to seek supervisory advice in any doubtful situation.

As a matter of policy, the *(Company)* seeks to resolve conduct and performance problems in the most informal and positive manner possible, such as through counseling, additional training or supervision, verbal cautions, and the like. However, under those circumstances when disciplinary action, including termination, becomes a necessary means of modifying undesirable situations, the *(Company)* has established the conditions and procedures that follow.

To ensure the equitable processing of disciplinary actions, the *(Human Resources Manager)* will be responsible for the proper handling of such matters, including the assurance that employee rights are protected, and that appropriate action is taken when circumstances warrant. Supervisory personnel should therefore consult with the *(Human Resources Manager)* prior to the implementation of discipline.

Disciplinary Illustrations

The illustrations of unacceptable conduct cited here are to provide specific and exemplary reasons for initiating disciplinary action, and to alert employees to the more commonplace types of employment conduct violations. However, because conditions of human conduct are unpredictable, no attempt has been made here to establish a complete list. Should there arise instances of unacceptable conduct not included in the following list, the *(Company)* may likewise fund it necessary and appropriate to initiate disciplinary action in accordance with these policies and procedures.[111]

---

[111]   Frequently the specific disciplinary infractions listed in personnel policies are construed as the employer's definition of "just cause." It is not the intent of employers to have the conditions under

Attendance

1. Improper or unauthorized use or abuse of paid leave
2. Excessive absenteeism, regardless of reason, the effect of which disrupts or diminishes operational effectiveness
3. Being absent without authorized leave or repeated unauthorized late arrival or early departure from work

Behavior

1. Willful or negligent violation of the *(Personnel Department)* policies and procedures, unit operating rules, or related directives
2. Failure to carry out a direct order from a superior, except where the employee's safety may reasonably be jeopardized by the order
3. Engaging in a conflict of interest activity
4. Conduct that discredits the employee or the *(Company)*, or willful misrepresentation of the *(Company)*
5. Conviction of a crime, including convictions based on a plea of nolo contendere or of a misdemeanor involving moral turpitude, the nature of which reflects the possibility of serious consequences related to the continued assignment or employment of the employee
6. Knowingly falsifying, removal, or destruction of information related to employment, payroll, or work-related records or reports
7. Soliciting outside work for personal gain during business hours; engaging in off-duty employment for any business under contract with the *(Company)*; participating in any off-duty employment that adversely affects the employee's performance of work for the *(Company)*; and engaging in unauthorized off-duty employment
8. Discourteous treatment of the public or other employees, including harassing, coercing, threatening, or intimidating others
9. Conduct that interferes with the management of the *(Company)* operations
10. Violation or neglect of safety rules, or contributing to hazardous conditions
11. Unauthorized removal or use of any *(Company)* property, or that of its *(clients, customers, agents, etc.)*
12. Physical altercations
13. Any act or conduct that is discriminatory in nature toward another person's race, creed, color, national origin, sex (including sexual harassment), age, religious beliefs, or political affiliations

---

111 *continued*   which discipline can occur so narrowly interpreted. For this reason, the language provided not only lists a fairly broad range of differing conditions, but also is preceded by language that expresses the employer's intent to be free to initiate disciplinary action in other circumstances where it is reasonable to do so. It is suggested that Chapter 29 be read to gain a more thorough understanding of the implications before modifying any of the basic policy language pertaining to discipline.

Performance

1. Inefficiency, incompetence, or negligence in the performance of duties, including failure to perform assigned tasks or training, or failure to discharge duties in a prompt, competent, and reasonable manner

2. Refusal or inability to improve job performance in accordance with written or verbal direction after a reasonable trial period

3. Refusal to accept reasonable and proper assignments from an authorized supervisor

4. Intoxication or incapacity on duty due to the use of alcohol or drugs

5. Driving under the influence of alcohol or drugs while on duty; suspension of driver's license where job duties require driving

6. Careless, negligent, or improper use of *(Company)* property, equipment or funds, including unauthorized removal, or use for private purpose, or use involving damage or unreasonable risk of damage to property

7. Unauthorized release of confidential information or official records

Alternative Policy: Disciplinary Conditions

It is the policy of the *(Company)* to maintain the most harmonious, pleasant, and positive work environment possible and thereby make work relations an enjoyable experience for all. It is believed that this objective can best be achieved by establishing specific standards of undesired conduct that are likely to result in disciplinary action, and to make them known openly and frequently to our employees.

Illustrative examples of the type of conduct, activities, and performance that the *(Company)* expressly wants employees to avoid include:

1. Destruction of, damage to, or unauthorized removal of company property or personal property of others without prior approval.

2. Inefficient or careless performance of job responsibilities or inability to perform duties successfully.

3. Failure to promptly report a work-related injury or accident.

4. Negligence that results in injury to an employee, self, or a visitor.

5. Intentional falsification of records required in the transaction of *(Company)* business.

6. Unauthorized punching or signing of another employee's time card or recording the time of another employee. Both employees may be subject to disciplinary action.

7. Irregular attendance: repeated tardiness, unreported or unexcused absence, abuse of sick leave, overstaying a leave of absence without written authorization.

8. Insubordination, including refusal or failure to perform assigned work.

9. Possessing or being under the influence of alcohol, narcotics, or drugs while on *(Company)* property.

10. Gambling on *(Company)* property.

11. Sleeping while on duty.

12. Fighting on *(Company)* property.

13. Making malicious, false, or derogatory statements that may damage the integrity or reputation of the *(Company)* or its employees.

14. Misrepresentation or withholding of pertinent facts in securing employment.

15. Refusal to follow instructions of authorized personnel, rude or discourteous conduct, or any action that endangers the health or safety of others.

16. Improper use of *(Company)* telephones.

17. Abuse of break times and lunch periods.

18. Accepting gratuities or tips.

19. Distributing or posting information that is detrimental to the general interest of the *(Company)*.

20. Use of *(Company)* vehicles without prior approval, or unlawful operation.

21. Possession, display, or use of explosives, firearms, or other dangerous weapons while on duty or on *(Company)* property.

22. Encouraging or engaging in any work stoppage, slowdown, walkout, cessation of work, or any other activity designed to restrict or delay the production, shipment, delivery, or receipt of goods or services by the *(Company)*.

23. Directly or indirectly, either for one's personal benefit or for the benefit of any other person or company, revealing any *(Company)* trade secrets or any other *(Company)* or employee information.

24. Discriminatory conduct or actions against any other person. Violation of any policy, rule, procedure, or practice established by the *(Company)*.

Types and Progression of Discipline

Depending on the nature and circumstances of an incident, discipline will normally be progressive and bear a reasonable relationship to the violation.[112] The types of discipline that may occur are as follows in general order of increasing formality and seriousness:

OPTIONAL AND RECOMMENDED INVESTIGATIVE SUSPENSION

If the offense, violation, or infraction requires investigative action to ascertain an employee's wrongdoing prior to the imposition of disciplinary action, an employee may be suspended temporarily with pay during the conduct of such investigation. If so informed, the effected employee will be notified by the *(Company)* as to the conclusions reached as a result of the investigation and any further action to be taken by the *(Company)*.

VERBAL REPRIMAND

A verbal statement by the supervisor to an employee, usually pointing out an unsatisfactory element of job performance, is intended to be corrective or cautionary. A verbal reprimand informally defines the area of needed improvement, sets up goals for the achievement of

---

[112]   It is important for employers to establish and follow the principle of progressive discipline, not only because it is the fairest approach to take when dealing with these matters, but also because it can be an important element in an employer's defense against a wrongful discharge suit. That is, it serves to demonstrate the employer's intent to correct a situation through progressively more strenuous forms of modifying undesirable behavior prior to a termination decision.

improvement, and informs the employee that failure to improve may result in more serious actions.[113]

WRITTEN REPRIMAND

This is the first level of *formal discipline.* The written reprimand is issued by the supervisor with approval of the *(Department Head),* and a copy to the *(Human Resources Manager)* for placement in the employee's personnel file.

PAY REDUCTION

As used for disciplinary purposes, an employee may be reduced in pay rate upon recommendation of supervisory personnel and approval of the *(Department Head).* A copy of such written notice will be given to the affected employee and the *(Human Resources Manager)* for placement in the employee's personnel file.

DISCIPLINARY DEMOTIONS

Under circumstances of demotion for disciplinary reasons, an employee may be reallocated from a present job to one having lower responsibilities, skill requirements, performance standards, and rate of pay upon recommendation of supervisory personnel and approval of the *(Department Head).* A copy of such written notice will be given to the affected employee and the *(Human Resources Manager)* for placement in the employee's personnel file.

SUSPENSION

An employee may be suspended from work without pay for up to *(five (5))* working days by authority of the *(Department Head).* Suspensions of a longer duration require approval by the *(President/General Manager).*[114]

Under certain circumstances, it may be necessary to restrict an employee immediately from performing duties at the work site. The circumstances usually involve potential danger to the employee, coworkers, or the public, or the employee's inability to discharge assigned duties satisfactorily. Because of the need for immediate action, the decision to suspend an employee is typically the responsibility of the supervisor. In these situations, the following procedure is to be followed:

---

[113] The verbal reprimand should, when reasonably possible, be delivered confidentially and not in the presence of other persons. The supervisor should record the date and content of the reprimand, but no record should be placed in the employee's personnel file. The employee receiving a verbal reprimand should be given the opportunity at the time of the reprimand to offer evidence in mitigation of the actions leading to the reprimand.

[114] Suspensions should be avoided as much as possible; they are harmful to the organization in terms of lost productivity than to an employee given today's predominance of two-income families.

In all cases of suspension, the management employee authorizing the suspension should prepare, or have prepared, a written account of the circumstances relating to the suspension, including available evidence. A copy should be given to the affected employee, and one placed in the employee's personnel file. Generally, such notice should be given to the employee prior to the implementation of a suspension.

- The supervisor taking the action to suspend an employee will immediately notify the *(Department Head and/or Human Resources Manager)* and, as soon as possible, prepare a written statement of the action taken and the reasons for such action.
- The *(Department Head)* will prepare, together with the supervisor, the statement of charges and document any supporting evidence.
- As soon as possible after the initial action, but not later than *(three (3))* working days, the *(Department Head)* will prepare written notification to the affected employee.

In no event will the use of paid time be allowed during a period of suspension without pay. Should a paid holiday occur during a period of suspension without pay, the suspension period will be extended by the number of holidays occurring during the suspension period.

DISCHARGE

Employees should be aware that their employment relationship with the *(Company)* is based on the condition of mutual consent to continue the relationship between the employee and the *(Company)*. Therefore, the employee or *(Company)* is free to terminate the employment relationship at will, with or without cause, and at any time. Recommendations to discharge an employee are to be made to, and authorized by, the *(Department Head)*.

Similarly, the *(Company)* reserves the right, at its sole discretion, to utilize forms of discipline less severe than termination in differing circumstances in order to effectuate positive changes in employee behavior and performance. Although one or more of these disciplinary measures may be taken in connection with a particular employee, no formal order or system is necessary, and the *(Company)* may terminate employment whenever such action is deemed necessary.

Initiating Discipline: Considerations and Notice

Supervisory and management personnel should be guided in their consideration of disciplinary matters by the following illustrative, but not exclusive, conditions.[115]

- The degree of severity of the offense
- The number, nature, and circumstances of similar past offenses
- Employee's length of service

---

[115] While it is true an element of consistency is needed in the application of penalties to particular violations of policy, supervisors should be aware that differences in the fact patterns associated with a particular violation can create "circumstantial distinctions," and they serve as justification in some cases for levying different penalties for two similar events. Simply stated, this means that if the same or a similar incident is created by two different employees, they can receive different penalties for the offense if the circumstances (fact pattern) surrounding the offense are reasonably different. An example of this difference may be that one employee has violated a particular rule two or three times, while the other employee violated the same rule for the first time. Documentation of disciplinary events is crucial, in this example for purposes of defending against perceived discrimination or retaliation, where an employer chooses two different penalties for a disciplinary event that is seemingly the same.

- Provocation, if any, contributing to the offense
- Previous warnings related to the offense
- Consistency of penalty application
- Equity and relationship of penalty to offense

Disciplinary notices to regular employees should, as a general rule, contain the following information:

- A statement of the disciplinary action to be taken and its effective date
- A statement of the reason(s) for imposing the discipline and the nature of the violation
- Attachment of any supporting material or evidence where appropriate

Service of disciplinary notice will be deemed to have been made upon personal presentation, or by depositing the notice, postage prepaid, in the U.S. mail, addressed to the employee's last known address on file.

Upon receipt of disciplinary notices for placement in a regular employee's personnel file, the *(Human Resources Manager)* may assign a recall date to the document at which time it may be reviewed for a determination of continued retention, assigned a new recall date, or mailed to the employee as evidence of removal from the employee's file.[116]

---

[116] It has now become a common practice for employers to remove disciplinary notices from an employee's personnel file after a sufficient period of time has lapsed during which the employee has not repeated the same or a similar act.

DISPUTE RESOLUTION POLICY

It is the policy of the *(Company)* to treat employees in a fair and impartial manner. The *(Company)* is firmly committed to the belief that undisclosed problems will remain unresolved, and eventually lead to a decay of work relationships, dissatisfaction in working conditions, and a decline in operational efficiency. The *(Company)* has therefore established the dispute resolution system that follows, the intent of which is to solve problems as quickly, fairly, and informally as possible, and it should not be interpreted by any person as anything more than a method of solving problems before they reach damaging proportions.[117]

This policy will be applicable only to regular nonsupervisory/nonmanagement employees, as management and supervisory personnel have a more direct means of resolving matters related to their employment.

Employees who seek resolution of employment situations by using established procedures are assured that they will not be subjected to discrimination or retaliation, or be penalized in any way for their use of these procedures.

Matters Covered by Dispute Resolution System

Eligible employees who have complaints, problems, concerns, or disputes with another employee, the nature of which causes a direct adverse effect upon the aggrieved employee, may initiate a dispute resolution according to established procedures. Such matters must have to do with specific working conditions, safety, unfair treatment, disciplinary actions, compensation, job classification, reassignments, or any form of alleged discrimination.

Informal Dispute Resolution Procedures

An employee having a problem, complaint, or dispute as defined is to make every effort to resolve the matter through informal discussion with the immediate supervisor within *(ten (10)) (working)* days of the occurrence or cause of such matter. If the employee's work unit structure is such that the immediate supervisor is subordinate to another supervisor, the aggrieved employee may request a discussion with both supervisors within this time period. The supervisor(s) will take the matter under consideration and attempt to resolve it verbally or provide a satisfactory explanation within *(five (5)) (working)* days, unless additional time is needed to gather adequate information.

---

[117] It is becoming increasingly important for employers to adopt procedures such as this in an effort to show reasonable attempts to give employees "due process" by having an internal mechanism to adjudicate grievances. Employers should bear in mind that the courts continue to search for an answer to the wrongful discharge issue and in the absence of a lower and less formal method of resolving differences between an employer and employee, the courts are likely to relieve the burden of their dockets by referring such cases to arbitration. Historically, employers do not fair well in the arbitration process. Aside from the legal implications of due process, contemporary management practices suggest that providing employees with a forum in which they can freely and comfortably pursue a fair resolution of employment matters, is a prudent measure that need not threaten the sanctity of management's decision-making prerogatives.

Formal Dispute Resolution Procedures

If the employee's matter is unresolved, or not resolved to the employee's satisfaction through informal procedures, the aggrieved employee may file a written Dispute Resolution Request with the *(Department Head or Human Resources Manager)* within *(five (5))* *(working)* days following the supervisor's informal response. Within *(five (5))* *(working)* days of receiving the employee's written request, the *(Department Head or Human Resources Manager)* may arrange a meeting with the employee to allow the employee to present a personal and complete description of the situation. Thereafter, the *(Department Head or Human Resources Manager)* will take the matter under consideration, including any necessary investigation or evaluation of the facts related to the situation, and render a written decision, response, or explanation as expeditiously as possible, but not to exceed *(fifteen (15))* *(working)* days.

If an employee is not satisfied with the outcome of the *(Department Head's or Human Resources Manager's)* response, the employee may file a copy of the same written request to the *(President/General Manager)* within *(five (5))* *(working)* days of such response. The *(President/General Manager)* or designee will discuss the matter with the employee and investigate the basis of the problem within *(fifteen (15))* *(working)* days after receipt of the request. Thereafter, the *(President/General Manager)* or designee will provide the employee with either a verbal or a written response, or both, within an additional *(ten (10))* *(working)* days. Such a decision or response will be final and conclusive.

Exceptions to Procedural Steps

The *(Company)* recognizes that there may arise certain circumstances in which it may be inappropriate for employees to pursue the resolution of a problem in the prescribed sequence. Consequently, the following exceptions are instances where an employee may bypass steps to seek resolution of a situation by the next higher authority. Employees who are uncertain as to the proper authority, or the method, should discuss the matter confidentially with the *(Human Resources Manager)*:

1. If the complaint or problem involves a known or suspected violation of law;
2. If the complaint or problem is clearly not within the authority of the employee's superior to resolve;
3. If the employee and superior mutually agree to bypass the superior's step; or
4. If the nature of the complaint, problem, or dispute involves or has been caused by the employee's superior, and the employee has reason to believe the superior may be less than impartial.

Alternative Policy: Dispute Resolution

In consideration of the possibility that a dispute, complaint, or problem may arise periodically concerning working conditions, policies and practices, or decisions made by *(Company)* representatives that affect an employee's job, the *(Company)* has established the following dispute resolution procedure. It is the intent of this policy and procedure to afford employees a voice in those matters that have a potential adverse, unjust, or inequitable effect on their employment conditions. Such issues may be honest differences of opinion, or judgment situations, but the *(Company)* acknowledges the importance of their expression. The *(Company)* is desirous of solving problems as promptly and justly as possible, objectively and confidentially, and free from any concern over reprisal or recrimination.

The three steps involved in the dispute resolution procedure are:

1. Let your supervisor know your wish to use the dispute resolution procedure by describing verbally the issue, the nature of your concern, and what you feel is an appropriate remedy. Experience has shown that most, if not all, problems can be resolved by honest and cooperative discussion between employees and their supervisor. If a satisfactory solution cannot be reached, or if the nature of the problem is not within the supervisor's authority, the employee should proceed to step 2.

2. Present the issue in writing to the *(Department Head)*, who will carefully investigate, examine, and evaluate the factual basis of the situation in an attempt to reach a satisfactory solution. Every effort will be made to provide the employee with a written decision, and the reasons thereof, within *(ten (10)) (working)* days. If the *(Department Head's)* decision is not satisfactory to the employee, proceed to step 3.

3. Within *(five (5)) (working)* days following receipt of the *(Department Head's)* decision, the employee should arrange an appointment to present and discuss the issue with the *(President/General Manager)*. On the basis of information provided in this meeting, or related written documents, the *(President/General Manager)* may conduct further inquiries to consider fully all relevant facts and circumstances, followed by a final written decision to the employee and others concerned generally within *(fifteen (15)) (working)* days.

Employee Suggestions

The *(Company)* welcomes new ideas and employee suggestions on how to improve our organization. Employees are therefore encouraged to communicate their ideas, comments, and suggestions to supervisors and managers. Such suggestions will be investigated and forwarded to the *(President)* for review and implementation consideration.

Suggestions that eliminate safety hazards, prevent lost workday accidents, improve operational methods or the efficiency of work procedures, and increase productivity and save time, labor, or materials are especially welcomed. Employees whose suggestions are implemented with cost-saving results may be eligible for an award by the *(Company)* in recognition of their contribution.

EMPLOYMENT SEPARATION

Resignations

An employee wishing to leave employment with the *(Company)* in good standing must file a written resignation with the immediate supervisor at least *(two (2))* weeks prior to the effective date, stating specific reason(s) for the resignation. The employee's resignation shall be promptly forwarded to the *(Human Resources Manager)* with a statement by the supervisor as to the employee's service performance and any other information pertinent to the resignation. Failure of the employee to give such notice will be noted on the employee's service record and may result in denial of future employment by the *(Company)*. [118]

Reductions-in-Force[119]

The *(Company)* works very hard to avoid the reduction of our work force; however, an employee may be subject to a nondisciplinary and involuntary layoff which is typically in connection with the national economy, periodic trends in our business, reorganization of the *(Company)* or a department, abolition of a position, a general lack of work to be performed by an employee or group of employees, or other factors that may influence employment.

When a general reduction in force is necessary, the *(Company)* will normally lay off any temporary employees first, followed by new hires in their introductory period, before laying off regular-status employees. However, it shall be the *(Company's)* sole discretion to determine which positions and employees are to be layed off, and in which order, based on the best interests of the *(Company's)* continuing operations. *(It shall further be the option of the company to provide some regular status employees with severance pay in consideration of their length of service, position in the company, and other circumstances determined by the company to be relevant).*

Alternative Policy: Reductions-in-Force

The *(Department Head)*, with the approval of the *(President/General Manager)*, may lay off a regular employee because of material change in duties, or organization, or shortage of work or funds. The *(Department Head)* is to notify the *(Human Resources Manager)* of the intended action at least *(fifteen (15))* calendar days before the effective date and provide a statement whether or not the employee gave satisfactory service. Other general layoffs may occur, usually as a result of business conditions, in which a larger segment of the work force may be affected.

Whenever it becomes necessary in the sole opinion of the *(Company)* to reduce the work force through layoffs, the *(Company)* will endeavor to provide affected employees with

---

[118] Many employers use this practice as a means of encouraging terminating employees to provide advance notice of their intended departure, giving the employer lead time to seek a replacement and avoid operational disruption.

[119] Employers must comply with the Workers Adjustment and Retraining Notification Act (WARN), which generally requires employers to give employees at least sixty days' notice of layoff if the employer is closing or reducing operations that affects one hundred or more employees in one or multiple locations. California employers are urged to consult with labor counsel and related advisors concerning any sizable reduction-in-force.

at least *(ten (10)) (working)* days' notice. In each class of position, employees shall be laid off according to employment status in the following order: temporary, provisional, part-time, probationary, and regular. Temporary, provisional, and probationary employees shall be laid off according to the needs of the service as determined by the *(President/General Manager)*.

An employee affected by layoff shall have the right to displace a similarly classified employee within the department who has less seniority in a lower position, or in another job within the *(Company)* in which the affected employee once had regular status. Seniority includes all periods of full-time *(Company)* service at or below the position level where layoff is to occur. To retreat to a former or lower position, an employee must have more seniority than at least one of the incumbents in the retreat position, and request displacement action in writing to the *(Human Resources Manager)* within *(five (5)) (working)* days of receipt of notice of layoff.

The names of employees who either are laid off or continue employment in a lower position will be placed on a reemployment list giving the position held at the time of layoff. The reemployment list will be maintained for a period of *(two (2))* years from the date of placement on the list. When a vacancy occurs in a position for which a reemployment list exists, persons appearing on the list will be considered for reemployment, in inverse order of their layoff dates, prior to consideration of other persons for employment.

Discharge

The *(Company)* strives to provide all employees with fair and reasonable conditions of employment at all times. However, to carry out its business obligations and priorities in the most efficient manner possible, the *(Company)* adheres to the principles of at-will employment whereby the *(Company)* and employees alike can terminate the employment relationship at any time, for any reason, and with or without notice.

Death of Employee

In the event of an employee's death, regardless of circumstances, the person receiving such notification is to promptly inform the *(President, Human Resources Manager)* of known details surrounding the employee's death. The *(President, Human Resources Manager)* or designee will verify this information and oversee the timely completion of necessary payroll, benefit, and other records to ensure that the beneficiaries of the employee receive all due funds and information pertaining to the conversion of benefit plans. Payroll and other funds will only be released to the beneficiaries designated on *(Company)* records by the applicable employee, or a person having the employee's legal power of attorney for this purpose.

Exit Interviews

An exit interview is generally conducted at the time of each employment separation, however they are not mandatory of employees. Exit interviews when scheduled are intended to provide employees with an opportunity to comment on *(Company)* operations, job requirements, working conditions, and any other information the employee considers beneficial to *(Company)* awareness. Employees may be asked to complete an exit interview questionnaire with or without disclosing their name. These records give the *(Company)* an opportunity to evaluate patterns of employment conditions and make adjustments accordingly. Additionally, exit interviews provide departing employees the opportunity to have questions answered about benefit conversions and to return any *(Company)* property that has been issued to the employee. It should be noted by employees that the return of *(Company)* property is mandatory, and an employee's refusal to do so will be reflected in the *(Company's)* records as an employee not in good standing at the time of separation, and the *(Company)* may pursue legal action against such employee.[120]

Employment Inquiries on Former Employees

All inquiries concerning former employees are to be directed to the *(President, Human Resources Manager)* for response. When such inquiries are made by another employer for the purpose of an employment reference, the *(Company)* maintains as its policy to provide only factual and pertinent information to the nature of the inquiry such as dates of employment, position and duties held, wages, and relevant performance characteristics of the employee known to be objectively truthful statements of fact. However, a detailed disclosure of employment records and information will only be provided to those outside the *(Company)* who possess written authority of the applicable employee to receive such information, or those who possess legal authority to observe or receive employment information relevant to the nature of their inquiry.[121]

Checkout upon Separation

Employees who resign, retire, or are discharged or laid off will be required to turn in any *(Company)*-owned property or working materials to their supervisor not later than their final workday. Employees may also be asked to complete and discuss details provided by the exit interview form with their supervisor or the *(President/General Manager or Human Resources Manager)*.

---

[120]   Exit interviews are strongly encouraged, as they can provide important information on employees' reasons for leaving, which can be checked against statements of reasons for leaving when the employees file for unemployment insurance. If the reason an employee gives for unemployment insurance purposes is different from that given to the employer, an employer would be well advised to report the discrepancy. Additionally, employers can gain useful information through the exit interview concerning particular problems that were encountered by the employee, how he or she felt about pay and benefits, the quality of supervision, and other suggestions for improvement within the organization. When it is done with interest and sincerity, the exit interview is a useful tool, not only to gain the employee's perspective of employment experience and inform the employee about converting insurance plans and filing for unemployment insurance, but also to provide the opportunity for the employer representative to conclude the employment relationship constructively.

[121]   Employers should exercise considerable caution when giving, or refusing to give, reasonable and employment-relevant reference information about former employees. In either case, employers can be held liable; for unreasonable withholding of reasonable information that precludes a former employee an employment opportunity, or for the improper invasion of the employee's right to privacy, defamation, false impression, and the like. For these reasons, employers should consult with qualified labor counsel when in doubt or in uncertain cases.

Chapter 3

MISCELLANEOUS, OPTIONAL, AND SUGGESTED PERSONNEL POLICIES AND PRACTICES FOR DIFFERING COMPANY OPERATIONS

The policies and procedures in this chapter represent an assortment of special-interest or condition topics that may serve as useful supplements to essential policies. For the most part, they are intended to be thought-generating rather than an exhaustive listing, or particularly comprehensive in content.

For easy reference, these policies have been arranged in alphabetical order within four subject area headings: Compensation, Benefits, Leaves and Schedules, and various Conditions of Employment. When incorporating these policies into basic policies, it is important to place them under the proper headings in order to maintain the logical continuity of topics presented. Also, be sure that these policies are added to the contents page of your manual or handbook, and that such additions do not change internal references to page or section numbers that may be affected by these additions. It may be helpful to have another person read your final draft for any internal inconsistencies.

COMPENSATION POLICIES AND PRACTICES

Pay in Lieu of Notice[1]

When it is deemed in the best interest of the *(Company)*, and as a strictly voluntary measure, an employee may receive pay in place of advance termination notice. Only those regular employees who have completed a minimum of *(one (1))* continuous year of service will be eligible for consideration, except where the termination resulted from any form of misconduct.

Employees granted pay in lieu of notice will receive at least the equivalent of *(one (1))* week's regular pay computed on the basis of the employee's average regular pay during the preceding *(twelve-(12-)month)* period. Employees may be granted additional weeks of pay in lieu of notice depending on such circumstances as the employee's length of service and performance record, the cause for termination, and the *(Company's)* ability to grant additional pay.

Preparation Time Pay

Employees designated by their supervisors to be at work prior to the employee's official starting time for the purpose of preparing to commence work will either be compensated at their *(straight time)* hourly rate or leave work early by an equivalent amount of time to that required for preparation. Such employees must notify their supervisors of the amount of preparation time put in each day so that the supervisor can determine the pay or time-off option, and record it on the employee's time sheet accordingly.[2]

---

[1]   Pay in lieu of notice should not be confused with severance pay. Severance pay is typically used by employers to benefit employees, and emanates from the employer's perceived moral and financial obligation to an employee who is being released because of lack of work, change of technology, or other neutral reason. Pay in lieu of notice, on the other hand, is used by many employers to compensate an employee for income that would have been earned had the employer given the employee the customary two-week notice of discharge. By using such a pay-in-lieu-of-notice policy, employers can more freely exercise the option to give an employee advance notice or release the employee immediately, and thereby avoid the prospect of the employee's working with lesser commitment and sincerity during the final period of employment.

Neither severance pay nor pay in lieu of notice is required under the Fair Labor Standards Act (FLSA). In the absence of any such state requirements, employers are free to adopt such policies at their own discretion. The one area of vulnerability to such policies is the employer's practice with regard to the potential for discriminatory effect; for example, granting pay in lieu of notice to one employee and not another under the *same* set of circumstances.

[2]   Policies of this type are generally written to be specifically applicable to a designated group of employees, the nature of whose duties requires some form of preparation such as changing clothes or preparing equipment that takes between fifteen and thirty minutes each workday. Where an employer compensates employees for preparation time, the employer need pay only at the straight-time hourly rate if the total number of compensating hours in that workday is less than the legally required number of hours for overtime.

Shift Differential Pay

Employees assigned to work normally scheduled work hours between *(8:00 P.M.)* and *(4:00 A.M.)* will be paid *(flat-rate amount)* per shift in addition to their regular wages. Eligible employees will be paid the shift differential in the paycheck following the close of the payroll period in which the shift was worked.[3]

Standby Pay

Some employees may be periodically or rotationally assigned to standby duty during weekends or other off-duty hours. The purpose of having employees on a standby status is to provide prompt service to the *(Company's)* *(customers, clients, etc.)* during irregular hours, where such response can prove instrumental to the success of the services provided by the *(Company)*.

    An employee assigned to standby duty will be paid *(flat-rate amount)* per *(week)* in addition to regular wages, provided the employee remains available and is responsive to duty calls. If the standby employee receives a duty call requiring the employee to report to another location to perform work, the employee *(will/will not)* be paid at the regular *(straight-time)* hourly rate from the time between leaving and returning from the location where the call was received. Calls received and time worked by a standby employee must be reported to the employee's supervisor on the next regular workday. The nature and amount of time worked during standby duty are subject to verification by supervisors. Where discrepancies occur, standby employees may be required to justify the details of their reports.

Tips and Gratuities

The acceptance of tips and gratuities of monetary value from *(customers, patrons, etc.)* is allowed by the *(Company)* so long as they are not expressly or covertly solicited. Such forms of additional personal income will not be accounted for or reportable to the *(Company)*, but employees will be individually responsible for reporting this income on personal income tax returns, as well as for the consequences for not reporting.

    Where it is determined by the *(Company)* that one employee collected and retained a tip known to be intended for another employee, and the collecting employee made no attempt to give the tip to the rightful employee, the collecting employee may be subject to disciplinary action including termination.

---

[3]   The clock hours noted here are arbitrary and can be modified in accordance with each employer's determination of what clock hours should constitute a workshift in which a premium differential pay is offered. It is recommended, however, that the amount of premium paid for shift differentials be a flat-rate amount rather than a percentage of each employee's hourly rate. Not only are percentages more difficult to deal with from a bookkeeping and administrative standpoint, but they are also more costly in terms of salary growth.

Weekend Work Premium

Employees whose work schedule requires the routine performance of work from *(6:00 A.M.)* Saturday to *(10:00 P.M.)* Sunday will be paid *(ten (10))* cents per hour in addition to the established wage rate for the position. Such premium pay will be added to the regular rate, and the combination of regular and premium pay will be used for the purpose of calculating overtime pay.

This policy is applicable only to those employees who work an entire weekend day or shift within the specified period of premium pay; it does not apply to employees whose work schedule overlaps into the prescribed period.

BENEFIT POLICIES AND PRACTICES

Bonuses

As a means of special recognition for the contribution of employees toward the success of the *(Company)*, year-end bonuses may be granted to some regular employees in the first December payday. The amount of the year-end bonus may vary between employees depending on such considerations as the employee's service length, performance record, special merit or uniqueness of the employee's contribution, and the *(Company's)* overall financial condition.

As a discretionary benefit, employees should understand that the year-end bonus is necessarily a year-to-year option of the *(Company)* and that its absence in a particular year should not be construed as the *(Company's)* dissatisfaction with general or individual employee performance. It is far more likely to result from the *(Company's)* need to dedicate available funds toward growth and stability of the *(Company)*, and therefore employee jobs, a more pressing interest.

Check Cashing

The *(Company)* does not keep sufficient currency available to cash employee payroll checks. However, the *(Company)* may cash a regular nonexempt employee's personal check up to the maximum amount of *(twenty-five dollars ($25))* on an infrequent basis and for reasonable purposes. An employee needing a personal check cashed must have the supervisor initial the check before taking it to the *(Cashier)*, who may deny the check on the basis of limited available cash.

Checking Accounts

Regular employees are eligible to receive a personal checking account without cost, including monthly service or check charges. Employees using this no-cost checking account benefit will be expected to keep their personal funds on a continuous credit basis. Overdrafts may be sufficient reason for a discontinuation of an employee's no-cost checking account, particularly if they are not corrected promptly when brought to the employee's attention. Customer rates will be charged for drawing against uncollected funds, late deposits, and similar servicing costs related to account maintenance.

Upon employment separation, the employee's checking account will be removed from employee status and will be treated as a normal customer account thereafter.

Child Care

As a means of allowing and encouraging the greatest cross section of employees possible, the *(Company)* has established a child care program for employees who might otherwise be unavailable for work because of limiting parental responsibilities.[4] Employees

---

[4]   No doubt employers are beginning to wonder if their role is not becoming "all things to all people." Nevertheless, an employer's involvement to some degree in child care programs is rapidly

who request participation in the program will be required to sign a waiver of liability against the *(Company)*, thereby relieving the *(Company)* of any form of responsibility for problems resulting from, or in connection with, providing child care services. Any employee is eligible to participate in the child care program if the dependent child:

- Is a natural or legal child normally dependent on the employee for care;
- Is between the ages of two and *(nine)* years of age; and
- Does not require specialized physical care.

Participating employees will be limited to use of the child care program for not more than *(two (2))* children at any one period of care, and such care will be provided only from *(Monday)* through *(Friday)*, *(8:00 A.M.)* to *(6:00 P.M.)*. Participating employees may use the child care program exclusively during those program hours when the employee is at work.

Information concerning enrollment, forms, rules, and other requirements of the child care program is available by contacting the *(Human Resources Manager)*.

Credit Cards

As the need arises, employees may be provided with a credit card issued to the *(Company)* for the purpose of such business-related expenses as gasoline or service on *(Company)* vehicles or equipment, nominal supplies, airfare, lodging, meals, or other approved purchases. *(Company)* credit cards may not be used to purchase personal items for an employee under any circumstance. Any employee found to abuse or misuse a *(Company)* credit card will be considered to have engaged in intentional theft of *(Company)* funds and will therefore be subject to immediate discharge. Lost or stolen *(Company)* credit cards should be reported to *(Controller/Finance Manager)* immediately.

Educational Assistance

In recognition of the long-range contribution that additional job-related education can make to the *(Company)*, a program of educational assistance has been established for regular *(full-time)* employees whereby a limited amount of the employee's costs for tuition and books can be reimbursed by the *(Company)* upon proof of successful course work completion, defined as receiving a grade of either "credit" or "C" or better. The *(Company)* also believes that it is incumbent upon every employee to self-initiate and be independently responsible for any continuous or periodic education required to maintain existing job skills and knowledge or to acquire the standards of promotional positions.

---

4 *continued*   becoming fashionable, at least for those employers who draw upon a work force consisting largely of single parents or those in child-rearing years. It is usually only the larger companies that can afford to pay for, reimburse, or sponsor in-house child care programs. Smaller organizations that choose to establish child care programs for their employees characteristically will either pool their resources with other employers to establish a common program or provide a designated portion of the business facility whereby employees operate the child care program by donating a predetermined number of hours each week.

Therefore, course work that qualifies for educational assistance will be considered on a case-by-case basis in advance of the employee's enrollment, the determination of which will be at the sole discretion and in the best interest of the *(Company)*.

Courses approved for educational assistance will be eligible for reimbursement of the following:

- *Tuition, Registration, and Laboratory Fees:* reimbursement of *(fifty percent (50%))* of the employee's actual and necessary expenses up to a maximum of reimbursement of *(one hundred dollars ($100))* per term (receipts required).

- *Required Textbook:* reimbursement of the necessary amount up to a maximum of *(thirty-five dollars ($35))* per term (receipts required).

Maximum annual educational assistance per employee is *(four hundred and five dollars ($405))*. Eligible employees wishing to have course work at an accredited educational institution considered for educational assistance should complete the Application for Educational Assistance form, and submit the form to the *(Human Resources Manager)* prior to enrollment. If approved, the employee will be required to show proof of expenses and successful completion before reimbursement is authorized.

Employees who separate employment with the *(Company)* within *(six (6))* months of receiving educational assistance may have the last amount of educational assistance deducted from their final paychecks, or otherwise be obliged to repay the *(Company)* in that amount.

Employee Assistance Program

The *(Company)* is mindful of the fact that everyone experiences personal difficulties from time to time and that these situations can be emotionally, physically, and mentally disruptive to an employee's otherwise well-balanced and fulfilling life. In recognition of these circumstances, and as a means of minimizing any potential adverse effect on the employee's job performance, the *(Company)* has established an employee assistance program whereby employees can acquire a limited amount of confidential assistance in dealing with such matters as family or marital conflicts, divorce, death, *(serious financial difficulties, and chemical dependency)*. Employees wishing to use the services of the employee assistance program should contact the *(Human Resources Manager)* for a confidential discussion of this program and referral.[5]

---

[5] Employers are finding benefit in treating employees as a human resource. Employee Assistance Programs (EAP's), are in their initial stages of growth as an employer-sponsored benefit and are worth consideration even if on a limited basis. For example, some employers will dedicate a specified amount of money each year for EAP services and establish a limit to the number of hours each employee may utilize these services. Employers who do not see the practical wisdom of this expense to keep employees productive on the job should examine the costs more commonly associated with the causes of lost productivity, such as absenteeism, declining performance, discipline, and turnover.

Employee Discounts

Regular employees are eligible for a discount of *(ten to twenty-five percent (10–25%))* of the *(retail)* price of *(Company)* products up to a maximum of *(two hundred and fifty dollars ($250))* in purchases per month. Discount purchases must be made from the employee's personal resources. Payroll deduction of purchases is disallowed.

Discount purchases will be extended only to the employee, and only for the immediate use and benefit of the employee. Consequently, employees may not use the *(Company's)* discount purchase privilege to acquire products for relatives, friends, or resale.

Loans and Advances

The *(Company)* generally does not extend payroll advances on prospective income and is not equipped to provide personal loans. For this reason, employees are encouraged to establish at least minimal personal savings accounts to accommodate the periodic or unforeseen need of additional finances. However, should the employee's financial need be relatively small, immediate, and serious, the employee may wish to consult with the *(Human Resources Manager)* to discuss the possibility of alternative methods of resolving the temporary financial difficulty.

Lockers

Employees who are assigned lockers are required to supply their own combination locks and must register the combination numbers and sequence with their superior. Lockers must be kept in good working order and undamaged by the employee's use. Food and beverages may be stored in the employee's locker only for the duration of the work *(day, shift)* in which it is brought to the workplace. Lockers are not to be used for the storage of such items as hazardous materials, alcoholic beverages, nonprescription drugs, contraband, or any other items not specifically authorized by the employee's supervisor.

Employees who enter or attempt to enter another employee's locker without supervisory authorization, or who abuse locker privileges, may be subject to disciplinary action including discharge.

Parking

The *(Company)* provides a designated parking area for the convenience and efficiency of employees, and to better enable employees to report to work on time. Employees using their personal vehicles for work travel are encouraged to arrange transport pools with other employees and utilize only the designated employee parking area.

Personal Property Repair/Replacement

Employees may be reimbursed for the repair or replacement of personal property damaged by unusual, unforeseen, or extraordinary circumstances that arise in the course of employment and performance of assigned duties. The option to repair or replace damaged items, and decide whether replaced property will be returned to the employee, will be at the sole discretion of the *(Company)*. This policy does not apply to normal depreciation or what may reasonably be construed as normal hazards to an employee's personal property during customary job performance.

Other exclusions include:

- Precious or semiprecious gems or metals;
- Vehicles of any type;
- Property in the care and control of another person;
- Money, notes of monetary value, or facsimiles;
- Property damage due to negligence or deliberate destruction; and
- Property valued at more than *($50)*.

Employees applying for repair or replacement of damaged personal property will be required to report the specifics of the incident causing damage and certify that repair or replacement of the item(s) *(is/are)* not recoverable through the employee's personal insurance policy.

The provisions of this policy shall not apply if the employee has concealed or misrepresented any material fact or circumstance.

Uniform Allowance

Those employees designated as required to wear uniforms in accordance with *(Company)* specifications will be reimbursed for the initial purchase of their uniforms, upon proof of purchase by receipt, up to *($)*. Thereafter, employees will receive a semi-annual allowance of *($)* in consideration of the cleaning, care, and replacement of uniforms to an acceptable condition of appearance according to *(Company)* standards as imposed by supervisory personnel.

Uniforms

Uniforms supplied by the *(Company)* will be kept in a neat, clean, and properly maintained condition at the employee's expense. Such uniform apparel may not be used as personal attire outside the work location. Uniforms whose condition no longer meets *(Company)* standards of appearance should be turned in for replacement. Employees who separate employment with the *(Company)* will be required to turn in *(Company)* supplied uniform apparel in a clean and neat condition.

LEAVE AND SCHEDULE POLICIES AND PRACTICES

Flexible Work Schedule

The *(Company)* recognizes that employees do not function best on the same clock hours, or may have personal preferences for the time they start their workday.[6] In response to this employee desire for a flexible method of scheduling work hours, the *(Company)* has adopted a flexible work schedule program available to employees whose work routine does not necessitate a precise schedule. Employees working a flexible schedule will ultimately be required to work their assigned number of hours in each workweek and complete assigned work tasks, and they may not exceed the maximum number of hours in a workday at straight-time pay without supervisory approval.

The *(Company's)* flexible work schedule will consist of *(six (6))* "core" hours from *(9:00 A.M.)* to *(3:30/4:00 P.M.)*, inclusive on assigned days. Flexible hours will be from *(7:30 A.M. to 9:00 A.M.)* and from *(3:30/4:00 P.M. to 5:30 P.M.)*. The following illustration is intended to give examples of actual work hour arrangements under the flexible schedule program.

	Report Time	Core Hours	Finish Time	Total Hours
Employee A	7:30 A.M.	9:00 A.M.–3:30 P.M.	4:00 P.M.	8
Employee B	8:30 A.M.	9:00 A.M.–4:00 P.M.	5:00 P.M.	8
Employee C	9:00 A.M.	9:00 A.M.–3:30 P.M.	5:30 P.M.	8

Employees on an approved flexible work schedule will be responsible for reporting their start and finish times to their immediate supervisor for the purpose of payroll record

---

[6]   More and more, workplace studies are concluding that flexible work schedules create a positive influence on employee attitude, behavior, and overall performance. While flexible work schedules are not suitable in all work routine circumstances, they can prove highly beneficial in other situations where work routines can be somewhat staggered. Given the nature of today's work force, employers may do well to examine their ability to accommodate flexible work schedules on a work unit-by-unit basis.

Another variation of flexible scheduling is the four-day workweek, or what is commonly referred to as the 4/10 Plan. Here, employees are scheduled to work four ten-hour days rather than the customary five eight-hour days, thereby getting three days off per week rather than two. Four-day workweeks became very popular in the early 1970s, not only because of growing employee interest in having more available free time, but also because of metropolitan transportation patterns and energy conservation. However, in recent years, studies are beginning to conclude that fatigue and a decline in productivity during the last two hours of each workday are common by-products of the four-day workweek schedule. These results will, of course, vary from employer to employer and work setting conditions depending on such factors as the degree of physical and mental exertion required in the performance of job duties. Employers wanting to examine the possibility of a four-day workweek for some or all employees should consult with a competent counsel or the state labor commissioner's office to ensure compliance with all applicable state laws pertaining to overtime pay and filing requirements.

keeping. Additionally, as the need arises based on the best interests of the *(Company)*, an employee's flexible schedule privileges may be modified or withdrawn at any time.

Floating Holidays

In addition to recognized holidays in which *(Company)* operations are closed for normal business, the *(Company)* provides *(one, two, or three (1, 2, or 3))* paid "floating" holidays each calendar year for regular employees continuously employed for at least *(three (3))* months.[7] Floating holidays are supplemental paid days off in which the employee may elect the date of use during the year with advance notice and approval of the supervisor. Floating holidays, like designated holidays, will not be considered hours worked for the purpose of calculating overtime. Floating holidays do not accrue from year to year and must therefore be taken or forfeited unless they are canceled by supervisory personnel, in which case the floating holiday should be rescheduled before year end.

General Leave

The *(Company)* has adopted a paid general leave program for regular employees which incorporates such forms of leave as vacation, sickness, personal emergency, bereavement, and *(any other)* leave. It is the intent of the general leave program to allow eligible employees greater flexibility in the use and application of paid absence from work while maintaining necessary and appropriate operation levels. It is also intended that the general leave program should serve to eliminate elaborate scrutiny of the employee's use of paid absence due to illness.[8]

Therefore, use of general leave will be subject to advance approval of the *(Department Head)*, except for personal illness or emergency in which case the employee's need to use general leave for this purpose will be communicated to the supervisor. However, nothing in this section is to be construed as limiting the supervisory personnel from requiring reasonable proof of personal illness or emergency in instances where supervision has cause to believe the use of general leave should have been subject to advance approval. In such cases, the *(Department Head)* may require the employee to provide sufficient proof of a bona fide

---

[7] Floating holidays can be useful for employers to supplement their paid holiday policy that is limited necessarily by the nature of their business. Conversely, some employers have added many holidays to their policy over the years that are no longer customary for business closure and may wish to eliminate some of those designated holidays by replacing them with floating holidays.

[8] General leave, similar to personal leave in Chapter 2, is a newer form of combining different leave types into one policy. Most general leave policies consist of combining vacation, sick leave, floating holidays, compensatory time off, and similar discretionary forms of paid leave into one policy. It has the advantages of being easy to administer and less paternal in terms of monitoring sick leave use, and it receives greater acceptance among employees who want to be dealt with as responsible adults. One disadvantage, if it can be seen in that light, is that general leave policies often transform otherwise noncompensable sick leave time upon termination to compensable time based on the actual number of accrued general leave hours. To offset this cost, employers who include sick leave as a form of general leave usually will discount the former number of days or hours granted under its separate sick leave policy. For example, if an employer has a sick leave policy allowing up to eight days of paid sick leave per year, the employer is likely to cut that time in half when including it in a general leave policy.

personal illness or emergency, or other reason the employee could not have acquired advance approval. In the absence of sufficient proof, the *(Department Head)* may charge the employee with an unauthorized leave without pay and, in cases of fraudulent use of general leave or deception in its use, may effectuate appropriate disciplinary measures.

Probationary employees will not be eligible for use of general leave, but will have credit applied retroactively upon achieving regular status. Employees will accrue general leave credit according to the following schedule:

Service Length	Monthly Credit Hours	Annual Days	Maximal Accrual Days
New employee—end of year 4	8	12	18
Start of year 5—end of year 9	10	15	23
Start of year 10—end of year 14	12	18	27
Start of year 15	14	21	32

Hours accrued in excess of the maximum will be forfeited by the employee. Eligible employees are entitled to use general leave only to the extent such leave has been accrued as of the date it is requested. General leave will be taken in minimum increments of one workday, except in cases of personal illness or emergency when leave may be taken in minimum increments appropriate to the circumstance.

Upon employment separation, eligible employees will be paid for accrued general leave based on their average pay rate over the preceding *(twelve (12))* months, unless the employee is discharged for gross misconduct whereby payment for general leave will be forfeited by the employee.

Inclement Weather Schedule

Employees whose routine work requires exposure to severe outdoor conditions may be assigned an inclement weather schedule as determined necessary and appropriate by supervisory personnel. During days of inclement weather, designated employees will receive normal pay if they are held by the supervisor for emergency calls; to receive first aid, safety, or other training; or to perform maintenance and other required work in sheltered locations.

Voting Time Off

Employees who would not be able to vote in a national, state, or local election because of the length of their work schedule, will be paid for up to *(two (2))* hours upon supervisory approval. Approval can be obtained by providing the supervisor with a valid voter's registration card for release and a voter's receipt upon return to work.[9]

---

[9]   Paid time off to vote is not required by the Fair Labor Standards Act, but is by many state laws. Typically, such policies are included only for those employers who conduct shift work for abnormal durations. Employers who feel they should include a voting time-off policy in their manuals should consult with competent counsel or the state labor commissioner's office to determine if such a law exists, and the minimum or maximum number of hours an employee is entitled to be paid for such an absence.

CONDITIONS OF EMPLOYMENT POLICIES AND PRACTICES

Affirmative Action Program

Affirmative action is not a matter of passive nondiscrimination or a neutral merit hiring policy. It is a deliberate results-oriented program aimed at the identification, recruitment, employment, and training of minorities, physically disabled persons, and women. It is intended to be a positive action that will equalize employment opportunities and fully utilize the greater pool of human resources and skills that exist among minorities, the physically disabled, and women. In adopting such a program, the *(Company)* recognizes the potential of all individuals who wish to participate in or seek entrance to the work force.

In undertaking affirmative action, the *(Company)* will not practice reverse discrimination by giving undue preferential treatment of minorities, the physically disabled, or women, by using quotas or other unequal opportunity devices. Rather, the affirmative action program has been developed to reinforce and enhance merit employment concepts by ensuring that all segments of the community have an opportunity to enter employment on the basis of open competition and to advance according to their relative ability and fitness.

The *(Company)* has developed, and maintains, a comprehensive affirmative action plan covering all elements of personnel policy and practice to remove discriminatory employment barriers when and where they are found to exist, and to enable all individuals to compete for employment opportunities on an equal basis, regardless of race, color, national origin, age, sex, handicap, or religious affiliation, unless there exists a bona fide occupational qualification.

Alternative Policy: Affirmative Action[10]

In furtherance of the *(Company's)* policy on equal employment opportunity, the *(Company)* additionally adopts this policy on affirmative action measures that may be taken from time to time as a means of ensuring that all people have a reasonable access and consideration with the *(Company)*. In adopting this policy, the *(Company)* gives recognition to the potential of all individuals who wish to participate in or seek entrance into the active work force.

In carrying out its affirmative action efforts, the *(Company)* shall periodically take the following steps as a means of making jobs known to the greater pool of human resources who might be qualified for employment, and to improve continuously upon any practice that is found or tends to be discriminatory in any known respect:

1. Develop and recommend any policies, procedures, practices, or programs that are in the *(Company's)* best interest to consider as a means of strengthening equal employment opportunities and the validity of employment decisions.
2. Develop and use recruitment sources that would provide information about *(Company)* job opportunities to all sectors of the available labor market.
3. Develop and use contemporary selection testing methods and standards that are determined appropriate for differing employment conditions.

---

[10] Levesque, *The Complete Hiring Manual,* pp. 51–52.

4. Monitor hiring results to evaluate the effectiveness of nondiscriminatory employment practices and attempts to achieve and maintain a representative work force.

5. Review and update job descriptions to ensure that they are relevant in all respects to actual job duties, requirements, and qualifications.

6. Investigate internal complaints or reports of discrimination and take the appropriate corrective action where warranted.

Management and supervisory personnel are expected to become aware of, and all employees are expected to abide by, the *(Company's)* policies and efforts concerning equal employment and affirmative action. Specifically, supervisors are expected to cooperate with the development of valid job descriptions and selection tests; to be responsible for making objective employment decisions and to report any condition that has the appearance or effect of discrimination solely on the basis on an individual's race, color, national origin, religion, age (over 40), sex, marital status, pregnancy, or physical disability.

Business Conduct

The reputation of the *(Company)* for its honesty, fairness, and business integrity is vital to success and therefore of paramount concern. The very nature of our *(customer, client)* relationship, and the confidential and private information provided in the course of our business places a special responsibility on each employee. The accountability for the manner in which employees conduct business extends equally to *(shareholders/directors)*, community members, and other employees.

In meeting these responsibilities, the *(Company)* expects its management, supervisory, and general staff to be free of influential interests and activities that may serve as a prevention from acting in the *(Company's)* best interest. It is incumbent on all employees to conduct their business and personal activities in a manner that does not adversely reflect upon the reputability of the *(Company)*. Compliance can be achieved only when business conduct conforms to the highest standard of ethical and lawful behavior.

In the conduct of *(Company)* business, no bribes, kickbacks, or similar improper payments or considerations are to be given or offered to any individual or organization. Political contributions are never made in a manner designed to circumvent the law.

In its many business activities, *(Company)* engages in a vigorous but fair and ethical competition, stressing the merits of our service and products. The *(Company)* does not undertake to make disparaging statements about competitors or their products and services or to engage in unfair actions to intentionally damage competitors.

Employees who have questions about the application of this policy, or who are uncertain in a particular circumstance, should seek the counsel and guidance of the *(Department Head or Human Resources Manager)* before proceeding.

Employee Relations[11]

The *(Company)* favors providing a work environment and conditions of employment that are both flexible and responsive to the needs of employees. The *(Company)* is therefore

---

[11] This is a good way of alerting employees to the employer's recognition of prevailing labor law, and of informing them that they cannot be legally barred from organizing or engaging in collective

opposed to the influence of outside representation and is aware of its management responsibilities as an employer to maintain a strong, healthy relationship with employees. The *(Company)* is continually interested in providing the best possible pay, benefits, and working conditions for the mutual betterment of employees and the *(Company)*. The ability and desire of the *(Company)* to continue in this manner is dependent on our freedom from outside intervention, and the restraints caused by collective representation, despite the *(Company's)* recognition of the lawful rights of employees to organize.

Employer Rights[12]

To ensure that *(Company)* reserves to itself, solely and exclusively, those functions necessary for the efficient and effective operation of the *(Company)*, the following employer rights are listed for illustrative purpose and are not intended to be limited by the existence of any other right:

- To manage the *(Company)* generally and to determine the issues of policy.
- To determine the existence of facts on which management decisions are based.
- To determine the necessity for, and organization of, any service or activity conducted by the *(Company)*, and to expand or diminish services.
- To determine the nature, manner, means, technology, and extent of services to be provided.
- To determine the *(Company)* budget, number and classification of employees, and methods of financing.
- To determine types of equipment or technology to be used.
- To determine and change the facilities, methods, technology, means, organizational structure, and size and composition of the work force and to allocate and assign the work by which *(Company)* operations are to be conducted.
- To determine and change the number of locations, relocations, and types of operations, processes, and materials to be used in carrying out all *(Company)* functions, including, but not limited to, the right to contract for or subcontract any work or operation of the *(Company)*.
- To direct, assign work to, and schedule employees in accordance with requirements as determined by the *(Company)* and to establish and change work schedules and assignments.

---

[11] *continued*   representation. However, it also lets employees know that the employer does not favor a union relationship, and thereby intends to manage the organization and treat employees in a humane manner.

[12]   Management or employer rights policies are usually found only in organizations having a unionized setting, and then they are found more frequently in the collective bargaining agreement. However, some employers may want to consider inclusion of this type of policy in their manuals, particularly where the employer has been teased with unionization, or in a nonunion business where the industry type is customarily unionized. Should an employer become unionized with this policy in place, it is considerably more difficult for the union to change existing policy than it would be for a union to initiate employer limitations.

- To lay off employees from duties because of lack of work or funds or under conditions where continued work would be ineffective or nonproductive.
- To establish and modify productivity and performance programs and standards.
- To discharge, suspend without pay, demote, reprimand, withhold salary increases, or otherwise discipline employees.
- To determine minimum qualifications, skills, abilities, knowledge, selection procedures and standards, and job classifications, and to reclassify employees.
- To hire, transfer, promote, and demote employees for nondisciplinary reasons.
- To determine policies, procedures, and standards for selection, training, and promotion of employees.
- To establish reasonable employee performance standards including, but not limited to, quality and quantity standards and to require compliance therewith.
- To maintain order and efficiency in *(Company)* facilities and operations.
- To establish, publish, and modify rules and regulations to maintain order, safety, and health in the *(Company)*.
- To take any and all necessary action to carry out the mission of the *(Company)* in emergencies.

Gifts and Gratuities

No employee shall accept or receive any benefit from any gift, gratuity, present, property, or service of any kind or nature regardless of value, which may be directly or indirectly offered as a result of, or in anticipation of, an employee's position or performance of duties with the *(Company)*.
Exceptions include:

- Unsolicited advertising or promotional materials of nominal intrinsic value such as pens and calendars;
- Awards for meritorious civic service contributions; and
- Unsolicited consumable items that are donated to an entire work group during holidays, and are consumed on the premises.

Investments—Conflict of Interest

It is the policy of the *(Company)* to conduct each and every business transaction with impartiality as to employee personal gain. Therefore, all employees are prohibited from making, directly or indirectly, investments that create, or have the appearance of creating a conflict of interest between the employee and *(Company)*, its *(customers, clients)*, or suppliers. Included in this policy is the use of private or confidential information related to the *(Company's)* business transactions used by employees for personal gain through employee investments in behalf of the employee, relatives, friends, or acquaintances.

Employees who have questions about the application of this policy, or who are uncertain in a particular circumstance, should seek the counsel and guidance of the *(Department Head or Human Resources Manager)* before proceeding.

Job Posting

The *(Company)* is generally committed to providing promotional opportunities to employees who have demonstrated exemplary job progress and self-motivation. In an attempt to advise employees of job openings, bulletins will be posted announcing job vacancies as the need arises. Employees who meet the standards and are interested in being considered for posted jobs should contact the *(Human Resources Manager)* for application details and further information about the job. Those employees selected for consideration of the posted job will be contacted by the *(Human Resources Manager)*.

Jobs posted are not necessarily reserved or held exclusively for internal consideration of employees. The *(Company)* may concurrently advertise or otherwise recruit qualified persons in the appropriate labor market.

Personal and Business Telephone Calls

Generally, personal telephone calls made or received by employees are discouraged due to their disruptive effect on *(Company)* operations. However, the *(Company)* recognizes that under certain circumstances it becomes necessary or important for an employee to communicate with a family member concerning a pressing matter. In such cases, the employee should seek supervisory approval to initiate or receive *(local)* calls, unless a pay telephone is available to employees during a scheduled break or meal period. Personal long-distance calls approved by a supervisor that are made on business lines as a matter of unavoidable necessity are to be reimbursed by the employee to the *(Company)*.

Employees may be contacted through the *(Company's)* business line any time an emergency exists that requires immediate notification of the employee. Employees so contacted will be allowed the opportunity to respond to the personal emergency, providing the situation is a legitimate emergency.

Whenever business-related telephone calls are initiated or received, employees should exercise customary business conversation, etiquette, and follow-up by use of these procedures:

- The call should be answered promptly by saying, "Good *(morning, afternoon, evening)*, this is *(state your name)*, may I help you?"
- Use a pleasant, welcoming, and courteous voice tone. Messages should be taken accurately and completely.
- Calls should be transferred to the appropriate person promptly and carefully, explaining to the caller why and to whom you are transferring their call. If you are unsure where to transfer the call, or cannot answer their question, the caller's name and telephone number should be taken and they should be told their call will be

returned. The person receiving such calls is responsible for ensuring that the caller is responded to as soon as possible.

- Calls should be concluded by letting the caller end the conversation, then pleasantly saying, "thank you" and "good-bye."

Predisciplinary Procedures:[13]

The imposition of discipline greater than suspension, without pay for *(five (5))* days, of an employee is subject to the following predisciplinary notice and review procedures.

1. The person recommending that discipline be imposed will give written notice to the affected employee of the proposed action at least *(five (5)) (working)* days prior to the proposed date of implementation of discipline. Such notice will contain

   a. A statement of the discipline proposed and its effective date;

   b. A statement of the reasons for imposing it, or the particular personnel policy violated;

   c. Any supporting material or documentation and a statement of the employee's right to review all relevant documents and materials; and

   d. An explanation of the employee's right to respond to the charges and proposed action, either verbally or in writing to the *(Human Resources Manager or President/General Manager)* within *(five (5)) (working)* days from receipt of the disciplinary notification.

2. Upon timely request of the affected employee, the *(Human Resources Manager or President/General Manager)* will meet with the employee, review the disciplinary recommendation, and evaluate any materials, documents, or arguments submitted on behalf of the affected employee in determining whether to impose discipline as recommended.

   Failure on the part of the affected employee to respond to the predisciplinary notification shall be grounds for immediate implementation of the proposed action.

3. Following the predisciplinary review by the *(Human Resources Manager or President/General Manager)*, the affected employee shall be promptly served a notice as to the decision to dismiss, modify, or implement the proposed disciplinary recommendation.

4. Service of any notice upon employees required by discipline provisions will be deemed to have been made upon personal presentation of such notice, or upon

---

[13]   Predisciplinary procedures are another method being used by some employers to avoid or reduce the chances of wrongful discharge suits, as well as to enhance the employer's stance on due process prior to initiating disciplinary action against employees. In essence, predisciplinary procedures provide advance notice to the employee who is being recommended for moderate or greater disciplinary action and give the employee an opportunity to informally meet with the person responsible for initiating disciplinary measures in an effort to mitigate the charges. These procedures can prove very useful in weeding out improper disciplinary actions by poorly trained supervisors.

depositing the notice, postage prepaid, in the U.S. mail, addressed to the employee at the last address of the employee as on file with the *(Company)*.

5. Exception: Under certain circumstances, it may be necessary to restrict an employee immediately from performing duties at the work site. The circumstances usually involve potential danger to the employee, coworkers, or the public; or the employee's inability to discharge assigned duties satisfactorily. Because of the need for immediate action, the decision to suspend an employee is typically the responsibility of the supervisor. In these situations, the following procedure shall be used:

   a. The supervisor taking the action to suspend an employee will immediately notify the *(Department Head)* and, as soon as possible, prepare a written statement of the action taken and the reasons for such action.

   b. The *(Department Head)* will, together with the supervisor, prepare the statement of charges and document supporting evidence.

   c. Within *(four (4))* days of the employee's suspension, the *(Department Head)* will prepare written notification to the affected employee in accordance with sections 1a–d.

Romantic or Sexual Liaisons

Although the *(Company)* generally confines its involvement in the private lives of employees, there may be some circumstances in which it becomes necessary for the *(Company)* to intervene. Romantic or sexual liaisons that develop in the workplace are instances that the *(Company)* sees as potentially disruptive to performing one's job, affecting the working conditions of others, damaging to business relationships, and adverse to careers and the *(Company's)* reputation as a harmonious workplace. Those employees who become involved in this regard should be aware that serious risks and consequences can develop as a result of its effect on business matters, at which time the *(Company)* may intervene by discussing the issue with affected employees, or taking remedial measures when, in the *(Company's)* opinion, it is necessary to do so to maintain the integrity of work relationships.

Further, it is expressly prohibited for management employees to date or become similarly involved privately with any nonmanagement employee of the *(Company)*, or for any married employee to establish a romantic or sexual relationship with any other employee. Should these kinds of relationships become known to *(Company)* officers, the *(Company)* will determine an appropriate course of action on a case-by-case basis. Such action may include counseling, transfer, demotion, or termination. The *(Company)* would rather avoid these situations altogether, and we therefore encourage employees to use common sense judgment in managing their work relationships so that this type of awkwardness does not develop.[14]

---

[14]   This discussion is from Joseph D. Levesque, *The Human Resource Problem-Solver's Handbook* (New York: McGraw-Hill, 1992), pp. I.4.126–127. Used with permission.

Seniority[15]

For full-time regular employees, seniority will be first based on an employee's length of uninterrupted service in the position occupied, and second, on an employee's length of service with the *(Company)* from the date of original full-time employment. Where two or more employees have the same length of service in the same position, the employee with greater *(Company)* service will be senior. Conflicts in the likeness of service length will be resolved by the determination that the employee having the better performance record, attendance, and skill development as evaluated by the *(Human Resources Manager)* will be considered senior.

Time Changes[16]

Employees subject to work shifts during the hours of daylight saving or standard time changes will work schedules on the basis of clock hours rather than total number of hours worked on these occasions. This policy will thereby constitute an even exchange of hours due to these time changes each year.

Use of Business Property

To avoid potential misunderstandings and problems, the *(Company)* has established the following policy concerning the use of business property and services.

Care of Business Property All employees are expected to exercise due care when using *(Company)* property and to utilize the property only for authorized purposes. Negligence in the care and use of *(Company)* property may be cause for disciplinary action including termination. Additionally, unauthorized removal of *(Company)* property from the premises, or its conversion to personal use, will be considered cause for termination.

Return of Business Property *(Company)* property issued to an employee must be returned to the *(Company)* at the time the employee separates employment or when its return is requested. It is the employee's responsibility to reimburse the *(Company)* for the value of any such property issued to the employee that is not returned upon request.

Personal Property on Business Premises The *(Company)* assumes no responsibility for the loss or damage to personal property of any employee who is brought on to *(Company)* premises. Also, it is prohibited for employees to carry personal property in *(Company)* vehicles without the express permission of the employee's supervisor.

---

[15]   This policy is reserved for unionized employers or those who feel that unionization may one day be a prospect. Other employers may best be served by avoiding this type of policy in their manuals altogether, unless there exists some compelling reason to include it. For that reason, this policy reflects a conservative, management-oriented approach to the issue.

[16]   This policy is optional and applicable to employers who have work activities being performed by employees during the hours and in time zones subject to clock changes as a result of daylight or standard time changes. This policy presumes that shifts will not rotate and that an employee subject to one change will also be subject to the corresponding time change.

Management will additionally have the right to request any employee to open for inspection any package or other container brought onto or taken from *(Company)* premises.

Use of Business Vehicles The use of *(Company)* vehicles for personal use by employee is prohibited. If an employee who normally operates a *(Company)* vehicle has a situation that must be taken care of during work time, prior approval from the employee's supervisor must be obtained, but approval will be restricted to unusual circumstances.

All employees using *(Company)* or personal vehicles during, and in the course of, performing assigned duties will be required to wear seat belts any time the vehicle is in use.

Use of Business Mail Employees are not permitted to make use of the *(Company's)* mail system, services, or postage materials for private use. If an employee is uncertain about the application of this policy to a particular situation, the employee should consult with his or her supervisor for clarification and proper authorization.

GLOSSARY

The following terms and their definitions as used in this manual apply where used unless otherwise defined within the manual. The notation "syn." means "synonymous" or "same as."

Acting Appointment — The temporary assignment of a person to a vacant position in the absence of an employee who normally fills such position. Persons receiving acting assignments must possess the minimum qualifications of the position.

Affirmative Action — Policies, procedures, and practices adopted to assure equal employment opportunities for all persons.

Allocation — The assignment of a single position to its proper class in accordance with the duties performed and the authority and responsibilities exercised.

Anniversary Date — The date upon which an employee first appears on the payroll due to original or promotional appointment and on which the employee establishes eligibility for salary advancement consideration. Anniversary dates may be changed by promotion, demotion, or reclassification. The anniversary date for salary step advancement eligibility shall be on that date which concludes service in the lower salary step.

1. For employees with anniversary dates between the *(first (1st)) and (fifteenth (15th))* of the month, inclusive, anniversary dates shall be adjusted to the *(first (1st))* day of the month.

2. For employees with anniversary dates between the *(sixteenth (16th))* and the end of the month, inclusive, anniversary dates shall be adjusted to the *(sixteenth (16th))* day of the month.

The base anniversary date is the date of original employment, in most cases probationary, to a regular position (also called "Date of Employment").

Appointing Authority — The position responsible for hiring, firing, directing work, scheduling, and supervising work for each position.

Appointment — The selection of, and acceptance by, a candidate to a position.

Bona Fide Occupational Qualification — A job-related requirement of a position that precludes employment of applicants on the basis of sex or physical handicap.

Bridged Service Credit — The linking or connecting of reinstated employees' prior time in a position where regular status was held, to present accrual of time in the same position for purposes of determining seniority, pay, and vacation accrual rate.

Candidate	An applicant who fulfills the requirements of a given position, who has successfully completed the required examination(s) for such a class of work, and whose name has been listed as eligible for employment.
Certification	Formal, written verification of eligibility for employment.
Class (**Syn.** *Classification*)	A group of positions sufficiently similar in respect to the duties and responsibilities that (1) the same descriptive title may be used with clarity to designate each position allocated to the class; (2) common requirements as to education, experience, knowledge, ability, and other qualifications exist for all incumbents; (3) common tests of fitness may be used to choose qualified employees; and (4) the same schedule of compensation can be made to apply with equity under the same or substantially the same employment conditions.
Classification Plan	A listing of job titles and descriptions in regular service.
Compensation (**Syn.** *Salary, Wages, Pay*)	The amount of cash payment made to employees by payroll check in consideration of the number of hours worked in accordance with payment schedules, including pay for overtime, work in a higher class (acting), educational incentive, and other forms of payment in connection with the performance of job assignments. Total compensation refers to that amount of cash pay plus employment-related benefits received by employees, including contributions to the employee's medical and dental programs, retirement, personal leave, vacation, and other similar benefits of monetary value.
Continuous Service	Employment without interruption, excluding authorized vacation, military leave, or other paid leaves.
Day	Calendar day unless otherwise noted.
Demotion	A change in employment status resulting in (1) movement from one position to another that requires fewer minimum qualifications and is assigned a lower pay range or (2) movement from one pay step to a lower pay step within the same salary range assigned to a particular position.
Discharge (**Syn.** *Dismissal; See Also Termination*)	Involuntary separation or termination of employment.
Employees	1. *Initial/Introductory Employee:* An employee who has not completed the initial trial period for a particular position. 2. *Management Employee:* Any employee having significant responsibilities for formulating and administrating policies and programs and for directing the work of subordinates by lower-level supervision; any employee having authority to exercise independent judgment or effectively to recommend

Employees (continued)   any action to hire, transfer, suspend, lay off, recall, promote, discharge, assign, reward, or discipline other employees, or to direct them or adjust their grievances, if the exercise of such authority is not of a merely routine or clerical nature, but requires the use of independent judgment and discretion.

3. *Professional Employee:* An employee engaged in work requiring specialized knowledge and skills attained through completion of an academic course of instruction, usually leading to the attainment of an academic degree, or a specialized course of instruction.

4. *Regular Employee:* An employee who has successfully completed the prescribed initial/introductory employment period. (1) A regular full-time employee provides full-time services and is compensated at full pay and benefits for the assigned position; (2) A regular part-time employee provides less than full-time service and is compensated in proportion to the amount of service provided.

5. *Supervisory Employee:* An employee who exercises responsibility for training, evaluating, assigning, and overseeing work, and who has the authority to recommend discipline.

6. *Temporary Employee:* An employee who possesses the minimum qualifications established for a particular position, and has been appointed to the position in the absence of available eligibles, or who has been appointed to a position of limited scope and duration.

Employment List   A list of names of persons, ranked in order of scores achieved, who have successfully passed all phases of the examination process for a class of employment.

Equal Employment Opportunity   A condition of equality in all employment-related actions brought about by unbiased personnel practices, procedures, and methods.

Examination   The process of measuring and evaluating the relative ability and fitness of applicants by job-related testing procedures.

1. *Assembled Examination:* An examination conducted at a specified time and place at which applicants are required to appear for competitive examination under the supervision of an examiner.

2. *Unassembled Examination:* An examination consisting of an appraisal of training, experience, work history, or any other means for evaluating other relative qualifications without the necessity for personal appearance at a specified place.

Flexible Schedule   A schedule of work hours and days during which an employee is to be present at work, the time of which shall consist of a specified period during the normal work schedule (core time) with

Flexible Schedule (continued) the prescribed balance of hours to be worked by arrangement of the employee and supervisor.

Increment One of a series of salary rate steps in a range between the minimum and maximum salary specified for a job classification.

Initial/Introductory Employment The trial period of employment during which the employee is trained and evaluated on fitness and ability to perform the duties of the appointed position. The final phase of the selection process for regular service.

Initial/Introductory Employment Period A designated period of time, and any extension thereof, in which an employee, upon original or promotional appointment, is trained and evaluated for suitability to a position.

Initial/Introductory Employment Release The discharge of an employee during the trial period. Where the employee has been promoted to a higher-level position and is being released while serving an introductory period in such position, the employee may be demoted to the lower level position previously held if regular status was obtained in the lower-level position.

Job Description (Syn. Class Specification) A detailed written description of the essential factors that distinguish one job from another; it includes a job title, duties and responsibilities, examples of work performed, and minimum or desirable qualifications.

Job Title A descriptive name given to a classification, listed on all official records of the employee.

Layoff (Syn. Reduction-In-Force) Involuntary separation from employment for nondisciplinary reasons including, but not limited to, lack of funds or work, abolition of position, reorganization, or the reduction or elimination in service levels.

Merit Increase (Syn. Pay Advancement, Step Increase) Advancement of an employee's base pay from one salary step to a higher salary step within the same salary range based on satisfactory demonstration of individual efficiency and performance.

Modified Duty Schedule The assignment of an employee, who has been injured on or off the job (except in connection with off-duty employment) and has been medically released to perform limited employment tasks, to a job in which the employee can perform tasks based on physical restrictions for a designated period of time.

Off-Duty Employment (Syn. Moonlighting) The simultaneous holding of more than one paid employment by an employee (full-time employment and a supplementary job with another employer or self-employment).

Performance Evaluation A formal system to evaluate performance factors related to an employee's job duties, responsibilities, and related employment characteristics on a regular and systematic basis by supervisory personnel.

Performance Test	A selection or retention test technique having as its primary objective the evaluation of relative ability to perform a job task or series of tasks based on a demonstration of the job task(s) or its reasonable simulation.
Position	A job defined by specific responsibilities, title, and locational assignment, and whose full description is contained in a job description.
Promotion	A change in employment status from one position to another position that requires higher minimum qualifications, is assigned more difficult duties and responsibilities, and is assigned a higher pay range.
Prorata	The proportional calculation of equivalency to the whole or full amount; an equivalent level of benefits based on the relationship of hours worked to earned benefit credits over any given period of time.
Protected Group Members	Ethnic and racial minorities, women, the physically disabled, and persons aged 40 years and over.
Reclassification	The modification of job duties due to a material difference between the existing job description and the actual job duties required to perform functions of a position.
Reduction (Syn. Pay Reduction)	A pay decrease within the limits of the pay range established for a position.
Reinstatement	The employment without examination of a former employee who has resigned or been laid off in good standing from regular service, and who within two years requests to be reinstated in the same job in which regular status was formerly held.
Resignation	Voluntary separation from employment.
Service Year	Twelve (12) calendar months from the date of hire. Every year from that date will be considered another "service year."
Selection Process	The sequence of examinations leading to the establishment of an eligible list and ultimately to placement as a regular employee.
Suspension	The temporary removal of an employee from service, without pay, for disciplinary reasons and for a specified period of time.
Termination	The involuntary separation of an employee from employment.
Third-Degree Kinship	A relative of the employee by blood or marriage, except spouse, within the third degree to include the employee's parents, children, grandparents, grandchildren, brothers, sisters, aunts, uncles, nephews, and nieces.
Transfer	A change of employment status from one position to another position where it is either (1) a voluntary or involuntary transfer to a position having the same or similar qualifications,

Transfer (continued)   duties and responsibilities, which does not result in reductions of salary, benefits, or privileges; or (2) a voluntary transfer to a position having the same, similar or lesser qualifications, duties, or responsibilities which may or may not result in a reduction of salary, benefits, or other privileges.

Validated Test   A selection examination whose elements are directly related to the significant and specific requirements and duties of the job class.

Workday   The number of hours of work within a *(twenty-four (24))*-hour period. For full-time employees, the workday shall generally consist of *(eight (8))* compensable hours of work. Part-time employees shall have a workday defined by the number of hours normally scheduled in a prescribed day of work.

Work Schedule   A listing of the specific days and hours each employee is assigned to perform normal work duties as determined by the supervisor.

Workweek   The number of days and hours assigned to an employee to perform normal duties. Full-time employees shall work a *(forty (40))*-hour workweek consisting of *(five (5))* days of *(eight (8))* hours' work within a calendar week.

Part Two

SETTING UP A COMPLETE PERSONNEL RECORDS SYSTEM

There is no mystery connected with the proper use and storage of employment records. As with most aspects of managing personnel operations, common sense should prevail.

Record keeping will be covered in this introductory section, as it does not require elaborate explanation or detail, even if an automated recordkeeping system is to be used. This part provides ready-to-use forms and sample employment letters. Whether forms or letters are being used for this manual, caution should be exercised to ensure that content fits the situation. Considerable effort has gone into designing these forms for generic use and overall utility in most personnel operations—and for dealing with most personnel situations likely to arise.

Employers, particularly smaller businesses with limited time and staff, should be careful about the number of forms they use to process personnel information. There is a general tendency among employers inexperienced in personnel matters to create a form for virtually every *separate* type of personnel transaction as the need surfaces. This adopt-a-form-as-you-go approach to personnel records will eventually create a mountain of confusing paperwork, it will annoy supervisors or others who have to fill out the forms, and it will overburden any available personnel staff with clerical processing tasks instead of leaving them free for meaningful professional-level work that can contribute to the organization's productivity.

In most cases, only one form has been provided in this manual for each differing situation commonly associated with the three stages of employment: the hiring process, transactions that should be recorded during employment, and outprocessing. Where possible, and in keeping with the theme (such as leaves and change of status), several different, yet related, transactions have been combined in one form, thus reducing the need for individual forms. Employers wishing to design their own forms may refer to the reference reading list at the end of this manual for other sources on personnel forms and forms design.

As a general rule, forms should not contain nor elicit any information that is not justifiably needed by the employer for a job-related purpose. It is therefore incumbent upon employers to understand the legalistic implications of asking for some kinds of information, and to consider the practical purpose for which the information will be used in the context of the employment relationship. For example, it is not prudent for employers to use an employment application form requesting information about the applicant's age, sex, height and weight, or marital status because these questions *imply* that the answers *may* aid the employer's discretionary *use* of such information. Such information should be avoided before employment, but it is essential for records upon employment.

The information, forms, and sample letters contained in this part are intended to aid the employer with a few of the more confusing, least publicized aspects of setting up a thorough yet simplified personnel program. These consist of the kinds and methods of records to be kept for both legal and good management practice reasons, the forms needed to document the more important and frequently encountered employment events, and the kind of wording to be used in employment-related letters.

There are four categories of forms in this part:

1. Preemployment forms
2. New-hire setup forms
3. During employment forms
   a. Compensation and benefit forms
   b. Classification, performance, and transfer forms
   c. Work schedule and leave forms
   d. Safety and industrial injury forms
   e. Discipline and employee relations forms
4. Miscellaneous forms

Each form is preceded by a brief notation or explanation of its use. The forms are designed for ready-to-use application by reproducing them in the desired quantity and size and by giving them a customized appearance when the employer's stylized name and logo are imprinted on the form.

Chapter 4

EMPLOYMENT RECORDS AND RECORDS SYSTEMS

LEGALLY REQUIRED RECORDS[1]

In compliance with the Fair Labor Standards Act (FLSA), Equal Employment Opportunity (EEO) laws, and various state laws that regulate mandatory record keeping by employers, you should attend to the following on new and rehired employees.

1. Secure a completed, verified, and lawfully acceptable I-9 form that attests to the individual's lawful right to be in the United States and obtain employment.

2. File all applications and selection testing records applicable to the hiring process that resulted in the employment of the person you hired, but not in their file folder.

3. In the case of employers with one hundred or more employees, record the personal characteristics of each employee by designated equal employment opportunity categories to prepare and submit the annual EEO-1 report to the Equal Employment Opportunity Commission (EEOC).

4. Compile and maintain a record of the employee's general personal information to include their:

    a. Name, address, phone number, and emergency notification information;

    b. Date of birth, social security number, and driver's license number;

    c. Marital status and dependent and beneficiary information; and

    d. Job title, classification status, and pay rate.

5. Complete W-4 form (declaration of income tax withholding) and payroll processing information.

6. Complete the applicable forms and records that would add the new or rehired employee to your workers' compensation plan and unemployment insurance account.

---

[1]   From Joseph D. Levesque, *The Complete Hiring Manual* (Englewood Cliffs, N.J.: Prentice Hall, 1992), p. 78.

POSTING NOTICES

There are specific posters and notices that *must* be posted by all employers in a place conspicuous to employees such as a bulletin board where employees pass by or congregate at each separate business location. These notices do not have to be in public view, although some employers prefer to display various antidiscrimination posters where applicants appear. Legally required posters and notices will vary from state to state, usually depending on distinctions in labor, safety, and fair employment laws. Employers should check with their nearest state labor commissioner's office or other knowledgeable advisors on the particular posting requirements in their state.

The typical posters and notices that are legally required for prominent display in the work place include the following:

1. Wage and Hour Notice (state or federal)
2. Occupational Safety and Health Act—Forms 101 and 200 (state or federal)
3. Workers' Compensation Carrier Notice (state or private carrier)
4. Equal Employment Opportunity and Nondiscrimination in Employment Notices (state and federal)
5. Unemployment Insurance Notice (state)

Employers may, of course, post any other notices such as the year's holidays and vacation schedule, activity reports, employee of the month, and newsletters. However, employers should guard against allowing the posting of offensive cartoons, sexually oriented photographics (centerfolds or pinups), and any derogatory material—particularly (disciplinary) notices or correspondence to a specific employee. Some employers have posted an employee's disciplinary or termination notice hoping that other employees would take note of the example being made of the employer's unwillingness to tolerate certain conditions, only to learn later, and for a painful price, that such a posting violated the employee's privacy rights.

PERSONNEL FILES AND CONTENTS

Setting up proper personnel files is essential not only because of privacy and other legal considerations connected to thorough record keeping, but also because it is an efficient management practice to maintain orderly business records. For most smaller businesses, a manual personnel records and file system will serve the intended purpose of employment record keeping rather than an automated (computer) system, which is discussed in the next section.

Most employment and personnel documentation must be readily available on an as-needed basis in hard copy—one of the major advantages of using a manual system, at least until processing of employment documents becomes inefficient, at which time it may prove useful to convert some records processing to an automated system.

Perhaps one of the most frequently asked questions is, "How should personnel files be set up, and what should they contain (and not contain)?" The answers to these questions depend on such factors as the nature of the business, kinds of employees, pay plans, and a host of other considerations, as well as operational preference for the form in which records are kept. Regardless of form, certain records must be kept in personnel files while other records or data may be considered optional—records that provide useful information for research, collective bargaining, or preparing annual reports on personnel matters, or that have some bearing on operations. Examples of these optional records are sick leave logs, turnover tabulations, and summaries of annual wage increases.

One of the best and most widely used methods of establishing personnel files is the use of heavy-duty legal-sized file folders with Acco fasteners at the top of both covers. An excellent folder is available from Universal Paper Goods in Los Angeles. The product is called a pressboard folder, has a two-inch expansion (#253F26), and may be ordered through most office supply companies. Regular legal files are normally not strong enough for the frequency of handling that personnel files receive. These heavy-duty legal folders have the added convenience of an expandable spine to accommodate growth of personnel records. They can be used as stand-alone files, be placed in individually marked Pendaflex® folders so that when the file is removed it is easier to locate its replacement order in the drawer. The name of the employee should be on both the file folder and the Pendaflex® folder.

Personnel files can be arranged in alphabetical order of employees' last names with full-time employee tabs on the left edge of folders, and part-time employee tabs on the right. Another method is to use color-coded tabs, or symbols on the tabs (self-adhesive colored dots for example), for easy identification of a certain group or class of workers (e.g., exempt/nonexempt, plant employees, or shift personnel).

It is suggested that the inside left folder flap be used for such in-processing and benefits documents as:

1. Application form and/or resume;
2. Preemployment tests (including interview, physical exam, and reference check/ employment verification forms);
3. Letter of employment (notification of hire);
4. New Employee Orientation Checklist form;
5. Declaration of Income Tax Withholding form;
6. Benefit (insurance) enrollment forms; and
7. Employee Information Log form.

Items 1–4 and 7 are available in Chapter 5. These documents represent the items most often referred to on a routine basis. Using the left flap makes them easy to find and rarely subject to reordering or lengthy search. With the Employee Information Log form on top, ongoing summary information can be logged on one form representing several types of personnel transactions such as leaves, pay and benefit changes, changes in job classification, training taken, and performance evaluation reports. The inside right folder flap is then used for those forms, records, and letters that serve as supporting documentation of data entered on the Employee Information Log. These supporting documents should be placed in the right flap as various situations arise *during the course of employment,* and they consist of such items as:

1. Leave request forms or notices;
2. Medical notices and records (except workers' compensation reports, which should be set up in a separate file);
3. Performance evaluation forms and reports;
4. Pay change notices;
5. Job classification change notices;
6. Job injury reports (unless a workers' compensation claim has been filed, then file the injury report in the workers' compensation file with related claims documents);
7. Request to Engage in Off-Duty Employment form (if applicable);
8. Disciplinary notices; and
9. Request for Administrative Review form.

Place these documents in chronological order with the most current document on top. To increase the efficiency of finding certain key right flap documents, copy the forms or letters onto colored paper. For example, pay change notices could be on green paper, evaluation reports on blue, disciplinary notices on goldenrod. The farsighted employer will appreciate the long-range wisdom of such a time-saving device as the business grows in number of employees or their length of service. I-9 forms, on the other hand, may be placed in one file folder for all employees.

Official personnel files *must* be stored in a locking file cabinet or other secured repository at the business location. Virtually *all* employment records should be considered *confidential* documents of the business and handled accordingly. The employer should not allow supervisors, employees, or any other person to drop paperwork into an employee's personnel file unless it has been reviewed and approved for placement in the file by someone familiar with the implications of personnel file contents.

Individual employee documents are private records, and many states have enacted laws protecting employee privacy rights, allowing employees' review of their own personnel files, restricting employment-related use of arrest and conviction records, and protecting employees from wage garnishments. In consideration of the confidentiality and privacy of personnel file records, most organizations restrict access to the following:

1. Human resources manager or official custodian of personnel records;
2. Individual employees;
3. Only those supervisors and managers in the organization who have a "legitimate *need* and *right* to know"; and
4. "Outsiders" possessing legal authority for access to *particular* personnel file information, such as by written approval of the employee or court order (subpoena).

CHECKLIST: HIRING, EMPLOYMENT, AND PERSONNEL FILE RECORDS[2]

Setting Up Employment and Personnel File Records

☐ Review state laws to determine the need to establish, file, and/or report different employment records than required by federal law.

☐ Place file cabinets in a private location but where their use can be observed.

☐ Ensure that file cabinets are fireproof and equipped with locks to which only designated staff have keys.

☐ Designate a management-level person officially as the "employment records custodian."

☐ Designate staff who are to prepare hiring, employment, and personnel file documents as "confidential" employees.

☐ Acquire file folders, fasteners, and tabs to set up personnel records, employment forms, and job description files.

☐ Determine if state law permits the keeping of secondary personnel files for sensitive documents; if so, set up these file folders.

☐ Gather and place employment forms in file folders.

☐ Prepare a policy on the handling, access, use, and disclosure of hiring, employment, and personnel file documents.

☐ Set up file folders for the storage of completed application forms, submitted resumes, and (if used) job interest and transfer request forms.

Completing and Filing Hiring Records

☐ Keep a separate file on all completed applications and test materials for each job subjected to a hiring process.

☐ Have new employees complete the I-9 form and file these in a single folder with other employment records.

☐ Complete the EEO identification characteristics of each new hire on a compiled log of all employees, and file in a separate folder with other employment records.

☐ Complete the Employee Information Log (or facsimile) form, or record basic personal, job, and payroll information about the new employee and place it in the employee's personnel file.

☐ Complete the W-4 form, forward a copy to the person handling payroll, and place the original copy in the employee's personnel file.

☐ Complete the appropriate forms and records to add the new employee to payroll, benefit plans, workers' compensation, and unemployment insurance policies.

☐ Complete and place in the employee's personnel file:
  • Application/resume and qualifications documents
  • Testing records
  • Background and medical examination reports and information (store in secondary file if permitted by state law)
  • Employee's acknowledgment forms verifying receipt of company property and employment handbook
  • Notices from the company's insurance carriers applicable to the employee
  • Orientation Checklist form
  • Job description
  • Employment (hiring) confirmation letters

☐ Prepare a master list of what hiring, employment, and personnel records need to be retained for designated periods of time and use this list as a guide to your company's records retention practices.

---

[2] Levesque, *The Complete Hiring Manual*, p. 97.

CONTROLLING ACCESS AND DISCLOSURE OF EMPLOYMENT AND PERSONNEL RECORDS INFORMATION[3]

While employment records and personnel files are the private property of the company that prepares them for their own purposes, the contents are not necessarily the sole domain of authorized company officials and representatives. *All* employment records pertaining to specific employees are discoverable through the acquisition powers of a subpoena. Also, the courts have determined that certain third parties such as governmental representatives (law enforcement and compliance agency personnel), union business agents, and the courts themselves can obtain certain kinds of employment records. Moreover, many states have adopted laws enabling employees to inspect their personnel files at convenient times and locations within a reasonable distance of their work location.

So, on the one hand, there are individuals who have the need and right to access employment records and personnel file information, while, on the other hand, there are individuals who may not gain access or knowledge of this information because of the employer's obligation to protect each employee's privacy rights. Here are some guidelines that should help you better understand and formulate your operating practice to control the inappropriate access and disclosure of employment records.

Internal Access and Disclosure

First, you should recognize the obvious fact that particular individuals in your organization do have legitimate need-to-know right to access, review, and modify file documents during the normal course of processing a variety of employment matters. These internal company representatives usually consist of:

1. The human resources manager who has ultimate internal responsibility for establishing and maintaining employment records and personnel files.
2. Human resources office staff whose jobs require access to files for storage and processing actions.
3. The employee's supervisor, department manager, or senior management personnel, each of whom must have some relevant and stated purpose for accessing these files.
4. Company advisors such as attorneys, consultants, and insurance company representatives whose work necessitates access and review of these files to acquire the information needed for some legitimate company interest.

Second, you should avoid making many of the mistakes commonly associated with employment records access and disclosure. One such mistake is to allow a file

---

[3]   Levesque, *The Complete Hiring Manual*, pp. 79–81.

to leave the area (human resources office) in which it is stored. To accommodate internal access by those who have the right to these records and files, you should have available a desk or table where those individuals can review this material—but within eyeshot of the person responsible for monitoring those allowed access (yours would not be the first company to have an employee or supervisor conceal their removal of a file document).

Another common mistake made is to allow supervisors to use an employee's personnel file as a repository for assorted handwritten notes. Rather, every supervisor should make use of a "supervisor's desk log" to record casual employment events until such time as the information is acted on in a more official fashion and thereupon made a formal part of the employee's file. And, finally, you should never allow co-workers or indirect managers access to employment records or personnel files, even if the co-worker is a union steward attempting to represent the employee's (grievance) interest. In each of these cases, access to the file should be denied and disclosure protected.

Third-Party Access and Disclosure

The access to employment records and improper disclosure of their contents is where most privacy rights problems arise, largely because third parties are taking immediate, visible, and often damaging action on the basis of information they receive. Consequently, access and disclosure should be severely controlled under advice of qualified legal counsel. However, those third-party representatives that are generally entitled to *limited* access to employment records are as follows.

1. Those representing the employee's interests and who present proper identification, purpose, and/or authority:
   a. Union business agent with identification, legitimate purpose, and the employee's written authorization to view records applicable to the nature of representation
   b. Private attorney representing a stated employment matter that *directly* concerns an employee and who has proper subpoena authority to access those records applicable to the cause of representation
2. Those representing employment compliance agencies who present proper identification, purpose, and authority:
   a. Labor Standards Enforcement personnel conducting routine audits or investigating records in relation to a claim made by an employee
   b. Occupational Safety and Health Administration (OSHA) or National Institute for Occupational Safety and Health (NIOSH) personnel conducting audits or investigations
   c. Equal Employment Opportunity Commission personnel conducting audits or investigations
   d. Similar state compliance agency personnel performing the same functions

3. Those representing law enforcement activities who present proper identification, documented proof of reasonable purpose, and advice from your company's legal counsel to cooperate:

    a. Federal Bureau of Investigation (FBI) or the Department of Justice (DOJ)

    b. State or local law enforcement representatives

    c. Court order having authoritative jurisdiction

It should be understood that not all these representatives have an automatic right to access any employment record or personnel file document they wish. One of the first things that you should establish is what document(s) are pertinent to their purpose and do they possess proper authority to access, view, and/or photocopy certain documents. Second, if access and disclosure are given, you or your company's authorized records custodian should participate in the examination and disclosure process with the external person acquiring information *after* reviewing the file to mark pertinent documents and thereby omit sensitive or inapplicable documents from being viewed out of context.

Developing an Employment and Personnel Records Access and Disclosure Policy

For those employers who truly desire a forthright yet controlled approach to matters of the confidentiality, security, access, and disclosure of employment records (rather than leaving these issues subject to quizzical or suspicious minds), it can prove worthwhile to publish and disseminate a company policy that addresses each of these major concerns—see Chapter 2 sample policies. Prior to adoption and release of such a policy, you should enlist the help of qualified legal and human resources advisors, as well as internal key managers, to identify various components and conditions related to employment documents, their access, use, and disclosure. It is important for you to consult with these individuals to consider all the prospective scenarios of records access and disclosure, to obtain current and clear information about applicable state laws and legal decisions, and to consider that company policies do not apply only to those over whom the company controls or wants a particular outcome.

Each employer's development of an employment records and personnel files access and disclosure policy may differ because of unique conditions within the company or the nature of its business, state laws, or the philosophical approach management takes to regulating this practice. As a means of at least starting the deliberation of what component and conditions might be included in your access and disclosure policy, the following are some preliminary items for you to consider.

1. What employment, personnel, and personal information does the company obtain in the course of its hiring and employment processes? Make a list of the types of information either required or acquired during the hiring process, and note which information should be designated "sensitive." Your list should

include those employment records and personnel file documents mentioned earlier in this chapter.

2. Describe and list the personnel file information that employees can have access to for the purpose of reviewing the contents of their own files. How often, where, and under what conditions can employees review their personnel files? Are employees prohibited from reviewing their files any time after employment separation, or will they be given a short period thereafter to do so?

3. Determine whether employees can have copies of the contents of their files. A recommended approach is to *insist* that employees be given copies of documents placed in their personnel file at the time such documents are produced and then charge them a small fee for preparing copies from their file.

4. Determine whether employees have the right to rebut or challenge statements made in file documents; if so, by when and how?

5. Determine whether state law allows the keeping of two official personnel files, the second of which can be used for the (employee or others) nonaccessible storage of sensitive information. If so, consider including the fact that these records exist but are nonaccessible, other than to company representatives who have a need and right to know.

6. Consider identifying in your policy what other individuals, such as third parties, may have access to employment records and under what conditions.

7. Determine what information will be disclosed to a verified, prospective future employer upon a reference inquiry and if this information is to be given with or without the employee's signed authorization and release to do so.

CHECKLIST: PRIVACY CONTROL SYSTEM[4]

Personnel Policies

☐ Have a written and well-disseminated policy on preparing, handling, use, and access of confidential employment information.

☐ Have a preemployment medical testing policy that assures only job valid testing will be conducted, including the reserved right of management to require medical testing when circumstances warrant (e.g., return to work, contagious condition absence, and workers' compensation disability).

☐ Have a drug/alcohol testing policy for new hires related only to sensitive, hazardous, or other legitimate business interest jobs and based on the presence of a reasonable suspicion for all other employees.

☐ Have a policy on the obtaining and giving of employment references, including letters of recommendation and requiring written authorizations to obtain/give references.

---

[4] Levesque, *The Complete Hiring Manual*, pp. 470–471.

Personnel Files

- ☐ Have a designated "records custodian" who is the ultimate authority on control, access, and use of filed documents.
- ☐ Have a list of designated staff whose jobs necessitate access and use of file documents.
- ☐ Have a procedure for the access and review of file documents by employees and authorized supervisory and management staff.
- ☐ Highly personal and sensitive documents are kept in a second or sealed file (if allowed by state law).

Applicant/Employee Authorizations

- ☐ Have an authorization form for the applicant's authorization to obtain any desired prior employment information and release of liability for the former employer.
- ☐ Have an authorization form for employee's written release of pertinent work history information and release of liability.

Application Form and Interviews

- ☐ List no inquiries on the employment application form that solicit information concerning the applicant's identification of protected privacy right details.
- ☐ Do not ask questions during preemployment interviews concerning an applicant's relationship with existing employees, mode of living, addictive habits, law enforcement violations, or other types of protected privacy right information.

Employment References

- ☐ Have only well-trained human resource or management personnel provide these.
- ☐ Confine references to factual and objective work history about the applicant's (if acquiring) or employee's (if giving) job performance characteristics, job scope, behavior and relationships, adherence to policies and instructions, and attendance.
- ☐ Verify that the requestor is duly authorized and the former employee's written release has been obtained and verified.

Performance Appraisals and Discipline Notices

- ☐ Verify that information is factual, objectively stated, honest, and reviewed by departmental management before discussion/copies to the employee.
- ☐ Have documents reviewed by a human resources professional prior to deposit in personnel files.
- ☐ Give employees an opportunity to write their own comments or rebuttal to statements or ratings that are disagreeable.
- ☐ Inform employees—preferably in writing—of their right to appeal adverse actions (denial of pay increase, suspension, demotion, etc.); providing the company has an established appeal mechanism.

Supervisory Training

☐ Provide frequent and in-depth training to all supervisory and management personnel on all pertinent aspects of applicant/employee privacy rights, including the limits of their authorities.

AUTOMATED RECORDS SYSTEMS[5]

The arduous process of hiring and conducting related employment transactions has become burdened with repetitive paperwork and tasks that absorb valuable time—if the job is being done correctly. In fact, largely due to the time required to perform quality hiring processes, many employers have progressively created shortcuts that damage the quality of end results rather than look for more efficient ways of *adding* qualitative and creative measures to improve results while actually decreasing the amount of time it takes to hire the best people. This requires one thing—automation of the entire hiring program, including recruitment, applicant flow, selection testing, and most if not all of the records processing function.

Smaller-sized organizations that do not need or use a larger "mainframe" computer system to accommodate other aspects of their operations will want to consider purchasing a micro (personal) computer. Software programs are designed for both Macintosh and IBM and IBM-compatible systems and so you will want to acquire a system with a large memory capacity to handle the hiring and employment software programs and information that is placed in those programs. One advantage of the microcomputer is that security of file data can be easily maintained by merely isolating the computer from use by others and storing informational software in a secured place. Mainframes, on the other hand, require a password to access programs, but private employment information is still available through the mainframe's information storage bank.

Selection and Use of Microcomputer Systems by Smaller-Sized Organizations

Use of computers for the storage, retrieval, and manipulation of employment data and records has been refined considerably. Computers now offer smaller-sized organizations with an easy alternative to manual record keeping by simply modifying standardized software programs to fit the organization's special needs. Acquiring a computer to handle the hiring, employment, and personnel functions is an investment that will have enduring returns. The initial investment will be the time it takes to select a suitable computer, software programs, and vendor support; train staff; work with a programmer to think through carefully needed customizing of standardized programs; and transform existing records into computer memory. Clearly, microcomputers have made it possible for smaller organizations to operate with the same efficiencies as their larger competitors, and the success of business

---

[5] Levesque, *The Complete Hiring Manual*, pp. 82–84.

will require efficiencies where the element of time is involved. For the 1990s and beyond, time cannot be wasted nor misdirected.

Initially, you will want to use your computer system to handle the recordkeeping aspects of employment transactions and personnel file documents, even though hard copies of many personnel file contents must be maintained as well. Once these records become a matter of routine computer handling, you should begin to develop a computerized method of dealing with all hiring process activities to simplify and streamline these tasks. For example, organizations required to (or interested in) tracking applicant characteristics for compilation of EEO and affirmative action reports will want to acquire software programs available for this purpose, and similar to the information contained on the Applicant Flow Data form at the end of Chapter 5. Additionally, computers can be very effective devices for preparing job announcements from stored job description information; for planning and layout of recruitment and testing activities; for the design of recruitment advertisements; for the development of specific, job-related selection tests, including interview rating forms and sample questions; and for payroll processing.

There is almost no limit to the type of information that can be created, stored, and used more wisely by organizations of all sizes to enhance the cost effectiveness of employment information. After all, for most organizations, employees represent the single largest cost of doing business and computers are the answer to managing those cost factors more precisely.

Ultimately, however, the decision to acquire and use a computer system to manage the hiring and employment functions must be based on overall efficiency versus the costs to initiate and operate the system. It should be remembered that efficiency is a long-range measure, while cost is generally measured as a short-range investment. As a fundamental rule, automated hiring, employment, and personnel records systems may not be efficient for employers with fewer than 25 to 50 employees unless (1) the nature of employment in the organization requires an extraordinary amount of data to be dealt with (high turnover, diverse jobs, etc.); (2) the organization has other business applications that necessitates the acquisition of computers, and the added costs associated with employment related software programs would be nominal; or (3) the organization anticipates growth beyond the current number of employees and desires to convert to computerized recordkeeping in advance of the growth.

Listing of Computer Program Vendors and Software Characteristics

To assist you in the selection of a computer system and software programs that are suitable to the hiring, employment, and personnel processing of information needs of your business, a listing of vendors is provided on the following pages for your investigation. However, since computer technology is ever changing and being improved upon with great frequency, you should not rely solely on these sources. Your best approach may be to acquaint yourself with these products, retain the services of a computer consultant with expertise in human resources operations (but who does not sell products), and work with this individual to select the most appropriate hardware and software to meet your immediate needs, but adaptable to your long-range "add-on" needs.[6]

Americans with Disabilities Act

The Avant Group
3804 Highland Drive
Suite B-9
Salt Lake City, UT 84106
(801) 278-5937

Applicant Tracking

Abra Cadabra Software
5565 Ninth Street North
St. Petersburg, FL 33703
(813) 525-4400

Allied Business Systems, Inc.
18350 Mt. Langley Street
Suite 211
Fountain Valley, CA 92708
(714) 963-5554

CompuServe/Collier-Jackson
3707 W. Cherry Street
Tampa, FL 33607
(813) 872-9990

The Consulting Team, Inc.
1655 Palm Beach Lakes Boulevard
Suite 200
West Palm Beach, FL 33401
(407) 478-0022

Corporate Education Resources, Inc.
P.O. Box 2080
Fairfield, IA 52556
(515) 472-7720

Drew Software
P.O. Box 101
Joplin, MO 64802
(417) 781-4248

Edge Information Management, Inc.
1901 S. Harbor City Boulevard
Suite 401
Melbourne, FL 32901
(407) 722-EDGE

Exxis Corporation
6232 North 7th Street
Phoenix, AZ 85014
(602) 274-2865

Focused Solutions, Inc.
1518 Dolphin Terrace
Corona del Mar, CA 92625
(714) 760-1292

Greentree Systems, Inc.
201 San Antonio Circle
Suite 120
Mountain View, CA 94040
(415) 948-8844

Human Resource MicroSystems, Inc.
101 California Street
Suite 410
San Francisco, CA 94111
(800) 972-8470; (415) 362-8400

lawrence-ray, inc.
265 South Anita Drive
Suite 230
Orange, CA 92668
(714) 939-9704

MicroTrac Systems, Inc.
20 Wells Avenue
Newton, MA 02159
(617) 965-4660

---

[6] "Buyer's Guide to HRIS," *HR Magazine*, May 1992, pp. 101–108, 110–111. Reprinted by permission.

Novaware Systems, Inc.
3800 Steeles Avenue West
Suite 117
Woodbridge, ONT
Canada L4L 4G9
(416) 851-7011

RESUMate
P.O. Box 7438
Ann Arbor, MI 48107
(800) 530-9310

Resumix, Inc.
2953 Bunker Hill Lane
Third Floor
Santa Clara, CA 95054
(408) 988-0444

Revelation Technologies
Two Park Avenue
New York, NY 10016
(800) 377-HRMS

Science & Engineering Associates, Inc.
SEAVIEW™ Information &
Image Management Software
SEA Plaza
6100 Uptown Boulevard, N.E.
Albuquerque, NM 87110
(800) SEA-1452; (505) 884-2300

Sigma Data Systems, Inc.
6375 E. Tanque Verde
Suite 250
Tucson, AZ 85718
(800) 677-1275

SPECTRUM Human Resource Systems
  Corporation
1625 Broadway
Suite 2700
Denver, CO 80202
(800) 334-5660

Attendance

Abra Cadabra Software
5565 Ninth Street North
St. Petersburg, FL 33703
(813) 525-4400

The Consulting Team, Inc.
1655 Palm Beach Lakes Boulevard
Suite 200
West Palm Beach, FL 33401
(407) 478-0022

Datamatics
330 New Brunswick Avenue
Fords, NJ 08863
(908) 738-9600

lawrence-ray, inc.
265 South Anita Drive
Suite 230
Orange, CA 92668
(714) 939-9704

Awards and Incentives

Seiko Time
1111 MacArthur Boulevard
Mahwah, NJ 07430
(800) 545-2783

Benefit Communication Software

Benefit Software, Inc.
212 Cottage Grove Avenue
Suite A
Santa Barbara, CA 93101
(800) 533-1388

DATAIR Employee Benefit Systems, Inc.
415 E. Plaza Drive
Westmont, IL 60559
(708) 325-2600

Dun & Bradstreet Software
3445 Peachtree Road, N.E.
Atlanta, GA 30326
(404) 239-INFO

On-Line Benefits
370 East 500 South
Salt Lake City, UT 84111
(800) 274-0503

Benefits Administration

ClaimsWare, Incorporated
P.O. Box 6125
Greenville, SC 29606
(803) 234-8200

The Consulting Team, Inc.
1655 Palm Beach Lakes Boulevard
Suite 200
West Palm Beach, FL 33401
(407) 478-0022

Coopers & Lybrand
1251 Avenue of the Americas
New York, NY 10020
(800) 232-2717

Corporate Systems Ltd.
P.O. Box 31780
1212 Ross Street
Amarillo, TX 79120
(800) 858-4364

DATAIR Employee Benefit Systems, Inc.
415 E. Plaza Drive
Westmont, IL 60559
(708) 325-2600

Dun & Bradstreet Software
3445 Peachtree Road, N.E.
Atlanta, GA 30326
(404) 239-INFO

Eldorado Computing Company
2880 E. Northern Avenue
Suite 4
Phoenix, AZ 85028
(602) 493-0288

Employee Benefits South, Inc.
1936 North Druid Hills Road
Atlanta, GA 30319
(404) 321-5110

lawrence-ray, inc.
265 South Anita Drive
Suite 230
Orange, CA 92668
(714) 939-9704

Logical Solutions, Inc.
425 Broad Hollow Road
Melville, NY 11747
(516) 293-7730

Novaware Systems, Inc.
3800 Steeles Avenue West
Suite 117
Woodbridge, ONT
Canada L4L 4G9
(416) 851-7011

PEAK 1 Resources, Inc.
15701 E. 1st Avenue
Suite 210
Aurora, CO 80011
(303) 366-5500

PRO*Systems, Inc.
26361 Curtiss Wright Parkway
Building 2F
Richmond Heights, OH 44143
(800) 377-5007

Reed Publications
3200 Cherry Creek So. Drive
Suite 650
Denver, CO 80209
(800) 347-7443

Resource Information Management
  Systems, Inc.
P.O. Box 3094
Naperville, IL 60566-7094
(708) 369-5396, ext. 271

Science & Engineering Associates, Inc.
SEAVIEW™ Information &
Image Management Software
SEA Plaza
6100 Uptown Boulevard, N.E.
Albuquerque, NM 87110
(800) SEA-1452; (505) 884-2300

Software 2000, Inc.
1 Park Center, Drawer 6000
Hyannis, MA 02601
(508) 778-2000

Travis Software Corp.
1001 S. Dairy Ashford
Suite 206
Houston, TX 77077
(713) 496-3737

Vision Service Plan
100 Howe Avenue
Suite 100 South
Sacramento, CA 95825
(800) 852-7600, ext. 4811

WTR Data Services, Inc.
630 Third Avenue
New York, NY 10017
(212) 949-8989

Career Development

Acumen International
3950 Civic Center Drive
San Rafael, CA 94903
(415) 492-9190

BENSU, INC.
211 Gough Street
Suite 201
San Francisco, CA 94102
(415) 626-6200

Human Resource Systems Professionals
P.O. Box 801646
Dallas, TX 75380-1646
(214) 661-3727

International Training Consultants, Inc.
P.O. Box 35613
Richmond, VA 23235
(804) 320-2415

SkillSearch Corporation
104 Woodmont Boulevard
Suite 306
Nashville, TN 37205
(615) 383-4700

Claims Auditing

IPRO National Medical Review
1979 Marcus Avenue
First Floor
Lake Success, NY 11042
(516) 326-7767, ext. 535

COBRA

Benefit Plan Systems Corporation
16 Technology
Suite 161
Irvine, CA 92718
(800) 523-8047

CompuServe/Collier-Jackson
3707 W. Cherry Street
Tampa, FL 33607
(813) 872-9990

Computing Management, Inc.
2346 South Lynhurst Drive
Suite C-101
Indianapolis, IN 46241
(317) 247-4485

Dun & Bradstreet Software
3445 Peachtree Road, N.E.
Atlanta, GA 30326
(404) 239-INFO

KPMG Peat Marwick
1601 Elm Street
Suite 1400
Dallas, TX 75201
(214) 754-2561

Compensation Administration

Coopers & Lybrand
1251 Avenue of the Americas
New York, NY 10020
(800) 232-2717

Mind Design Systems
883 East 2850 North
North Ogden, UT 84414
(801) 782-2965

Princeton Management Consultants, Inc.
99 Moore Street
Princeton, NJ 08540
(609) 924-2411

Rustan Systems
883 East 2850 North
North Ogden, UT 84414
(801) 782-2965

William M. Mercer, Incorporated
1500 Meidinger Tower
Louisville, KY 40202
(502) 561-4569

Computer-Based Recruiting

SkillSearch Corporation
104 Woodmont Boulevard
Suite 306
Nashville, TN 37205
(615) 383-4700

Computer-Based Testing

ADD Enterprises, Inc.
1552 Lost Hollow Drive
Brentwood, TN 37027
(615) 370-9646

Drew Software
P.O. Box 101
Joplin, MO 64802
(417) 781-4248

KEE Systems
9135 Guilford Road
Columbia, MD 21046
(800) 846-0932

ORION SYSTEMS
One Summit Plaza
5727 S. Lewis
Suite 705
Tulsa, OK 74105
(800) 824-4298

QWIZ, Inc.
120 W. Wieuca Road
Suite 101
Atlanta, GA 30342
(800) 367-2509; (404) 843-1124

Wonderlic Personnel Test, Inc.
820 Frontage Road
Northfield, IL 60093
(800) 323-3742

Computer-Based Training

ADD Enterprises, Inc.
1552 Lost Hollow Drive
Brentwood, TN 37027
(615) 370-9646

Commodore Business Machines, Inc.
1200 Wilson Drive
West Chester, PA 19380
(215) 431-9100

FinnTrade, Inc.
2000 Powell Street
Suite 1200
Emeryville, CA 94608
(510) 547-2281

QWIZ, Inc.
120 W. Wieuca Road
Suite 101
Atlanta, GA 30342
(800) 367-2509; (404) 843-1124

Data and Survey Analysis

APIAN SOFTWARE
P.O. Box 1224
Menlo Park, CA 94026
(415) 694-2900; (800) 237-4565

Coopers & Lybrand
1251 Avenue of the Americas
New York, NY 10020
(800) 232-2717

Creative Research Systems
15 Lone Oak Court
Petaluma, CA 94952
(707) 765-1001

Cybernetic Solutions
3479 West 7480 South
Salt Lake City, UT 84084
(800) 359-3386

Information Retrieval Methods, Inc.
1525 North Stemmons
Carrollton, TX 75006
(800) 533-2312; (214) 242-2312

ORION SYSTEMS
One Summit Plaza
5727 S. Lewis
Suite 705
Tulsa, OK 74105
(800) 824-4298

William Steinberg Consultants, Inc.
P.O. Box 1754
Champlain, NY 12919
(514) 483-6954

Disability Certification/Management

The Precertification Center
P.O. Box 898125
Camp Hill, PA 17089
(800) 441-2333

Document Imaging

Science & Engineering Associates, Inc.
SEAVIEW™ Information &
Image Management Software
SEA Plaza
6100 Uptown Boulevard, N.E.
Albuquerque, NM 87110
(800) SEA-1452; (505) 884-2300

EAP Evaluation Software

Innergy Comprehensive Limited
4757 Donovan Court
Ottawa, ONT
Canada K1J 8W1
(613) 749-9661

EEO/AA

About Management, Inc.
630 Camp Street
New Orleans, LA 70047
(504) 596-2706

Abra Cadabra Software
5565 Ninth Street North
St. Petersburg, FL 33703
(813) 525-4400

ALLIED BUSINESS SYSTEMS, INC.
18350 Mt. Langley Street
Suite 211
Fountain Valley, CA 92708
(714) 963-5554

C. Alexander and Associates, Inc.
460 Vista Roma
Newport Beach, CA 92660
(714) 644-5829 Inside CA
(800) 433-3761 Outside CA

Copeland Griggs Productions
302 23rd Avenue
San Francisco, CA 94121
(415) 668-4200

Criterion Incorporated
9425 North MacArthur Boulevard
Irving, TX 75063
(214) 401-2100

Human Resources Management Services
9240 N. Meridian
Suite 220
Indianapolis, IN 46260
(317) 848-9614

PRI Associates, Inc.
1905 Chapel Hill Road
Durham, NC 27707
(919) 493-7534

SkillSearch Corporation
104 Woodmont Boulevard
Suite 306
Nashville, TN 37205
(615) 383-4700

Yocom & McKee P.C.
855 Lupine Street
Second Floor
Golden, CO 80401
(303) 277-0692

Employee Accident/Illness Record Keeping and Analysis

Pro-Am Software
P.O. Box 1290
4432 Route 910
Gibsonia, PA 15044
(800) 852-7316

Employee Assessment and Selection

Bigby, Havis & Associates
12201 Merit Drive
Suite 420
Dallas, TX 75251
(214) 233-6055

Drew Software
P.O. Box 101
Joplin, MO 64802
(417) 781-4248

HRStrategies, Inc.
P.O. Box 36778
Grosse Pointe, MI 48236
(800) HRS-SKIL; (313) 881-8885

Hartford
6 Forest Park Drive
Farmington, CT 06032
(203) 677-1236

Houston
1521 Green Oak Place
Suite 208
Kingwood, TX 77339
(713) 358-7588

Los Angeles
170 Newport Center Drive
Suite 240
Newport Beach, CA 92660
(714) 640-2904

New York
1281 Main Street
First Floor
Holly Pond Plaza
Stamford, CT 06902
(203) 323-1055

ORION SYSTEMS
One Summit Plaza
5727 S. Lewis
Suite 705
Tulsa, OK 74105
(800) 824-4298

Proudfoot Reports Incorporated
Nassau North Corporate
Center I
70 Glen Street
Glen Cove, NY 11542
(516) 674-4800

QWIZ, Inc.
120 W. Wieuca Road
Suite 101
Atlanta, GA 30342
(800) 367-2509; (404) 843-1124

Science & Engineering Associates, Inc.
SEAVIEW™ Information &
Image Management Software
SEA Plaza
6100 Uptown Boulevard, N.E.
Albuquerque, NM 87110
(800) SEA-1452; (505) 884-2300

Wonderlic Personnel Test, Inc.
820 Frontage Road
Northfield, IL 60093
(800) 323-3742

Employee Background Screening

Factual Business Information/
  Employment Screening
8300 Executive Center Drive
Suite 204
Miami, FL 33166
(305) 592-7600

Employee Communications Services

Coopers & Lybrand
1251 Avenue of the Americas
New York, NY 10020
(800) 232-2717

Employment/Recruitment/Assessment

Career Expo Division of RSI
2367 Auburn Avenue
Cincinnati, OH 45219
(513) 721-3030

Electronic Selection Systems Corp.
2300 Maitland Center Parkway
Suite 302
Maitland, FL 32751-4129
(407) 875-1102

kiNexus
640 N. LaSalle Street
Suite 560
Chicago, IL 60610
(800) 828-0422, ext. 236

LaFountain Research Corporation
One Palmer Square
Suite 300
Princeton, NJ 08542
(609) 683-9191; (609) 683-1750 (FAX)

National Employment Screening
  Services
8801 South Yale
Tulsa, OK 74137
(918) 491-9936

ORION SYSTEMS
One Summit Plaza
5727 S. Lewis
Suite 705
Tulsa, OK 74105
(800) 824-4298

Wonderlic Personnel Test, Inc.
820 Frontage Road
Northfield, IL 60093
(800) 323-3742

Empowerment Training and Development

International Training Consultants, Inc.
P.O. Box 35613
Richmond, VA 23235
(804) 320-2415

Expatriate Management

Copeland Griggs Productions
302 23rd Avenue
San Francisco, CA 94121
(415) 668-4200

Price Waterhouse
55 E. Monroe Street
30th Floor
Chicago, IL 60603
(312) 419-1565

SkillSearch Corporation
104 Woodmont Boulevard
Suite 306
Nashville, TN 37205
(615) 383-4700

Flexible Benefits Administration

Alexander & Alexander Consulting Group
2540 North First Street
San Jose, CA 95131
(800) 962-4423

Business Information Technology, Inc.
1011 Centre Road
Suite 400
Wilmington, DE 19805
(302) 996-0720

Comerica, Inc.
ComeriCOMP Benefits
Consulting Services
Detroit, MI 48275-2125
(313) 370-7381

Computing Management, Inc.
2346 South Lynhurst Drive
Suite C-101
Indianapolis, IN 46241
(317) 247-4485

The Consulting Team, Inc.
1655 Palm Beach Lakes Boulevard
Suite 200
West Palm Beach, FL 33401
(407) 478-0022

Coopers & Lybrand
1251 Avenue of the Americas
New York, NY 10020
(800) 232-2717

DATAIR Employee Benefit Systems, Inc.
415 E. Plaza Drive
Westmont, IL 60559
(708) 325-2600

Dun & Bradstreet Software
3445 Peachtree Road, N.E.
Atlanta, GA 30326
(404) 239-INFO

FlexBen Corporation
900 Wilshire Drive
Suite 304
Troy, MI 48084
(313) 362-2120

FLX Corportion
220 Willowbrook Lane
West Chester, PA 19382
(215) 696-6600

Magnus Software Corporation
2500 Windy Ridge Parkway
Suite 1400
Marietta, GA 30067
(404) 952-7854

Mayer Hoffman McCann
420 Nichols Road
Kansas City, MO 64112
(800) 433-2292

P&W Software
5655 Lindero Canyon Road
Suite 403
Westlake Village, CA 91362
(818) 707-7690

SBC Systems Corporation
30 Perimeter Center East
Suite 203
Atlanta, GA 30346
(404) 399-6321

SLI-Select Software
3350 Founders Road
Indianapolis, IN 46268
(317) 876-4741

Software 2000, Inc.
1 Park Center, Drawer 6000
Hyannis, MA 02601
(508) 778-2000

SPECTRUM Human Resource Systems
   Corporation
1625 Broadway
Suite 2700
Denver, CO 80202
(800) 334-5660

Group Management

Experience In Software, Inc.
2000 Hearst Avenue
Suite 202
Berkeley, CA 94709
(510) 644-0694

HR/General Business Software

KnowledgePoint
1311 Clegg Street
Petaluma, CA 94954
(800) 727-1133

HR Management

Abra Cadabra Software
5565 Ninth Street North
St. Petersburg, FL 33703
(813) 525-4400

Abra MacDabra Software
485 Pala Avenue
Sunnyvale, CA 94086
(408) 737-9454

Business Information Technology, Inc.
1011 Centre Road
Suite 400
Wilmington, DE 19805
(302) 996-0720

CompuServe/Collier-Jackson
3707 W. Cherry Street
Tampa, FL 33607
(813) 872-9990

HarrisData
611 N. Barker Road
Waukesha, WI 53186-0500
(800) 225-0585

lawrence-ray, inc.
265 South Anita Drive
Suite 230
Orange, CA 92668
(714) 939-9704

Microcast Systems, Inc.
P.O. Box 35353
Tulsa, OK 74153
(918) 492-6988

MST Software
#1 Tierra Vista
Laguna Hills, CA 92653
(714) 837-3664

Novaware Systems, Inc.
3800 Steeles Avenue West
Suite 117
Woodbridge, ONT
Canada L4L 4G9
(416) 851-7011

Radford Associates/Alexander &
   Alexander Consulting Group
2540 North First Street
Suite 400
San Jose, CA 95131
(800) 962-4423

Science & Engineering Associates, Inc.
SEAVIEW™ Information &
Image Management Software
SEA Plaza
6100 Uptown Boulevard, N.E.
Albuquerque, NM 87110
(800) SEA-1452; (505) 884-2300

Software Plus, Inc.
301 Route 17 North
Rutherford, NJ 07070
(800) 343-6844

HRIS Consulting Services

Business Information Technology, Inc.
1011 Centre Road
Suite 400
Wilmington, DE 19805
(302) 996-0720

The Consulting Team, Inc.
1655 Palm Beach Lakes Boulevard
Suite 200
West Palm Beach, FL 33401
(407) 478-0022

The Eddon Corporation
6421 Arbor Drive
New Port Richey, FL 34655
(800) 272-4884

HDC Consulting Services
1200 MacArthur Boulevard
Mahwah, NJ 07430
(201) 825-8887

The Hunter Group
11 East Chase Street
Suite 8E
Baltimore, MD 21202
(410) 576-1515

Nardoni Associates, Inc.
1465 Route 31 South
Annandale, NJ 08801
(908) 730-9444

Ryder Move Management
3600 N.W. 82nd Avenue
Miami, FL 33166
(800) 421-1234

Interactive Voice Response

Cascade Technologies, Inc.
1430 Broadway
New York, NY 10018
(212) 768-7380

Computer Communications
 Specialists, Inc.
6529 Jimmy Carter Boulevard
Norcross, GA 30071
(800) 536-8321

Coopers & Lybrand
1251 Avenue of the Americas
New York, NY 10020
(800) 232-2717

InnOvation Voice Technologies, Inc.
P.O. Box 3555
2417 Brewery Road
Cross Plains, WI 53528
(800) 424-6757, ext. 200

InterVoice
17811 Waterview Parkway
Dallas, TX 75252
(214) 669-3988

Syntellect Inc.
15810 North 28th Avenue
Phoenix, AZ 85023
(602) 789-2828

Job Analysis

The Avant Group
3804 Highland Drive
Suite B-9
Salt Lake City, UT 84106
(801) 278-5937

Drew Software
P.O. Box 101
Joplin, MO 64802
(417) 781-4248

ORION SYSTEMS
One Summit Plaza
5727 S. Lewis
Suite 705
Tulsa, OK 74105
(800) 824-4298

Job Descriptions

Human Resources Management Services
9240 N. Meridian
Suite 220
Indianapolis, IN 46260
(317) 848-9614

Intelliware, Inc.
P.O. Box 2139
Stow, OH 44224
(216) 686-0711

William M. Mercer, Incorporated
1500 Meidinger Tower
Louisville, KY 40202
(502) 561-4569

HOW LONG SHOULD EMPLOYMENT RECORDS BE RETAINED?

A frequently confusing area for most employers dealing with the hiring of employees and accumulation of paperwork involved is not only what to do with these records, but also how long do we have to keep what kind of records on those employees we hire. Retention requirements of employment records are controlled by both federal and state laws. Because state laws vary considerably, no attempt is being made here to identify the records retention requirements of the various states, but generally they follow similar periods as corresponding federal law. Nevertheless, it is advisable to conduct a little research or consult with qualified labor counsel in your state to determine specific record retention requirements applicable to state laws dealing with employment matters.

There are, however, five federal laws that have particular recordkeeping requirements in the absence of more stringent, corresponding state requirements you should incorporate into your hiring records management program. You should also bear in mind that these laws focus primarily on general hiring and employment records rather than those kinds of documents typically stored in individual personnel files. The federal law sources, records types, and specific retention periods you should use as a starting point in your employment records management system are as follows.[7]

A. **Verification of Right to Work in the United States—Immigration Reform and Control Act**

The Immigration Reform and Control Act (IRCA) requires that employers complete the I-9 form for each employee hired to verify and determine whether the person is a lawful resident of the United States and has the legal right to obtain employment. *Retain records for three years or one year after employment separation.*

B. **Basic Employee Data, Pay Records, Work Hours, and Training—Fair Labor Standards Act**

1. Basic records containing employee information, work schedules including overtime and premium rate hours, payrolls, individual contracts or collective bargaining agreements, and sales and purchase records (if any employee is paid by commission). *Retain records for three years.*

2. Supplementary basic records including basic employment and earnings records and wage rate tables. Also work time schedules including order, shipping, and billing records, records of additions to or deductions from wages paid, and documentation of basis for payment of any wage differential to employees of the opposite sex in the same establishment (Equal Pay Act). *Retain records for two years.*

---

[7]   Levesque, *The Complete Hiring Manual*, pp. 81–82.

3. Certificates of age. *Retain until termination of employment.*

4. Written training agreements. *Retain for duration of training program.*

C. **Discriminatory Practices or Actions—1964 Civil Rights Act, Title VII; 1991 Civil Rights Act**

1. Any personnel or employment record made or kept by the employer, including application forms and records having to do with hiring, promotion, demotion, transfer, layoff, or termination; rates of pay or other terms of compensation; and selection for training or apprenticeship. *Retain records for eighteen months from date of making the record or taking the personnel action involved, whichever occurs later.*

2. Personnel records relevant to charge of discrimination or action brought by the Attorney General against an employer, including, for example, records relating to charging party and to all other employees holding similar positions, application forms, or test papers completed by unsuccessful applicant and by all other candidates for the same position. *Retain records for three years from date of final disposition of charge or action.*

3. For apprenticeship programs:

   a. A chronological list of names and addresses of all applicants, sex, and minority group identification or file of written applications containing same information and other records pertaining to apprenticeship applicants (e.g., test papers and interview records). *Retain records for two years or period of successful applicant's apprenticeship, whichever is later.*

   b. Any other record made solely for completing the EEO-2 report or similar document. *Retain records for one year from due date of report.*

4. Copy of EEO-1 (Employer Information Report) for employers with one hundred plus employees. *Retain records for three years from date of preparation.*

D. **Age Discrimination—Age Discrimination in Employment Act**

1. Payroll records containing each employee's name, address, date of birth, occupation, rate of pay, and compensation earned per week. *Retain records for duration of employment.*

2. Personnel records relating to (a) job applications, resumes, or other replies of job advertisements including records pertaining to failure or refusal to hire; (b) promotion, demotion, transfer, selection for training, layoff, recall, or discharge; (c) job orders submitted to employment agency or union; (d) test papers in connection with employer-administered employment tests; (e) physical examination results considered in connection with personnel action; and (f) job advertisements or notices to the public or employees regarding openings, promotions, training programs, or opportunities for overtime work. *Retain records for one year from date of personnel action to which record relates, except ninety days for application forms and other preemployment records of applicants.*

3. Employee benefit plans and written seniority or merit rating systems. *Retain records for the duration the plan or system is effective plus one year.*

4. Personnel records, including the foregoing, relevant to an enforcement action commencement against the employer. *Retain records until final disposition of the action.*

E. **Workplace Safety and Health—Occupational Safety and Healthy Act**

1. Log and Summary of Occupational Injuries and Illnesses briefly describing recordable cases of industrial injury and illness, the extent and outcome of each incident, and summary totals for the calendar year. *Retain records for five years following the end of the year to which they relate.*

2. Supplementary Record containing more detailed information for each occurrence of injury or illness. *Retain records for five years following the end of the year to which they relate.*

Chapter 5

MODEL PERSONNEL AND PREEMPLOYMENT FORMS

PERSONNEL REQUISITION FORM[1]

The primary functions of this form are to document internal approvals to fill jobs, to create a record of vacancies and new jobs, to give advance notice to your employment office that an employee is leaving the company, and to provide a mechanism by which operating managers must justify the creation of new positions. The form used for these purposes should contain all four elements, so if your preference is to modify this form for your company's use, be sure to include each of these elements. The use of personnel requisition forms also has the advantage of taking the surprise out of job vacancies, miscommunications between operating departments and the employment/human resources office, and provides those in the company's decisional chain an opportunity to consider any desired alternative decisions with each vacancy or new job.

Follow these guidelines in requesting approval of a new position:

1. Submit a Personnel Requisition form.
2. In addition to a job description, submit the following information:
   a. Estimated salary and benefits costs.
   b. Economic factors to be considered:
      (1) Number of overtime hours to be reduced weekly
      (2) Increase in revenue to be generated annually
      (3) Other cost savings
   c. Consideration for the quality of services rendered and customer satisfaction.
   d. The effect on operations should this position not be filled.
   e. The anticipated date that the new position must be filled.
3. Notify the (*Human Resources Manager*) at the earliest possible time if salary or benefits surveys will be required.
4. When the foregoing justification items are satisfactorily completed, forward the request to the (*Human Resources Manager*) to submit to the Personnel Committee for review at the next regularly scheduled meeting.

---

[1]   Levesque, *The Complete Hiring Manual*, p. 284.

PERSONNEL REQUISITION FORM*

POSITION TITLE _____

DEPARTMENT _____ WORK LOCATION _____

_____ New Position   _____ Replacement for _____

_____ Full Time   _____ Part Time   _____ Regular   _____ Temporary/On-Call

Work Hours and Days: _____

REASON NEEDED (If replacement, state why employee is being replaced. If new position,

attach separate justification.) _____

_____

PLEASE ATTACH <u>CURRENT</u> JOB DESCRIPTION.

SPECIAL REQUIREMENTS (special training/experience, driver's license, etc.):

_____

_____

Requested by: _____   Date _____
              Signature

Approvals: _____   Date _____
              Department Head

              _____   Date _____
              Human Resources Manager

_____

For Human Resources Department Use

Disposition:

Person Hired:
Offer Date: Budget Code:
Start Date: Range:

_____

*   From G. Beach, Human Resources Manager, Radiological Associates of Sacramento Medical
Group. Levesque, *The Complete Hiring Manual,* pp. 319–320.

EMPLOYMENT APPLICATION FORM

It should be noted that potentially illegal (discriminatory) information has been omitted from this form, while information essential to screening applicants on the basis of job-related background remains.

Employers who do not want to accept employment applications until and unless job openings exist, or who receive a large number of job inquiries, may want to use the Job Interest Form as an alternative.

EMPLOYMENT APPLICATION

**PLEASE PRINT
IN INK OR TYPE**

EQUAL OPPORTUNITY EMPLOYER: It is our policy to abide by all Federal and State laws prohibiting employment discrimination solely on the basis of a person's race, color, creed, national origin, religion, age (over 40), sex, marital status, or physical handicap, except where a reasonable, bona fide occupational qualification exists.

PERSONAL

NAME	(LAST)	(FIRST)	(MIDDLE)	TELEPHONE (AREA CODE AND NO.)

ADDRESS	(STREET)	(CITY)	(STATE)	(ZIP CODE)

PREVIOUS ADDRESSES DURING THE LAST FIVE YEARS

STREET ADDRESS	CITY	STATE	ZIP	FROM	TO
STREET ADDRESS	CITY	STATE	ZIP	FROM	TO

OTHER EMPLOYMENT-RELATED INFORMATION

CHECK THE FOLLOWING OPTIONS WHICH YOU WOULD CONSIDER:	LIST ANY RELATIVES WORKING FOR THIS ORGANIZATION
☐ Full-Time ☐ Part-Time ☐ Temporary	Name Department
IF MINOR, AGE	

CAN YOU, AFTER EMPLOYMENT, SUBMIT A BIRTH CERTIFICATE OR OTHER PROOF OF U.S. CITIZENSHIP?   Yes ☐   No ☐

IF NOT A U.S. CITIZEN, CAN YOU, AFTER EMPLOYMENT, SUBMIT VERIFICATION OF YOUR LEGAL RIGHT TO WORK PERMANENTLY IN THE U.S.?   Yes ☐   No ☐

WERE YOU PREVIOUSLY EMPLOYED BY THIS ORGANIZATION? Yes ☐ No ☐ Date(s) _____	HAVE YOU EVER BEEN CONVICTED OF A FELONY, OR PLEADED NO CONTEST IN A FELONY, OR BEEN CONVICTED OF A MISDEMEANOR RESULTING IN IMPRISONMENT OR A FINE OVER $500 DURING THE LAST TEN YEARS? (Conviction will not necessarily disqualify an applicant.) Yes ☐ No ☐ If yes, explain _____
DO YOU HAVE ANY PHYSICAL LIMITATIONS TO PERFORM THE JOB APPLIED FOR? (IF YES, EXPLAIN THE TYPE OF ACCOMMODATION REQUIRED.) Yes ☐ No ☐ ACCOMMODATION _____	HAVE YOU RECEIVED WORKERS' COMPENSATION DURING THE LAST TEN YEARS? Yes ☐ No ☐ IF YES, STATE THE NATURE AND DATE OF INJURY, RECURRING EFFECTS, AND DEGREE OF DISABILITY (APPLICANTS MAY BE REQUIRED TO PASS A JOB-RELATED PHYSICAL EXAM).

EDUCATION & TRAINING

HIGH SCHOOL	COMPLETE ADDRESS		Graduated: Yes ☐ No ☐
COLLEGE OR UNIVERSITY	COMPLETE ADDRESS	MAJOR	DEGREE/YEAR
COLLEGE OR UNIVERSITY	COMPLETE ADDRESS	MAJOR	DEGREE/YEAR
TRADE SCHOOL	COMPLETE ADDRESS	SUBJECTS	Completed: Yes ☐ No ☐ YEAR:
APPRENTICE SCHOOL	COMPLETE ADDRESS	SUBJECTS	Completed: Yes ☐ No ☐ YEAR:

LIST ANY OTHER EDUCATION, TRAINING, SPECIAL SKILLS, OR CERTIFICATES/LICENSES THAT YOU POSSESS RELATED TO THIS JOB:

LIST ANY MACHINES OR EQUIPMENT THAT YOU ARE QUALIFIED AND EXPERIENCED AT OPERATING:

LIST ANY LANGUAGES THAT YOU FLUENTLY:

SPEAK: READ: WRITE:

REFERENCES

LIST BUSINESS PERSONS KNOWN, BUT NOT RELATED, TO YOU FOR AT LEAST THREE YEARS

	NAME	TITLE	BUSINESS	PHONE	YEARS KNOWN
1.					
2.					
3.					

POSITION APPLIED FOR: DATE: LAST NAME: FIRST NAME: INITIAL:

continued

EMPLOYMENT APPLICATION—*continued*

EXPERIENCE

List the last 10 years' work experience beginning with most recent.

NAME OF EMPLOYER		TYPE OF BUSINESS	

ADDRESS	CITY	STATE	ZIP	PHONE ( ) —

DATES EMPLOYED FROM TO	STARTING TITLE	LAST TITLE

NAME AND TITLE OF SUPERVISOR	MAY WE CONTACT? YES ☐ NO ☐	WAS EMPLOYMENT FULL-TIME ☐ PART-TIME ☐	REASON FOR LEAVING

BRIEF DESCRIPTION OF DUTIES

NAME OF EMPLOYER		TYPE OF BUSINESS	

ADDRESS	CITY	STATE	ZIP	PHONE ( ) —

DATES EMPLOYED FROM TO	STARTING TITLE	LAST TITLE

NAME AND TITLE OF SUPERVISOR	MAY WE CONTACT? YES ☐ NO ☐	WAS EMPLOYMENT FULL-TIME ☐ PART-TIME ☐	REASON FOR LEAVING

BRIEF DESCRIPTION OF DUTIES

NAME OF EMPLOYER		TYPE OF BUSINESS	

ADDRESS	CITY	STATE	ZIP	PHONE ( ) —

DATES EMPLOYED FROM TO	STARTING TITLE	LAST TITLE

NAME AND TITLE OF SUPERVISOR	MAY WE CONTACT? YES ☐ NO ☐	WAS EMPLOYMENT FULL-TIME ☐ PART-TIME ☐	REASON FOR LEAVING

BRIEF DESCRIPTION OF DUTIES

DRIVERS

DO YOU HAVE A VALID DRIVER'S LICENSE IN THIS STATE?   YES ☐   NO ☐

IF YES, LICENSE NO.:

_____

LIST ANY MOVING VIOLATIONS DURING THE LAST FIVE YEARS UNDER "COMMENTS."

COMMENTS

LIST ANY COMMENTS OR QUALIFYING STATEMENTS YOU CARE TO MAKE.

_____
_____
_____
_____
_____

APPLICANT'S CERTIFICATION

Please read carefully before signing. If you have any questions regarding the following statements, please ask for assistance.

I certify that, to the best of my knowledge and belief, the answers given by me to the foregoing questions and the statements made by me in this application are correct and complete. I understand that any false information contained in this application may result in my discharge.

I authorize you to communicate with all my former employers, school officials and persons named as references. I hereby release all employers, schools and individuals from any liability for any damage whatsoever resulting from giving such information.

I understand that as this organization deems necessary, I may be required to work overtime hours or hours outside a normally defined work day or work week. If employed, I understand and agree that such employment may be terminated at any time and without any liability to me for any continuation of salary, wages, or employment related benefits.

Date_____   Signature_____

VOLUNTARY APPLICANT
IDENTIFICATION FORM

Employers with fifty or more employees, or who are the recipients of federal grants, or who have adopted a voluntary affirmative action plan should ask that each job applicant complete this form at the time the Employment Application is completed. This form *must* be removed and kept separate from the Employment Application *at the time applications are screened for qualifications*. The applicant data from this form is used to compile the Applicant Flow Data Form, which demonstrates the composition of applicants through the selection process.

VOLUNTARY APPLICANT IDENTIFICATION FORM

This organization is an Equal Opportunity/Affirmative Action employer.

The information below is needed to measure the effectiveness of our recruitment efforts and is in conformity with federal government guidelines which require us to compile statistical information about applicants for employment. You are not required to furnish this information, but are encouraged to do so. The law provides that an employer may neither discriminate on the basis of this information, nor on whether you choose to furnish it. However, if you choose not to furnish it, under federal regulations, this employer is required to note race and sex on the basis of visual observation or surname.

This Voluntary Applicant Identification Form will be kept in a confidential file separate from the Employment Application.

Position Applied for: _____

I wish to furnish this information _____ (please print name) _____

I do not wish to furnish this information _____ (please print name) _____

Please check the appropriate box: ☐ Male   ☐ Female

ETHNIC CATEGORY (Check One)

_____ WHITE (not of Hispanic origin)—All persons having origins in any of the original peoples of Europe, North Africa, or the Middle East.

_____ BLACK (not of Hispanic origin)—All persons having origins in any of the black racial groups of Africa.

_____ ASIAN OR PACIFIC ISLANDER—All persons having origins in any of the original peoples of the Far East, Southeast Asia and Indian Subcontinent, or the Pacific Islands. This area includes, for example, China, Japan, Korea, the Philippine Islands, and Samoa.

_____ AMERICAN INDIAN OR ALASKA NATIVE—All persons having origins in any of the original peoples of North America, and who maintain cultural identification through tribal affiliations or community recognition.

_____ HISPANIC—All person of Mexican, Puerto Rican, Cuban, Central or South American, or other Spanish culture or origin, regardless of race.

Please check if the following categories are applicable:

_____ HANDICAPPED INDIVIDUAL—Any person who (1) has a physical or mental impairment that substantially limits one or more of his or her major life activities, (2) has a record of such impairment, or (3) is regarded as having such an impairment. A handicap is "substantially limiting" if it is likely to cause difficulty in securing, retaining, or advancing in employment.

_____ VETERAN ELIGIBILITY—Served in armed forces between August 5, 1964, and May 7, 1975.

_____ DISABLED VETERAN ELIGIBILITY—A veteran with a disability, service connected or otherwise.

AFFIRMATIVE ACTION DATA RECORD

This form should be used by employers required to maintain an affirmative action plan and program and by those employers who voluntarily establish an affirmative action program. This form allows such employers to track the characteristics of applicants for entry and promotional jobs through each phase of the hiring process as documented evidence of nondiscriminatory selection practices. Applicant characteristics are thus taken from the Voluntary Applicant Identification Form, or facsimile, or by visual identification (if available) of the applicant by the person who receives applications.

AFFIRMATIVE ACTION DATA RECORD

Employees are treated during employment without regard to race, color, religion, creed, gender, national origin, age, disability, marital or veteran status, sexual orientation, or any other legally protected status.

As an employer with an Affirmative Action Program, we comply with government regulations, including Affirmative Action responsibilities where they apply.

The purpose for this Data Record is to comply with government record keeping, reporting, and other legal requirements. Periodic reports are made to the government on the following information. The completion of this Data Record is optional. If you choose to volunteer the requested information please note that all Data Records are kept in a Confidential File and <u>are not</u> a part of your Application for Employment or personnel file. <u>Please note</u>: YOUR COOPERATION IS VOLUNTARY. INCLUSION OR EXCLUSION OF ANY DATA WILL NOT AFFECT ANY EMPLOYMENT DECISION.

(Please Print)

Last Name	First Name	Middle Name
Address Number Street	City	State Zip Code
Telephone Number(s)	Social Security Number

REFERRAL SOURCE:

___ Advertisement   ___ Employee   ___ Relative   ___ Private Employment Agency

___ Friend   ___ Walk-in   ___ Government Employment Agency   ___ Other _____

	Complete Only The Sections Below That Have Been Checked
	Current Job
	Check One: ☐ Male ☐ Female
	Check One Of The Following: (Ethnic Origin) ☐ White ☐ Hispanic ☐ American Indian/Alaskan Native ☐ Black ☐ Other ☐ Asian/Pacific Islander
	Check If Any Of The Following Are Applicable ☐ Vietnam Era Veteran ☐ Disabled Veteran ☐ Handicapped Individual
	Birthdate

This Affirmative Action Data Record is sold for general use throughout the United States. Amsterdam Printing and Litho Corp. assumes no responsibility for the use of said form or any questions which, when asked by the employer of the job applicant, may violate State and/or Federal Law.

FOR POST HIRE USE ONLY

AFFIRMATIVE ACTION DATA RECORD—*continued*

FOR AFFIRMATIVE ACTION PROGRAM USE ONLY

Position(s) Applied For Is Open: ☐ Yes   ☐ No

Position(s) Considered For: _____

_____

Date _____

Hired .... ___YES ___NO

Start Date .... ___/___/___

Position .... _____

EMPLOYMENT ANALYSIS REGISTER

Gender:	
Race:	
Disability:	
Other:	
Referral Source:	
EEO1 Category:	
Disposition:	

NOTES:

Completed By _____   **Date** ____/____/____

EMPLOYMENT ELIGIBILITY VERIFICATION (I-9) FORM[2]

This is the form required by the U.S. Immigration and Naturalization Service (INS) to be completed by *all* employers on *all* employees hired after November 6, 1986, as a condition of the Immigration Reform and Control Act of 1986. Completed and verified forms should be placed in a single (I-9 Form) file where you store other general confidential employee records. Failure to use this form, or failure to obtain verifying proof of legal presence and employment in the United States as specified on the form, can result in severe fines and penalties.

---

[2]   Levesque, *The Complete Hiring Manual*, p. 322.

EMPLOYMENT ELIGIBILITY VERIFICATION

U.S. Department of Justice
Immigration and Naturalization Service

OMB No. 1115-0136
Employment Eligibility Verification

Please read instructions carefully before completing this form. The instructions must be available during completion of this form. ANTI-DISCRIMINATION NOTICE. It is illegal to discriminate against work eligible individuals. Employers CANNOT specify which document(s) they will accept from an employee. The refusal to hire an individual because of a future expiration date may also constitute illegal discrimination.

Section 1. Employee Information and Verification. To be completed and signed by employee at the time employment begins

Print Name: Last	First	Middle Initial	Maiden Name

Address (Street Name and Number)		Apt. #	Date of Birth (month/day/year)

City	State	Zip Code	Social Security #

I am aware that federal law provides for imprisonment and/or fines for false statements or use of false documents in connection with the completion of this form.	I attest, under penalty of perjury, that I am (check one of the following): ☐ A citizen or national of the United States ☐ A Lawful Permanent Resident (Alien # A_____) ☐ An alien authorized to work until ____/____/____ (Alien # or Admission #_____)

Employee's Signature	Date (month/day/year)

Preparer and/or Translator Certification. *(To be completed and signed if Section 1 is prepared by a person other than the employee.) I attest, under penalty of perjury, that I have assisted in the completion of this form and that to the best of my knowledge the information is true and correct.*

Preparer's/Translator's Signature	Print Name

Address (Street Name and Number, City, State, Zip Code)	Date (month/day/year)

Section 2. Employer Review and Verification. To be completed and signed by employer. **Examine one document from List A OR examine one document from List B and one from List C** as listed on the reverse of this form and record the title, number and expiration date, if any, of the document(s)

	List A	OR	List B	AND	List C
Document title:	_____		_____		_____
Issuing authority:	_____		_____		_____
Document #:	_____		_____		_____
Expiration Date (if any):	___/___/___		___/___/___		___/___/___
Document #:	_____				
Expiration Date (if any):	___/___/___				

CERTIFICATION - I attest, under penalty of perjury, that I have examined the document(s) presented by the above-named employee, that the above-listed document(s) appear to be genuine and to relate to the employee named, that the employee began employment on (month/day/year) ____/____/____ **and that to the best of my knowledge the employee is eligible to work in the United States.** (State employment agencies may omit the date the employee began employment).

Signature of Employer or Authorized Representative	Print Name	Title

Business or Organization Name	Address (Street Name and Number, City, State, Zip Code)	Date (month/day/year)

Section 3. Updating and Reverification. To be completed and signed by employer

A. New Name (if applicable)	B. Date of rehire (month/day/year) (if applicable)

C. If employee's previous grant of work authorization has expired, provide the information below for the document that establishes current employment eligibility.

Document Title:_____ Document #:_____ Expiration Date (if any): ___/___/___

I attest, under penalty of perjury, that to the best of my knowledge, this employee is eligible to work in the United States, and if the employee presented document(s), the document(s) I have examined appear to be genuine and to relate to the individual.

Signature of Employer or Authorized Representative	Date (month/day/year)

Form I-9 (Rev. 11-21-91) N

EMPLOYMENT ELIGIBILITY VERIFICATION—*continued*

LISTS OF ACCEPTABLE DOCUMENTS

LIST A		LIST B		LIST C
Documents that Establish Both Identity and Employment Eligibility	**OR**	**Documents that Establish Identity**	**AND**	**Documents that Establish Employment Eligibility**

LIST A — Documents that Establish Both Identity and Employment Eligibility

1. U.S. Passport (unexpired or expired)

2. Certificate of U.S. Citizenship (*INS Form N-560 or N-561*)

3. Certificate of Naturalization (*INS Form N-550 or N-570*)

4. Unexpired foreign passport, with *I-551 stamp or* attached *INS Form I-94* indicating unexpired employment authorization

5. Alien Registration Receipt Card with photograph (*INS Form I-151 or I-551*)

6. Unexpired Temporary Resident Card (*INS Form I-688*)

7. Unexpired Employment Authorization Card (*INS Form I-688A*)

8. Unexpired Reentry Permit (*INS Form I-327*)

9. Unexpired Refugee Travel Document (*INS Form I-571*)

10. Unexpired Employment Authorization Document issued by the INS which contains a photograph (*INS Form I-688B*)

LIST B — Documents that Establish Identity

1. Driver's license or ID card issued by a state or outlying possession of the United States provided it contains a photograph or information such as name, date of birth, sex, height, eye color, and address

2. ID card issued by federal, state, or local government agencies or entities provided it contains a photograph or information such as name, date of birth, sex, height, eye color, and address

3. School ID card with a photograph

4. Voter's registration card

5. U.S. Military card or draft record

6. Military dependent's ID card

7. U.S. Coast Guard Merchant Mariner Card

8. Native American tribal document

9. Driver's license issued by a Canadian government authority

For persons under age 18 who are unable to present a document listed above:

10. School record or report card

11. Clinic, doctor, or hospital record

12. Day-care or nursery school record

LIST C — Documents that Establish Employment Eligibility

1. U.S. social security card issued by the Social Security Administration (*other than a card stating it is not valid for employment*)

2. Certification of Birth Abroad issued by the Department of State (*Form FS-545 or Form DS-1350*)

3. Original or certified copy of a birth certificate issued by a state, county, municipal authority or outlying possession of the United States bearing an official seal

4. Native American tribal document

5. U.S. Citizen ID Card (*INS Form I-197*)

6. ID Card for use of Resident Citizen in the United States (*INS Form I-179*)

7. Unexpired employment authorization document issued by the INS (*other than those listed under List A*)

Illustrations of many of these documents appear in Part 8 of the Handbook for Employers (M-274)

INSTRUCTIONS FOR COMPLETING FORM I-9[3]

These are the bulk of the instructions provided by INS for employer's guidance on how the I-9 Form is to be filled out and what types of documents can be used for verifying proof. You should note that proof documents are to be photocopied and attached to each I-9 Form. If you wish to obtain the entire instructional booklet, write to the imprinted address at the upper left corner of the first page and request a (free) copy along with a small supply of forms.

---

[3]   Levesque, *The Complete Hiring Manual*, p. 322.

EMPLOYMENT ELIGIBILITY VERIFICATION

U.S. Department of Justice
Immigration and Naturalization Service

OMB No. 1115-0136
Employment Eligibility Verification

INSTRUCTIONS
PLEASE READ ALL INSTRUCTIONS CAREFULLY BEFORE COMPLETING THIS FORM.

Anti-Discrimination Notice. It is illegal to discriminate against any individual (other than an alien not authorized to work in the U.S.) in hiring, discharging, or recruiting or referring for a fee because of that individual's national origin or citizenship status. It is illegal to discriminate against work eligible individuals. Employers **CANNOT** specify which document(s) they will accept from an employee. The refusal to hire an individual because of a future expiration date may also constitute illegal discrimination.

Section 1 - Employee. All employees, citizens and noncitizens, hired after November 6, 1986, must complete Section 1 of this form at the time of hire, which is the actual beginning of employment. **The employer is responsible for ensuring that Section 1 is timely and properly completed.**

Preparer/Translator Certification. The Preparer/Translator Certification must be completed if Section 1 is prepared by a person other than the employee. A preparer/translator may be used only when the employee is unable to complete Section 1 on his/her own. However, the employee must still sign Section 1 personally.

Section 2 - Employer. For the purpose of completing this form, the term "employer" includes those recruiters and referrers for a fee who are agricultural associations, agricultural employers, or farm labor contractors.

Employers must complete Section 2 by examining evidence of identity and employment eligibility within three (3) business days of the date employment begins. If employees are authorized to work, but are unable to present the required document(s) within three business days, they must present a receipt for the application of the document(s) within three business days and the actual document(s) within ninety (90) days. However, if employers hire individuals for a duration of less than three business days, Section 2 must be completed at the time employment begins. **Employers must record:** 1) document title; 2) issuing authority; 3) document number, 4) expiration date, if any; and 5) the date employment begins. Employers must sign and date the certification. Employees must present original documents. Employers may, but are not required to, photocopy the document(s) presented. These photocopies may only be used for the verification process and must be retained with the I-9. **However, employers are still responsible for completing the I-9.**

Section 3 - Updating and Reverification. Employers must complete Section 3 when updating and/or reverifying the I-9. Employers must reverify employment eligibility of their employees on or before the expiration date recorded in Section 1. Employers **CANNOT** specify which document(s) they will accept from an employee.

- If an employee's name has changed at the time this form is being updated/ reverified, complete Block A.

- If an employee is rehired within three (3) years of the date this form was originally completed and the employee is still eligible to be employed on the same basis as previously indicated on this form (updating), complete Block B and the signature block.

- If an employee is rehired within three (3) years of the date this form was originally completed and the employee's work authorization has expired **or** if a current employee's work authorization is about to expire (reverification), complete Block B and:
  - examine any document that reflects that the employee is authorized to work in the U.S. (see List A **or** C),
  - record the document title, document number and expiration date (if any) in Block C, and
  - complete the signature block.

Photocopying and Retaining Form I-9. A blank I-9 may be reproduced provided both sides are copied. The Instructions must be available to all employees completing this form. Employers must retain completed I-9s for three (3) years after the date of hire **or** one (1) year after the date employment ends, whichever is later.

For more detailed information, you may refer to the INS Handbook for Employers, (Form M-274). You may obtain the handbook at your local INS office.

Privacy Act Notice. The authority for collecting this information is the Immigration Reform and Control Act of 1986, Pub. L. 99-603 (8 U.S.C. 1324a).

This information is for employers to verify the eligibility of individuals for employment to preclude the unlawful hiring, or recruiting or referring for a fee, of aliens who are not authorized to work in the United States.

This information will be used by employers as a record of their basis for determining eligibility of an employee to work in the United States. The form will be kept by the employer and made available for inspection by officials of the U.S. Immigration and Naturalization Service, the Department of Labor, and the Office of Special Counsel for Immigration Related Unfair Employment Practices.

Submission of the information required in this form is voluntary. However, an individual may not begin employment unless this form is completed since employers are subject to civil or criminal penalties if they do not comply with the Immigration Reform and Control Act of 1986.

Reporting Burden. We try to create forms and instructions that are accurate, can be easily understood, and which impose the least possible burden on you to provide us with information. Often this is difficult because some immigration laws are very complex. Accordingly, the reporting burden for this collection of information is computed as follows: 1) learning about this form, 5 minutes; 2) completing the form, 5 minutes; and 3) assembling and filing (recordkeeping) the form, 5 minutes, for an average of 15 minutes per response. If you have comments regarding the accuracy of this burden estimate, or suggestions for making this form simpler, you can write to both the Immigration and Naturalization Service, 425 I Street, N.W., Room 5304, Washington, D. C. 20536; and the Office of Management and Budget, Paperwork Reduction Project, OMB No. 1115-0136, Washington, D.C. 20503.

Form I-9 (Rev. 11-21-91) N

EMPLOYERS MUST RETAIN COMPLETED I-9
PLEASE DO NOT MAIL COMPLETED I-9 TO INS

JOB INTEREST FORM

This form can be used instead of the Employment Application when job seekers express an interest in employment during periods of no vacancies. When recruitment becomes necessary, the employer uses the Job Interest Form as a given pool of interested applicants and notifies them when vacancies occur. Most employers will do this by mailing a cover letter announcing the vacancy and an Employment Application Form.

JOB INTEREST FORM

To help _____ understand your job interests, please indicate what type of jobs interest you. Checking "Yes" or "No" will not exclude you from being considered for any job for which you are qualified.

PLEASE INDICATE YOUR INTEREST:

Check (✔) your interest for each item below:

	Yes	No
1. Are you interested in overtime work?		
2. Are you interested in performing routine tasks daily?		
3. Are you interested in jobs having rotating days off including week-ends and holidays?		
4. Are you interested in the following types of work?		
(a) Office work?		
(b) Out of doors?		
(c) Shop or plant?		

5. Are you interested in one or more kinds of work having the following physical demands?

(a.) **Sedentary Work (very light):**
Lifting 10 lbs. maximum and occasionally lifting and/or carrying such articles as dockets, ledgers and small tools. Although a sedentary job is defined as one which involves sitting, a certain amount of walking and standing is often necessary in carrying out job duties. Jobs are sedentary if walking and standing are required only occasionally and other sedentary criteria are met.

(b.) **Light Work:**
Lifting 20 lbs. maximum with frequent lifting and/or carrying of objects weighing up top 10 lbs. Even though the weight lifted may be only a negligible amount, a job is in this category when it requires walking or standing to a significant degree, or when it involves sitting most of the time with a degree of pushing and pulling of arm and/or leg controls.

(c.) **Medium Work:**
Lifting 50 lbs. maximum with frequent lifting and/or carrying of objects weighing up to 25 lbs.

(d.) **Heavy Work:**
Lifting 100 lbs. maximum with frequent lifting and/or carrying of objects weighing up to 50 lbs.

(e.) **Very Heavy Work:**
Lifting objects in excess of 100 lbs. with frequent lifting and/or carrying of objects weighing 50 lbs. or more.

List below titles of jobs in which you're most interested:

1. _____   4. _____

2. _____   5. _____

3. _____   6. _____

Name (last) _____ (first) _____ (initial)

Address (street) _____ (city) _____ (state) _____ (zip code)

Day telephone (area code and no.)

Date filed

continued

JOB INTEREST FORM—*continued*

CERTIFICATION:

I understand that the purpose of this form is to advise _____ of my interest in employment in the jobs I have listed, and that _____ will make every effort to notify me of job vacancies for the listed jobs for a period of one year from the date of filing of this form. I further understand that this form does not constitute a job application, that I must file a job application to be considered for any vacancy, and that _____ does not accept job applications except for current vacancies.

Signed:_____ Date:_____

FOR OFFICE USE ONLY:

Dates contacted applicant	Position	Application received?
1. _____	_____	_____
2. _____	_____	_____
3. _____	_____	_____
4. _____	_____	_____
5. _____	_____	_____

_____is an Equal Opportunity Employer, and does not discriminate on the basis of a person's race, color, creed, national origins, religion, age (40-70)), sex, marital status or physical handicap. Thus, every job applicant considered is for employment into jobs for which they are qualified.

EMPLOYMENT INTERVIEW RATING FORM

Interview rating forms can be designed in an almost unlimited number of ways. Some use points and some are weighted based on the most pertinent tasks performed, but nearly all use some sort of scale to evaluate distinctions in skill, knowledge, experience, and other job-related factors between differing applicants. The use of such rating forms can provide the employer with documentation in defending against a discrimination claim. These forms also serve as useful reference sources for later or delayed hiring decisions.

See Chapter 25 for a discussion on conducting the selection interview.

EMPLOYMENT INTERVIEW RATING FORM

INSTRUCTIONS: Assign a number from __ to __ for each scale below. In rating each scale, check the area above a phrase if you feel the phrase adequately summarizes your evaluation of the applicant. If, on the other hand, you feel that your evaluation of the applicant falls between two of the phrases along the scale, check the area between the phrases.

Please write relevant comments in the space provided above each scale. Try to give a rating for the applicant on each dimension. If you feel that you do not have sufficient information to make a rating on a certain dimension, write "Cannot Rate" in the comment space.

Applicant's Name: _____   Date: _____

Position Title: _____   Time: _____

Interviewer's Name: _____   Interviewer's Title: _____

_____

I. *Relevant Knowledge and Skills:* | Weight (Points) |
    Demonstrates possession of required technical competencies
    and expertise acquired through past experience, education,
    and record of achievement to date. Ability to successfully
    apply knowledge.

Low (_____ | _____ | _____ | _____) High

| Lacking in scope and grasp of technical knowledge. Some areas severely deficient or out-of-date. | Generally good grasp of job technical knowledge requirements. Some gaps in information and currency of knowledge. | Has thorough, complete and up-to-date knowledge of technical skills and abilities needed by the job. |

II. *Oral Communication Skills:* | Weight (Points) |
    Speaks in a clear and understandable manner so listener
    grasps message. Is able to persuade verbally, summarize, and
    justify effectively. Elicits feedback and is able to draw others
    into conversation. Listens attentively to others.

Low (_____ | _____ | _____ | _____) High

| Articulation poor, mumbled a great deal, extremely difficult to understand. | Articulation good, used appropriate language. Listened attentively but some | States ideas very clearly. Speaks in complete, organized sentences. Uses |

continued

EMPLOYMENT INTERVIEW RATING FORM—*continued*

Poor listener— numerous questions had to be repeated.	questions needed to be repeated. Responded appropriately.	adequate and/or job-related vocabulary. Good listener— no repeated questions. Quick and appropriate responses.

III. *Interpersonal Sensitivity Skills:*

Weight (Points)

Ability to interact with individuals without eliciting negative or hurt feelings. Awareness of the needs and feelings of other individuals. Ability to make appropriate statements or actions in order to pacify hostile persons or situations. Answers questions diplomatically and avoids excessive argumentation. Maintains open and approachable manner.

Low (_____|_____|_____|_____) High

Would be insensitive and uncooperative. Would antagonize and alienate co-workers and employees.	Would get along well with most people. Would provide support and enthusiasm to co-workers and employees. Would be liked and respected.	Very sensitive, good listener. Very effective in conflict/awkward interpersonal situations. Provides excellent support and enthusiasm to co-workers and staff.

IV. *Planning and Organization:*

Weight (Points)

Ability to set priorities, and to coordinate and schedule tasks or events in a logical manner to maximize staff and material resources, increase efficiency, and anticipate problems. Ability to meet a predefined goal with a prescribed timetable. Anticipates problems and is proactive rather than reactive to problems. Takes steps to alleviate problems.

Low (_____|_____|_____|_____) High

Unable to set priorities in an efficient manner. Lacks time-management skills. Would be poor decision maker, indecisive and missing critical elements. Would use old solutions for new and different problems. Little initiative and poor work under pressure.	Sets priorities most of the time. Would generally make good decisions using relevant information. Adapts well to new problems. Shows initiative and flexibility. Works well in organization, even under pressure.	Always plans work and sets priorities in accordance with reasonable time schedules. Would use all pertinent information to make excellent decisions. Good common sense. Adapts quickly and efficiently to new situations. Copes efficiently with pressure.

continued

EMPLOYMENT INTERVIEW RATING FORM—*continued*

V. *Management Control Skills:*

Coordinates and delegates work within office. Able to assess capabilities and skills in order to optimize utilization of staff personnel. Able to train and develop staff members. Keeps staff members informed on new developments, and handles/prevents personnel problems.

Weight (Points)

Low (_____|_____|_____|_____) High

Unable to delegate work in an efficient manner. No follow-through. Cannot explain requirements clearly.	Delegates work most of the time. Follows up and provides training assistance when required. Effective evaluator.	Always assigns work to appropriate person and provides training. Excellent and fair evaluator. Always follows up.

VI. *Summary and Recommendations:*

Add Ratings: I ( ) II ( ) III ( ) IV ( ) V ( ) = TOTAL ( )

( ) I do not feel this applicant is suited for this kind of work. I would definitely not recommend hiring.

( ) The applicant might do well in this kind of work, but I would have some reservations about hiring.

( ) I would endorse this applicant. I feel the individual should do well in this type of work.

( ) I would endorse this applicant with confidence. Applicant is a high-level performer and would do very well in this kind of work.

Notes/Comments:

_____   _____
(Date)   (Interviewer's Signature)

TELEPHONE REFERENCE CHECK FORM[4]

This form should be used for informal, yet documented, conversations with former employers concerning reference information on applicants under final hiring consideration. You should follow the information on this form when talking to former employers, and write in responses during your conversation. The form itself should be placed in (1) a confidential folder with other employment reference documents (if permitted by state law), (2) a personnel file folder on the employee but not accessible for the employee's review (if permitted by state law), or (3) a sealed envelope marked "To Be Opened Only by *(name of company officers)* before deposit into the employee's personnel file."

---

[4]   Levesque, *The Complete Hiring Manual,* pp. 321–322.

TELEPHONE REFERENCE CHECK

By: _____ Date: _____

Name of
Applicant: _____ S.S. No. _____
     (Last)   (First)   (Middle Initial)

Position
Applied For: _____

Name of Person   Title and
Being Contacted: _____   Department: _____

                                     Telephone
Company: _____   Number: _____

INFORMATION STATED

Employment
Dates: From _____ To _____

Leaving
Salary: $ _____ Per _____

Leaving
Position: _____

Reason(s)
for Leaving: _____
_____

REFERENCE CHECK

From _____   To _____

$ _____   Per _____

Started
Position: _____

Leaving
Position: _____

Reason(s)
for Leaving: _____
_____

PERFORMANCE FACTORS

Major
Duties: _____
                                          How
_____ Long: _____

Application of   Quality of
Skills and Knowledge: _____   Work: _____

Ability to Plan   Supervision:
and Follow Through: _____   How much required: _____

Comparison to Other Employees
in the Same Classification: _____

continued

TELEPHONE REFERENCE CHECK—*continued*

SUPERVISORY ABILITY/POTENTIAL

No. of People
Supervised: _____
How
Long _____
Ability to Select,
Motivate, Discipline _____

Evaluation of
Supervisory Potential: _____

_____

PERSONAL FACTORS

Ability to Work
with Others: _____
Work
Habits: _____

Strength or
Strong Points: Technical _____
General _____

Negative or   (Note: Probe
Weak Points: suspected fault) _____

Attendance: Good _____ Average _____ Poor (state reason) _____

Were There Any Personal Reasons
that Affected Job Performance: _____

OVERALL EVALUATION

Eligible
for Rehire: Yes _____ No (state reason) _____
(Note: Describe position under
consideration and its requirements) _____

_____

Would You Consider
Applicant Suitable: Yes _____ No (state reason) _____

Any Additional
Comments: _____

_____

(ATTACH TO EMPLOYMENT APPLICATION AFTER COMPLETION)

AUTHORIZATION FOR EMPLOYMENT REFERENCE FORM[5]

This form is very similar to the Telephone Reference Check Form, but it is used to mail to former employers and has the advantage of explaining how you use this information, its confidentiality, and the former employee's signed authorization to release this type of employment related information. By including information concerning the individual's performance, strengths and weaknesses, and functional abilities, it provides you with much-needed information about the person's competence or training/supervision needs relative to the job for which they are being considered. The completed form should be handled in the same way as the Telephone Reference Check Form, inasmuch as they contain very similar confidential information that should not be accessible to persons who do not have a need and right to know its contents.

---

[5]   Levesque, *The Complete Hiring Manual*, p. 322.

AUTHORIZATION FOR EMPLOYMENT REFERENCE*

To:

Reference Name _____ Title _____

Organization _____ Phone ( ) _____-_____

Address _____ City _____

State _____ _____ Zip _____

From:

(Name and title of person form to be returned to)

(Company name)

(Company address)

(City, state, Zip code)

The person whose signature appears below has applied to this company for employment as a _____. To complete our determination of this person's overall suitability for employment in this position and with this company, it is important to us to obtain prior employment, education, and other related information about prospective employees.

While we recognize that prior employers and others having confidential information on their people are reluctant to divulge such information to "outsiders" due to privacy rights laws, we would like to assure you that the contents of this document is treated by us as confidential, is stored separately from an employee's normal personnel file in accordance with (state name) law, and is not allowed to be reviewed by applicable employees under routine access policy established by (state name) law. In addition, to assure your further comfort in supplying us with the information requested below, we have obtained the reference person's written authorization allowing you to release the information requested.

Thank you in advance for your help and cooperation in this matter, and please use the confidential envelope enclosed for the return of your response.

APPLICANT IDENTIFICATION DATA

Applicant's Name _____ Position _____

Date of Birth _____ Social Security No. _____-____-_____

Current Address _____ City/State _____

Prior Address _____ City/State _____

Home Phone ( ) _____-_____ Driver's Lic. No. _____ State _____

PRIOR EMPLOYMENT INFORMATION

Date of Hire _____ Position Title _____

Pay Rate $_____/_____

Previous Positions Held _____ Date _____ Rate$_____/_____

Last Position Held _____ Date _____ Rate$_____/_____

Reason for Leaving _____

_____

_____ Last Work Date _____

What was this person's most noteworthy job responsibilities? _____

_____

---

* Levesque, *The Complete Hiring Manual*, pp. 335–336.

AUTHORIZATION FOR EMPLOYMENT REFERENCE—continued

Performance Strengths Were? _____
_____
_____

Performance Weaknesses Were? _____
_____
_____

Date and Nature of Disciplinary Problems (prior three years) _____
_____
_____

Notable Recognitions, Awards, or Achievements _____
_____

BASED ON OVERALL EMPLOYMENT **HOW WOULD YOU RATE THIS PERSON'S PERFORMANCE?**				
	Superior	Good	Fair	Poor
Job Knowledge and Use of Skills				
Attention to Detail and Memory				
Use of Time/Efficiency				
Relations with Coworkers				
Relations with Superiors				
Customer Relations				
Compliance with Rules and Policies				
Tardiness				
Honesty and Trustworthiness				
Personal Grooming				
Absenteeism				
_____ hours absence during last twelve months of employment				

DISCLOSURE AUTHORIZATION AND RELEASE

I hereby authorize (Name of former employer or school) and its employees and representatives to provide any and all information they deem appropriate regarding my employment and job performance to (Name of your company) and any of its employees, representatives, and agents. This information may be provided either verbally or in writing. In addition to authorizing the release of any information regarding my employment, I hereby fully waive any rights or claims I have or may have against (Name of your company) and its employees, representatives, and agents, and I release (Name of your company) and its employees, representatives, and agents from any and all liability, claims, or damages that may directly or indirectly result from the use, disclosure, or release of any such information by any person or party, whether such information is favorable or unfavorable to me.

Signature _____ Date _____

Typed or Printed Full Name _____

AUTHORIZATION TO ACQUIRE
CREDIT REPORT FORM[6]

This form should be used by those employers whose business necessitates an evaluation of an applicant's credit and/or character worthiness. Even then, it should be used only for those applicants whose job responsibilities provide them with access to, handling of, or use of monetary transactions related to the employer's business or its customers. As the form indicates, applicants who request copies of the report are entitled to obtain them when such reports are conducted by a consumer credit reporting agency.

---

[6]   Levesque, *The Complete Hiring Manual*, p. 322.

APPLICANT AUTHORIZATION TO ACQUIRE CREDIT REPORT*

Personal Identification Information

Applicant Name _____   Birthdate _____

Current Address _____   How Long? _____

City _____   State _____ Zip _____

Previous Address _____   How Long? _____

City _____   State _____ Zip _____

Social Security No. _____   Driver's Lic. No. _____

Financial and Credit References

BANK AND SAVINGS ACCOUNTS   **CREDIT ACCOUNTS**

Name _____   Company _____

Branch _____   Address _____

Account No. _____   Account No. _____

Account Type _____   Account Type _____

Name _____   Company _____

Branch _____   Address _____

Account No. _____   Account No. _____

Account Type _____   Account Type _____

Name _____   Company _____

Branch _____   Address _____

Account No. _____   Account No. _____

Account Type _____   Account Type _____

(Company) has determined that the job for which you are being considered requires that an investigation be made about your credit history, personal character, and general reputation prior to confirming your employment. This notice is given to you in compliance with Public Law 91-508, otherwise known as the Fair Credit Reporting Act, to inform you that a routine inquiry may be made concerning your credit, character, general reputation, personal characteristics or mode of living, and we expect to receive a report thereon. Further information on the nature and scope of such report, if one is made, will be available to you upon your written request that we, or the reporting agency, provide you with a copy.

I HEREBY AUTHORIZE *(Company)* TO ACQUIRE INFORMATION FROM THE SOURCES PROVIDED ABOVE, AND OTHER APPLICABLE SOURCES DEEMED SUITABLE, CONCERNING MY CREDIT, CHARACTER, REPUTATION, AND MODE OF LIVING.

Signature _____   Date _____

---

*   Levesque, *The Complete Hiring Manual*, p. 337.

APPLICANT FLOW DATA FORM

Use this form to list the names and equal employment opportunity (protected class) characteristics of qualified applicants who make application for *each separate position title* in which a hiring decision is made. These data are almost always requested by fair employment compliance agencies during the investigation of a discrimination claim.

APPLICANT FLOW DATA

APPLICANT FLOW DATA
(Print All Information)

Position Title: _____ Process Period: _____

EEO-1 Category*: _____

Prepared By: _____

Name of Applicant	Sex		Age	EEO Identification*											Disposition*	Complete this Section if Hired		
	M	F	40+	W	B	HP	API	AI	HCI	VE	DVE					Hire Date	Position Title	Pay Rate
Total																		

CODES*

EEO-1 Categories
1. Officials and Managers
2. Professionals
3. Technicians
4. Sales Workers
5. Office and Clerical
6. Crafts—Skilled
7. Operatives—Semiskilled
8. Laborers—Unskilled
9. Service Workers

EEO Identification

W — WHITE (Not of Hispanic origin)—All persons having origins in any of the original peoples of Europe, North Africa, or the Middle East.

B — BLACK (Not of Hispanic origin)—All persons having origins in any of the Black racial groups of Africa.

HP — HISPANIC—All persons of Mexican, Puerto Rican, Cuban, Central or South American, or other Spanish culture or origin, regardless of race.

API — ASIAN OR PACIFIC ISLANDER—All persons having origins in any of the original peoples of the Far East, Southeast Asia and Indian Subcontinent, or the Pacific Islands. This area includes, for example, China, Japan, Korea, the Philippine Islands and Samoa.

AI — AMERICAN INDIAN OR ALASKA NATIVE—All persons having origins in any of the original peoples of North America, and who maintain cultural identification through tribal affiliations or community recognition.

HCI — HANDICAPPED INDIVIDUAL—Any person who (1) has a physical or mental impairment that substantially limits one or more of his or her major life activities; (2) has a record of such impairment; or (3) is regarded as having such impairment. A handicap is "substantially limiting" if it is likely to cause difficulty in securing, retaining or advancing in employment.

VE — VETERAN ELIGIBILITY—Served in armed forces between August 5, 1964 and May 7, 1975.

DVE— DISABLED VETERAN ELIGIBILITY—A veteran with a disability, service connected or otherwise.

Disposition

A—Hired

B—Applicant rejected offer of employment

C—Qualified applicant, but no vacancy

D—Failed to complete application

E—Insufficient educational background or equivalent experience

F—Unsatisfactory work history

G—Unfavorable interview

H—Unfavorable reference check

I—Inadequate transportation

J—Did not meet other job requisites

K—Under consideration

Chapter 6

NEW-HIRE SETUP FORMS

EMPLOYEE INFORMATION LOG FORM

This form is designed to be used for recording a wide variety of common employment data, including changes that typically occur during the employment period, often referred to as personnel transactions. The form can be used in one of two ways: it can be affixed to each employee's personnel file (inside left flap), or it can be kept in a confidential file by alphabetical order of employee's last name.

EMPLOYEE INFORMATION LOG

_____
Date prepared

Attach Photograph Here

EMPLOYEE

Print Name	Last	First	Middle		Sex
Address	Number	Street	City	State	Zip	Telephone No. ( )
Social Security number — —	Driver license (state/no.)	Marital Status	Fingerprints Taken Record
Date of Birth	Date Verified	Place of Birth	U.S. Citizen
Handicap (nature)			

DEPENDENTS

No. of dependents	Spouse	Children	Parents	Other

Name	Relationship	Sex	Age
1.			
2.			
3.			
4.			
5.			

EMERGENCY

In case of emergency notify	Relationship
Name	
Address	Day Phone No. ( )
	Evening Phone No. ( )

DATA

Date Hired	Position	Location/Department/Office
Full-time/Part-time (No. of Hours)	Exempt/Non-Exempt	Starting salary	Employee (payroll) Number	EEO No.

EMPLOYMENT

Education Record	Years	Graduated	Date Verified	Vocational or special training
Elementary School				
High School				
College		Years Completed		
Major Subject		Graduated?		
Degree		Date Left		
Hobbies or avocational skills				
Relative employed in this company				

INITIAL

Military Record	Rank of Rating	Branch of Service	Period of Service	Date of Transfer or Discharge
Active Service				
Reserve Status				Until

Test	Range	Range	Init.
Clerical			
Mechanical			
Verbal			
Nonverbal			
Dexterity			
Electricity			
Language			
Typing	Speed	Errors	
Dictation	Speed	Errors	
Others (list)			

REFERENCES	DATE VERIFIED	INITIALS

COMMENTS

continued

EMPLOYEE INFORMATION LOG—*continued*

Checklist of Required Forms

FORMS	DATE GIVEN TO EMPLOYEE OR SENT	DATE RETURNED	MISSING INFORMATION	DATE SENT BACK TO EMPLOYEE	FOLLOW-UP	FINAL RETENTION DATE	COMMENTS
Application							
Application Supplement							
Preemployment Medical History							
Payroll Authorization Form							
W-4 Form							
Acknowledgment of Employee Handbook							
Security Form							
Insurance Enrollment Form						Effective Date	
Reference Verification							
Others (list)							

Company Service Record

Date Effective	Job Title	Exempt Nonexempt	Hours	Rate	Location	Nature of Change

Employee Educational Record

Date	Title of Class or Course	Remarks

Performance Evaluation Reports

Date	Date	Date	Date	Date	Date

Employee Leave Record

Date	Code	Days	Date	Code	Days

CODE:
DF = Death in Family
J = Jury Duty
S = Sick Leave
V = Vacation
FH = Floating Holiday
X-1 = Excused Absence-
       Other (with pay)
X-2 = Excused Absence-
       Other (without pay)
U = Unexcused Absence
     (without pay)
M = Military Leave

continued

EMPLOYEE INFORMATION LOG—*continued*

Pre-Employment Medical History

Date Prepared

(to be completed by applicant)

Name	Last	First	Initial	Social Security Number
				— —

Have you had or do you now have any of the following: (Check yes or no)

YES	NO		YES	NO		YES	NO	
		Abdominal Pain			Gall Bladder Trouble or Gall Stones			Rupture
		Alcoholism			Goiter			Serum Reaction
		Allergy			Hearing Impairment			Severe Eye, Ear, Nose, or Throat Trouble
		Arthritis			Hernia			Shortness of Breath
		Asthma			High or Low Blood Pressure			Sinusitis
		Back Injury			Jaundice			Skin Disorders
		Bone, Joint, or Other Deformity			Kidney Disease, Nephritis			Sleeplessness
		Chest or Lung Disease			Kidney Stone or Blood in Urine			Spitting of Blood
		Chronic Back Trouble			Loss of Memory			Stomach, Liver, or Intestinal Trouble
		Chronic Cough			Marked Fatigue			TB
		Constipation			Marked Increase or Decrease in Weight			Tumor, Growth, Cyst, or Cancer
		Depression			Menstrual Difficulty			Undue Worry or Fear
		Diabetes			Nervous or Mental Trouble			Veneral Disease
		Discharging Ear			Pain or Pressure in Chest			HAVE YOU EVER:
		Dizziness or Unconsciousness			Painful or Trick Shoulder, Elbow, or Knee			Worn Glasses
		Drug or Narcotic Addiction			Palpitation or Heart Disease			Worn an Artificial Eye
		Epilepsy or Convulsions			Paralysis (Including Infantile)			Worn Hearing Aids
		Family History Diabetes			Piles or Rectal Disease			Worn a Brace or Support
		Female Disorders			Pleurisy			Had Foot Trouble
		Fracture			Pneumonia			Lived with Anyone Who Had TB
		Frequent Headaches			Pregnancy			Had a Heart Murmur
		Frequent or Painful Urination			Rheumatic Fever			

1. Have you had illness other than those listed above?_____No _____Yes if yes, describe and indicate dates below:

   Illness_____ Date _____

   Illness_____ Date _____

2. Have you been under a doctor's care within the past 5 years?_____No _____ Yes if yes, give details:_____

3. Have you ever had an injury at work elsewhere covered by Workmen's Compensation Insurance? _____No _____Yes if yes, describe below

   Injury_____Date_____Employer_____

4. Was permanent disability awarded?_____No _____Yes if yes, give percent_____

5. Are you allergic to any drugs? _____No _____Yes if yes, what?_____

6. Are you currently taking medication? _____No _____Yes if yes, what?_____

7. Is vision good in both eyes? _____Yes _____No if no, explain below:
   Corrected by Glasses_____Contact Lenses_____Other_____

8. Is hearing good in both ears? _____Yes _____No if no, explain:_____

9. Do you have any physical limitations/restrictions? _____No _____Yes if yes, explain below:

   _____

   _____

I certify that information given above is accurate to the best of my knowledge. I understand that any misstatement of fact is grounds for dismissal.

_____   _____

SIGNATURE   DATE

NEW EMPLOYEE ORIENTATION
CHECKLIST FORM

New employees should be systematically integrated into the organization and the work force. To assure that all employees receive at least the same basic orientation, have supervisors use this form as a guide when conducting new employee orientations. It is also a useful document to demonstrate that an employee did receive certain information that may later be in question (note that the employee is required to sign and date the form).

NEW EMPLOYEE ORIENTATION CHECKLIST

NOTE: All appropriate information must be discussed with each new employee.

Employee's Name: _____   Social Security
Number: _____

Job Title: _____   Date: _____

PERSONNEL DEPARTMENT: In order to avoid duplication of instructions, the information checked ( ) below has been given or explained to the employee by the Personnel Department.

I. *Compensation and Benefits*
- Time sheet/card ( )
- Payroll procedures ( )
- Insurance Program Booklet ( )
- Pension Plan Booklet ( )
- Educational Assistance ( )
- Credit Union ( )
- Stock Purchase Plan ( )
- Savings Bond Plan ( )
- Sick Benefits, A&S,
  Limitations, etc. ( )

II. *Leaves, Promotions, and Transfers*
- Probationary Period ( )
- Performance Evaluations ( )
- Promotions ( )
- Transfers ( )
- Vacations ( )
- Holidays ( )
- Absences or Tardiness ( )
- Jury Duty ( )
- Leaves of Absence —
  Maternity/Medical, etc. ( )

III. *General*
- Employee Handbook/Labor Agreement/Rules Booklet ( )
- Disciplinary Procedures ( )
- Difficulties, Complaints, Discrimination, and Grievance Procedures ( )
- Patient Agreement ( )
- ID Card ( )
- Introduction to Guards ( )
- Transportation ( )
- Parking Facilities ( )
- Safety Booklet ( )
- First Aid and Requirements of Reporting Injury ( )
- Bulletin Boards/Company Newsletters ( )
- Voluntary Resignation Notice ( )
- (Others) ( )

continued

NEW EMPLOYEE ORIENTATION CHECKLIST—*continued*

SUPERVISOR: The following is a checklist of information necessary to orient the new employee to the job in your department. Please check off each point as you discuss it with the employee and return to the _____ within _____ days following employee placement in the job.

I. *Receive the New Employee*
- Review copy of employee's application. Be familiar with employee's experience, training, and education. ( )
- Review job description with employee, including the duties, responsibilities, and working relationships. ( )
- Discuss with the employee the unit organization and the department division organization. Explain the function of your department/division as related to the total organization and how the employee fits in. ( )
- Discover the employee's career goals and objectives. Relate them to the goals and objectives of the department. ( )
- Confirm that employee has a copy of employee handbook. Set aside one hour in first week for employee to read employee handbook and to understand it. ( )

II. *Welcome the New Employee*
Introduce Employee to Co-workers:
- Indicate to each co-worker the new employee's position. ( )
- Explain the functions of each person as you introduce the new employee. ( )

Show New Employee Around:
- Tour the department, plant, or company. ( )
- Explain where lavatories, coffee areas, and parking facilities are located. ( )
- Explain the various departments within the organization. ( )

III. *Introduce the New Employee to Job*
- Ensure that new employee's working area, equipment, tools, and supplies are prepared and available. ( )
- Explain the levels of supervision within the department. ( )
- Provide new employee with necessary or required training. ( )
- Explain use of: Telephones (personal/company calls) ( )
  - Copy machines ( )
  - Company vehicles ( )
  - Mail procedures ( )
  - Supply procedures ( )
- Explain hours of work, overtime, call-in procedures. ( )
- Give new employee department telephone number. ( )
- Review location of department's first aid equipment. ( )
- Explain housekeeping responsibilities. ( )

continued

NEW EMPLOYEE ORIENTATION CHECKLIST—*continued*

IV. *Follow-Up:*
- Set date and time within one week to cover any questions or concerns of the new employee.   ( )
- Inform employee of date for first probationary review.   ( )

_____
Supervisor's Signature

_____
Supervisor's Title

_____
Department

_____
Date

_____
Employee's Signature

_____
Date

**UPON COMPLETION, FILE ORIGINAL IN EMPLOYEE'S PERSONNEL FOLDER,
WITH A COPY TO THE EMPLOYEE**

PERSONNEL MANUAL/EMPLOYEE HANDBOOK ACKNOWLEDGMENT FORM

Some employers have found that employees periodically dispute receiving a copy of the organization's employee handbook (personnel policies). More often than not, this situation arises when an employee is charged with violating a policy, rule, or condition of employment, whereupon the employee claims lack of knowledge. This form serves as verification that the employee received and assumed responsibility for becoming familiar with the contents of the employee handbook.

PERSONNEL MANUAL/EMPLOYEE HANDBOOK
ACKNOWLEDGMENT FORM*

This will acknowledge my receipt of *(Company)* personnel handbook and my responsibility to become familiar with its contents. I further understand and agree to the following:

- This handbook represents a brief summary of some of the more important *(Company)* policies relative to employment, but not intended to be all inclusive of company policies or practices.

- The *(Company)* retains the sole right in its business judgment to modify, suspend, interpret, or cancel in whole or part at any time, and with or without notice, any of the published or unpublished personnel policies or practices.

- This *(Company)* does not recognize verbal or implied contracts for employment. Only the *(President)* of the *(Company)* has the authority to enter into any agreement of employment for specified durations. Such employment agreements will only be valid and binding on the *(Company)* when the agreement is set forth in a written document signed by the employee and *(President)*, or other authorized agent, of the *(Company)*.

- The contents of this handbook does not constitute an expressed or implied contract of employment.

- I have the right to end my employment relationship with the *(Company)*, with or without advance notice or cause, and I acknowledge that the *(Company)* has the same right.

Employee's Name (Print or type): _____

Employee's Signature: _____

Date: _____   Witness: _____

Title: _____   Date: _____

---

*   Levesque, *The Complete Hiring Manual,* p. 158.

PROPERTY ISSUANCE FORM

This form should be used whenever new or continuing employees are issued *any* form of tangible company property, particularly where such should be returned upon employment separation.

PROPERTY ISSUANCE*

Employee's Name: _____

Job Title: _____

Date of Issuance: _____

    I acknowledge receipt of the company-owned equipment and materials listed below. In accordance with company policy, it is my understanding and agreement that I am responsible for maintaining these items in good condition, and to promptly return each listed item at the time I separate from active employment, or earlier upon request. I also understand and agree that it is my responsibility to promptly report any loss or damage to these items.

Receipt			Return	
Item	Quantity	Serial #	Returned To	Date
_____	_____	_____	_____	_____
_____	_____	_____	_____	_____
_____	_____	_____	_____	_____
_____	_____	_____	_____	_____
_____	_____	_____	_____	_____
_____	_____	_____	_____	_____

Employee's Signature _____

Date _____

Issued by _____

---

* Levesque, *The Complete Hiring Manual*, p. 159.

PROPERTY INSPECTION CONSENT FORM

This form authorizes company officials to inspect each employee's assigned or personal property—when it is deemed the company has a legitimate business interest to do so, including reasonable suspicion of drug and/or alcohol use, sale, and the like. Therefore, this form should be signed by each new hire.

PROPERTY INSPECTION CONSENT*

It is my understanding that *(Company)* maintains policies that reserve the right of the *(Company)* to inspect desks, lockers, and similar furnishings at any time, with or without notice, and that any personal property I bring on to *(Company)* premises may be subject to inspection, including searches, in connection with the *(Company's)* investigation of stolen property, hazardous materials, or controlled substances.

I therefore acknowledge the existence of these policies and the assertion of the *(Company's)* rights to conduct such inspections and investigations, and I am agreed to cooperate in all respects during any such proceeding.

Employee's Name: _____

Job Title: _____

Date: _____

Witnessed by: _____

---

*   Levesque, *The Complete Hiring Manual,* p. 154.

Chapter 7

COMPENSATION AND BENEFIT FORMS

NONEXEMPT EMPLOYEE TIME RECORD

This is a simple form to use for recording work hours of *individual* nonexempt employees. It is particularly useful for employers who have fewer than twenty-five employees, and who choose not to record work hours and exempt personnel. The form can also be modified, if desired, to enter other status codes at the bottom such as those shown on the Payroll Time Report Form. The form can be further simplified by deleting the last two categories of in-and-out times; these blocks can be used instead to enter the names of three employees and their workday start and ending times. Many employees resent clocking in and out so often, and it becomes an administrative headache.

NONEXEMPT EMPLOYEE TIME RECORD

Payroll Period of: _____ to: _____

Employee Name: _____ Position Title: _____

☐ Full time ☐ Part time   Soc. Sec. # _____-____-_____

DATES								NOTES
	SUN.	MON.	TUE.	WED.	THUR.	FRI.	SAT.	
Morning Coded Hours								
Afternoon Coded Hours								
Overtime From / To								
TOTAL* Regular								
Overtime								Weekly Total: _____ regular _____ overtime

*Employee: Total each day's column using coded hours and weekly total. Examples of coded hour entries are:

5R	= 5 hrs. regular	WC = workers' compensation leave
4V/4R	= 4 hrs. vacation/	8H = 8 hours holiday
	4 hrs. regular	LOA = leave of absence without pay
4.5 S/L	= 4½ hrs. paid sick leave	

Employee's Signature: _____ Date: _____

SUPERVISOR: Indicate total number of overtime hours to be paid: _____ hrs. @ 1½ regular rate _____ hrs. @ 2 times regular rate. *Note: Overtime is determined on the basis of hours worked, not payroll hours.*

Supervisor's Signature: _____ Date Approved: _____

PAYROLL TIME REPORT
(EXEMPT EMPLOYEES)

This is the standard payroll report form used by most employers to record the hours worked and other status of employees for each payroll period. It is usually completed by the unit supervisor and approved by the next higher (departmental) manager as the final certification to the person who prepares payroll checks. It is advisable to record payroll hours and status of both nonexempt and exempt personnel, given the chance that an employer may one day be challenged on the exempt classification of a particular position(s).

EXEMPT EMPLOYEE TIME REPORT

Payroll Period of: _____ to: _____

Employee Name: _____ Position Title: _____

☐ Full time   ☐ Part time   Soc. Sec. # _____-____-_____

DATES	SUN.	MON.	TUE.	WED.	THUR.	FRI.	SAT.	NOTES
_____								
Morning Coded Hours								
Afternoon Coded Hours								
Additional Hours Worked								
TOTAL * Regular								
Additional								Weekly Total: _____ regular _____ overtime

*Employee: Total each day's column using coded hours and weekly total. Examples of coded hour entries are:

5R	= 5 hrs. regular	WC	= workers' compensation leave
8V	= 8 hrs. vacation	LOA	= leave of absence without pay
8H	= 8 hrs. holiday		
4.5 S/L	= 4½ hrs. paid sick leave		

Note: Exempt employees are ineligible for overtime compensation. However, the company wishes to track hours worked that are "additional" to normal scheduled workdays and work hours, and unscheduled work hours as a matter of considering those hours relating to performance effectiveness and types of hours used by employees throughout the year.

Employee's Signature: _____ Date: _____

Supervisor's Signature: _____ Date Approved: _____

PAY RATE REVIEW AND HISTORY CHART

This is a useful form if the employer does not use the Employee Information Log Form to maintain an ongoing record of each employee's change in job classification or pay rates. Like the Employee Information Log, this form can be kept in each employee's personnel file (inside left flap) or in a single alphabetical file. Additionally, data can be collected from this form on all employees to determine the employer's annual increase in direct and indirect payroll costs.

PAY RATE REVIEW AND HISTORY CHART

(Confidential)

Name: _____   Hire Date: _____

Social Security Number: _____   Beginning Job Title: _____

Payroll/I.D. Number: _____   Beginning Pay Rate: _____

Effective Date	Change Code*	JOB TITLE From	To	PAY RATE From	To	%	$	Performance Rating	Date

Change Codes

PI   – Promotion Increase   RC   – Reclassification
MI   – Merit Increase   RH   – Rehire
COL – Cost of Living Increase   DM – Demotion
NI   – Negotiated Increase   B   – Bonds
LSI – Length of Service Increase (longevity)

DETERMINATION OF EXEMPT
CLASSIFICATION STATUS

Use this form as a means of documenting the conditions under which each different position qualifies for exempt status in any one of the three categories (executive, administrative, or professional) as defined in the Fair Labor Standards Act.

DETERMINATION OF EXEMPT CLASSIFICATION STATUS

An exempt classification, as provided under wage and hour provisions of the Fair Labor Standards Act, is hereby claimed on the position of _____ and any incumbents of such position whose employment conditions may be affected by exempt classification status. The determination to classify this position in exempt status is based on direct observation of the work performed, duties and responsibilities of the position as illustrated on the job description, and the information provided below.

Executive Employee (check all applicable statements)

1. (   ) The primary duty consists of the management of a department, or subdivision thereof.

2. (   ) The incumbent customarily and regularly directs the work of two or more other persons.

    a. What percent of time is spent in the supervision of these employees?

    _____

    b. What types of work are performed by subordinates?

    _____

3. (   ) The position has the authority to hire or fire, or recommendations carry considerable weight.

4. (   ) The position customarily exercises discretion and independent judgment.

    a. Does anyone assist in supervising the work of subordinates?

    _____

    b. What position supervises this position?

    _____

5. (   ) The incumbent spends less than 20 percent of the workweek doing nonexempt work.

    a. Does the incumbent perform work of a similar nature to that of nonexempt subordinates?

    _____

    b. Does the incumbent perform manual or routine clerical work?

    _____

    (The note taking involved in preparing a report that affects the policy making of a firm, is not normally an executive ability, but may be considered such in this instance if directly and closely related to exempt functions.)

6. (   ) The incumbent is paid at least $8,060 annually ($155 weekly) on a salary basis. (Requires items 1 through 5.)

    a. Approximately how many hours does the incumbent work in normal weeks? _____ Busy weeks? _____

7. (   ) The incumbent is paid at least $13,000 annually ($250 weekly) on a salary basis. (Requires items 1 and 2 only.)

continued

DETERMINATION OF EXEMPT CLASSIFICATION STATUS—*continued*

Administrative Employee (check all applicable statements)

1. (   ) The primary duty is the performance of office or nonmanual field work directly related to management policies or general business operations.

    a. Describe briefly each major responsibility the position carries in addition to those in description.

      Daily _____

      Periodically _____

      Occasionally _____

2. (   ) Work involves the customary and regular exercise of discretion and independent judgment.

    a. What important types of decisions are normally made that affect the work, policies, or management of the company or the incumbent's department?

    _____

    b. What work does the incumbent perform or review that is not approved or further reviewed by anyone else?

    _____

3. (   ) The incumbent regularly and directly assists an officer or department head.

    a. Who assigns work to the incumbent? _____

    b. Who reviews this work? _____

4. (   ) The incumbent performs, under only general supervision, work along specialized or technical lines requiring special training, experience, or knowledge.

5. (   ) The incumbent executes, under only general supervision, special assignments and tasks.

6. (   ) The incumbent does not spend more than 20 percent of the workweek doing nonexempt work.

    a. Approximately what percentage of each workweek is spent on the duties described in item 1a of this section?

    _____

    b. Is any of this work of a similar nature to that of nonexempt co-workers?

    _____

7. (   ) The incumbent is paid at least $8,060 annually ($155 weekly) on a salary basis. (Requires items 1, 2, and 6, plus either 3, 4, or 5.)

    a. Approximately how many hours does the incumbent work in normal weeks? _____ Busy weeks? _____

8. (   ) The incumbent is paid at least $13,000 annually ($250 weekly) on a salary basis. (Requires items 1 and 2 only.)

continued

DETERMINATION OF EXEMPT CLASSIFICATION STATUS—*continued*

FOR DEPARTMENT SUPERVISOR:

I agree to inform the Personnel Department promptly in writing: (1) if changes in the above statements make an exemption invalid, or (2) if a temporary assignment requires payment for overtime.

Date: _____ Signed: _____ (Department Supervisor)

FOR EMPLOYEES:

I understand and agree with the statements checked above as a basis for my exemption from requirements of the Federal Wage and Hour Law. *I agree to inform my Department promptly in writing:* (1) if changes in my duties make my exemption invalid, or (2) if a temporary assignment requires me to do nonexempt work.

Date: _____ Signed: _____ (Employee)

FOR PERSONNEL DEPARTMENT:

Above claim approved this date.

Date: _____ Signed: _____ (Personnel Department)

OVERTIME HOURS WORKED REPORT

Use this form, or a simplified facsimile, to record any and all overtime hours worked. See Chapter 12 for a discussion of overtime hours and wage provisions under federal and state laws.

REPORT OVERTIME WORKED

Read instruction on reverse side before completing

EMPLOYEE REQUEST (Employee complete, print or type)	
1. Employee's Name	2. Department or Division
3. Overtime Worked	4. Name of Supervisor who gave prior approval

3. Overtime Worked

Date	Day

		Total Hours Worked
From _____	A.M. / P.M.	
TIME TO _____	A.M. / P.M.	___ Hrs. ___ Mins.

5. Purpose for overtime (Explain)

6. Employee's Signature	Date Submitted

7. **SUPERVISORY ACTION**					
A.	Supervisor Receiving Report from Employee Credit Overtime to: ( ) **COMPENSATORY TIME OFF (CTO)** ( ) **TIME AND ONE-HALF PAY**				
	Approve	Disapprove	SIGNATURE	DATE
B.				

continued

REPORT OVERTIME WORKED—*continued*

8. CLERICAL EMPLOYEE COMPLETE		(✔) Completed
A.	Verify figures; To calculate for proper overtime credit: round actual time to nearest half hour, then multiply at rate specified by supervisor (item 7-A)	
B.	Enter hours as calculated here: AMOUNT: _____	
C.	Enter hours (item 8-B) to "Payroll Form" with "OVERTIME WORKED" KEY LETTER "W"	
D.	File REPORT in department file	

INSTRUCTIONS

OVERTIME HOURS WORKED REPORT

Each eligible employee must receive prior Supervisory approval before overtime can be worked. This report must be submitted to the Supervisor within twenty-four (24) hours upon completion of the overtime. Actual overtime worked as reported by an employee will be rounded to the nearest half hour interval by the designated clerical employee, then multiplied at the rate (straight-time or time and one-half) as specified by the Supervisor.

EMPLOYEE COMPLETE ITEMS 1–6

1. and 2. Self-explanatory.
3. Show date and day that overtime was worked in excess of normal workday or shift. Show time period (from/to) and the total hours worked.
4. Show name of Supervisor who gave prior approval for this overtime.
5. Describe in detail the purpose for the overtime. Show: case or project number, type of overtime (i.e., training, court, call-back) and any other appropriate information.
6. Certify that this report is correct by signing and dating. Submit to Supervisor for action.

DEPARTMENT COMPLETE ITEMS 7 AND 8

7. As designated by Department Head: First Supervisor to receive report shall check appropriate box that overtime is to be credited (either compensatory time off or time and one-half), sign, date, and forward to other Supervisors to review, as specified, and forward to clerical employee.
8. Clerical employee shall process, make appropriate calculations, and file.

COMPENSATORY TIME OFF REQUEST

This form, or a close facsimile, should be used to document the request and use of compensatory time off (CTO) by nonexempt employees for payroll and related recordkeeping purposes. Where an employer uses CTO as an alternative to repaying overtime hours worked, this form is usually used in conjunction with the Overtime Hours Worked Report and serves as backup documentation for the Payroll Time Report.

It is advisable for employers to use this form for exempt employees. Keep in mind that exempt employees are salaried and, as such, receive consistent pay regardless of hours worked, unless they are in an unpaid status such as a leave of absence. The official recording and giving of CTO to exempt employees demonstrates that they are being treated as a nonexempt employee. If an employer wants to reward exempt employees who work excessive hours by giving them paid time off, this should be done by informal permission and time records, and not reported on payroll records.

COMPENSATORY TIME OFF REQUEST

Read Instructions on reverse side before completing

EMPLOYEE COMPLETE (Print or Type)	
1. Employee's Name	2. Department or Division

3. Compensatory Time Off Requested		TOTAL HOURS REQUESTED OFF (Minimum in half-hour intervals)
Date(s)		
Days(s)		_____
Time(s)	From:	
	To:	_____HOURS

4. Employee's Signature	Date Submitted

5. **SUPERVISORY ACTION**				
Approve	Dis-approve	SIGNATURE	DATE	(✔) EMPLOYEE NOTIFIED

6. **CLERICAL EMPLOYEE COMPLETE**		(✔) COMPLETED
A.	Verify figures; hold request until time off is taken	
B.	Verify actual time taken off; (if discrepancy in amount actually taken off with item 3, refer to supervisor for action)	
C.	Enter approved hours here (round to half-hour interval) HOURS: _____	
D.	Enter hours (item 6-C) to "TIMEROLL" with "COMPENSA-TORY TIME OFF" KEY LETTER "T"	
E.	File REQUEST in department file	

continued

COMPENSATORY TIME OFF REQUEST—*continued*

INSTRUCTIONS

COMPENSATORY TIME OFF REQUEST

Each eligible employee must receive prior Supervisory approval before taking compensatory time off. This request must be submitted to the Supervisor at least three (3) working days or shifts prior to the date that compensatory time off is requested. Minimum time that can be taken off is intervals of one-half (1/2) hour.

If an unusual situation occurs that requires an employee to request compensatory time off with less than three (3) days' or shifts' notice, the Department Head shall review the merits of the special request and the staffing requirements of the Department, and take the appropriate action.

EMPLOYEE COMPLETE ITEMS 1–4

1. and 2. Self-explanatory.
3. Show date(s); day(s) of week; time period(s), (from/to); and total hours of time off requested, (MINIMUM INTERVALS OF ONE-HALF (1/2) HOUR).
4. Certify that information is correct by signing and dating. Submit to Supervisor for action.

DEPARTMENT COMPLETE ITEMS 5 and 6

5. As designated by Department Head, Supervisors shall review; take appropriate action: if employee request is modified or disapproved, Supervisor shall notify employee and check (✔). Upon approval, sign, date, and forward to clerical employee.
6. Clerical employee shall process, make appropriate entries, and file.

EMPLOYEE ATTENDANCE LOG
AND ANNUAL SUMMARY

Use this form as a supplement to, or in lieu of, the Employee Information Log. This form provides a quick and easy reference document for recording various types of paid and non-paid leaves, as well as tardiness and absence data that the employer may use for disciplinary, pay denial (docking), and retention decisions.

EMPLOYEE ATTENDANCE LOG AND ANNUAL SUMMARY

Employee Name: _____ Social Security Number: _____ Date Hired: _____

SUMMARY

	TARDY			ABSENT			LEAVES/VACATION		
Date	Arrival Time	Reason/ Codes*	Date	Number of Days	Reason/ Codes*	Date	Amount	Reason/ Codes*

YEAR 19___	TARDY	ABSENT	PAID LEAVES	UNPAID LEAVES	VACATION
Jan					
Feb					
Mar					
Apr					
May					
Jun					
Jul					
Aug					
Sep					
Oct					
Nov					
Dec					
Total					

CODES*

AP — Personal Time Off (with pay)	V — Vacation Time	C — Comp. Time
LOA — Leave of Absence (without pay)	H — Holiday	J — Jury Duty
	FH — Floating Holiday	MR — Military Leave
X-1 — Excused Absence (with pay)	WC — Worker Compensable Leave	PD — Personal Disability
X-2 — Excused Absence (without pay)		TC — Training/ Conference
UA — Unexcused Absence (without pay)		

Vacation: _____
_____
_____
_____
_____

LEAVE REQUEST/RETURN
FROM LEAVE FORM

This form is used to document the reason and type of leave requested and taken by employees and the respective dates of leave. It is used as backup documentation for payroll accounting, including the deduction of accrued leave entitlement or other types of leave allowed by the employer or required to be available to employees by law (military).

LEAVE REQUEST/RETURN FROM LEAVE FORM

Date _____

Employee's   Social Security
Name _____   Number _____

Job Title _____   Date Hired _____

EMPLOYEE REQUEST

REASON FOR LEAVE:

( ) Personal Disability   ( ) Family Illness (name) _____
( ) Military   ( ) Family Death (name) _____
( ) Training/Conference
( ) Compensatory Time Off   ( ) Other (Explain) _____
( ) Jury Duty
                                  _____
                                  _____

LEAVE REQUESTED:

                                    A.M.   Total Number of
From: Date _____ Time _____   P.M.   Hours Requested: _____
                                    A.M.   Total Number of
To: Date _____ Time _____   P.M.   Days Requested: _____

Indicate Regular
Work Shift: _____

_____

Employee Signature: _____   Date: _____

I recommend that this   ( ) With Pay
leave be approved: ( ) Without Pay

Authorized Signature: _____   Date: _____

RETURN AFFIRMATION

ABSENT:

                                    A.M.
From: Date _____ Time _____   P.M.   Total Number of
                                    A.M.   Working Days Absent: _____
To: Date _____ Time _____   P.M.

( ) Excused/Warranted
( ) Not Excused/Not Warranted (Explain) _____

EMPLOYEE:

( ) Resumed Part-Time Work
( ) Resumed Full-Time Work
( ) Resumed Modified Duty (Explain) _____

( ) Other (Explain) _____

Affirmed By: _____   Date: _____

JURY DUTY ATTENDANCE AND COMPENSATION FORM

Self-explanatory for purposes of paying employees serving on jury duty for prescribed periods of such service.

JURY DUTY ATTENDANCE AND COMPENSATION FORM*

Instructions to Employee: In accordance with *(Company)* policy, you may be entitled to receive your normal base pay for a predetermined period during which you are required to serve as a juror. To receive normal pay, eligible employees must complete and submit this form at the end of each payroll period during which jury duty is served and payable under *(Company)* policy entitlements. Completion also consists of signed entries of your attendance at jury duty by the court clerk and in other respects that you adhered to *(Company)* policy.

Instructions to Court Clerk: To process the payroll of the undersigned employee in a timely and correct manner, it is important that we have documented proof of this employee's selection as a juror and dates/hours of attendance in connection with jury duty. Please enter the requested information on a daily basis and return to the requesting employee promptly. We appreciate your cooperation.

Employee's Name: _____

Job Title: _____

Social Security No.: _____

- The above-named person has been selected to serve on jury duty. Jury duty service is expected to last approximately _____ calendar days.
- The above-named person has appeared for jury duty consideration, but is not being impaneled at this time.

Attendance Dates and Hours

Date	*From*	*To*	*Clerk's Initials*
_____	_____	_____	_____
_____	_____	_____	_____
_____	_____	_____	_____
_____	_____	_____	_____
_____	_____	_____	_____
_____	_____	_____	_____
_____	_____	_____	_____

I certify that the above information is true and correct to the best of my knowledge:

Employee's Signature　　　　　　　　　　　Court Clerk's Signature

_____　　　　　_____

Date _____　　　　　Date _____

_____

* 　　Levesque, *The Complete Hiring Manual,* p. 172.

PHYSICIAN'S RELEASE FOR WORK FORM

Use this form in conjunction with an employee's return from extended (see policies, Chapters 2 and 3) sick leave, long-term disability, or workers' compensation disability absences.

PHYSICIAN'S RELEASE FOR WORK*

Instructions to Employee: In accordance with *(Company)* policies, this form must be completed by the licensed physician who treated, or will treat, you for the illness or injury that resulted in your absence from work. If the disability is to be an extended one, or one of unknown duration, ask your physician to estimate the duration of your absence from work in connection with the disability.

Instructions to Physician: We are anxious to have our employees returned to work promptly and in a healthy state so that they can continue to perform the full scope of their work in a safe manner. We ask that you consider the nature of their job when examining and treating this person, and that you complete this form, including the expected duration of disability based on medical facts. You may either give the completed form to the employee or mail it directly to *(Name of person, company name, and company address)*. If you have questions or explanations in connection with this employee, please feel free to call the *(Company)* representative. Thank you!

This is to certify that _____ *(employee)* has been under my professional care since _____.

Having examined or otherwise treated this individual, it is my opinion that he/she:

- may return to normal work activities on _____ without restriction;
- may not be expected to resume normal work activities until _____ because (state diagnosis and prognosis).

  _____
  _____
  _____
  _____
  _____

  The technical designation of this individual's condition is _____ commonly known as _____.

  _____
  Signature of Physician

  Please Print Physician's Name, Address, and Phone Number
  _____
  _____
  _____
  _____

---

*   Levesque, *The Complete Hiring Manual,* p. 163.

Chapter 8

JOB CLASSIFICATION, PERFORMANCE EVALUATION, AND TRANSFER FORMS

POSITION DESCRIPTION FORM

Employers wanting to study jobs to prepare job descriptions, or to determine if a position should be reclassified, will need to record certain job content information otherwise known as job analysis. This form is the simplified version of a job analysis questionnaire (discussed in more detail in Chapter 20), as compared to the more detailed Job Analysis Questionnaire that follows. Both forms include self-explanatory instructions to the employee, but accuracy is enhanced by supplementing the written instructions with verbal explanations.

POSITION DESCRIPTION FORM

NOTE: Information on this form will be used to help classify or set the salary for your job. Please answer clearly, accurately, and completely.

Employee's
1. Name _____   2. Department _____

3. Payroll Title _____   4. Division _____

5. Who is your immediate supervisor? _____
   (Name)   (Payroll Title)

6. I directly supervise the following employees:

   Name   Payroll Title

7. I supervise through subordinates (show numbers and titles only)

   Number of Employees   Payroll Title

8. List any machines, equipment, or motor vehicles you are *required* to use. Indicate whether use is occasional, frequent, or constant:

   _____

   _____

   _____

9. For Office Positions Only: (please check)

	Typing	Stenography
Regularly Required:	_____	_____
Occasionally Required:	_____	_____
Not Required:	_____	_____

10. Explain with whom (other than co-workers) you have business contacts in your work:

11. In what way and how often is your work assigned and reviewed? List the kind and amount of work guidance you receive from supervisors, manuals, or established procedures.

12. How long have you been performing your current duties?

13. Describe your own job in your own words. *This is the most important item on this form.* List your most important duties first. Using percentages, *estimate the amount of your working time spent on each duty.* **Attach extra sheets if more space is needed.**

_____
PERCENT OF TIME SPENT

continued

POSITION DESCRIPTION FORM—*continued*

14. In your opinion, what is the most difficult part of your job?

_____

15.   **CERTIFICATE OF EMPLOYEE**

I certify that the answers to all questions are my own and that to the best of my knowledge they are complete and correct.

Date: _____, 19___   Signed: _____

CERTIFICATE OF IMMEDIATE SUPERVISOR	**CERTIFICATE OF DEPARTMENT HEAD**
A. I agree entirely with employee's statement. _____	A. I agree entirely with employee's statement. _____
B. See attached memo for comments. _____	B. See attached memo for comments. _____
C. Contact me for further information. _____	C. Contact me for further information. _____
Signed _____	Signed _____
Position Title _____	Position Title _____
Date _____	Date _____

INSTRUCTIONS FOR COMPLETING THE POSITION DESCRIPTION FORM

Please read these instructions carefully before filling out your Position Description Form.

The Position Description Form is used to obtain detailed information about your duties and to assist in the classification of your job and determination of your pay.

After completion of the attached forms, hand all copies to your immediate supervisor. The blue copy will be returned to you for your personal file. If you need additional space, extra pages may be attached, and should be identified by your name and department.

This form is intended for general use and some of the questions may not apply to your job. Skip them. If the questions do apply, answer them completely, be specific, and illustrate your statements with examples.

Your supervisor and department head will review your Position Description for completeness and accuracy and to clarify or give additional information concerning your duties and responsibilities. *Under no circumstances*, however, should the supervisor or the department head change the answers as given and certified by you.

The following numbered instructions or comments relate to corresponding items on the Position Description Form:

Item 6:   Answer this item only if you are actually responsible for directing the work of others. Inspecting, checking, or proofreading the work of others does not in itself constitute supervision. These types of duties should be described in Item 13.

continued

POSITION DESCRIPTION FORM—*continued*

Item 11: In this space explain the kind of instructions, written or oral, given you. For example, "I follow a prescribed procedure set forth in the accounting manual," or "I am shown how to operate the equipment and then work on each job as it is given to me," or "I am given a project with instructions as to the results expected and general methods, but details are left to me." This item should also be used to explain whether your work is reviewed in detail or only for overall results. Is your work reviewed for the way you do it as well as for what you accomplish? Is it a personal review by observation of your work or a review of a written report? How frequently is your work reviewed, for example: every day, once a week, at periodic intervals, or only on completion of a total project?

Item 13: The answer to this item is an exact account of what you do. Describe your "whole job" or year-round duties; not just those which might be performed during rush or peak periods of activity, or when you are substituting for other persons. Start with your most important duties and describe your occasional or infrequent duties last. Use a separate paragraph for each major duty.

Examples of Good and Poor Duties Statements

<u>Poor Statement</u>	<u>Good Statement</u>
Assist in handling correspondence	Receive, open, time stamp, and route incoming mail.
Maintain grounds and landscape areas	Mow lawns with power mower and hand mower. Rake and weed grounds. Trim trees from ground and from ladder, using power saws. Lubricate mowers.
Perform skilled mechanical work on automotive equipment	Repair shock absorbers and transmissions. Check and balance wheels and adjust clutches. Overhaul and test generators.
Keep claim registers	Prepare registers of all claims showing allocation of budget expenditures and total amount of expenditures for month in which claims are made.
Unit is responsible for keeping all purchasing records	Compare invoices with purchase orders. Review requisitions submitted by different departments for accuracy, then give them to the Purchasing Agent for OK

Item 14: Indicate here the part of your job which demands the greatest care and thought or the most skill and understanding. Which duty would be most difficult for another person taking your place to learn? Tell us what makes it difficult and give one or two specific examples.

Item 15: This section is to be signed and dated by you after the form is typed. Your signature indicates that the answers are your own and to the best of your knowledge complete and correct. Do not sign the certificate until you have reread your statements.

JOB ANALYSIS QUESTIONNAIRE

This form is the more detailed, and therefore more complex, questionnaire completed by employees whose jobs are being studied for the purpose of preparing job descriptions, comparing pay rates, or developing testing and performance evaluation criteria. Emphasis in this job analysis methodology is on the frequency and importance of tasks performed.

JOB ANALYSIS QUESTIONNAIRE

General Instructions

(Please read *all* instructions carefully before completing your form)

This form is used to obtain information about your duties, the requirements of your job, and to determine your job classification. Complete the form in your own words. Be clear, accurate, and complete. You may answer "N/A" to each question that does not apply to your position. For additional space, attach extra pages, *identified with your name, the name of your department, and the question number or page number which is being continued on the additional page.*

Please read the complete instructions for each page before completing any information for the page. Then go back and review the instructions for each item on the page as you complete the item.

WE RECOMMEND THAT YOU FIRST PREPARE YOUR ANSWERS ON SCRATCH PAPER. When you believe your answers are accurate and complete, copy your statements neatly on this working copy and give it to your supervisor. He or she will have copies typed (or you may ask to type it yourself) and returned to you for your *signature*. Your handwritten copy will be returned to you for your keeping.

Your immediate supervisor and your department or division head will go over your form. They will attach a separate review sheet to your form, and will use that sheet to give us any extra information or explanations about your duties and responsibilities. *Under no circumstances* should any supervisor change the answers as given and certified by you.

Instructions for Completing Part 1 of the Form

Item 1:	Your name as it appears on organization records, i.e., Mary B. Jones, *not* Mrs. Philip Jones; John Brown, *not* "Sparks" Brown.
Item 2:	The name of the department in which you work and the name of your work location.
Item 3:	Your job title as it appears on official records, such as the salary schedule.
Items 4 & 6:	Show address where you work or report for duty, even though your department's main office may be elsewhere. Show phone number where you can be contacted during work hours.
Items 5 & 7:	Show the name and title of your *official* immediate supervisor. Your supervisor is generally the person who completes and signs your performance evaluation form, has the authority to approve absences and vacations, and may recommend discipline and promotion. Please ask the head of your organizational unit for assistance if you are not sure of the answer to item 6.
Item 8:	Show how long you have been working for your present employer— performing other duties as well as your present job.
Item 9:	Show how long you have been performing your *present* duties as listed on this form.

continued

JOB ANALYSIS QUESTIONNAIRE—*continued*

Item 10:   Show the official title(s) of any other job(s) you have held for *this* employer prior to your current job.

Item 11:   Show any courses, training programs, or previous experience that has been particularly helpful to you in performing your current duties.

Item 12:   Circle the number that indicates schooling completed. Example: 8 means eighth grade, 13 means one year of college, 16 means a bachelor's degree, 18 means a master's degree, 20 means a doctorate.

Item 13:   List *only* equipment you are *required* to operate in the performance of your current duties. *Exclude* equipment you know how to operate but do *not* use to do your own work.

Item 14:   List *only* licenses or certificates *required* for your present position. *Exclude* licenses you possess which are *not* required for your current assignment.

Item 15:   Put "N/A" if you are not a supervisor. Checking or proofreading the work of others, or even giving others tasks to do, does not necessarily mean you are a supervisor. An immediate supervisor generally does the performance evaluations on employees under him or her; approves vacations, sick leave, and overtime, and can recommend hiring or firing workers. It is likely that if you are a supervisor, the employees you list to answer this question will have written your name as their answer to item 5 on this page. List *only* paid, regular employees. Use "Vacant" as the name if a position you supervise is vacant right now.

                If you are sometimes called on to oversee others' work, but are not a supervisor, list this responsibility as one of your tasks.

Item 16:   Answer this question *only* if you supervise employees who are supervisors of other employees. Indicate how many employees you direct through subordinate supervisors. Example, as a Maintenance Supervisor who supervises a section composed of two units, each supervised by a Foreman, you might answer this question as follows: 7 Carpenters; 2 Cabinetmakers; 3 Maintenance Workers.

1. Name _____   2. Department and location _____

   _____   _____

3. Official job title _____   4. Address where you work _____

   _____   _____

5. Immediate supervisor's name: _____   6. Work telephone number: _____

   _____   ext. _____

7. Immediate supervisor's title: _____

8. How long have you been working for this organization? _____

9. How long have you been performing your *current* duties in this organization? _____

10. What other jobs have you had in this organization? _____

   _____

   _____

continued

JOB ANALYSIS QUESTIONNAIRE—*continued*

11. What training/preparation/experience do you have that help you do your present job?
_____
_____
_____

12. What is the highest grade of your formal schooling: 1 2 3 4 5 6 7 8 9 10 11 12
    13 14 15 16 17 18 19 20   (circle one)

13. List any machines, equipment, office appliances or vehicles that you are *required* to operate in doing your job.
_____
_____
_____

14. List the licenses or certificates *required* to do your job.
_____
_____
_____

15. What employees do you directly supervise?

Name	Title
_____	_____
_____	_____
_____	_____
_____	_____
_____	_____
_____	_____
_____	_____
_____	_____

16. What number of employees do you supervise through subordinate supervisors?

Number	Job Titles
_____	_____
_____	_____
_____	_____
_____	_____
_____	_____
_____	_____
_____	_____
_____	_____

INSTRUCTIONS FOR COMPLETING
WRITING TASK STATEMENTS

List tasks you perform throughout a whole year, *not* just those which are performed during rush or vacation periods. Do *not* list tasks performed when you are substituting for other employees. Be sure to include duties you perform only once or twice a year in your list of tasks.

Each task statement should be a *clear* description of the task and should start with a verb (action word). For example:

Good Task Statement	*Poor Task Statement*
1. Place forms for concrete walks and curbs.	1. I do concrete work for walks and curbs.
2. Mix and pour concrete.	
3. Finish concrete.	

continued

JOB ANALYSIS QUESTIONNAIRE—*continued*

4. Receive, open, date stamp and distribute mail.

2. Handle correspondence.

5. Compose correspondence.
6. Type letters and memoranda from drafts.

7. Mow lawns with power mowers.

3. Maintain grounds and landscaped areas.

8. Rake and weed grounds.
9. Trim trees from ground.

WORDS TO AVOID: Please try not to use words like *assist, help, coordinate, handle, communicate,* and *maintain* as they do not tell us *exactly* what you do. Be very detailed and specific.

Use additional pages if you have more tasks than can be listed in the space allotted. Begin task numbers with 35.

RATING YOUR TASKS

Be sure to list all of your tasks first, before you begin rating any of them.

I. *TIME SPENT RATING:* Please rate each of your tasks by considering the amount of time you spend on the task over a one-year period. The task which takes more of your time than any other task should be rated "9." Tasks which take that same amount of time should also be "9"; those which take a little less "8." Tasks which take about half as much time as a task rated "9" should be rated "5." The task which takes the very least amount of time should be a "1," etc. Enter the appropriate rating number in Column I on pages 2 and 3.

(1) *Very Little:* You do the task, but it does not take much of your time.

(2) *Little:* The task takes some of your time, but it is still a minor part of the time.

(3) *Below Average:* This task takes more than just a little time, but considerably less than the average time for all tasks.

(4) *Slightly Below Average:* You do this task slightly less than the average time for all tasks.

(5) *Average:* This task and other tasks like this each take the medium amount of time of any of your work activities; each of these takes the most "normal" or typical amount of time.

(6) *Slightly Above Average:* You do this task just slightly more than the average involvement for all tasks.

(7) *Above Average:* You do this task more than the average involvement for all tasks.

(8) *Much Above Average:* You are involved with this task a major portion of your time.

(9) *Very Much Above Average:* This task is one you are very involved with; it takes the largest part of your time every time you must do it.

II. *FREQUENCY RATING:* How often is this task *typically* performed on the job? Enter the appropriate rating in Column II.

(1) *Seldom* — (quarterly to yearly)
(2) *Occasionally* — (monthly)
(3) *Frequently* — (weekly)
(4) *Continuously* — (daily)

continued

JOB ANALYSIS QUESTIONNAIRE—*continued*

III. *CONSEQUENCE OF A MISTAKE:* The immediate consequences of inadequate performance of some tasks are much more serious than for others. The failure to "frisk" a suspect could be fatal to a police officer, while writing up a traffic ticket improperly would be little more than embarrassing.

What are the consequences, to you, co-workers, or the organization, if this task is not performed or not performed correctly? Enter the appropriate rating in Column III.

(0) *Not Critical:* error easily detected by employee and easily corrected. No significant delay or financial implications.

(1) *Slightly Critical:* may result in minor injury or may cause operating delays, but is easily corrected. Financial/legal implications, if any, are minimal.

(2) *Moderately Critical:* may result in more serious injury or may cause operating difficulties that are correctable, but should be avoided; financial/legal implications may exist to some degree.

(3) *Critical:* may result in serious injury or may cause operating difficulties to the point that work is stopped. Very difficult to correct; financial/legal implications are serious.

(4) *Very Critical:* may result in extremely serious injury or may create such operating difficulties that all work must be redone. Noncorrectable errors; financial/legal implications are far-reaching and damaging to the organization.

TASK STATEMENTS

Please list each task that you perform in your job. Start each task statement with an "action word" such as: Type, Clean, Operate, Repair, . . . etc. Each task statement should be brief.

III. CONSEQUENCE OF A MISTAKE: SEE INSTRUCTIONS	I. Time	II. Frequency	III. Consequence of a mistake
II. FREQUENCY RATING: How often do you perform this task? SEE INSTRUCTIONS			
I. TOTAL TIME: How much job time is spent on this task? SEE INSTRUCTIONS			
TASKS:			
1. _____			
_____			
2. _____			
_____			
3. _____			
_____			
4. _____			
_____			
5. _____			
_____			
6. _____			
_____			
7. _____			
_____			

continued

JOB ANALYSIS QUESTIONNAIRE—*continued*

8. _____

_____

9. _____

_____

10. _____

_____

11. _____

_____

12. _____

_____

13. _____

_____

14. _____

_____

15. _____

_____

16. _____

_____

17. _____

_____

TASK STATEMENTS

Please list each task that you perform in your job. Start each task statement with an "action word" such as: Type, Clean, Operate, Repair, . . . etc. Each task statement should be brief.

	I. Time	II. Frequency	III. Consequence of a mistake
III. CONSEQUENCE OF A MISTAKE: SEE INSTRUCTIONS			
II. FREQUENCY RATING: How often do you perform this task? SEE INSTRUCTIONS			
I. TOTAL TIME: How much job time is spent on this task? SEE INSTRUCTIONS			
TASKS:			
18. _____			
19. _____			
20. _____			

continued

JOB ANALYSIS QUESTIONNAIRE—*continued*

21. _____

22. _____

23. _____

24. _____

25. _____

26. _____

27. _____

28. _____

29. _____

30. _____

31. _____

32. _____

33. _____

34. _____

continued

JOB ANALYSIS QUESTIONNAIRE—*continued*

INSTRUCTIONS FOR COMPLETING
SKILLS, KNOWLEDGE, AND ABILITIES (SKA's)

1. Please list the Skills, Knowledge, and Abilities (SKA's) *necessary* to perform tasks *adequately* in the course of performing your job:

   a) What SKA's are required? (i.e., skill at what? knowledge of what? ability to do what?)
   b) To what degree of accuracy or at what level?

   Skill statements should state the skill needed and, if required, the specific level of skill necessary. Examples:

   > Brazing and welding at a level sufficient to install air conditioner components.
   > Freehand lettering.
   > Type accurately at 60 WPM.

   Knowledge statements should state whether a person would need general knowledge, working knowledge, or detailed knowledge and should list the specific areas of knowledge needed. Here are some examples:

   > General knowledge of cleansers and equipment used in custodial work.
   > Working knowledge of standard office procedures.
   > Detailed knowledge of the materials, tools, and methods of carpentry.
   > Basic mathematics

   Ability statements should state what an applicant should be able to do, and how well. Examples:

   > Ability to operate an offset duplicating machine to do two-color printing.
   > Ability to read blueprints.
   > Ability to operate a typewriter.

PHYSICAL CHARACTERISTICS

Physical Characteristics covers the requirements and physical demands placed on you by your work assignment, including, for example, specific agility and dexterity requirements, and physical activities such as climbing, lifting, pushing, balancing, stooping, kneeling, crouching, crawling, or reaching. Think also about how often or for how long the activity must be done; a job requiring prolonged standing, for example, requires more physical effort than a job requiring standing only off and on.

Please be specific!

Here are some examples:

Mobility to:	stoop to lower file drawers
	crawl in tight spaces
	climb stairs (three flights at a time)
	climb extension ladders
Strength to:	lift and carry 100 pounds three or four times daily
	sit for prolonged periods of time
	bend and stoop
Stamina to:	stand for eight hours straight, except for lunches and breaks
	run for prolonged periods of time
Tolerance to be exposed to:	dust
	pollen
	specific chemicals, gases, and toxic substances
	cleansers
	foul smells

continued

JOB ANALYSIS QUESTIONNAIRE—*continued*

Other:　　　　Be available for frequent evening meetings
　　　　　　　Travel within county
　　　　　　　Be on 24-hour call two weekends each month
　　　　　　　See well enough to read fine print
　　　　　　　Distinguish minor differences in shades of color
　　　　　　　Speak well enough to make oral presentations before large
　　　　　　　groups

MINIMUM REQUIREMENTS TO DO THE JOB

Skills

1. _____
2. _____
3. _____
4. _____
5. _____
6. _____
7. _____
8. _____

Knowledge

1. _____
2. _____
3. _____
4. _____
5. _____
6. _____
7. _____
8. _____

Abilities

1. _____
2. _____
3. _____
4. _____
5. _____
6. _____
7. _____
8. _____

continued

JOB ANALYSIS QUESTIONNAIRE—*continued*

PHYSICAL CHARACTERISTICS

List below the physical characteristics your job requires. Use an example of what you do on your job to show the need for the physical characteristics. (See instructions for examples.) List the number of the task that requires the characteristic in the column to the right. column to the right.

	Task Number
Mobility — Stoop, reach, crawl, or climb to:	
Strength — Lift and carry _____ pounds? How often?	
Stamina — To stand as long as: or To work without protection from weather:	
Tolerance — To be exposed to:	
Others:	

AMPLIFYING INFORMATION

The top portion of this page *is all yours*. It is your chance to clarify any terminology or task you feel is not fully described by the previous task statement(s). If there is anything about your job that you would like to tell us or feel was not adequately covered in other areas of the form, please explain those points here. Attach extra pages if necessary.

TASK/PAGE

OTHER: _____

_____

_____

_____

_____

_____

_____

_____

continued

JOB ANALYSIS QUESTIONNAIRE—*continued*

EMPLOYEE CERTIFICATION

Please review your completed typewritten or final copy of the Job Analysis Questionnaire for completeness and accuracy before affixing your signature. Remember this information will be used to clarify your position.

I certify that the answers to all questions are my own and that to the best of my knowledge they are complete and correct.

Date: _____ 19___ (Signed) _____

JOB ANALYSIS INTERVIEW FORM

Job analysis for any purpose is most thorough when it includes a personal interview with the employee whose job is being studied. Because these interviews are often unstructured, it is advisable for the person conducting the study (the job analyst) to use an interview form consisting of predetermined questions about the employee's job as a means of clarifying or embellishing information provided on the questionnaire completed by the employee. If a predetermined series of questions is followed, the analysis of job content information is easier because the information flows in consistent order for each employee interviewed.

JOB ANALYSIS INTERVIEW FORM

Position Title: _____   Department: _____

Incumbent: _____   Time in Job: _____

Interviewer: _____   Date: _____

1. Describe briefly *what* you do and, if possible, *how* you do it. Include duties in the following categories:

   a. daily duties (those performed on a regular basis every day or almost every day)

   b. periodic duties (those performed weekly, monthly, quarterly, or at other regular intervals)

   c. duties performed at irregular intervals

2. Describe the successful completion and/or end results of the job.

3. What do you feel is the most important part of your job? Why?

4. What do you feel is the most difficult or complicated part of your job? Why?

5. Has your job changed since you were hired? How?

continued

JOB ANALYSIS INTERVIEW FORM—*continued*

6. Are you performing duties you consider *unnecessary?* If so, describe.

7. Are you performing duties not presently included in the job description? Describe?

8. Describe your repetitive job tasks. Are you frequently bored on the job?

9. Are there any exceptional problems you encounter in performing the job under normal conditions? If so, describe.

   a. What is *the degree* of independent action you are allowed to take?

   b. What decisions are you permitted to make?

10. What kinds of problems or questions would you ordinarily refer to your supervisor?

11. Are you responsible for any confidential data? State the type of confidential data handled (personnel files, salary information, business secrets, etc.).

12. Are you responsible for money or things of monetary value? State the type of responsibility and the approximate amount you must safeguard.

continued

JOB ANALYSIS INTERVIEW FORM—*continued*

13. What kinds of contacts do you have with others? Describe.

    a. Internal

    b. External

14. To what extent is your work supervised?

    a. How do you receive instruction?

    b. How often does your supervisor check your work?

    c. What written material do you have to read in the course of your job?

15. How many employees do *you* supervise directly? _____ indirectly? _____

16. What do you feel is necessary in terms of formal education or its equivalent to perform this job satisfactorily?

_____ No formal education required	_____ 4-year college degree (or equivalent)
_____ Eighth grade education	_____ Graduate work or advanced degree (specify: _____)
_____ High school diploma (or equivalent)	
_____ 2-year college degree (or equivalent)	_____ Professional license (specify: _____)

continued

JOB ANALYSIS INTERVIEW FORM—*continued*

17. Can you specify the training *time* needed on the job to arrive at a level of competence?

18. What job duty took the longest time to learn? The shortest?

19. How much job experience (in terms of weeks, months, or years) is needed to perform the job satisfactorily? Where can this type of experience be obtained (inside the organization or elsewhere)?

_____ None	_____ One to three years
_____ Less than one month	_____ Three to five years
_____ One to six months	_____ Five to ten years
_____ Six months to one year	_____ More than ten years

Check the location of one job

_____ Outdoor	_____ Underground
_____ Indoor	_____ Other _____

20. Check any objectionable conditions found on the job and note afterward how frequently each is encountered (rarely, occasionally, constantly, etc.).

_____ Dirt _____	_____ Wetness/humidity	_____
_____ Dust _____	_____ Vibration	_____
_____ Heat _____	_____ Sudden temperature changes	_____
_____ Cold _____	_____ Darkness or poor lighting	_____
_____ Noise _____	_____ Other (specify)	_____
_____ Fumes _____		_____
_____ Odors _____		_____

21. Check any undesirable health and safety conditions under which you must perform and note how often they are encountered.

_____ Elevated work place _____	_____ Fire hazards	_____
_____ Mechanical hazards _____	_____ Radiation	_____
_____ Explosives _____	_____ Other (specify)	_____
_____ Electrical hazards _____		_____

continued

JOB ANALYSIS INTERVIEW FORM—*continued*

22. Describe briefly what machines, tools, equipment, or work aids you work with on a regular basis.

23. Are there any personal attributes (special aptitudes, physical characteristics, personality traits, etc.) required by the job?

24. Describe those activities that are part of your supervisory duties.

    Work assignments

    Instruction/training/coaching

    Hiring/placement

    Performance appraisal

    Discipline

    Grievance handling

    Work or material flow

    Follow-up/follow-through

    Cost reduction

continued

JOB ANALYSIS INTERVIEW FORM—*continued*

Quality control/improvement

Developing new products or patterns

Troubleshooting

Incentives

Methods

Reports

Other

25. If you think there are other relevant facts we should know about your job, please describe them.

EMPLOYEE TRANSFER REQUEST FORM

Employers having more than twenty-five employees may want to formalize the periodic request of employees to transfer from one position to the same (or substantially the same) position at another location or work unit. Typically, such requests are approved only when (1) a vacancy exists and (2) the supervisors of both locations agree to the transfer.

EMPLOYEE TRANSFER REQUEST

Date: _____

Employee's Name: _____

Position Title: _____

Hire Date: _____

SSN or Employee
Payroll Number: _____

Current Pay Rate: _____

The following transfer is requested:

	FROM (current job)	TO
Position		
Location		
Department		
Hourly Status	Full-Time _____ or Part-Time _____	Full-Time _____ or Part-Time _____ (hrs. per) (week)

Employee Qualifications: _____

_____

_____

Reason's for Request: _____

_____

Employee Signature: _____

Note: Separate forms must be filed for each separate request of transfer to other positions, locations, or departments.

EMPLOYEE PERFORMANCE EVALUATION REPORT

This is a standardized and universal performance evaluation form using the more common graphic rating scale method. It is an enhanced evaluation instrument by virtue of defining each rating element category at each of three rating standards. It can be used for both introductory and regular employees with authorizations for merit pay increases. The second copy shown here with the black box may be used to transmit pay increase information to your accounting office without divulging performance ratings.

    The Employee Development Plan is optional for those employers desiring such a supplement to the evaluation process.

    See Chapter 28 for a detailed discussion of developing and conducting performance evaluations.

GENERAL EMPLOYEE PERFORMANCE REPORT

SECTION I. INSTRUCTIONS
This performance evaluation report on the employee listed below is to be completed by the employee's supervisor, then discussed with the employee. Each must sign in succession as indicated in Section V. The employee, if in disagreement with the evaluation, may attach comments regarding such disagreements and discuss with the department head. RETURN ALL COPIES TO THE INDUSTRIAL RELATIONS MANAGER.

SECTION II. EMPLOYEE INFORMATION

1. Name (Last, First, Init.)/Payroll No.	2. Job Title	3. Dept./Divis. (Name & No.)	4. Present Range & Step

5. Rating Period From: _____ To: _____	6. Merit Increase Scheduled? ☐ Yes Effect. Date: _____ ☐ No To $_____	7. Type of Report ☐ Probationary: No: _____ ☐ Regular: ☐ Annual	☐ Final ☐ Special

SECTION III. PERFORMANCE RATING/COMMENTS

Giving careful consideration to the employee's performance during the entire evaluation period, assign the employee a rating based on the rating factor elements listed below using the attached rating definitions. After completing the individual rating factor elements, assign a weighted overall rating based on the importance of the individual elements to the employee's particular job. Under **Comments** section, note specific performance deficiencies and/or the means by which the employee can improve (include needed training through the company or through the employee's own initiative). All ratings of Below Satisfactory are to be clarified under **Comments** in terms of required performance levels or standards.

Rating Factor	Rating Element	Below Satis.	Satis-factory	Superior		Rating Factor	Rating Element	Below Satis.	Satis-factory	Superior
Work Quantity	Amount	☐	☐	☐		Work Habits	Punctuality/Attendance*	☐	☐	☐
	Promptness						Compliance	☐	☐	☐
	Completion/						Initiative	☐	☐	☐
	Thoroughness	☐	☐	☐			Behavior	☐	☐	☐
Work Quality	Skill/Accuracy	☐	☐	☐			Equip. Usage	☐	☐	☐
	Knowledge	☐	☐	☐			Safety	☐	☐	☐
	Communications	☐	☐	☐		Personal Relations	Co-Workers	☐	☐	☐
	Judgment/						Public	☐	☐	☐
	Decision Making	☐	☐	☐			Habits/Appearance	☐	☐	☐
						Adaptability	Job Progress	☐	☐	☐
							New/Unusual			
*Number of hours, sick leave, tardy, or leave of absence							Situations	☐	☐	☐
S/L _____ L/A _____ Tardy _____							Responsiveness	☐	☐	☐

WEIGHTED OVERALL PERFORMANCE RATING ▬

BELOW SATISFACTORY	SATISFACTORY	SUPERIOR

Comments: _____
_____
_____
_____
_____
_____
_____
_____

SECTION IV. RECOMMENDATIONS

I recommend that this employee ☐ receives ☐ does not receive the scheduled merit increase.

I certify that this employee ☐ has ☐ has not successfully completed the probationary period.

I certify that this employee ☐ is ☐ is not meeting probationary standards.

SECTION V. SIGNATURES

	Signature	Date
1. Supervisor: This evaluation represents my considered judgment of the employee's performance during the rating period, and I have discussed this report with the employee.	_____	_____
2. Department Head: Reviewed and concur with evaluation.	_____	_____
3. Employee: I have reviewed my performance rating; for the period cited. I ☐ do ☐ do not wish to discuss this rating further. (Employee may attach comments.)	_____	_____
4. President: Reviewed and approved for recommended pay increase.	_____	_____
5. Industrial Relations Manager: Reviewed and processed.	_____	_____

DISTRIBUTION: White — Personnel   Yellow — Finance   Pink — Employee   Blue — Department

continued

GENERAL EMPLOYEE PERFORMANCE REPORT—*continued*

SECTION I. INSTRUCTIONS

This performance evaluation report on the employee listed below is to be completed by the employee's supervisor, then discussed with the employee. Each must sign in succession as indicated in Section V. The employee, if in disagreement with the evaluation, may attach comments regarding such disagreements and discuss with the department head. RETURN ALL COPIES TO THE INDUSTRIAL RELATIONS MANAGER.

SECTION II. EMPLOYEE INFORMATION

1. Name (Last, First, Init.)/ Payroll No.	2. Job Title	3. Dept./Divis. (Name & No.)	4. Present Range & Step

5. Rating Period
From: _____
To: _____

6. Merit Increase Scheduled?
☐ Yes Effect. Date: _____
☐ No   To $_____

7. Type of Report
☐ Probationary: No: _____
☐ Regular: ☐ Annual
☐ Final
☐ Special

SECTION IV. RECOMMENDATIONS

I recommend that this employee ☐ receives ☐ does not receive the scheduled merit increase.

I certify that this employee ☐ has ☐ has not successfully completed the probationary period.

I certify that this employee ☐ is ☐ is not meeting probationary standards.

SECTION V. SIGNATURES

	Signature	Date
1. Supervisor: This evaluation represents my considered judgment of the employee's performance during the rating period, and I have discussed this report with the employee.	_____	_____
2. Department Head: Reviewed and concur with evaluation.	_____	_____
3. Employee: I have reviewed my performance rating; for the period cited. I ☐ do ☐ do not wish to discuss this rating further. (Employee may attach comments.)	_____	_____
4. President: Reviewed and approved for recommended pay increase.	_____	_____
5. Industrial Relations Manager: Reviewed and processed.	_____	_____

DISTRIBUTION: White — Personnel   Yellow — Finance   Pink — Employee   Blue — Department

continued

GENERAL EMPLOYEE PERFORMANCE REPORT—*continued*

RATING FACTOR/ELEMENT		BELOW STANDARDS	MEETS STANDARDS	EXCEEDS STANDARDS
1. Work Quantity	Amount	Does not produce a sufficient volume of work for alloted time of effort; overlooks customary time saving techniques; work volume is often inconsistent.	Productive worker in terms of providing a proper amount of work; uses proper work techniques that produce an expected volume of work.	Produces an exceptional level of work output; utilizes innovative or cost effective work techniques that enables consistently high levels of work output or efficiency.
	Promptness	Starts/completes assignments irregularly on time, erratic or unreliable about doing work within alloted time.	Starts/completes assignments on time; conducts work within prescribed time; usually will complete all aspects of assigned work prior to due dates.	Has demonstrated willingness to use own time to complete work on time to meet schedules; frequently starts/completes work ahead of schedules; uses time effectively to complete difficult tasks.
	Completion/ Thoroughness	Often does not carry out work activities in the required or appropriate detail; tends to leave work in marginal conditions; will often do only what instructed to do.	Consistently performs work with desired level and amount of detail; utilizes the most effective procedures or process to insure thoroughness; provides clean, neat and well organized work product; does not leave loose ends.	Performs work in exemplary detail without sacrificing efficiency or economy; work product is always complete beyond standard expectations in every detail.
2. Work Quality	Skill/Accuracy	Does not demonstrate a proper level of work skill proficiency; requires repetitive instructions; produces errors in work that result in inefficiency or ineconomy.	Performs work with requisite skills; does work accurately without repetitious performance to achieve; has full range of skills required for competent performance; absence of continuous or serious errors in work.	Work is always accurate and orderly; performs work with superior skill and execution of duties; rarely has to repeat the same tasks due to error; has developed an advanced proficiency in the full range of work skills.
	Knowledge	Possesses marginal or inadequate state of the art job, program, and/or Company knowledge including policies, regulations, and operating procedures; does not ask questions or seek information to learn about unfamiliar job aspects.	Possesses and exercises the requisite job knowledge; understands and uses new information as it becomes available; willing to spend time and effort to maintain current and thorough knowledge.	Has developed and uses outstanding job knowledge; keeps abreast of changes and new developments in the job; uses Company and own resources to improve job knowledge; shares knowledge with others.
	Communications	Has difficulty in explaining and understanding instructions and information; shows antagonism or other negative traits in conversations; is offensive to others; has weak writing, grammar, and articulation skills related to the job.	Expresses concerns, ideas and other information clearly and concisely; speaks without unusual disruption of thought or offensive manner; provides accurate information using vocabulary and grammar appropriate to each situation. Creates sense of confidence and friendliness in conversation; has good command of written/oral communication skills.	Extremely articulate and clear in conversation; possesses advanced writing skills; able to communicate effectively with a wide range of persons; keeps others informed of important information; considers behavioral effect of proper communications.
	Judgment/ Decision Making	Has difficulty separating important and unimportant work tasks; avoids decisions; does not apply logic to work situations; avoids taking responsibility for results of work.	Has sense of priority; uses common sense; makes logical decisions; able to distinguish importance or impact of decisions; takes responsibility for decisions and actions on the job.	Possesses a keen sense of work priorities and approaches work tasks in a logical, practical, and pragmatic manner at all times; willing and eager to make decisions, and accepts responsibility for consequences.
3. Work Habits	Punctuality/ Attendance	Frequently late to work or has had an excessive number of missed work hours; reports to assignments late; abuses leave or time off privileges.	Reports on time to work and assignments; is free from excessive absence; is consistent in reporting to work and in attendance on time or as otherwise required.	Always punctual and commences work activities on time; has exemplary attendance; by example, discourages others from excessive use of leave and absences.
	Compliance	Breaks or deviates from prescribed rules, procedures or work instructions; is not responsive to instruction or work or other conditions regulating work or employment; fails to take responsibility for adherence to work conditions.	Responds to work assignments and directions of supervisors; adheres to work rules, methods, procedures, and other Company requirements; takes responsibility for and corrects minor infractions.	Complies with Company work conditions, and encourages compliance by others; makes constructive suggestions on rules, methods, or procedures that would enhance productivity or Company operations in general.
	Initiative	Does not pursue job related improvement in skills or knowledge; fails to initiate routine work; has to be told or reminded what work has to be done; does not use work hours efficiently, does not volunteer to assist others or pursue opportunities to self develop.	Self-motivated; contributes ideas or work improvement methods; demonstrates desire for job related self-improvement; does work without being told; uses work hours effectively and efficiently; assists others where and when needed.	Genuinely interested in and actively pursues new methods, tools, information or knowledge; self-initiates obvious, routine, or needed work; plans work activities carefully to insure maximum efficiency; observes others in need and readily assists.

continued

3. Work Habits (continued)	Behavior	Displays behavior that is not conducive to good working relations, morale, productivity, cooperation, or other generally accepted standards of Company services.	Understands and works according to the need for teamwork and cooperation; has a positive orientation toward job and a positive approach toward requirements of the job; uses appropriate behavior effectively in varying situations.	Exemplary in behavior towards others; cooperative and teamwork oriented at all times; makes extra effort to serve others and maintains an organizational perspective; possesses command in dealing with a wide range of situations requiring strong behavioral skills.
	Equip./Mat'ls. Usage	Fails to use proper procedures, care, skill or accuracy in use of equipment and materials; does not apply sound safety practices or precautions; manner of use has resulted in loss, damage, or excessive wear.	Exercises care and caution toward equipment and material use; uses only required and proper amount of material to get job done adequately; performs daily maintenance of equipment to prolong its use; practices preventive maintenance or use of equipment/materials.	Promotes or provides efficient use of equipment/materials resulting in cost savings or increased productivity; carefully maintains and repairs equipment to prolong its use; carefully examines cost and efficiency of office products in selection among choices.
	Safety	Does not demonstrate proper knowledge or practice of safety related to job; has caused avoidable accident to self or others; does not participate conscientiously in safety concerns or activities; takes unnecessary risks.	Follows established safety rules and safe work practices; considers safety implications of work performance procedures, methods, and the use/operation of applicable equipment and materials; advises supervision of hazards.	Eliminates hazards when observed or found and/or makes safety suggestions; encourages others to use safe work practices and procedures; helps identify or prepare safety practices.
4. Interpersonal Relations	Co-Workers	Fails to exercise principles of teamwork; lacks cooperation or courtesy; is a loner or makes others uncomfortable when present; practices territorialism or work unit prejudices; does not attempt to resolve conflicts.	Exercises adequate interpersonal skills and understands human behavior such that working relationships are smooth and conflicts are resolved by mature and responsible means; makes visible effort to get along well with co-workers and superiors.	Possesses sound understanding of interpersonal relations and is effective in its application with individuals or groups; resolves conflicts congenially; takes a positive and mature approach in dealing with co-workers and superiors.
	Public Contact	Deliberately avoids public contact; expresses little interest in or regard to concerns of public; discourteous, unfriendly or intolerant of public contacts; tends to have an abrasive manner.	Demonstrates positive Company service behavior; shows interest in and concern for questions or concerns; is helpful and friendly toward the public; demonstrates tolerance, respect, and control in public contact; follows through to completion on questions or concerns.	Consistently demonstrates good judgment and strong rapport in public contacts; listens to public concerns and resolves problems or refers to proper source; handles adverse or pressure situations in an ideal manner; always follows up with public inquiries.
	Habits/ Appearance	Possesses specific habits that are incompatible with the job or related requirements; grooming or attire is substandard for job; possesses personal manners not conducive to desirable representation of the Company.	Free from poor work or personal habits that could otherwise tend to interfere or adversely influence performance; maintains proper and acceptable attire and grooming appropriate to job.	Exemplary work habits that aid high performance including work product and efficient use of time; personal appearance is at all times appropriate to position and commendable to Company representation.
5. Adaptability	Job Progress	Has not met standards of job progress in one or more areas given the time in service or amount of training; is not learning job responsibilities at expected rate or level; has not made adequate effort to improve competency; resists constructive criticism.	Demonstrates an appropriate and expected level of knowledge, skill, and adaptation to the job requirements given the time in service and training; has shown self-motivation to keep abreast of changes in the work and to improve competency in areas needing some development; has clear goals in mind.	Performs consistently higher, and progresses faster than required standards of the skills and knowledge related to position; demonstrates well above average adaptation to the job, work rules, and other conditions of employment; remains self-motivated and motivates others to improve their job skills and knowledge; seeks new challenges and goals.
	New/Unusual Situations	Is indifferent to or avoids changes, new ideas and approaches, or suggesting improvements; has difficulty adjusting to new or unusual work conditions; resists the introduction of new or unusual situations.	Presents a positive attitude towards, and diligently works at learning new work situations; is free from restrictive or narrow views/approaches to unusual work tasks, priorities, or operating procedures.	Behavior is supportive of, and encourages new work methods, changes in procedures that improve work, new approaches or responsibilities; is always available to participate or help in unusual situations.
	Responsiveness	Avoids work under adverse or pressure conditions; unreliable in response to work conditions or Company needs; avoids or uncooperative about overtime work requirements; unwilling to make personal sacrifices in times of work need; avoids or resists assignments dealing with travel, meeting, or related disruptions to personal priorities.	In situations requiring long working hours or work under adverse conditions, is reliable and responsive to work needs and related demands of the Company to accomplish goals; is willing to sacrifice own time and personal convenience when demands of work require response; is prompt in responding and follows direction in a positive manner despite circumstances.	Is always ready to serve needs of the Company; volunteers when overtime or work under adverse conditions exists; makes suggestions to improve responses or reduce the need/impact; performs work efficiently and effectively under short notice, demanding, or adverse conditions.

continued

GENERAL EMPLOYEE PERFORMANCE REPORT—*continued*

Employee Development Plan

The Employee Development Plan is designed to assist the evaluating supervisor and employee to identify specific abilities and potentials upon which higher-level skills can be developed for the purposes of meeting promotional requirements, career goals, and organizational objectives, and of achieving greater efficiency in present job responsibilities. The Development Plan may therefore relate to some aspects of the Performance Evaluation Report, but it is not necessary that it do so. In completing the Development Plan, evaluating supervisors should consider the employee's skill, knowledge, methods, and any other individual characteristics illustrative of specific job-related activities that demonstrate particular strengths, deficiencies, and results. Emphasis should also be given to how the employee can achieve each separate area of development, whether by the employee's or Company's means, or a combination thereof.

Present Position

Evaluating Supervisor: Consider the employee's skills, knowledge, abilities, and other characteristics in performing job tasks in each performance dimension relative to the five rating factors.

STRENGTHS

CONTRIBUTIONS

DEFICIENCIES

WAYS TO INCREASE EFFECTIVENESS

Employee's Performance/Career Goals

Employee: Consider particular abilities, tasks, and work assignments in which you would like to improve, change, or accomplish when identifying your Performance Goals. When identifying Career Goals, consider both short- and long-range events that would demonstrate accomplishment, and the method(s) by which they can be achieved.

PERFORMANCE GOALS

HOW ACHIEVED

CAREER GOALS

HOW ACHIEVED

Organizational Development Suggestions

Employee: In what way(s) do you feel you could be better utilized by the Company to improve the efficiency or effectiveness of our operations? Do you have any other suggestions that would contribute to the Company or your employment situation?

Evaluating Supervisor

Name _____

Title _____ Date _____

Employee

Name _____

Title _____ Date _____

MANAGEMENT PERFORMANCE APPRAISAL AND RESULTS REPORT

The Management Performance Appraisal and Results Report form is a combined rating scale, essay, and objectives-oriented format. In the first column the rater is to write in the most significant responsibilities (or goals) of the position. These are typically taken from the job description.

Under the column "Methods and Results" the rater should designate *how* each major responsibility should be carried out in terms of skills, methods, traits, and so on and what the desired results should be.

The "Action Plan" column is used to note accomplishments, additional work needed, and any problems that arose.

The last set of columns is used for an overall qualitative rating of each major responsibility, which can be the basis of such decisions as awarding pay increases, promotion, and job redefinition.

The last page is used for documentation and discussion with the employee concerning achievements during the evaluation period, areas of performance requiring additional concentration, and goals for the next evaluation period.

MANAGEMENT PERFORMANCE APPRAISAL AND RESULTS REPORT

Manager's Name _____ Position Title _____ Dept./Division _____

Location _____ Hire Date _____ Service Length _____ yrs. _____ mo. Evaluation Period

Completed by _____ Title _____ Date _____ From _____ To _____

Operations Responsibility				Methods and Results	Action Plan	Rating				
List the more significant functional operations responsibilities of the position and the overall importance of each responsibility.	Significance Level E – essential I – important R – routine			Comment on the particular skills, aptitudes, traits, performance standards, methods, and expected or desired results during the evaluation period for each operational responsibility. Place emphasis on how the job was performed and results.	Comment on current status of performance as it relates to short- and long-range responsibilities, developments, and goals noting particular milestones. Include comments on the manager's contribution to the organization.	Outstanding	Commendable	Successful	Needs Improving	Unacceptable
	E	I	R							

continued

MANAGEMENT PERFORMANCE APPRAISAL
AND RESULTS REPORT—*continued*

Notable Areas of Strength, Achievement, and Other Performance Attributes	Notable Areas of Needed/Potential Improvement, Development, or Emphasis to Be More Effective
_____	_____
_____	_____
_____	_____
_____	_____
_____	_____
_____	_____
_____	_____
_____	_____
_____	_____
_____	_____

Goals During Next Appraisal Period	Long-Range Goals
1. _____	_____
2. _____	_____
3. _____	_____
4. _____	_____
5. _____	_____
6. _____	_____

Employee Comments: _____

_____

_____

_____

This report has been discussed with me, and I have been given a copy.

_____

Employee's signature

_____
Date

This report represents my true and complete appraisal of this management employee during this appraisal period.

_____ _____

Appraiser's Signature   Date

Recommended Action: _____

_____

_____

EMPLOYEE COUNSELING FORM—
SUPERVISORY DESK NOTE

This form can be used by supervisors as a means of documenting performance or behavior problems that arise or begin to develop where the nature of the situation is inappropriate for disciplinary measures. The form should be completed *after* the counseling session or discussion with the employee has taken place. While the contents (date, nature of situation, etc.) can become an important reference source citation later if the situation worsens to a disciplinary action, *the form itself should not be placed in the employee's personnel file*—to avoid giving the appearance of a written reprimand.

EMPLOYEE COUNSELING FORM—SUPERVISORY DESK NOTE

Counseling Date: _____

Supervisor: _____

**Employee's
Name:** _____

**Position
Title:** _____

Nature of Condition, Inquiry, or Incident:
(Describe the incident/issue in detail to allow for ready interpretation by other concerned parties. Cite subject of counseling, time, and date.)

_____

_____

_____

_____

_____

_____

_____

_____

Conclusion/Action to Be Taken:
(Describe what remedy was requested of the employee to improve performance or change behavior. BE SPECIFIC.)

_____

_____

_____

_____

_____

_____

_____

_____

_____

_____

_____

_____

_____

_____

_____

EMPLOYEE WARNING NOTICE

Utilizing the principle of progressive discipline, this form serves as more formal notice to an employee who has violated some provision of employment, but the nature of the circumstance is just short of formal discipline. Often, when minor violations occur, employees are more prone to compliance if they are warned or informally noticed than if the initial notice is formal discipline. Again, this form should be kept by the supervisor (copied to the employee of course), unless it is a repeat warning, whereupon the form can be placed in the employee's personnel file with the notation "Second Warning."

EMPLOYEE WARNING NOTICE

EMPLOYEE NAME: _____

Social Security
Number: _____

POSITION TITLE: _____

Date of
Warning: _____

TYPE OF　( ) Tardiness　　( ) Quality of Work　( ) Carelessness
VIOLATION ( ) Absenteeism　 ( ) Quantity of Work ( ) Safety
　　　　　　( ) Insubordination ( ) Neatness　　　　( ) Intoxication or Drinking
　　　　　　( ) Other: _____

_____

_____

VIOLATION: Date
VIOLATION: Time　A.M.　P.M.
PLACE VIOLATION OCCURRED: _____

_____

WARNING ( ) First Date: _____
NOTICE:　 ( ) Second Date: _____
　　　　　　( ) Final

COMPANY STATEMENT	**WARNING DECISION**
1. Describe in detail what the employee has done.	1. Explain in detail what employee must do to improve performance or change behavior.
2. Cite how this interferes with work environment, employee performance, business operations or the well-being of other employees.	2. Cite date that improvements are to be required.
3. Cite verbatim the rule, policy, law, standard, or regulation that was violated.	3. Cite consequences if improvements are not achieved by date specified.
	APPROVED BY: _____
	TITLE: _____
	DATE: _____

ATTACH SEPARATE PAGE IF NEEDED FOR MORE DETAILED EXPLANATIONS

EMPLOYEE COMMENTS: _____

_____

_____

_____

_____
Employee's Signature　　　　　Date

_____

REQUEST FOR DISPUTE
RESOLUTION REVIEW

Otherwise known and commonly referred to as a grievance or complaint form (dispute resolution sounds less adversarial), this form can be used by employers as an internal appeal mechanism to resolve problems, concerns, or disputes raised by employees who feel aggrieved about some decision or action related to them. The form should be readily available—put in their orientation packet when hired—and completed by the employee. The form should be copied by the employee; the original goes to the person (or level) to whom the employee is appealing for a review of the situation and a decision on the matter.

REQUEST FOR ADMINISTRATIVE REVIEW

The following is a statement of my grievance, which I hereby request to be reviewed.

Name: _____

Position Title: _____

Immediate Supervisor: _____

Department: _____

The reason for my grievance is as follows: _____
_____
_____

I discussed this grievance with my immediate supervisor on _____

My supervisor's response was as follows: _____
_____
_____

I believe this response was incorrect for the following reasons: _____
_____
_____
_____

I believe the appropriate resolution of my grievance would be: _____
_____
_____

Witnesses who can confirm my statements are: _____
_____

_____   _____
          Date   Employee Signature

Chapter 9

SAFETY AND INDUSTRIAL INJURY/ILLNESS FORMS

SAFETY SUGGESTION FORM

For employers having a work environment other than office or limited risk surroundings, use of a safety suggestion form can be an effective way to reduce accident hazards. Employers need to be aware of any workplace hazard or condition that might cause injury (which gives rise to lost workdays and increases in workers' compensation costs).

SAFETY SUGGESTION

EMPLOYEE'S SUGGESTION

Date _____

Facility/Location _____

Nature of Problem _____

_____

_____

_____

Your suggested remedy _____

_____

_____

_____

_____

(Employee's Signature)

SUPERVISOR'S REPLY TO EMPLOYEE

Date _____

_____

_____

_____

_____

_____

_____

(Supervisor's Signature)

Safety Committee: Checked _____   Signed _____
                                    (date)

SUPERVISOR'S REPORT OF WORK INJURY

This form is a must, and it should be completed by the immediate supervisor in consultation with the injured employee *at the earliest possible opportunity* after the injury takes place. Supervisors should be informed of this responsibility and emphasis placed on promptness, detail, and completeness of information. This form is used as the basis for completing the Employer's Report of Occupational Injury or Illness Form, which is sent to the employer's workers' compensation carrier, and most states levy penalties for late payments to employees (most often caused by slow internal reporting of injuries).

SUPERVISOR'S REPORT OF WORK INJURY

The unsafe acts of persons and the physical conditions that contribute to accidents can be corrected only when they are known in detail. As Supervisor, it is your responsibility to *find* and *describe* them, and to *state* the *remedy* for them in this report.

Name of Injured Person (Last, First, Middle)	Social Security No.
Home Address	Phone Home ( ) No. Work Ext. ( )

Job Title	Date of Employment	Time on Present Job
Department of Section in Which Employee Works	Location of Accident	Date and Hour of Accident

Describe the injury. (Be specific—burned forearm, cut left thumb, etc.)

How did injury occur? (State what the injured was doing and the circumstances leading to the injury.)

Who gave first aid, if any?

Names of Witnesses

Physical Condition (Describe as poor light, broken steps, lack of guards on belts.)

Remedy (What steps have been taken to prevent a similar injury?)

Supervisor (report prepared by)	Date Report Prepared	Report Reviewed and Approved By

FIRST AID REPORT LOG

Some employers may not want to use the Supervisor's Report of Work Injury to record minor injuries where only first aid was rendered on the job without lost work time. In these cases, the incident should be reported on a log such as this form in the event the employee's condition worsens at some later time (a minor cut treated with a bandage may become infected, resulting in a serious workers' compensation claim).

FIRST AID REPORT LOG

This form is for the purpose of profiling routine occurrence of minor injuries—small cuts, bruises, etc., which do not require medical treatment or lost work hours.

Date of Injury	Time of Injury	Name of Employee	Description of Injury or Illness (Specify part of body affected)	Injury/Illness		Treatment Administered	Administered by Whom	Injury Report Filed	
				New	Re-ccuring			YES	NO

*Advisable that minor injuries be recorded on the "Supervisor's Report of Work Injury."

OCCUPATIONAL INJURY/ILLNESS
REPORT LOG

Use this form as an *annual* log of work-related injuries/illness. Entries should be taken from either the Supervisor's Report of Work Injury or the Employer's Report of Occupational Injury or Illness. This form is used as an easy resource for completing the Annual Summary of Occupational Injury/Illness Incident Report (OSHA 200). It also provides the employer with a quick and easily understood reference to what causes and types of injuries are resulting in lost workdays. Such diagnostic information can be valuable to abate hazards or point out needed safety training.

OCCUPATIONAL INJURY/ILLNESS REPORT LOG

This form is used in work injury cases where the employee had to leave the work premises to seek medical attention, or to go home, resulting in lost work hours or days.

Date of Injury	Employee Name	Job/Position Title	Description of Injury/Illness	Location of Injury	Number of Lost Work Hrs./Days	Date Returned to Work	Disposition of Employee (Enter Code)
TOTAL							

Code: PT – Resumed Part-Time Work
FT – Resumed Full-Time Work
MD – Resumed Modified Duty
RH – Rehabilitated to New Position
O – Other (Explain)

*This information is legally required under OSHA standards and is the source document upon which the Annual Summary of Occupational Injury/Illness Incident Report is obtained.

EMPLOYER'S REPORT OF OCCUPATIONAL INJURY OR ILLNESS

Under state workers' compensation law, this form must be completed by the employer and mailed promptly to the employer's workers' compensation insurance carrier for handling, processing, or investigating. The form is shown here for illustrative purposes only, and every employer should obtain a supply of these forms from the particular workers' compensation insurance carrier.

EMPLOYER'S REPORT OF OCCUPATIONAL INJURY OR ILLNESS

EMPLOYER'S REPORT OF OCCUPATIONAL INJURY OR ILLNESS		OSHA Case or File No. _____

law requires an employer to report <u>within five days</u> every industrial injury or occupational disease which: (a) Results in lost time beyond the day of injury, or (b) requires medical treatment other than first aid. PLEASE NOTE: In addition, if death results or if the injury or illness: (a)Requires inpatient hospitalization of more than 24 hours for other than medical observation, or (b) results in loss of any member of the body; or (c) produces any serious degree of permanent disfigurement, then the nearest district office of the Division of Occupational Safety and Health also must be notified <u>immediately</u> by telephone or telegraph. This notification is not required, however, if the injury or death results from an accident on a public street or highway.

EMPLOYER

1. FIRM NAME	1A. POLICY NUMBER	**PLEASE DO NOT USE THIS COLUMN**
2. MAILING ADDRESS (Please include City, ZIP)	2A. PHONE NUMBER	**CASE NO.**
3. LOCATION IF DIFFERENT FROM MAILING ADDRESS		
4. NATURE OF BUSINESS e.g., painting contractor, wholesale grocer, sawmill, hotel, etc.	5. State Unemployment Insurance Acct. No.	**OWNERSHIP**

EMPLOYEE

6. NAME	7. DATE OF BIRTH _____ Month Day Year	**INDUSTRY**
8. HOME ADDRESS (Number and Street, City, ZIP)	8A. PHONE NUMBER	**OCCUPATION**
9. SEX ☐ MALE ☐ FEMALE 10. OCCUPATION (Regular job title, not specific activity at time of injury)	11. SOCIAL SECURITY NUMBER	**SEX**
12. DEPARTMENT IN WHICH REGULARLY EMPLOYED	12A. DATE OF HIRE _____ Month Day Year	**AGE**
13. HOURS USUALLY WORKED EMPLOYEE WORKS_____HOURS PER DAY FOR _____ DAYS PER WEEK 13A. WEEKLY HOURS 13B. Under what class code of your policy were wages assigned?		**DAILY HOURS**
14. GROSS WAGES/SALARY EMPLOYEE EARNS $_____PER ☐ HOUR ☐ DAY ☐ WEEK ☐ EVERY TWO WEEKS ☐ MONTH ☐ OTHER_____		**DAYS PER WEEK**

INJURY OR ILLNESS

15. WHERE DID ACCIDENT OR EXPOSURE OCCUR? (Number, and Street, City) 15A. COUNTY 15B. ON EMPLOYER'S PREMISES? ☐ YES ☐ NO	**WEEKLY HOURS**
16. WHAT WAS EMPLOYEE DOING WHEN INJURED? (Please be specific. Identify tools, equipment or material the employee was using.)	**WEEKLY WAGE**
17. HOW DID THE ACCIDENT OR EXPOSURE OCCUR? (Please describe fully the events that resulted in injury or occupational disease. Tell what happened and how it happened. Please use separate sheet if necessary.)	**COUNTY**
18. OBJECT OR SUBSTANCE THAT DIRECTLY INJURED EMPLOYEE e.g., the machine employee struck against or which struck him; the vapor or poison inhaled or swallowed, the chemical that irritated his skin; in cases of strains, the thing he was lifting, pulling, etc.	**NATURE OF INJURY**
	PART OF BODY
19A. DESCRIBE THE INJURY OR ILLNESS e.g., cut, strain, fracture, skin rash, etc. 19B. PART OF BODY AFFECTED e.g., back, left wrist, right eye, etc.	**SOURCE**
20. NAME AND ADDRESS OF PHYSICIAN (include phone number)	
21. IF HOSPITALIZED, NAME AND ADDRESS OF HOSPITAL	**ACCIDENT TYPE**
22. DATE OF INJURY OR ILLNESS _____ Month Day Year 23. TIME OF DAY ____a.m. ____p.m. 24. Did employee lose at least one full day's work after the injury? ☐ Yes, date last worked_____ ☐ No	**A.O.S.**
25. HAS EMPLOYEE RETURNED TO WORK? ☐ Yes, date returned_____ ☐ No, still off work 26. DID EMPLOYEE DIE? ☐ Yes, date_____ ☐ No	**EXTENT OF INJURY**
27. WAS ANOTHER PERSON RESPONSIBLE? ☐ ☐ 28. WAS INJURED AN EXECUTIVE OFFICER? ☐ ☐ 29. WAS INJURED A PARTNER? ☐ ☐ (IF PUBLIC AGENCY EMPLOYER, CITY, COUNTY, SCHOOL, ETC. PLEASE OMIT QUESTIONS 28 & 29) Yes No 30. HAVE YOU GIVEN THE INJURED EMPLOYEE WRITTEN NOTICE OF WORKERS COMPENSATION BENEFITS WITHIN 5 WORKING DAYS OF YOUR KNOWLEDGE OF THE INJURY? ☐ Yes ☐ No	**CODED BY**

Completed by (type or print)	Signature	Title	Date

FILING OF THIS REPORT IS NOT AN ADMISSION OF LIABILITY

ANNUAL SUMMARY OF OCCUPATIONAL INJURY/ILLNESS INCIDENT REPORT

Otherwise known as the OSHA 200 report, this form must be completed by the employer for each calendar year. A copy must be sent to either the state agency overseeing occupational safety or, if no state agency, to the nearest federal OSHA office. The completed form must also be posted on (employee) bulletin boards during the minimum period of February 1 to March 1.

ANNUAL SUMMARY OF
OCCUPATIONAL INJURY/ILLNESS INCIDENT REPORT

For Calendar Year 19_____   Page_____of_____

Company Name

Establishment Name

Establishment Address

Extent of and Outcome of INJURY						Type, Extent of, and Outcome of ILLNESS												
Fatalities	Nonfatal Injuries					Type of Illness							Fatalities	Nonfatal Illness				
Injury Related	Injuries with lost workdays				Injuries without lost workdays	CHECK Only One Column for Each Illness *(See other side of form for terminations or permanent transfers.)*							Illness Related	Illnesses with lost workdays				Illnesses without lost workdays
Enter DATE of death. Mo./Day/Yr.	Enter a CHECK if injury involves days away from work, or days of restricted work activity, or both.	Enter a CHECK if injury involves days away from work.	Enter number of DAYS away from work.	Enter number of DAYS of restricted work activity.	Enter a CHECK if no entry was made in columns 1 or 2 but the injury is recordable as defined above.	Occupational skin diseases of disorders	Dust diseases of the lungs	Respiratory conditions due to toxic agents	Poisoning (systemic effects of toxic materials)	Disorders due to physical agents	Disorders associated with repeated trauma	All other occupational illnesses	Enter DATE of death. Mo./Day/Yr.	Enter a CHECK if illness involves days away from work, or days of restricted work activity, or both.	Enter a CHECK if illness involves days away from work.	Enter number of DAYS away from work.	Enter number of DAYS of restricted work activity.	Enter a CHECK if no entry was made in columns 8 or 9.
(1)	(2)	(3)	(4)	(5)	(6)	(a)	(b)	(c)	(d)	(e)	(f)	(g)	(8)	(9)	(10)	(11)	(12)	(13)
									(7)									

Certification of Annual Summary Totals By_____ Title_____ Date_____

OSHA No. 200   **POST ONLY THIS PORTION OF THE LAST PAGE NO LATER THAN FEBRUARY 1.**

Chapter 10

MISCELLANEOUS FORMS

PERSONNEL TRANSACTION/CHANGE
OF STATUS NOTICE

This is one of the more common forms used by employers, and it has universal applications. It is recommended for all employers. A review of the form will show that it is used by the supervisor and/or departmental manager to transmit such information as changes in personal data, pay or job classification, transfer, leaves, and employment separations. Therefore, it can take the place of several single-purpose forms used to transmit this type of information. The person completing the form need only fill in the basic (identifier) information at the top, then the detail in the particular section applicable to the situation.

PERSONNEL TRANSACTION/CHANGE OF STATUS NOTICE

Employer Name		EEO Code	Date Prepared
Effective Date	SSN	Position Title	Dept./Office

TYPE OF TRANSACTION:
( ) Employee Personal Information Change ( ) Transfer/Job Assignment Change
( ) Classification/Pay Rate Change ( ) Leave of Absence/Vacation
( ) Employment Separation

EMPLOYEE PERSONAL INFORMATION CHANGE

	FROM	TO
Name* Change		
Address Street City & Zip		
Telephone ( )	( )	
Marital Status Change*	( ) Single ( ) Married	( ) Single ( ) Married

If marital status is changed from single to married, give full name of spouse (maiden name of wife)

Name of Spouse: First Name   Middle Name   Last Name

DEPENDENTS*	Last Name	First Name	Initial	Date of Birth Mo	Day	Yr	Relationship to Employee
( ) Add ( ) Cancel							
( ) Add ( ) Cancel							
( ) Add ( ) Cancel							

BENEFICIARY*	Name	Address	Relationship to Employee
( ) Add ( ) Cancel			
( ) Add ( ) Cancel			

* Employee may wish to change state and/or federal declaration of exemptions (W-4 Forms), Beneficiary, Declaration, and Benefit Enrollment forms.

TRANSFER/JOB ASSIGNMENT CHANGE

	FROM	TO
Transfer Location		
Job Title		
Pay Rate		
Supervisor		
Office/ Dept.		
Hours	( ) Regular Full-Time ( ) Part-Time (# of hrs/wk)	( ) Regular Full-Time ( ) Part-Time (# of hrs/wk)
Status	( ) Permanent ( ) Temporary	( ) Permanent ( ) Temporary

( ) NOTICE that your present scheduled shift is changed as shown in the new schedule.
( ) REQUEST for present schedule to be changed as shown on the new schedule.

PRESENT								NEW							
	M	T	W	T	F	S	S		M	T	W	T	F	S	S
Date															
Day															
Swing															
Gr Yd															

Signed _____ Date_____

Approved _____ Date_____

CLASSIFICATION CHANGE

( ) Promotion   ( ) Demotion   ( ) Reclassification
( ) Pay Rate Recommendation Initiated
( ) No Immediate Pay Rate Action Planned

	FROM	TO
Classification Title		
Pay Rate Range		
Dept.		
Supv.		
Shift		

PAY RATE CHANGE

( ) Merit Increase   ( ) Longevity Increase   ( ) Bonus
( ) Negotiated Increase   ( ) COL Increase
( ) Salary Reduction

	FROM	TO
Job Title		
Pay Rate	$	$
	( ) Exempt ( ) Non-Exempt	( ) Exempt ( ) Non-Exempt

Reasons:_____

_____

continued

PERSONNEL TRANSACTION/CHANGE OF STATUS NOTICE—*continued*

Page two

LEAVES OF ABSENCE

( ) Personal Disability Leave   ( ) With Pay

( ) Military Leave   ( ) Without Pay

( ) Worker Compensable Leave

( ) Other (Specify) _____

_____

_____

Days Requested: _____

Starting Date: _____

Return Date: _____

Last Day Worked: _____

VACATION

Date Hired:

19____ vacation days due: _____

Accumulated days not yet taken: _____

Vacation days completed: _____

Days Requested: _____

First Date of Vacation: _____

Last Date of Vacation: _____

Balance Due: _____

EMPLOYMENT SEPARATION

( ) Resignation   ( ) Probationary

( ) Layoff   ( ) Retirement

( ) Discharged   ( ) End of Temp. Empl.

( ) Disability   ( ) Deceased

( ) Other (specify) _____

Eligible For Rehire: ( ) Yes   ( ) No

Replacement Requirements: ( ) Yes   ( ) No

If yes, specify: _____

_____

Check appropriate box for each attribute and leave boxes blank that do not pertain to this individual's present duties.

WORK RECORD	OUTSTANDING	ABOVE AVERAGE	SATISFACTORY	LESS THAN SATISFACTORY
Job Knowledge				
Quality				
Quantity				
Service of Responsibility/Work				
Service of Responsibility/Others				
Communication Skills—Oral				
Communication Skills—Written				
Others (list)				

COMMENTS: _____

_____

_____

REMARKS: Complete in all cases to give circumstances and considerations relevant to the mentioned actions.

Authorization Signature   Title   Date

REQUEST TO ENGAGE IN
OFF-DUTY EMPLOYMENT

Employers having a bona fide business reason for adopting certain restrictions or conditions through their personnel policies (see Chapter 2), should keep records of approved off-duty employment requests in the employee's personnel file. The top portion should be completed by the employee, signed by authorizing supervisors, and a copy given to the employee.

REQUEST TO ENGAGE IN OFF-DUTY EMPLOYMENT

Date: _____

Name of Employee: _____ Dept./Div. _____

Job Title: _____

_____

Name of Outside Employer or Enterprise: _____

Address of Outside Employer or Enterprise: _____

_____

Phone: _____ Days and Hours per Week: _____

Duration of Employment: _____

Type of Employment and Duties to be Performed: _____

_____

_____

_____

Your department head has the authority to prohibit any outside employment which:

1. Involves the use of *(Company)* time, facilities, equipment, or supplies for your private gain;
2. Involves the acceptance of money from any person for any work which you would be expected to do as part of your employment;
3. Involves such time demands that you would be less efficient in performing your duties.

You should also know that you are not eligible for workers' compensation benefits for injuries incurred in your outside employment. Failure to complete this form, or failure to provide complete and accurate information, may subject you to disciplinary action.

I have read the above information. The information I have provided is accurate and complete.

Employee's Signature: _____ Date: _____

Supervisor: _____ Date: _____

Approved (   )

Disapproved (   )

MILEAGE REIMBURSEMENT REPORT

This form is for employees required to use their personal vehicles in the course of employment business where the employer has agreed to reimburse this expense to the employee at a predetermined fixed rate per mile traveled. The form can be easily modified to serve the purpose of logging business travel using business-owned vehicles.

MILEAGE REIMBURSEMENT REPORT

Name of Employee _____ Driver's License No. _____

Type of Vehicle _____ License Number _____

Department _____ Month of _____

Date	Beginning Reading	Ending Reading	Total Mileage	Reason for Travel (place)

Total Mileage for Month _____ @ $.__ __ per Mile = $_____

Approved by: _____

Title: _____

Date: _____

TRAVEL AND EXPENSE
REIMBURSEMENT REQUEST

This form can be used not only as an accounting by employees returning from out-of-area business travel, but also as a request for advance funds to pay for certain larger expense items (air fare, lodging, conference fees, etc.) that employees should not be expected to pay out of pocket.

TRAVEL AND EXPENSE REIMBURSEMENT REQUEST

Name_____ Date _____

Position Title _____

Purpose of Travel _____

MEAL AND LODGING EXPENSES (Attach Receipts)

Date	Type of Expense	Location	Amount

Subtotal Meals and Lodging $_____

TRANSPORTATION EXPENSES (Attach Receipts)

1. Air Fare (if paid by company, do not claim) $_____

2. Rental Vehicle $_____

3. Private Vehicle Use ($.__ __/mile) ____ miles $_____

4. Company Vehicle (actual expense only) $_____

5. Cabs and Public Transit $_____

Subtotal Transportation $_____

OTHER EXPENSES (Attach Receipts)

1. Registration Fee (if paid by Company, do not $_____
    claim)
2. Incidentals and Phone Calls $_____

Subtotal Other $_____

continued

TRAVEL AND EXPENSE REIMBURSEMENT REQUEST—*continued*

CLAIM AMOUNT

1. Total of Meals, Lodging, Transportation and
   Other Expenses $_____

2. Less Amount Advanced $_____

3. Net Amount Due Claimant $_____

4. Net Amount Owed by Claimant $_____

   I certify this to be a true and correct statement of expenses incurred on official business.

   _____
   Signature of Claimant

Approved:

_____
Signature

_____
Title

APPLICATION FOR REIMBURSEMENT
OF EDUCATIONAL EXPENSES

This form can be used by employers who have adopted an educational assistance program (usually reimbursing all or a part of the employee's tuition and/or books) in their personnel policies as a discretionary employment benefit similar to the policy in Chapter 3.

APPLICATION FOR REIMBURSEMENT OF EDUCATIONAL EXPENSES

Date _____

Please print or type

Name	Social Security Number

Job/Position Title	Date Employed	Salary Status ( ) Exempt ( ) Nonexempt

Work Unit	Circle Last Year Completed	High School 10 11 12	College 1 2 3 4	Graduate 1 2 3 4

Name and Address
of Accredited School

Title of
Courses (Attach a copy of the school catalogue course description for each course.)

1. _____   3. _____

2. _____   4. _____

Field of Study	Present Academic Standing ( ) Undergraduate	Present Academic Goal ( ) Degree Program
Number of Credits per Term	( ) Graduate ( ) Other	( ) Non-Degree Program ( ) Other

Date Course Begins	Date Course Ends	Full Tuition Amount $	Book/ Lab Fees $	Total $	___ % of Total $

Brief description of
Employee's Job Assignment

Brief description of reason for taking course(s)—how it relates to present job or future predictable job.

continued

APPLICATION FOR REIMBURSEMENT OF EDUCATIONAL
EXPENSES—*continued*

Work Schedule
While Attending School: _____ hours/week

I hereby apply for reimbursement of tuition and book/laboratory fees for the course(s) specified above. I understand that, upon completion of the course(s) with a Grade "__" or better ("Pass" if not graded), I will be reimbursed ___% of the cost of the tuition and book/laboratory fees. I also understand that the maximum reimbursement for courses taken in any one calendar year is $_____, and that my work performance must not suffer as a result of spending time taking classes.

Employee Signature _____ Date _____

Supervisor Approved _____ Date _____

_____ Date _____
Division/Department Manager Approval

EMPLOYEE EXIT INTERVIEW FORM

This form should be completed by the person conducting the interview, except for Part II, which should be completed by the employee. If an employee is being discharged under circumstances in which the employer-employee relationship is less than ideal, and inappropriate to eliciting employee cooperation in completing the form, it may be advisable to have the supervisor complete the form, except for Part II, with a written reference to the circumstance.

EMPLOYEE EXIT INTERVIEW FORM

Confidential

Date: _____   Social Security
Name: _____   Number: _____

Location/Department: _____   Supervisor: _____

Hire Date: _____   Termination Date: _____

Starting Position: _____   Ending Position: _____

Starting Salary: _____   Ending Salary: _____

PART I: Reasons For Leaving

More than one reason may be given if appropriate; if so, circle primary reason.

- **RESIGNATION**
  - ( ) Took another position
  - ( ) Pregnancy—Home/Family needs
  - ( ) Poor health—physical disability
  - ( ) Relocation to another city
  - ( ) Travel difficulties
  - ( ) To attend school
  - ( ) No response to recall from layoff
  - ( ) Other (Specify) _____

  - ( ) Dissatisfaction with salary
  - ( ) Dissatisfaction with type of work
  - ( ) Dissatisfaction with supervisor
  - ( ) Dissatisfaction with co-workers
  - ( ) Dissatisfaction with working conditions
  - ( ) Military leaves of absence (6 mo. or more)
  - ( ) Failure to return from leave of absence

  _____

- **LAID OFF**
  - ( ) Lack of work
  - ( ) Plant/facility closure
  - ( ) Abolition of position
  - ( ) Lack of funds

- **RETIREMENT**
  - ( ) Voluntary retirement
  - ( ) Compulsory retirement

- **DISCHARGE**
  - ( ) Absenteeism
  - ( ) Violation of rules, policies, etc.
  - ( ) Unsatisfactory work performance
  - ( ) Intoxication
  - ( ) Other (Specify) _____

  - ( ) Tardiness
  - ( ) Dishonesty
  - ( ) Insubordination
  - ( ) Drug addiction

  _____

Plans after Leaving:

_____

_____

_____

continued

EMPLOYEE EXIT INTERVIEW FORM—*continued*

PART II: Comments/Suggestions for Improvement

We are interested in our employees' comments about their work experience with _____.
Please complete this form. **YOUR ANSWERS WILL BE HELD CONFIDENTIAL.**

1. What did you like *most* about your job?

2. What did you like *least* about your job?

3. How did you feel about pay and benefits?

	Excellent	Good	Fair	Poor
• Rate of pay for your job	( )	( )	( )	( )
• Paid holidays	( )	( )	( )	( )
• Paid vacations	( )	( )	( )	( )
• Retirement plan	( )	( )	( )	( )
• Medical coverage for self	( )	( )	( )	( )
• Medical coverage for dependents	( )	( )	( )	( )
• Life insurance	( )	( )	( )	( )
• Sick leave	( )	( )	( )	( )

4. How did you feel about the following?

	Very Satisfied	Slightly Satisfied	Neutral	Slightly Dissatisfied	Very Dissatisfied
• Opportunity to use your abilities	( )	( )	( )	( )	( )
• Recognition for the work you did	( )	( )	( )	( )	( )
• Training you received	( )	( )	( )	( )	( )
• Your supervisor's management methods	( )	( )	( )	( )	( )
• The opportunity to talk with your supervisor	( )	( )	( )	( )	( )
• The information you received on policies, programs, projects, and problems	( )	( )	( )	( )	( )
• The information you received on departmental policies and organizational structure	( )	( )	( )	( )	( )
• Promotion policies and practices	( )	( )	( )	( )	( )
• Discipline policies and practices	( )	( )	( )	( )	( )
• Job transfer policies and practices	( )	( )	( )	( )	( )
• Overtime policies and practices	( )	( )	( )	( )	( )
• Performance review policies and practices	( )	( )	( )	( )	( )
• Physical working conditions	( )	( )	( )	( )	( )

Comments: _____

_____

_____

continued

EMPLOYEE EXIT INTERVIEW FORM—*continued*

5. a) If you are taking another job, what kind of work will you be doing?

   b) What has your new place of employment offered you that is more attractive than your present job?

6. Could *(Business Name)* have made any improvements that might have influenced you to stay on the job?

7. Other remarks: _____

_____

_____

(Optional)

_____

Employee's Signature   Date

_____

Do not write below this line: Office Use Only

EXIT CHECKLIST

( ) All *(Business Name)*-issued property returned:
List of property _____

_____

_____

_____

( ) Discussed with Employee

    ( ) Right to file for Unemployment Benefits

    ( ) Conversion of Insurance Benefits

( ) Recommend Rehire: ( ) Yes   ( ) No

( ) Special Comments: _____

_____

_____

_____   _____ _____

Interviewer's Signature   Title   Date

Chapter 11

SAMPLE HUMAN RESOURCES AND EMPLOYMENT LETTERS TO MAKE YOUR JOB EASIER AND MORE EFFICIENT

This chapter provides a variety of sample letters, memoranda, and similar correspondence to employees concerning situations that are more conducive to this format than to a form. A letter is a more personal way to notify employees of a unique or changed employment condition, and allows for a customized explanation of the matter.

The writing style and tone of personnel and employment letters should fit the situation(s). Many such letters may be merely informative, and therefore rather neutral sounding. Others may require a conciliatory style (response to a discrimination complaint), while others may be more appropriately expressed in firm, directive language (disciplinary warning).

Employers should be extremely cautious of the manner in which statements are made to employees, and this is particularly true when statements are made in writing. While it is important for employers to document various employment situations, such documents can be used against an employer as evidence of an illegal or inappropriate act, whether intentional or unintentional on the employer's part, if a poor choice of words is used.

Copies of employment letters distributed to the entire work force should be filed in a "general employee correspondence" file or the file pertaining to the topic of the letter (e.g., group health insurance). Letters to specific employees should be filed in the employee's personnel file (right folder flap), with the original copy sent to the applicable employee(s).

Selection Process Letters

- Employment Rejection
- Notice of Employment Examination
- Employment Verification

- Employment Offer/Confirmation Letter 1
- Employment Offer/Confirmation Letter 2

Employment Process Letters

- Nondisclosure Agreement
- Regular Employment Status
- Performance/Service Recognition
- Promotion
- Warning
- Written Reprimand
- Suspension/Reduction/Demotion

Separation Process Letters

- Initial/Introductory Employment Release
- Reduction in Work Force
- Recommendation to Terminate Employment
- Termination—Intoxication
- Termination—Excessive Absenteeism
- Termination and Conversion of Insurance Benefits

SELECTION PROCESS LETTERS

[Business Letterhead]   <u>**EMPLOYMENT REJECTION LETTER**</u>

_____ (Date)

_____ (Name)

_____ (Address)

_____ (City, State, Zip)

Dear _____,

    Thank you very much for your interest in our _____ position.

    As our announcement indicated, we anticipated and received an impressive number of highly qualified applicants for this position. This, of course, makes the examination and selection process a difficult choice; however, it is our intention at this time to process those applications which reflect the most extensive preparation for this position. While your background and experience meet some or most of our requirements, there were other applicants whose qualifications more closely fit our particular needs. If we have a similar opening in the near future, we would be happy to consider you again, or you may wish to apply for other positions for which your background would qualify.

    We appreciate your interest in employment with the *(Company)*, and we wish you success in your employment goals.

Sincerely,

_____ (Signature)

_____ (Title)

[Business Letterhead]   **NOTICE OF**
                                                    EMPLOYMENT EXAMINATION

_____ (Date)

_____ (Name)

_____ (Address)

_____ (City, State, Zip)

RE: NOTICE OF EMPLOYMENT EXAMINATION

Dear _____,

    After reviewing your qualifications, we would like you to take our employment tests for the position of _____.

    Please appear in our office on _____, at _____ (A.M., P.M.).

    Please bring this letter, personal identification, and the following items to the exam:

                _____

                _____

                _____

If you are unable to make this appointment, please telephone _____.

Sincerely,

_____
(Position Title)

[Business Letterhead]   **EMPLOYMENT VERIFICATION**

_____ (Date)

TO: _____ (Name of Company)

_____ (Address)

_____ (City, State, Zip)

ATTN: EMPLOYMENT VERIFICATION

The person identified below is being considered for employment and has signed a statement authorizing this inquiry. We would appreciate a statement of your opinions and experiences with this person. Please provide the information requested on the attached form, and return to us in the enclosed envelope at your earliest opportunity. Your reply will be considered confidential. We sincerely appreciate your cooperation.

AUTHORIZATION: I hereby authorize _(Company)_ to request verification of statements made by me on my employment application, and any other job-related information. I also give permission to the company addressed above to release the information requested by _(Company)_.

	Applicant Signature Date
Name of Applicant	Dates of Claimed Employment
Social Security Number	Final Rate of Pay
Position Last Held	Reason for Leaving

1. Is the above information correct? Yes _____ No _____ If not, please make corrections.
2. What is your opinion as to this person's:

Rating	Excellent	Good	Fair	Poor	Comments
Application of Knowledge					
Quality of Work					
Attendance					
Supervisory Ability					

3. Is there anything in your experience with the Applicant to indicate any disloyalty to the United States? Yes _____ No _____

4. To what extent was the applicant granted access to classified information?
    Top Secret _____ Secret _____ Confidential _____ None _____ Other _____

5. Would the Applicant be eligible for rehire? Yes _____ No _____

6. Your further comments on any personal or professional strengths and weaknesses will be appreciated.

_____

_____

_____

Signature   Position   Date

EMPLOYMENT OFFER/CONFIRMATION LETTER 1*

[Business Letterhead]

_____ (Date)

_____ (Name)
_____ (Address)
_____ (City, State, Zip)

Dear *(First name)*:

On behalf of *(Company)*, I am pleased to inform you that you have been selected for employment in the position of (*Job Title*) at a starting salary of approximately $*(2,145)* per *(month)*. Since your position is classified as nonexempt by the company, your actual pay rate is *($12.375)* per hour, and this is the amount used as the basis of calculating your regular overtime rate for such required work. As agreed during our telephone conversation on *(Date)*, your employment will commence on *(Date)* when you report to *(Specify location and title of person)*. Please make arrangements to report at 8:30 A.M. on that day. Your initial work schedule will be Monday through Friday, 8:00 A.M. to 5:00 P.M. *(or other specified schedule)*, excluding holidays in which the office is closed.

As you know, your immediate supervisor will be *(Name)*, who is the Processing Services Supervisor for your unit. I am confident you will enjoy your working relationship with *(Name)*, and it may interest you to know that *(he/she)* has been with the company for over five years. *(He/She)* also takes a great deal of pride in the abilities of *(his/her)* staff, most of whom you will meet during your first day with us.

(Insert any contingencies or special information about employment here).

During your first *(day, days, week)* of employment, you will be given an orientation to the company, its people and their activities, our personnel and operating policies, and the benefits which you will be entitled to as a full-time employee. The orientation is also intended to allow you an opportunity to have any of your questions answered concerning employment matter with *(Company)*.

Once again, *(Employee's name)*, we are delighted about your decision to accept employment with *(Company)*, and we hope that your experience here is a mutually gratifying one. If I can be of any further assistance to your employment interests, please do not hesitate to contact me.

Sincerely,

_____ (Signature)
_____ (Title)

---

*   Levesque, *The Complete Hiring Manual*, p. 232.

EMPLOYMENT OFFER/CONFIRMATION LETTER 2*

[Business Letterhead]

_____ (Date)

_____ (Name)
_____ (Address)
_____ (City, State, Zip)

Dear *(First name)*:

    This letter will confirm your employment with this company in the position of *(job title)* effective *(date)* when you are to report for work. Please appear at 8:00 A.M. to this location to complete your initial in-processing of employment documents. Shortly thereafter, we will direct you to your supervisor, *(Name and title)*, who will provide you with an additional orientation to your job and other operational matters of mutual interest to you and the company.

    As agreed in our telephone conversation on *(date)*, your starting salary will be *(amount)* per *(month, week, hour)*. Since your position is classified as nonexempt, you will be entitled to overtime pay for applicable hours worked at your equivalent hourly rate of regular pay. Additionally, advancement to regular employment status is contingent upon successful completion of a *(six-month)* initial employment period during which time both you and the company can better evaluate the employment relationship. However, as noted on the company's employment application form, *(Company)* is an at-will employer, and therefore allows either employees or the company the right to terminate employment whenever and for whatever reason is deemed suitable. Naturally, we hope that such an event will only arise in cases of a positive outcome.

    Since we are anxious to receive your confirmation accepting this employment opportunity, we would appreciate learning of your decision by *(date)*. Please do so by signing below and returning the attached copy to me. Once again, we are pleased at the prospect of having you join our company, so do not hesitate to contact me if I can be of further assistance to you at this time or during your employment with us.

Sincerely,

_____ (Signature)
_____ (Title)

---

*   Levesque, *The Complete Hiring Manual*, p. 233.

EMPLOYMENT PROCESS LETTERS

[Business Letterhead]   **NONDISCLOSURE AGREEMENT**

1. Introduction:

   This is an agreement between _____ *(Employee/Agent) (Company)* in which the Employee/Agent agrees not to disclose trade secrets or other Confidential Information belonging to the *(Company)* hereafter referred to as the *(Company)*.

2. Agreement:

   In consideration of Employee's/Agent's association with the *(Company)*, Employee/Agent agrees to keep all Confidential Information, including but not limited to all trade secrets and/or proprietary information of the *(Company)* in strict confidence and to take all reasonable precautions against accidental disclosure of the same. This agreement encompasses all Confidential Information and *(Company)* trade secrets known to Employee/Agent as well as Confidential Information and/or trade secrets that shall become known to Employee/Agent during his or her tenure at the *(Company)*. In addition, Employee/Agent agrees that he/she will not utilize the Confidential Information or trade secrets of the *(Company)*, either directly or indirectly, for any purposes except performance of the Employee/Agent responsibilities in furtherance of the *(Company's)* business, unless otherwise expressly authorized by the *(Company)* in writing in advance.

3. Confidential Information:

   "Confidential Information" is any information, process, or idea that is not generally known in the industry; that the *(Company)* considers confidential; that gives the *(Company)* a competitive advantage; or that affects or relates to the *(Company)*, its business, or its methods of operation. Examples of Confidential Information include, but are not limited to, the following:

   • Computer program listing, source code, and object code.
   • Customer lists, marketing information, price lists, cost information, business forms, and financial records.
   • Product design, contents, formulas, packaging, marketing, or anything related to the unique character of products.

   Employee/Agent understands that the list is intended to be illustrative rather than comprehensive and that other Confidential Information covered by this Agreement may currently exist or arise in the future. In the event that Employee/Agent is not sure whether certain information is Confidential Information within the scope of this Agreement, Employee/Agent will treat that information as confidential unless informed in writing by the *(Company)* to the contrary. In the event of any dispute or lawsuit relating to use or disclosure of Confidential Information, Employee/ Agent agrees that he or she shall have the burden of proof in establishing that the information was not confidential or that its disclosure was authorized.

   Employee/Agent agrees to surrender to the *(Company)* all notes, records, and documentation that was supplied to Employee/Agent by the *(Company)* or was used, created, or controlled by Employee/ Agent during association with the *(Company)* upon request by the *(Company)*, and in any event upon termination of Employee's/Agent's association with the *(Company)*. This includes all materials whether in written or machine-readable form. Employee/Agent agrees that he or she shall not, by virtue of his or her association with the *(Company)*, acquire any rights in any Confidential Information, goodwill, or other asset or property of the *(Company)*, whether tangible or intangible, and whether or not created by Employee/Agent. If any such rights become vested in Employee/Agent by operation of law or otherwise, Employee/Agent agrees to assign the same to the *(Company)* without further consideration immediately upon the *(Company's)* request.

4. Attorney Fees:

   If any legal action arises relating to this agreement, the prevailing party shall be entitled to recover all costs, expenses, and reasonable attorney's fees incurred because of the legal action.

5. Duration:

   This agreement is considered by both parties to be a binding contract, and shall remain in effect throughout the period of association between Employee/Agent and the *(Company)* and for _____ years following the termination of association.

6. Execution:

   This agreement is executed this _____ day of _____, 19___.

AUTHORIZED REPRESENTATIVE: AUTHORIZED REPRESENTATIVE:

_____   _____
Employee/Agent

[Business Letterhead]   **REGULAR EMPLOYMENT STATUS**

_____ (Date)

_____ (Name)

_____ (Address)

_____ (City, State, Zip)

Dear _____,

    On _____, 19____, you successfully completed your *(length of time)* probationary period as *(Position/Title)*.

    You are now considered a *(full time/part-time)* regular employee with all rights and privileges attendant thereto contingent, of course, upon your continued satisfactory performance.

    Please allow me to extend my congratulations to you. The *(Company)* looks forward to a continuation of our mutually rewarding employment relationship.

Sincerely,

_____ (Signature)

_____ (Title)

[Business Letterhead]   <u>**PERFORMANCE/SERVICE RECOGNITION**</u>

_____ (Date)

_____ (Name)

_____ (Address)

_____ (City, State, Zip)

Dear _____,

    On behalf of the *(Company)* I would like to take this brief opportunity to express our appreciation for your *(years of service as a [Position/Title] or description and meaningfulness of performance contribution.)*

    The work you performed during this period in the *(Operative Name Department/Division/Section)* has enhanced the achievement of their goals and has materially contributed to the success of the *(Company)*. We would like you to know that your contribution has been acknowledged and appreciated, and we hope you are as proud of this achievement as we are. We look forward to your continued interest and dedication to making the *(Company)* a progressive, successful endeavor.

Sincerely,

_____ (Signature)

_____ (Title)

[Business Letterhead]   **PROMOTION**

_____ (Date)

_____ (Name)

_____ (Address)

_____ (City, State, Zip)

Dear _____,

Congratulations on your recent promotion to the position of *(Position/Title)* in the *(Operational Name/Department/Division/Section)*. In an effort to make your move a little easier, I will take this opportunity to review some information about your new position. In addition, I have enclosed a copy of the job description covering those more essential duties and responsibilities.

Your immediate supervisor will be *(Supervisor's Name)*, *(Supervisor's Title)*, who will orient you to your new position when you report on *(date)* at *(time)* to *(reporting location)*. Your starting salary will be $_____ per _____, and because your position is classified as *(exempt/nonexempt)*, you *(will/will not)* be eligible for overtime pay. The probationary period will be *(number of months)*.

Again, congratulations on your promotion. If I can be of any assistance to you in your new position, please let me know.

Sincerely,

_____ (Signature)

_____ (Title)

[Business Letterhead] **WARNING**

_____ (Date)

_____ (Name)

_____ (Address)

_____ (City, State, Zip)

Dear _____,

    This letter is to serve both as a warning regarding _____

_____

_____ as well as a

confirmation of our discussion on this matter in my office on _____, 19____.

    This cautionary warning is based upon the following:

1. _(State time and date of incident/issue.)_
2. _(Describe the incident/issue in sufficient detail to allow for ready interpretation by other concerned parties.)_
3. _(Cite how the incident/issue interferes with the work environment and operations, employee performance, or the safety and well-being of other employees.)_

    Your actions in this matter constitute a violation of the following policy(ies) of the _(Company)_ which state(s):

_____

_____

    You are strongly advised to heed this warning, resolve to change your behavior, and improve your performance. In order to avoid further disciplinary measures, it is recommended that you:

1. _(Explain what the employee must do to improve performance or change behavior.)_
2. _(Cite a time limitation.)_

    If you fail to change or improve, there may be no alternative but to consider more stringent disciplinary measures, including possible termination.

    It is my opinion that one day you will make an excellent _(Position/Title)_ if you employ these criticisms as a growth opportunity. Should you have any questions in this matter, please feel free to contact me for further discussion.

Sincerely,

_____ (Signature)

_____ (Title)

[Business Letterhead]   **WRITTEN REPRIMAND**

_____ (Date)

_____ (Name)

_____ (Address)

_____ (City, State, Zip)

Dear _____ ,

This letter is to advise you that you are hereby reprimanded in your position as a(n) *(Position/Title)*, with the *(Company)*. This action is based on the following facts:

1. *(State time and date of incident/issue.)*
2. *(Describe the incident/issue in sufficient detail to allow for ready interpretation by other concerned parties.)*
3. *(Cite how the incident/issue interferes with the work environment and operations; employee performance or the safety and well-being of other employees.)*

Your actions in this matter constitute a violation of the following policy(ies) of the *(Company)* which state(s):

_____

_____

Your conduct as described above constitutes sufficient cause for disciplinary action. In addition, you have been disciplined in the past as follows:

(List prior violations in chronological order)

1. _____   _____   _____
       Violation   Type of action taken   Date of action

2. _____   _____   _____
       Violation   Type of action taken   Date of action

A copy of this letter will be placed in your personnel file. You have the right to respond in writing to present information or arguments rebutting this disciplinary measure. The written response must be received by _____, 19___ (date of letter plus five working days) or earlier.

You are strongly advised to heed this notice, resolve to change your behavior, and improve your performance. In order to avoid further disciplinary measures, it is recommended that you:

1. *(Explain what the employee must do to improve performance or change behavior.)*
2. *(Cite a time limitation.)*

If you fail to change or improve, there may be no alternative but to consider more stringent disciplinary measures, including possible termination.

Should you have any questions in this matter, please feel free to contact me.

Sincerely,

_____ (Signature)

_____ (Title)

[Business Letterhead]   **SUSPENSION/REDUCTION/DEMOTION**

_____ (Date)

_____ (Name)

_____ (Address)

_____ (City, State, Zip)

Dear _____ ,

     This letter is to inform you that you are hereby disciplined in your position as a _____ with the *(Company)* as of *(effective date)*. This disciplinary action will take the form of *(suspension without pay/withholding of merit increase/in-grade salary reduction/demotion)* and is based on the following facts:

1. *(State time and date of incident/issue.)*
2. *(Describe the incident/issue in sufficient detail to allow for ready interpretation by other concerned parties.)*
3. *(Describe what is requested of the employee to effect proper performance in the future.)*
4. *(State that the employee failed to give proper performance.)*

     Your actions in this matter are in violation of the following policy(ies) of the *(B)* which state(s):

_____

_____

     Your conduct as described above constitutes sufficient cause for disciplinary action. In addition, you have been disciplined in the past as follows:

(List prior violations and formal discipline in chronological order)

1. _____   _____   _____
        Violation   Type of action taken   Date of action

2. _____   _____   _____
        Violation   Type of action taken   Date of action

Your formal disciplinary action is:

☐ Suspension without pay for ___ consecutive working days beginning _____, 19___.

☐ Withholding of merit increases to __*(range)* – *(step)*__ and will be due for consideration on _____, 19___.

☐ In-grade salary reduction from __*(range)* – *(step)*__ to __*(range)* – *(step)*__ .

☐ Demotion from _____ to _____ effective _____, 19___.

     A copy of this letter will be placed in your personnel file. You have the right to respond in writing to present information or arguments rebutting this disciplinary action. If you choose to respond, you have until 5:00 P.M. on _____, 19___ (date of letter plus five working days). Your response, if any, will be considered prior to the imposition of the proposed disciplinary action. It will be assumed that you have waived the right to respond if you do not take advantage of the above alternative.

     The purpose of this *(suspension/withholding of merit increase/in-grade salary reduction/ demotion)* is to impress upon you the seriousness with which the *(Company)* regards the above violation of employment conditions, and to give you the opportunity to reflect upon your future compliance with these and other employment standards. Should you choose to continue violating the conditions of your employment, you will be subject to further disciplinary action, including termination consideration.

Sincerely,

_____ (Signature)

_____ (Title)

SEPARATION PROCESS LETTERS

[Business Letterhead]   **INITIAL/INTRODUCTORY
                                          EMPLOYMENT RELEASE**

_____ (Date)

_____ (Name)

_____ (Address)

_____ (City, State, Zip)

Dear _____,

This letter is to inform you that you will be released from your position as
(Position/Title) with the *(Company)*, effective at the end of the working day on
(date).

The reason for this release is that you have failed to meet the requirements
for this position during your initial/introductory employment period. Please meet
with *(Title)* to discuss out-processing matters sometime prior to the above date.

We wish you success in your future employment goals.

Sincerely,

_____ (Signature)

_____ (Title)

[Business Letterhead]   **REDUCTION IN WORK FORCE**

_____ (Date)

_____ (Name)
_____ (Address)
_____ (City, State, Zip)

Dear _____,

    It is with regret that we find it necessary at this time to take a most difficult step and reduce the number of our employees due to *(state reason(s))*. Unfortunately, *(Name of Employee),* you are one of the affected employees in this work force reduction, and your last date of employment will be _____, 19____. However, the *(Company)* will pay you for (an additional _____ days, through _____, 19____, all unused and accrued vacation, and regular company severance pay). In addition, we have made arrangements to provide continued medical and hospitalization coverage through _____, 19____. The *(Company)* will also provide workshops on job search procedures, résumé writing, and interviewing techniques to those employees who request them. If you are interested in the training, or if you have any further questions regarding these actions, please contact _____, _____, before _____, 19____.

Sincerely,

_____ (Signature)
_____ (Title)

[Business Letterhead]   **RECOMMENDATION TO TERMINATE EMPLOYMENT**

_____ (Date)

_____ (Name)

_____ (Address)

_____ (City, State, Zip)

Dear _____,

    This letter is to inform you of my recommendation to the _(title of person who will impose termination)_ that you be terminated from your position of _____, with the _(Company)_, effective _____, 19____. You are hereby notified of your rights to a pretermination meeting with the _(title of person who will impose termination)_ prior to the effective date, and your subsequent right to appeal this action.

    This termination action is based upon the following facts:

1. _(State time and date of incident/issue.)_
2. _(Describe the incident/issue in sufficient detail to allow for ready interpretation by other concerned parties.)_

    Your actions in this matter constitute a violation of the following policy(ies) of the _(Company)_ which state(s):

_____

_____

    Additionally, you have been disciplined in the past for the following reasons:

      (List prior violation and formal discipline in chronological order)

1.		
Violation	Type of action taken	Date of action
2.		
Violation	Type of action taken	Date of action

    I feel that your conduct described above constitutes sufficient cause for termination.

    All written materials, reports, and documents upon which this action will be based are attached for your review.

    You have the right to respond either orally or in writing, or both, to present information or arguments rebutting the proposed disciplinary action. If you choose to respond, you have until 5:00 P.M. on _____, 19____ (date of letter plus five working days). Your response, if any, will be considered prior to the imposition of the proposed disciplinary action. It will be assumed that you have waived the right to respond if you do not take advantage of the above alternative.

Sincerely,

_____ (Signature)

_____ (Title)

[Business Letterhead]   **TERMINATION—INTOXICATION**

_____ (Date)

_____ (Name)

_____ (Address)

_____ (City, State, Zip)

Dear _____,

    This is to advise you that I am terminating your employment effective _____
_____. This decision is based upon the incident report of _____,
19____, submitted to me by *(Name), (Title),* and the recommendation to terminate your employment due to your intoxication during duty hours.

    As you know, the first reported occurrence of your intoxication on duty was
(date), the report of which was entered into your personnel file. You were also
advised at that time that a recurrence would result in disciplinary action or could
result in dismissal, even though no disciplinary action was taken other than sending you home for the remainder of your work schedule. Both reports of your intoxication on duty will be made available to you upon request.

    You intoxication on duty is in violation of the following policy of the *(Company)*
which states:

_____

_____

    In addition, your intoxication is a circumstance that threatens the safety of
other employees, as well as adversely affecting the operational efficiency and effectiveness in your work unit.

    Your final paycheck, including all forms of compensation due you, is being
placed in the mail today to your last known address. As required by *(Company)* policy, you are to return *(list items in employee's possession)* not later than *(date).*

Sincerely,

_____ (Signature)

_____ (Title)

[Business Letterhead]　　　**TERMINATION—EXCESSIVE ABSENTEEISM**

_____ (Date)

_____ (Name)

_____ (Address)

_____ (City, State, Zip)

Dear _____,

As stated in my letter to you of _____, 19____, your record of absence from work at that time precluded you from performing the full schedule of assignments for your position. I further indicated that a continuation of that pattern of absences could lead to my recommendation for your termination.

A current review of your attendance indicates that you have been absent from work, on sick leave or leave without pay, for _____ (days/hours) of the last _____ (days/hours) since my letter of _____, 19_____.

In view of your attendance record and the consequent lowering of operational effectiveness, I am recommending to *(person imposing termination)*, *(Title)*, by copy of this letter, that your employment with the *(Company)* be terminated effective _____, 19____.

Should you desire to meet with either me or the *(title of person imposing termination)* for the purpose of discussing this intended action, please notify me or *(Title)* within _____ working days after receipt of this letter.

Sincerely,

_____ (Signature)

_____ (Title)

[Business Letterhead]   **TERMINATION AND CONVERSION**
                                              OF INSURANCE BENEFITS

_____ (Date)

_____ (Name)

_____ (Address)

_____ (City, State, Zip)

Dear _____,

    As you are aware, your last day of employment will be _____, 19____.
As a result, your employee benefits under the group plan will be terminated as outlined
below. Upon separation, you may request a life or health conversion as shown. Whether
you _do_ or _do not_ desire to convert your coverage, this letter MUST be signed and returned
to the _(Human Resources Manager)_ promptly.

    Your _Group Term Life Insurance_ may be converted to an individual policy without a
health evidence statement within 31 days from your last day of employment and provided
you pay the required premium within this period. During this time, your life insurance will
remain in force under the group plan. (Note: _____ insurance ceases on
the employee's termination date and may not be converted.)

    Dependent Life Insurance for your spouse may be converted to an individual policy
under the same provisions and time period as indicated above. Life insurance for dependent children may _not_ be converted on an individual basis.

    Your _group health_ coverage will continue to the end of the calendar month in which
you terminate. You may convert your health coverage to an individual policy for yourself
and any eligible dependents without a medical examination at your option and expense
within the time limit noted below. (You were covered under the group health plan checked
below at the time of your termination.)

☐   _(Name of Health Plan):_ You have 31 days from your date of termination to convert to
    an individual policy.

    If you are interested in converting your health or life insurance to an individual policy,
you are responsible for contacting the group insurance carrier to obtain the necessary
forms to complete the conversion process and to arrange for premium payments. Any
questions you may have regarding the coverage under an individual policy can also be answered by the insurance company.

    Your _Long-Term Disability_ coverage, if applicable, ceases on the date of your termi-
nation and may not be converted.

Sincerely,

_____ (Signature)

_____ (Title)

I acknowledge receiving a copy of this statement.

Signed: _____ Date: _____

I also acknowledge receiving notification of my Unemployment Insurance Benefits.

Signed: _____ Date: _____

Part Three

KEEPING UP WITH EMPLOYMENT LAWS AND COURT DECISIONS

Labor attorneys and personnel consultants alike would probably agree that describing the current state of employment law on any given day is difficult; it is constantly changing, and has been doing so for the last thirty years. The laws and judicial decisions of the separate states differ, sometimes quite widely, and even the U.S. Supreme Court reverses its position on long-standing employment matters. The federal and state administrative compliance agencies responsible for enforcement of these laws are almost constantly engaged in rewriting the rules of the game, and the only obvious result has been to keep employers off balance in their attempts to comply and still accomplish business objectives.

In the absence of clear, uniform guidance from our lawmakers and the courts, we are forced to turn to our own devices—our best judgment, based on understanding existing law, deciphering trend-setting legal decisions, and being cognizant of how social evolution influences this relatively new arena of legalistic involvement in the employment relationship known as quasi-contractual law. Ultimately, the rightness or wrongness of employment decisions and actions will be tested on two fronts: (1) the present laws and legal climate (for example, consider the issue of comparable worth) and (2) whether the decision proves to be beneficial to business operations. To increase our chances of making right decisions on the legal front, it is imperative to gain at least a fundamental understanding of a few of the more significant employment laws, and to look into the shaping of current judicial trends.

As a general rule, the basic legal concepts used with greatest frequency in employment law matters are:

1. That people have the right to expect fair and reasonable treatment from others and that this expectation should not be diminished by one's status as an employee.

2. That people have the right to speak out on matters of concern and legitimate interest to them.

3. That people should have equal opportunities available to them, and the freedom to make individual choices.

4. That people have a right to protect their property and liberty, and that this right cannot be infringed upon without due process of law.

These concepts became particularly apparent during three significant periods. The first was the 1930s to mid-1940s period, when union activism took root as a so-called balance-of-power mechanism between employers and employees with the inauguration of collective bargaining and bilateral decision making on employment matters. This period also saw the growth of the employer's social welfare role through introduction of government statutes requiring employers to contribute to social security and unemployment compensation. Child labor laws also came into being at this time.

In the second period, the 1960s and 1970s, the country witnessed a sociocultural revolution resulting in a wave of antidiscrimination laws reaching into nearly every employment practice. In many instances, the diversity of antidiscrimination laws and affirmative action requirements created a paradox for employers—whenever one person was hired, promoted, paid more, or fired, there would be at least one other person who could perceive discrimination. Further, with governmental attention given to social and economic conditions related to employment, this period subjected employers to yet more regulatory controls by the introduction of the health maintenance organization (HMO) requirements (see reference notes on benefits policies), the Employee Retirement Income Security Act (ERISA), and the Occupational Safety and Health Act (OSHA).

The third period began in 1980 when various state courts began to entertain the notion that mere longevity of employment could create an "implied" contract of employment, thereby providing employees with a property interest in their jobs, terminable only for just and fair reasons. The result is popularly known as *wrongful discharge,* and it has produced some legal theorems threatening the doctrine of at-will employment. Conversely, the early 1990s have given renewed attention and redefinition to the tenets of antidiscrimination laws, largely through the vying for societal power between the U.S. Supreme Court and Congress, with enactment of the Americans with Disabilities Act (ADA) and the 1991 Civil Rights Act (CRA).

The outcome of the regulations imposed in these three periods has been the limiting of many freedoms previously enjoyed by employers, an increase in employment recordkeeping requirements, the addition of the element of *control* to personnel management operations, and the alteration of fundamental philosophies by which human resources are managed. No longer can the employer of a contemporary work force afford to approach its personnel program as either a clerical business function or a mere inspirational service to operating managers. Effective personnel management today requires both.

To further aid employers' understanding of at least some of the more significant legal aspects of operating a contemporary personnel program, the chapters that follow provide important background and trend-setting employment law information. If used as a periodic reference source, these chapters will give you confidence to make informed decisions.

An abbreviated overview of applicable laws is illustrated on the next two pages.

SUMMARY OF FEDERAL LAWS AND REGULATIONS
DEALING WITH EMPLOYMENT MATTERS

	LAW	POSTING REQUIREMENT	AGENCY	COVERAGE	SUMMARY
WAGES, HOURS, AND CONDITIONS OF EMPLOYMENT	Fair Labor Standards	Yes—Work Location	U.S. Department of Labor; Wage & Hour Div.; Public Contracts Div.	Employers engaged in interstate commerce	Provides: employee minimum wages ($4.25 hr. in nonagricultural work, $3.61/hr. in agricultural work); *overtime* pay after 40 hours a week at not less than time and 1/2. Executive, administrative, professional and outside sales employees are exempt. Exemption test includes, among others, salary requirement of $250/wk. (short test). Equal pay for equal work *regardless of sex.* Child labor protection.
	Walsh-Healy Act	Yes—Work Location	Same as above	Employers w/govt. contracts in excess of $10,000	Employers must pay the prevailing minimum wage, time and 1/2 after 8 hours per day and 40 hours per week.
	McNamara-O'Hara Service Contract Act	Yes—Work Location	Same as above	Employers w/govt. contracts in excess of $2,500	Employers required to notify employees of statutory wage rights.
	Davis-Bacon Act	Yes—Work Location	Same as above	Public works contractors on contracts in excess of $2,000	Employers must pay *specified minimum hourly rates.*
	State Labor Code	Yes—Work Location	State Department of Industrial Relations; Division of Industrial Welfare	All employers	Basic state law governing employment relationships and conditions such as wages, hours, minimum hours guarantee, record keeping, payment, facilities, child labor, and apprenticeship. Working conditions and rates of pay governed by applicable industry order. Minimum wage is $4.25/hr. except for learners, minors, students, and agricultural workers.
FAIR EMPLOYMENT PRACTICES	Civil Rights Act, Title VII 1964	Yes—Hiring and Work Location	U.S. Department of Labor; Equal Employment Opportunity Commission	Employers engaged in interstate commerce with 15 or more employees	Employers required to treat job applicants and employees without discrimination regardless of color, religion, sex, or national origin.
	Age Discrimination in Employment Act 1967	Yes—Hiring and Work Location	U.S. Department of Labor; Wage and Hour and Public Contracts Division	Employers engaged in interstate commerce with 20 or more employees	Prohibits discrimination in employment based on ages *40–70.*
	Federal Military Selective Service Act	No	U.S. Department of Labor; Office of Veterans' Reemployment Rights	Employers in interstate commerce	Employers must give an employee returning from U.S. military service the same wages, benefits, and rights as the employee would have received had he or she not left.
	Fair Credit Reporting Act	No	Federal Trade Commission	Employers in interstate commerce	Employers must disclose to applicants and employees intent to use, and results of, credit reports.
	Rehabilitation Act of 1973, Section 503	No	U.S. Department of Labor; Employment Standards Division	Employers w/govt. contracts in excess of $2,500	Employers are required to provide employment opportunities for *handicapped persons.*
	Exec. Orders 11598 & 11701 Public Listing of Jobs by Government Contractors	No	U.S. Department of Labor	Employers w/govt. contracts of $2,500 or greater	All employment openings paying up to $18,000 per year must be listed with the State Employment Service. Quarterly reports must be filed.

SUMMARY OF FEDERAL LAWS AND REGULATIONS
DEALING WITH EMPLOYMENT MATTERS—*continued*

	LAW	POSTING REQUIREMENT	AGENCY	COVERAGE	SUMMARY
TAXES, INSURANCE, AND EMPLOYEE BENEFITS	Social Security Act (FICA)	No	U.S. Social Security Administration	Employers who pay over $50/quarter in wages	Employers required to withhold 7.65 percent of employee wages up to $57,600 and to contribute a comparable amount to fund paying Social Security retirement, disability, life insurance, and Medicare benefits.
	Federal Unemployment Tax Act (FUTA)	No	U.S. Internal Revenue Service	Employers who employ 1 or more persons 20 or more weeks annually	Employers required to contribute 0.5 percent up to $4,200 of each employee's wages to finance federal unemployment insurance.
	Unemployment Insurance Code	Yes—Work Location	State Employment Development Department		
	Unemployment Disability Compensation (State Disability Insurance)	Yes—Work Location	Same as above		
	Employee Retirement Income Security Act of 1974	No	U.S. Department of Labor; Office of Labor-Management and Welfare Pension Reports	Employers in interstate commerce	Requires extensive pension and welfare plan information and disclosure of information to plan participants.
	Health Maintenance Organization Act	No	U.S. Department of Health, Education and Welfare	Employers subject to the Fair Labor Standards Act with 25 or more employees	Employer must offer employees health-plan coverage option of membership in a qualified HMO (health maintenance organization) if one is available where employees live.
LABOR RELATIONS	Labor Management Relations Act	No	National Labor Relations Board	Employers in interstate commerce	Employers required to recognize and deal with union desired by a majority of employees in bargaining unit. Unfair labor practices prohibited.
	Agricultural Labor Relations Act	No	Agricultural Labor Relations Board	Employers engaged in agriculture meeting commerce tests	Same as above.
SAFETY AND WORKERS' COMP.	Workers' Compensation insurance	Yes—Work Location	State	All employers	Employer must provide insurance (or self-insure) covering accidents and illnesses arising from employment.
	OSHA	Yes—Work Location	Department of Labor	All employers, regardless of number of employees	Employers required to furnish safe employment according to designated work-place standards.
GARNISH-MENT	Consumer Credit Protection Act, Title III	No	U.S. Department of Labor; Wage and Hour and Public Contracts Division	All employers under the wage and hour law	Restricts garnishment withholding to 25 percent of disposable income. Limits employers' actions relative to discharge.
VOT-ING	F.L.S.A.	Yes—Work Location		All employers	Employers must grant employees up to two hours off with pay to vote, if needed.

Chapter 12

COMPLYING WITH WAGE AND HOUR LAWS

PERSPECTIVES ON SMALL-BUSINESS EMPLOYERS

Without employees, business is simpler, but it is limited, as one person must wear too many hats at once. Subtle changes occur when the business makes the transformation to employer. Hiring employees to contribute to the success and growth of a business is an investment of trust on the part of employers who expect employees to represent the business in an appropriate manner and not to take advantage of the employer in any way.

Employees may not approach their jobs with the employer's dedication, but most employees do a good job and present few problems. However, in the personnel management profession, there is an old adage that 10 percent of the employees take up 90 percent of the employer's time. *Consequently, like it or not, employers must recognize that absenteeism, personal problems, differences in perception of fairness, work injuries, turnover, compensation equity, and a host of other employee-related issues are just as much a part of business operations as are business development, buying office equipment, and preparing tax records.*

Managing a business's human resources is a difficult task for most people because of the complexities commonly associated with situations that are beyond the employer's control but have an effect on the business—and because such employee-related matters are not seen as being connected to production of revenue. In short, many employers regard personnel matters as a necessary evil, and therefore avoid or disregard routine management tasks until a problem arises. We often forget that "an ounce of prevention is worth a pound of cure."

One of the areas of employment law that sometimes takes employers by surprise is that of wage and hour laws. This occurs when an employer receives an official-looking *Notice of Claim Filed* or *Notice of Hearing* from the state labor commissioner's office, which is responsible in most states for enforcement of the state labor code, particularly wage and hour provisions. The employer's surprise is usually that (1) the wage claim was not anticipated, (2) the basis for and amount of wages being claimed as due the employee seem ridiculous, (3) no known violation of wage law that would give rise to such a claim is apparent, and (4) the employer thought this particular employee would not have cause to allege unfair treatment after being treated so well during employment.

The amount of time and money expended by employers in defense and settlement of wage claims is a tremendous liability that detracts from primary business concerns. However, there are some ways of avoiding such business losses; one must know some basics about wage and hour laws and keep good records.

BASICS OF WAGE AND HOUR LAWS

Under the Fair Labor Standards Act (FLSA), individual states may adopt their own labor laws, which can be enforced within the state's jurisdiction so long as the provisions of such laws are not in conflict with or less stringent than their federal counterparts.

Minimum Wage

States may require an equal or higher minimum wage than the current $4.25 per hour prescribed by federal law. Minimum wages must be paid to all employees regardless of the pay plan used by employers as production incentives such as commission, percentage, piece rate, or some other variation from the hourly wage rate. Ultimately, the pay received by an employee must be equivalent to at least the minimum wage rate for the initial forty hours per week.

Exceptions to minimum wages apply to minors and learners, and have differing definitions under federal and many state laws, but permit employers to pay 85 percent of the minimum wage to such conditional employees.

Other minimum wage laws apply to employers with federal contracts exceeding $10,000 (Walsh-Healy Act) and public works contracts exceeding $2,000 (Davis-Bacon Act).

Child Labor

Federal and some state labor laws have strict provisions concerning an employer's use of child labor. The following detail is for general information, as there are too many variables influencing child labor laws to delineate here. *Employers having specific questions should seek advice from a qualified advisor.*

1. Minimum age
   a. Sixteen years under federal laws; 18 years under some state laws.
2. Maximum hours
   a. Under age 18, hours are limited to eight hours per day, forty-eight hours per week. Such minors cannot work before 5:00 A.M. or later than 10:00 P.M. (12:30 A.M. if next day is not a school day), and overtime pay must be paid on the sixth consecutive workday.

b. Minors age 16 or 17 who are on a bona fide school work experience program may work to 12:30 A.M., as long as the employer has written parental permission and is paying the minor at the adult minimum wage.

3. Work permits
   a. Should be required by the employer for minors under 18 years old unless the minor has graduated from high school or is working in parents' business. Work permits normally expire five days after the scheduled start of the next school year.

Time and Place of Wage Payments

Federal law does not place restrictions on time and place of payments, however, many state laws have strict provisions and frequently impose penalties on employers for noncompliance up to thirty days of wages.

1. Exceptions
   a. "White collar" (executive, administrative, and professional) can be paid monthly if paid before the twenty-sixth of the month in which work was performed or within seven days after close of month in which work was performed (not covered by FLSA or collective bargaining agreement and not eligible for overtime pay).
   b. Union employees must be paid at times specified in their labor agreement.
   c. Weekly or biweekly payrolls must provide for paydays within seven days of payroll period closure.

2. Termination of employment
   a. State laws differ concerning discharged and resigning employees. About one-fourth of the states require payment in full on the last day worked, another one-fourth require payment within seventy-two hours of the final workday, and the other one-half of the states allow for final payment to occur by the next regular payday.
   b. Place of payoff should be the work location, or it can be mailed to the employee's last known address (at the written request of the employee). *Employers are advised not to give payroll checks to anyone but the employee.*

Overtime Pay

The issue of overtime wage calculations has become one of the most complex and confusing areas of wage and hour laws. Because each case may vary depending on a number of specific and variable pay conditions, employers may wish to seek professional advice on nonroutine situations.

1. Federal law requires overtime pay at one and one-half (1½) times the employee's regular hourly rate after forty hours' work each week. State laws can be different and more restrictive. The federal "regular rate" for overtime

calculations consists of the employee's *base* hourly rate *plus* such additions as premiums, bonuses, shift differentials, and the like.

2. Exceptions to overtime pay apply to bona fide white-collar employees, and employees covered by a labor agreement that provides for more liberal calculations of overtime pay.

3. Neither federal nor most state laws require overtime pay for work performed on weekend days or holidays unless such hours would exceed forty for the workweek. Employers paying premium wage rates for weekend or holiday work usually do so as a liberal voluntary practice, or under provisions of a collective bargaining agreement, and not by statutory requirements. Additionally, there is nothing legally binding on employers to pay employees for hours not worked so long as the employer has reasonable documentation of scheduled, but not worked, hours. Therefore, if an employer provides paid holidays off and requires an employee to work on the holiday, the employer may deduct hours not worked during the same week for the purpose of calculating the over-forty overtime pay. Verbal agreements and *written policies*, to the contrary, may compel the employer to pay overtime or other premium rates when a holiday is worked.

Compensatory Time Off

Federal law does not provide for compensatory time off (CTO) per se, but allows employers discretion in modifying the length of an employee's daily work schedule. Employers should consider the following elements that may establish a legitimate CTO program if:

- It is agreed, at the employee's request, that overtime be compensated in the form of paid time off;
- The paid time off is taken in the same workweek it is earned; and
- As an overtime payment the employee receives one and one-half hours paid time off for every one hour of overtime worked. Employers should have precise and clearly written policies on overtime and compensatory time off, in addition to well-documented time and payroll records.

Rest and Meal Periods

Rest periods are not required by federal law but usually are under state laws which, in most cases, provide that employees must be *allowed* a paid ten-minute break for each consecutive four hours worked.

Under federal law, employers do not have to pay for meal period if:

- The employee is relieved of duty and the duty station;
- The employee is free to leave the employer's premises; and
- The period is at least thirty minutes.

If an employer *requires* an employee to remain at the work station while consuming a meal, or be available for emergencies, the employer must pay for the meal period.

General Employee Rights

There are a number of rights extended to employees through various federal and state laws. The following cover some of the most important for employers to be aware of and abide by, thus avoiding punitive measures.

1. *Filing Claims:* Freedom from employer coercion, obstruction, intimidation, harassment, or retaliation in filing claims pertaining to job safety, workers' compensation, discrimination, or wages and hours.

2. *Union Representation:* The uninhibited opportunity to petition and vote for union representation in employment relations with the employer and, if unionized, the right to have such a representative present in disciplinary matters.

3. *Privacy:* The right to have personal or nonjob-related information held in strictest confidence by employer (those who "have a need to know"), to be treated with respect and dignity, to be counseled and disciplined in privacy, to have employment records maintained in confidence, and to be free of rumor and false accusation.

4. *Records:* Employees' right to review their personnel records at convenient times and places.

EMPLOYER DEFENSE OF WAGE AND HOUR CLAIMS

Employers need not be represented by legal counsel; they can represent themselves or they can utilize the representation services of a personnel consultant or any other professional advisor unless otherwise prohibited by state law. Ideally, representatives should be knowledgeable about state labor commission practices and procedures, wage and hour laws, the adequacy of records and supporting documents, and the employer's business and work practices. *Employers should recognize their own tendencies to become emotionally involved in their own defense of such claims, as well as to become overzealous about the principles of the wage dispute brought up by an employee.* For these reasons, employers would be well advised to secure experienced representation of their interests.

As disheartening as it may appear to employers, claimants (employees) usually need only present superficial proof to justify filing a wage claim with the state labor commissioner's office. In fact, the language of many state labor laws tends to promote an employee advocacy rule for administrative compliance agencies such as the labor commissioner's office, and almost compels them to accept nearly any verbal or written allegation of unfair or unlawful treatment by an employer. Therefore, as a practical matter the burden of proof falls upon the employer to establish clearly innocence or inaccuracy of the alleged claim.

Once a claim is accepted, the labor commissioner's office will send a Notice of Claim Filed to the employer. Such notice is intended to alert the employer to the existence of and basis for the wage claim, and to encourage the employer to contact the local commissioner's office for an informal discussion. This step affords the employer an opportunity to provide specific evidence in dispute of the claim and to have a voice in its settlement. If it becomes apparent to the commissioner and the employer that back wages are due the employee at this informal discussion stage, it may be worthwhile to work out a conciliation agreement (no-fault negotiated settlement).

If the employer fails to respond to the initial notice, or if the matter is not resolved at the informal stage, it is then scheduled for a formal hearing by a labor commissioner with about thirty days' notice to both parties. During the hearing, the commissioner alone will determine the rules and procedures of testimony and the propriety of evidence. Hearings are recorded, witnesses placed under oath, and the ebb and flow of testimony determined by the commissioner hearing the matter. *In most wage claims, the key to sound employer defense lies in the form, accuracy, and legibility of work-hour and payroll records.* They should be recorded in ink (or typed), with clear notations of the employee's name, dates, work hours and days/hours not worked (including holidays and vacations), and wage payments and adjustments made. Copies should be submitted to the commissioner and employee, along with a summary that outlines all supporting evidence.

Most hearings are scheduled for about one hour, and both parties should be prepared to submit all their evidence within as brief a period as possible. Ultimately, the issue(s) will be decided on the relative merit of *facts* presented by both parties. In the absence of defensible facts, or if the employer's is weak, the commissioner is most likely to lean toward the claimant. Should the employer wish to appeal the commissioner's decision, the employer must retain legal counsel and file the case in municipal or superior court within specified time limits of the commissioner's decision. Again, the burden of proof remains with the employer in a court defense and, under certain circumstances, it may well be the hearing commissioner (or legal representative) who shows up to act as counsel in behalf of the claimant. It is thus well worth the time of employers to familiarize themselves with basic employment laws, to maintain accurate employee records, to develop specific employment policies, and to seek professional advice on how to prevent such time- and cost-consuming matters as wage claims.

DEFINITIONS OF "WHITE-COLLAR" EXEMPT STATUS

Federal (FLSA 13 (a.1) and Wage and Hour Division Regulations)

Definitions can be found in 29 C.F.R. 541.1-541.3 and 541.99-541.315. Focus is on the employee's duties and salary. The following are streamlined tests.

1. Executive
   a. *Primary* duties must consist of the management of the enterprise or of a customarily recognized department or division thereof.
   b. *Primary* duties must include the customary and regular direction of the work of two or more other employees therein, including the responsibility to control or participate in hiring and firing decisions.
   c. Must be paid *at least* $250 per week on a *salary basis*.

2. Administrative
   a. *Primary* duty must consist of the performance of (1) office or nonmanual work directly related to management policies or general business operations of the employer or the employer's customers or (2) functions in the administration of a school system.
   b. *Primary* duty must include work requiring the exercise of discretion and independent judgment.
   c. Must be paid *at least* $250 per week on a *salary basis*.

3. Professional

   Must be paid *at least* $250 per week on a *salary basis*, and

Learned Profession	**Artistic Profession**
Primary duty must consist of the performance of work requiring advanced knowledge in a field of science or learning, or work as a teacher. The advanced knowledge contemplated by the regulations is customarily acquired by a prolonged course of specialized intellectual instruction and study, as distinguished from a general academic education or from an apprenticeship, or from training in the performance of routine mental, manual, or physical processes.	*Primary* duty must consist of the performance of original and creative work requiring invention, imagination, or talent in a recognized field of artistic endeavor, such as music, writing, theater, or the plastic and graphic arts. Such work is distinguished from work that can be produced by a person endowed with general manual or intellectual training.
Primary duty must include work requiring the consistent exercise of discretion and judgment.	

Note: When a variation in the application of the state and federal exemption exists, the exemption imposing comparatively higher standards generally applies.

Employers can combine exemption categories in order to meet exemption eligibility standards under most state and federal definitions.

Determinations of exemption status are made on the basis of duties, responsibilities, and salary.

Collective bargaining agreements can, and often do, preclude otherwise lawful exemptions.

CHECKLIST: HOURS WORKED

Nonexempt employees are paid overtime on the basis of actual hours worked, not total paid hours such as including paid holidays, vacation, and sick leave. Employers will have to determine whether the hours recorded for payroll purposes are subject to overtime pay, subject to recording as hours worked, or merely paid hours not worked.

Hours Worked Excludes

- ☐ Paid leave time (holiday, vacation, sick leave, etc.).*
- ☐ Compensatory time off with pay.
- ☐ Meal periods when completely relieved of all duties and free to leave premises.
- ☐ Work performed contrary to direction or instructions by the employer (supervisor).
- ☐ Normal travel to and from residence to job location.

Hours Worked Includes

- ☐ Preparatory activities (early arrival) that are an integral part of the job such as servicing tools, opening the business, and so on.
- ☐ Rest and break periods.
- ☐ Waiting time associated with the job.
- ☐ Work "volunteered" by the employee, unless directed by the employer not to perform work. If employer knew, or should have known, work was being performed, the work time is considered hours worked.
- ☐ Training time, unless it is outside work hours, is purely voluntary on the employee's part *and* is not directly related to the job, and no productive work for the employer is performed during the training.
- ☐ Standby time, unless the employee is merely required to advise the employer where the employee can be reached if needed.

---

* Unless forfeited by the employer through a collective bargaining agreement.

CHECKLIST: "REGULAR" PAY RATE

The general overtime standard of the FLSA requires that a nonexempt employee who works overtime must be compensated for those overtime hours at least one and one-half times the "regular rate" at which the employee is *actually* employed. The regular rate, then, is the basis of all overtime calculations and, because regular rate is different from base rate (normal hourly rate), the FLSA regulations are reasonably precise as to what forms of compensation are either added to or excluded from base rates to derive the regular rate. While the FLSA does not require employers to pay nonexempt employees based on an hourly rate, the regular rate should always be expressed as an hourly rate, and is based on the normal, nonovertime workweek for which the employee performs work.

To calculate the *base* hourly rate for salaried employees, take the weekly, biweekly, or monthly salary, and divide it by the number of hours which the salary is intended to compensate.

Regular Rate Excludes

- [ ] Paid time not worked, including vacation, holidays, sick leave.
- [ ] To extent pay exceeds time worked, such a minimum call-out pay, show-up time, minimum time between shifts.
- [ ] End-of-year bonuses that are totally discretionary as to whether awarded consistently and amount paid.
- [ ] Travel, uniform, and other bona fide expense reimbursements.
- [ ] Suggestion system awards.
- [ ] Premium payments for working more than eight hours per day or working more than another number of scheduled hours per day, or for working more than a weekly number of hours less than forty.
- [ ] Premium payments, if premium is at least half the regular rate, for working Saturdays, Sundays, holidays, regular day off.
- [ ] Premium payments if premium is at least half the regular rate and if pursuant to a collective bargaining agreement, for working other than the employer's normal, basic work schedule.

Note: The premium exclusions under the last three items are also creditable against FLSA overtime due. Such credit not allowable for paid time not worked items.

Regular Rate Includes

- [ ] Any pay for work actually performed, or for productivity or efficiency pay.
- [ ] Shift differentials, unless differential is paid for working all hours outside of basic workday, and unless differential is at least half the regular rate.
- [ ] Retroactive pay adjustments.
- [ ] Educational or other incentive payments.
- [ ] "Uncontrolled" standby time payments.
- [ ] Hazard, dirty work pay.
- [ ] Bilingual pay.
- [ ] Special assignment pay.

Chapter 13

AN OVERVIEW OF FAIR EMPLOYMENT LAWS AND VULNERABLE PERSONNEL PRACTICES

INTRODUCTION

It is often said that few employers intentionally discriminate against certain job applicants or employees, yet nearly thirty years after adoption of the 1964 Civil Rights Act barring employment discrimination, state and federal compliance agencies are still receiving thousands of formal complaints each year. Only a small percentage of these claims advance to formal hearing; most are settled through conciliation agreements by the agency's administrative staff. Conciliation agreements are often arrived at through negotiated settlements (similar to out-of-court settlements) of past wages and possibly agreements to hire due to the employer's defense weakness, litigation costs, damage to reputation, or other compensatory damages and affirmative relief. All too frequently, the action of the employer, including managers and supervisors, that gives rise to a discrimination complaint stems from a lack of understanding of the laws, their intent, and how violations can occur in routine employment practices most vulnerable to discrimination.

The following discussion, together with the information contained in Chapters 14 and 18, is therefore intended to serve as a guide for employers to avoid costly, time-consuming, and unnecessary employment-related discrimination. The focus of this chapter is on very basic discrimination law; it will identify the most common employment practices in which violations occur and show how to correct vulnerable practices.

For a more thorough understanding of the legal issues and trends in various fair employment matters, the reader is encouraged to review and use as a reference source the synopses of laws and court decisions in Chapters 14 and 18.

PURPOSE OF ANTIDISCRIMINATION LAWS

Historically, employment laws have been adopted by the federal and state governments as a means of forcing employer compliance with some aspect of public interest, welfare, or protection of individual rights granted by the doctrines that have framed a democratic society. Usually, such laws and their subsequent court interpretation are a reaction to a pervasive social or economic condition that runs counter to democratic doctrines or English common law. Clear examples are laws that have been established by such historical events as the hazardous nature of work during the Industrial Revolution (workers' compensation), the Depression (social security and unemployment insurance), the American labor movement (collective bargaining laws), racial unrest (early discrimination law emphasis), and categorical inequities (ERISA, HMOs, comparable worth pay).

To say that today's work force is unparalleled in its diversity of interests, values, and perceptions is to make an obvious understatement. Given trends in the last two decades, the increased diversification is not likely to reverse markedly short of some national peril. It should not, therefore, be surprising to note that employers have been bombarded with complex and legalistic do's and don'ts during the last two decades of the most recent onslaught of employment laws. It is interesting to note that since the mid-1970s, the U.S. Supreme Court has dealt with more issues on, or related to, employment law than any other single area of law. Additionally, because employment conditions are so intertwined with intrinsic human conditions, many of the high courts of this land have begun to embody new, quasi-contractual doctrines into legal thought. New legal theories have evolved; for example, the idea that employees can conditionally gain a property interest in their employment (wrongful discharge), or should not be accused of some wrongdoing in front of other employees (stigmatizing and deprivation of "dignity" rights). This is not to say that the inclination or positioning of the courts is without justification; rather, it merely points to the court's trends in dealing with alleged human inequities in employee relationships with employers, who are being held immensely more accountable for their actions.

So employers are confronted with innumerable laws and court decisions prohibiting employment discrimination on the basis of race, color, creed, national origin, sex, age, and physical handicap. The essence of these prohibited forms of discrimination is contained in the following federal laws.

Year	Law	Coverage
1866	Civil Rights Act	National origin
1871	Civil Rights Act	National origin and sex
1963	Equal Pay Act	Equal pay for equal work
1964	Civil Rights Act, Titles VI and VII	Race, color, national origin, sex (including sexual harrassment), religion
1967	Age Discrimination in Employment Act	40–65 age group
1972	Equal Employment Opportunity Act	Strengthened 1964 coverage; EEOC more authority

1973	Vocational Rehabilitation Act	Physical handicap
1974	Veterans Readjustment Act	Physical handicap; preference hiring
1975	Age Discrimination in Employment Act (amendments)	40–70 age group
1978	Pregnancy Discrimination Act (amendment to 1964 Act, Title VII)	Pregnancy and leaves
	Consumer Credit Act	Marital status
1985	Consolidated Omnibus Budget Reconciliation Act	Extension of group plan health care benefits
1988	Worker Adjustment and Retraining Notification Act	Dubbed the "Plant Closure" bill, it requires sixty days' advance notice to employees of a layoff where fifty or more employees work at an employer's facility
1989	Omnibus Budget Reconciliation Act	Lifted the age 70 limit on age discrimination
1990	Americans with Disabilities Act	Applied the essence of redefined 1973 Vocational Rehabilitation Act to private sector employees
1991	Civil Rights Act	Broadened the scope of discriminatory claims and damages available

Enforcement of these laws is usually through the regulatory authority of either a single state's fair employment department, or by the federal Equal Employment Opportunity Commission (EEOC) with regional offices in most major cities. In certain cases, where employers are engaged in such activities as interstate commerce, performing public works contracts, or receiving federal grants, these employers can be subject to yet additional fair employment and affirmative action requirements by such regulatory agencies as the Departments of Commerce, Justice, Labor, Health and Human Services, and Education.

Keep in mind that these various regulatory agencies are often allowed by law to establish their own regulations, which are sometimes found by the courts to exceed the authority provided by law. Because of the intent of fair employment laws, these compliance agencies frequently adopt procedural authority that seems to result in an "employee advocate" role when dealing with employers; that is, the employer is considered guilty until and unless irrefutable evidence establishes innocence. Some strides have been made in recent years among these agencies to investigate and process claims alleging unfair treatment by employers with greater objectivity. In fact, some of these agencies have even created advisory brochures, telephone consultation, and review of employer documents on a no-fault basis in an effort to prevent discrimination—a novel idea! If such services exist near the employer's location, the employer can call to have questions answered or personnel policies reviewed.

VULNERABLE EMPLOYMENT PRACTICES

The most frequently contested areas of employment include hiring (principally employment applications, tests, and medical evaluations), training, promotion, pay and benefits, discipline, and layoff and discharge. The focus is on whether various employment decisions and actions are based upon proof of job nexus (direct relatedness to job duties), common business practices, and bias-free judgment. In other words, once a person establishes a prima facie (surface evidence) case of alleged discrimination, the burden shifts to the employer to prove that the action was fair and reasonable, based on legitimate standards and past practice, and without discriminatory effect.

Unintentional discrimination, or its effect upon a particular person, is not an acceptable defense for employers. If the employer cannot establish clear evidence of the validity and nondiscriminatory effect of its employment practice under challenge, the employer is left with only two rather weak defenses; those being the "business necessity" of its action, or that its action was a bona fide occupational qualification (BFOQ). A third defense, used most often by employers in cases of alleged physical handicap discrimination, is financial hardship where the employer can reasonably demonstrate that workplace accommodation of an applicant's handicap would present a burdensome cost.

For the complainant, there are three primary forms of discrimination for which an allegation can be filed, and they are:

- *Disparate Treatment:* The (adverse) treatment of a person or class of persons differently from that of others under the same or similar set of circumstances.
- *Disparate Impact:* The (adverse) consequence of an employment practice or condition. Two examples of an adverse impact complaint are (1) a preemployment test insufficiently related to actual job performance and (2) the absence of ramps and other accommodations for workplace access by the physically handicapped.
- *Present Effect of Past Discrimination:* The composition of the present work force which, if not fully representative of the available labor market demographics (parity) can be used as *prima facie* evidence that the employer is doing or has done something in the past, to exclude underrepresented persons from the work force.

Let's examine the three most vulnerable areas of employment—the selection process, pay and benefits, and discharge—with some attention given to correction measures.

Selection Process

Discriminatory or invalid hiring practices act to bar certain "protected" classes of persons from employment who might have otherwise succeeded in securing the job based upon their qualifications as compared with those of other applicants.

Typically, employers are found to have the following discriminatory practices in connection with the selection process.

1. *Employment applications* that require a response to such information as age, date of birth, sex, year of graduation from schools, and physical disabilities are regarded by many state fair employment compliance agencies as illegal. Additionally, it is nearly impossible for employers to prove that their knowledge of this information did not influence their decision to hire someone else, particularly if the hired person had characteristics different from the complainant's. For this reason, most employers are eliminating such potentially discriminatory questions from their application forms.

2. *Job descriptions* should avoid such unintentional or artificial discriminatory characteristics as sex-based job titles; height, weight, or unrealistic lifting requirements; and minimum qualifications that inappropriately exclude qualified persons.

3. *Interview questions* that are substantially different among applicants for the same job, are outright discriminatory in nature (e.g., marital status), or lack clear relatedness to the job or employment conditions are illegal. Employers would be well advised to remember that applicants are informed about possibly discriminatory questions today and will perceive them accordingly.

4. *Written tests* used to evaluate prospective employees are also illegal if they fail to measure the applicant's skill, knowledge, or abilities based on job-related questions or situations. Written tests have been among the heaviest areas of employment discrimination litigation. For example, two early landmark decisions by the U.S. Supreme Court (*Griggs* v. *Duke Power Co.*, 1971, and *Albermarle Paper Co.* v. *Moody*, 1975) clearly set forth the high court's intent to see that employment decisions were henceforth based on job-related criteria.

5. *Medical evaluations* conducted *either* for preemployment or during consideration for hiring or retention are the most recent area of emphasis by the EEOC. Here, employers should guard against using components of a medical examination insufficiently related to the job under consideration and speculating on the *future* outcome of a *current* physical condition which does not *presently* limit or preclude the applicant from proper job performance. Consider, for example, the California Supreme Court decision in *American National Insurance Co.* v. *FEHC* (32 Cal. 3rd 603, 1982) wherein the employer was barred from firing an employee with high blood pressure, the condition of which did not manifest itself in any diminishment of the employee's present job performance. The employer was merely trying to protect a potential liability should the condition lead to a stroke, heart attack, or death during the performance of work.

Pay and Benefits

Discriminatory practices related to an employer's pay and benefit plans have become a formidable issue in recent years as evidenced by numerous court decisions concerning such issues as the equality and comparability (worth) of pay, mandatory retirement age, maternity leave, insurance benefit payments disfavoring unmarried employees, and life insurance premiums set by sex-based mortality tables.

1. *Pay plans* and pay-related decisions are predominantly a sex-based issue where women are paid less than male counterparts who perform substantially the same work. Comparable worth has likewise been heralded as sex-based wage discrimination where the emphasis shifts from "equal pay for equal work" to "equal pay for work of comparable value." The issue has gained national and statewide recognition.

   Another recent state Supreme Court decision (*Kouba*) disallows employers from using a person's former wage as a *primary* determinant in setting a hire wage, pointing out that the sex of an employee is not the only condition that can establish a form of discrimination or other unlawful practice.

2. *Benefit plans* having different levels or types of benefit provisions that adversely affect "protected" employees are in general regarded as an illegal practice. A noteworthy exception to this exists when an employer has granted more or a different level of benefits to a class of employees (say, executive management) or where the benefit will inherently vary conditional to an employee's rate of pay (pension plan contributions).

   More specifically, compliance agencies and the courts have been actively scrutinizing age, marital status, and sex-based forms of discrimination like requiring retirement at specified ages (not necessarily a determinant of performance capacity); contributing more money to married employees or those with dependents than single employees; and offering such other benefit plans as maternity coverage or life insurance payments that provide differing amounts of benefits. Although such considerations are controlled by federal law, it is interesting, if not paradoxical, to note that Social Security allows such marital status reduction of benefits (death of covered spouse).

   Because of discriminatory effects of benefit plans and practices, many employers have initiated flexible (insurance) benefit programs whereby the employer contributes a fixed dollar contribution for all employees to use among discretionary plans of their choosing with excess costs, if any, paid by the employee. Some employers have also adopted general leave programs in lieu of separate allotments of paid vacation, sick and disability leave (including maternity), and compensatory time off.

   Employers should also be aware that many states have yet additional statutes prohibiting such forms of discrimination as harassment, retaliation, and coercion under the mandatory benefit laws covering workers' compensation and occupational safety.

Discipline and Discharge

Employers are cautioned against allowing the many forms of targeted discrimination from entering into, or having evidence within, their decision making in discipline and discharge matters. Employers will need to possess sound, bias-free, and preferably written documentation of events to support a nondiscrimination contention. In discipline matters, it is common to have the employer's past practices carefully reviewed to determine if (and why) the employer acted differently with another employee in similar circumstances.

One of the most glaring, and possibly most costly, cases of discriminatory discharge in recent years was the 1982 decision of the Ninth Circuit Court of Appeals in *Cancellier* v. *Federated Department Stores* (I. Magnin), wherein three long-term, over age 40, executive employees were terminated as a result of the company's change in fashion and marketing strategies to appeal to younger women. Damages in this case were $1.26 million for compensatory damages to plaintiffs and $640,000 in punitive damages and $400,000 in attorney fees, or collectively $2.3 million, which served the intended purpose—to get the attention of employers about the court's intent when confronted with apparent arbitrary, capricious, and malicious employment practices.

Generally, then, the trend in discrimination law and its interpretation and application by the courts is toward the abolition of virtually any form of judgment or action taken by an employer that adversely affects the person's employment conditions based on personal characteristics rather than sound, consistent, and reasonable management practices. Such laws and their subsequent application have differentiated and will continue to differentiate, specific personal characteristics where discrimination occurs among a sufficiently identifiable group of persons. Among the categorical forms of discrimination, future emphasis is likely to shift toward the physically handicapped and the use of preemployment medical standards that may result in artificial preclusion from employment.

DISCRIMINATION AVOIDANCE

As a rule-of-thumb, employers must carefully examine all their employment practices where there is possible discrimination to ensure that their practices, processes, decisions, and employment provisions are based exclusively on objective, *job-related* criteria. Specific attention should be given to the following sources of potential weakness.

Managerial Philosophy and Attitudes

Without firm and well-communicated commitment to a discrimination-free work place by the employer's top-ranking managers, it is doubtful that the organization will rid itself of the problem. The atmosphere, and the thoughts and actions of people in organizations are largely shaped by top officials. If those officials fail to be clear and concise about their position on employment discrimination, others in the organization will feel free to use their own divergent attitudes and methods.

Personnel Rules and Policies

Personnel rules and employment policies should be reviewed for overall legal and operational accuracy at least every three to five years. The best approach is to regard personnel rules and procedures as dynamic rather than static and to make necessary changes as they become apparent to keep practices current.

Personnel rules and policies should specifically address the nature and type of prohibited activities of its employees (ethnic jokes, sexual harassment, etc.), as well as elucidate the ways in which personnel practices are intended to support the concept of equal employment opportunity (e.g., test validation, removal of artificial barriers from job descriptions, employment standards, recruiting efforts to fill vacancies). While there is always a certain amount of risk to employers who commit themselves to things in written rules and handbooks, they are generally better off addressing such issues as discrimination openly to get some measure of control over these matters and to establish defensible intent.

To reduce the chances of "outsider" involvement by compliance agencies and the courts, have an internal complaint or grievance mechanism whereby persons who feel that discrimination of some sort has occurred can lodge such concerns with a sufficiently high-ranking and objective company official who will review and attempt to resolve such matters before they become costly problems. Although compliance agencies have not yet given much weight to requiring that complainants exhaust internal (company) remedies where they exist, the courts are beginning to support employer efforts to resolve these matters at the lowest, most informal level (particularly where collective bargaining agreements are in force).

Job Descriptions and Performance Evaluation Systems

Job descriptions often provide the catalyst for decisions and actions in the same areas in which discrimination most commonly occurs (i.e., recruiting, testing, pay setting, performance evaluation, and the like) and, as such, are receiving considerable attention by compliance agencies and the courts. Employers should not be dissuaded from preparing job descriptions, as they are an essential tool for the organization in developing a meaningful structure, maintaining proper work flow and assignment of tasks, and making the many employment-related decisions that require clarity about what employees are hired to do.

Job titles and description content should be desexed. They should state general responsibilities, tasks, authorities, and accountabilities. These are followed by a more detailed description of exemplary duties that reflect the most frequent, difficult, and critical functions of the position, including the notation "and other *related* duties as may be required" which has been upheld in the courts so long as employers can show that the other duties were in fact reasonably related to the illustrative duties.

Another highly vulnerable area of job descriptions is the employment standards section, where entry or minimum qualifications specifications are given.

These are under heavy attack by compliance agencies and courts simply because employers will too frequently use arbitrary standards or allow them to fluctuate depending on the available labor market. Although every employer wants to hire the person who will contribute the most for the least output, specifying "college degree" for a job that clearly does not require it is not allowable, for example, nor is there adequate evidence that such requirements are a valid measure of job success. There is, however, substantial evidence that these artificial barriers exclude otherwise capable people, and therefore the requirement tends to discriminate. Employers need to think more critically about the variations of job standards that will realistically measure an applicant's success in performing the job. Performance evaluations can also be discriminatory; that is, most evaluation forms have criteria (rating factors) that are poorly defined, are completely unrelated to particular jobs, and foster scoring more on personalities than performance results. If a rater (supervisor) is biased against an employee, it is sure to come through in the performance evaluation if there is latitude for it. Other problems can surface if the evaluation system fails to distinguish adequately between levels of performance (leniency and central tendency—seeing the employee as average in all categories), or it is too easy to get a good rating if the boss likes you (halo effect). If performance evaluations are to serve the organization well for its intended purposes of employee feedback, development, salary increases, and promotion, then the system needs to have clarity of job relatedness and performance levels, and methods of improving weaknesses in performance. Emphasis also needs to be placed on training raters to observe, record, counsel, and write meaningful statements on the performance of employees in a proactive rather than reactive manner. In short, either develop a good performance evaluation system, or have none at all. (See also Chapters 20 and 28.)

Discipline and Discharge

Many disciplinary actions and all discharges constitute an adverse effect on the employee by virtue of taking away wages, seniority accrual, or means of a livelihood. Once again, the emphasis of these actions is on the adverse effect upon the employee who may perceive, or have the right to feel, that the employer's action is unfair, unreasonable, or different from that handed down to other employees in similar situations. For this reason, employers should try to deal with disciplinary issues before they lead to such harsh or formal measures as suspension or demotion by using preventive measures (ongoing communication, counseling, performance evaluations), have all the facts gathered and reviewed by a top-ranking company official before action is taken, and provide an internal appeal mechanism for employees. Most important, discipline and discharge actions must be predicated on sound, unbiased judgment, and the completeness and accuracy of material facts having a direct job or employment relationship.

Employers must manage their personnel operations with careful thought and defensible motives, not only from the standpoint of compliance defense, but even more because objective judgment and technical precision produces better results.

Ultimately, we must bear in mind that personnel involves the management of an organization's human resources, and humans have frailties. (See also Chapter 29.)

DEFINITION OF OTHER FAIR EMPLOYMENT TERMS

Establishing a Defense

1. *Prima Facie:* An allegation of discrimination that, on the surface of initial information or evidence, appears to have merit.

2. *Burden of Proof:* Borne by the party responsible for providing evidence of wrongdoing or innocence. The hearing process starts with complainant's establishing a *prima facie* case of discrimination after which the burden shifts to the employer to articulate a legitimate, nondiscriminatory reason for the employer's action. If the employer successfully articulates its defense, then the ultimate burden of proof shifts to the complainant. Most cases are decided on this shifting defense and the ultimate preponderance of factual evidence.

3. *Business Necessity:* A *justifiable,* compelling, business-related need for an employer to discriminate knowingly as a result of the unique nature of the business, which would otherwise be adversely affected.

4. *Bona Fide Occupational Qualification:* Special requirements of a job, usually unique to one sex (e.g., physical education teachers, detention guards, rest room attendant).

Employment Test Validity

1. *Parity:* Substantial equivalency of work force composition with that of the labor market area concerning race, sex, color, national origin, and physically handicapped persons.

2. *Test Validity:* Employment tests, regardless of type, accurately measure the significant aspects of the actual duties and responsibilities of the job under consideration; accurate and appropriate measures of job performance.

3. *Job Nexus:* Related *directly* to the duties, responsibilities, and employment standards of a particular job.

4. *80 Percent (or 4/5) Rule:* The passing score level at which the validity of a test is achieved; that is, 80 percent or more of *each* of the protected groups ought to pass the test, otherwise the test *or* employment standards are not valid to the job.

Chapter 14

SUMMARIES OF THE CIVIL RIGHTS ACTS

CIVIL RIGHTS ACTS

Civil Rights Act of 1866, Found at 42 U.S. Code Section 1981[1]

Section 1981. Equal rights under the law.

"All persons within the jurisdiction of the United States shall have the same right in every state and territory to make and enforce contracts, to sue, be parties, give evidence, and to the full and equal benefit of all laws and proceedings for the security of persons and property as is enjoyed by white citizens, and shall be subject to like punishment, pains, penalties, taxes, licenses, and exactions of every kind, and to no other."

There is some question as to whether this section applies to national origin discrimination. The courts have held that Section 1981 requires proof of intent to discriminate, and that the "disparate impact" proof model is inapplicable. Such a holding has been overturned by congressional enactment of the Civil Rights Act of 1991. This act is enforced by either federal or state courts.

Civil Rights Act of 1871, Found at 42 U.S. Code Section 1983

Section 1983. Civil action for deprivation of rights.

"Every person who, under color of any statute, ordinance, regulation, custom or usage, of any state or territory of the District of Columbia, subjects, or causes to be subjected, any citizen of the United States or other person within the jurisdiction thereof to the deprivation of any rights, privileges, or immunities secured by the Constitution and laws, shall be liable to the party injured in an action at law, suit in equity, or other proper proceeding for redress. For the purposes of this section, any act of Congress applicable exclusively to the District of Columbia shall be considered to be a statute of the District of Columbia."

---

[1] The short summaries accompanying quoted statutes are not intended as comprehensive discussions. There are hundreds of issues involved in cases brought under any of those statutes, and in many cases there are administrative regulations issued by the compliance agency.

This section is remedial in nature, and does not constitute a *substantive* anti-discrimination statute. However, it embraces all alleged violations of the U.S. Constitution and federal laws that do not have entirely independent remedial provisions. Plaintiffs routinely ask for relief under Section 1983 in Title VII suit. This act is enforced by either the federal or state courts. It applies to all forms of discrimination.

Title VI of the Civil Rights Act of 1964, Found at 42 U.S. Code Sections 2000d et seq.

Section 2000d. Prohibition against exclusion from participation in, denial of benefits of, and discrimination under federally assisted programs on grounds of race, color, or national origin.

"No person in the United States shall, on the grounds of race, color, or national origin, be excluded from participation in, be denied the benefits of, or be subjected to discrimination under any program or activity receiving federal financial assistance."

This section requires "federal funding" for its operation. Ninth Circuit case law has interpreted Title VI to mean that the federal funding must be earmarked for employment, and the plaintiff must be an intended beneficiary of the funding in the particular program or activity involved. The Supreme Court has not ruled on these issues. Title VI is enforceable by funding agencies and by the courts. While legally it appears to apply only to race, color, or national origin, the various federal funding acts enforced through Title VI have their own nondiscrimination provisions. The result is that virtually all forms of discrimination are reachable under Title VI.

Title VII of the Civil Rights Act of 1964, Found at 42 U.S. Code Sections 2000e et seq.

Section 2000e-2. Unlawful Employment Practices—Employer Practices

"1. It shall be an unlawful employment practice for an employer:

"a. To fail or refuse to hire *or to discharge* any individual, *or otherwise* to discriminate against any individual with respect to his compensation, terms, conditions or privileges of employment, because of such individual's race, color, religion, sex including sexual harassment, or national origin; or

"b. To limit, segregate or classify his employees or applicants for employment in any way which would deprive or tend to deprive any individual of employment opportunities or otherwise adversely affect his status as an employee, because of such individual's race, color, religion, sex, or national origin."

Title VII is applicable to all employers with fifteen or more employees, notwithstanding federal funding. Contrary to Title VI which is program specific,

Title VII is pervasive and affects any and all employment practices, screening devices, policies, and procedures. Title VII is enforced by the Equal Employment Opportunity Commission and provides for a mandatory specific and highly technical administrative enforcement scheme, the end product of which varies. The EEOC will issue a "right to sue" letter upon completion of the process. It may additionally proceed against the employer on its own, if the issue is controversial or significant, or if it ascertains a "pattern or practice" of discrimination on the part of an employer. *Title VII deals with all forms of discrimination, except for age and handicap discrimination.*

The Civil Rights Act of 1991[2]

The Civil Rights Act of 1991 (S.B. 1745) was passed by Congress and signed into law by President Bush in November 1991. The act was clearly intended to broaden the scope of the 1964 Civil Rights Act and express congressional discontent with eight recent U.S. Supreme Court cases. The Civil Rights Act of 1991 contains five separate titles.

- Title I. Section 101 et seq.
  - Extends the coverage of Title VII of the Civil Rights Act of 1964 to extraterritorial employment (¶ 104).
  - Extends the application of Title VII to the House of Representatives and to the instrumentalities of Congress (¶ 701).
  - Clarifies that Title VII prohibits the discriminatory use of test scores, but not the use of lawful affirmative action (¶ 201).
  - Reverses *Patterson* v. *McLean Credit Union* by clarifying that 42 U.S.C.S. Section 1981 applies to race discrimination in the performance and termination of employment contracts in addition to the formation of such contracts (¶ 202).
  - Expands the types of relief recoverable for violations of Title VII, the Americans with Disabilities Act of 1990 (ADA), and the Rehabilitation Act of 1973 (¶ 504).
  - Reverses *Library of Congress* v. *Shaw* by establishing the availability of prejudgment interest in Title VII claims against the federal government (¶ 505).
  - Reverses *Crawford Fitting Co.* v. *J. T. Gibbons, Inc.* and *West Virginia University Hospital, Inc.* v. *Casey* by removing the limit on recoverable expert fees (¶ 506).
  - Reverses *Lorance* v. *AT&T Technologies, Inc.* by specifying the starting point of Title VII's charge-filing period for challenging discriminatory seniority systems (¶ 301).

---

[2] From *Special Study: Analysis of the Civil Rights Act of 1991*, by Warren Gorham Lamont, 210 South St., Boston, MA 02111. Reprinted with permission. All rights reserved.

- Mandates the establishment of the Equal Opportunity Commission's Technical Assistance Training Institute and enhances Title VII's provisions regarding education and outreach (¶ 303).
- Standardizes Title VII's limitations period for filing civil complaints against the federal government and the Age Discrimination in Employment Act's limitations period for filing civil complaints after completion of the EEOC's administrative process (¶s 401, 711).
- Reverses *Martin* v. *Wilks* by clarifying the circumstances under which litigated or consent judgments or orders may be challenged (¶ 402).
- Reverses *Wards Cove Packing Co.* v. *Antonio* and *Price Waterhouse* v. *Hopkins* by establishing the respective burdens of proof in disparate impact and mixed motive disparate treatment cases under Title VII (¶s 404, 405).

- Title II. Section 201 et seq., entitled the Glass Ceiling Act of 1991 (GCA), establishes the Glass Ceiling Commission to study the manner in which business fills management and decision-making positions and establishes an annual award for excellence in promoting a more diverse skilled work force at the management and decision-making levels.
- Title III. Section 301 et seq., entitled the Government Employee Rights Act of 1991 (GERA), provides procedures to protect the rights of Senate and other government employees to be free from discrimination on the basis of race, color, religion, national origin, sex, and disability (¶ 701 et seq.).
- Title IV. Section 401 et seq. contains general provisions regarding severability and the effective date of the Civil Rights Act of 1991.
- Title V. Section 501 makes minor amendments, unrelated to employment discrimination in the Civil War Sites Study Act of 1990.

SUMMARY OF THE CIVIL RIGHTS ACT OF 1991

The following highlights the most significant aspects of the new law.

Topic	What the New Law Does
Title VII coverage	Specifies that Title VII covers extraterritorial employment.
Employment testing	Bars discriminatory use of test scores to favor any protected group over any other group (e.g., "race norming").
Seniority systems	Broadens potential time frame for challenging discriminatory seniority systems.
Race discrimination	Ensures that Section 1981 applies to race discrimination in all aspects of employment.
Burdens of proof	Mandates that employer defending a Title VII disparate impact challenge to an employment practice show that practice is "job related" for the particular position and consistent with "business necessity"; also creates new burden of proof for "mixed motive" disparate treatment cases.

Topic	What the New Law Does
Damages	Permits specified amounts of compensatory and punitive damages to be awarded to victims of intentional job bias.
Government employees	Extends Title VII antibias principles to Congress.
Consent decrees	Limits the circumstances under which consent decrees may be challenged.
Fees and costs	Removes limit on fees recoverable for use of experts in job bias cases.
Prejudgment interest	Makes prejudgment interest available in suits against federal government.

¶ *102. Effective dates*   The CRA of 1991 and the amendments made by the CRA of 1991 are effective on the date of enactment (Section 402).
Other dates affect:

- Employment conduct covered by the CRA of 1991's provisions regarding extraterritorial employment (¶ 104);
- The deadline for preparation and submission of the Glass Ceiling Commission's report to the president (¶ 304);
- The expiration of the Glass Ceiling Commission and the authority to present the National Award for Diversity and Excellence in American Executive Management (¶ 304); and
- The application of the CRA of 1991 to disparate impact cases (¶ 404).

¶ *103. Effect on other laws*   The CRA of 1991 amends Title VII by adding or amending provisions pertaining to:

- The types of employees protected (¶ 104);
- The use of test scores and lawful affirmative action (¶ 201);
- The types of remedies available to persons aggrieved by discrimination in federal employment (¶ 504);
- The period of limitations for filing administrative charges (¶ 301);
- Technical assistance, education, and outreach (¶ 303);
- The period of limitations for filing civil complaints against the federal government (¶ 401);
- Collateral attacks on litigated or consent judgments or orders (¶ 402); and
- The burdens of proof in disparate impact (¶ 403) and mixed motive disparate treatment (¶ 404) cases.

The CRA of 1991 also amends the ADEA with respect to the limitations period for filing civil complaints (¶ 401).

The CRA of 1991 adds language to Section 1981 regarding its application to private and state government employment (¶ 105) and to conduct occurring after the formation of employment contracts (¶s 202, 203).

The CRA of 1991 adds language to the Civil Rights Attorney's Fees Act of 1976 regarding the inclusion of expert witness fees in attorney's fee awards (¶ 506).

¶ 104. Extraterritorial employment under Title VII and the ADA   The Supreme Court held earlier in 1991 that Americans working abroad for U.S. firms were not protected by Title VII (*EEOC* v. *Arabian American Oil Co.*).

The CRA of 1991 expands the definition of employees protected by both Title VII and the Americans with Disabilities Act. Title VII and the ADA now protects citizens of the United States employed by businesses in foreign countries. If an employer controls a corporation incorporated in a foreign country, a violation of Title VII or the ADA engaged in by the corporation is presumed to be engaged in by the employer (Section 109(a), (b)).

However, it is not unlawful for an employer to take any action that would otherwise be unlawful under Title VII or the ADA with respect to an employee working in a foreign country if compliance with the Title VII or the ADA would cause the employer to violate the law of the country in which the employee works. Furthermore, the prohibitions of Title VII and the ADA do not apply to the foreign operations of an employer that is a foreign person not controlled by an American employer. This applies to employers, corporations controlled by employers, labor organizations, employment agencies, and joint management committees (Sections 109(b)(1)(B), 109(b)(2)(B)).

The determination of whether an employer controls the corporation must be based on:

- The interrelation of operations;
- The common management; and
- The centralized ownership or financial control of the employer and the corporation (Sections 109(b)(1)(B), (b)(2)(B)).

The CRA of 1991's amendments regarding coverage of extraterritorial employment do not apply to conduct occurring before the date of enactment of the CRA (Section 109(c)).

¶ 105. Application of Section 1981 to private and state government employment   The Supreme Court has ruled previously that the right to be free from racial discrimination in the making and enforcement of contracts, guaranteed under 42 U.S.C.S. Section 1981, applies to private action, whether it is in the context of education (*Runyan* v. *McCrary*) or employment (*Patterson* v. *McLean Credit Union*). As amended by the CRA of 1991, Section 1981 now expressly provides that this right is protected against impairment by nongovernmental discrimination as well as against impairment under "color of state law" (Section 101(2)). The amendment is

intended to codify the *Runyan* decision and, to the extent it affirms *Runyan*, the *Patterson* ruling as well.

Observation: Although neither *Runyan* nor *Patterson* expressly stated that Section 1981 prohibits racial discrimination in public employment, this type of discrimination has been treated as actionable under Section 1981, subject to state's immunity form suits for damages under the Eleventh Amendment. This had meant that actions against state employers could be maintained only to recover equitable relief, while actions for damages resulting from discrimination in public employment could be maintained only against local employers in accordance with certain requirements for establishing municipal liability. Thus the addition of language to Section 1981 referring to nongovernmental discrimination and impairment under color of state law does not change the type of employers covered by Section 1981 as interpreted by the Court prior to enactment of the CRA of 1991.

PROHIBITED EMPLOYMENT PRACTICES

¶ 201. Alteration of test scores and other discriminatory employee selection procedures   As amended by the CRA of 1991, Title VII now contains a ban on the discriminatory use of test scores in connection with the selection or referral of applicants or candidates for employment or promotion. It is unlawful for a covered business to adjust the test scores, use different cutoff scores, or otherwise alter the results of employment-related tests on the basis of race, color, religion, sex, or national origin (Section 106).

Observation: The new Title VII language referring to employment tests prevents the practice of "race norming" and other practices that give unfair advantages to classes protected by Title VII, but does not alter existing legal requirements that employment tests operate fairly without regard to sex or minority status. Furthermore, since it applies only to employment-related tests, it has no bearing on disparate impact cases where the employment relatedness of tests is at issue and therefore not established.

However, nothing in the amendments mandated by the CRA of 1991 (Title II) may be construed to affect lawful affirmative action (Section 116), whether the affirmative action is mandatory or voluntary.

Observation: The CRA of 1991 reiterates that lawful affirmative action measures are not subject to challenges alleging discrimination against classes other than those the measures are designed to benefit. However, modification of test scores or use of different cutoff scores for the benefit of a class protected under Title VII is not a lawful affirmative action measure.

¶ 202. Application of Section 1981 to posthiring terms and conditions of employment and discharge   The Supreme Court held in 1989 that the right guaranteed under 42 U.S.C.S. Section 1981 (¶ 105) was limited in the employment context to hiring and promotion decisions that involved the formation of new contracts and did not apply to breaches of contracts or to such postformation conduct as racial harassment on the job (*Patterson* v. *McLean Credit Union*).

The CRA of 1991 reverses *Patterson* by amending Section 1981 to cover the making, performance, modification, and termination of employment contracts, as well as the enjoyment of all benefits, privileges, terms, and conditions of the contractual relationship (Section 101(2)). This list is intended to be illustrative rather than exhaustive and is intended to cover promotion, transfer, demotion, harassment, and discharge.

Before *Patterson*, federal courts routinely held that Section 1981 prohibited racial discrimination in connection with the performance of employment contracts, including discriminatory wages, denial of promotion, denial of training, downgrading, harassment, discharge, and other working conditions.

¶ 203. Retaliation, reprisal, and intimidation   The courts have been split regarding the effect of the *Patterson* decision (¶ 202) on claims alleging retaliation for opposing employment discrimination that was unlawful under Section 1981. The CRA of 1991's amendment of Section 1981 is intended to cover such retaliation.

As is the case with most new or revised employment laws having such a sweeping impact, the 1991 CRA is being subjected to interpretive lawsuits and further congressional redefinition. For example, at the time of this writing a lawsuit is pending by the National Treasury Employees Association which desires to have the act's November 21 effective date apply to any lawsuit (under the 1964 CRA) pending court review at the time of enactment of the 1991 Act in difference to an existing EEOC field policy to the contrary. Additionally, under original legislation, the 1991 act placed a "cap" on the combined compensatory and punitive damages that could be recovered under both *Title VII* and *ADA* cases based on the employer's number of employees as follows:

Number of Employees	Maximum Award of Compensatory and Punitive Damages
15–100	$ 50,000
101–200	100,000
201–500	200,000
501 or more	300,000

However, three congressional bills were introduced in 1991 that would alter the original caps on compensatory and punitive damages. Such legislation would eliminate the caps altogether under the theory that those who claim sex, religious, or disability discrimination should be afforded the same access to remedies (awards) currently available to those who claim race or national origin discrimination under the Civil Rights Act of 1866. Obviously, there are two ways to approach this discrepancy, but the most liberal approach has been advanced first. Another bill (S.2053), on the other hand, would lift all caps, excluding employers with fewer than 50 employees who would retain a $50,000 cap on compensatory and punitive damages.

Due to the ever-changing legal environment in which employers must operate, it becomes imperative for *all* employers, and their human resource representatives, to stay abreast of changes in federal and state laws, court decisions, and contemporary practices. For that reason you may wish to establish affiliation with one or more of the professional associations listed in the references at the end of the manual. Likewise, the use of qualified and duly credentialed human resource management consultants and labor attorneys can be instrumental and cost efficient in the *prevention* of complicated liability matters.

EMPLOYER LIMITATIONS ON RETALIATION AGAINST EMPLOYEES WHO FILE TITLE VII ACTIONS

The following case citations are intended to warn employers that there is substantial precedence, and a harsh legal view, concerning an employer who takes *any form* of retaliatory measure against an employee who files a discrimination claim while still employed. Examples of retaliation, or retaliatory actions by an employer, consist of such things as telling employees they will sacrifice future promotional consideration, or they can (or will) get fired; suggesting that they're trouble-makers; and any other threatening, harassing, or coercive acts to impede employees' unprejudiced freedom to file a complaint.

Employers are further cautioned that most states impose the same nonretaliation principles, with varying degrees of penalty costs, concerning employer infringements upon an employee's right to file OSHA safety hazard claims, workers' compensation claims (and hearing requests), and wage and hour claims. Because of these sanctioned employee rights, the best defense for employers is a strong offense—establish and encourage the use of internal mechanism (grievance system) for employees to air their questions and complaints and to eliminate their need to use external resources.

1. 42 USC § 2000e-3(a):

   § 704(a):

   "It shall be an unlawful employment practice for an employer to discriminate against any of his employees or applicants for employment, for an employment agency to discriminate against any individual, or for a labor organization to discriminate against any member thereof or applicant for membership because he has opposed any practice made an unlawful employment practice by this title, or because he has made a charge, testified, assisted, or participated in any manner in an investigation, proceeding, or hearing under this title."

2. *Pettway* v. *American Cast Iron Pipe Co.*, 411 F.2d 998, 1 FEP Cases 752 (5th Cir., 1969).

3. EEOC Compliance Manual, § 491.2.

4. EEOC Decision No. 71-1804, CCH Employment Practices Guide ¶ 6264 (1971).

5. *Pettway,* supra.

6. EEOC Decision No. 71-2338, CCH Employment Practices Guide ¶ 6247, 3 FEP Cases 1249.

7. EEOC Compliance Manual, ¶ 493.3.

8. EEOC Decision No. YME 9-068, CCH Employment Practices Guide ¶ 6039 (5/28/69).

9. *Barela* v. *United Nuclear Corp.*, 462 F.2d 149, 4 FEP 831 (CA, 10th Cir., 1972).

10. EEOC Compliance Manual, § 493.5.

11. EEOC Decision No. 71-310.

12. EEOC Decision No. 71-2312, CCH Employment Practices Guide ¶ 6248 (1971).

13. *EEOC* v. *United Assoc. of Journeymen*, 311 F. Supp. 464 (DC Ohio 1974).

14. EEOC Decision No. 71-1151, 3 FEP Cases 387 (January 14, 1975).

15. EEOC Decision No. 74-121, 8 FEP Cases 703 (April 22, 1974).

16. Schlei & Grossman, *Employment Discrimination Law*, Ch. 15, p. 424.

17. *EEOC* v. *C & D Sportswear Corp.*, 398 F. Supp. 300, 10 FEP 1131 (M.D. Ga. 1975).

18. Schlei, supra at p. 430.

19. *McDonnell-Douglas Corp.* v. *Green*, 411 U.S. 792, 5 FEP 965 (1973).

20. *Green* v. *McDonnell-Douglas Corp.*, 318 F. Supp. 846, 3 EPD 8014, 2 FEP Cases 997 (ED Mo. 1970).

21. EEOC Compliance Manual, § 494.1

22. EEOC Decision No. 74-56, 10 FEP Cases 280 (1973).

23. EEOC Decision No. 71-1804, 3 FEP Cases 955 (1971).

24. *Hochstadt* v. *Worchester Foundation*, 545 F.2d 222, 13 FEP Cases 804 (1st Cir., 1976).

25. *Garrett* v. *Mobil Oil Corp.*, 531 F.2d 892, 12 FEP Cases 397 (8th Cir., 1976).

26. See generally 11 ALR Fed. 315 and EEOC Compliance Manual § 495 and Schlei, pp. 433–36.

27. *Francis* v. *American Tel. & Tel. Co.*, 55 F.R.D. 202, 4 FEP Cases 777 (D., DC 1972).

28. EEOC Decision No. 71-1000, CCH Employment Practices Guide ¶ 6194 (1970).

29. EEOC Decision No. 70-547, CCH Employment Practices Guide ¶ 6123 (1970).

30. EEOC Decision No. 71-573, CCH Employment Practices Guide ¶ 6183 (1970).

31. *McDonnell-Douglas Corp.* v. *Green*, 411 U.S. 792, 5 FEP Cases 965 (1973).

32. *Brown* v. *Rollins, Inc.*, 397 F. Supp. 571 (W.D., N.C. 1974).

33. Schlei, supra, pp. 438–39.

34. *Tidwell* v. *American Oil Co.*, 332 F. Supp. 424, 3 FEP 1007 (D. Utah 1971).

Chapter 15

LAWS PERTAINING TO RACE, NATIONAL ORIGIN, GENDER, AND AGE DISCRIMINATION

RACE, COLOR, AND NATIONAL ORIGIN VIOLATIONS[1]

The discriminatory rejection of applicants during the hiring process because of the physical differentiation on the basis of their race, color, or national origin continues to be a predominant violation of antidiscrimination laws. The Equal Employment Opportunity Commission (EEOC) reports that violations of prohibited forms of race, color, and national origin discrimination occur most frequently during the hiring process. More specifically, the greatest tendency to discriminate for these physical and language differences is during recruitment, defining job standards (physical qualifications such as height and weight or language skills in the job description, advertisements, and testing), and during the employment interview(s). These and other hiring process errors commonly lead to violations of law that can be avoided by taking a few simple affirmative steps. The first step is gaining a better understanding of what the laws and their prohibited employment practices are.

What Are Hiring Practice Violations?

Like most forms of employment related discrimination, there are usually two levels of law with which employers should gain a basic understanding, and they are federal law and state law. Since state law is normally fashioned after federal law, and each state enacting its own version of antidiscrimination laws makes these publications easily available to local employers, the focus here will be on federal laws. Among the federal laws covering race, color, and national origin discrimination, there are two federal statutes applicable to most employers and two Executive Orders applicable to federal contractors and financial recipients that provide at least fundamental guidance on what constitutes prohibited hiring practices and violations thereof.

---

[1]   Levesque, *The Complete Hiring Manual*, pp. 430–433.

CIVIL RIGHTS ACT OF 1964 (42 U.S.C. 2000 et seq.)

This act contains several "titles" dealing with various types of discriminatory prohibitions in an effort to establish a national policy on the illegality of differential treatment of "protected group" members in our society. For employment purposes, it is Title VII, Section 703 (a) of the act that makes it an unlawful practice for employers:

1. To fail or refuse to hire or to discharge any individual, or otherwise to discriminate against any individual with respect to his compensation, terms, conditions or privileges of employment, because of such individual's race, color, religion, sex including sexual harassment, or national origin; or

2. To limit, segregate, or classify his employees or applicants for employment in any way which would deprive or tend to deprive any individual of employment opportunities or otherwise adversely affect his status as an employee, because of such individual's race, color, religion, sex, or national origin.

As you can see from this definition of prohibited employment practices, Title VII deals with protecting most differentiation characteristics except age and physical handicap discrimination which are covered in separate federal statutes. In 1972, the Equal Employment Opportunity Act modified applicability of Title VII to public and private employers with fifteen or more employees. Further, Title VII is more pervasive than other titles in the act inasmuch as Title VII affects virtually all employment practices, policies, and procedural decisions. Title VII is administered and enforced by the EEOC through its fifty-nine regional and district offices.

Complaints may be resolved by the EEOC; they may find insufficient grounds to proceed but issue a "right to sue" letter to the complainant, or they may proceed against the employer on its own by filing a lawsuit in the respective federal district court—usually in cases where there is a controversial or significant issue they want judicially tested, or if they ascertain the existence of a pattern or practice of obvious discrimination on the employer's part. The few exceptions to Title VII are:

1. It does not prohibit an employer from giving veterans' preference to qualified job seekers.

2. It does not prohibit discrimination when deemed necessary to protect the interests of national security.

3. It does not prohibit employers from using bona fide occupational qualifications (BFOQ) for jobs that are reasonably necessary to the operation of the business, such as black actors to portray a black person's role or Mexican food servers in a restaurant specializing in Mexican food. However, the employer bears the burden of proof of the "business necessity," and the courts have viewed these conditions narrowly. Mere preference to hire people with particular personal characteristics is irrelevant in the scope and intent of Title VII.

4. It does not prohibit seniority systems or intend to interfere with lawful collective bargaining agreements. Seniority and merit pay systems are lawful so long as they are not the result of an intention to discriminate. Therefore, seniority that accrues within a job or operating department of the company may be seen perpetuating past practices of (unintentional) discrimination, while companywide seniority would be less vulnerable to such a conclusion.

In summary then, as Title VII pertains to hiring practice violations, it is unlawful for employers to reject applicants or treat them any differently during the entire hiring process as a result of their race, color, or national origin—except in those rare jobs where there exists a BFOQ or business necessity to make some personal characteristic a job requirement, including foreign or English language skills. Care must not only be exercised with each phase of the hiring process (e.g., recruitment, screening, and testing), but also with the development, communications, enforcement, and adherence to the company's personnel policies and practices that guide hiring decisions.

IMMIGRATION CONTROL AND REFORM ACT OF 1986 (P.L. 99-603)

President Reagan signed this law into effect placing regulatory authority with the Attorney General and administrative and enforcement authority with the Immigration and Naturalization Service (INS). The purpose of the act is twofold: (1) to curb the economic incentive for illegal aliens to enter the United States to secure employment by making it unlawful to employ such persons and (2) to provide a one-time opportunity for those unauthorized aliens working for American employers prior to enactment of the law to obtain legal employment status. Sanctions and penalties against noncomplying employers include civil fines for each illegal alien hired, but does not apply to simple, unintentional mistakes made in the hiring process. However, blatant disregard of the law or repeated violations may result in criminal penalties including jail terms for up to six months.

This law dramatically strengthens the prohibition against national origin discrimination under Title VII while simultaneously requiring that employers obtain preemployment (at the time of job offer) identification information concerning the applicant's eligibility for employment—if the applicant has the legal right to be in and remain in the United States, and whether that right includes employment. Under this act, employers with four to fourteen employees are prohibited from engaging in *national origin discrimination*, while employers with three or more employees are prohibited from discriminating on the basis of *citizenship*, with one exception: a U.S. citizen may be preferentially hired over an alien if their qualifications are equal. The other important elements of national origin discrimination include specific definitions and prohibitions.

NATIONAL ORIGIN DEFINED

National origin discrimination has been defined by the EEOC under Title VII to include but not be limited to the denial of equal employment opportunity because of an individual's, or their ancestors', place of origin or because such person possesses the physical, cultural, or linguistic characteristics of a national origin group. Examples of national origin associations include:

- Marriage to, or association with, persons of a national origin group;
- Membership or association with an organization seeking to promote the interests of a national origin group;
- Attendance or participation in schools, churches, temples, or mosques generally used by persons of a national origin group; and
- The name of an individual, or spouse's name, that is associated with a national origin group.

PROHIBITIONS

The Immigration Control and Reform Act specifies that it is unlawful for an employer to knowingly hire, recruit, or refer for a fee any alien not authorized to work in the United States, or to continue employing an alien once the employer knows that the alien is not authorized to work in the United States. Likewise, employers may not refuse to hire or discharge from employment an individual because of his or her national origin, or because of the individual's status as "citizen" or "intending citizen." Citizen is defined as a citizen or national of the United States, whereas an intending citizen is one who is a permanent resident alien, a newly legalized alien, a refugee, or an alien who has been granted asylum, and who has completed a Declaration of Intention to Become a Citizen. The types of documentation acceptable to establish an applicant's employment eligibility are provided in the appendix.

EXECUTIVE ORDERS 11246 AND 11375

These two laws are issued by the Executive branch of the federal government, and their respective prohibitions as they relate to the hiring process and practices (see Levesque, *The Complete Hiring Manual*, P-H, 1991, Appendix C). These laws are limited in scope to require specific prohibitions against race, color, and national origin discrimination in hiring and other employment conditions for contractors and subcontractors of the federal government, and those organizations that are the recipients of federal grants or funds. These laws also set forth particular requirements and standards by which such employers must adopt formal affirmative action plans and activities to assure that all possible measures are being taken to remedy any imbalances of minorities in their work force.

How to Avoid Violations of Race, Color, and National Origin Discrimination

Depending on the locale of your company, the particular ethnic mix of your available labor force will vary considerably from other geographic zones that determine the yet different population characteristics. You should remember that the underlying intent of antidiscrimination laws based on an individual's race, color, or national origin is to not only prohibit their unreasonable exclusion from employment opportunities, but also to mandate that each employer's work force should strive toward parity representation in their available labor force composition. Consequently, the closer an employer's work force is to the parity representation of their geographic region with regard to the race, color, and national origin mix of the available labor supply, the greater are the chances of defeating any allegations of discriminatory violations. By having and maintaining a balanced work force, this condition alone suggests that the company is using nondiscriminatory measures to hire and otherwise treat employees in an impartial manner.

So, the first step to take in your efforts to avoid violations of race, color, or national origin discrimination is to assess those characteristics of your present work force compared to the available labor supply in your region to determine what categories you do, or do not, have a representative balance of these characteristics in your work force. Where imbalance exists, you should then prepare an *informal* plan to correct the situation through such measures as more directed recruitment, reviewing job descriptions and personnel practices for potential forms of bias, and other conditions in your company that may be contributing to the underrepresentation of a particular group of people.

Here, you should give special attention to such details as reviewing how many applicants of this group you have had in the past and why they did not succeed in getting the job—precisely where did they fail in the hiring process and who or what was involved in the process at that time. If you find that few individuals from this underrepresented group have applied for positions in the past, this fact alone suggests that the problem begins with insufficient recruitment of these individuals. If, however, a sufficient number of these individuals apply but are not hired, then something or someone involved in your testing process may be creating a discriminatory impact on these applicants and the source of this flaw will put your company in court, and perhaps the newspapers, sooner or later. Some other measures that can help you avoid race, color, and national origin discrimination violations are:[2]

1. Make your organization color and racially blind by adopting firm philosophies that communicate the organization's commitment to employing any individual who demonstrates desired abilities.

2. Hire and promote into supervision and management jobs only those people whose inclinations toward others are positive and without strong proclivity toward adverse forms of discrimination.

3. Provide thorough and regular training of supervisors and mangers on human relations, legal issues associated with employment discrimination, organizational policies, and how to handle discrimination problems.

---

[2]   Levesque, *The Complete Hiring Manual*, pp. 430–433.

4. Make it clear to supervisors and managers that it is their job to ensure a discrimination free workplace and that they are to confront and promptly resolve acts of discrimination including jokes, harassment (however mild), and investigate rumors and complaints.

5. Ensure that job descriptions, recruiting standards and selection examinations, and all job conditions do not arbitrarily create artificial barriers for minority employment.

6. Rather than develop a voluntary (formal) affirmative action plan (AAP), prepare an annual audit report reflecting the work force composition compared to the available labor market composition, where improvements in work force parity could be made and by what measures, and identify other efforts that ought to be taken to achieve the goal of meaningful equal employment opportunity.

7. Review personnel policies and operating standards periodically in light of the potential for discriminatory effect, particularly with regard to hiring, and other practices that often give rise to discriminatory events, however unintentional they may be.

8. Determine if English-only rules serve a legitimate business interest. Establish them only where they are valid and can be defended from a business necessity point of view, then communicate the policy to all employees but allow some forgiveness for minor infractions.

9. Require that all personnel actions are centrally reviewed and approved by a human resource professional or other knowledgeable person to ensure objectivity and consistency of decisions, particularly as they relate to new hires.

10. Use the human resource department as an internal consulting service, or external sources when qualified staff is not available, to obtain advice and assistance on vulnerable personnel actions *prior* to deciding or acting on them. Most human resource professionals prefer the service role over the control role, and they are trained in ways to make organizations run smoothly.

11. Establish an "administrative review" procedure that encourages employees to take complaints to higher management and requires them to bring forth any condition related to discrimination including harassment, and you may want to add the required reporting of such conditions as malfeasance, dishonesty, theft, and the like to this "whistle-blowing" type of policy.

12. Ensure that both federal and state antidiscrimination posters are displayed on bulletin boards at each work location in a prominent place.

Additional attention should be given to your applicant intake and flow record keeping to ensure a well-documented account of your company's selection process performance and the thorough training of those who interview applicants and possess hiring authority to ensure they do not ask illegal kinds of questions or use ethnic factors as a determinant in the hiring or rejection decision.

RELIGIOUS DISCRIMINATION[3]

Religious discrimination in the hiring context is much the same as physical hand-icap violations inasmuch as both require the employer to not only abandon preju-dicial hiring practices, but also accommodate the applicant's personal needs. In the case of religious discrimination, accommodation means allowing religious fol-lowers to observe the customs of their religion on the applicable Sabbath.

What Are Religious Discrimination Violations?

Employer prohibitions against discrimination based on an individual's religious beliefs, observances, and practices are codified in Title VII of the 1964 Civil Rights Act. Although religious violations are the least litigated areas of discrimi-nation law, it is nevertheless a potential vulnerability in the hiring process used by many employers that can carry formidable consequences.

The reason for much of the inattention given to religious discrimination vio-lations is fairly straightforward. First, the law's primary focus is upon employer accommodation of religious observances, meaning the ability and willingness to arrange job assignments and work schedules to allow for Sabbath and other dates of religious observances. Typically, this does not present a major problem for those employers using the customary Monday through Friday workweek, except for an occasional religious holiday that may be observed within a particular reli-gion but not by the employer. For many other employers who operate under shift, weekend days, or seven-day work schedules, their vulnerability to potential viola-tions is ever present and are likely to encounter the accommodation condition eventually—which should not be skirted by merely refusing to hire a religious fol-lower, or terminating one who makes such requests.

Second, complaints and litigation over religious discrimination are unusual because the two major prohibitions are easily complied with by discerning em-ployers, namely, don't refuse to hire primarily due to the applicant's religion, or to avoid the prospect of religious accommodation unless there exists a very good business or job reason to do so, and don't arbitrarily deny an employee's request for taking a particular day off for a religious observance—the time of which does not have to be paid by the employer unless allowed by the employer's own policies. Typically, neither of these two conditions presents major obstacles for manage-ment in the way of business disruption or economic hardship. Absent willful or negligent violation of the law, both the courts and EEOC have generally used back pay and reinstatement orders as the penalty for employer wrongdoing. The fact that litigation costs far exceed the remedy for alleged violations serves as sage ad-vice to employers when confronted with the opportunity to conciliate, or even ar-bitrate, settlements where there exists some elements of wrongdoing in the hiring process.

---

[3]   Levesque, *The Complete Hiring Manual,* pp. 441–442.

In evaluating the sincerity of an applicant's religious attachments, there is a degree of judgment that must be exercised. Even compliance agencies and the courts have been skeptical of the sincerity of an individual's beliefs in cases where:

1. The applicant had advance knowledge of the employer's required work schedule, but said nothing until after acceptance of the job.

2. The employee worked the assigned work schedule for some length of time without notice or objection to the employer.

3. The evidence suggests that the employee's (or applicant's) religious belief is more "circumstantial convenience" than sincere since the employee's notice has been in conjunction with such employment changes as shift changes, reassignments, or unpleasant work assignments.

How to Avoid Discriminatory Hiring and Employment Practices

Based on prevailing federal law and those employment practices addressed by the courts during their most active decade (1978–1988) when religious discrimination became more clearly defined, the following are suggested approaches that should be taken by employers who wish to avoid the principal violations.

1. Do not refuse or otherwise avoid hiring an applicant merely because of the individual's religious beliefs, observances, or practices unless there exists a very practical business necessity associated with the job that would adversely reflect upon the company, nature of their business, or unreasonably interfere with the rights of other employees.

2. Remove any reference concerning the identification of an applicant's religion on your employment application form.

3. Be careful about framing interview questions that elicit or indirectly prompt information about the applicant's religious affiliation or beliefs such as asking, "Are there any particular days during the year that your absence would be necessary?" or "Do you attend any organized activities with your family?"

4. If you reject an applicant on the grounds of a religious conflict with the nature or schedule of the job (assuming the applicant volunteered the information of course), you should be certain that the reason your company cannot make an accommodation is because doing so would cause an *undue* (unreasonable) hardship such as the requiring of considerable overtime costs, a significant operational disruption, or inconsistent with the legitimate business interests of the organization as in the partial exemption that exists for religious institutions and businesses.

5. Take employee requests for religious accommodation seriously, at least until evidence proves otherwise. Ask the employee to provide you with a written statement attesting to the specific name, requirements, and conditions of their religion; what, in particular, is the job or employment conflict; and what is their requested or preferred accommodation.

Before making a decision, consult with experienced advisors concerning the company's (policy) position and implications of a decision. If the request is determined to be legitimate, then you should try to identify and offer one or more ways of easily alleviating the conflict. If the employee rejects your offer of accommodation, your obligation is complete and you can notify the employee—in writing is best—of your offer, their rejection, and an order to perform their job under existing conditions or find other employment.

6. Deal with each religious accommodation request in a thorough and expeditious manner, and handle each one on an individual basis. Blanket policies and practices that openly disfavor any applicant or employee due to their religious observances and practices should be carefully reexamined for revision, or better yet abandoned.

TYPE-SPECIFIC NONDISCRIMINATION ACTS

Pregnancy Discrimination

Pregnancy discrimination is now actually covered by the Title VII sex discrimination prohibition. It is separately set out here because of its relatively recent (1978) addition to Title VII and because it is currently the subject of substantial controversy. The 1978 amendment added pregnancy discrimination to Title VII coverage by virtue of an amendment to the definition of sex discrimination.

> (k)   The terms "because of sex" or "on the basis of sex" include, but are not limited to, because of, or on the basis of pregnancy, childbirth or related medical conditions; and women affected by pregnancy, childbirth or related medical conditions shall be treated the same for all employment-related purposes, including receipt of benefits under fringe benefit programs, as other persons not so affected but similar in their ability or inability to work, and nothing in Section 2000e-2(h) of this title shall be interpreted to permit otherwise. This subsection shall not require an employer to pay for health insurance benefits for abortion, except where the life of the mother would be endangered if the fetus were carried to term, or except where medical complications have arisen from an abortion: *Provided*, that nothing herein shall preclude an employer from providing abortion benefits or otherwise affect bargaining agreements in regard to abortion.

Because this act is part of Title VII, it is enforced by the EEOC and is subject to the Title VII administrative process.

Age Discrimination

The Age Discrimination in Employment Act (ADEA) prohibits age-based employment discrimination against individuals 40 and more years of age, as amended. According to the act, its purpose is "to promote the employment of older persons based on their ability rather than age; to prohibit arbitrary age discrimination in employment; to help employers and workers find ways of meeting problems arising from the impact of age on employment."

The age limit for individuals protected by the act was raised by 1978 amendments from 65 to 70 and again in 1988 to remove the upper age limit altogether. Those amendments also removed the upper age limit of 70 for act coverage of federal employees.

The Equal Employment Opportunity Commission is charged with administration and enforcement of the ADEA. The EEOC has issued interpretations on most of the act's provisions, with one exception: the permissibility of benefit differentials based on age under employee benefit plans. Until the EEOC issues an interpretation of this provision, employers may rely on the Department of Labor's notices or advertisements for employment and may operate a seniority system or employee benefit plan that requires or permits the involuntary retirement of an employee under age 70.

Employment agencies serving covered employers and labor unions with twenty-five or more members are also included under the provisions of the act. Employment agencies are forbidden from refusing to refer individuals for employment because of age and from classifying or referring for employment on the basis of age. Unions are forbidden from excluding or expelling individuals from membership on the basis of age.

To make a *prima facie* (presumably true) case of age discrimination, employees must first show that they belong to the protected age group (40 and over) and that they were adversely affected by the action of an employer, union, or employment agency. An employee may demonstrate adverse effect by pointing to (1) a direct act against his or her employment status based on the employee's age, (2) an act that has specific and different impact on workers aged 40 and over than on younger employees, or (3) the employer's work force, if it does not reflect the available interpretative statement.

Employers, employment agencies, and labor unions are required to maintain certain records and to make them available to the EEOC. The Age Discrimination Act of 1975 extends the prohibitions against age discrimination to recipients of federal assistance, including recipients of federal revenue sharing funds.

PROHIBITIONS AND GUIDELINES

Employer   Under the act, private employers of twenty or more persons are forbidden to

- Fail or refuse to hire, to discharge or otherwise discriminate against, any individual with respect to compensation, terms, conditions, or privileges of employment because of such individual's age.
- Limit, segregate, or classify an employee in any way that would deprive such employee of job opportunities or adversely affect employment status because of age.

- Reduce the wage rate of an employee to comply with the act.
- Indicate any "preference, limitation, specification, or discrimination" based on age in any labor pool's percentage of workers aged 40 and over.

Once an individual makes out a *prima facie* showing of age discrimination, the burden of proof shifts to the employer who must show, with some exceptions, that the employment decision was not made on the basis of age. Some defenses an employer might offer are:

- The employment decision was based on factors other than age.
- Age is a bona fide occupational qualification.
- The employment decision was made pursuant to the terms of a seniority system.

An exception to the act's requirement that employers not treat older workers differently from younger workers arises under the provision permitting benefit differentials under bona fide employee benefit plans.

Advertisements and employment applications   Help-wanted notices or advertisements that contain terms that deter employment of older persons are prohibited under the act. Such terms or phrases include "age 25 to 35," "young," "college student," "recent college graduate," "boy," or "girl." Other phrases such as "40 to 50," "age over 65," "retired person," or "supplement your pension" discriminate against others in the protected age group of 40 and over, and are therefore not permissible either.

Asking for date of birth or age on a job application form does not, by itself, violate the act. But in the case of help-wanted ads, such a request could deter older persons from applying, and therefore would be closely scrutinized to ensure a lawful purpose. The EEOC's interpretations instruct an employer to make clear on the application that the purpose for requesting the information is not prohibited under the act. One way this may be done is by including the phrase on the application, "The Age Discrimination and Employment Act of 1967 prohibits discrimination on the basis of age with respect to individuals who are at least 40," or some similar phrase that would indicate that age information will not be used unlawfully. The EEOC has noted that "employment application" refers to all written inquiries concerning a job or promotion, including resumes, preemployment inquiries, and inquiries by employees concerning terms, conditions, and privileges of employment.

Involuntary retirement   The 1978 amendments to the act provide that no seniority system or employee benefit plan can permit the forced retirement of any individual because of age. The EEOC's interpretations provide the following:

- All new and existing systems and plans are prohibited from forcing or permitting involuntary retirement, regardless of whether the plan's provisions were in effect before the enactment of ADEA or the enactment of the 1978 amendment.

- Before January 1, 1979, the provision protected individuals between 40 and 65. After that date, it applies to individuals between 40 and 70.

- Collective bargaining agreements that were in effect on September 1, 1977, were exempt from the provision until the expiration of the agreement or until January 1, 1980, whichever was earliest.

- Plans may permit individuals to elect early retirement at a specified age or at their option.

- Early retirement for reasons other than age may be required by a plan.

The following two cases exemplify court decisions in this area. The U.S. Court of Appeals at Cincinnati ruled that a 59-year-old executive who accepted a "sweetened" early retirement package when a company reorganization eliminated his job did not have a legitimate discrimination claim.

The executive's job, under the reorganization plan, was divided between two former subordinates, one in his late thirties and the other in his early fifties. At the time of the reorganization, a company official suggested to the executive that he take early retirement, with a package of benefits that amounted to more than he would have received had he been terminated. A month after being offered the early retirement package, the executive signed an agreement accepting the company's terms. He later filed suit against the company, claiming that he was discharged in violation of the ADEA.

Finding no ADEA violation, the appeals court ruled that the decision to eliminate the executive's job was made to "increase corporate efficiency" and was not reviewable by the court. The executive's decision to retire was voluntary, the court stated, citing the employee's admission that he signed the agreement of his own free will. In reaching this decision, the court asserted, "The ultimate issue is whether age was a factor" in the employer's decision to terminate the employee. In conclusion, the evidence indicated that the company had a legitimate business reason for its action.

A second decision involved a jury's $2.3 million age discrimination award to three former department store executives. This decision was upheld by the U.S. Court of Appeals (San Francisco).

Three executives, all in their fifties, brought suit against the I. Magnin Department Store chain, claiming that it violated the ADEA by pursuing a corporate policy of replacing older and highly paid executives with younger workers. They presented evidence at the trial showing that the proportion of over-40 employees in the executive work force fell from 68 percent to 24 percent between 1971 and 1980. The jury rejected the company's argument that the executives had been fired for good reason or had left voluntarily, and awarded the three executives damages ranging from $500,000 to $800,000. The company appealed the award, claiming that the jury had been improperly instructed.

Although the lower court's jury instructions were indeed erroneous, the appeals court found that the errors were harmless and did not affect the outcome. In

ADEA cases, juries should be told that there may be more than one factor in a decision to terminate an older employee and that a worker is entitled to recover if age is a factor that "made a difference" in the employer's decision. In this case, there was ample evidence that consideration of age made a difference in the company's decision to terminate the executives.

EXEMPTIONS

Bona fide executives   The ADEA permits compulsory retirement for certain executives and individuals in policy-making positions, provided certain conditions are met.

- The employee must be at least 65 but not yet 70 years of age;
- For the two-year period before retirement, the employee must have been employed in a bona fide executive or high policy-making position; and
- The employee must be entitled to immediate nonforfeitable annual retirement benefits from a pension, profit sharing, or compensation plan which amounts to at least $44,000.

An employer is free to compel retirement of an employee falling within this exemption, but is also free to keep the employee either in the same position or in a different position. According to the EEOC's interpretations, an employer may offer a position of lesser status or a part-time position to an individual who falls in the exemption provision, provided the employee is not treated "less favorably" in the new position than a younger employee.

DEFENSES

Factors other than age   An employer who can show that employment decisions with respect to older workers are based on reasonable factors other than age is not in violation of the ADEA. Like the EEOC's treatment of bona fide occupational qualifications, whether a differentiation is based on factors other than age will be decided individually, based on the following:

- An employer using age as a factor in making employment decisions may not argue that the practice is justified by a reasonable factor other than age.
- When an employment practice, including tests, is shown to have an adverse impact on individuals protected by the ADEA, it must be justified as a business necessity.
- A differentiation may not be made on the grounds that it costs more to employ older workers.
- An employer who asserts that reasonable factors other than age are the basis for employment decisions bears the burden of proving that those factors do in fact exist.

Bona fide occupational qualifications   An employer will not be in violation of the ADEA if its job classifications or qualifications are based on bona fide occupational qualifications. Whether a BFOQ exists will be determined upon an examination of the facts of a particular situation. However, the EEOC stresses that, as this is an exception to the act, the concept of a BFOQ will have "limited scope and application" and "must be narrowly construed." Thus an employer who successfully argues that a job qualification as a BFOQ must prove that

- The age limit is necessary to the essence of the business;
- Substantially all the individuals excluded from the job because of the BFOQ are in fact disqualified; or
- Some of the excluded individuals possess a disqualifying trait that cannot be determined except by reference to age.

If an employer asserts that public safety is the reason for making age a factor in employment decisions, the employer must prove that elimination of those individuals who were not within the allowable age group does in fact effectuate the goal of public safety, and that there is no alternative that would advance the goal with less discriminatory impact. State laws conflicting with the ADEA's provision for BFOQs are superseded by the federal law.

The courts have said an airline's rule barring anyone over 35 from consideration for a flight officer's job was not based on a bona fide occupational qualification. In this particular case, the U.S. Court of Appeals at Richmond rejected the company's claim that the rule was based on safety considerations because the hiring of older pilots would have impeded its crew operations and raised the risks of medical emergencies during flights. To justify a refusal to hire under the BFOQ exception, the employer must show that the BFOQ is reasonably necessary to the essential operation of its business and that there is reason to believe substantially all persons over the age limit would be unable to perform the job, or that it would be impracticable to deal with persons over the age limit on an individual basis. In this particular case, the employer did not provide sufficient evidence to prove that employing flight officers over the age of 35 would violate air safety standards. It was found that the airline's physical examination program could effectively detect potentially disabling medical conditions.

In another decision, a different federal appeals court upheld American Airline's age limit for new pilots. It was decided that the limit was based on valid safety considerations and was "reasonably necessary to the normal operations" of the airline.

The court accepted the airline's contention that the safest captain "will be experienced" with "as much of that experience as possible" with American and stressed that an airline must be accorded "great leeway and discretion" in determining safe operating procedures.

Another example is helpful in understanding this problem. A mandatory retirement age of 65 for a uniformed fire department employee was found to have violated the ADEA when applied to the job of district fire chief. The age requirement could be a proper BFOQ for other departmental jobs, but it did not meet the BFOQ requirement when applied to the district chief's job. The purpose of the ADEA is to promote employment of older persons based on their ability rather than on age. Consistent with this purpose, it is clear that the plain meaning of the phrase "bona fide *occupational* qualification" indicates age can be considered relevant in an occupation within a particular business. It would be inconsistent with the purpose of ADEA to allow a city to retire a fire chief or police chief completely able to fulfill his duties because he was unable to fulfill the duties of another position within the department such as fire captain or patrolman.

This decision is at odds with that of a Chicago appeals court in a similar case involving the forced retirement of a police chief at age 55. In that case the court, reasoning that the language of the BFOQ provision requires consideration of the particular business, not a particular occupation within that business, ruled that the proper inquiry was into the general class of law enforcement personnel rather than into the position of police chief.

Bona fide seniority systems   Employment decisions made in observance of the terms of a bona fide seniority system are exempt from challenge under the act. This exemption applies so long as the system is not a subterfuge to circumvent the purposes of the ADEA. However, the act does prohibit involuntary retirement of an employee because of age even if prescribed by a seniority system. To be considered bona fide, a system:

- Must be communicated to all employees and be applied uniformly;
- May take into account merit, capacity, and ability, but must make length of service the primary criterion for making employment decisions; and
- Should not give employees with longer service fewer rights, as such a system may, depending on the circumstances, be considered a "subterfuge to evade the purposes of the act."

EXCEPTIONS

Employee benefit and pension plans   Under the ADEA, it is not unlawful for an employer to provide lower benefits for older workers, when such a practice is dictated by the terms of a bona fide employee benefit plan which is not a subterfuge to evade the purposes of the act. However, no plan can legally prohibit the hiring of an individual or compel early retirement because of age.

A plan that permits differentials in benefits based on age to be judged nondiscriminatory under the ADEA, must satisfy three requirements.

1.   It must be a "bona fide plan"; that is, its terms must have been accurately described in writing to all participants and it must actually provide the benefits to participants. The plan must provide employees "fringe benefits" and not

wages as lower compensation to older employees based on age is strictly prohibited under the act.

2. The lower benefits must be provided in observance of "the terms of" the plan. Where a plan does not expressly require that lower benefits be provided to older workers, the exception does not apply. According to the Labor Department's interpretations, this requirement has two justifications:

   a. When the policy is an express term of a plan, employees have the opportunity to know of the policy and act accordingly.

   b. An express provision that prescribes discrimination will necessarily be applied to all employees of the same age and therefore will not allow for individual acts of discrimination.

3. It must not be a subterfuge to evade the purposes of the ADEA. In general, a plan that can justify lower benefits for older workers on the basis of age-related cost considerations will not be considered a subterfuge. In addition, there are several other requirements that a plan must meet in order not to be considered a subterfuge. An example follows.

The U.S. Court of Appeals at New York has ruled that a "bona fide" retirement plan still cannot be used as a subterfuge. In a case involving an employer who lowered mandatory retirement age from 65 to 62, seven years after the ADEA's enactment, the court placed the burden on the employer to disprove the possibility that the revised retirement plan was not a subterfuge for age discrimination. The New York appeals court found that the justification by the employer did not disprove the possibility of subterfuge. In particular, one of the reasons given, that is, improving employee morale by increasing promotional opportunities for younger workers, would, "if proved a motivating factor, justify a decision against the employer."

Apprenticeship programs   Age limits for entry into bona fide apprenticeship programs are not banned by the ADEA. The EEOC has stated there have traditionally been age limits for entry into such programs and apprenticeship "is an extension of the educational process to prepare young men and women for skilled employment." However, at the time of this writing, the EEOC is reviewing potential new regulations on age limitations for apprenticeship programs, so employers involved in bona fide apprenticeships should check on the status of new age requirements by calling their regional EEOC office.

Chapter 16

SUMMARY OF THE AMERICANS WITH DISABILITIES ACT AND OTHER LAWS PERTAINING TO DISABLED EMPLOYEES

HANDICAPPED DISABLED PERSONS DISCRIMINATION[1]

The two most essential legal violations involving handicapped applicants in the hiring process are (1) employer failures to consider reasonable accommodation needs of the handicapped and (2) failure to recruit (or rejection of) handicapped applicants solely on the basis of preferring applicants without handicaps. Prohibitions against this type of discriminatory treatment now exists for nearly every employer, and these prohibitions have been established by law because the employment community has shown little willingness to set aside prejudicial exclusion of otherwise qualified workers from employment opportunities.

Able and eager to work, handicapped job seekers are undoubtedly one of the most frequently overlooked sources of valuable applicants in the labor force pool. The social stigma attached to people with various kinds of physical and mental impairments has been in existence for decades, even centuries, and it has created bias imprints into the minds and judgments of those who do not bear the burden of such impairments. Clearly, not all people with handicaps or certain types of disabilities are capable of participation in the work force. However, studies have shown that as many as 60 percent of those with handicaps can easily adapt to normal working conditions; they are capable of being productive employees when given the opportunity to demonstrate their abilities; they are highly motivated to do a good job for those who provide meaningful employment opportunities; most require only nominal forms of accommodation (average cost is only $500); and they tend to have fewer accidents, less turnover, better attitudes, and create no impact on an employer's cost for workers' compensation insurance.

---

[1]   Levesque, *The Complete Hiring Manual*, pp. 437–438.

Like other forms of visible bias, the key to overcoming attitudinal barriers to accepting handicapped people for consideration of employment opportunities is looking at the person's skills, abilities (rather than disabilities), and motives instead of mere appearances. A major shortcoming of employers is that their human resources planning, including recruitment of workers with particular skills, has not given much thought to ways in which those with physical, sensory, or mental impairments *can* be used in their employment settings. Rather, employers have been lulled into favoring applicants who are without any form of handicap based on a continuously sufficient supply of nonhandicapped workers. Not understanding how to evaluate the minor limitations of many handicapped job seekers, job requirements, and workplace conditions, most managers have felt inadequately equipped to accommodate the handicapped employee in an accepting, comfortable way from the perspective of workplace interaction or productivity measurement.

Given these kinds of "unconscious" considerations that accompany the thought of hiring a handicapped applicant, it has simply been easier for employment decision makers to give preference to the nonhandicapped applicant even if they possess lesser skills, abilities, and experience. As you have probably learned in your own career by now, easier is not always the most prudent course of action. Further, from the purely legal point of view, giving undue preference to one applicant over another who has some protected personal characteristic is referred to as *prima facie* evidence of prohibited discrimination. But, before we get into the legal aspects of rejecting handicapped applicants in the hiring process, let's take a brief look at just a few of the evolutionary events that led up to the current type of legal protectionism applied to this group of job seekers aimed at the eradication of employment discrimination. Here are some of those events which may provide you with some additional insight into their struggle for recognition as able employees, and desire to regain independence and self-esteem.

1918	*Smith-Sears Veteran's Rehabilitation Act:* First law mandating rehabilitation for disabled veterans and providing vocational training.
1920–1965	*Smith-Fees Act:* Provided services for the physically handicapped, vocational training, placement, and counseling.
1960s	Social attitudes and national awareness began to transform from a parochial treatment (services and benefits) of the handicapped and disabled to that of providing rights and advocacy. During this period medical advances also surged in the areas of treatment methods, drugs, therapy, and prosthetic devices enabling more handicapped persons to participate actively and fully in society.
1968	*Architectural Barriers Act:* Required modifications to transportation and building facilities that would provide more accessible accommodation of the physically handicapped.
1972	*Title XVI of the Social Security Act:* Added disability benefits for disabled workers.
1973	*Vocational Rehabilitation Act:* Required federal contractor, grant recipients, and those organizations receiving federal financial

assistance to develop affirmative action plans to increase the utilization of handicapped workers and established prohibited hiring and employment practices that tended to disfavor handicapped workers.

1978 *Developmental Disabilities Act:* Provided at least partial funding of advocacy services in each state for persons with developmental disabilities which necessitated the assistance of trained professionals to help them deal with legal and administrative remedies for the protection of their rights and benefits.

Executive Order 12106: Established the EEOC as the monitoring agency to ensure that the hiring, placement, and promotion of handicapped workers in federal service met nondiscriminatory standards.

1982 Forty-five states had adopted physical handicap nondiscrimination laws; among these states only five of them excluded private sector employers, and those states are Alabama, Arkansas, Idaho, Mississippi, and South Dakota. The five remaining states without laws equivalent to federal standards were Arizona, Delaware, North Dakota, South Carolina, and Wyoming.

1990 *Americans with Disabilities Act:* Supplemented the 1973 Vocational Rehabilitation Act (which only applied to public sector employers and those contractors or financial recipients of federal funds) by requiring that all other employers comply with nondiscrimination employment standards and practices concerning disabled and otherwise handicapped, yet qualified, applicants and employees.

How to Avoid Physical Handicap/Disability Violations[2]

There are four principal hiring process areas in which employers tend to find it particularly difficult to refrain from discriminatory violations:

1. *Employment Office:* Make sure that your personnel or employment office location where applications are filed is easily accessible to those with walking and climbing disabilities.

2. *Assistance:* Identify employees or others who can provide assistance to applicants with sight, hearing, and writing impairments during the application, testing, and interviewing process.

3. *Interviewing:* Refrain from asking questions about the existence of handicaps or disabilities, but rather focus on the distinguishing type and level of each applicant's ability to perform essential job functions.

4. *Physical Examinations:* Do not require that an applicant undergo a preemployment medical examination merely because of their handicap or disability when you would not require the same examination of any other applicant. You may, however, wish to let all applicants know that an offer of employment is

---

[2] Levesque, *The Complete Hiring Manual,* pp. 441–442.

conditional on passing a job-related physical exam and other preemployment considerations concerning their suitability to the job and your company (such as satisfactory results of driving records, prior employment, and the like).

If you have any doubt or concern about a handicapped or disabled applicant's ability to perform the job being applied for, an alternative to having the applicant undergo a physical exam would be to contact prior employers to ascertain the existence of *significant* difficulties in performing a similar job.

What Are the Violations Resulting in Discrimination Against the Physically Handicapped/Disabled?[3]

There are two primary sources of federal law that create the legal standards for determining what hiring and other employment practices constitute employer violations: the 1973 Vocational Rehabilitation Act and the 1990 Americans with Disabilities Act. The 1973 Rehabilitation Act has been applicable to state and local public entities, as well as federal contractors and grant recipients, since its inception. Since then, public pressure has mounted concerning discriminatory treatment of persons with various handicaps or disabilities by private sector employers. Consequently, in 1990, Congress enacted the Americans with Disabilities Act (ADA) to bring private sector employers (with twenty-five or more employees by July 1992 and fifteen or more employees by July 1994) into compliance. The ADA also gave Congress the opportunity to redefine (liberalize) distinctions between "handicapped persons" under the 1973 act and "disabled persons" under the 1990 act, incorporate 1973 act applicability to public entities (broadening their scope of compliance), and establish dates and standards for correction of architectural "facilities" barriers.

An overview of these two laws should provide you with a better understanding of how to examine your company's present hiring efforts and practices, and thereby determine if there exists internal conditions that are likely to prompt violations. Similar state laws should also be fully considered with respect to legal requirements and prohibited employment practices.

1973 VOCATIONAL REHABILITATION ACT

Within this law, there are two sections and three definitions with which you should gain familiarity:

Section 503 requires the development and pursuit of affirmative action hiring plans for contractors or subcontractors receiving federal funds in excess of $2,500 per year; it compels employer consideration of hiring and promoting "qualified handicapped individuals"; and such requirements are enforceable by the Office of Federal Contract Compliance Programs (OFCCP) within the Department of Labor (DOL). The courts have determined that legal suits cannot be brought against employers who violate provisions of the act, however the courts have upheld the right of DOL to discontinue funding if *any* part of a recipient employer's action violates

---

[3]   Levesque, *The Complete Hiring Manual*, pp. 438–439.

this section, even if the violation involves employment outside the area of the program or project being funded.

Federal regulations further require that *any* federal contractor or subcontractor having a federal contract of $50,000 or more, and having fifty or more employees, must prepare and maintain an affirmative action plan (AAP) for the employment of handicapped persons at each of its work locations. Unlike AAP requirements under Executive Order 11246, applicable employers are not required to establish goals and timetables for hiring handicapped workers, but rather they must periodically review personnel procedures, examine the validity of physical and mental requirements of jobs, and to provide reasonable accommodation and workplace accessibility.

Section 504 applies to recipients of federal financial assistance (grants, loans, services, and property) and prohibits discrimination against qualified handicapped individuals in programs or activities supported by such federal assistance. The major objective of this section is to ensure accessibility for *qualified* handicapped persons, rather than all forms of handicaps or disabilities. This section is administered by the departments of Health and Human Services, and Education, and violations are enforceable in court when not resolved at the administrative level.

A *handicapped person* is any person who:

- Has a physical or mental impairment that substantially limits one or more major life activities (e.g., caring for oneself, performing manual tasks, walking, seeing, hearing, speaking, learning, and working);
- Has a record of such an impairment (has a history of, or has been misclassified as having, a physical or mental impairment that substantially limits one or more major life activities); or
- Is regarded as having such an impairment, which may mean:
    —Having a physical or mental impairment that does not substantially limit major life activities but is treated by an employer as constituting such a limitation;
    —Having a physical or mental impairment that substantially limits major life activities only as a result of the attitudes of others toward such impairment; or
    —Having no physical or mental impairment but is perceived or treated by an employer as having such an impairment.

A *physical or mental impairment* is defined as a condition that weakens, diminishes, restricts, or otherwise damages the individual's physical or mental ability to perform the requisite functions of a given job. Impairment need not affect the individual's general employability—only that it serves as a bar to employment—nor does it have to be a current condition (epilepsy, prior history of drug addiction, previous back ailments, etc.). Federal regulations define impairment as:

- Any physiological disorder or condition, cosmetic disfiguration, or anatomical loss affecting a body system.

- A mental or psychological disorder, including mental retardation and specific learning disabilities.
- Various disabling and debilitating diseases and conditions (tuberculosis, cancer, AIDS, etc.), and (current) drug addiction and alcoholism.

A *qualified handicapped individual* is the primary person for which legal protection applies and consists of persons who can perform the essential functions of a job with reasonable accommodation. In this regard, employers are not expected to abandon legitimate job requirements or suffer burdensome sacrifices in their effort to provide the kind of accommodation that may be needed by some qualified handicapped workers. Rather, employers are expected to make reasonable changes in order to accommodate the otherwise qualified handicapped applicant, and there is a three-part analysis employers should go through when considering handicapped applicants for employment:

1. Whether the applicant is capable of performing the job (possesses required skills, training, experience, etc.).
2. If not, whether the applicant would be able to perform the job if the employer provides some type of reasonable accommodation.
3. Whether these circumstances would impose an undue economic hardship, unsafe working conditions for the applicant or other employees, or any other reason to reject the applicant on the basis of a sound bona fide occupational qualification (e.g., a blind person applying for the position of bus driver).

Reasonable accommodation is not defined per se but rather requires some subjective judgment on the part of employers as to the kinds and costs of accommodation (devices or architectural changes) necessary for the employment of a particular qualified handicapped applicant. However, examples are provided in federal guidelines, and they include such actions as making facilities accessible to and usable by handicapped persons (a *prima facie* case could be made if a handicapped applicant cannot gain access to your employment office to fill out an application form), acquiring or modifying equipment or devices to be used by handicapped persons for job performance, redesigning job tasks, instituting part-time or modified work schedules, and introducing similar methods that would allow these individuals to perform work in a normal fashion. Accommodation need not be provided if the employer can establish that doing so would present an undue economic or other significant employment hardship.

Consequently, the four reasons (defenses) an employer may refuse to hire a handicapped applicant are:

1. The handicap is such that the applicant is *unable to perform essential functions of the job* and is therefore not protected by law since they are not an "otherwise qualified" individual.

2. The handicap would prove to be threatening or dangerous to the *health and safety* of the applicant and/or other employees in the work unit.

3. The necessary scope, nature, and responsibilities of the job itself creates a bona fide occupational qualification that prohibits the hiring of a person with certain types of impairments.

4. The applicant's accommodation would prove to create an *undue hardship* on the employer with respect to the type, cost, or delay in acquiring the kind of accommodation needed.

1990 AMERICANS WITH DISABILITIES ACT

For all practical purposes, this federal law is much the same as the 1973 Vocational Rehabilitation Act, but it expands coverage to *all* employers with twenty-five or more employees as of July 1992, and employers with fifteen or more employees as of July 1994. Signed into law in July 1990, the provisions of the act essentially create a national policy governing public accommodation and employment treatment of handicapped disabled persons.

The ADA is comprised of five sections:

Title I makes it illegal to discriminate against a qualified individual with a disability in employment and imposes an obligation for employers to make reasonable accommodation to the disability unless doing so would impose an undue hardship.

Regulations and Interpretive Guidelines to implement Title I were published by the EEOC on July 26, 1991 (29 Code of Federal Regulations Part 1630).

Title II makes it illegal for state or local governments to discriminate against a qualified individual with a disability in the provision of public services. Title II also includes requirements regarding the accessibility of public transportation for individuals with disabilities.

Title III makes it illegal for public accommodations to discriminate against individuals with disabilities in the provision of goods, benefits, services, facilities, privileges, advantages, or accommodations. Public accommodations must be accessible to persons with disabilities. Examples of public accommodations covered by the ADA are places of lodging; restaurants; places of public gatherings like an auditorium; sales or retail establishments such as a bakery or clothing store; offices of health care providers; places of recreation such as amusement parks or health spas; and social service establishments such as homeless shelters and adoption agencies.

Title III requires existing public accommodations to be made accessible and architectural barriers to be removed where it is "readily achievable" or where it is easily accomplishable and able to be carried out without much difficulty or expense by January 26, 1992. Commercial facilities and public accommodations which are designed and built for first occupancy later than January 26, 1993, must be accessible and usable by individuals with disabilities, unless doing so would be structurally impracticable.

Regulations implementing Title III were promulgated by the Department of Justice on July 26, 1992 (28 Code of Federal Regulations Part 36).

Title IV requires common carriers engaged in interstate communication to insure that telecommunications systems are available to individuals with hearing and speech impairments and to provide various technological accommodations.

Title V is the "catch-all" title. Among other provisions, retaliation against individuals who exercise their rights under the Act is made illegal, and the federal Rehabilitation Act of 1973 is amended to exclude current users of illegal drugs from the protections of the Rehabilitation Act.

Due to the significant impact Title I of the ADA has on employees, the following summary of its provisions and employer obligations is provided for your reference and use as a compliance/implementation tool. This summary is part of a paper prepared by Orrick, Herrington & Sutcliffe, and distributed to members of the Sacramento, CA, Human Resource Management Association.

THE ADA: NEW FEDERAL RIGHTS FOR DISABLED EMPLOYEES[4]

I. INTRODUCTION

A. Purpose of the ADA

Title I of the Americans with Disabilities Act of 1990 (ADA), the employment-related provisions of which become effective on July 26, 1992, prohibits workplace and employment discrimination against individuals with disabilities. The purpose of the ADA is to provide a clear and comprehensive national mandate with enforceable standards for the elimination of discrimination against the estimated 43 million Americans with disabilities.

The ADA is fundamentally different from earlier civil rights legislation. Unlike Title VII and the Age Discrimination in Employment Act, the ADA not only prohibits discrimination but also requires employers to provide, at their own expense, "reasonable accommodation" for disabled employees.

In addition, unlike the Federal Rehabilitation Act of 1973, 29 U.S.C. Section 701 et seq. (Rehabilitation Act), which applies only to federal contractors and employers that are recipients of federal assistance, the ADA covers private employers generally, without regard to their dealings with the federal government.

The ADA is not a crystal-clear model of legislation, and employers may find it difficult to determine in advance whether they are complying with the ADA. This is because each case will require a detailed factual analysis of the essential functions of the job as they relate to the individual capabilities of the applicant or employee. Trying to

---

[4]   From a paper prepared by Orrick, Herrington & Sutcliffe, Sacramento, CA, 1992. All rights reserved. Reprinted with permission.

determine if an accommodation is reasonable adds yet another layer of complication.

Administration of the employment provisions of the ADA is placed in the Equal Employment Opportunity Commission (EEOC), which has now promulgated final regulations interpreting the provisions of the ADA (29 C.F.R. Part 1630), a memorandum giving further interpretative guidance, and a Technical Assistance Manual. The regulations define key terms under the ADA, but they also make clear that they are only guidelines for the case-by-case determinations that must be made under the ADA. The Technical Assistance Manual provides guidance on the practical application of legal requirements established in the statute and the regulations, as well as a directory of outside resources which offer employers assistance in effecting ADA compliance.

Even though most states and many cities and counties have their own antidiscrimination statutes, the ADA may differ significantly from those laws, both as to the scope of the conditions to which it applies and as to the remedies available. Employers are now faced with evaluating their job decisions under federal, state, and local law to make sure no prohibited discrimination takes place.

This review will focus on both the new legal rules imposed by the ADA and the practical problems employers may face in complying with this new law.

B. Basic Discrimination Rules Under the ADA

1. Which Employers Are Covered

Title I of the ADA, governing employment, takes effect July 26, 1992. At that time, all employers with twenty-five or more employees will be covered and required to comply. Employers with fifteen to twenty-four employees will come under the act on July 26, 1994—an extension designed to help smaller businesses to manage the costs of compliance. Employers with fewer than fifteen employees are exempt from the ADA, although they may be covered by state and local disability discrimination laws.

2. What Is Prohibited

The ADA prohibits discrimination against a qualified individual based on his disability with regard to application, hiring, advancement, compensation, training, discharge or other terms, conditions, and privileges of employment.

The final EEOC regulations further specify that such discrimination is unlawful with respect to:

a. Recruitment and job application procedures;

b. Hiring, promotion, transfer, termination, and layoff and similar status changes;

c. Rates of and changes in compensation;

    d. Job assignments and classifications, organizational structures, position descriptions, progression and seniority;

    e. Leaves of absence, sick leave, or any other leave;

    f. Fringe benefits, whether or not administered by the employer;

    g. Selection and financial support for assorted training procedures and programs;

    h. Activities sponsored by a covered entity, including social and recreational programs;

    i. Any other term, condition, or privilege of employment.

Other prohibited activities include limiting, segregating, and classifying disabled applicants or employees in ways that adversely affect employment opportunities and making contractual or other arrangements that have the effect of subjecting applicants or employees with disabilities to prohibited forms of discrimination.

3. What Is Required

Employers must make *reasonable accommodations* to the known disability of an otherwise qualified individual, unless the employer can demonstrate that the accommodation would impose an *undue hardship* on the employer. *Undue hardship* is defined by the ADA as "an action that is excessively costly, extensive, substantial or disruptive, or that would fundamentally alter the nature or operation of the business."

II. WHO IS DISABLED?

A. The Basic Definitions of the Act

Employers may find it frustrating trying to determine who is "disabled" within the meaning of the ADA. Unlike gender or age, disability is not necessarily subject to an easy and objective standard.

Under the ADA, a "disability" is defined as:

- A physical or mental impairment that "substantially limits" one or more of the "major life activities" of such individual;

- A record of such an impairment; or

- The perception that one has such an impairment.

This definition is the same as the Rehabilitation Act's definition of a "handicap." Whether a person has a disability is determined in the first instance without regard to the availability of mitigating measures, such as reasonable accommodations or auxiliary aids.

Each of the major terms of the statutory definitions has now been further addressed by the EEOC's regulations:

1. Physical or Mental Impairment

"Physical or mental impairment" is defined as (1) any physiological disorder or cosmetic disfigurement or an anatomical loss affecting a major body system or (2) any mental or psychological disorder, such as mental retardation, emotional illness, or specific learning disabilities.

These categories do not include pregnancy or characteristic predisposition to illness or disease. Similarly, advanced age is not in itself an impairment within the regulation's definition, although various medical conditions commonly associated with advanced age might be.

A physical or mental impairment does not constitute a disability unless its severity results in a "substantial limitation" of one or more "major life activities."

2. Major Life Activities

Under the final regulations, "major life activities" are defined as "functions, such as caring for oneself, performing manual tasks, walking, seeing, hearing, speaking, breathing, learning, and working."

For example, a paraplegic will have difficulty in the major life activity of walking; a deaf person will have substantial difficulty in hearing, another major life activity. By contrast, persons with minor problems, such as an infected finger, are not impaired in a major life activity and therefore are not considered "disabled" under the ADA.

3. Substantial Limitation

An impairment "substantially limits" a major life activity if the disabled individual is either unable to perform that activity or is "significantly restricted as to the condition, manner or duration under which she/he can perform that activity." In both cases, the individual's level of disability is measured against that of an average person performing the same activity. Such determinations must be made on a case-by-case basis, focusing on the disabled individual's inherent capacity, irrespective of mitigating medicines, devices, or other measures.

To make such determinations, employers should take into account: (a) the severity and nature of the impairment, (b) the duration or expected duration of the impairment, and (c) the permanent or long-term impact of or resulting from the impairment.

Although an individual need not to be completely incapable of working to be considered substantially limited in that major life activity, the inability to perform a particular job for a specific employer, or to perform a specialized job, does not constitute a substantial limitation. However, a disabled person is substantially limited in working if he is "significantly restricted in the ability to perform either a class of jobs or a broad range of jobs in various classes as compared to an average person."

Such determinations should only be made if the individual is not disabled in any other major life activity. Employers must make these determinations on a case-by-case basis, and they may consider: (a) the worker's geographical area, (b) the job from which the disabled person has been disqualified and the number and types of similar jobs from which the disabled person would be disqualified in the geographical area, and/or (c) the job from which the disabled person has been disqualified and the number and types of dissimilar jobs in the geographic area from which the individual would be disqualified.

A person is considered as having a disability when the individual's major life activities are restricted as to the manner, conditions or duration of performance in comparison to most people. For example, just because an individual cannot walk continuously for 10 miles does not mean that he is "disabled," inasmuch as few of us can walk that far without taking a rest.

4. Perceived Impairments

The perception that one has an impairment that substantially limits a major life activity is otherwise stated as "being regarded as having such an impairment." 29 C.F.R. § 1630.2(g). An example would be severe physical disfigurement.

The EEOC regulations adopted under the ADA reflect the encompassing view of the Senate Labor and Human Resources Committee, which suggested that regulations implementing the Rehabilitation Act should also apply to the ADA. This has largely been the effect of the new ADA regulations. Under this approach, a physical or mental impairment is any physiological disorder or condition, cosmetic disfigurement, or anatomical loss affecting one or more of the body systems, or any mental or psychological disorder, such as mental retardation, organic brain syndrome, emotional or mental illness, and specific learning disabilities. Certain diseases included are orthopedic, visual, speech, and hearing impairments; cerebral palsy; epilepsy; muscular dystrophy; multiple sclerosis; infection with HIV; cancer; heart disease; and diabetes.

By including as a "disability" the perception that one is disabled, the ADA means to protect persons who do not have an impairment but, by virtue of stereotyping and prejudices, are considered impaired. Serious burn victims with scarred faces come under this category, as do those with controlled medical conditions, such as certain diabetics and epileptics.

B. Exclusions from the Definition of Disability

1. Various Excluded Matters

Statutorily excluded from the ADA's protection are homosexuality, bisexuality, transvestism, transsexualism, pedophilia, exhibitionism, voyeurism, gender identity disorders not resulting from physical impairments, compulsive gambling, kleptomania, pyromania, or psychoactive substance use disorders resulting from current illegal use of drugs. The regulations specifically exclude these phenomena from the definitions of "disability" and "qualified individual with a disability."

Also, physical characteristics, such as blue eyes or black hair, are not covered. Neither are environmental, cultural, or economic disadvantages.

2. Drugs and Alcohol—Specific Provisions

The ADA has explicit provisions that address alcohol and drug abuse or addiction. An individual who is currently engaging in the illegal use of drugs is not protected by the ADA when the employer acts on the basis of the illegal drug use. The regulations specifically exclude such persons from the definitions of "disability" and "qualified individual with a disability." In fact, an employer can refuse to hire an individual solely on this ground. Furthermore, an employer may seek reasonable assurances that applicants or employees are not current users of illegal drugs.

Under the ADA, "drugs" means controlled substances prescribed under the Controlled Substances Act, and illegal drug use includes possession or distribution. It does not include the use of a drug taken under supervision by a licensed health care professional, or other uses authorized by federal law.

However, an employer cannot discriminate against an individual who has successfully completed or is participating in a supervised drug rehabilitation program and is no longer using illegal drugs, or who has otherwise been rehabilitated successfully. It is not a violation for an employer to adopt or administer reasonable policies or procedures, including drug testing, designed to ensure that an individual who has or is undergoing rehabilitation is no longer using the illegal drugs. Drug testing is not considered a "medical examination" under the ADA.

The ADA explicitly allows an employer to prohibit the illegal use of drugs and the use of alcohol at work by all employees, to require that employees not be under the influence of alcohol or illegal drugs at work, and to require that employees behave in conformance with the requirements established under the Drug-Free Workplace Act of 1988. The employer can require that employees comply with the standards established by the various federal agencies if the employees are employed in an area subject to those regulations.

An employer cannot discriminate against addicts and alcoholics because of their status, but an employer may hold an employee who engages in the illegal use of drugs or who is an alcoholic to the same qualification standards for employment or job performance and behavior to which it holds other employees, even if any unsatisfactory performance or behavior is related to the drug use or alcoholism of the employee. For example, the employer can require an alcoholic to be sober at the workplace and to meet required job performance standards. If the alcoholic employee comes to work inebriated, he can be disciplined. However, the employer cannot refuse to hire an applicant on the basis of the applicant's alcoholic past.

III. THE REQUIREMENT OF QUALIFICATION

Under the ADA, an individual with a disability is qualified for a job if, with or without reasonable accommodation, he can perform the essential functions of the job. This avoids the ongoing debate under the Rehabilitation Act on whether the accommodation should be considered in evaluating a person's qualifications.

A. Qualification Standards

The final regulations define "qualification standards" as "personal and professional attributes including the skill, experience, education, physical, medical, safety, and other requirements established by a covered entity as requirements which an individual must meet" to be eligible for the position held or desired.

Although an employer is not permitted to use such standards if they screen out or tend to screen out disabled individuals on the basis of their disability, qualification standards may be applied if they are shown to be job related for the position in question and consistent with business necessity.

To qualify for protection under the ADA, individuals with disabilities need satisfy only "the requisite skills, experience, education, and other job-related requirements of the employment position" held or desired. Determinations of whether an individual with a disability is qualified within the meaning of the ADA must be made at the time of the employment action in question.

The chance of future incapacity does not make an individual unqualified. Nor does speculation that insurance premiums may rise as a result of hiring or maintaining disabled employees have any allowable role in the determination process, although the regulations do not address the issue, and the EEOC has stated it will continue to analyze it.

B. Essential Functions of the Job

"Essential functions" are defined in the regulations as the fundamental, nonmarginal duties of the employment position either held or desired by a disabled individual. A job function may be regarded as essential if the employment position exists for the performance of that function, the function may be distributed to a limited number of employees available to perform it, or the function is so highly specialized that an expert is specially hired to perform it.

Employers may consider various factors as evidence that a particular function of a job is essential. The list includes the employer's own judgment, written job descriptions, the amount of time the function requires, the consequences of not requiring the incumbent to perform the function, and the past or current experience of past incumbents on the job.

Notably, the terms of a collective bargaining agreement may also be considered as evidence that a function is essential.

Although the list is not intended to be exhaustive, all of the enumerated factors are relevant and must be considered when available. Furthermore, although written job descriptions are relevant, an employer is not required to maintain them. Finally, the regulations are not intended to "second-guess an employer's business judgment regarding production standards, whether qualitative or quantitative."

The ADA provides that the employer's judgment "is considered" as to what functions of a job are essential. This means the employer's opinion as to what is an essential function of a particular job should be given some deference. But how much deference is unclear.

The ADA is not intended to undermine an employer's ability to choose and maintain qualified workers. An employer is still free to select the most qualified applicant available and to make decisions based on reasons unrelated to the existence or consequence of a disability. According to the Senate Labor and Human Resources Committee,

> Suppose an employer has an opening for a typist and two persons apply for the job, one being an individual with a disability who types 50 words per minute and the other being an individual without a disability who types 75 words per minute. The employer is permitted to choose the applicant with the higher typing speed. On the other hand, if the two applicants are, one, an individual with a hearing impairment who requires a telephone headset with an amplifier and the other, an individual without a disability, both of whom have the same typing speed, the employer is not permitted to choose the individual without a disability because of the need to provide the needed reasonable accommodation. The employer would be permitted to reject the applicant with a disability and choose the other applicant for reasons not related to the disability or the accommodation or otherwise prohibited by this legislation.

C. Relationship Between Job Criteria and Applicant Ability

Three requirements attempt to assure a fit between job criteria and an applicant's actual ability to do the job:

1. Persons with disabilities are not to be disqualified because of the inability to perform nonessential or marginal functions of the job;

2. Any selection criteria that screen out or tend to screen out must be job related and consistent with business necessity; and

3. Reasonable accommodation to assist persons with disabilities to meet legitimate criteria must be provided.

For example, an employer may deny a job to an individual with a disability if the individual fails to meet any one selection criterion that concerns any essential, nonmarginal aspect of the job. However, that criterion must have been carefully tailored to determine the individual's actual ability to perform that essential aspect of the job. If the criterion meets this test, it is nondiscriminatory on its face and otherwise lawful under the ADA. The criterion, however, may not be used to exclude an applicant with a disability if the criterion can be satisfied by the applicant with a reasonable accommodation.

An employer cannot conduct a medical examination or make inquiries of an applicant as to whether the applicant is an individual with a disability or as to the nature or severity of any disability. The final regulations also include extensive sections regarding medical examinations and inquiries, and employment entrance examinations. The most significant of these is the new requirement that employers may not ask questions about a job applicant's workers' compensation history at the preoffer stage. The employer can, however, make preemployment inquiries into the ability of an applicant to perform job-related functions, and as to whether an individual who has a history of illegal drug abuse is no longer using illegal drugs.

After an employment offer, an employer may require a medical examination and may condition an offer of employment on the results of the examination, if all entering employees are subjected to the same examination regardless of disability.

Information so obtained must be collected and maintained separately and confidentially. Disclosure is permitted to supervisors and managers with a legitimate need to know about necessary restrictions or accommodations for the employee, to first aid and safety personnel if the disability might require emergency treatment, and to government officials investigating compliance with the ADA. In addition, an employer may conduct voluntary medical examinations, including taking voluntary medical histories, which are part of an employee health program available to employees at that work site.

Note that these restrictions may require employers to change their application procedures and forms. A careful review of those currently in place is required to avoid problems under the ADA.

The qualifications to be assessed are those that exist when the employment decision is being made and not, in most circumstances, those that may occur in the future.

IV.   COMPARISON TO REHABILITATION ACT OF 1973

The Rehabilitation Act applies to only a small subset of employers. Section 503 of that act applies only to federal contractors with contracts of at least $2,500.00. These contractors must have an affirmative action plan and nondiscrimination clauses in their contract. Section 504 covers only those employers who receive federal assistance, usually in the forms of grants. Section 504 does not require affirmative action, but does prohibit discrimination against any individual with a disability.

The definitions, obligations, and policies are otherwise the same as those in the ADA. Throughout the ADA and embedded in its legislative history are references to the Rehabilitation Act, with explicit instructions to follow examples of the Rehabilitation Act and its implementing regulations and consequently the case law interpretations as guidance in understanding and fleshing out the ADA. At no place are the standards of the ADA to be construed as less stringent than those of the Rehabilitation Act.

Except for the limited coverage of certain employers, and the affirmative action obligations of federal contractors, the two statutes are the same. Those with federal contracts or federal assistance now have to abide also by the ADA, but for the reasons discussed above, this should not result in additional costs or obligations.

V. THE DUTY TO MAKE REASONABLE ACCOMMODATION SHORT OF UNDUE HARDSHIP

Employers are required to make reasonable accommodation for otherwise qualified individuals for their "known" physical or mental limitations unless "undue hardship" is shown. The obligation is generally triggered by a request from the individual with the disability. Indeed, the ADA's legislative history states that it would be inappropriate to accommodate absent a request, especially where it might adversely affect the individual.

The following procedure for identifying a reasonable accommodation is suggested:

- Look at the particular job involved and determine its purpose and its essential functions;
- Consult with and involve the individual in deciding on possible accommodations;
- If unable to agree on a solution (perhaps because of inadequate information), distinguish between essential and nonessential job tasks and aspects of the work environment;
- Propose the accommodation that is most appropriate and that does not pose an undue hardship on the employer's operation, or, if there is undue hardship, permit the employee to provide his own accommodation.

In situations where there is more than a single effective accommodation, the employer may choose the accommodation that is less expensive or easier for the employer to implement so long as the selected accommodation provides meaningful equal employment opportunity.

Reasonable accommodation is not defined in the ADA. Instead, the statute provides some nonexhaustive examples of what may be considered reasonable accommodation:

- Making existing facilities used by employees readily accessible to and usable by individuals with disabilities; and
- Job restructuring, part-time or modified work schedules, reassignment to a vacant position, acquisition or modification of equipment or devices, appropriate adjustment or modifications of examinations, training materials or policies, the provision of qualified readers or interpreters, and other similar accommodations for individuals with disabilities.

The reference above to "reassignment to a vacant position" appears to mean that bumping another employee out of a position is not required. These examples are reflected in the EEOC's final regulations.

The final regulations define "reasonable accommodations" as (1) modifications to the application process that enable qualified applicants with disabilities to be considered for the positions they desire, (2) modifications to the work environment or to the manner in which positions are performed that enable qualified individuals with disabilities to perform the essential functions of those positions, or (3) modifications that enable a covered entity's disabled employees to enjoy equal benefits and privileges of employment as are enjoyed by all employees.

Under the regulations, reasonable accommodations may include improved accessibility to the facility, improved usability and accessibility in work areas and nonwork areas (including rest rooms), various forms job restructuring, including reassignment to positions that become vacant in a reasonable time, acquisition or modification of equipment, examinations, training materials, or policies, the provision of readers or interpreters, and possibly even the provision of personal assistants to help disabled employees with specified job-related duties.

In order to fulfill the requirements of the final regulations, employers may need to "initiate informal, interactive process[es]" with qualified individuals with disabilities in need of the accommodations. This process "should identify the precise limitations resulting from the disability and potential reasonable accommodations that could overcome those limitations." Nevertheless, the accommodation should be made with the employee's consent or at his request; it should not be imposed upon an unwilling recipient.

The Senate Committee noted that many individuals with disabilities do not require any reasonable accommodation. Instead, the only change necessary for such persons to achieve equal employment opportunity is a change in employer attitudes about them.

A. Case Examples of Reasonable Accommodation Under the Rehabilitation Act

Under Sections 503 and 504 of the Rehabilitation Act, a handicap discrimination inquiry does not end with a finding that a person is unable to perform the essential functions of the job. Instead, the investigating agency or the reviewing court must also "consider whether any 'reasonable accommodation' by the employer would enable the handicapped person to perform those functions." *School Bd. of Nassau County, Fla.* v. *Arline*, 480 U.S. 273, 287 n.17 (1987).

1. Job Restructuring

   a. Accommodation Required

      (1) *Davis* v. *Frank*, 711 F. Supp. 447 (N.D. Ill. 1989): Davis, a U.S. Postal Service ("USPS") employee, was deaf since birth. USPS

denied her applications for time- and attendance-clerk positions because she would not be able to answer the telephone. However, USPS never suggested any alternative procedure to accommodate Davis.

The court held that Davis's deafness posed no health or safety risks to others within the workplace. The "essential functions" of the clerical job did not include answering the phone; it was just the habit of Davis's branch. Therefore, Davis could perform the paperwork duties required even though she was deaf. Further, the court suggested the following "inexpensive accommodations" to perform the communication duties required:

- Laminated cards containing phrases Davis would need to use frequently;
- Prepared lists of terms and questions frequently encountered by the time and attendance clerk, to allow people to point to the topic they want to discuss and thereby make lip-reading easier;
- Elementary training that could be given at no cost to the Postal Service to make hearing employees aware of common mistakes in communicating with deaf employees;
- Training in basic signs and finger spelling for those few hearing employees who might come into contact with Davis on a frequent basis, training that could be completed in about one hour; and
- Expanding the use of a TTY keyboard (purchased for minimal cost) for the hearing impaired as a means of making written communication faster. 711 F. Supp. at 454.

The court concluded that these accommodations did not rise to the level of "undue hardship" and ordered USPS to institute the accommodations.

b. Accommodation Not Required

(1) *DiPompo* v. *West Point Military Academy*, 770 F. Supp. 887 (S.D.N.Y. 1991): DiPompo, a dyslexic, was refused hire as a structural firefighter at the U.S. Military Academy, West Point, because he could not read at a 12th grade level. The ability to read at a 12th grade level was a requirement imposed by West Point on all applicants for the position of structural firefighter.

The court held that West Point could not reasonably accommodate DiPompo's dyslexia so as to enable him to perform the essential duties of the position. The duties of a structural firefighter required substantial reading, including the ability to identify chemically dangerous and hazardous materials through words, numbers, and symbols, in both emergency and nonemergency settings, and to consult an extensive guidebook containing the proper procedures to be followed in the event a dangerous material was encountered. A structural firefighter also had to dispatch equipment to the scene of a fire while working alone on "housewatch" duty, a function which could not be performed absent the ability to obtain essential information from a computer terminal or printed cards. It was not reasonable to expect West Point to engage in a major restructuring of the position by hiring a full-time dispatcher in order to eliminate housewatch duty, nor was it feasible to have another firefighter read the contents of the hazardous materials manual to DiPompo as the need arose, accommodations proposed by DiPompo. Further, in light of the potentially disastrous consequences inherent in firefighting, even if these steps could be taken to alleviate the reading burden faced by DiPompo, his dyslexia could not be accommodated without creating an unreasonable safety risk to himself and others.

(2) *Guice-Mills* v. *Derwinski*, 772 F. Supp. 188 (S.D.N.Y. 1991): Guice-Mills suffered from clinical depression during her employment as a head nurse for a Veterans Administration hospital. When her symptoms of depression and severe anxiety persisted despite several medical leaves of absence, Guice-Mills took disability retirement after the hospital denied her request to alter her work schedule. As an alternative, the hospital had proposed to Guice-Mills that she be reassigned to a staff nursing position with no reduction in pay, but she considered such a move to be a demotion and refused the position.

   The district court rejected Guice-Mills' claim that the hospital had failed to reasonably accommodate her by refusing to modify her daily hours from 8:00 A.M. to 4:30 P.M. to 10:00 A.M. to 6:30 P.M. for an indefinite period. It was critical for a head nurse to work an "administrative work week," that is, commence work at 7:00, 7:30, or 8:00 A.M., to properly supervise her unit. Creating an exception for Guice-Mills would have imposed an unreasonable administrative burden on the hospital to attain adequate staffing prior to 10:00 A.M. Moreover, the hospital's proposed transfer of Guice-Mills to a staff nurse position at the later shift, with no reduction in pay, was deemed by the court to constitute a reasonable accommodation.

(3) *Fields* v. *Lyng*, 705 F. Supp. 1134 (D. Md. 1988), *aff'd*, 888 F.2d 1385 (4th Cir. 1989): Fields, who was employed as a labor relations specialist for the U.S. Department of Agriculture Research Service, suffered from "Borderline Personality

Organization," with side effects of anxiety over travel and kleptomania.

The district court found that the Service could not accommodate Fields's handicap because his position required extensive travel. Additionally, his kleptomania had weakened his reputation for integrity, undermining his effectiveness in negotiations. To accommodate these handicaps would have required "creating an entirely new position or restructuring his duties." 705 F. Supp. at 1137. *(Note that kleptomania is specifically excluded as a disability under the ADA.)*

2. Reassignment or Transfer to Another Job

"Although [employers] are not required to find another job for an employee who is not qualified for the job he or she was doing, they cannot deny an employee alternative employment opportunities reasonably available under employer's existing policies." Furthermore, an employer is not required to create a job for a handicapped person unable to perform the present job functions. *Arline,* 480 U.S. at 289 n.19, *citing* 45 CFR § 84.12 (1985).

a. Accommodation Required

Rhone v. *U.S. Dept. of Army,* 665 F. Supp. 734 (E.D. Mo. 1987): Rhone was a twenty-four-year civilian employee of the U.S. Army. He was four years short of his retirement. In 1980, Rhone was diagnosed as having sarcoidosis, and he became anorexic, lost weight, and was easily fatigued. As a result, Rhone's doctor recommended various changes and restructuring of Rhone's duties, such as limiting him to a position that required work on only one shift.

Although the Army attempted to accommodate Rhone by transferring him to another department, the court held that the Army's efforts were insufficient because: (1) he was assigned to a position requiring work on more than one shift, (2) he was passed over for a position of higher rank, and (3) he was not selected for other positions for which he was qualified. The court relied on the *Handbook on Reasonable Accommodation* published by the Office of Personnel Management, which states:

> In cases of current Federal employees who become disabled after employment, agencies have a responsibility to make every effort for their continued utilization. An employee who, because of illness or injury, is unable to continue to perform the duties of his or her current position should not automatically be retired on disability. Alternatives include [retraining and reassignment]. 665 F. Supp. at 743–44.

The court concluded that while an employer "should not be required to conduct an endless hit-and-miss job search for a handicapped employee in hopes of finding a suitable position, agencies are under a *substantial obligation* to accommodate their employees." 665 F. Supp. at 735 (emphasis supplied).

    b. Accommodation Not Required

Adams v. *Alderson,* 723 F. Supp. 1531 (D.D.C. 1989): Adams had physically assaulted his supervisor and subsequently damaged office equipment. Adams's doctor found that he suffered from "maladaptive reaction to a psychosocial stressor," in this case, the antagonizing supervisor. After a lengthy review process, the U.S. General Services Administration ("GSA") fired Adams for his conduct. Adams claimed that GSA had failed to make reasonable accommodation for his handicap.

The court rejected Adams's claim and stated that "the 'reasonable accommodation' plaintiff proposes be extended him is to distance him from the offending supervisor, by transferring either or both of them elsewhere within the agency. Though such a course would surely be an accommodation to plaintiff, it is clearly not one reasonably to be expected of GSA. An agency is entitled to assign its personnel as the needs of its mission dictate. It is not obliged to indulge a propensity for violence—even if engendered by a 'handicapping' mental illness—to the point of transferring potential assailants and assailees solely to keep peace in the work place." 723 F. Supp. at 1532.

  3. Acquisition or Modification of Devices

    a. Accommodation Required

Crane v. *Dole,* 617 F. Supp. 156 (D.D.C. 1985): The Federal Aviation Administration (FAA) violated the act by refusing to hire a former air traffic controller because of his physical handicap, a hearing loss. The court concluded that the FAA never considered any possible accommodation to make the necessary equipment or devices usable by someone with such a handicap. The court stated that "[s]uch accommodations may include, but are not limited to, a phone designed to amplify voices." 617 F. Supp. at 163.

    b. Accommodation Not Required

Carter v. *Bennett,* 840 F.2d 63 (D.C. Cir. 1988): Carter, a blind employee whose duties consisted of analyzing and answering correspondence from members of Congress and the public, was reasonably accommodated by his employer, the Department of Education ("DOE"). The DOE had provided two part-time readers and "special equipment" that consisted of a Visualtek machine, tape recorder, and a Braille typewriter and reduced his work load to one-half that of other nonhandicapped employees.

The court rejected Carter's request for additional accommodations that included a voice synthesized computer and two floppy disk drives. The court stated that an employer "is not obligated under the statute to provide [an employee] with every accommodation he may request, [the employer] must, at a minimum, provide reasonable accommodation as is necessary to enable him to perform his essential functions." 840 F.2d at 67. The court concluded that the accommodation provided by the DOE satisfied this requirement.

4. Rearranging Office Seating

   a. Accommodation Required

Arneson v. *Sullivan*, 946 F.2d 90 (8th Cir. 1991): An employee who suffered from apraxia, a neurological disorder which adversely affected his motor skills and prevented him from concentrating on his job at the Social Security Administration when distracted by activity near him in the workplace, would have been reasonably accommodated by being afforded a private area in which to work. The employee had performed successfully in a distraction-free environment when previously assigned to a different office. Special assistance in the form of a "reader" was also required to benefit the employee where the agency had instituted a similar program for blind employees.

   b. Further Accommodation Not Required

Vickers v. *Veterans Administration*, 549 F. Supp. 85 (W.D. Wash. 1982): The employer reasonably accommodated an employee's hypersensitivity to smoke by physically separating desks of smokers and nonsmokers, obtaining voluntary agreement from co-workers in same and adjacent rooms not to smoke in those areas, installing ceiling vents, and giving the complainant the opportunity to move his desk closer to a window. Further accommodation was not required.

VI. UNDUE HARDSHIP AND OTHER EMPLOYER DEFENSES

A. Undue Hardship

An employer is not required to make an accommodation that is an "undue hardship." Undue hardship is defined as an action requiring "significant difficulty or expense incurred by a covered entity." Various financial factors may be considered to determine whether reasonable accommodations will cause undue hardship, including:

- The nature and overall cost of the accommodation needed under the ADA;

- Availability of tax credits by reason of the expense;

- The overall financial resources of the facility or facilities involved in the provision of the reasonable accommodation;

- The number of persons employed at such facility;
- The effect on expenses and resources;
- The impact of such accommodation upon the operation of the facility, including the impact on the ability of other employees to perform their duties and the impact on the facility's conduct of its business;
- The overall financial resources of the covered entity;
- The overall size of the business of a covered entity with respect to the number of its employees;
- The number, type, and location of its facilities; and
- The type of operation or operations of the covered entity, including the composition, structure, and functions of the work force of such entity, the geographic separateness or administrative, or fiscal relationship of the facility or facilities in question to the covered entity.

Inability of a covered entity to afford the costs of reasonable accommodations does not permit the covered entity to avoid its obligations under the ADA if funding is available from other sources, such as state vocational rehabilitation agencies. However, if such funding is not available, a qualified individual with a disability should be given the opportunity to pay a portion of the costs that may constitute the undue hardship.

If there is a determination that a particular reasonable accommodation will result in undue hardship, the employer must pay for that portion of the accommodation that would not cause an undue hardship if anyone else, be it the prospective employee or an agency, will pay the remainder.

Costs to businesses for reasonable accommodation are predicted by some to be less than $500 per worker for 30 percent of workers needing an accommodation, with 51 percent of those needing an accommodation requiring no expenses at all. A Louis Harris national survey of people with disabilities found that among those employed, accommodations were provided in only 35 percent of the cases.

According to a report prepared by the GAO for Congress on accommodations made by a select group of federal contractors, 51 percent cost nothing, another 30 percent cost less than $500, and 8 percent of the workers received accommodations costing more than $2,000.00. The greatest costs incurred were on behalf of persons receiving audiovisual aids. The lowest costs incurred were associated with relocating worksites; changing hours, work procedures, and task assignments; transferring the workers to a new job; and orienting co-workers.

1. Case Examples

    Courts have rejected the contention that an employer may justify its handicap discrimination on the basis of increased costs of workers' compensation, sick leave, rehabilitation, expenses of replacing injured workers, or other economic factors associated with a higher potential of future injury to presently handicapped applicants or employees. For example, in *OFCCP* v. *E.E. Black, Ltd.*, 19 FEP Cases (BNA) 1624, 1635 (1979), the court rejected employer's argument that "back injuries present a greater risk of economic loss to employers and workers alike than do other types of injuries generally, with the result that defendant's costs of providing workers' compensation coverage to employees justify the selection out of potential employees presenting such physical conditions."

B. Safety

An employer is not required to hire or keep individuals who pose a "direct threat" to the health or safety of other individuals in the workplace or to property. The regulations have given further definition to this defense.

Employers may either refuse to hire an applicant or may discharge an employee if he poses a "direct threat" or a significant risk of substantial harm to himself or others that cannot be eliminated or reduced by reasonable accommodation. The duration of the risk, the nature and severity of the potential harm, the likelihood of that harm occurring, and the imminence of the harm are all factors that must be considered.

The direct threat standard must be applied equally to all applicants and employees. Moreover, a slightly increased risk of harm will not meet the standard, and case-by-case determinations of direct threat must be based on objective, factual evidence. Furthermore, the determination must be based on "an individualized assessment of the individual's present ability to safely perform the essential functions of the job."

The burden is on the employer to show a safety risk. The determination that an individual with a disability will pose a safety threat to others must be made on a case-by-case basis; it may not be based on generalizations, misperceptions, ignorance, irrational fears, patronizing attitudes, or pernicious mythologies. The employer must identify a risk that is real and specific, not speculative or remote. For people with mental disabilities, the employer must identify the specific behavior on the part of the individual that would pose the anticipated direct threat.

The ADA does not protect individuals with an infectious or communicable disease that is transmitted to others through the handling of food if the individual's position requires handling food. (A proposed amendment to the ADA that would have treated AIDS as a disease transmitted to others in the handling of food was eventually rejected by Congress.)

1. Case Examples of the Breadth of the "Safety" Defense

In *Mantolete* v. *Bolger*, 767 F.2d 1416 (9th Cir. 1985), the Court established the following standard to determine whether a sufficient health or safety risk exists so that reasonable accommodation is not required:

In order to exclude such individuals, there must be a showing of a reasonable probability of *substantial harm*. Such a determination cannot be based merely on an employer's subjective evaluation or, except in cases of a most apparent nature, merely on medical reports. The question is whether, in light of the individual's work history and medical history, employment of that individual would pose a reasonable probability of substantial harm. 767 F.2d at 1422 (emphasis supplied).

Based on this standard, the court reversed and remanded the trial court's ruling against an epileptic applicant who was denied a position with the postal service based on her physical handicap. The trial court erroneously held that the applicant was not a qualified handicapped person because her employment as a letter-sorting machine operator would pose an *elevated risk* of injury. As discussed above, a more demanding legal standard is required.

One common area of concern to employers is employees with infectious diseases. "A person who poses a significant risk of communicating an infectious disease to others in the workplace will not be otherwise qualified for his or her job if reasonable accommodation will not eliminate that risk." *Arline*, 480 U.S. at 287 n.16.

Arline sets out a test for determining whether a contagious individual is otherwise qualified. The court must analyze the following four factors to assess the threat to others:

(1) the nature of the risk (how the disease is transmitted),

(2) the duration of the risk (how long the carrier is infectious),

(3) the severity of the risk (what is the potential harm to third parties), and

(4) the probability that the disease will be transmitted and will cause varying degrees of harm. 480 U.S. at 285.

This test has been applied by the courts in AIDS and other similar types of cases. See, for example, *Martinez v. School Board of Hillsborough County, Fla.*, 861 F.2d 1502 (11th Cir. 1988) ("remote theoretical possibility" of transmission from tears, saliva, and urine of mentally handicapped child with AIDS did not support segregation of child from regular trainable mentally handicapped classroom); *Kohl v. Woodhaven Learning Center*, 865 F.2d 930 (8th Cir. 1989) (exclusion of handicapped individual from rehabilitation residence due to fact that he was a carrier of infectious hepatitis B was enjoined); *Doe v. Washington University*, 780 F. Supp. 628 (E.D. Mo. 1991) (dismissal of dental student with human immunodeficiency virus (HIV) upheld because of some, albeit minimal, risk of transmission of HIV during the performance of invasive dental procedures).

C. Collective Bargaining Agreements

An employer cannot use a collective bargaining agreement to accomplish what it otherwise would be prohibited from doing under the ADA. A collective bargaining agreement can be considered when determining whether or not a given accommodation is reasonable.

VII. ENFORCEMENT AND REMEDIES

The ADA adopts the powers, remedies, and procedures of Title VII of the Civil Rights Act of 1964, 42 U.S.C. Section 2000e et seq., as amended by the Civil Rights Act of 1991. Prior to the Civil Rights Act of 1991, Title VII provided for injunctive and other equitable relief, including back pay, attorneys' fees, and costs. Now, punitive and compensatory damages may also be available to victims of intentional discrimination, up to certain maximum amounts depending on the size of the employer. In cases concerning reasonable accommodation, compensatory or punitive damages may not be awarded if an employer can demonstrate that "good faith" efforts were made to provide reasonable accommodation.

The ADA encourages the voluntary use of alternative means of dispute resolution, including settlement negotiations, conciliation, facilitation, mediation, fact-finding, mini-trials, and arbitration. However, an arbitration clause in a collective bargaining agreement or other employment contract cannot prevent an individual from pursuing his rights under the ADA.

VIII. CONCLUSION

Like any new law, the ADA once effective will likely generate substantial litigation over its meaning and scope. In order to comply fully with the ADA, however, employers should now make sure that they evaluate each applicant or employee on the basis of ability to perform the particular job, and that they not reject people on the basis of generalizations with respect to a particular physical or mental condition.

Employers should also bear in mind that the ADA does not require an employer to prefer a disabled employee over a nondisabled employee or to create a new job for an individual with a disability. Like the other civil rights laws, the ADA is designed to make irrelevant in employment decisions a disability that, with reasonable accommodation, does not prevent the employee from doing the job.

FEDERAL AGENCIES RESPONSIBLE FOR ENFORCEMENT OF ADA PROVISIONS

Title I
Employment

U.S. Equal Employment Opportunity Commission
1801 L St., N.W., Washington, DC 20507
ADA Helpline (800) 669-EEOC (Voice) or (800) 800-3302 (TDD)

Enforces Title I provisions prohibiting discrimination in employment against qualified individuals with disabilities. Provides information, speakers, technical assistance, training, and referral to specialized resources to employers and people with disabilities, through headquarters and district offices.

Publications: *Title I Regulations; ADA Technical Assistance Manual* ("how to" information on Title I compliance and resource directory); booklets on employer responsibilities and rights of individuals with disabilities; questions and answers on ADA employment and public accommodation provisions; fact sheets on ADA and tax credits and deductions for ADA accommodations; video series on key aspects of Title I compliance.

*Note: EEOC will issue additional policy guidance through its internal interpretive *Compliance Manual* prior to and following the effective date of the ADA. The manual is available to the public at Commission headquarters and field offices and at public libraries. It also is available through two commercial services: (1) Bureau of National Affairs, 1231 25th St., N.W., Washington, DC 20037, (800) 372-1033; (2) Commerce Clearing House, 4025 West Peterson Ave., Chicago, IL 60646, (312) 583-8500.

Title II
State and Local
Government
Services

U.S. Department of Justice
Civil Rights Division
Office on the Americans with Disabilities Act
P.O. Box 66118, Washington, DC 20035-6118
(202) 514-0301 (Voice) or (202) 514-0381 (TDD)
(202) 514-6193 (Electronic Bulletin Board)

Title III
Public
Accommodations
and Commercial
Facilities

Enforces ADA provisions prohibiting discrimination on the basis of disability in state and local government services (Title II) and in public accommodations and commercial facilities (Title III). Provides technical assistance to those with rights and responsibilities under the law. (See Technical Assistance Grant Projects, Section II.)

Publications: *Title II and Title III Regulations; ADA Technical Assistance Manual;* books, brochures, and fact sheets focusing on Title II and Title III requirements.

*Note: An *ADA Handbook,* a joint publication of EEOC and the Department of Justice, containing the text of the ADA, Regulations for Titles I, II, and III, Accessibility Guidelines, Uniform Accessibility Standards, and other useful resources is for sale by the Government Printing Office. Serial No. 052-015-00072-3. Available at Government Book Stores or by calling (202) 783-3238.

Title II
Public Mass
Transportation

U.S. Department of Transportation
400 7th St., S.W., Washington, DC 20590
(202) 366-9305 (Voice) or (202) 755-7687 (TDD)

Title III
Private Mass
Transportation

Enforces ADA provisions that require nondiscrimination in public (Title II) and private (Title III) mass transportation systems and services.

Publications: *Transportation for Individuals with Disabilities, Regulations; ADA Paratransit Handbook* for implementing complementary paratransit service requirements; other technical assistance materials available in 1992.

Title IV
Tele-
communications

Federal Communications Commission
1919 M St., N.W., Washington, DC 20554
(202) 632-7260 (Voice) or (202) 632-6999 (TDD)

Enforces ADA telecommunications provisions, which require that companies offering telephone services to the general public must offer telephone relay services to individuals who use text telephones or similar devices. Also enforces requirements for closed captioning of federally produced or federally funded television public service announcements. Maintains database of state telecommunications relay service facilities.

Publications: *Telecommunications Services for Hearing and Speech Disabled, Regulations; Telecommunications Relay Service—An Informational Handbook.*

FEDERAL AGENCY PROGRAMS PERTAINING TO DISABILITY AND EMPLOYMENT

Centers for Independent Living Program
Rehabilitation Services Administration
U.S. Department of Education
Mary E. Switzer Building, 330 C St., S.W., Washington, DC 20202

Approximately four hundred independent living centers, most funded by this program, provide local services and programs to enable individuals with severe disabilities to live and function independently. Centers offer individuals with disabilities a variety of services, including independent living skills training, counseling and advocacy services on income benefits and legal rights, information and referral, peer counseling, education and training, housing assistance, transportation, equipment and adaptive aid loans, personal care attendants, and vocational and employment services. Assistance available to employers includes: accessibility surveys; job analyses; advice on job accommodations, job modifications, and assistive devices; recruitment; job training; job placement and support services; information and referral to specialized technical assistance resources.

Clearinghouse on Disability Information
Office of Special Education and Rehabilitation Services
U.S. Department of Education
Switzer Bldg., Rm. 3132, Washington, DC 20202-2524
(202) 732-1241 or (202) 732-1723 (Voice/TDD)

Provides information on federal disability legislation, funding for programs serving individuals with disabilities, and programs and services for people with disabilities on the national, state, and local levels.

Publications: Quarterly newsletter on federal activities affecting people with disabilities; guides to disability legislation and federal resources for people with disabilities; employment information package listing public and private organizations that assist individuals with disabilities who are seeking employment.

Client Assistance Program (CAP)
Office of Program Operations
Rehabilitation Services Administration
U.S. Department of Education
Mary E. Switzer Building, 330 C St., S.W., Washington, DC 20202
(202) 732-1406 (Voice) or (202) 732-2848 (TDD)

Programs in each state provide information and assistance to individuals seeking or receiving services under the Rehabilitation Act of 1973. Investigate, negotiate, and mediate solutions to problems of applicants and clients of programs, projects, or facilities funded under the act regarding services. Offer advice and assistance to governmental agencies and service providers, and provide legal counsel and litigation services to persons unable to obtain adequate legal services.

Developmental Disability Councils
Administration on Developmental Disabilities
U.S. Department of Health and Human Services
200 Independence Ave., S.W., Rm. 349-F, Washington, DC 20201
(202) 245-2890 (Voice/TDD)

Councils in each state provide training and technical assistance to local and state agencies, employers, and the public on improving services to people with developmental disabilities; provide information on the ADA; and make referrals to appropriate agencies.

Education and Assistance Program for Farmers with Disabilities
USDA Extension Service
U.S. Department of Agriculture
Washington, DC 20250-0900
(202) 720-3377

Eight projects serving ten states provide education and technical assistance to farmers, ranchers, and other agricultural workers with disabilities for accommodating disability in agricultural operations. Provide on-site technical assistance for designing, adapting, modifying, and restructuring agricultural equipment and tools. Assist in modifying work site operations, locations, and buildings, and with utilizing assistive technology.

Publications: Manuals on modified and restructured agricultural tools, equipment, machinery, and buildings for agricultural workers with physical disabilities; technical articles on health and safety risks, hand controls for agricultural equipment, improving work site mobility, prosthetic and work site modifications, chairlift attachments, all-terrain vehicles for physically impaired individuals, and manlift attachments for tractors and combines.

Internal Revenue Service
U.S. Department of the Treasury
1111 Constitution Ave., N.W., Washington, DC 20224
(202) 566-3292 (Voice) or (800) 829-4059 (TDD)
(800) 829-3676 (Publications and Forms)

Provides information on *tax credits* and *tax deductions* available to business for costs in complying with accommodation and accessibility requirements of the ADA and tax information for people with disabilities. For information on the Targeted Jobs Tax Credit Program, which offers tax incentives for hiring individuals with disabilities referred by state vocational rehabilitation or Veterans Administration programs, call (202) 566-4741.

Publications: Publication #907, "Tax Information for Persons with Handicaps and Disabilities," Form 8826 (ADA "Access Credit" and instructions), and information on Section 190 tax deduction may be obtained by calling the toll-free number.

Job Training Partnership Act (JTPA) Programs
Office of Job Training Programs
Employment and Training Administration
U.S. Department of Labor
200 Constitution Ave., N.W., Rm. N-4709, Washington, DC 20210
(202) 535-0580

Established by the Job Training Partnership Act (JTPA) of 1982 to train and place "economically disadvantaged" adults and youth facing significant barriers to employment, including persons with disabilities, in permanent, unsubsidized jobs. More than 600 local JTPA programs offer individuals with disabilities who meet the act's eligibility criteria a range of employment services, including occupational and basic skills training, job development, counseling, job search assistance, school-to-work transition, on-the-job training, and follow-up services. Programs act as a recruitment source for employers and may offer partial funding for training costs.

Publications: Brochure on the Job Training Partnership Act.

National AIDS Clearinghouse
P.O. Box 6003, Rockville, MD 20849-6003
(800) 458-5231 (Voice)

Primary information, publication, and referral service of the Centers for Disease Control on HIV infection and AIDS. Offers information on AIDS in the workplace, employee education programs, small-business concerns, infection control, first aid, insurance, employee rights and legal issues related to the ADA. Makes referrals to providers of HIV- and AIDS-related services, AIDS in the workplace programs, and legal services for people with AIDS.

National AIDS Hotline
Centers for Disease Control
Public Health Service
U.S. Department of Health and Human Services
(800) 342-2437 (Voice) or (800) 243-7889 (TDD/TTY)

Operates a toll-free, twenty-four-hour, national AIDS hotline that offers free confidential information and publications on HIV infection and AIDS. Accesses database of over 10,000 local and national organizations for referrals.

Publications: Free information on HIV, AIDS, and HIV/AIDS in the workplace.

National Clearinghouse for Alcohol and Drug Information
Office for Substance Abuse Prevention
Alcohol, Drug Abuse, and Mental Health Administration
U.S. Department of Health and Human Services
P.O. Box 2345, Rockville, MD 20852
(800) 729-6686 (Voice) or (800) 487-4889 (TDD)

Maintains largest federal collection of alcohol and other drug abuse material. Operates twenty-four-hour hotline providing direct information, publications, and referral on alcohol and other drug abuse. Coordinates regional alcohol and drug prevention information centers which offer support to local prevention efforts.

Publications: Bimonthly information service offering current information about abuse prevention; hundreds of guides, videos, and booklets on alcohol and drug abuse issues, including employee education, substance abuse programs, drug testing, and workplace-related issues.

National Technical Information Service
U.S. Department of Commerce
5285 Port Royal Rd., Springfield, VA 22161
(703) 487-4650

Maintains worldwide database of research, development, and engineering reports on a range of topics, including architectural barrier removal, employing individuals with disabilities, alternative testing formats, job accommodations, school-to-work transition for students with disabilities, rehabilitation engineering, disability law, and transportation. Provides referral to local institutions and vendors that will perform database searches. Distributes requested publications in paper and microfiche.

Publications: Alternative testing publications include *Guide for Administering Examinations to Handicapped Individuals for Employment Purposes: A Federal Employment Test Modified for Deaf Applicants; Statistical Characteristics of the Written Test for the Professional and Administrative Career Examination (PACE) for Visually Handicapped Applicants; Testing the Handicapped for Employment Purposes: Adaptations for Persons with Motor Handicaps.*

Office of Financial Assistance
U.S. Small Business Administration
409 Third St., S.W., Eighth Fl., Washington, DC 20416
(202) 205-6490

Administers the Small Business Act of 1953, which provides loan programs to assist small-business owners with physical disabilities. Offers loans to individuals with disabilities to establish, acquire, and operate small businesses, and loans to small businesses owned or to be owned by individuals with disabilities. Provides special small-business loans to disabled and Vietnam-era veterans, to nonprofit sheltered workshops and similar organizations employing people with disabilities. Provides technical assistance to individuals with disabilities, including help with bookkeeping and accounting services, production, engineering and technical advice, feasibility and marketing studies, advertising expertise, and legal services.

Publications: Brochures on the Handicapped Assistance Loan Program.

President's Committee on Mental Retardation
330 Independence Ave., S.W., Rm. 5325, North Bldg., Washington, DC 20201-0001
(202) 619-0634

Advises and assists the president and the secretary of Health and Human Services on issues related to mental retardation. Evaluates national, state, and local programs for individuals who are mentally retarded. Provides information and publications to the public on mental retardation and related issues.

Publications: Reports on attitudinal barriers, employment of individuals who are mentally retarded, and community integration.

Projects with Industry
Inter-National Association of Business, Industry and Rehabilitation (I-NABIR)
P.O. Box 15242, Washington, DC 20003
(202) 543-6353

More than 125 federally funded local *Projects with Industry*, which involve small businesses, major corporations, labor organizations, trade associations, foundations, voluntary agencies, and the rehabilitation community create and expand job opportunities for individuals with disabilities. Provide training and supportive services to individuals with disabilities in commercial and industrial work settings. Contact the Association for information on local projects.

Protection and Advocacy for Individual Rights (PAIR)
Office of Developmental Programs
Rehabilitation Services Administration
U.S. Department of Education
Switzer Building, Rm. 3038
330 C St., S.W., Washington, DC 20202-2375

Program established by the Rehabilitation Act of 1973 to protect the rights of individuals with severe disabilities receiving services from federally funded independent living centers who are not eligible for services provided by other protection and advocacy programs, and whose request for services cannot be addressed by a Client Assistance Program. Currently operating in eleven states (Arkansas, Colorado, Louisiana, Maine, Michigan, New Hampshire, New Mexico, New York, Rhode Island, South Dakota, Wisconsin) to assist qualified individuals with severe disabilities in pursuing remedies under the ADA, the Rehabilitation Act, and the Fair Housing Act.

Protection and Advocacy for Mentally Ill Individuals (PAMII)
National Institute of Mental Health
Alcohol, Drug Abuse and Mental Health Administration
U.S. Department of Health and Human Services
5600 Fishers Ln., Rm. 11-C-22, Rockville, MD 20857
(301) 443-3667

Established by the Protection and Advocacy of Mentally Ill Individuals Act of 1986 (reauthorized with amendments 1988, 1991) to protect the rights of persons with mental illness in public and private residential treatment facilities, including homeless shelters and jails. Independent agencies in each state pursue administrative, legal, and other appropriate remedies, and investigate incidents of abuse and neglect. Provide technical assistance, information, and referral on the ADA and other disability and mental health laws. Provide legal counsel and litigation services to mentally ill persons unable to obtain adequate legal services.

Protection and Advocacy for Persons with Developmental Disabilities (PADD)
Administration on Developmental Disabilities
U.S. Department of Health and Human Services
(202) 245-2897 (Voice) or (202) 245-2890 (TDD)

Established by the Developmental Disabilities Assistance and Bill of Rights Act of 1975 to protect the rights of individuals with developmental disabilities under federal and state statutes. Provides legal, administrative, and other appropriate remedies to individual problems, including those involving employment discrimination and accessibility issues. Offer technical assistance, information, and referral on the ADA and other disability law.

Social Security Administration
6401 Security Blvd., Baltimore, MD 21202
(800) 772-1213

Provides information on Social Security Disability Insurance (SSDI) and Supplemental Security Income (SSI) disability programs that provide financial support and Medicaid or Medicare coverage to individuals with disabilities who are returning to work.

Publications: Pamphlets and fact sheets on SSI and SSDI programs.

State Technology Assistance Projects
National Institute on Disability and Rehabilitation Research
330 C St., S.W., Washington, DC 20202-2572
(202) 732-5066 (Voice) or (202) 732-5079 (TDD)

Projects funded in thirty-one states provide information and technical assistance on technology, related services, and devices for individuals with disabilities. Specific services and activities of individual state projects vary considerably; they include technical assistance and public awareness programs related to assistive technology, training seminars, the development of curricula/training materials and model programs, and the provision of information and referral on assistive technology.

State Vocational Rehabilitation Services Program
Rehabilitation Services Administration
Office of Special Education and Rehabilitative Services
U.S. Department of Education
Switzer Building, 330 C St., S.W., Rm. 3127, Washington, DC 20202-2531
(202) 732-1282 (Voice/TDD)

State and local vocational rehabilitation agencies provide comprehensive services of rehabilitation, training, and job-related assistance to people with disabilities and assist employers in recruiting, training, placing, accommodating, and meeting other employment-related needs of people with disabilities.

Agencies conduct workplace accessibility surveys, job analyses that match functional abilities, and limitations of individuals with disabilities to needed accommodations and provide assistance in job restructuring, job modification, and assistive technology. Agencies may fund all or partial costs of needed training, assistive technology, or other accommodations for eligible individuals. Employment-related services to individuals with disabilities include evaluation and assessment, vocational counseling and guidance, referral to appropriate rehabilitation technology services, physical and mental restoration services, vocational training, on-the-job training, job placement, job development, and services necessary to obtain or maintain employment.

U.S. Employment Service
Employment and Training Administration
Department of Labor
200 Constitution Ave., N.W., Washington, DC 20210
(202) 535-0189

Through more than seventeen hundred state and local offices nationwide, provides employment services to job seekers, including employability assessments, job counseling, occupational training referral, job placement, and trained specialists to work with the specific needs of job seekers with disabilities. Circulates information about local, state, and national job openings, training opportunities, and occupational demand and supply information within particular labor markets. Assists employers in filling job vacancies with qualified individuals with disabilities, and performs eligibility certification for targeted jobs tax credit.

Publications: Fact sheet on employment-related services for people with disabilities.

The Wage and Hour Division
Employment Standards Administration
U.S. Department of Labor
200 Constitution Ave., Rm. S 3516, N.W., Washington, DC 20210
(202) 523-8727

Administers regulations governing the employment of individuals with disabilities in sheltered workshops and the disabled workers industries.

Publications: Fact sheets and guides on the employment of disabled individuals in sheltered workshops; sheltered workshop certification.

ADA ASSISTANCE AND SUPPORT ORGANIZATIONS

Architectural and Transportation Barriers Compliance Board
1111 18th St., N.W., Suite 501, Washington, DC 20036-3894
(800) USA-ABLE (Voice/TDD)

Sets guidelines adopted as accessibility standards under Titles II and III of the ADA. Provides information on technical and scoping requirements for accessibility and offers general technical assistance on the removal of architectural, transportation, communication, and attitudinal barriers affecting people with disabilities.

Publications: *ADA Accessibility Guidelines for Buildings and Facilities; ADA Accessibility Guidelines for Transportation Vehicles; ADA Accessibility Guidelines for Transportation Facilities;* manuals on ADA accessibility guidelines for transportation vehicles; ADA Accessibility Guidelines Checklist for buildings and facilities; Uniform Federal Accessibility Standards Accessibility Checklist; design bulletin series explaining various provisions of ADA accessibility guidelines for buildings and facilities; booklets and guides on barrier-free design, accessible rest rooms, wheelchair lifts and slip resistant surfaces, transit facility designs, assistive listening devices, visual alarms, airport TDD access, and air carrier policies affecting people with disabilities.

Centers for Disease Control
Public Health Service
U.S. Department of Health and Human Services
Mail Stop C09, 1600 Clifton Rd., N.E., Atlanta, GA 30333
(404) 639-2237

Publishes an annually updated list of infectious and communicable diseases transmitted through the handling of food in accordance with Section 103(d) of Title I.

Publication: *Diseases Transmitted Through the Food Supply.*

Department of Justice ADA Technical Assistance Grant Projects

The following organizations were funded by the Department of Justice in September 1991 to provide technical assistance on Titles II and III of the ADA. Some of these projects will also provide assistance on aspects of Title I compliance.

ADA Clearinghouse and Resource Center
National Center for State Courts
300 Newport Ave., Williamsburg, VA 23185
(804) 253-2000

Will disseminate information on ADA compliance to state and local court systems. Will develop a diagnostic checklist, strategies for compliance specifically relevant to state and local courts, and a model curriculum for use in the education of future judges and court administrators.

American Foundation for the Blind (AFB) and
Gallaudet University—National Center for Law and the Deaf (NCLD)
1615 M St., N.W., Suite 250, Washington, DC 20036
(202) 651-5343 (NCLD) or (202) 223-0101 (AFB)

Through voice and TDD telephone information lines, will provide advice and technical assistance on a case-by-case basis to consumers and covered entities on overcoming communications barriers resulting from hearing and vision loss. Will develop and distribute pamphlets targeted at restaurants, the hospitality industry, places of assembly, health care providers, and consumers.

American Speech-Language-Hearing Association
10801 Rockville Pike, Rockville, MD 20852
Consumer Help (301) 897-5700 or (800) 638-8255 (Voice)
Consumer Help (301) 897-0157 (TDD)

Will disseminate information on the ADA to people with communications disabilities, professionals in the disability field, and covered entities, including retail stores, day care centers, places of assembly, and emergency service providers. Will provide telephone information lines on communications access issues for businesses, audiologists, and persons with disabilities, and will develop and conduct a national workshop addressing these issues.

The Association for Retarded Citizens of the United States (ARC)
500 East Border, S-300, Arlington, TX 76010
(817) 261-6003

Will disseminate information regarding the ADA as it applies to individuals with mental retardation. Will establish a national information center to develop and disseminate educational brochures to restaurants, hotels and motels, retail stores, and places of public assembly on how to provide cognitively accessible, integrated services. Will also conduct national training for ARC chapters on Title III and for organizations representing child care facilities, and develop and disseminate a resource book for child care centers.

The Association on Handicapped Student Service Programs in Postsecondary Education (AHSSPPE)
P.O. Box 21192, Columbus, OH 43221-0192
(614) 488-4972
ADA Hotline (800) 247-7752 (Voice/TDD)

In collaboration with the National Clearinghouse on Licensure Enforcement and Regulations (CLEAR), will develop a manual on testing accommodations and ADA compliance by boards of licensure and certification. Also, will provide a telephone hotline to respond to ADA information requests from CLEAR members.

Council of Better Business Bureaus' Foundation
4200 Wilson Blvd., Suite 800, Arlington, VA 22203-1804
(703) 276-0100 (Voice) or (703) 247-3668 (TDD)

Through its network of 177 Better Business Bureaus, will educate small- and medium-sized business members on their obligations as public accommodations under Title III of the ADA. Will also provide specialized resources and training in ADA alternative dispute resolution. In collaboration with the Disability Rights Education and Defense Fund (DREDF) and Barrier Free Environments (BFE), will conduct meetings with business and disability groups, and develop and disseminate industry-specific business "advisories," technical assistance guidelines for conducting ADA seminars, and instructional options for dispute resolution managers.

Disability Rights Education and Defense Fund (DREDF)
2212 Sixth St., Berkeley, CA 94710
ADA Hotline: (800) 466-4ADA (Voice/TDD)
(415) 644-2555 (Voice) or (415) 644-2625 (TDD)

Has established a telephone information line to answer ADA questions (emphasis on Titles II and III) and respond to requests for ADA materials.

Will also conduct a seminar to train regional community-based representatives as technical assistance specialists to assist individuals with rights and responsibilities under the ADA and provide further training and resources for groups nationwide.

Information Access Project
National Federation of the Blind
1800 Johnson St., Baltimore, MD 21230
(301) 659-9314

Will assist entities covered by the ADA in finding methods for converting visually displayed information, such as flyers, brochures, and pamphlets, to formats accessible to individuals who are visually impaired. Will also serve as a resource for other grantees who are required under the terms of their grants to provide materials in nonvisually accessible formats.

Institute for Law and Policy Planning
P.O. Box 5137, Berkeley, CA 94705
(415) 486-8352

Will produce a thirty-minute broadcast-quality video and a ten-minute video on readily achievable barrier removal in places of public accommodation. Both videos will be available at the ADA Regional Disability and Business Technical Assistance Centers and other technical assistance and training projects.

National Association of Protection and Advocacy Systems
900 2nd St., N.E., Suite 211, Washington, DC 20002
(202) 408-9518 (Voice) or (202) 408-9521 (TDD)

Will conduct three regional "train-the-trainer" seminars that will focus on nonlitigatory dispute resolution techniques, self-advocacy, and voluntary compliance. Will provide funding to twelve state protection and advocacy systems that will conduct statewide training. Will provide materials on ADA to national network of protection and advocacy service centers and client assistance programs to provide direct technical assistance.

National Conference of States on Building
Codes and Standards
505 Huntmar Park Dr., Suite 210, Herndon, VA 22070
(703) 437-0100

In conjunction with the Paralyzed Veterans of America (PVA), will promote the certification of state codes for equivalency with ADA standards, and encourage the development of alternative dispute resolution procedures within the existing state regulatory framework. Will promote voluntary compliance with the new construction and alterations requirements of the ADA, develop models for certification and dispute resolution, and hold a national seminar on the ADA, certification, and appeal and complaint procedures.

National Rehabilitation Hospital
102 Irving St., N.W., Washington, DC 20010
(202) 877-1000 (Voice) or (202) 877-1450 (TDD)

Through seminars and written materials, will provide information on the ADA to doctors, hospitals, health care facilities, and health care consumers. Will produce an accessibility checklist, a compliance handbook for facility managers, and a brochure describing consumers rights to health care services as part of these materials.

Job Accommodation Network
P.O. Box 6123, 809 Allen Hall, Morgantown, WV 26506-6123
(800) 526-7234 (Accommodation Information) (Out of State Only/Voice/TDD)
(800) 526-4698 (Accommodation Information) (In State Only/Voice/TDD)
(800) ADA WORK (800) 232-9675 (ADA Information) (Voice/TDD)
(800) DIAL JAN (800) 342-5526 (ADA Information) (Computer Modem)

Free consultant service funded by the President's Committee on Employment of People with Disabilities. Through telephone consultation with professional human factors counselors, provides information and advice to employers and people with disabilities on custom job and worksite accommodations. Performs individualized searches for workplace accommodations, based on the job's functional requirements, the functional limitations of the individual, environmental factors, and other pertinent information. Assists employers and individuals with disabilities in the use of a variety of public programs dealing with disability, including the Job Training Partnership Act, Projects with Industry, Supported Employment, Targeted Jobs Tax Credit, and barrier removal incentives. ADA Work Line is staffed by people experienced in discussing the application of the ADA, especially as it relates to accommodation and accessibility issues.

Videotape: "Bridging the Talent Gap," features a variety of individuals with disabilities successfully employed as a result of vocational rehabilitation and on-the-job accommodation; descriptive literature on JAN services.

National Council on Disability
800 Independence Ave., S.W., Suite 814, Washington, DC 20591
(202) 267-3846 (Voice) or (202) 267-3232 (TDD)

Required by Section 507 of the ADA to conduct a study and report on the effect of wilderness designations and wilderness land management practices on the ability of people with disabilities to use and enjoy the National Wilderness Preservation Systems. Conducts **ADA Watch** to monitor the implementation of the ADA in employment, public accommodations, transportation, and telecommunications. Develops recommendations for federal disability policy. Provides ongoing advice to the president, the Congress, the Rehabilitation Services Administration, and other federal agencies on programs authorized by the Rehabilitation Act. Establishes general policies for reviewing the operation of the National Institute on Disability and Rehabilitation Research. Reviews and approves standards for Independent Living and Projects with Industry programs.

Publications: Quarterly newsletter; special reports on federal laws and programs affecting persons with disabilities, the ADA, and education for students with disabilities.

National Institute on Disability and Rehabilitation Research
400 Maryland Ave., S.W., Washington, DC 20202-2572
(202) 732-5801 (Voice) or (202) 732-5316 (TDD)

Provides funding for three major programs to assist ADA compliance:

1. **ADA Regional Disability and Business Technical Assistance Centers** (see above).

2. **Materials Development Projects.** During 1992 and 1993, a variety of written and audiovisual materials on employment, public accommodations, public services and communications aspects of ADA compliance will be developed and made available to the Regional Disability and Business Technical Assistance Centers for distribution to the public. These materials will include fact sheets, brochures, manuals, self-assessment guides, training modules, slides, and video and audiotapes and will be designed as self-instructional training resources for employers and other organizations, as well as for the peer training projects.

3. **"Peer Training" Projects.** Two national training programs will be funded and conducted in 1992: (a) training for all persons in the fields of Independent Living and disability advocacy on all aspects of the ADA and (b) training for people with disabilities, their families, and organizations representing them on rights under the ADA. Both projects will develop trainers who can conduct additional training for other interested groups.

NIDRR also funds research projects that provide information on assistive technology and employment.

The President's Committee on Employment of People with Disabilities
1331 F St., N.W., Washington, DC 20004
(202) 376 (Voice) or (202) 376-6205 (TDD)

Provides information and advice on employment of people with disabilities. Conducts training conferences on ADA, and an annual meeting which offers training opportunities on many aspects of employing people with disabilities. Works with state organizations (President's Committee Partners) which include governors, mayors, local committees, and disability rights advocacy organizations to increase employment opportunities for people with disabilities. Involved in programs with business, industry, and labor to educate and inform through local and national initiatives. President's Committee Partners provide technical assistance on employment and information on assistive technology and workplace accommodations for people with disabilities. Funds the Job Accommodation Network which provides free consultation on specific accommodation issues (see above).

Publications: Provides a range of informational materials on the ADA and practical guidance on job analysis, job accommodation and modification, hiring and training people with disabilities, job placement, supervising employees with mental retardation, vocational rehabilitation, disability legislation and regulations, and working with people who have specific disabilities such as multiple sclerosis, blindness, diabetes, cerebral palsy, and cystic fibrosis.

Chapter 17

AFFIRMATIVE ACTION REGULATIONS AND PROGRAMS

FEDERAL AFFIRMATIVE ACTION REQUIREMENTS[1]

There are three primary sources requiring that certain employers adopt and carry out affirmative action plans. The types of employers required to do so include federal agencies, all public funded organizations, federal contractors and subcontractors, and recipients of federal funds, grants, and material endorsements. The three sources of "law" establishing the requirements and standards of affirmative action plans (AAPs) consist of Executive Orders 11246, 11375, and 11478.

EXECUTIVE ORDER 11246

In September 1965, President Johnson signed this order whose central purpose was to advance the employment opportunities of minority group members. This was to be accomplished by requiring that employers take affirmative action to ensure that minorities were given equal opportunity to apply and compete for jobs within the federal government and its contracting or grant agent employers. For employers with grants or contracts of $10,000 or more per year, the employer merely has to demonstrate that it was taking "affirmative" measures to provide employment to minority members. Contractors receiving $50,000 or more per year are additionally required to prepare and follow a written affirmative action plan in accordance with federal guidelines. 41 CFR, Part 60-2. Employers covered by Executive Order 11246 must:

1. Refrain from discrimination against any employee or job applicant because of race, color, religion, or national origin;
2. Take affirmative action to ensure that applicants are employed, and employees are treated, without regard to race, color, religion, national origin (the

---

[1] Levesque, *The Complete Hiring Manual*, pp. 405–407.

obligation extends to working conditions and facilities such as rest rooms, as well as hiring, promotions, compensation, and firing/layoffs);

3. State in all solicitations and advertisements for employment and contracts that all qualified applicants will receive consideration without regard to race, color, religion, or national origin;

4. Advise each labor union with which the employer deals of their commitments under the order;

5. Include the obligations under the order in every subcontract or purchase order unless specifically exempted;

6. Comply with all provisions of the order, its rules, and regulations; furnish all information and required reports; permit access to books, records, and accounts for the purpose of investigations to ascertain compliance; and

7. File regular compliance reports describing hiring and employment practices.

Further, the mandatory starting point for affirmative action programs in analysis of areas in which the employers may be underutilizing "protected" group persons. Such employers must consider at least the following factors:

1. Minority population of the labor area surrounding the employer's work site;

2. Size of the minority unemployment force in the labor area;

3. Percentage of minority work force compared with the total work force in the immediate area;

4. General availability of minorities having requisite skills in the immediate labor area;

5. Availability of minorities having requisite skills in the area in which the employer can reasonably recruit;

6. Availability of promotable minority employees within the employer's labor force;

7. Anticipated expansion, contraction, and turnover in the labor force;

8. Existence of training institutions capable of training minorities in the requisite skills; and

9. Degree of training the employer is reasonably able to undertake to make all job classes available to minorities.

Unlike Title VII of the 1964 Civil Rights Act, Executive Orders relating to employment are the administrative responsibility of the federal Department of Labor, Office of Federal Contract Compliance Programs (OFCCP). In addition to enforcement of Executive Orders 11246 and others, the OFCCP also requires covered employers to prepare AAPs for veterans, disabled veterans, and handicapped persons under authority of Section 503 of the 1973 Vocational Rehabilitation Act and the 1974 Veteran's Readjustment Act. Since the legal standards of these two laws are different with respect to the protected groups under Executive Order 11246 (which merely requires *good-faith* recruitment, hiring, and accommodation, but not quotas and timetables), many covered employers prepare a separate AAP for veterans and handicapped people.

EXECUTIVE ORDER 11375

In 1967, Executive Order 11375 was issued having the singular effect of adding sex-based discrimination to the list of protected characteristics covered by Executive Order 11246. Therefore, in addition to making it unlawful to discriminate on the basis of an applicant's or employee's sex, the OFCCP also requires in its guidelines that covered employers take affirmative action to recruit women for jobs in which they had previously or traditionally been excluded. The guidelines also prohibit employers from:

1. Making any distinction based on sex in employment opportunities, wages, hours, and other conditions;
2. Advertising for workers in newspaper columns headed "male" and "female" unless sex is a bona fide occupational qualification for the job;
3. Relying on state protective laws to justify denying a female employee the right to any job that she is qualified to perform; and
4. Denying employment to women with young children or making a distinction between married and unmarried persons, unless the distinctions are applied to both sexes.

EXECUTIVE ORDER 11478

This order was issued in 1969 by President Nixon. Among other effects pertaining to the affirmative hiring of jobs in the federal government, it also prescribed that companies who advertise job openings must specify that they are an equal opportunity employer, and they must post antidiscrimination notices on company bulletin boards.

Employers are cautioned about the fact that there remains considerable debate among various courts, including changing positions on the part of the U.S. Supreme Court, concerning the manner in which affirmative action plans or similar agreements (e.g., collective bargaining) can or should be used in the making of hiring and other employment decisions. It is advisable for employers to consider precedent legal decisions in the area of their decision before development of AAP commitments or acting on the specific terms of AAP obligations. Simply stated, what many of the past U.S. Supreme Court cases have conveyed to employers concerning the use of their affirmative action plans is:

1. That *voluntary* affirmative action developments are aimed at remedying present minority and other imbalances in the employer's work force.
2. That employment decisions made in light of the affirmative action plan goals do not infringe upon, or otherwise displace, nonminority employees.

3. That fixing of hiring quotas without an official determination (court decree) of present imbalance due to past discrimination under voluntary AAP's is unwarranted and unlawful. For reference to some of these precedent cases, see:

Bakke v. *Regents of the University of California, Davis* (1978)

Weber v. *Steelworkers* (1981)

Stotts v. *Fire Fighters Local 1984* (1984)

Wygant v. *Jackson Board of Education* (1986)

Martin v. *Wilks* (1989)

For employers not required to develop, implement, and use affirmative action plans to guide their employment decision making, these court cases imply that *voluntary* AAPs are inadvisable if for no other reason than the courts will hold employers who use them accountable for their resultant decisions. While the courts have generally held that discriminatory *hiring* decisions or actions are less detrimental to the party discriminated against, as opposed to say the effect of a discriminatory layoff where the damaged employee holds a greater property interest in the job, the net result for employers remains the same—costly potential liability even if it was unintentional. For this reason, those employers who are not compelled to use AAPs should probably refrain from doing so on a voluntary basis. If you are truly interested in remedying past or potentially present effects of discriminatory hiring practices, you should consider an annual audit of your practices, work force composition characteristics, and other pertinent factors, then prepare an informal report that suggests proposed changes for the next year or so.

For those employers who are required to prepare and use affirmative action plans, you may wish to obtain the reference manual entitled *How to Write an Affirmative Action Plan* published by Business & Legal Reports, Inc. (1989). Meanwhile, you can use the Affirmative Action Program Checklist provided at the end of this chapter to begin your evaluation of what parts of your programs will need attention or full development.

FEDERAL REGULATIONS AND CONSTITUTIONAL PROVISIONS

The EEOC and other agencies have issued regulations supplementing the various statutes they are required to enforce. The principal sets of regulations, all of which are found in the Code of Federal Regulations, are enumerated as follows:

1. EEOC Guidelines on Affirmative Action, 29 CFR, Part 1608.

2. Office of Federal Contract Compliance Programs, Guidelines for Affirmative Action Programs, 41 CFR, Part 60-2 (Implementation of Executive Order 11246).

3. Department of Labor, 29 CFR, Part 32.4 (handicap discrimination).

4. EEOC Interpretations of the Age Discrimination in Employment Act, 29 CFR, Part 1625.

5. EEOC Sex Discrimination and Pregnancy Guidelines, 29 CFR, Part 1604. *Note: The EEOC has guidelines on sexual harassment, found at 29 CFR, Part 1604, Section 1604.11.*

6. EEOC National Origin Discrimination Guidelines, 29 CFR, Part 1606.

7. EEOC Testing Guidelines, 29 CFR, Part 1607.

8. EEOC Regulations on the Age Discrimination Act of 1975, 29 CFR, Part 1616.

Overlying all these statutes and regulations are the provisions of the U.S. Constitution. Two clauses of the Fourteenth Amendment are involved—the equal protection clause and the due process clause.

Between the various forms of discrimination, these constitutional provisions are *not* applied in a uniform fashion. For example, a classification of individuals based upon *race* cannot survive constitutional scrutiny; however, a classification based on age may be constitutionally permissible, given a "legitimate state interest."

FEDERAL UNIFORM GUIDELINES ON EMPLOYEE SELECTION PROCEDURES[2]

Shortly following the U.S. Supreme Court's 1971 landmark decision in *Griggs* v. *Duke Power Company* in which the employer was held to have conducted a discriminatory preemployment written examination, the federal government required that several of its departments prepare regulations and guidelines for employers to follow to validate such preemployment "tests." By 1976, several federal departments had published and distributed various interpretations of what they regarded as reasonable regulations for public agencies and private companies having federal contracts and subcontracts or receiving federal grants or financial assistance. However, considerable confusion ensued because the regulations from each department were notably different making compliance nearly impossible for employers having to deal with more than one such department. As a result of this disparity, the departments were ordered to collaborate and devise a singular set of regulations and guidelines by which employers could rely for compliance. The result was the 1978 Uniform Guidelines on Employee Selection Procedures, and they are administered by the Department of Labor.

The Uniform Guidelines are aimed at controlling the use of any type of preemployment "test" that results in a discriminatory effect on those people having

---

[2] Levesque, *The Complete Hiring Manual*, pp. 407–408.

protected characteristics (women, minorities, handicapped, etc.). The regulatory portion of the Guidelines is the government's way of recognizing that employers have been using their own or purchased tests to determine who should be hired or promoted based on their test results, and that many of these tests were not valid for the job in question. Such was the case in *Griggs*, wherein a black male applied for a maintenance job and was rejected for failing to pass a general aptitude test. The high court eventually determined that the test was illegal due to its discriminatory effect upon *Griggs* case because it was insufficiently related to the particular job for which the applicant was seeking employment.

In essence, the Uniform Guidelines require that all employers who use pre-employment tests must determine that each such test does not discriminate (does not have adverse effect or impact) against any group of people having protected characteristics. Test, as defined in the Guidelines, means any paper-and-pencil instrument or other measurement of a person's skill, knowledge, ability, or fitness. Given the scope of this definition, it is easy to see that virtually every conceivable type of preemployment test likely to be given by employers is covered as a regulated test under the Guidelines. For preemployment tests to be lawful, and therefore allowable, each element of the test must bear a direct relationship to the job (be valid), be administered equally for all taking the test, and otherwise not result in a discriminatory effect upon any protected group of people. The latter point means that, as a general rule, a test will be considered invalid if fewer than 80 percent of any protected group fails to pass the test—referred to as the 4/5ths or 80 percent rule.

Validating preemployment tests is a time-consuming, complex, and costly proposition for most employers, but that fact should not deter you from making some effort to take at least informal validation measures. Formal validation procedures require administering the test to a statistically significant cross section of people, then analyzing the results using prescribed statistical formulas. If those results determine the test to be invalid, the problem questions (or components of other types of tests) must be changed and retested for validity. To avoid this elaborate procedure, yet demonstrate your interest in complying with the intent of this legal requirement, you should design each preemployment test based solely on the exact and more prevalent features of each separate job being tested.

Have your test reviewed by someone with adequate credentials, meaning someone who would represent a credible source to a court, before you administer it to applicants or employees. Also, you should keep a record of the characteristics of those who take your test and your respective test results as a means of determining possible bias within each test. You should compile these records on such tests as written examinations, performance tests, interviews, medicals, drug/alcohol tests, and any other selection device your company uses to make hiring decisions. If you purchase tests, you should request that the test developer provide you with proof of their validation effort and results pertaining to the test you are acquiring, and consider whether their information would hold up against the scrutiny of a court or compliance agency. Remember, *any* test you give is considered to be *your* test, and you will therefore be held liable for its results.

CHECKLIST: AFFIRMATIVE ACTION PROGRAM

☐ Issue a written equal employment policy and affirmative action commitment.

☐ Appoint a top official with responsibility and authority to direct and implement your program.

    1. Specify responsibilities of the program manager.

    2. Specify responsibilities and accountability of all managers and supervisors.

☐ Publicize your policy and affirmative action commitment.

    1. Internally: To managers, supervisors, all employees, and unions.

    2. Externally: To sources and potential sources of recruitment, potential minority and female applicants, to those with whom you do business, and to the community at large.

☐ Survey present minority and female employment by department and job classification.

    1. Identify present areas and levels of employment.

    2. Identify areas of concentration and underutilization.

    3. Determine extent of underutilization.

☐ Develop goals and timetables to improve utilization of minorities, males, and females in each area where underutilization has been identified.

☐ Develop and implement specific programs to achieve goals.

This is the heart of your program. Review your entire employment system to identify barriers to equal employment opportunity; make needed changes to increase employment and advancement opportunities of minorities and females. These areas need review and action:

    1. Recruitment: all personnel procedures.

    2. Selection process: job requirements; job descriptions, standards and procedures. Preemployment inquiries; application forms; testing; interviewing.

    3. Upward mobility system: assignments, job progressions; transfers; seniority; promotions; training.

    4. Wage and salary structure.

    5. Benefits and conditions of employment.

    6. Layoff, recall, termination, demotion, discharge, disciplinary action.

    7. Union contract provisions affecting above procedures.

☐ Establish internal audit and reporting systems to monitor and evaluate progress in each aspect of the program.

☐ Develop supportive in-house and community programs.

Chapter 18

PRECEDENT FAIR EMPLOYMENT COURT CASES

GENERAL—ADMINISTRATIVE PRECEDENCE

As was pointed out in the introduction to Part Three, employers can gain a better understanding of some employment laws by examining various court decisions related to a particular concern. They can begin to see certain trends in legal thinking emerge—trends that can be important for policy or situation decision making. This may be especially true with respect to fair employment (antidiscrimination) laws, as this realm of employment law depends on so many circumstantial variables. Therein lies some danger for you: court decisions, even those landmark or precedent-setting ones at the state or U.S. Supreme Court level, can be overturned by a subsequent decision or law. In a sense, then, the condition of employment law on any specific matter is like a photograph—it depends on conditions that exist at that moment.

To render the best available decision, an employer must ask:

1. What are the particular circumstances (fact pattern) surrounding the situation at hand?

2. What are the *present* conditions of (state and federal) laws and applicable court decisions on this matter?

3. What legal precedence and trend-setting thinking has been applied to this or similar situations in the past?

4. What is the legal and operational outcome of this situation likely to be if I do A, B, or C?

Bear in mind: the following case summaries should not be your sole source of advice or legal condition, but they do represent various cases of significance to the topics illustrated.

In formulating a decision on any of the topics presented, employers would be well advised to consult with a qualified employment law (labor) attorney who is abreast of the laws and court decisions in their state and at the federal level.

Texas Dept. of Community Affairs v. Burdine, 101 S. Ct. 1089 (1981)

Burden of proof/ hiring most qualified

Joyce Burdine brought an age discrimination suit when a male was hired in the position she occupied for an interim (acting) period. The U.S. Supreme Court found no evidence of discrimination, but did clarify that burden of proof to establish *prima facie* evidence is initially on plaintiff, while the defendant bears only the burden of clearly showing the nondiscriminatory reasons for its actions. It also determined that "the employer has discretion to choose among equally qualified candidates, provided the decision is not based upon unlawful criteria."

EEOC v. Associated Dry Goods Corp., S. Ct. 817 (1981)

Employer obligation to disclose information to charging party

U.S. Supreme Court held that employer must honor the subpoena of charging party records by the duly authorized compliance agency. Title VII forbids disclosure of employment discrimination charges (records) to the public, but nondisclosure does not apply to compliance agencies. However, such agencies are not automatically authorized access to other charging party files against the same employer.

Nuss v. Pan American World Airways, Inc., et al., 24 FEP 1184, Ninth Circuit (1980)

Timely filing

Under Title VII of the 1964 Civil Rights Act, a charge must be filed with the Equal Employment Opportunity Commission (EEOC) within 180 days of the alleged occurrence of the unlawful employment practice. However, states where discrimination charges are regulated by state compliance agencies are referred to as "deferral" states, meaning that the state has statutory prohibitions against employment discrimination to the same or greater extent than federal law, these state laws are investigated and enforced by a state compliance agency, and the EEOC will "defer" a charge that has been filed to the appropriate state agency. Typically in deferral states, the state agency requires that a claim be filed in 180 days, and thereafter with the EEOC within 300 days from the date the employee (or person) feels the alleged discriminatory act occurred.

State of Connecticut et al., 102 S. Ct. 2525 (1982)

Bottom-line defense invalid

Supreme Court ruled in a 4–5 decision that the "bottom-line" hiring result does not provide an employer with a valid defense against a claim of racial discrimination in violation of Title VII of the 1964 CRA. Under the "bottom-line" defense provided for in the federal regulations, employers have been able to assert that individual components of a selection process should not be reviewed for adverse impact if the final selection resulted in no adverse impact.

Statistics of Case

	Took Test	Passed Test		Promoted	
		Number	Percentage	Number	Percentage
Whites	259	206	79.5%	35	13.5%
Blacks	48	26	54.0	11	22.9

Ford Motor Company v. EEOC, 458 US 219, 102 S. Ct. 3057, 73 L. Ed. 2d721 (1982)

Employer back pay liability

Claimants were three unemployed women who applied for positions with the Ford Motor Company. All were experienced. However, Ford selected men for the vacant positions. Two of the women subsequently were rehired by General Motors. When another vacancy occurred at Ford, the two women were offered positions unconditionally and without prejudice to their Title VII action seeking back pay. They refused because Ford would not also grant seniority retroactive to the date claimants first applied to Ford for jobs.

The U.S. Supreme Court after reviewing 42 U.S.C. 2000e-5(g) notes that back pay is not automatic or mandatory, and that the court's discretion is to be guided by meaningful standards. The primary objective of Title VII is to end discrimination and remove employment barriers, and the preferred means of accomplishing the objective is through cooperation and voluntary compliance. Therefore, to implement the objective, a policy encouraging employers promptly to make curative unconditional job offers on a voluntary basis is to be preferred to costly and interminable litigation. The court concludes:

> When a claimant rejects the offer of the job he originally sought, as supplemented by a right to full court-ordered compensation, his choice can be taken as establishing that he considers the ongoing injury he has suffered at the hands of the defendant to have been ended by the availability of better opportunities elsewhere. For this reason, we find that, absent special circumstances, the simple rule that the ongoing accrual of back pay liability is tolled when a Title VII claimant rejects the job he originally sought comports with Title VII's policy of making discrimination victims whole.

Kauffman v. Sidereal Corporation, Ninth Circuit, 695 Fd 343 (1982)

Back pay—not offset by unemployment insurance payments

Kauffman brought an action against her employer alleging unlawful retaliation in response to her filing a sex discrimination complaint with EEOC. Title VII makes it unlawful to discriminate against an employee because she has made a charge against her employer. The court found that Kauffman clearly demonstrated that her Title VII complaint played some part in her discharge and that the termination would not have occurred but for her complaint. The Title VII back pay remedy (42 U.S.C. 2000e-5(g)) provides, "Interim earnings or amounts earnable with reasonable diligence by the person or persons discriminated against shall operate to reduce the back pay otherwise allowable." There was nothing in the legislative history to assist in determining whether Congress intended that unemployment benefits be deducted. The court rejected arguments involving collateral source, double recovery, and punitive damages and held that "unemployment benefits received by a successful plaintiff in an employment discrimination action are not offset against a back pay award."

RACE DISCRIMINATION

Griggs v. *Duke Power Co.*, 401 U.S. 424 (1971)

Hiring on basis of job-related test

Griggs, a black male, applied for a maintenance position. He was rejected after failing to achieve a sufficiently high score on a general aptitude written test which contained subject matter and educational level questions unrelated to the position he sought. The court concluded that tests and other instruments used in hiring decisions must bear a reasonable job relationship to the position under consideration, and that inappropriately related tests constitute invalid artificial barriers to employment, particularly with regard to one's race.

Gomez v. *Alexian Bros. Hospital of San Jose*, Ninth Circuit Court of Appeals (1983)

Discrimination of contractors

A minority contractor who is discriminated against on the basis of race can bring suit against a potential employer under Title VII of the 1964 Civil Rights Act. This expands employer liability of discrimination to potential employees (contractors), as the effect of the discriminatory act is to bar the contractor from gainful employment.

RELIGIOUS DISCRIMINATION

Nottleson v. *Smith Steel Workers*, Seventh Circuit Court of Appeals (1981)

The U.S. Court of Appeals for the Seventh Circuit upheld the constitutionality of Section 701(j) of the Civil Rights Act of 1964, as amended, which requires employers and unions to accommodate reasonably the religious beliefs and practices of employees. The court also found that the accommodation provision of the act was not preempted by the National Labor Relations Act (NLRA). The case arose when the plaintiff joined a church which teaches that it is morally wrong to be a member of or pay dues to a labor organization. He notified the union of this and requested it to accommodate his beliefs by permitting him to pay

an equivalent sum to a non-union, nonreligious charity. The union refused and notified the plaintiff that if he did not pay his dues he would
be discharged. The employer indicated that it was willing to make an
accommodation but not without the consent of the union (which was
not forthcoming). The plaintiff filed suit under Title VII, alleging religious discrimination and the trial court found in his favor.

The union argued on appeal that the religious accommodation
provision of Title VII is preempted by those provisions of the NLRA,
which require enforcement of union security clauses. The union maintained that these provisions represent a congressional determination
of the balance to be struck between the national policy of promoting
labor peace and the national policy protecting the religious needs of
individual employees and, therefore, constitutes an exception to the
duty to accommodate otherwise imposed by Title VII.

The Court of Appeals, disagreeing, found that the balance struck
by the NLRA was between the abuses of compulsory unionism and the
problem of "free-riders" and that the question of religious accommodation was not addressed by the NLRA. The court stressed that there
is no national labor policy of higher priority than the elimination of
discrimination in employment. Furthermore, it noted that the union's
claim that the NLRA established an overriding policy favoring union
security provisions is belied by the fact that such provisions are unen-
forceable in states where state law is to the contrary. The court held
that the union security provisions of the NLRA do not relieve an employer or a union of the duty to accommodate the individual religious
needs of the employee. The employer and the union both argued on appeal that accommodating the plaintiff's beliefs in this case would create "undue hardship" which would result in discrimination against
other employees. The court found that the union presented no evidence suggesting that the loss of the employee's dues would require an
increase in the dues of other employees and that by contributing to
charity, the plaintiff was bearing an equal financial burden.

The employer argued that it could not unilaterally accept plaintiff's suggestion for accommodation in disregard of the union security
clause of the collective bargaining agreement. The court reasoned,
however, that Title VII rights cannot be bargained away and that a collective bargaining agreement does not, in itself, provide a defense for
Title VII violations. The court of appeals upheld the trial court's ruling that both the union and the employer violated Title VII in that they
failed to show undue hardship.

Finally, the court rebuffed the challenges of the employer and
the union that the religious accommodation provision of Title VII
was an unconstitutional establishment of religion in violation of the
First Amendment. Using the three-part test enunciated by the U.S.
Supreme Court, the court of appeals found that Title VII serves a
secular purpose (the elimination of discrimination), and does not
have the primary effect of advancing the interests of "religionists"
over "nonreligionists" or the beliefs of one sect over another.

It does not confer a benefit on those accommodated, but rather relieves those individuals of a special burden that others do not suffer by permitting them to fulfill their societal obligations in a different manner . . .

The court found that some religions' having more or different religiously dictated observances than other religions does not invalidate the law that applies to all faiths equally. Finally, the court found that the provision does not foster an "excessive governmental entanglement" with religion. The government is required only to determine whether a belief is religious within the meaning of the statute and whether it is sincerely held. The court accordingly upheld the constitutionality of the religious accommodation provision in affirming the trial court's decision in favor of the plaintiff.

SEX, SEXUAL HARASSMENT, MARITAL STATUS, AND PREGNANCY DISCRIMINATION

Harriss v. *Pan American World Airways, Inc.,* 24 FEP Cases 947, Ninth Circuit (1980)

Pregnancy leave

The Appellate Court held that Pan Am's mandatory policy requiring female flight attendants to take maternity leave upon their learning of their pregnancy was justified by safety considerations under both business necessity and bona fide occupational qualification (BFOQ) defense.

EEOC v. *Lockheed Missiles and Space Co., Inc.,* 680 F2d 1243 (1982)

Pregnancy medical benefits

The U.S. Court of Appeals for the Ninth Circuit has ruled that the Pregnancy Discrimination Act of 1978, which is an amendment to Title VII of the Civil Rights Act of 1964 does not apply to spouses of male employees. The Ninth Circuit stated that the Pregnancy Discrimination Act applies to women employees and the "exclusion of pregnancy-related medical expenses of spouses of male employees was not gender-based discrimination in violation of Section 703(a) of Title VII."

Lockheed offered its employees a medical benefit plan that covered the medical expenses of the dependents of its employees with the exception of pregnancy. The EEOC alleged that this plan discriminated against male employees in violation of Title VII. EEOC believed the *spouses of male employees* would not be covered for medical expenses resulting from pregnancy while *female employees* would be covered. The district court ruled in favor of the company; it believed that the Pregnancy Discrimination Act applied only to *women employees*.

On appeal, the Ninth Circuit noted that the Pregnancy Discrimination Act was passed by Congress to overturn the 1976 Supreme Court ruling in the case of *General Electric Company* v. *Gilbert.* In that case, the Supreme Court held that, in providing insurance benefits to employees, an employer could exclude pregnancy-related disabilities from the coverage. Title VII prohibits discrimination based on an individual's sex and the Pregnancy Discrimination Act expanded the definition of sex discrimination to include pregnancy. The Ninth Circuit believed that Congress intended to cover only women employees.

The U.S. Court of Appeals for the Fourth Circuit reached the opposite conclusion in a similar case *(Newport News Shipbuilding and Dry Dock Company* v. *Equal Employment Opportunity Commission)*. In that case, the Fourth Circuit believed that a health insurance plan which provided larger pregnancy benefits to female employees than were provided to the spouses of male employees violated Title VII. The Fourth Circuit ruled that the Pregnancy Discrimination Act contained "no intimation that benefits payable with respect to the disability of a spouse are excluded from the statute's reach." It is possible that the Supreme Court will decide to review these cases in order to resolve the conflict that exists between the Fourth Circuit and the Ninth Circuit.

Wambheim v. J. C. Penney Co., Inc., Ninth Circuit Court of Appeals (1981)

Head of household— disparate impact

The appellate court reversed the district court decision, holding that the plaintiff established a *prima facie* case of disparate impact based on a showing that Penney's "head of household" rule resulted in only 37 percent of the female employees' receiving dependent medical coverage compared to 95 percent for male employees.

Gunther v. County of Washington, 101 Supreme Court 2242 (1981)

Sex-based pay discrimination can be brought as a Title VII action

Plaintiff was a jail matron seeking remedy for differential pay between female *matrons* and *male* guards whose duties were substantially similar in nature. Case was an attempt to get the U.S. Supreme Court to decide on the doctrine of "comparable-worth" pay. Rather, the high court upheld the state supreme court's finding that sex-based pay discrimination could be sought as a joint violation of the 1963 Equal Pay Act and Title VII of the 1964 Civil Rights Act.

Kouba, EEOC v. Allstate Insurance Co., 691 F. 2nd., Ninth Circuit (1982)

Equal pay— prior salary as a factor

Allstate Insurance Company computes minimum salary for new sales agents on the basis of ability, education, experience, and "prior salary." Kouba, representing a class of females, contended that use of "prior salary" as a factor discriminates against women because women traditionally have been paid less than men. In other words, the use of prior salary results on the average in female agents making less than males. Allstate contended that the use of "prior salary" is a factor "other than sex" and therefore an exception to the equal pay requirement. When positions require equal skill, effort, and responsibility and are performed under similar working conditions, an employer must provide equal pay regardless of the sex of the person occupying the position. However, there are four exceptions where such payment is made, pursuant to (1) a seniority system, (2) a merit system, (3) a system that measures earnings by quantity or quality of production, or (4) a differential based on any other factor other than sex.

The court of appeals first indicates it has held that the *employer* bears the burden of showing that the wage differential resulted from a factor other than sex. The court also notes that:

> An employer cannot use a factor which causes a wage differential between male and female employees absent an acceptable business reason. Conversely, a factor used to effectuate some business policy is not prohibited simply because a wage differential results.

To prevent an employer from using business reasons as a pretext for a discriminatory objective, the court suggests that the employer use the factor reasonably in the light of the employer's stated purpose as well as its other practices. While it is held that the Equal Pay Act does not impose a strict prohibition against the use of prior salary, the trial court must find that the business reasons given by the employer do not reasonably explain its use of that factor before finding a violation of the act.

Jurgens v. *EEOC*, USDC, Texas (1982)

Reverse discrimination— males

Jurgens was a trial attorney in the EEOC Dallas office and claimed a woman was appointed to a position he had applied for because of her sex. The U.S. district court held that the EEOC had established a policy of preference for females and that the "preferences were not remedial because jobs were not traditionally closed to women and minorities."

Chronology of Legal Events Leading to Current Definitions and Prohibitions of Sexual Harassment

1975   First reported lawsuit in Arizona (*Corne* v. *Bausch & Lomb*), wherein two female employees resigned due to repeated verbal and physical advances by their supervisor; rejected by court as mere proclivity of supervisor not serving policy interest of employer.

1977   First case to determine that sexual harassment affects job conditions and is therefore an act of sex discrimination under Title VII (*Barnes* v. *Costle, Dist. of Columbia*). Similarly, the Third Circuit Court of Appeals found (*Tomkins* v. *Public Service Electric and Gas Co.*) that the employer did not take "prompt and appropriate action" when advised of a supervisor's dismissal of a female employee who wouldn't submit to his demands for sexual favors.

1979   A mere policy prohibiting sexual harassment is no defense (*Miller* v. *Bank of America*, Ninth Circuit).

1980   EEOC releases Guidelines on Sexual Harassment Discrimination.

1982   Quid pro quo theory of sexual harassment established (*Hensen* v. *City of Dundee*, Eleventh Circuit).

1986   Hostile work environment theory established in first sexual harassment case to reach the U.S. Supreme Court (*Meritor Savings Bank* v. *Vinson*).

            Off-duty harassment by supervisor toward a female employee did not relieve the employer of liability because such acts are an extension of company vested authority (*Schroeder* v. *Schock*, Kansas Dist. Court).

1987   Workers' compensation not exclusive remedy where physical or emotional damage done to victim, and lack of timely handling by employer is sufficient evidence for finding of *intentional* infliction of emotional distress (*Ford* v. *Revlon*, Arizona Supreme Court).

1991   Application of court-defined "reasonable woman" rule (*Ellison* v. *Brady*, Ninth Circuit) with regard to perception of harassment by alleged victim.

            Employer may sue employee who sexually harassed a female employee as determined by an Oklahoma state appeals court (*Biggs* v. *Surrey Broadcasting Co.*).

Sexual harassment in the workplace has become a prominent issue for employers since the Equal Employment Opportunity Commission issued its November 1980 guidelines (Section 1604.11); this form of workplace conduct was brought within the meaning of sex discrimination under Title VII of the 1964 Civil Rights Act in at least two 1978 precedent court decisions. This is not to say that the issue of uninvited sexual conduct was less than prominent prior to regulatory involvement. Quite the contrary, for it is a well-researched and long-standing fact that the workplace provides a diverse range of opportunities for men and women to develop an affinity, but it also provides unique problems that would not exist in situations other than the workplace. It is important for employers to gain a more complete understanding of what constitutes sexual harassment in the workplace, how to prevent it or recognize it when it happens, and how it should be handled if a complaint emerges.

The issuance of the 1980 EEOC guidelines on sexual harassment was in response to an alarming number of complaints by female employees that they were being sexually harassed and threatened with termination or other retaliatory measures by male supervisors. The intent of the guidelines was to establish the definitions, standards, and conditions of sexual harassment so that employers would understand how to initiate remedial measures, and to establish methods of processing complaints. Yet the definition of sexual harassment remains something of a problem for employers because of the seemingly subjective aspect of a person's perception, and the fact that some courts recognize the right of the alleging person to define harassment in many instances. However, the general trend in legal thinking is that sexual harassment is more often the insensitivity of the initiating person than it is the sensitivity of the recipient, but even the courts acknowledge that perceptions of such abusive treatment as sexual harassment vary widely among individuals. More precisely, the guidelines define sexual harassment as follows:

> Unwelcome sexual advances, requests for sexual favors, and other verbal or physical conduct of a sexual nature constitute sexual harassment when (1) submission

to such conduct is made either explicitly or implicitly a term or condition of an individual's employment; (2) submission to or rejection of such conduct by an individual is used as the basis for employment decisions affecting such individual; or (3) such conduct has the purpose or effect of unreasonably interfering with an individual's work performance or creating an intimidating, hostile, or offensive working environment.

To offer some reassurance to employers and employees alike that claims will be viewed within the context of guideline intent on the facts and merit of individual cases, the guidelines go on to state:

> In determining whether alleged conduct constitutes sexual harassment, the Commission will look at the record as a whole and at the totality of the circumstances, such as the nature of the sexual advances and the context in which the alleged incidents occurred. The determination of the legality of a particular action will be made from the facts, on a case-by-case basis.

Additionally, the guidelines hold employers liable for the acts of their "agents," regardless of whether the conduct was forbidden by the employer, or whether the employer "knew or should have known" of the occurrence of sexual harassment.

Employers are again reminded that the burden of proof in any type of discrimination case rests with them. In defending a claim of sexual harassment, it is advisable to be able to demonstrate an awareness of law, taking preventive measures such as distributing policies and training supervisors in sexual harassment prohibitions, and being prepared to take immediate corrective action if such a condition surfaces.

Sexual harassment law is equally applicable to males and females, and to heterosexuals and homosexuals alike. It applies primarily to superior-subordinate relationships, but also includes harassment occurring between peer employees *and* between nonemployee and an employee. Historically, and based on sociocultural conditioning of role behavior, women have been the predominant victims of sexual harassment. To them, the issue is ever present, while many men have difficulty believing the issue is a serious one (or that it exists in their organizations) simply because they don't behave in those ways and don't see those traits in other men. Denial that sexual harassment is taking or might take place, whether a conscious or unconscious attitude, will undoubtedly complicate the matter for employees, or impede the resolution of a situation that emerges; the fact that a complaint hasn't emerged doesn't mean that sexual harassment isn't going on.

It should also be pointed out that the guideline prohibitions on sexual harassment do not include friendship or even romance among employees. The key here, and the likely reason for its exclusion, is that friendship and romance are assumed to be conditions *mutually* entered into and fostered by both persons. While this "romance in the office" situation may represent a wholly new type of problem for some employers as disclosed in many recent business magazine articles, it remains outside the scope of prohibited harassing conduct unless the romantic attraction takes a *one-sided* turn and subsequently becomes harassing in nature. The three most common factors examined to determine sexual harassment are:

1. *Unwelcome/Offensive Behavior:* Exchanges of sexually suggestive conversations, jokes, and the like among employees is not, in itself, considered unwelcome or offensive behavior if everyone participates, but even these situations can lead to offensiveness and should therefore be discouraged. In the stricter sense of unwelcome and offensive behavior, the perpetrator has used bad judgment by making explicit sexual remarks, gestures, invitations, or some act that the recipient did not invite and does not want continued. Often, the recipient won't say anything for fear of reprisal from the perpetrator (termination, poor evaluations, denial of pay increases or promotion). However, studies have shown that in the case of a male perpetrator and female recipient, most men would have discontinued their behavior if they were told by the woman that their interest was not mutual or pleasing. The point to be made here is that the law does not require the recipient to confront the perpetrator—only to bring it to the employer's attention, then it is up to the employer to take corrective action quickly (in a discreet manner).

2. *One-Sided versus Mutual Interest:* If one's behavior is unwelcome or offensive, the situation is also one-sided. If it is, the employer should act to correct the condition. If, on the other hand, the situation started as a mutual one, then later became one-sided, both parties should be held responsible to some degree in the employer's resolution. Additionally, while (implied) mutual consent between employees who are engaging in sexually oriented behavior (touching, inuendos, etc.) is not considered harassment within the legal meaning, employers should consider eliminating this behavior early, as it can, and often does, become offensive or interfere with the work of other employees, or it becomes a one-sided attraction that creates other problems.

3. *Authority:* Sexually harassing conduct can be initiated by a subordinate, a coworker, a superior, or an outsider. The most serious case is that in which the harassment is initiated by a superior toward a subordinate, because of the decision-making authority held, directly or indirectly, by the superior, providing a more intimidating work condition for the subordinate. The existence of authority over another person's job and related work conditions presents a particularly threatening situation for subordinates, and for this reason it is imperative that employers adopt an internal complaint mechanism that provides discreet handling of these situations, without fear of reprisal.

In summation, then, sexually harassing behavior (1) is unwelcome or offensive, (2) is one-sided and repetitive (except in cases of sexual assault), (3) involves authority that produces an intimidating environment, and (4) makes the recipient feel powerless to stop the behavior. The existence of a sexually harassing situation is dependent on the recipient's perception of these conditions, not the initiator's intent or perception. Here are some specific examples of conduct that should be communicated to *all* employees as unacceptable by the employer.

- Verbal:
  - —Sexually oriented compliments, remarks, inquiries, or manner of referring to another person; personal or telephone pressuring for dates (dinner, drinks, etc.) or sexual encounter, and jokes of a sexual nature.
  - —Referring to another as honey, sweetheart, doll, girl/boy, dear, and the like.
  - —"You turn me on" . . . "Don't be afraid to show your merchandise" . . . "You seem tense—aren't you getting enough?" . . . "You'd have a better chance for promotion if we got to know each other better" . . . "I enjoy watching you when you wear (tight clothes, low-cut blouses)" . . . "Did you hear the one about the lesbian who . . ."
- Nonverbal: Flirting, leering (visually undressing); protruding tongue in a sexual expression; leaving notes of a sexual nature on a desk or in a mailbox; allowing the display of nude or sexually suggestive photos, centerfolds, or cartoons; touching—particularly on the waist, hips, leg, and buttocks—or restricting the movement of another (blocking passage or physically restraining); pinching; and unsolicited neck or back rubs.

Given the diversity of the work force, their differences in life-styles, preferences, and perceptions, and the nature of workplace interaction between men and women that can set the stage and provide the countless opportunities for a sexually harassing situation, employers can no longer rely on unwritten or implied standards of sexual conduct. Nor should employers take a passive position merely because they recognize that most of their employees behave in a responsible manner. The time has come for employers to address this problem of workplace conduct openly by stressing its unacceptability, the complaint and investigative methods, and types of corrective action, including possible termination, in written policies, communications with employees, and training for those in positions of authority. Failure to do so will only perpetuate the problem, leaving the employer with a greater potential for unproductive employees; loss of credibility, respect, and trust in those with authority; and the persistent threat of litigation. Prevention has always been the best solution.

The number and variety of court cases dealing with sexual harassment in the workplace since its public notoriety began in the mid-1970s is too extensive to provide comprehensive legal detail here. However, it may prove helpful to list a few of the more trend-setting cases that have led various courts, state legislatures, and compliance agencies to formulate the conditions under which violations of prohibited activities occur, and the extent of the employer's liability in the way of monetary damages.

Williams v. Saxbe, 413 F. Supp. 654, 11 E.P.D. 10,840 (D.D.C. 1976)

Significance of the problem

The court ruled that gender is a factor contributing to discrimination in a substantial way and that the charge of sexual harassment had a cause of action under Title VII of the Civil Rights Act.

Tomkins v. Public Service Electric and Gas Co., 568 F. 2d 1044 (3rd Cir. 1977)

Failure to take prompt and appropriate action

This appellate court ruled that Title VII was violated because the employer did not take "prompt and appropriate action" when advised of a supervisor's dismissal of a female employee who did not submit to his demands for sexual favors. See also **Heslan v. Johns-Manville Corp., 29 FEP Cases 251 (DC Col. 1978)**

Miller v. Bank of America, 600 F2d 211 (9th Cir. 1979)

Mere policy prohibition is no defense

Even though the bank had an established policy prohibiting sexual harassment, the court did not hold the bank harmless from charges of sexual harassment when a bank supervisor discharged a female employee because she refused to submit to his requests for sexual favors.

Minnesota v. Continental Can Co., 23 E.P.D. 30,997 (Minn. S. Ct. 1980)

Employer obligation to prohibit coworker harassment

The Minnesota Supreme Court held that the employer is also responsible for the behavior of coworkers in ensuring that the work environment is free of sexual harassment.

Bundy v. Jackson, 641 F2d 934 (C.A.C.D. 1981); see also Gan v. Kepro Circuit Systems, 28 FEP 639 (E.C. Mo. 1982)

Proof of harassment not dependent on job loss

Court ruled that sexual harassment, in and of itself, is unlawful. For a complaint to be valid, proof that loss of a job or job benefit would occur is not needed.

1980

Equal Employment Opportunity Commission releases Guidelines on Sexual Harassment Discrimination

Hensen v. City of Dundee, 682 F2d 897 (11th Cir. 1982); see also Morgan v. Hertz Corp., 542 F. Supp. 123 (WD Tenn. 1981)

Quid pro quo theory established

The court in this case clarified the quid pro quo (something given for something exchanged, that is job security or advancement in exchange for sexual favors) theory of sexual harassment.

Meritor Savings Bank v. Vinson, 477 U.S. 57 (1986)

Hostile work environment theory established

The first U.S. Supreme Court case heard on the issue of sexual harassment established the theory and general parameters of sexual harassment having the effect of creating a hostile work environment. However, the court rejected the EEOC's orientation that the employer is automatically liable for hostile environment harassment when such conduct is precipitated by managers and supervisors;

rather, the court determined that each should be examined in light of all factual information including contributory involvement factors of the person being harassed (e.g., provocative dress, lewd joke telling, suggestive conversation, and the like). Notwithstanding these issues, the employer was found liable in this case since upper management knew of the "victims" complaints for an extended period of time and choose to do little about it. At trial, it was made known that the victim and harasser (her supervisor) had had sexual contact forty to fifty times in a two-year period, but that it was an ongoing and nonconsensual relationship based on the supervisors' promise of a promotion.

Ford v. *Revlon,* Az. Sup. Ct. (1987)

Workers' compensation not exclusive remedy

The Arizona Supreme Court ruled in this case that workers' compensation is not the exclusive remedy where physical or emotional damage is done to an employee subjected to sexual harassment (rape, physical assault, battery, etc.) and lack of timely handling by the employer is sufficient evidence for a finding of *intentional* infliction of emotional distress.

Ellison v. *Brady,* 924 F2d 871 (9th Cir. 1991); see also *Rabidue* v. *Osceola Refining Co.,* 805 F. 2d 611 (6th Cir. 1986)

Reasonable woman rule established

This case set the standard on whether sexual harassment is determined solely by the perception of the victim or by what other similar victims would regard as offensive behavior or hostile conditions. Both cases essentially determined that the trier of fact should evaluate the totality of all circumstances in light of how a "reasonable person" would react to similar circumstances under the same or similar conditions.

Robinson v. *Jacksonville Shipyards,* (M.D. Fla. 1991)

Explicit photos violates women's rights

This case determined that the posting by men of explicit photos of women was an overt form of sexual harassment, the nature of which abridges the men's right to "freedom of expression."

Biggs v. *Surrey Broadcasting Co.,* 56 FEP Cases 289 (1991)

Employer may seek indemnification suit against harasser

This Oklahoma appellate court determined that it was lawful for an employer to seek indemnification recovery of damages for sexual harassment of a supervisor brought by a female employee victimized by her supervisor. The employer agreed to a $65,000 settlement and terminated the supervisor for his outrageous conduct. Then the supervisor filed suit against the employer for severance and vacation pay. The employer filed a counterclaim against the harasser for indemnification in the amount of the settlement of the sexual harassment case. The court, in agreeing with the employer's right to bring suit for indemnification, noted that (in Oklahoma) there exists an implied contract of indemnity between one who is vicariously liable for a tort (the employer) and the person who commits the wrong (the harasser).

Employers may also want to consider the potential unemployment insurance liability issue connected to sexual harassment. Should an employee quit because of unsatisfactory response from the employer, or perhaps even the existence of an intimidating work environment due to sexual overtures, an Unemployment Insurance Appeals Board may determine that the employee had good cause to voluntarily terminate the employment relationship, and thereby award a claim in behalf of the employee and against the employer.

CHECKLIST: SEXUAL HARASSMENT PREVENTION AND COMPLAINT PROCESS

☐ Has a written, comprehensive policy prohibiting sexual harassment been adopted and communicated to all employees?

☐ Does the policy name a specific company officer to whom complaints of sexual harassment should be filed? Is the complaint procedure clearly stated, practical, and does it assure employees that complaints will be handled with the utmost confidentiality and discretion?

☐ Are complaints investigated promptly, thoroughly, and in an unbiased fashion?

☐ Does the complaint constitute:

　☐ Behavior or an act that can reasonably be construed as unwelcome, offensive, or intimidating?

　☐ Sexual assault or repetitive conduct of a harassing nature?

　☐ An exercise (abuse) of authority by the perpetrator over the complainant?

　☐ Implied or expressed conditions of sexual favors in consideration of job retention, promotion, or any other benefit of employment?

　☐ Contributing behavior on the part of the complainant?

☐ Are all the circumstances of the complaint, including responses of the alleged perpetrator and witnesses, documented in detail?

☐ Has corrective action, if warranted, been taken, including discipline or termination of the perpetrator (or the complainant in the case of a falsified complaint or contributory behavior)?

☐ Have the complainant and other *directly* involved persons been served notice of the employer's disposition of the matter?

Sex-Based Pay Discrimination Cases

Angelo v. Bacharach Instrument Co., 14 FEP Cases 1778

Similarity of work content

This case arose because the defendant company was paying male and female bench assemblers different rates of pay. The court ruled that before equal pay standards—equal skill, effort, and responsibility under similar working conditions—apply, it must be shown that jobs done by men and women have substantially the same content (i.e., terms and conditions of work).

Bourque v. Powell Electrical Manufacturing Co., 19 FEP Cases 1524

Similarity of work content

A female buyer established that she was discriminated against when she showed that she performed work substantially equal to that of male buyers but for less compensation. A male buyer eventually performed other duties, but these were never assigned to the female buyer even though she had the qualifications to perform them.

Christensen v. State of Iowa, 16 FEP Cases 222

Market pay a factor in setting pay/comparable worth

The court found for the defendant, although it was paying its female clerical force less pay than its male maintenance workers and even though the results of a point factor job evaluation plan determined the jobs to be essentially equal by assigned points. The court ruled that the market must be taken into consideration when making final pay determinations and that jobs are considered equal only when assignments are similar.

DiSalvo v. Chamber of Commerce of Greater Kansas City, 13 FEP Cases 636

Higher pay for replacement employee/ sex-based discrimination

In this case, the defendant was found guilty of unfair employment practices because it paid a female associate editor considerably less than it did the male communications specialist hired to replace her. They performed substantially the same duties, and the additional duties assigned to the male replacement, such as photography, were considered inconsequential. The female received $8,200 a year, and the male received $12,000 a year.

Howard v. Ward County, North Dakota, 14 FEP Cases 548

Equal pay act violation

A female deputy sheriff performing work substantially equal to that of higher-paid deputies in skill, effort, and responsibility was unlawfully discriminated against. The award to the plaintiff for back pay was predicted on the pay received by a major in the sheriff's office as uncontroverted evidence that the female deputy did work equal to that performed by the major.

Marshall v. Hodag Chemical Corp., (N.D. Ill., 1978), 16 EPD #8323

Equal Pay Act violation

The court found against a chemical manufacturing company that was paying higher wages to a male analytical chemist than to a female analytical chemist, even though they had equal job duties. Although the male had performed some supervisory duties and had more academic credentials, the Equal Pay Act does not require jobs to be identical, only substantially equal.

Lemons v. City & County of Denver, 22 FEP Cases 959

Market wage comparison/ comparable worth

The court found the defendant not guilty of violating Title VII despite the contention that it paid nurses (a female-dominated occupation) less than it pays persons doing comparable work in male-dominated occupations. The defendant used the market to set wage rates of nurses.

Marshall v. Farmers Insurance Co., (N.D. Kan. 1978), 17 EPD #8581

Equal pay violation

A female promoted to policywriter supervisor began at a lower pay level than males similarly promoted and was never granted salary parity with her male peers. Although on several occasions, the female received raises equal to or grater than those of her male peers, her lower starting salary kept her at a pay disadvantage, which was considered a discriminatory practice.

Peltler v. City of Fargo, 12 FEP Cases 945

Equal pay violation

This ruling held that although male police officers were more skilled than their female counterparts, the job content for issuing tickets for parking and other nonmoving violations did not justify higher pay for the males.

Taylor v. Weaver Oil & Gas Corp., 18 FEP Cases 23

Validity of pay differential when job requirements are different

Female draftspersons received lower starting salaries and lower pay increases than their male counterparts. The pay differentials were justified by the extra duties of some employees and by differences in experience and job performance. Pay differentials were held to be substantively valid based on content differences, and the defendant prevailed by a showing of its intent to introduce female employees into this nontraditional occupation.

From these court rulings, it is evident that the courts, when involved in pay discrimination cases, place considerable emphasis on:

1. Job content.
2. Ordering of jobs by such compensable factors as skill, effort, and responsibility, or their equivalent.
3. Actual duties performed and quality of job performance.
4. Relating of actual pay received by incumbents to preset limits of the jobs.
5. Education and skills actually required in the performance of current assignments.
6. Influence of the market on the actual pay assigned to a particular job.

PHYSICAL HANDICAP DISCRIMINATION

American National Insurance Co. v. FEHC, 32 Cal. 3d. 603 (1982)

High blood pressure—FEHC coverage as physical handicap

An insurance company that had terminated a sales and debit agent on account of his elevated blood pressure sought judicial review of an administrative decision that the company had violated the California Fair Employment and Housing Act (FEHA), which prohibits employment discrimination against one with a physical handicap (Gov. Code, Section 12940; former Lab. Code, Section 1420). Although the agent's high blood pressure did not impair his ability to work, the employer believed, on medical advice, that it would expose him to a greater than normal risk of disability or death. Concluding that high blood pressure was a protected physical handicap under the act and that the findings of the Fair Employment and Housing Commission were supported by the evidence, the trial court denied the company's petition for administrative mandamus.

The Supreme Court affirmed. The Court held that high blood pressure may be a "physical handicap" under the FEHA, as the statutory definition of such term (Gov. Code, Section 12926, subd. (h)) is not restrictive, thus permitting consideration of all handicaps that are physical, and as the legislature did not intend to cover only those health problems that are presently disabling. For purposes of the FEHA, the Court held that a physical handicap is a condition of the body which has the disabling effect of making achievement unusually difficult. The Court also held that the trial court properly employed the substantial evidence test, as the right to establish employment practices and procedures could not be termed a fundamental vested right and properly found as a fact that the record did not support the company's contention that the employee could not perform his duties in a manner that would not endanger his health or safety.

Simon v. St. Louis County, Missouri, 8th Circuit Court of Appeals No. 80-1667 (1981)

BFOQ— reasonable, legitimate necessary job requirements

An employer was required to review the physical requirements of a job to determine if they were "reasonable, legitimate, and necessary" and would not discriminate against a handicapped individual. According to the Eighth Circuit Court of Appeals, a review must be made to determine whether the accommodation required to employ a handicapped individual was reasonable. The plaintiff in this case was a police officer who was paralyzed as a result of having been shot. St. Louis County terminated him from his job on the ground that he was unable to fulfill the required duties. The plaintiff sued, alleging a violation of the Rehabilitation Act of 1973. The district court dismissed the case, as it did not believe that he could perform all of the department's physical requirements and that substantial modification would have to be undertaken for Mr. Simon to be employed. The district court had concluded that, based on the Supreme Court decision in the case of *Southeastern Community College* v. *Davis*, Mr. Simon was not an otherwise qualified handicapped individual.

The court of appeals remanded the case, as it believed the court applied too rigid a standard. The court of appeals believed the *Davis* case referred to those handicapped persons who could satisfy all the "legitimate physical requirements of a program." The Appellate Court believed there must be an examination as to whether the requirements of St. Louis County were reasonable and necessary for the job. These requirements consisted of being able to effect a forcible arrest and render emergency aid in addition to having the capacity to be transferred to any position within the police department. The court of appeals believed that substantial evidence existed to demonstrate that the physical requirements "were not in fact necessary and were not required of all officers." The court also stated that consideration should be given to the plaintiff's actual physical condition in addition to his police experience and a determination should be made as to which functions within the department the plaintiff had the physical capacity to perform.

OFCCP v. E.E. Black, Ltd., 19 FEP Cases 1624 (DOC) (1979)

Perceived handicap—future limitations invalid

The definition of handicap was liberally construed in this Department of Labor ruling. The case involved a carpenter apprentice with a history of back problems who was perceived by a government contractor as predisposed to future back disease or injury. The person was denied employment even though he could presently perform all the necessary job skills and was within the definition of a "qualified handicapped individual." The contractor was found to be in violation of Section 503 of the Rehabilitation Act and was ordered to offer the carpenter a job in addition to providing back pay. In so holding, the department defined "impairment" as a condition that weakens, diminishes, restricts, or otherwise damages the individual's physical or mental ability. Further, it is not necessary for the impairment to affect the general employability of the applicant but only that the impairment is a current bar to the employment of the applicant's choice with a federal contractor. The department cautioned, however, that Section 503 does not protect persons with conditions of impairment that are of no consequence in their securing, retaining, or advancing in a particular job.

Duran v. City of Tampa, 17 FEP Cases 914 (USDC Fla.) (1977)

"Impairment" does not have to be actual current disability

Duran was an applicant rejected for the position of police officer due to a past medical history of epilepsy. The district court held that a person capable of performing the duties of a police officer as demonstrated by physical tests and medical opinion could not be barred from employment merely because of past medical history if such a person is in all other respects qualified.

Note: A Florida district court later held under a case alleging violation of constitutional equal protection rights that there was violation where the U.S. Postal Service refused to hire a person with a history of epilepsy for the position of postal clerk, which required driving a vehicle, because the post office's ban on hiring epileptics served a valid and important interest in preventing harm to other employees and the public. *Courts* v. *U.S. Postal Service,* 17 FEP Cases 1161 (USDC Fla.) (1978)

Davis v. Bucher, 17 FEP Cases 919 (USDC Penn.) (1978)

Drug abuse— impairment of "life activity"

This district court held that persons with histories of drug use were handicapped individuals within the meaning of the Rehabilitation Act and therefore employers could not absolutely refuse to hire persons because of their former drug abuse.

Note: Although Section 503 and the Veterans' Act have this common purpose, their scope and applicability differ. Section 503 sets forth certain requirements applying to both public and private employers who employ persons to work under a contract or subcontract with any federal department or agency for the procurement of goods or nonpersonal service. Such requirements often include the formulation of an affirmative action program to aid the employment of handicapped individuals. A "handicapped individual" is broadly defined under the Rehabilitation Act to include any person who:

1. Has a physical or mental impairment that substantially limits one or more of such person's major life activities;
2. Has a record of such impairment; or
3. Is regarded as having such an impairment.

"Life activities" are interpreted (by Section 504 regulations) to include such activities as self-care, communicating, walking, seeing, breathing, performing manual tasks, learning, working, and socializing. This definition reaches not only those who have a present impairment, including alcoholism and drug addiction, but also those persons who have a history of, or have been misclassified as having, a handicap.

Carmi v. St. Louis Sewer District, 20 FEP Cases 162 (USDC Mo.) (1979)

Reasonable accommodation— capable of performing job

This district court held that the Rehabilitation Act prohibits nonhiring of handicapped workers only when their disabilities do not prevent them from performing the job. In that case, the complainant's charges of discrimination were dismissed because his rare hereditary disease caused muscle and nerve deterioration, weakness of grip, uneven gait, and inability to lift over forty pounds and thus he could not show that he could perform on a daily and continued basis the requisite job-related skills of a storeroom keeper. In addition to meeting the definition of handicapped, to qualify as an "otherwise qualified applicant," such individual must be able to prove that he is capable of performing the particular job with reasonable accommodation to his handicap.

Note: A similar finding was made by a California federal district court in holding that a school board did not violate Section 504 when it refused to hire a blind teacher for an administrative position because the board determined that the individual lacked necessary administrative skills and had not demonstrated requisite experience or leadership ability. Although the court's holding was based on its finding that the teacher was not a "qualified handicapped person," it went on to say that it was proper for the board to consider the teacher's handicap in determining whether he was qualified. Further, the court stated that the Rehabilitation Act's requirement to reasonably accommodate handicapped workers does not require the school district to hire an assistant to aid the handicapped person.

Rogers v. *Frito-Lay, Inc.,* **14 FEP Cases 1752 (USDC Texas) (1977)**

Qualification of federal grant recipient

This district court found that handicapped persons could not maintain an action under Section 504 against an employer that received federal funds under a procurement contract. Similarly, a Virginia district court held that a woman who was fired because of failing eyesight did not have a cause of action under 504 merely because the Medicaid, welfare, and medical payments received by the employer were not grants but rather payments for services rendered. See also *Trageser* v. *Libbie Rehabilitation Center,* 17 FEP Cases 938 (1979).

Coleman v. *Darden,* **19 FEP Cases 137 (10th Circuit Ct. of Appeals) (1979)**

Failure to meet job qualifications

This appellate court upheld the EEOC's rejection of a blind law clerk on the basis that the EEOC did not automatically exclude the applicant from consideration, but rather made an individual determination that he was not qualified for the requirements of the position. Plaintiff in this case brought the action as an alleged violation of the Due Process Clause in the Fifth Amendment as applied to the states through the Fourteenth Amendment of the U.S. Constitution.

AGE DISCRIMINATION

Smallwood v. *United Airlines, Inc.,* **Fourth Circuit Court of Appeals (1981)**

BFOQ held invalid

In August, 1977, Gerald E. Smallwood who was then 48 years old sought employment as a pilot with United Airlines. He was rejected by United Airlines since the airline was accepting applications only from individuals 21 through 35 years of age. Mr. Smallwood had been a pilot for ten years. Mr. Smallwood filed suit against United Airlines alleging a violation of the ADEA.

At the trial in the district court, United Airlines alleged that hiring pilots over the age of 35 would have an adverse effect on flight safety. United Airlines based its contention on the belief that hiring pilots who were over the age of 35 would disrupt its "crew concept" and would increase the chance of a medical emergency occurring during a flight. The district court for the Eastern District of Virginia held that denying employment to pilot applicants over the age of 35 constituted a bona fide occupational qualification and therefore did not violate ADEA. On appeal, the Fourth Circuit reversed and remanded the district court's decision, as it did not believe that United Airlines met the two-part test required to establish a bona fide occupational qualification. This test had first been adopted by the Fourth Circuit in the case of *Arritt* v. *Grisell*. The two-part test required that an employer demonstrate that the bona fide occupational qualification is reasonably necessary to the essence of its business and that the employer have reasonable cause for believing that "all or substantially all persons within the class would be unable to perform safely and efficiently the duties of the job involved or that it is impossible or impractical to deal with persons over the age limit on an individualized basis."

Ginsberg v. *Burlington Industries*, 24 FEP Cases 426 (1980)

*Remedy—
liquidated
damages/denial
of reinstatement*

Plaintiff was employed as a salesman for twenty-seven years and filed a claim of violation of the ADEA following his termination. After the jury of this New York federal district court returned a verdict in favor of the plaintiff, he attempted to amend his complaint to include reinstatement. The court denied the request both on the basis of timely filing and because evidence demonstrated that his superiors considered him incompetent.

The court conceded that the jury verdict necessarily represents a finding that age was indeed a factor in the employer's decision to terminate the employee. However, the evidence also showed that the officers of the company sincerely entertained doubts about the employee's ability to perform his job. The employee had also become embittered against the employer and his superiors and did not genuinely wish to work for them, and the two reasons justified his termination from employment.

The court also refused to award the ex-employee damages for lost compensation which he would have earned until his date of retirement at the age of 70. Even if the court had authority to grant such relief, such an award would be inappropriate under the circumstances. However, the court did award the employee liquidated damages. Liquidated damages are a specific amount of money set forth in the provisions of a contract or statute designed to offset any monetary loss that a party or individual who is covered may suffer as a result of a breach or violation. If the amount of liquidated damages is reasonably related to the amount of damage actually suffered, it will be enforced by a court of law.

Such an award is authorized by the ADEA, which provides that "liquidated damages shall be payable only in cases of willful violation of this chapter" (29 USC Sec. 626 (b)). As the jury found in this case that a willful violation had occurred, the liquidated damages clause in the ADEA could be invoked. In its decision, the court noted that while the employer may have acted more out of ignorance than malice, and while the jury was undoubtedly impressed with the unfairness of review procedures of the employee's performance, the case was ultimately based on the employee's claim that he was intentionally replaced by a younger man.

Lyons v. *Allendale Mutual Insurance Co.,* 23 FEP Cases 537 (1980)

Remedy—denial of general, punitive, and compensatory damages

Lyons asserted that he was discharged because of his age, and therefore had been forced to secure employment in another state and sell his Georgia home, and that he had incurred consequential damages. The employee sued under the Age Discrimination Employment Act of 1967 (ADEA). He sought recovery for such losses as moving expenses, the difference in interest rates between his new and old home mortgages, and the difference in commuting expenses.

The court ruled that consequential damages of the nature sought by the employee may not be awarded under the act. It was not the purpose of the act to allow recovery of either these general damages or punitive damages. Although a few previous cases ruled to the contrary, the court's prohibitive interpretation reflects the most recent attitude concerning the better view.

Thus any monetary recovery is limited to the amount of unpaid minimum wages, unpaid overtime compensation, or an additional equal amount in liquidated damages. Both punitive damages and compensatory damages for such items as pain and suffering, humiliation, mental or emotional distress are not recoverable in ADEA actions.

The court's rationale for such a ruling was that liquidated damages are available as an alternative to compensatory and punitive damages. To allow compensatory and punitive damages, plus statutory liquidated damages, would be to permit double recovery, an impermissible result under the act.

Cancellier v. *Federated Department Stores,* Ninth Circuit Court of Appeals (1982)

Age/Wrongful Discharge—$2.3 million damages

Three employees with twenty-five, seventeen, and eighteen years of service were discharged for an alleged corporate policy that favored younger executive personnel to appeal to the youth retail market. Punitive and compensatory damages awarded ($2.3 million total).

EEOC v. *Missouri State Highway Patrol,* U.S. District Court (1982)

Mandatory retirement age

Mandatory retirement at age 60 violated ADEA.

Orzel v. *City of Wannatosa Fire Department,* Seventh Court of Appeals (1983)

Mandatory retirement age

Mandatory retirement at age 55 violated ADEA.

EEOC v. *State of Wyoming,* 460 US 226, 103 S. Ct. 1054, 75 LEd 2d 18 (1983)

Mandatory retirement age

Determined that mandatory retirement age requirements were arbitrary and illegal; must be based on ability to perform work tasks.

Steckl v. *Motorola,* **Ninth Circuit Court of Appeals (1983)**

*Age
discrimination
rebutted*

Steckl worked fifteen years for Motorola in various management positions. A new position was created for which Motorola selected a younger person. Steckl contended he was refused promotion in violation of the ADEA. Motorola was able to show evidence that the younger person had substantially more education, training, and experience in circuit design and systems—a basic qualification of the position. The court stated that complainants in ADEA cases must tender a genuine issue of material fact as opposed to pretext to avoid summary judgment (sole decision of judge deciding a case before it goes into a full evidenciary hearing).

*Written
Agreements—
Releases*

Employers should be cautious about entering into prelitigation settlements involving releases of potential discrimination claims by employees, as some courts may not feel that an employee's waiver to file a claim thereafter is enforceable (e.g., *Runyan* v. *National Cash Register Corp.,* F.2d 83-3862 (1985)).

AFFIRMATIVE ACTION

Bakke v. *Regents of the University of California, Davis,* **Cal. Sup. Ct., (1978)**

*Reverse
discrimination—
affirmative
action*

University of California, Davis, Medical School allowed admissions on the basis of applicants' obtaining high enough scores by two separate committee ratings: a regular admissions program considering comprehensive academic achievement, and a special admissions program considering economic, educational, or minority disadvantages (sixteen out of one hundred slots were "reserved" for such persons). After achieving significantly higher academic and combined scores in 1973 and 1974 than did minority applicants who were accepted to the school, Bakke filed in state court for mandatory injunctive and declaratory relief to compel his admission to Davis, alleging that the special admissions program operated to exclude him on the basis of his race in violation of the Equal Protection Clause of the Fourteenth Amendment, a provision of the California Constitution, *and* Section 601 of Title VI of the Civil Rights Act of 1964, which provides, interalia, that no person shall, on the ground of race or color, be excluded from participating in any program receiving federal financial assistance. Davis cross-claimed for a declaration that its special admissions program was lawful. The trial court found that the special program operated as a racial quota, because minority applicants in that program were rated only against one another, and sixteen places in the class of one hundred were reserved for them. Declaring that Davis could not take race into account in making admissions decisions, the court ruled that the program violated the federal and state constitutions and Title VI. Bakke's admission was not ordered, however, for lack of proof that he would have been admitted but for the special program. The California Supreme Court, applying a strict-scrutiny standard, concluded that the special admissions program was not the least intrusive means of achieving the goals of the admittedly compelling state interests of integrating the medical profession and increasing the number of doctors willing to serve minority patients. Without passing on the state constitutional or federal statutory grounds, the court held that Davis's special admissions program violated the Equal Protection Clause. As Davis could not demonstrate that Bakke, absent the special program, would not have been admitted, the court ordered his admission to Davis, invalidated the special admissions program, but reversed the lower court's decision prohibiting Davis from taking race into account in future admission decisions.

The Davis program may be reflective of aggressive affirmative action programs voluntarily adopted by employers in an effort to comply with Title VII of the U.S. Constitution. Four *Bakke* justices would seemingly allow such voluntarily created race-conscious programs to remedy the effects of past societal discrimination where certain conditions are met, and thus may approve such an affirmative action program created by an employer. Four other *Bakke* justices read the nondiscrimination language of Title VI literally, finding that race cannot be the basis of excluding *anyone* from participation in a federal program. These justices, applying the same literal analysis, may conclude that Title VII or the U.S. Constitution is equally "colorblind" and cannot be relied upon to support voluntarily created job quotas established pursuant to an affirmative action plan like the one at Davis.

Finally, we are left with the pivotal view of Justice Powell. Indirectly, he tells us in *Bakke* that race-conscious programs may be lawful if created to remedy past discrimination where a determination of past discrimination is made by a responsible legislative, administrative, or other governmental body with the authority and capability to establish, in the record, that the plan is responsive to the identified discrimination.

Note: Two other significant cases have determined that *voluntary* affirmative action plans fixing hiring quotas were invalid in the absence of an official determination of past discrimination.[1] Therefore, the courts seem to be saying that preferential hiring may be lawful only under circumstances of a court order (consent decree) or a negotiated settlement with a state or federal compliance agency where past discrimination has reasonably been substantiated by such an investigatory agency.

---

[1]   *Detroit Police Officers Association* v. *Young*, 16 FEP Cases 1005, and *Weber* v. *Kaiser Aluminum & Chemical Corp.*, 16 FEP Cases 1.

Stotts v. Fire Fighters Local 1984, 104 S. Ct. 2576 (1984)

*Layoff seniority—
constitutionality
of affirmative
action*

Referred to as the "Memphis case," this precedent case of the U.S. Supreme Court began in 1980 when Stotts and Jones, both black employees, challenged hiring and promotion policies of the Memphis Fire Department on the grounds that they were racially discriminatory. Later, the firefighters and the city settled on a consent decree (instead of a court battle) designed to remedy the situation. Under the terms of the agreement, thirteen black firefighters were promoted, and eighty-one were awarded back pay. The city adopted the goal of increasing the number of blacks in each job classification to approximately the same percentage as that of blacks in the labor force in the surrounding county. In coming to this agreement, the city acknowledged no guilt, and, for their part, the plaintiffs waived further relief apart from the terms of the decree. The U.S. District Court was given continuing jurisdiction over the agreement. The agreement made no mention of layoffs.

In May 1981, the City of Memphis faced a budget deficit and had to lay off some employees. It decided that the fairest policy was to use the "last hired, first fired" seniority rule and give senior employees the right to "bump down" to lower positions if their own job classifications were eliminated. On hearing of this plan, Stotts appealed.

The appeals court adopted three arguments on behalf of the lower court order. It decided, first, that the lower court decree was permissible under general contract law. By this reasoning, the city had, in effect, contracted under the consent decree to increase black personnel, and layoffs would interfere with that agreement. It decided, second, that the district court was authorized to do what it did "because new and unforeseen circumstances had created a hardship for one of the parties of the decree," and, finally, it rejected counter-arguments that the seniority system was authorized by Title VII of the Civil Rights Act of 1964.

When the case was appealed from the circuit court to the Supreme Court, the issue was, in the words of the Supreme Court, "whether the District Court exceeded its powers in entering an injunction requiring white employees to be laid off when the otherwise applicable seniority system would have called for the layoff of black employees with less seniority."

On the substantive issue of the relationship between affirmative action and seniority systems, the Supreme Court majority responded to the arguments advanced by the lower courts. The majority began by rejecting the argument that the district court order was permissible under general contract law and was simply a "necessary" and "appropriate" way of enforcing the consent decree. Instead, it decided that, as the original decree did not mention layoffs, the district court order was not, in fact, part of the decree.

The Supreme Court noted that there was no proof that either the intent of the seniority system or the layoffs was discriminatory. Moreover, the Supreme Court decided that the lower court had erred in overstating "the authority of the trial court to disregard a seniority system in fashioning a remedy." On the one hand, the Court acknowledged that minority members who could prove that they were specific victims of discrimination "may be awarded competitive seniority and given their rightful place on the seniority roster." On the other hand, the Court argued that "mere membership in the disadvantaged class is insufficient to warrant a seniority award . . ."

The Supreme Court obviously believes that seniority systems are legitimate ways of providing employees with protection. While the Court might award retroactive seniority to individual minority-group members who can show that they are specific victims of discrimination, it is unlikely that the Court will sanction an affirmative action plan eliminating a seniority system altogether. Without specific language in a consent decree or clear evidence of discriminatory intent, the courts will almost surely *not* interfere with an ongoing seniority plan.

EEOC v. American Telephone & Telegraph Co., 14 FEP Cases 1210 (1973)

Largest damage settlement— five-year cost of $68 million

Reading *Bakke, Detroit Police Officers*, and *Weber* together, employers may reasonably conclude that without an official finding of past discrimination, they proceed at their own risk in creating affirmative action plans, including preferential treatment of women or minorities. Indeed, the following language of Title VI specifically states that they need not do so:

> Nothing contained in this title shall be interpreted to require any employer . . . to grant preferential treatment to any individual or to any group because of the race, color, religion, sex, or national origin of such individual or group on account of an imbalance which may exist with respect to the total number or percentage of persons of any race, color, religion, sex, or national origin employed by the employer . . . in comparison with the total number or percentage of persons in such race, color, religion, sex, or national origin in any community . . . or in the available work force in any community . . . (42 USCS Sec. 2000e-2(j)).

Steelworkers v. Weber, 16 FEP Cases 1 (1981); and McLaughlin v. Great Lakes Dredge & Dock Co., 23 FEP Cases 1295 (1980)

Effect of affirmative action plan

In the landmark decision of *Weber*, the U.S. Supreme Court endorsed the adoption of voluntary affirmative action plans by employers. The court rejected the argument that Congress intended in Title VII to prohibit all race-conscious affirmative action plans, presumably because of the harmful exclusions that resulted to nonminority applicants. It was concluded that Title VII did not prohibit all voluntary, race-conscious, affirmative action efforts on the part of employers and unions.

The court's rationale in that case for justifying certain affirmative action plans applies to a recent case involving a government contractor that hired a black crane operator who had worked for the contractor on a seasonal and temporary basis. However, he was not an employee of the contractor and did not have any reasonable expectation of renewed employment at the time of the alleged discrimination.

A conflict arose with a white crane operator who had obtained a job with a contractor through a union hiring hall. The job was on a seasonal basis. Once the work was finished, the operator was unemployed again. The next spring he was again sent to work for the company. It was his understanding that the company had specifically requested the union to have him fill the opening. A pattern of periodic employment and unemployment with the company continued over the next several months. However, when the 1976 season opened, the white operator was not hired. The individual hired for the job that the white operator had performed the previous year was black.

Subsequently, the white operator filed a charge that the company had discriminated against him on the basis of his race. The facts revealed that one of the provisions in the contract between the contractor and the federal government required the company to comply with Executive Order 11246. This Executive Order requires all federal contractors to take affirmative action to hire employees without regard to race, color, religion, sex, or national origin. It was assumed by the court that the black engineer hired obtained his position by virtue of the requirements imposed by the order.

The court noted the difficulty in reconciling Title VII, whose central purpose is to eliminate invidious or pervasive racial discrimination in employment, and the Executive Order, which may require an employer to take race into consideration as a factor in making employment decisions. The *Weber* decision made this problem less difficult. It was decided in *Weber* that Title VII did not prohibit an employer from voluntarily agreeing upon bona fide affirmative action plans that accord racial preferences in hiring.

In allowing the plan in *Weber*, the Supreme Court outlined what makes a particular plan acceptable. The Court noted that the purposes of the plan must mirror those of Title VII. In *Weber*, both purposes were designed to break down old patterns of racial segregation and hierarchy. Both were structured to open employment opportunities for blacks in occupations that had been traditionally closed to them.

At the same time, the plan did not unnecessarily trammel the interests of the white employees. The plan did not require the discharge of white workers and their replacement with new black hires; nor did the plan create an absolute bar to the advancement of white employees, as half of those trained in the program would be white. Also, the plan was a temporary measure, and was not intended to maintain racial balance, but simply to eliminate an obvious racial imbalance.

Chapter 19

AT-WILL EMPLOYMENT AND PRECEDENT WRONGFUL DISCHARGE CASES

Employers have long been familiar with the term *at-will* employment, or at least they knew they had the right to hire and fire whom they wanted, when they wanted, for their own reasons. In just about all states, the at-will employment provision has been codified in labor laws, and it typically specifies that both the employer and employee can terminate the employment relationship at the discretion of either party without advance notice. However, the practice of at-will employment—emanating from a nineteenth-century legal theory of the master-servant relationship—has been modified substantially since 1980 by various courts across the country taking the position that employers do not enjoy a completely unfettered right to fire an employee *for any reason or under any condition,* hence the emergence of the "doctrine of wrongful discharge."

The emergence of yet another realm of employment law, adding to the existing burden of legal do's and don'ts for employers, stems from changes in the way employee rights have been viewed over the years. Consider the following:

- Servants may not have had many rights, but once emancipated their rights were immensely broadened under constitutional protections, including the right to due process of law as a protection of property interests.

- The United States experienced a major sociocultural revolution in the 1960s. It began to focus national attention on the issue of civil rights, the result of which produced sweeping reforms in the legality of many employment practices.

- This "new society" has become sensitive to the equity and equality of the human condition in general, and specifically to the individual as employee, where certain rights should be enjoyed no less than for a private citizen.

- Employees today are educated, likely to be thoroughly exposed to events and trends by the media, and less subdued about a perceived wrong against them by the threat of losing their jobs. They are also more aggressive about due process remedies.

- Members of this "new society" are judges, jurors, state and federal compliance agency officers, arbitrators, legislators, and employees, all of whom are in positions to bring about rapid change in traditional employment laws, practices, and conditions.

LEGAL THEORIES OF WRONGFUL DISCHARGE

Recent cases on the issue of wrongful discharge stem from the precedent 1959 *Petermann* v. *International Brotherhood of Teamsters* case in which an eighteen-year employee was fired for refusing to lie. The court concluded that he had obtained "just cause" rights due to the implied contract of long-term employment, and thereby accumulating a property interest in his employment.

Once a property right is established, be it through the length of one's employment service or by lawful possession of real property, the person's interest in the property has Constitutional protection. There must be sufficient and reasonable cause to take the property away from the person (termination), and the person must be afforded due process of law. Unlike most types of employment law where damages against an employer are limited to perhaps back pay and minor penalties (equity law), wrongful discharge is being viewed by the courts as a breach of contractual law, thereby giving rise to a tort action (civil wrongdoing), which can result in heavy compensatory and punitive damages and costly attorney fees.

Note: Employers should be aware that business insurance policies do *not* generally cover punitive damages, so such assessments become out-of-pocket expenses for the employer assessed with this form of damages.

The onslaught of litigation began about 1980 and spread quickly from one coast to the other. Characteristic of a new form of law, the courts began to emerge with new tenets that would set certain limits on, if not redefine, the historic right of employers to terminate employment at will. Generally, the courts have established a two-part test, where at least one part must be present to determine whether an employee was discharged wrongfully and, in either part, the terminated employee's length of employment can be a considerable influence on juries.

1. **Breach of Contract**

   The courts will examine both expressed and implied covenants made by the employer that create, or could reasonably be construed by the employee as creating, a belief in the assurance of long-term employment and termination *only* for just cause. The most common document used and cited by the courts for this assessment is the employer's personnel policies and rules, or employee handbooks. Employment letters, contracts, and even verbal comments such as "As long as you keep doing the same fine work, you'll never have to worry about being terminated," can extend a contractual obligation to the employee.

2. **Violation of "Public Policy"**

Evidence supplied to the court that an employer—or any representative, officer, or agent of the employer—was moved to terminate an employee because of the employee's refusal to lie, steal, falsify records or information, or perform any other act that violates common laws will put the last nail in the employer's coffin, even if the first two didn't! This is also one of those rare areas of law where a supervisor or line manager can lose personal immunity as a company representative, and therefore be held individually liable for misconduct (including criminal prosecution) if he or she is found responsible for initiating the order to lie, steal, or otherwise violate laws.

ILLUSTRATIVE COURT CASES

From the illustrative cases provided, it should become increasingly clear that the courts are now recognizing that a person's job is a significant part of the person's ability to enjoy opportunities in a free and democratic society, to earn a living and be a productive participant, and to be dealt with in a fair and reasonable manner throughout the course of employment, including its termination. In context of the potential liability for wrongful discharge, employers should examine their employment practices in light of the following examples of "actionable cause" for an employee to bring suit.

- Breach of contract; expressed or implied term of employment, longevity, indeterminate employment based on satisfactory performance.
- Requiring employee to steal, lie, falsify, participate in any illegal activity.
- Willful or negligent discrimination practices (race, national origin, age, sex, sexual harassment).
- Breach of expressed employment conditions such as personnel policies and collective bargaining agreements. Such cases may be preempted by the National Labor Relations Act (NLRA) or the Employee Retirement Income Security Act (ERISA).
- Distortion, falsifying, or altering performance evaluations.
- Malicious or capricious conduct of employer that damages the employee's right to fair and reasonable treatment.

It is beyond the scope of this manual to deal with the monumental number and variety of state and federal court cases. However, for the purpose intended, it may be helpful for the employer to learn a little about a few cases that may serve as precedent-setting decisions in this relatively new area of employment law and about the conditions of present legal tests in these cases.

Tameny v. Atlantic Richfield Co., 27 Cal. App. 3d. 167 (1980)

Public policy violation breach of good faith and fair dealing

Employee refused to be involved in a price-fixing scheme; because of "malicious conduct" of employer, employee could bring tort suit—employee was not limited to breach of contract (employment) damages and could recover compensatory *and* punitive damages (designed to punish defendant based on net worth of malicious conduct).

Cleary v. American Airlines, 111 Cal. App. 3d. 443 (1981)

Breach of implied contract

Cleary was accused of stealing and was fired. Cleary sued, because of absence of due process. Court found that Labor Code 2922 (at will) does not apply to vested interests right of employment due to this length of service. Employee could not only sue in tort, but court created a new legal theory—breach of implied-in-law covenant of good faith and fair dealing. Mere longevity of service (eighteen years in this case) created an implied-in-law covenant, and employer had to show just cause for discharge or employee could recover compensatory *and* punitive damages.

Cancellier v. Federated Department Stores, Ninth Circuit Court of Appeals (1982)

Age discrimination and public policy violation

(Federalized California discharge laws.) Three employees of I. Magnin (twenty-five, seventeen, and eighteen years' employment) brought suit under Age Discrimination in Employment Act of 1967, California State Law for breach of the implied covenant of good faith and fair dealing and intentional infliction of emotional distress. They alleged that they were forced out of I. Magnin in 1979 because of a deliberate corporate policy to replace them with younger executive personnel who would supposedly appeal to the youth market targeted in its retail policy. Damages were awarded to plaintiffs in the amount of $800,000, $600,000, and $500,000, respectively ($640,000 in punitive damages), another $400,000 in attorney's fees for a total of $2.3 million.

Hentzel v. The Singer Co., 138 Cal. App. 3d. 290 (1982)

Public policy violation

Hentzel had been employed by the Singer Company for five years as a senior patent attorney when she was terminated, allegedly in retaliation for her complaints about other employees' smoking in her workplace—intentional infliction of emotional distress. Hentzel further alleged that Singer implied she would not be discharged so long as her services were satisfactory. Her services had been rated superior.

The court of appeals notes the common law rule codified in Section 2922 (California Labor Code) to the effect that "an employment contract of indefinite duration is in general terminable at the will of either party." However, the court observes:

> Under both common law and the statute, an employer does not enjoy an absolute or totally unfettered right to discharge even an at-will employee. In a series of cases arising out of a variety of

factual settings in which a discharge clearly violated an express statutory objective or undermined a firmly established principle of public policy, courts have recognized that an employer's traditional broad authority to discharge an at-will employee may be limited by statute . . . or by consideration of public policy.

Pine River State Bank v. Mettille, 333 N.W.2d 622 (Minn. 1983)

Employee handbook— implied contract

The Minnesota Supreme Court held that procedural restraints on termination of employees that were contained in an employee handbook were contractually binding on the employer. The court followed *Pugh* v. *Sees Candies*.

Ferraro v. Koelsch, 368 N.W. 2d 666 (Wis. 1985)

Employee handbook

The State Supreme Court held that an employment handbook may convert an employment at-will relationship into one that can be terminated only by adherence to terms contained in the handbook. The court cited *Pugh*. In this case, the court still upheld the termination because the employee *had* violated the terms of the handbook.

Palmater v. International Harvester, 85 Ill. 2d 124, 421 N.E.2d 876 (1981)

Retaliatory discharge—public policy

An employee who was discharged after sixteen years of service alleged he was fired for supplying information to the police regarding another IH employee who was possibly involved in criminal conduct, and for agreeing to cooperate in the police investigation. The court reversed a dismissal of the employee's claim and held that a valid cause of action for retaliatory discharge was presented. The court cited *Tameny*.

Magnan v. Anaconda Industries, 479 A.2d 781 (Conn. 1984)

Employment contract— condition of good faith and fair dealing

This Connecticut court decision held that the covenant of good faith and fair dealing applies *only* where there is an employment contract and *not* in cases of employment at will.

Delaney v. Taco Time, 681 P.2d 114 (Ore. 1984)

Public policy

This Oregon court decision followed *Tameny* in holding that an employee who was wrongfully discharged for refusing to sign a false and potentially fortuitous statement filed an action based on public policy. The false statement allegedly cast aspersions on the work habits and moral behavior of a former employee.

Weiner v. McGraw-Hill, 443 N.E.2d 441 (1982)

Employment contract—not implied obligation

This New York Court of Appeals decision held that there was no implied obligation of good faith and fair dealing in at-will employment agreements. However, the court did recognize the possibility of a wrongful termination cause of action.

Leikwold v. *Valley View Community Hospital,* 688 P.2d 170 (Ariz. 1984)

Personnel manual

The Arizona Supreme Court reversed a summary judgment ruling for the employer, holding that representations in the personnel manual can become part of a contract and limit an employer's ability to discharge. The court held that it was an issue of material fact as to whether the personnel manual was incorporated into the contract. This case appears to apply only to situations where an employment contract exists, and not to at-will employees.

Sabine Pilot Service Inc. v. *Hauck,* 119 L.R.R.M. 2187 (1985)

Texas joins public policy violation

The case arose when an individual employed as a deckhand refused an instrument to pump the bilges of the boat on which he worked into the water because it was illegal to do so. The Texas Supreme Court noted that the sole issue before it was "whether an allegation by an employee that he was discharged for refusing to perform an illegal act states a cause of action." The court first observed that employment for an indefinite term may be terminated at will and without cause in Texas. However, the court also observed that twenty-two other states have recognized exceptions to the employment-at-will doctrine in recent years. In light of its perception of the "changes in American society and in the employer/employee relationship," the court held that "public policy, as expressed in the laws of (Texas) and the United States which carry criminal penalties, requires a very narrow exception to the employment-at-will doctrine." The court hastened to limit its ruling, however, by indicating that the "narrow exception covers *only* the discharge of an employee for the *sole* reason that the employee refused to perform an illegal act. We further hold that in the trial of such a case it is the plaintiff's *burden to prove* by a preponderance of the evidence that his discharge was for *no reason other than* his refusal to perform an illegal act." Although limited to the violation of public policy, Texas joins the growing number of states recognizing the merits of wrongful discharge through employment conditions that can serve as exceptions to the doctrine of at-will employment.

Thompson v. *St. Regis Paper Co.,* 102 Wash. 2d, 219 685, P.2d, 1081 (1984)

Washington adopts public policy and handbook exceptions to at-will employment

In this Supreme Court of Labor Report D-1 Washington case, the employee alleged that he had been fired for instituting an accurate accounting program in compliance with the Foreign Corrupt Practices Act of 1977, which prohibits employers from offering a bribe to foreign officials to obtain business and requires employers subject to the Securities Exchange Act of 1934 to devise and maintain a system of accounting that ensures compliance with the antibribery provisions of the law. The court found that these laws represented a clear expression of public policy regarding bribery of foreign officials. The court noted that the at-will employment doctrine is a court-developed legal principle taken from a nineteenth-century treatise on the subject of master and servant and went on to note statutory and judicial developments that serve as exceptions.

First, the court noted that a (employment) contract is terminable by the employer only for cause if:

1. There is an express or implied agreement to that effect; or
2. The employee does something different and beyond the intended (contractual) scope of the job.

The court noted, however, that "independent consideration" did not exist where an employee merely signed an employment agreement assigning any inventions or patents during his employment to his employer. Moreover, the court cited an earlier decision that properly held that a nonnegotiated unilateral grievance process did no more than implement a company policy to treat employees fairly, and that such provisions, as well as a provision establishing a probationary policy, merely implemented company policies to treat employees in a fair and consistent manner; it did not provide evidence of an implied contract that the employee can be discharged only for cause.

Second, the court concluded that policy or practice statements made in an employer's personnel handbook may, in certain situations, obligate the employer to act in accordance with those promises. Furthermore, "once an employer announces a specific policy or practice, especially in light of the fact that he expects employees to abide by the same, the employer may not treat its promises as illusory." However, the court identified several potential means by which *employers can attempt to confine their obligations* in employee manuals. For example, they "can specifically state in a conspicuous manner that nothing contained therein is intended to be part of the employment relationship and are simply general statements of company policy. Additionally, policy statements as written may not amount to promises of specific treatment and can merely be general statements of company policy, and thus, not binding. Moreover, the employer may specifically reserve the right to modify those policies or write them in a manner that retains discretion to the employer."

Third, the court determined that employers can be held liable in the discharge of an employee for reasons of violating a public policy mandate where the employer's conduct clearly imposes on the letter or purpose of a constitutional, statutory, or regulatory provision.

Chamberlain v. *Bissell, Inc.*, 547 F. Supp. 1067 (1982)

Negligence performance and performance evaluation

This case involves an employee with twenty-two years of adequate service who was discharged for performance-related deficiencies. Although this Michigan court found in behalf of the employer due to plaintiff's contributory negligence in his job performance, the court made special note of the employer's duty to use "reasonable care" in carrying out its performance evaluation process. The conclusion of the court was that as the employer had a contractual duty to review the employee's performance, the employer had a duty to use ordinary and reasonable care in performing the review. The court set the standard of care as being that of a reasonable person performing a review, and then the court questioned whether the reviewer conformed to the standard. The court concluded that a reasonable employer under the circumstances would have informed the employee that his discharge was being considered, or was possible, unless a rapid and drastic change in job performance came about before the time of subsequent evaluation. *A failure to warn the employee was equivalent to negligence on the part of the employer.*

This case raises the potential liability of an employer for wrongful discharge where the employee is terminated based on a formal performance evaluation instrument that is less than objective or insufficiently related to the employee's job standards of performance and where the employee is not warned that failure to correct performance deficiencies may result in termination.

Foley v. *Interactive Data Corp.*, 47 Cal. 3d. 654 (1988)

Tort damages limited

Tort damages cannot be recovered under the claim that the employer's action failed to constitute "good faith and fair dealing." Nor could such damages be made for claims of "intentional infliction of emotional distress," the condition of which was held by the California Supreme Court to be preempted by state workers' compensation as an exclusive remedy.

Fournier v. *United States Fidelity and Guarantee Co.*, Md. Ct. Spec. App. (1990)

At-will notice on application form protected employer

In this case, a Maryland appellate court rejected a terminated employee's claim of breach of contract. Here, the court notes that the employer's at-will employment statement on its application form, which was signed by plaintiff, nullified the employee's argument that the employer's handbook implied termination only for just cause. Several other states have held similarly such as *Slivinsky* v. *Watkins-Johnson Co.*, 90 Daily Journal, D.A.R. 7265, 1990.

Gantt v. *Sentry Insurance*, 1 Cal. 4th 1083 (1992)

Public policy violations limited to statutes or constitutional provisions/ employee wrongfully discharged for sexual harassment complaint

This case was decided by the California Supreme Court where a lower court's award of $1.3 million for wrongful discharge was upheld. Here, plaintiff established she was fired in retaliation for her support of a female coworker's sexual harassment claims. Also, as a matter of clarifying earlier decisions in California on the issue of what constitutes "public policy," the Supreme Court ruled that only those provisions of statute (state or federal) or constitution qualify as public policy.

States Adopting Legal Action for Breach of Implied Contract due to Personnel Policy Manuals, Employee Handbooks, and Other Written Representations of Job Security

Alabama	Maryland	New Jersey	South Dakota
Alaska	Massachusetts	New Mexico	Tennessee
Arizona	Michigan	New York	Utah
California	Minnesota	North Dakota	Washington
Idaho	Missouri	Ohio	West Virginia
Illinois	Nevada	Oregon	Wisconsin
Maine			

CHECKLIST: "AT-WILL" EMPLOYMENT

☐ Avoid use of the word "permanent" and "probationary" in handbook, personnel manuals, application form, and job description.

☐ Avoid suggestions that employment will continue as long as performance is satisfactory.

☐ Train persons interviewing and hiring employees to avoid such statements.

☐ Make sure evaluation processes provide for negative comments and a progressive grading system.

☐ Encourage supervisors to evaluate employees truthfully.

☐ Require approval of evaluations by personnel office or chief management officer. Require counseling of employees where necessary.

☐ Employment contracts with management personnel should contain provisions such as: reasons for termination (be flexible); employee not employed for a specified term; use of third party as a way to resolve the dispute; limit damages recoverable by either party in the event of a breach.

☐ Require thorough investigation of all discharges, including taking statements from witnesses and extensively cross-examining them as to the facts.

☐ Determine if discharge of a long-term employee is absolutely necessary. Would a jury think that discharge was appropriate?

☐ Give employee opportunity to respond to the charges.

☐ Termination interview—be flexible if new facts arise. (Consider suspending employee pending investigation.)

☐ Subjective comments, for example, "He was not a part of the management team," or "He could not take the pressure," should be translated into objective and specific problems.

☐ Do not be hostile or insulting toward discharged employee. (Consider a severance policy.)

☐ Review disciplinary policy and causes for termination. Is there consistency with actual events and stated policies?

☐ Does punishment fit the crime? Use progressive discipline principles when possible.

☐ Train supervisors and department managers in the area of documentation and employee discipline.

Employers are encouraged to seek qualified counsel from neutral advisors in all cases of discharge.

Part Four

HOW TO DEVELOP KEY SUPPORT SYSTEMS

Parts One, Two, and Three have been aimed principally at establishing legal and operational soundness of your personnel operation. Part IV provides the managerial "how-to" in six areas of critical value to the overall effectiveness of the organization's personnel programs. Chapter 20 explains why job descriptions are important to several aspects of personnel operations and how to go about preparing them, then gives format and content, and samples of job descriptions (Chapters 21–24) representative of several different job types. Chapter 25 gives the background and elements necessary for achieving the best results from interviewing job applicants. Chapters 26 and 27 set forth the ingredients for making wage and medical plan determinations, which are the two most costly employer expenses in relation to supporting a work force. Chapter 28 deals with the various techniques and effects of conducting performance evaluations, and employee development plans, and shows how evaluations serve as a useful management tool to achieve better performance results, enhance participative employee communications, and establish reliable criteria by which better pay and other decisions can be made. Chapter 29 presents a thorough discussion of the ways in which an employer can establish performance and conduct standards and, when necessary, how to deal with particular disciplinary problems, including the potential liability of wrongful discharge.

The focus of this part, then, is to give you the most practical background, suggestions, reasoning, and the "how-to's" of putting together the operational pieces of your personnel programs in a way that brings managerial soundness, business integrity, and employee confidence to the organization. Clearly, employers must recognize that the development of a personnel program goes well beyond the mere adoption of policies, rules, forms, and records. A support system should be established consisting of such things as designating one person to review all personnel matters, training those who make personnel decisions (supervisors and managers), periodically reviewing and updating (or improving) documents and methods, and maintaining open channels of communication among all employees such that the entire work force can participate in and contribute to the continued success of the organization. Thereafter, top management must ensure that personnel-related decisions are consistent with policies and past practices, fair and reasonable, and guided by the same sound, ethical business principles that distinguish a democratic society. If we believe in those freedoms to operate our businesses, why would we want to restrain employees' opportunity to be less than they might otherwise be? The chapters in this part will provide you with some insight and the means to manage the personnel program with successful results for both the business and those hired to contribute to it.

Chapter 20

PREPARING JOB DESCRIPTIONS FOR VALID PERSONNEL OPERATIONS

THE PURPOSE AND USE OF JOB DESCRIPTIONS

One of the more frequently posed questions of employers is, "Do I really need job descriptions?" or "Why are job descriptions necessary as long as I tell my employees what their job entails?" Typically, the real concern of employers is twofold: (1) that they will be confined to only a fixed number and type of duties they can require of employees and (2) that they will waste time writing job descriptions (usually meaning they aren't sure how to go about it!). Before an employer decides whether to spend the time and effort preparing job descriptions, it may prove worthwhile to examine how they are used and why they can be an important part of the effectiveness of a personnel program. If the following purpose and uses of job descriptions are even marginally convincing, then read on; you may discover that the task isn't that difficult after all, and you may even find that the sample job descriptions provided at the end of this section can get you started with only minor modification to tailor them to your business situation.

Testing and Hiring

This employment process is one of the most vulnerable to discrimination complaints with the Equal Employment Opportunity Commission (EEOC) and state compliance agencies. The problem for the employer arises when the employer has the "appearance" of discriminating against job applicants by requiring artificial employment standards such as a certain height, amount of education, or experience when, in fact, such requirements do not have a sufficiently direct correlation with the particular job (e.g., screening out any applicant who is not a high school graduate for the position of janitor). Jobs are fairly easy to define in terms of what they are and how they are done, but careful attention must be given to the requirements the applicant must possess to be eligible for consideration. Rest assured that the EEOC and other compliance agencies *always* demand that the employer provide them with a full description of the job when a complaint has been filed. If the employer's description of the job contains *any* requirements that have the appearance of being unrelated or superficially related to the job duties, the compliance agency will establish a charge of *prima facie* (on the surface) discrimination against the employer, and the employer may be required to pay up to two years' back pay to the claimant.

Pay and Status Determinations

Employers should be aware that there are two pay status classifications for employees: exempt employees, who are salaried and not eligible for overtime pay, and nonexempt employees, who can be either salaried or paid hourly and are eligible for overtime pay. More specific standards of exempt/nonexempt determinations are contained in another part of this manual, and they originate from the Federal Fair Labor Standards Act (FLSA) *and* state labor laws, which sometimes are different or more stringent than the FLSA requirements. Ultimately, the exempt/nonexempt classification of various jobs by the employer must be in conformance to these federal and state standards, which hinge on the amount of pay received and the type of job duties predominantly performed by all persons working in a particular job. When an employee, or former employee, files a wage claim with either the state labor commissioner or Wage and Hour Division of the Department of Labor, the employer will likely be asked to provide a thorough description of the claimant's job among other documents used as evidence in hearings. If it is found that the employer inappropriately classified the claimant's job as exempt, and thereby did not pay for overtime hours worked, the employer will be required to pay back overtime wages plus a penalty fine.

Written job descriptions are also essential in other kinds of pay determinations, such as conducting annual wage surveys or evaluating wage data in surveys taken by others. An important factor in any comparison of wages is comparability, which is discussed in greater detail in Chapter 26. Without thorough job descriptions, the employer may be using "skewed" wage information simply because other jobs having a similar job title may in reality have a diverse range of different tasks or level of responsibilities. With good job descriptions, the employer can compare wages paid by other employers among jobs having sufficiently similar content.

Workers' Compensation Insurance

Employers are often surprised to find that their insurance agent asks for job descriptions, or reasonable facsimile, when they call to inquire about the cost of workers' compensation insurance, which, by the way, is one of those mandatory employee benefits required of all employers—and don't try to avoid it by dubbing them contract employees! Each state has workers' compensation laws and regulations governing such matters as the definition of employer and employee, benefit provisions, conditions of job relatedness of injury or illness, and how employees are classified by type of work performed. These occupational categories determine the specific rate the insurance company (or state fund in the case of monopolistic states) will charge the employer (premium) for the policy. Since all insurance companies providing workers' compensation insurance in a particular state use the same rate chart, employers should shop for services (i.e., claims handling, timely payment, reports to employer, litigation representation) of the insurance carrier rather than premium rates. The surest way to be certain that the insurance agent is using the correct worker classification is to provide the agent with copies of job descriptions.

Performance Evaluations

Most employers agree that performance evaluations are instrumental in determining worker efficiency, job progress, training or development needs, pay increases, employee feedback, and the like. Yet the most common complaint by employees is that the categories used to rate their performance, and standards of different performance levels, don't relate to the particular tasks they perform in a reasonably meaningful way. Equally legitimate is the complaint that employees are often hired with a verbal description of the job, and thereafter their job either evolves to something entirely different (at the same pay rate) or it changes so frequently they lose a true picture of the job with respect to priorities, timing, and methods of performing work. If employers are to maintain their managerial credibility, some semblance of logic and order must be imposed when it comes to dealing with employees. The best way to establish and communicate job duties with employees is with written job descriptions, then use those descriptions as the basis of preparing individualized performance evaluations. If, during the course of a particular job, the employer has a need to modify a significant part of the job, rewrite the job description—preferably with the assistance of any affected employee(s).

There are a number of other reasons that could be cited for employers to prepare thorough job descriptions. Some of them include employee orientations, training, promotional considerations, discipline, terminations, Americans with Disabilities Act (ADA) compliance, and just good management practice. Suffice it to say that with accurate job descriptions, many problems can be avoided and workplace order enhanced. Without them there is uncertainty, inefficiency, and cost vulnerability.

INFORMAL VERSUS FORMAL METHODS

The informal method of preparing job descriptions is unquestionably the most common, but it is not very accurate. The reason: lack of trained staff, lack of priority for such administrative details, and lack of understanding of the catalyst nature of job descriptions on other personnel matters. With the informal method, a supervisor, manager, or sometimes even an incumbent employee, writes out a list of job duties felt to be most representative of the job. A title is typed at the top, duties listed numerically, and, with some extra effort, an education and experience level established for the job. Who should know better than the business owner, the supervisor, or an incumbent employee about the job? While these individuals are the best sources of job content, there are many other elements involved in preparing accurate as well as legally valid descriptions. First, let's examine what a job description is, and how the informal and formal methods work. By using the suggestions provided, the employer should be able to prepare good descriptions with minimal amount of time and effort.

A job description is a written profile of the duties, responsibilities, and qualifications of the job based on information provided by some form of job analysis. The duties and responsibilities are illustrative rather than exhaustive of the most frequent, important, and difficult tasks performed by an incumbent. Qualification statements, meaning employment requirements, are expressed in terms of minimums to be considered eligible for consideration. Job descriptions may also include such information as working conditions, tools or methods used, physical or special characteristics, and even relationships with other jobs. In the absence of such detail, many different jobs that possess some similarities become difficult to differentiate. Given this detail, jobs can be given accurate titles, classification status (exempt/nonexempt), pay assignment, and performance criteria.

Formal methods of preparing job descriptions are the most accurate in gathering, classifying, and analyzing job content information. They are also the most expensive because they require hiring professional staff (job analysts) or qualified consultants, and this level of attention to detail can take a considerable amount of time. Cost alone can range from $150 to $400 per job description for a consultant using formal methods. For these reasons, the remaining discussion will provide the employer with ways in which the informal method can be improved by adding a few of the more simplified approaches to the formal methods. The result will most certainly prove worthwhile to employer, supervisor, and employee alike.

GATHERING JOB INFORMATION

Job information can be gathered in a variety of ways, with varying degrees of accuracy and thoroughness. Here are five of the more commonplace methods used, from least to most formal (and accurate).

1. Itemize by random thought from someone familiar with performing the work. Employers should be discouraged from using this method if it is the only source of job information being relied upon to prepare a job description. The principal weaknesses of this method are that it tends to focus only on tasks, it is rarely thorough in descriptive detail, and it fails to prioritize the most meaningful aspects of a job. However, the exercise of listing job tasks independent of other information-gathering methods can be useful as a means of comparing this list against other sources.

2. Compile by a process of selection and elimination of statements made on similar job descriptions acquired from other employers. This can be a useful and

time-saving method, but it is not without its problems. Plagiarism of another's work, thought, and special conditions is always dangerous. One employer using another's information may be gaining the advantage of a quality product, or the disadvantage of incomplete work. For example, such jobs as typist clerk are considered "benchmark" jobs. That is, typist clerk positions generally perform the same basic tasks, require the same basic skills, and possess the same basic working conditions among most employers. Yet virtually every typist clerk has job duties, responsibilities, and conditions unique to each employer—training lower-level clerks, making decisions, using certain office equipment, or exposure to obnoxious odors. Using another's job descriptions as a source of gathering information is not necessarily discouraged, but each statement should be thoughtfully scrutinized for relatedness, accuracy, and thoroughness to the job in question. The same caution should be exercised with the sample job descriptions contained at the end of this chapter.

3. Obtain from the *Dictionary of Occupational Titles* (DOT) where over 20,000 jobs are described by brief task detail geared toward the jobholder's function and involvement with data, people, and things. Designed for use by the U.S. Employment Service, the DOT can be a valuable source of job information if used properly. The DOT groups jobs into occupational categories based on work content similarities resulting from comprehensive studies of how similar jobs are performed in different businesses across the country. Employers wishing to use this source of information can see if it is available in the nearest community or college library (reference section), the nearest government library, the local employment office, or by purchasing a copy from:

Superintendent of Documents
U.S. Government Printing Office
Washington, D.C. 20402

The only time such descriptions as those in the DOT are truly justified as the primary source of job information is when jobs are newly created by an employer or a new business is just getting started. In these cases, the DOT descriptions can be initially helpful for recruiting and wage-setting purposes. After employees are hired and their jobs evolve to a point of stabilization, a more thorough evaluation of the job and pay should be conducted, and a more detailed description prepared.

4. Develop from using such job analysis methods as incumbent questionnaires, incumbent or "subject expert" (supervisor) interviews, or direct observation of work being performed. The two most common and practical methods are questionnaires and interviews, and the best results are obtained when the information is provided by an incumbent employee and verified by a supervisor. Two samples of job analysis questionnaires—one brief and one detailed—have been provided in the forms section of Part Two, along with a sample job analysis interview form, each of which is self-instructive.

5. Gather from any combination of the preceding methods, which is typically how professional job analysts and consultants obtain comprehensive job detail.

ORGANIZING AND ANALYZING JOB CONTENT

Once job information has been gathered, it should be broken down into organized units consisting of duties and responsibilities by type of job function, distinguishing characteristics from related jobs, special requirements and conditions (e.g., licenses, fluency in a foreign language, physical working conditions), and employment eligibility *minimum* requirements. Here, it may be helpful to look ahead at the sample format of a job description to get a clearer picture of these descriptive units.

Next, arrange the duty and responsibility statements by function, beginning each separate function statement(s) with an action verb such as the following:

- *Supervises* assigned clerical employees including their assignment and evaluation of work, training, payroll record keeping, approval of requests, and recommendation of discipline; may be independently responsible for preparing and implementing work unit rules; is required to exercise independent decision making in routine work unit matters.

- *Reviews* records, reports, correspondence, and other written materials for accuracy of contents, spelling and grammatical errors, punctuation, brevity, and flow; reviews data and format to assure correctness of information and illustrative interpretation; and reviews final copy of materials to be used by media sources.

In these two examples, all duties and responsibilities related to the function of "supervision" and "review" are listed by brief statements within a single category that begins with the functional action verb.

After grouping the duty and responsibility statements under proper function action verbs, do the following:

1. Eliminate those tasks that can be easily mastered in less than eight hours of training—meaning they are insignificant for purposes of the job description in most cases.

2. Eliminate task statements where there would be little consequence of errors, where tasks are performed infrequently and are relatively unimportant, and where tasks are easily learned.

3. Examine the remaining statements and see if they represent an accurate and thorough cross section of the job scope. What should remain are those duties and responsibilities that are the most *frequently* performed, the most *important* or critical to the business, and the more *difficult* tasks to learn or carry out. If the job is not sufficiently represented by the remaining statements, some of those eliminated may have to be added back in, or more thought should be given to writing supplemental statements about weakly illustrated job functions.

In preparing the qualifications (sometimes called job specifications) for the job, special attention should be paid to developing a valid relationship between the duty and responsibility statements (what and how the job is performed) and what characteristics a person should *minimally* possess to be successful. Usually these characteristics are expressed in terms of education, experience, skills, knowledge, licenses (or credentials, certificates, etc.), and special requirements. Be careful of using "artificial" requirements such as excessive education or experience merely because such people are available. Compliance agencies are quick to find discriminatory intent against employers who use such excesses in screening people out. A better approach is to use equivalency examples like those in the sample job descriptions provided at the end of this chapter.

Additionally, merely stating education and experience requirements is no longer sufficient for the true purposes of job descriptions mentioned earlier. Each qualification section of the job description should also have a series of skill and knowledge statements directly corresponding to the tasks performed. Skills are those things people do (type, draw, analyze, etc.), and knowledge refers to ability to understand, apply, develop, and so forth.

One last point: To distill the fear some employers have about employees' viewing the job description as the entirety of the job and taking the "it's not in my job description" posture—particularly in a unionized environment where it seems to be most prevalent—it is advisable to add the following comments at the end of each job description.

> This job description should not be construed to imply that these requirements are the exclusive standards of the position. Incumbents will follow any other instructions, and perform any other related duties, as may be required.

FORMATTING THE JOB DESCRIPTION

There are many variations in the format of job descriptions. Over the years, many companies, college professors, and consultants have devised unique designs for job descriptions, but the information they contain is essentially the same. There is no one right or best format; it's a matter of preference as long as the essential ingredients are present. It is more important that the format selected be used consistently.

Two sample job description formats are provided on the following pages. Another version of sample 2 simplifies the format by omitting documentation detail at the bottom of the page.

JOB DESCRIPTION FORMAT: SAMPLE 1

TITLE

Date Approved: _____   **Status:** _____(exempt/nonexempt)_____

Revised: _____(dates)_____   **Rate:** _____$ (salary or hourly)_____

General Description

Describes under what level of supervision and control the general functions of the job are performed.

Exemplary Duties/Responsibilities

Describes by functional categories of the job those tasks and realms of responsibilities that are frequent, important, and difficult to perform.

Qualification Requirements

Describes the minimum requirements a person must have to be considered eligible, and characteristics a successful employee would possess.

Education:

Experience:

Skill at:

Knowledge of:

Licenses:

Special Requirements:

JOB DESCRIPTION FORMAT: SAMPLE 2

TITLE

Summary Description

Illustrative Duties/Responsibilities

Employment Standards

Education/Experience:

Skill at:

Knowledge of:

Statement of nonlimitation of requirement to perform other related duties.

Date Approved: _____   Dept./Division: _____

Revised: _____   Status: _____

Reports to: _____   Pay Grade: _____

Chapter 21

JOB DESCRIPTIONS FOR MANAGERIAL OCCUPATIONS

Executive Director
Controller
Human Resources Manager
Branch Manager
Store Manager
Data Processing Manager

JOB DESCRIPTION
EXECUTIVE DIRECTOR

Summary Description

Under policy direction of the Board of Directors, performs a wide range of difficult to complex administrative activities related to finances and accounting, marketing and promotion of services, staffing and personnel operations, and discretionary activities that serve to support effective business operations; uses considerable independent judgment in decisions that influence operations; advises and assists the Board of Directors in planning, policy, and operations matters.

Exemplary Duties/Responsibilities

Directs and participates in the development and implementation of goals, objectives, policies, and procedures; directs and ensures proper coordination of all administrative affairs; prepares and submits to the Board of Directors reports of finances, staffing, program, and other administrative activities; prepares agenda and documents and attends and participates in Board of Director meetings to receive general direction.

General Administration Develops and implements organizational and program plans; researches applicable laws, legislation, and regulations; prepares reports, correspondence, memos, records, and forms; evaluates activities and interacts with representatives of comparable firms; develops and prepares forms, records, charts, and other operational materials; implements operations systems to achieve effective work loads and work flow.

Prepares and delivers formal presentations before various public and private concerns; attends meetings, conferences, and seminars requiring periodic to frequent travel.

Secures the services and products of outside sources such as business insurance, security systems, vehicles and equipment, office supplies and furnishings, and legal or other advisory/support services.

Performs immediate supervision of department heads and key support staff and maintains official records.

Financial Administration Prepares the annual budget and approves subsequent modifications and transfers; monitors and evaluates accounting systems, audits of accounts, and internal control methods; establishes the method and means of determining fiscal accountability; reviews and approves accounts payable, payroll, and other financial warrants, requisitions, purchase orders, receipts, and records or reports.

Personnel Administration Develops and revises personnel policies, rules, procedures and directives, job specifications, performance evaluation methods, and all personnel forms and records; ensures compliance with applicable federal and state employment laws and regulations; makes hiring, performance, and disciplinary determinations; conducts staff meetings and wage surveys and initiates wage increases based on meritorious performance; hears and resolves complaints, problems, grievances; maintains employee personnel files and other confidential records.

Employment Standards

Education/Experience Any combination of education and experience providing the required skill and knowledge for successful performance would be qualifying. Typical qualifications would be equivalent to:

1. Possession of a bachelor's degree from an accredited college or university with major course work in business or public administration, political science, sociology, or closely related field; and
2. Three (3) years' experience performing responsible general administrative work.

Knowledge Principles and practices of business administration including personnel practices and employment laws, program budgeting, general accounting, and fiscal management practices; office procedures and business operating systems; the appropriate methods and means of dealing with human behavior situations in a variety of business circumstances.

Skill Communicating effectively, verbally and in writing, in a diverse range of audiences and settings; persuasion and negotiation of conflicts and problems; assessing operational, program, staffing, and fiscal needs; interpreting legal documents and government regulations; evaluating fiscal and financial reports, forms, and data; analyzing complex written documents; identifying and resolving administrative problems; working long and irregular hours, and under pressure conditions; delegating responsibility and achieving results through subordinates; maintaining order in an environment of changing priorities.

Licenses Possession of a valid _____ motor vehicle operator's license and willingness to use personal vehicle in the course of employment.

Note: This job specification should not be construed to imply that these requirements are the exclusive standards of the position. Incumbents will follow any other instructions, and perform any other related duties, as may be required.

JOB DESCRIPTION
CONTROLLER

Summary Description

Under general direction of the _____, oversees all operations in connection with financial matters, including accounts receivable and payable, payroll, and auditing; trains and supervises department staff; develops and initiates systems, policies, and procedures for transacting financial matters; ensures that the financial system is accurate, efficient, and in accordance with professional accounting practices and governmental regulations.

Exemplary Duties/Responsibilities

Develops and implements the Accounting Department's goals, projects, policies, procedures, methods, and controls; directs the general accounting activities including maintenance of general ledgers, analysis of computer printouts, and review of payroll records; prepares monthly and close-out reports as required by state and federal regulations; profit-loss statements, annual corporate tax returns, and special financial reports, studies, and analyses; develops and maintains internal audit control system; develops and administers the cash management program.

Provides data, reports, and other information to assist in the preparation of the annual budget; forecasts revenues, expenditures, and year-end balances; plans, designs, implements, and modifies the data processing system; prepares and revises the fiscal operations procedure manual; coordinates with other departments concerning short- and long-range fiscal needs and plans; responds to requests for information; supervises daily accounting operations, especially the verifying and signing of payroll and cash disbursements; selects, trains, supervises, and evaluates accounting staff.

Employment Standards

Education/Experience Any combination of education and experience providing the required skill and knowledge for successful performance would be qualifying. Typical qualifications would be equivalent to:

1. Possession of a bachelor's degree in accounting or business administration with an accounting concentration from an accredited college or university; and
2. Four (4) years' progressively responsible experience in accounting, of which two (2) years were in a supervisory capacity.

Knowledge Principles, practices, and methods of modern accounting and auditing; principles and practices of financial administration including budgeting and reporting; modern office practices, procedures, methods and equipment; modern principles and practices in operations procedures and data processing; application of data processing in the maintenance of accounting records and financial administration; budget preparation, program analyses, and revenue forecasting; principles and practices of organization, administration, budget, and management; reports accounting practices required by state and federal regulations.

Skill Planning, coordinating, and directing a complex financial operation; developing, revising and installing accounting systems and procedures; interpreting and applying appropriate laws and regulations; preparing varied financial statements, reports, and analyses; communicating clearly and concisely orally and in writing; selecting, supervising, training, and evaluating assigned staff.

Licenses Possession of a valid _____ motor vehicle operator's license and willingness to use personal vehicle in the course of employment.

Desirable Qualifications Possession of a Certified Public Accountant (CPA) Certificate.

Note: This job specification should not be construed to imply that these requirements are the exclusive standards of the position. Incumbents will follow any other instructions, and perform any other related duties, as may be required by their supervisor.

JOB DESCRIPTION
HUMAN RESOURCES MANAGER

Summary Description

Under general direction, plans, coordinates, and directs all functions of employee relations, including labor relations, recruitment and selection, classification and salary administration, safety, training, and fair employment; provides professional and technical staff assistance; performs related work as required.

Exemplary Duties/Responsibilities

Directs and participates in the formulation and implementation of goals, objectives, policies and priorities; administers and directs a comprehensive personnel program, formulates and recommends policies, regulations, and practices for carrying out the program; consults with and advises management and supervision to coordinate the various phases of the policies, practices, ordinances, and resolutions; directs, coordinates, and supervises the administration of the classification and compensation plan, recruitment and selection, safety, training, fair employment, employee performance rating and orientation programs; administers a system of employee service records and other personnel records; prepares and recommends to management revisions and amendments relating to personnel matters; conducts special studies, prepares reports and makes recommendations to management; serves in an advisory capacity to management and supervision.

Meets with shop stewards and supervisors to resolve grievances; represents management in matters of concern to employee organizations; acts as chief negotiator in negotiations with various employee organizations; prepares and administers budget for personnel operations; prepares personnel forecast to project employment needs; studies legislation, arbitration decisions, and collective bargaining contracts to assess current trends; selects, supervises, trains, and evaluates professional, technical, and clerical subordinates.

Employment Standards

Education/Experience Any combination equivalent to education and experience that provides the required skill and knowledge is qualifying. Typical qualifications would be equivalent to:

1. Possession of a bachelor's degree from an accredited college or university with major course work in business, public or personnel administration, or any other related field; and
2. Three (3) years' professional experience in personnel administration, including one (1) year in a supervisory or administrative capacity.

Knowledge Principles and practices of personnel administration, including methods and techniques used in recruitment and selection, classification, salary administration, training, safety, and affirmative action; proper safety programs and policies; training techniques and program development; applicable federal, state, and local laws, regulations, ordinances, and policies.

Skill Planning, organizing, assigning, and coordinating the activities of a technical and clerical staff; presenting ideas effectively, orally and in writing; dealing constructively with conflict and developing consensus; selecting, supervising, training, and evaluating subordinates.

Licenses Possession of a valid _____ motor vehicle operator's license and willingness to use personal vehicle in the course of employment.

Note: This job specification should not be construed to imply that these requirements are the exclusive standards of the position. Incumbents will follow any other instructions, and perform any other related duties, as may be required by their supervisor.

JOB DESCRIPTION
BRANCH MANAGER

Summary Description

Under general direction, performs a wide range of difficult to complex administrative activities; coordinates and directs operations and personnel to ensure efficient and profitable operations; uses independent judgment within the framework of established policies and objectives in decisions affecting branch activities; makes recommendations and assists in the formulation of branch objectives, policies, and plans.

Exemplary Duties/Responsibilities

Plans, examines, analyzes, and evaluates branch operations; prepares reports and records for management review; evaluates current procedures, practices, and precedents for accomplishing branch activities and functions; identifies and resolves operational problems; develops and implements alternative methods for work improvement; coordinates branch activities with interrelated activities of other branches or departments for optimum efficiency and economy; prepares periodic budget estimates and reports; orders supplies and equipment as needed, reviews branch audit reports to ensure operational efficiency and quality control; develops relationships with customers and businesses, community, and civic organizations to promote goodwill and generate new business.

Directs and coordinates, through subordinate personnel, branch activities and functions, utilizing knowledge of established policies, procedures, and practices; initiates personnel actions such as recruitments, selections, transfers, promotions, and disciplinary or dismissal measures; resolves work grievances or submits unsettled grievances to next in chain of command for action; prepares work schedules; assigns or delegates responsibilities; gives work directives; resolves problems; sets deadlines to ensure completion of branch operational functions; interprets and disseminates policy to workers; evaluates employee performance.

Employment Standards

Education/Experience Any combination of education and experience providing the required skill and knowledge for successful performance would be qualifying. Typical qualifications would be equivalent to:

1. Possession of a bachelor's degree in business administration with a management or financial concentration from an accredited college or university; and

2. Three (3) years' progressively responsible business experience of which two (2) years were in a supervisory and planning capacity.

Knowledge Principles, practices, and methods of accounting and financial administration including budgeting, auditing, reporting, and quantitative analysis skills; modern principles and practices of organization, administration, budget, and management; financial and personnel reports and practices required by state and federal regulations.

Skill Planning, coordinating, and directing varied and complex administrative operations; speaking clearly and effectively; writing legibly and effectively; collecting, analyzing, and interpreting data from a wide variety of sources and taking appropriate action; and selecting, supervising, training, and evaluating employees.

Licenses Possession of a valid _____ motor vehicle operator's license and willingness to use personal vehicle in course of employment.

Note: This job specification should not be construed to imply that these requirements are the exclusive standards of the position. Incumbents will follow any other instructions, and perform any other related duties, as may be required by their supervisor.

JOB DESCRIPTION
STORE MANAGER

Summary Description

Under general direction, performs a wide range of difficult to complex administrative duties; coordinates and directs store operations and personnel to ensure efficient and profitable store operations and merchandising objectives; performs other related duties as required.

Exemplary Duties/Responsibilities

Develops and implements policies and procedures for store operations, personnel, and community relations; plans, examines, analyzes, and evaluates store operations; prepares sales and inventory reports; reviews operating and financial statements and sales records to determine merchandising activities that require additional sales promotion, clearance sales, or other sales procedures to turn over merchandise.

Negotiates or approves contracts with suppliers of merchandise or other service-oriented establishments; orders merchandise or prepares requisitions to replenish merchandise; formulates pricing policies for sale of merchandise; implements policies according to established requirements for profitability of store operations; ensures that merchandise is correctly priced and displayed; keeps detailed operating records; reconciles daily cash with sales receipts; approves checks for payment of merchandise and issues credit, cash refunds, or returned merchandise; and takes periodic and annual inventory.

Directs and coordinates employees engaged in sales work, and may perform sales work; plans and prepares work schedules; assigns specific duties; trains employees in store policies and job duties; ensures compliance of employees with established sales, record keeping, and security procedures and practices; evaluates employees' work performance; initiates personnel actions such as recruitment, selection, promotions, transfers, and disciplinary or dismissal measures; resolves employees' work grievances; interprets and disseminates store policies to employees; investigates customers' complaints and attempts to resolve problems to restore and promote good public relations.

Employment Standards

Education/Experience   Any combination of education and experience providing the required skill and knowledge for successful performance would be qualifying. Typical qualifications would be equivalent to:

1. Possession of a bachelor's degree or equivalent from an accredited college or university with major course work in business, accounting, marketing, management, or any other related field; and
2. Two (2) years' professional experience in business administration, including one (1) year in a supervisory capacity.

Knowledge   Modern principles, practices, and methods of organization, administration, accounting, merchandising, record keeping, and personnel management; financial and personnel reports and practices required by state and federal regulations.

Skill   Planning, organizing, assigning, and coordinating varied and complex operations; presenting ideas effectively, orally and in writing; dealing constructively with conflict; collecting, analyzing, and interpreting data from a wide variety of sources and taking appropriate action; selecting, supervising, training, and evaluating employees.

Licenses   Possession of a valid _____ motor vehicle operator's license and willingness to use personal vehicle in the course of employment.

Note: This job specification should not be construed to imply that these requirements are the exclusive standards of the position. Incumbents will follow any other instructions, and perform any other related duties, as may be required by their supervisor.

JOB DESCRIPTION
DATA PROCESSING MANAGER

Summary Description

Under the general direction of _____, plans, coordinates, controls, supervises, and participates in the provision of activities and services relating to information system design, programming and documentation, data processing operations, and data communications; provides highly technical and responsible staff assistance.

Exemplary Duties/Responsibilities

Participates in the development and implementation of goals, objectives, policies, and priorities; plans, coordinates, and manages the activities involved in the study of problems, the development and analysis of alternative solutions, and the programming, testing, implementation, computer processing, procedures, and forms design of the selected solution.

Establishes work standards, assigns schedules, reviews staff work, directs training and interprets policies, purposes, and goals to subordinates; administers all work rules, disciplinary actions, and employment practices.

Establishes and maintains production schedules; maintains production records; consults with manufacturers' representatives to define equipment and software needs; prepares requests for proposals; reviews and evaluates proposals; prepares and administers the division budget; orders necessary supplies and materials.

Employment Standards

Education/Experience   Any combination of education and experience providing the required skill and knowledge for successful performance would be qualifying. Typical qualifications would be equivalent to:

1. Possession of a bachelor's degree in business administration or computer science from an accredited college or university; and
2. Three (3) years' increasingly responsible experience in computer operations, programming, and system development and design of which two (2) years were in a supervisory capacity.

Knowledge   Principles and techniques of systems analysis and programming; operating principles, methods, practices, and limitations of automatic data processing computers and related equipment; _____ and _____ programming language; principles of organization, administration, budget, and personnel management.

Skill   Planning, organizing, assigning, supervising, and reviewing data processing activities and services; designing systems and performing necessary programming and documentation; establishing and maintaining production schedules; operating computer equipment; communicating clearly and concisely, orally and in writing; selecting, supervising, training, and evaluating assigned staff.

Note: This job specification should not be construed to imply that these requirements are the exclusive standards of the position. Incumbents will follow any other instructions, and perform any other related duties, as may be required by their supervisor.

Chapter 22

JOB DESCRIPTIONS FOR CLERICAL OCCUPATIONS

Executive Secretary
Secretary I/II
Legal Secretary
Account Clerk I/II
Account Clerk III
Customer Service Representative (Teller) I/II
Data Entry Operator Trainee
Clerk Typist I/II
Clerk Typist III
Receptionist
Storekeeper
Inventory Clerk
Messenger/Stock Clerk
Cashier I/II

JOB DESCRIPTION
EXECUTIVE SECRETARY

Summary Description

Under general supervision of the Executive Director, performs a variety of complex, responsible, and confidential secretarial and administrative duties requiring a thorough knowledge of organizational procedures and precedents; supervises office clerical staff; provides clerical assistance to designated staff members; performs related work as required. This position requires the ability to work independently, exercising judgment and initiative.

Exemplary Duties/Responsibilities

Screens visitors, telephone calls, and mail directed to the Executive Director; independently responds to letters and general correspondence of a routine nature; responds to complaints and requests for information; relieves Executive Director of routine personnel, budget, payroll, and purchasing duties; researches, compiles, and analyzes data for special projects and prepares routine reports; maintains appointment schedules and calendars; makes travel arrangements and arranges meetings; assists in agenda preparation, gathers information and contacts meeting participants; trains, supervises, assigns duties to, and evaluates subordinates; provides clerical assistance to designated staff members; takes and transcribes dictation from shorthand notes or dictaphone recordings; takes, edits, and types minutes and distributes copies.

Employment Standards

Education/Experience Any combination of education and experience providing the required skill and knowledge is qualifying. Typical qualifications would be equivalent to:

1. Completion of the twelfth (12th) grade supplemented by specialized secretarial courses or graduation from an accredited business school/college; and
2. Three (3) years' increasingly responsible secretarial and clerical experience.

Knowledge Correct English usage, grammar, spelling, and punctuation; modern office methods and procedures, equipment and filing systems; business letter- and report-writing techniques; proofreading; statistical and recordkeeping principles and procedures; principles of supervision, training, and performance evaluation.

Skill Performing responsible secretarial and clerical work requiring independent judgment with speed and accuracy; learning, interpreting, and applying organizational policies, laws, rules and regulations; taking responsibility for the compilation and organization of reports; composing correspondence on own initiative; typing accurately from a clear copy at a speed of 65 words per minute; taking dictation at a speed of 100 words per minute and transcribing it accurately; making arithmetic calculations with speed and accuracy; meeting the public tactfully and courteously answering questions in person and over the telephone; communicating effectively with all segments of the community.

Licenses Possession of an appropriate _____ motor vehicle operator's license, vehicle insurance, a good driving record, and a willingness to utilize own vehicle as needed in connection with employment.

Desirable Qualifications Fundamental accounting and bookkeeping knowledge preferred.

Note: This job specification should not be construed to imply that these requirements are the exclusive standards of the position. Incumbents will follow any other instructions, and perform any other related duties, as may be required by their supervisor.

JOB DESCRIPTION
SECRETARY I/II

Summary Description

Under general supervision, performs a variety of complex, responsible, and confidential secretarial and administrative duties; performs related work as required.

Distinguishing Characteristics

SECRETARY I

Positions in this class perform varied secretarial and clerical work under general supervision within a framework of standard policies and procedures. Assigned tasks require initiative, organization, and independent judgment in solving routine problems. There may be leadership responsibilities.

SECRETARY II

Positions in this class are normally filled by advancement from the lower grade of Secretary I or, when filled from outside, require prior secretarial and administrative experience. Appointment to the higher class requires that the employee be performing substantially the full range of duties for the class and meet the qualifications standards for the class. A Secretary II performs varied complex, responsible, and confidential secretarial and clerical duties under limited supervision requiring a thorough knowledge of policies, procedures, and precedents. Reports, documents, and records prepared and maintained by employees in this class are often of a confidential nature. Assigned tasks require tact, independent judgment, initiative, and organization in solving a variety of problems. There may be leadership or supervisory responsibilities.

Exemplary Duties/Responsibilities

Reviews logs, determines priority of, and routes, correspondence; composes routine correspondence and independently prepares correspondence not requiring supervisor's personal attention; acts as receptionist, screens calls, visitors, and refers inquiries as appropriate; responds to complaints and requests for information in relation to the intent, coverage, and content of instructions, guides, precedents, and regulations; gathers, organizes, and prepares information for comprehensive reports; supervises, initiates, and maintains a variety of files and records of information such as payroll, attendance, budget, production, and cost records; recommends organizational or procedural changes affecting administrative clerical activities.

Takes and transcribes dictation from rough draft, shorthand notes, or taped recordings; takes, edits, and types minutes and distributes copies; researches, compiles, and analyzes data for special projects; supervises, trains, and evaluates subordinates.

Employment Standards

SECRETARY I

Education/Experience Any combination of education and experience providing the required skill and knowledge for successful performance would be qualifying. Typical qualifications would be equivalent to:

1. Completion of the twelfth (12th) grade, supplemented by specialized secretarial courses; and
2. One (1) year of responsible secretarial and clerical experience.

Knowledge Correct English usage, grammar, spelling, punctuation, and arithmetic; modern office methods, procedures and equipment, and business letter and report writing; fundamental recordkeeping principles and procedures; receptionist and telephone techniques, and filing systems.

Skill Following oral and written directions; working effectively with others; learning rapidly, interpreting and applying laws, rules, and office policies and procedures; typing accurately from clear copy at a speed of 60 words per minute; taking dictation at the rate of 100 words per minute; operating modern office equipment, including word processors, memory typewriters, and data entry equipment; communicating tactfully and effectively in both oral and written form; working independently in the absence of supervision; analyzing situations carefully and adopting effective courses of action; compiling and maintaining complex and extensive records and files; preparing reports; composing correspondence independently.

SECRETARY II

In addition to the qualifications for Secretary I:

Experience Four (4) years' increasingly responsible secretarial and clerical experience or three (3) years' experience performing duties comparable to those of Secretary I.

Knowledge Principles of supervision, training, and performance evaluation.

Skill Supervising and prioritizing the work of subordinates; training and evaluating subordinates; compiling and maintaining complex, extensive, and confidential records and files; preparing extensive and confidential reports.

Note: This job specification should not be construed to imply that these requirements are the exclusive standards of the position. Incumbents will follow any other instructions, and perform any other related duties, as may be required by their supervisor.

JOB DESCRIPTION
LEGAL SECRETARY

Summary Description

Under general supervision, performs difficult and responsible legal clerical and secretarial duties; performs related duties as required.

Exemplary Duties/Responsibilities

Types from draft, oral dictation, or tapes, a variety of correspondence and legal documents such as resolutions, opinions, contracts, briefs, leases, and agreements; compares dictated legal references with reference books to ensure accuracy; prepares and processes legal papers and documents requiring knowledge of legal format, terminology, and procedures; sets up and maintains files of court cases pending and in process; conforms, indexes, and files legal documents; maintains law library.

Screens telephone calls and answers requests for information or routes to appropriate staff; gathers, organizes, and prepares information for routine reports; independently responds to letters and general correspondence of a routine nature; maintains a variety of files and records.

Employment Standards

Education/Experience Any combination of education and experience providing the required skill and knowledge for successful performance would be qualifying. Typical qualifications would be equivalent to:

1. One (1) year of legal stenographic and related legal clerical work and possession of an associate of arts degree or its equivalent in legal secretarial science from an accredited college or university; and

2. Three (3) years' increasingly responsible legal stenographic and related legal clerical work and successful completion of at least four (4) college-level courses directly related to legal secretarial work.

Knowledge Technical legal terms and various legal forms and documents; legal procedures and practices involved in composing, processing, and filing a variety of legal documents; standard legal references and their contents; business English, grammar, spelling, vocabulary, and arithmetic; operation of standard office equipment.

Skill Performing complex legal clerical work involving independent judgment and requiring accuracy and speed; analyzing situations accurately and taking effective action; reading, interpreting, and applying laws, rules, and directions; communicating clearly and concisely orally and in writing; reading, writing, and speaking English at a level necessary for satisfactory job performance; typing at a speed of 60 words per minute; taking dictation at a rate of 100 words per minute and transcribing from a recorded copy.

Note: This job specification should not be construed to imply that these requirements are the exclusive standards of the position. Incumbents will follow any other instructions, and perform any other related duties, as may be required by their supervisor.

JOB DESCRIPTION
ACCOUNT CLERK I/II

Summary Description

Under general supervision, performs clerical recordkeeping work of average difficulty involving the typing, posting, verifying, and compilation of financial records and forms; receives and distributes mail and internal documents; collects and accounts for limited amounts of revenues and monies; prepares and processes invoices; responds to telephone and personal inquiries; performs related clerical work as required.

Distinguishing Characteristics

ACCOUNT CLERK I

This is the entrance level for clerical accounting employees. Employees in this class normally work under close and continuous supervision performing a group of repetitive or closely related duties according to established procedures. A variety of tasks may be assigned such as cashiering and financial and statistical record keeping. Each step usually fits a pattern which has been observed and reviewed both during its performance and upon completion and changes in procedure or exceptions to the rules are explained in detail as they arise. Under this training concept, positions assigned to the class of Account Clerk II, which became vacant, may responsibly be filled at the Account Clerk I level.

ACCOUNT CLERK II

Positions in this class are normally filled by advancement from the lower grade of Account Clerk I or when filled from outside, require prior clerical accounting experience. Appointment to the higher class requires that the employee be performing substantially the full range of duties for the class and meet the qualification standards for the class. An Account Clerk II works under general supervision and, within a framework of established procedures, is expected to perform a variety of difficult accounting duties such as the maintenance of financial or statistical records with only occasional instructions or assistance. An Account Clerk II is expected to work productively in the absence of supervision. Work is normally reviewed only on completion and for overall results.

Exemplary Duties/Responsibilities

Collects, records, verifies, and otherwise processes financial transactions and documents as required for the processing of accounts receivable, accounts payable, statements, purchase orders, and worksheets; maintains accounts records such as matching invoices to purchase orders, preparing data for computer input, spreading job detail on worksheets, posting job numbers, and filing financial records; prepares deposit and petty cash slips, and may make bank deposits; may assist in preparing material for data processing; maintains materials and supplies inventory for department; prepares new payroll-period time sheets and distributes.

Employment Standards

ACCOUNT CLERK I

Education/Experience   Any combination of education and experience providing the required skill and knowledge for successful performance would be qualifying. A typical way to obtain the knowledge and skills would be completion of the twelfth (12th) grade or its equivalent and course work in business math, typing, office procedures, and record keeping. No experience is needed.

Knowledge   Modern office methods, practices, procedures, and equipment; fundamentals of financial record keeping and methods of performing basic business mathematic calculations; the clerical methods, techniques, forms, and filing systems used in an accounting environment.

Skill   Posting data and making arithmetic calculations with speed and accuracy; using a calculator by touch; establishing and maintaining efficient filing and records retention of financial documents; using initiative and judgment in dealing with work flow and uncertain situations; working effectively under narrow time limitations to produce accurate results; comprehending and using basic accounting terminology, codes, and formats; operating data entry equipment and typing at a rate of 40 words per minute from clear copy; following verbal and written instructions; maintaining effective work relations with those encountered in the course of employment.

ACCOUNT CLERK II

In addition to the qualifications for Account Clerk I:

Education/Experience   Any combination of education and experience providing the required skill and knowledge for successful performance would be qualifying. A typical way to obtain the knowledge and skills would be one (1) year of experience performing duties comparable to those of Account Clerk I.

Skill   Working independently in the absence of supervision.

Note: This job specification should not be construed to imply that these requirements are the exclusive standards of the position. Incumbents will follow any other instructions, and perform any other related duties, as may be required by their supervisor.

JOB DESCRIPTION
ACCOUNT CLERK III

Summary Description

Under general supervision, performs responsible work involving the keeping of financial and statistical records; provides leadership and supervision to subordinate accounting clerical personnel; performs work as required.

Exemplary Duties/Responsibilities

Keeps complete set of financial transactions records; collects information, computes and prepares figures for journal entries; summarizes details in separate ledgers and transfers data to general ledger; balances books and compiles reports to show statistics, such as cash receipts and expenditures, accounts payable and receivable, profit-and-loss statements, and sales tax reports; closes and reopens book of accounts; prepares billing for accounts receivable following up on collection items.

May calculate employee wages from source material; compiles earnings log, change sheets, adjustment sheets, time cards, and control sheets to determine payroll information; may prepare payroll and fringe-benefit data; researches employees' permanent records for information requested by employees or others.

Coordinates and directs work of subordinate accounting clerical personnel; answers subordinates' inquiries; prepares and answers correspondence; prepares input for data processing; prepares and types financial and statistical reports; operates office and data processing equipment.

Employment Standards

Education/Experience Any combination of education and experience providing the required skill and knowledge for successful performance would be qualifying. Typical qualifications would be equivalent to:

1. Completion of the twelfth (12th) grade with concentration in business math, financial record keeping, or other job-related courses; and
2. Four (4) years' progressively responsible experience in maintenance of financial, fiscal, and related statistical records; comparable to that of an Account Clerk II.

Knowledge Principles, practices, and terminology used in financial and statistical record keeping; modern office methods, supplies, and equipment; principles of supervision, training, and performance evaluations.

Skill Planning, organizing, and acting as a leader in coordinating the work of others in the performance of financial record keeping and general clerical work; expressing ideas and giving instructions effectively; performing responsible financial record keeping requiring use of independent judgment and initiative; reading, interpreting, and explaining laws, rules, and regulations; preparing accurate financial and statistical reports and maintaining records; making arithmetical calculations with speed and accuracy; operating calculating machines and other office equipment; typing 40 words per minute.

Note: This job specification should not be construed to imply that these requirements are the exclusive standards of the position. Incumbents will follow any other instructions, and perform any other related duties, as may be required by their supervisor.

JOB DESCRIPTION
CUSTOMER SERVICE REPRESENTATIVE (TELLER) I/II

Summary Description

Under general supervision, performs a variety of clerical, recordkeeping, and consumer service duties concerned with receiving and disbursing money and recording transactions; answers customers' inquiries; performs related work as required.

Distinguishing Characteristics

CUSTOMER SERVICE REPRESENTATIVE I

This is the entrance level for clerical teller employees requiring basic business mathematic computation skills and little or no previous experience. Employees in this class work under close supervision performing a group of repetitive or closely related duties according to established procedures. While a variety of tasks may be assigned, each step usually fits a pattern that has been established and explained before work is started. Any changes in procedure or exceptions to rules are explained as they arise. Generally, work is observed and reviewed both during its performance and upon completion.

Under this training concept, as the difficulty and variety of work increase, positions may be assigned to the higher class of Customer Service Representative II as vacancies occur. Positions may remain in the Customer Service Representative I class if assignments remain limited, work continues to be closely supervised, or the difficulty of the work does not increase.

CUSTOMER SERVICE REPRESENTATIVE II

Positions in this class are normally filled by advancement from the lower class of Customer Service Representative I or, when filled from the outside, require prior teller experience. A Customer Service Representative II is expected to perform a wide variety of moderate-to-difficult clerical, recordkeeping, and customer service duties with only occasional instruction or assistance. Employees in this class are expected to solve routine problems by working within a framework of established procedures and by choosing among the number of limited alternatives. Judgment and initiative are required in making decisions in accordance with approved procedures and precedents. A Customer Service Representative II is expected to work productively in the absence of supervision and may have leadership responsibilities over others. Work is normally reviewed only upon completion and for overall results.

Exemplary Duties/Responsibilities

Receives and pays out money, and keeps records of money and negotiable instruments involved in transactions. Receives checks and cash for deposits, verifies amounts, and examines checks for endorsements; enters deposits in depositers' passbooks; issues receipts; cashes checks and pays out money upon verification of signature and customer balances; computes service charges, interest, and discounts; explains and sells additional services to customers, prepares and posts data to pertinent documents, logs, and forms; answers customers' inquiries or services customers' requests in person, by telephone, or through correspondence; operates office machines, such as typewriter, calculator, bookkeeping, and check-writing machines; balances daily monies.

Employment Standards

CUSTOMER SERVICE REPRESENTATIVE I

Education/Experience Any combination of education and experience providing the required skill and knowledge for successful performance would be qualifying. Typical qualifications would be completion of the twelfth (12th) grade or its equivalent, with course work in business math, business practices, and English usage. No experience necessary.

Knowledge Correct English usage; basic business mathematical computations; modern office equipment and practices.

Skill Following oral and written instructions; reading, writing, and performing mathematical calculations at the level required for successful job performance; operating calculating machine quickly and accurately; typing 40 words per minute from clear copy; learning rules, methods, policies and procedures of the workplace; communicating effectively, orally or in writing; working cooperatively with others; paying attention to detail.

CUSTOMER SERVICE REPRESENTATIVE II

In addition to the qualifications for Customer Service Representative I:

Experience Any combination equivalent to the experience providing the required skill and knowledge. Typical qualifications equivalent to:

1. One (1) year's experience performing duties comparable to Customer Service Representative I; or
2. Two (2) years' increasingly responsible recordkeeping and customer service duties.

Knowledge Working independently in absence of direct supervision; analyzing situations accurately and taking effective action; performing teller work of average difficulty; compiling statistical data for documents and reports.

Special Consideration Both Customer Service Representatives I and II will be working in a nonsmoking area.

Note: This job specification should not be construed to imply that these requirements are the exclusive standards of the position. Incumbents will follow any other instructions, and perform any other related duties, as may be required by their supervisor.

JOB DESCRIPTION
DATA ENTRY OPERATOR TRAINEE

Summary Description

Under direct supervision, learns and operates data entry equipment; performs related specialized clerical work; performs other related work as required.

Exemplary Duties/Responsibilities

Learns the operation of key data entry devices including key entry and verification methods. Types computer program from worksheet and inputs required data. Edits source data to ensure that they conform to predetermined specifications. Compares data on printout or screen with source data to detect errors. Maintains time log of jobs performed; performs routine clerical work as required.

Employment Standards

Education/Experience   Sufficient formal or informal education to provide the required skill and knowledge is qualifying. No experience is required.

Knowledge   Modern office practices and procedures, basic arithmetic, and basic business English.

Skill   Following oral and written instructions; typing accurately at the rate of 40 words per minute from copy; working quickly and accurately under pressure; learning to operate data entry equipment, using ten-key adding machine helpful but not essential.

Special Considerations   Must be willing and able to work any shift within a twenty-four-hour period and on holidays and weekends.

Note: This job specification should not be construed to imply that these requirements are the exclusive standards of the position. Incumbents will follow any other instructions, and perform any other related duties, as may be required by their supervisor.

JOB DESCRIPTION
CLERK TYPIST I/II

Summary Description

Under supervision, performs a variety of clerical duties including typing and the maintenance of a wide variety of records and materials.

Distinguishing Characteristics

CLERK TYPIST I

This is the entrance level for clerical employees, requiring typing skills and little or no previous clerical experience. Employees in this class work under close supervision performing a group of repetitive or closely related duties according to established procedures. While a variety of tasks may be assigned, each step usually fits a pattern that has been established and explained before work is started. Generally, work is observed and reviewed both during its performance and upon completion, and changes in procedure or exceptions to rules are explained in detail as they arise. As the difficulty and variety of work increase, positions are usually allocated to the higher class of Clerk Typist II. Positions may remain in this class if assignments remain of a limited variety, work continues to be closely supervised, or the difficulty of the work does not increase.

CLERK TYPIST II

Positions in this class are normally filled by advancement from the lower class of Clerk Typist I or when filled from the outside, require prior clerical experience. A Clerk Typist II is expected to perform a wide variety of typing and general clerical duties of moderate difficulty with only occasional instruction or assistance. Employees in this class are expected to solve routine problems by choosing among the number of limited alternatives and to work productively even in the absence of supervision. Judgment and initiative are required in making decisions in accordance with approved procedures and precedents. Work is normally reviewed only upon completion and for overall results. There may be leadership responsibilities over others.

Exemplary Duties/Responsibilities

Performs a wide variety of clerical work including typing, proofreading, filing, checking, and recording information; receives, screens, and refers telephone calls to the appropriate persons; types letters, memorandums, statistical information, and other material from oral direction, rough draft, taped or handwritten copy, or notes; receives, sorts, and distributes incoming and outgoing mail; operates adding machine and other office equipment; checks and tabulates statistical data; prepares simple statistical reports; sorts and files documents and records according to predetermined classifications, maintaining alphabetical, numerical index, and cross-reference files; supervises and trains others.

Employment Standards

CLERK TYPIST I

Education/Experience Any combination of education and experience providing the required skill and knowledge for successful performance would be qualifying. Typical qualifications would be completion of the twelfth (12th) grade or its equivalent with major course work in business practices and typing. No experience necessary.

Knowledge Basic elements of correct English usage, spelling, vocabulary, grammar, punctuation, and arithmetic; modern office equipment and practices; principles of letter and report writing; filing systems.

Skill Following oral and written instructions; performing routine clerical work; reading and writing at the level required for successful job performance; learning to operate standard office equipment; learning rules, methods, and policies of the workplace; spelling correctly, using correct English, and making arithmetic calculations; using correct letter and report formats; typing at a speed of not less than 45 words per minute from clear copy; working cooperatively with others.

CLERK TYPIST II

In addition to the qualifications for Clerk Typist I:

Education/Experience Any combination of education and experience providing the required skill and knowledge is qualifying. A typical way to obtain the skill and knowledge would be one (1) year of experience performing duties comparable to those of Clerk Typist I.

Knowledge Operating details, policies, and procedures of workplace; basic methods of supervision.

Skill Working independently in absence of direct supervision; analyzing situations accurately and taking effective action; performing clerical work of average difficulty; compiling data for reports; operating office equipment; typing at a speed of not less than 50 words per minute from clear copy.

Note: This job specification should not be construed to imply that these requirements are the exclusive standards of the position. Incumbents will follow any other instructions, and perform any other related duties, as may be required by their supervisor.

JOB DESCRIPTION
CLERK TYPIST III

Summary Description

Under general supervision, performs a variety of specialized and difficult clerical duties including typing and the maintenance of records and materials; supervises and directs the work of clerical staff; performs related work as required.

Distinguishing Characteristics

Positions in this class are distinguished from those of the next lower class, Clerk Typist II, by regularly performing a variety of the most difficult duties. Employees in this class are expected to exercise consistently a high degree of initiative, independence, responsibility, and working knowledge of detailed regulations, policies, and procedures of the workplace. The work at this level is rarely reviewed. Positions may supervise others and may have responsibility for functional guidance in training and assisting less experienced employees.

Exemplary Duties/Responsibilities

Performs a variety of specialized and difficult clerical work applying independent judgment, discretion, and initiative; types letters, memorandums, statistical and financial data, and other material from oral direction, rough draft, taped or handwritten copy, or notes; researches, compiles, and analyzes information for and prepares reports; maintains complex and confidential filing systems; answers inquiries in person or over the telephone, or refers to another source of information; composes correspondence, either independently or from oral instructions; operates a variety of office equipment; checks and tabulates statistical and financial data; coordinates, supervises, and reviews work assignments of clerical staff.

Employment Standards

Education/Experience   Any combination of education and experience providing the required skill and knowledge for successful performance would be qualifying. Typical qualifications would be equivalent to:

1. Completion of the twelfth (12th) grade with major course work in business practices and typing; and
2. Three (3) years' increasingly responsible typing and advanced clerical experience, of which one (1) year must have been in a supervisory capacity, or two (2) years' experience performing the duties of Clerk Typist II.

Knowledge   Operating details, policies, procedures, and precedents of workplace; correct business English usage, grammar, spelling, punctuation, vocabulary, and arithmetic; office equipment and operation; modern office methods and practices; letter- and report-writing techniques; basic methods of supervision, training, and performance evaluations; filing systems.

Skill   Performing specialized and difficult clerical work with speed and accuracy; preparing and maintaining accurate and complete records and reports; typing accurately from clear copy at a rate of 55 words per minute; making arithmetic calculations with speed and accuracy; working independently; supervising and prioritizing work of subordinates; training and evaluating subordinates; analyzing situations accurately and taking effective actions; operating office equipment including word processors, memory typewriter, data entry equipment, and adding machine; communicating tactfully and effectively both orally and in writing; composing correspondence independently; understanding and carrying out oral and written directions.

Note: This job specification should not be construed to imply that these requirements are the exclusive standards of the position. Incumbents will follow any other instructions, and perform any other related duties, as may be required by their supervisor.

JOB DESCRIPTION
RECEPTIONIST

Summary Description

Under direct supervision, operates a multiline telephone console, gives routine information to the public; greets the public; performs routine clerical work such as typing, filing, scheduling, and mail processing; performs related work as required.

Exemplary Duties/Responsibilities

Receives calls and gives information to callers; screens and routes calls to appropriate destination; obtains and records caller's name, time of call, nature of business, and person called upon; greets visitors, staff, and others in a professional courteous manner; ascertains nature of business and directs visitors or callers to appropriate department or person; types reports, business correspondence, memos, schedules, and other statistical and financial data; adds and checks columns of figures; checks and tabulates simple statistical or accounting data; maintains various files, listings, and records; reads and routes incoming mail; prepares outgoing mail; maintains records of long-distance calls and may schedule appointments; operates office equipment, including adding machine, copy machine, and other office equipment; runs errands.

Employment Standards

Education/Experience   Any combination of education and experience providing the required skill and knowledge is qualifying. Typical qualifications would be equivalent to:

1. Sufficient formal or informal education to assure the ability to read and write English and compute accurate business math at a level required for successful job performance; and
2. Six (6) months' experience in an organization performing duties comparable to those of a telephone switchboard operator and/or general clerk/typist; or graduation from an accredited business school/college with courses in business practices and typing.

Knowledge   Operation of a multiline telephone console; correct English usage, spelling, grammar, and punctuation; office practices, procedures, and equipment.

Skill   Operating a multiline telephone console; performing routine clerical work; learning to operate office equipment and learning office methods, rules, and policies; understanding and carrying out verbal and written directions; typing at a speed of not less than 40 words per minute from clear copy; making arithmetic calculations; maintaining working relations with staff and public; recognizing and maintaining confidentiality of work materials as appropriate; working independently in the absence of supervision.

Licenses   Possession of an appropriate _____ motor vehicle operator's license, vehicle insurance, a good driving record, and a willingness to utilize own vehicle as needed in connection with employment.

Note: This job specification should not be construed to imply that these requirements are the exclusive standards of the position. Incumbents will follow any other instructions, and perform any other related duties, as may be required by their supervisor.

JOB DESCRIPTION
STOREKEEPER

Summary Description

Under general supervision, receives, stores, and issues supplies, equipment, and materials; determines sources of supplies; interviews vendors; evaluates cost of purchase and materials' effectiveness; processes purchase requisitions; maintains adequate stock levels and inventory records; performs related work as required.

Exemplary Duties/Responsibilities

Receives, checks, stores, and issues supplies, materials, and equipment; receives and reviews purchase requisitions; investigates sources of supply; contacts vendors to determine price and availability of required supplies; reorders necessary supplies to maintain stock control; inspects deliveries for damaged goods or discrepancies; reconciles discrepancies with suppliers or shippers; receives authorized requests for supplies, materials, and equipment; issues supplies from stock; maintains inventory control records and participates in periodic inventories; cleans and maintains assigned work area; operates light equipment to pick up and deliver stock, mail, and other items.

Employment Standards

Education/Experience Any combination of education and experience providing the required skill and knowledge for successful performance would be qualifying. A typical way to obtain the knowledge and skill would be one (1) year of experience in storekeeping and inventory work.

Knowledge Storekeeping and inventory methods, practices, and recordkeeping procedures; nomenclature, grades, and classification of a variety of supplies, materials, and equipment; proper methods of storing supplies; operation and maintenance of stockroom equipment.

Skill Following oral and written instructions; maintaining records; performing mathematical calculations; applying department policies and procedures; speaking, reading, and writing English at a level necessary for satisfactory job performance; performing heavy physical work in lifting and moving stock; operating light equipment.

Licenses Possession of a valid _____ motor vehicle operator's license and willingness to use personal vehicle in the course of employment.

Note: This job specification should not be construed to imply that these requirements are the exclusive standards of the position. Incumbents will follow any other instructions, and perform any other related duties, as may be required by their supervisor.

JOB DESCRIPTION
INVENTORY CLERK

Summary Description

Under general supervision, inventories, requisitions, receives, stores, issues, and delivers materials, supplies, equipment, and services; plans and organizes mechanical maintenance and tool inventory services; maintains the supplies, storage, and inventory in an orderly manner; acquires office materials and equipment as needed; performs related work as required.

Exemplary Duties/Responsibilities

Maintains a perpetual inventory on all materials, supplies, and equipment; ascertains items to be ordered; determines where items may be obtained, secures price quotations, and compares prices; completes requisition forms and purchase order forms for those materials, supplies, and equipment items needed; receives deliveries, verifies items against printed order, checks quantity and description, and reports shortages, damages, or other discrepancies; shelves items in correct warehouse/storeroom locations; maintains a clean and orderly warehouse/storeroom by sweeping, dusting, removing packaging material and other debris; issues materials, supplies, and equipment to appropriate members as required; performs monthly inventories; arranges for repairs and replacement of equipment as needed; secures all needed material and equipment on a timely basis; orders, receives, and delivers various office supplies, equipment, and materials requested by designated staff; maintains related files and compiles periodic reports.

Employment Standards

Education/Experience Any combination of education and experience providing the required skill and knowledge is qualifying. Typical qualifications would be equivalent to:

1. Sufficient formal or informal education to ensure the ability to read, write, and compute accurately shop and business math at a level required for successful job performance; and
2. Three (3) years' increasingly responsible clerical, accounting, or record keeping experience preferable, including at least one (1) year in purchasing, storeroom, or inventory activities.

Knowledge Financial record keeping and basic purchasing principles, procedures, and documents; types and sources of materials, supplies, and equipment; commonly used correct English, grammar, spelling, and punctuation; proper letter-writing techniques and formats.

Skill Learning and interpreting established policies, methods, and procedures used for purchasing supplies and equipment; compiling and maintaining complex and extensive records, reports, and files; performing arithmetic calculations rapidly and accurately; performing account record keeping; performing responsible clerical work quickly and accurately; typing accurately from clear copy at a speed of 45 words per minute; establishing and maintaining cooperative relationships with those contacted during the course of work; lifting 40 pounds; following oral or written directions.

Licenses Possession of an appropriate _____ motor vehicle operator's license, vehicle insurance, a good driving record, and a willingness to utilize own vehicle as needed in connection with employment.

Special Requirement Must be capable of working flexible hours, including weekends.

Note: This job specification should not be construed to imply that these requirements are the exclusive standards of the position. Incumbents will follow any other instructions, and perform any other related duties, as may be required by their supervisor.

JOB DESCRIPTION
MESSENGER/STOCK CLERK

Summary Description

Under direct supervision, receives, inspects, records, stores, inventories, and delivers supplies; maintains the supplies storage and inventory in an orderly manner; collects and delivers mail, messages, paperwork, and other documents; sorts and processes mail; operates light vehicles; performs other related duties as needed.

Exemplary Duties/Responsibilities

Receives deliveries, assists in unloading trucks, operating forklifts when required; verifies goods against printed order, checking quantity and description and reporting shortages, damages, or other discrepancies; stores supplies by code descriptions or delivers to appropriate work sites; keeps logs of items received and delivered; maintains a clean and orderly storage area; assists in periodic and annual inventories; receives approved supply requisitions, selects stock, packages and delivers stock to requesting work site; opens, sorts, and distributes incoming mail and collects and stamps outgoing mail; provides additional related messenger and delivery services as directed by supervisor.

Employment Standards

Education/Experience   Any combination of education and experience providing the required skill and knowledge for successful performance would be qualifying. Typical qualifications would be equivalent to:

1. Successful completion of any formal or informal education providing training in high school–level basic mathematic and English usage; and
2. The equivalent to six (6) months' stock or storekeeping work including stock record keeping.

Knowledge   Methods and procedures involved in receiving, recording, storing, and issuing supplies and equipment, including fundamental record keeping and performing basic mathematical calculations and correct English usage; operation of forklift and delivery vehicles; warehousing safety standards.

Skill   Understanding and carrying out oral and written instructions; reading, writing, and performing mathematical calculations at the level required for successful job performance; setting work priorities and organizing work schedule; working cooperatively with others; operating forklift and delivery truck, with either manual or automatic transmission, safely; using good judgment in decision-making situations; reading and interpreting U.S. postal regulations covering special delivery, certified, insured, and registered mail, and parcel post.

Licenses   Possession of a valid _____ motor vehicle operator's license with a good driving record and willingness to use personal vehicle in the course of employment.

Personal Characteristics   Capable of lifting bulk objects or objects weighing up to 70 pounds; willing to work in varying weather conditions; willing to work split or variable work schedules.

Note: This job specification should not be construed to imply that these requirements are the exclusive standards of the position. Incumbents will follow any other instructions, and perform any other related duties, as may be required by their supervisor.

JOB DESCRIPTION
CASHIER I/II

Summary Descriptions

Under general supervision, performs any combination of duties to receive funds from customers in payment for goods or services, disburse funds, and record any monetary transactions.

Exemplary Duties/Responsibilities

Operates cash register to itemize and total customer's purchases; reviews price sheets to note price changes and sale items; records prices and departments, subtotals taxable items, and totals purchases on cash register; receives payment from customers, counts money to verify amounts and issues receipts for funds received; completes credit card charge transactions; gives cash refunds or issues credit memorandums to customers for returned merchandise; may weigh items, bag merchandise, and issue trading stamps.

Compares totals on cash register with amount of currency in register to verify balances; endorses checks and lists and totals cash and checks for bank deposit; prepares bank deposit slips; withdraws cash from bank accounts and keeps custody of cash fund; disburses cash and writes vouchers and checks in payment of company's expenditures; compiles collection, disbursement, and bank reconciliation reports.

Employment Standards

Education/Experience   Any combination of education and experience providing the required skill and knowledge for successful performance would be qualifying. Typical qualifications would be equivalent to:

1. Sufficient formal or informal education to assure the ability to read, write, and speak English; compute accurate business math; and keep accurate records, and
2. One (1) year's full-time paid work experience performing responsible cashier work and financial record keeping.

Knowledge   Modern business methods, practices, procedures, and office equipment; fundamentals of financial record keeping and methods of performing basic business mathematic calculations.

Skill   Performing responsible cashier work requiring independent judgment with speed and accuracy; maintaining records; posting data and making arithmetic calculations with speed and accuracy; using a calculator or register by touch; meeting the public tactfully and courteously and maintaining working relations; understanding and carrying out verbal and written directions; applying organization policies and procedures; recognizing and maintaining confidentiality of work materials as appropriate; working independently in the absence of supervision, and using initiative and judgment in dealing with work flow and uncertain situations.

Note: This job specification should not be construed to imply that these requirements are the exclusive standards of the position. Incumbents will follow any other instructions, and perform any other related duties, as may be required by their supervisor.

Chapter 23

JOB DESCRIPTIONS FOR PROFESSIONAL OCCUPATIONS

Accountant
Accounting Specialist
Administrative Assistant
Advertising Assistant
Computer Programmer/Operator
Construction Inspector
Operations Officer
Paralegal Assistant
Program Coordinator

JOB DESCRIPTION
ACCOUNTANT

Summary Description

Under general supervision, performs a variety of professional accounting work; compiles, prepares, and maintains financial data and records, ensuring that all financial data are recorded in accordance with generally accepted accounting principles and consistent with established policy and procedures.

Exemplary Duties/Responsibilities

Performs professional accounting work in accordance with prescribed accounting system and generally accepted principles of accounting; establishes and maintains accounts; prepares monthly journal entries and accounting corrections to ensure accurate accounting records and checks general ledger from books of detail entries; assists in the preparation, analysis, and review of estimates of revenues, reimbursements, expenditures, fund conditions, or other proprietary and budgetary accounts; analyzes and verifies financial reports and statements, accounts and records of expenditures and revenues; assists with the preparation of accounting and management control reports; handles assets transfers among activities; organizes, directs, and controls the retention of historical accounting and legal records, ensuring that all information is safely stored and available on short notice.

Employment Standards

Education/Experience Any combination of education and experience providing the required skill and knowledge for successful performance would be qualifying. Typical qualifications would be equivalent to:

1. Possession of a bachelor's degree in accounting or business administration from an accredited college or university; and
2. One (1) year's professional accounting experience.

Knowledge Principles, practices, and methods of modern accounting and auditing; principles and practices of financial administration including reporting; modern office practices, procedures, methods, and accounting equipment.

Skill Examining and verifying financial documents and reports; developing accounting procedures and forms; working independently from general instructions; communicating clearly and concisely, orally and in writing; assisting in supervision and training of clerical personnel.

Note: This job specification should not be construed to imply that these requirements are the exclusive standards of the position. Incumbents will follow any other instructions, and perform any other related duties, as may be required by their supervisor.

JOB DESCRIPTION
ACCOUNTING SPECIALIST

Summary Description

Under general and direct supervision of the _____, performs responsible and technical accounting work involving the keeping of statistical and financial records, recording transactions within established systems and procedures, exercising independent judgment in the processing of accounts, and providing supervision over subordinate staff as assigned.

Exemplary Duties/Responsibilities

Performs technical accounting work in accordance with established accounting systems and generally accepted principles of accounting; establishes and maintains accounts as assigned; prepares and balances monthly journal entries and accounting corrections, and verifies ledger entries from detailed records; assists in the preparation, analysis, and review of revenue estimates, program operating costs, fund conditions, or other proprietary or budget accounts; analyzes and verifies financial reports, statements, and records of expenditures and revenues; assists with the preparation of accounting reports; prepares monthly bank reconciliations.

Distributes material, labor, equipment and indirect costs and other documents, coding such costs according to functional and organizational classifications; edits time cards for accuracy, making changes as appropriate; deposits transfers and payroll; receives and processes invoices, purchase orders, and reimbursements; assists with annual budget and audit as assigned; maintains and reconciles petty cash.

Enters data and information into accounting records systems and modifies as needed; makes moderate-to-difficult arithmetic calculations; preaudits and codes various claims and purchase orders and prepares for payment; receives cash, issues receipts, and prepares various bank deposits; may assist in the preparation of, and explain to others, the financial procedures, programs, and accounting requirements; provides training and general supervision over subordinate staff.

Employment Standards

Education/Experience   Any combination of education and experience providing the required skill and knowledge for successful performance would be qualifying. Typical qualifications would be equivalent to:

1. Successful completion of a two- (2)-year accredited college curriculum in accounting equivalent to an associates of arts degree with course work up to advanced accounting, business math, and fundamental supervision; and
2. Two (2) years' responsible accounting or bookkeeping experience related to accounts payable, payroll, general ledger, and reconciliations. Additional experience of up to two years may be substituted for the education requirement.

Knowledge   Principles, procedures, and practices of general accounting; modern office practices, procedures, systems, and equipment relating to financial operations, including computerized accounting procedures; the regulatory requirements of processing payroll accounting transactions.

Skill   Planning, organizing, and completing assigned work in a timely manner; preparing financial reports, statements, documents, and entries in accordance with established procedures and requirements; working effectively and accurately under narrow time limitations; using time, equipment, and materials in the most efficient manner possible; assigning, evaluating, and generally supervising the work of other staff; working effectively with others; communicating clearly and concisely, verbally and in writing; reading, writing, and speaking English at a level required for satisfactory job performance; using a typewriter and calculator by touch.

Note: This job specification should not be construed to imply that these requirements are the exclusive standards of the position. Incumbents will follow any other instructions, and perform any other related duties, as may be required by their supervisor.

JOB DESCRIPTION
ADMINISTRATIVE ASSISTANT

Summary Description

Under general direction, performs staff assistance on difficult to complex projects and programs pertaining to administrative, organization, operation and budgeting considerations, and performs related work as required. This position requires the ability to work independently, exercising judgment and initiative.

Exemplary Duties/Responsibilities

Assists in the development and implementation of goals, objectives, policies, and priorities; prepares administrative studies of organizational and administrative policies, practices, and techniques; evaluates existing administrative policies and techniques; proposes new policies and procedures; prepares materials for, and assists in presentation of, data.

Collects, analyzes, and interprets statistical and other data; prepares written reports and makes recommendations regarding their necessity and feasibility based on studies, surveys, and analyses; may review and process such documents as contracts and agreements, bids, and petitions; may act as liaison with other concerned parties concerning the coordination of activities related to efficient operations.

Coordinates and supervises staff's daily work in support of goals and objectives; may assist in the selection, training, orientation and, evaluation of staff; interprets matters of policy/procedures and rules/regulations for staff; maintains appropriate files; prepares correspondence, reports, and other written documentation as necessary.

Employment Standards

Education/Experience   Any combination of education and experience providing the required skill and knowledge for successful performance would be qualifying. Typical qualifications would be equivalent to:

1. Possession of a bachelor's degree from an accredited college or university with major course work in business or public administration, or a closely related field; and
2. Two (2) years' experience performing responsible general administrative work.

Knowledge   Principles and practices of business administration, organization, general accounting, program budgeting, and personnel management and employment laws; common techniques and practices of training, supervision, and evaluation; research and report-writing methods, including basic quantitative analysis; administrative and management information systems; modern office practices and procedures, including efficient record keeping.

Skill   Independently planning, organizing, scheduling, coordinating, and making decisions and judgments relating to assigned projects and other responsibilities; applying sound analytical decision-making processes and approaches; communicating effectively, verbally and in writing, in a diverse range of audiences and settings; developing alternative solutions to problems; synthesizing, comparing, and analyzing data; interpreting legal documents and governmental regulations; preparing clear, concise, thorough, meaningful, and grammatically correct written reports, letters, memoranda, policies, and other written documents; establishing working relationships and interacting effectively with a wide range of people.

Note: This job specification should not be construed to imply that these requirements are the exclusive standards of the position. Incumbents will follow any other instructions, and perform any other related duties, as may be required by their supervisor.

JOB DESCRIPTION
ADVERTISING ASSISTANT

Summary Description

Under general supervision, performs media billing functions, including reconciliation of time changes and schedules, and monitors advertising.

Exemplary Duties/Responsibilities

Compiles advertising orders for submission to publishers; reviews order to determine specifications; may suggest changes to improve advertisement effectiveness; computes cost of advertisement, based on size, date, frequency, position, and other requirements using standard rate charts and data; maintains accurate records in changing rates for all media; determines cost of advertising space in various media in other areas; prepares and maintains accurate scheduling calendars for all media, reflecting air dates, times, rotations, insertions, and modifications; monitors radio and television commercials and print advertising, keeping track of tear sheets; prepares monthly budget summaries showing net expenditures; maintains files of all advertising material; may proofread and correct advertising proofs.

Employment Standards

Education/Experience   Any combination of education and experience providing the required skill and knowledge for successful performance would be qualifying. Typical qualifications would be equivalent to:

1. An associate of arts degree in marketing or related field with concentration in media billing; or
2. Three (3) years' progressively responsible experience in advertising or broadcasting, of which two (2) years must have included media billing functions.

Knowledge   Advertising, broadcasting, and newspaper terminology, methods, and equipment; principles of artistic design and their application to marketing; methods and procedures for scheduling advertisements to achieve the greatest effectiveness; accounting principles and procedures; general office procedures.

Skill   Examining and verifying financial documents and reports; developing billing procedures and forms; tracing and justifying billing discrepancies; obtaining cost estimates and coordinating printing and publishing of advertisements; estimating time and scheduling jobs; establishing cooperative working relationship with others; reading and writing at a level appropriate to duties of the position; working under deadlines.

Special Qualifications   Must not be colorblind.

Note: This job specification should not be construed to imply that these requirements are the exclusive standards of the position. Incumbents will follow any other instructions, and perform any other related duties, as may be required by their supervisor.

JOB DESCRIPTION
COMPUTER PROGRAMMER/OPERATOR

Summary Description

Under general supervision, performs a variety of technical and skilled tasks concerned with processing data using automatic data processing equipment and peripheral equipment; performs related work as required.

Exemplary Duties/Responsibilities

Develops and writes computer programs to classify, index, input, store, locate, and retrieve specific documents, data, and information to resolve questions and problems; writes computer programs from logic flow charts, record layouts, and input and report formats using language processable by computer; devises sample input and data to test and assure program accuracy; revises programs to increase operating efficiency, adapt to new requirements, and correct errors or omissions; prepares written instructions and documentation.

Operates computer and peripheral equipment that processes, records, stores, transfers, prints, or displays data according to operating instructions; operates related equipment including reproducer, sorter, and collator; loads computer equipment with proper files and forms for each computer run; maintains a record of computer jobs completed; separates and sorts printed data to prepare for distribution.

Employment Standards

Education/Experience   Any combination of education and experience providing the required skill and knowledge for successful performance would be qualifying. Typical qualifications would be equivalent to:

1. Possession of a bachelor's degree with major courses in computer and computer programming; and
2. Six (6) months' experience in the programming and operation of electronic automatic data processing equipment or three (3) years' increasingly responsible experience in computer operations, data management techniques, and data communication concepts; other related tasks as assigned to this position.

Knowledge   Computer and related equipment operations and principles; computer programming and processing techniques; computer theory and principles, practices, and methods of electronic data systems.

Skill   Analyzing complex problems by applying knowledge of computer capabilities, subject matter and symbolic logic; creating and writing computer programs for user ease; developing written instructions, flow charts, and documentation; operating data processing and peripheral equipment.

Note: This job specification should not be construed to imply that these requirements are the exclusive standards of the position. Incumbents will follow any other instructions, and perform any other related duties, as may be required by their supervisor.

JOB DESCRIPTION
CONSTRUCTION INSPECTOR

Summary Description

Under general supervision, inspects and oversees various types of construction work to ensure that procedures and materials comply with plans and specifications.

Exemplary Duties/Responsibilities

Observes work in progress to ensure that procedures followed and materials used conform to specifications; examines finished work to ensure compliance with regulations governing construction; maintains daily log of construction and inspection activities; prepares related reports and records; prepares samples of soil or other unapproved materials for testing; interprets blueprints and specifications; performs calculations relative to inspection requirements.

Employment Standards

Education/Experience   Any combination of education and experience providing the required skill and knowledge is qualifying. Typical qualifications would be equivalent to:

1. Sufficient formal or informal education to ensure the ability to read, write, and perform advanced mathematical calculations at a level required for successful job performance; and

2. Four (4) years' construction experience of which two (2) years must have been as a construction inspector, superintendent of construction, or construction lead worker.

Knowledge   State and local building codes, ordinances, and regulations; calculating functions of rectangles, triangles, circles, volumes, weights, lengths, percents, fractions, and decimals; building mode standards, terminology, and construction methods; occupational health and safety standards; inspection methods, procedures, and record keeping.

Skill   Reading and interpreting construction plans and specifications, permit requirements, special provisions, memorandums, and test reports; identifying nonconforming materials; workmanship or deviations from plans; using surveyor's transit to verify elevations relative to grades or construction; drawing to scale and maintaining as-built construction plans; establishing and maintaining effective working relationships with others; maintaining files, preparing and submitting reports in a timely and accurate manner; planning and organizing work activities, setting priorities; identifying alternative courses of action; anticipating and resolving problems using sound judgment; communicating effectively, orally and in writing.

Licenses

1. Possession of a valid _____ motor vehicle operator's license and willingness to use own transportation in the course of performing required duties.

2. Possession of a valid inspector's certificate.

Note: This job specification should not be construed to imply that these requirements are the exclusive standards of the position. Incumbents will follow any other instructions, and perform any other related duties, as may be required by their supervisor.

JOB DESCRIPTION
OPERATIONS OFFICER

Summary Description

Under general supervision, directs and coordinates daily activities and personnel involved in performing internal operations; uses independent judgment within the framework of established policies and objectives in decisions that influence operations.

Exemplary Duties/Responsibilities

Assists management in formulating administrative and operational policies and procedures; inspects operating functions to evaluate efficiency methods; compiles required and special reports and prepares recommendations on findings for management evaluations; may authorize requisition of equipment and supplies.

Supervises and coordinates activities of employees; initiates personnel actions such as promotions, transfers, discipline, and discharge; interviews, selects, and trains new personnel; determines work procedures, prepares work schedules, and expedites work flow; assigns duties and examines work for quality and quantity; interprets, implements, and enforces compliance with policies, procedures, and safety regulations; may advise or assist employees in performing duties; conducts staff meetings to discuss operational problems or explain procedural changes; investigates, analyzes, and resolves personnel and operational problems or complaints; may confer with workers' representative to resolve grievances; may keep time and personnel records, and oversee preparation of payroll.

Employment Standards

Education/Experience   Any combination of education and experience providing the required skill and knowledge for successful performance would be qualifying. Typical qualifications would be equivalent to:

1. Completion of the twelfth (12th) grade, supplemented with college-level courses in business, accounting, or other related areas; and
2. Three (3) years' progressively responsible operations experience, of which one (1) year must have been in a leadership capacity.

Knowledge   Principles and techniques of organization administration, budget, supervision, training, and performance evaluations; effective and efficient methods and procedures for scheduling and assigning work flow for greatest efficiency; basic operational functions and procedures of department or branch.

Skill   Planning, scheduling, and assigning work of subordinates; preparing reports and maintaining records; communicating clearly and concisely, orally and in writing; supervising, training, and evaluating subordinates.

Note: This job specification should not be construed to imply that these requirements are the exclusive standards of the position. Incumbents will follow any other instructions, and perform any other related duties, as may be required by their supervisor.

JOB DESCRIPTION
PARALEGAL ASSISTANT

Summary Description

Under general direction, performs a variety of complex and responsible legal, confidential, and administrative duties; supervises office clerical staff; performs related work as required.

Exemplary Duties/Responsibilities

Independently researches and analyzes law sources such as statutes, recorded judicial decisions, legal articles, treaties, constitutions, and legal codes to prepare legal documents such as briefs, pleadings, appeals, wills, contracts, deeds, and trust instruments for review and approval; performs administrative liaison duties for preparation of complex documents and litigation; files pleadings with court clerk; prepares affidavits of documents and maintains document files; interprets policies, rules, and regulations in response to inquiries; answers letters and general correspondence; processes confidential matters; may deliver subpoenas to witnesses and parties to action; assigns, supervises, and reviews work of clerical staff; maintains control of the flow of all documents and correspondence.

Employment Standards

Education/Experience Any combination of education and experience providing the required skill and knowledge for successful performance would be qualifying. Typical qualifications would be equivalent to:

1. Five (5) years' increasingly responsible legal secretarial experience in a law office and at least three (3) college courses in law; or
2. Four (4) years' increasingly responsible legal secretarial experience in a law office and possession of an associate of arts degree in a closely related field, including course work in law and report writing; or
3. Two (2) years' legal research and report-writing experience and possession of a bachelor's degree in a closely related field, including course work in law.

Knowledge Principles of civil and criminal procedures; legal terminology, forms, documents, procedures, and practices involved in composing, processing, and filing a variety of legal documents and reports; legal references and their contents; methods of legal research; English composition and office management techniques; principles of supervision, training, and performance evaluation.

Skill Communicating clearly and concisely, orally and in writing; working independently with little or no supervision; gathering, organizing, and analyzing data in formulating conclusions and recommendations; planning and assigning work of others; supervising, training, and evaluating subordinates; establishing and maintaining cooperative relationships with professional staff and the public in situations requiring tact, diplomacy, and poise; reading, interpreting, and applying laws, rules, and regulations; doing complex legal work involving considerable initiative, judgment, and responsibility; operating standard typewriting and word processing equipment; typing a variety of correspondence from draft, oral dictation, or tapes.

Note: This job specification should not be construed to imply that these requirements are the exclusive standards of the position. Incumbents will follow any other instructions, and perform any other related duties, as may be required by their supervisor.

JOB DESCRIPTION
PROGRAM COORDINATOR

Summary Description

Under general direction, plans, directs, and coordinates activities of designated program to ensure that established goals and objectives are accomplished in accordance with prescribed priorities, time limitations, and funding conditions; advises, makes recommendations, and assists in the formulation of goals and objectives; and exercises independent judgment in the course of carrying out overall responsibilities.

Exemplary Duties/Responsibilities

Reviews and evaluates the effectiveness of program proposal or plan; oversees feasibility studies; ascertains time frame and funding limitations to determine program methods and procedures, staffing requirements, and allotment of funds to various stages of program; authorizes, verifies, and keeps records of disbursements from the program account; assures mailing and receipt of funds; compiles and prepares monthly report of program activities; identifies and makes recommendations on the program's budgetary and operational requirements by collecting, analyzing, projecting, and drafting program information; prepares reports, records, charts, files, and related program documents as required; orders and acquires office supplies; conducts postaudits to ensure that original program goals and objectives are still being obtained and recommends corrective actions as needed.

Develops staffing plan, and establishes work plan and schedules for each stage of the program; assigns, monitors, and evaluates the work of program staff; interviews, orients, and trains new staff; makes recommendations on wage increases, discipline, and other employment-related decisions affecting staff; proposes changes to the level or type of staff required for effective operations; authorizes staff payroll records.

Employment Standards

Education/Experience Any combination of education and experience providing the required skill and knowledge for successful performance would be qualifying. Typical qualifications would be equivalent to:

1. Possession of a bachelor's degree with major course work in business administration, accounting, supervision, or a closely related field; and
2. Two (2) years' full-time work experience performing supervisory responsibilities or highly responsible administrative office work related to the tasks assigned to this position.

Knowledge Principles and practices of business administration, including program budgeting, general accounting, fiscal management practices, personnel practices, and employment laws. Principles and practices of supervision including assigning, evaluating, and modification of work; functions and processes of carrying out programs; content and format of reports, payroll records, and correspondence.

Skill Interpersonal communications, verbally and in writing, with a diverse range of people, including the proper handling of emotional situations; effectively using time and resources to accomplish program operations; supervising others and maintaining effective business relations with those encountered in the course of work; analyzing and independently solving a variety of moderately difficult situations and problems; assessing operational, program, staffing, and fiscal needs; evaluating fiscal and financial reports, forms, and data; analyzing complex written documents; identifying and resolving administrative problems; working long and irregular hours, under pressure; delegating responsibility and achieving results through subordinates.

Licenses Possession of a valid _____ motor vehicle operator's license and willingness to use personal vehicle in the course of employment.

Desirable Qualifications Fluency in reading, writing, and speaking _____.

Note: This job specification should not be construed to imply that these requirements are the exclusive standards of the position. Incumbents will follow any other instructions, and perform any other related duties, as may be required by their supervisor.

Chapter 24

JOB DESCRIPTIONS FOR TRADE OCCUPATIONS

Auto Shop Parts Clerk
Building Maintenance Helper/Worker
Equipment Service Worker
Heavy Equipment Mechanic
Janitor
Painter
Tree Trimmer

JOB DESCRIPTION
AUTO SHOP PARTS CLERK

Summary Description

Under general supervision, identifies, orders, receives, stores, issues and maintains automotive parts and materials; prepares records, reports, and correspondence related to automotive equipment repair; performs related duties as required.

Exemplary Duties/Responsibilities

Determines and investigates sources of automotive supplies; secures price quotations and compares prices; negotiates with suppliers to obtain best price and terms; orders, receives, checks, stores, and issues parts and supplies; compiles data and periodic reports; maintains catalogs and related filing systems; prepares period, special, or perpetual inventory of stock; compiles information concerning the receipt or disbursement of parts and supplies and computes inventory balance, price, and costs; prepares reports of inventory balance, prices, and shortages; traces history of item to determine reasons for discrepancies between inventory and stock control records.

May operate forklift or handtruck to move shipments from delivery area to storage area; drives vehicle to pick up incoming stock or to pick up and deliver parts or schedules to delivery routes; types correspondence and reports; answers telephones and provides shop information.

Employment Standards

Education/Experience   Any combination equivalent to education and experience that could likely provide the required skill and knowledge is qualifying. A typical way to obtain the knowledge and skills would be:

1. Sufficient formal or informal education to insure the ability to read and write at a level required for successful job performance; and
2. Two (2) years of experience performing the duties associated with automotive parts clerk, inventory or shipping and receiving clerk, or automotive equipment repair and parts usage.

Knowledge   Automotive terminology; a wide range of parts and supplies for automotive and mechanical equipment; sources of supply; automotive parts catalog use and interpretation; basic purchasing principles, procedures, and stock record systems; techniques of receiving, storing, and issuing parts and supplies; parts substitution; assembly and repair procedures for automotive and construction equipment; modern office methods, procedures, and equipment.

Skill   Developing and maintaining accurate records and reports; following oral and written instructions; developing and implementing inventory and records control systems; designing forms appropriate to inventory control and recordkeeping requirements; dealing effectively with vendors in situations requiring judgment, friendliness, tact, and firmness; performing responsible clerical work and arithmetic calculations quickly and accurately; typing accurately from clear copy; compiling and interpreting data; working independently and exercising initiative; communicating clearly and concisely, orally and in writing.

Licenses   Possession of a valid _____ motor vehicle operator's license and willingness to use personal vehicle in the course of employment.

Note: This job specification should not be construed to imply that these requirements are the exclusive standards of the position. Incumbents will follow any other instructions, and perform any other related duties, as may be required by their supervisor.

JOB DESCRIPTION
BUILDING MAINTENANCE HELPER/WORKER

Summary Description

Under general supervision, performs skilled and semiskilled building maintenance and repair requiring a working knowledge of carpentry, plumbing, and minor electrical work; performs related work as required.

Distinguishing Characteristics

Building Maintenance Helper This is the entry-level class in the maintenance worker series. Positions in this class normally perform a variety of unskilled or semiskilled physical tasks in construction and maintenance activities. Work is usually closely supervised and fits a pattern that has been established and explained before work is started. Work is observed and reviewed both during its performance and upon completion. Building maintenance helpers are normally considered to be on a training status. Under this training concept, the difficulty and variety of work increases, positions may be assigned to the class of Building Maintenance Worker should a position become vacant. There is no supervision over others.

Building Maintenance Worker Positions in this class are normally filled by advancement from the lower grade of Building Maintenance Helper or, when filled from the outside, require prior construction, carpentry, or electrical experience. A Building Maintenance Worker works under general direction within a framework of established procedures, is expected to perform a wide variety of skilled and semiskilled building maintenance and repair work. Judgment and initiative are required in making decisions in accordance with established guides. There may be supervision and training responsibilities over others.

Exemplary Duties/Responsibilities

Repairs and maintains machinery, plumbing, physical structure, grounds and electrical wiring and fixtures in accordance with blueprints, manuals, and building codes, using hand tools and carpenter's, electrician's, and plumber's tools; performs routine maintenance on machines; replaces or repairs machine belts; removes dust, dirt, grease, and waste materials from machines; paints machines or equipment to prevent corrosion.

Installs electrical equipment and repairs or replaces wiring, fixtures, and bulbs; repairs or replaces brick and plaster walls; paints walls, floors, ceilings, or fixtures; repairs and replaces gauges, valves, pressure regulators, and other plumbing equipment and opens clogged drains; repairs various types of furniture, doors, windows, floors, lockers, gates, roofs, and ceilings; builds sheds and other outbuildings; digs ditches, trenches, and post holes; patches and repairs sidewalks and streets; maintains grounds.

Employment Standards

BUILDING MAINTENANCE HELPER

Education/Experience Any combination of education and experience providing the required skill and knowledge is qualifying. A typical way to obtain the skill and knowledge would be sufficient formal or informal education to ensure the ability to read, write, and perform mathematical computations at a level required for successful job performance. No experience is necessary.

Knowledge Use and care of construction hand and power tools; safe work practices.

Skill Following oral and written instructions; performing unskilled and semiskilled tasks in a variety of construction and maintenance activities; learning to perform skilled carpentry, plumbing, and electrical work; performing heavy physical labor; working at a height of fifteen (15) to twenty (20) feet above the ground; establishing and maintaining cooperative relationship with those contacted in the course of work.

BUILDING MAINTENANCE WORKER

In addition to the qualifications for Building Maintenance Helper:

Education/Experience One (1) year of experience performing building maintenance and repair work.

Knowledge Standard tools, materials, methods, and practices involved in building, maintenance, and repair, including carpentry, plumbing, electrical, and painting; safe work practices; estimating materials and labor need; supervising and training others.

Skill Reading and interpreting blueprints, manuals, and building codes; analyzing and evaluating situations and using independent judgment and initiative in taking effective action; making mathematical calculations quickly and accurately; communicating clearly and concisely; operating and caring for electrical, carpentry, plumbing, and construction hand and power tools; setting priorities; training, supervising, and evaluating others.

Licenses Possession of a valid _____ motor vehicle operator's license and willingness to use personal transportation in the course of performing duties.

Note: This job specification should not be construed to imply that these requirements are the exclusive standards of the position. Incumbents will follow any other instructions, and perform any other related duties, as may be required by their supervisor.

JOB DESCRIPTION
EQUIPMENT SERVICE WORKER

Summary Description

Under general supervision, performs a variety of semiskilled work in servicing, maintaining, and repairing automotive and other mechanical equipment; performs related work as required.

Exemplary Duties/Responsibilities

Repairs, adjusts, services, and tests automotive and other equipment using hand and power tools; installs and services batteries, spark plugs, light bulbs, fan belts; mends damaged body and fenders by hammering out or filling in dents; replaces and adjusts headlights and brakes and installs and repairs accessories such as radios, heaters, mirrors, and windshield wipers; performs other simple mechanical repairs; greases and lubricates automobiles, trucks, and other automotive and mechanical equipment.

Tests repaired equipment; services automotive equipment with gasoline and oil; cleans tools and parts with cleaning compounds; assists in the general maintenance and cleanliness of automotive shop area; maintains detailed records of work performed, such as labor and material used; performs service calls; makes temporary repairs; tows equipment to shop area; picks up and delivers parts and equipment.

Employment Standards

Education/Experience Any combination of education and experience providing the required skill and knowledge for successful performance would be qualifying. Typical qualifications would be equivalent to:

1. Sufficient formal or informal education to ensure ability to perform at a level required for successful job performance; and
2. One (1) year's experience in automotive servicing work.

Knowledge Lubricating systems and oils, greases, and attachments used in lubricating automotive and related equipment; equipment operation, utilization, and repair methods; less complex components of automotive equipment; occupational hazards and standard safety precautions necessary in the work.

Skill Understanding and carrying out oral and written instructions; keeping detailed records; performing minor repairs and brake work as required; performing heavy physical labor; servicing heavy and light equipment.

Licenses Possession of a valid _____ motor vehicle operator's license at the time of appointment. Loss of license is cause for demotion or termination.

Special Qualifications Ability and willingness to work any shift during a twenty-four hour period, and on weekends and holidays.

Note: This job specification should not be construed to imply that these requirements are the exclusive standards of the position. Incumbents will follow any other instructions, and perform any other related duties, as may be required by their supervisor.

JOB DESCRIPTION
HEAVY EQUIPMENT MECHANIC

Summary Description

Under general supervision, performs skilled journey-level work in the mechanical repair and maintenance of light and heavy gasoline and diesel-driven automotive and other mechanical equipment; performs related work as required.

Exemplary Duties/Responsibilities

Operates and inspects automotive or mechanical equipment to diagnose defects; analyzes malfunctions and performs general overhaul, tune-up, and repair work on automobiles, light and heavy trucks, mowers, motor sweepers, and other automotive or mechanical equipment; estimates cost of repairs; dismantles and reassembles equipment, using hoists and handtools; plans work procedure, using charts, technical manuals, and experience; repairs, adjusts, and replaces necessary units and parts such as rods, valves, pistons, gears, bearings, fuel and exhaust components, assemblies and cooling; repairs, overhauls, and replaces brakes, ignition systems, transmissions, differentials, front and rear axle assemblies; repairs and installs hydraulic pumps and controls; inspects, repairs, overhauls, and assembles automotive electrical equipment such as generators, distributors, ignitions, and starters.

Performs gas and acetylene welding, brazing, and soldering; uses lathes, sharpeners, and drill presses; lubricates a wide variety of parts and auxiliary equipment; maintains detailed records of time and materials used in each job; inspects and tests repaired equipment.

Employment Standards

Education/Experience   Any combination of education and experience providing the required skill and knowledge for successful performance would be qualifying. Typical qualifications would be equivalent to:

1. Completion of a recognized apprenticeship in the automotive/equipment mechanic trade; or
2. Two (2) years' experience as a journey-level automotive mechanic.

Knowledge   Methods, materials, tools, and techniques used in the repair and maintenance of a variety of automotive and mechanical equipment; operating principles of gasoline and diesel engines and of mechanical repair of heavy trucks and construction equipment; occupational hazards and standard safety precautions necessary in the work; principles and methods of gas and electrical welding; basic machinery operations.

Skill   Locating, correcting, and adjusting defects in complex automotive and mechanical equipment; performing skilled work in repairing, overhauling, and maintaining gas- and diesel-powered automotive equipment; interpreting and working from charts, technical manuals, and diagrams; using and caring for tools used in automotive and mechanical repair work; maintaining detailed and routine records.

Licenses

1. Possession of a valid _____ motor vehicle operator's license at the time of appointment.
2. Possession of a current Class A smog, lights, and brakes certificate at the time of appointment. Loss of license or certificates is cause for demotion or termination.

Note: This job specification should not be construed to imply that these requirements are the exclusive standards of the position. Incumbents will follow any other instructions, and perform any other related duties, as may be required by their supervisor.

JOB DESCRIPTION
JANITOR

Summary Description

Under general supervision, performs cleaning tasks and operation of various types of cleaning equipment to care for and maintain assigned buildings and related facilities; performs related work as required.

Exemplary Duties/Responsibilities

Sweeps, mops, waxes, and polishes floor; dusts and polishes furniture, woodwork, fixtures, and equipment; washes windows and walls; vacuums and spot-cleans carpets; empties and cleans waste receptacles; cleans and maintains supplies in rest rooms; moves and arranges furniture and equipment; sets up tables and chairs for special meetings or events; picks up refuse from grounds; may shovel snow or cut and trim grass using power equipment or hand tools; maintains custodial supplies and equipment; notifies management concerning need for major repairs or additions.

Employment Standards

Education/Experience   Any combination of education and experience providing the required skill and knowledge for successful performance would be qualifying. Typical qualifications would be equivalent to:

1. Completion of the eighth (8th) grade; and
2. One (1) year's experience in janitorial work desirable.

Knowledge   Methods, materials, and equipment used in custodial work; safe work practices.

Skill   Understanding and carrying out oral and written directions; cleaning and caring for assigned areas and equipment; operating cleaning equipment; using a variety of custodial materials; setting work priorities; working independently in the absence of supervision; establishing and maintaining cooperative relationships with those contacted in the course of work; lifting up to 40 pounds.

Note: This job specification should not be construed to imply that these requirements are the exclusive standards of the position. Incumbents will follow any other instructions, and perform any other related duties, as may be required by their supervisor.

JOB DESCRIPTION
PAINTER

Summary Description

Under general supervision, performs various duties in preparation and performance of both interior and exterior painting tasks; performs related duties as assigned.

Exemplary Duties/Responsibilities

Applies coats of paint, varnish, stain, enamel, or lacquer to decorate and protect interior or exterior surfaces, trimmings, and fixtures; prepares surfaces for painting, removes old paint from surfaces, conditions surfaces, and fills nail holes and joints with filler; repairs cracks and holes; applies paints using brushes, spray guns, or paint rollers; erects scaffolding and sets up ladders to perform required tasks; may hang wallpaper and fabrics.

Employment Standards

Education/Experience Any combination of education and experience providing the required skill and knowledge for successful performance would be qualifying. Typical qualifications would be equivalent to:

1. Completion of the eighth (8th) grade; and
2. One (1) year's experience performing painting duties.

Knowledge Fundamental tools, practices, maintenance, and procedures to prepare and paint a variety of surfaces; standard safety rules and regulations governing normal products and chemicals of the industry.

Skill Understanding and carrying out oral and written directions; paying attention to detail; operating and maintaining a variety of painting equipment and tools; conditioning surfaces for paint application; applying various types of paints, stains, and varnishes; setting work priorities; working independently in the absence of supervision; establishing and maintaining cooperative working relationships with those contacted on a day-to-day basis; lifting heavy loads of 30 pounds or more.

Note: This job specification should not be construed to imply that these requirements are the exclusive standards of the position. Incumbents will follow any other instructions, and perform any other related duties, as may be required by their supervisor.

JOB DESCRIPTION
TREE TRIMMER

Summary Description

Under general supervision, performs a wide variety of tree maintenance and trimming work such as pruning, trimming, topping, and felling; performs related work as required.

Exemplary Duties/Responsibilities

Transplants, trims, prunes, sprays, repairs, and removes trees; operates a variety of equipment used in tree trimming maintenance activities; climbs trees with ropes and rigging; trims trees to clear right-of-way for electric power lines; prunes treetops, using saws or pruning shears; repairs damaged trees by trimming jagged stumps and painting them to prevent bleeding of sap; removes broken or dead limbs from wires, using hooked extension poles, fells trees using chainsaw. Prepares reports relating to work activities; may be assigned leadership and training duties.

Employment Standards

Education/Experience Any combination of education and experience providing the required skill and knowledge for successful performance would be qualifying. Typical qualifications would be:

1. Specialized training in tree trimming and tree surgery; and
2. Two (2) years' increasingly responsible experience in tree trimming and tree surgery work.

Knowledge Modern methods, materials, equipment, and tools used in the trimming, pruning, transplanting, spraying, and removal of trees; types and characteristics of trees common to the area; tree pests and diseases, and methods of their control and eradication; safe work practices; principles of supervision and training.

Skill Communicating clearly and concisely, orally and in writing; understanding and carrying out oral and written instructions; pruning, trimming, felling, and topping trees; performing fundamental tree surgery tasks; recognizing and identifying various trees and tree diseases common to the area; operating a variety of equipment of the tree trimming trade; analyzing and evaluating work situations using independent judgment, initiative, and firmness; climbing and doing work in high and hazardous locations; providing supervision and training to subordinates.

Licenses Possession and maintenance of a valid _____ motor vehicle operator's license.

Note: This job specification should not be construed to imply that these requirements are the exclusive standards of the position. Incumbents will follow any other instructions, and perform any other related duties, as may be required by their supervisor.

Chapter 25

INTERVIEWING JOB APPLICANTS TO ENSURE PROPER HIRING

The personal interview of job applicants is the most widely used method of testing interested persons for their qualifications to fill job vacancies. This is particularly true for smaller businesses that lack the time and expertise to develop more objective and valid testing methods. Without question, the greatest faults of the personal interview are its tremendous vulnerability to violations of fair employment (discrimination) laws by asking illegal or nonjob-related questions and the inherent weakness in judging a person's ability to perform certain work merely by evaluating answers to the interviewer's questions. A brief review of the fair employment court case summaries in this book will clearly illustrate the legal implications of a poorly conceived interview process.

In principle, the purpose of the personal interview is to give several applicants who are competing for a job the opportunity to provide evidence of possessing the personal qualities, characteristics, and capacities necessary to perform the job under consideration. While the burden of selling themselves rests with the applicants, it is the interviewer's responsibility to conduct and direct the interview process in a way that is legal, thorough, and consistent and that accomplishes the overall goal of distinguishing clearly between applicant's job-related qualifications. Questioning and observing of job applicants should be directed toward gathering evidence of their suitability to the job.

The application form is the place to begin compliance with legal requirements for hiring employees. In recent years, the courts and enforcement agencies have taken the position that anything on an application that elicits information about a person's race, color, religious creed, national origin, sex, marital status, age, physical handicaps, or religious beliefs is generally held to be illegal. For this reason, there is considerable danger in purchasing the preprinted application forms found in stationery stores or office suppliers or using another employer's form merely because it looks good. As an alternative to designing a customized application form, a sample application form has been provided in Chapter 4.

THE INTERVIEW SETTING/OPENING

One of the most frequently observed failings of employers is conducting applicant interviews in a noisy, uncomfortable, and public location. This is not the proper manner to set up a private, well-represented conversation with an interested job seeker and decidedly not conducive to getting a lot of explanatory information from the applicant. To gain the most productive results from a personal interview, give some thought to setting up proper environmental conditions. A location should be selected that is easy to find, private, quiet, and without distracting interruptions; lighting and temperature should be comfortable.

In opening the interview, the interviewer should be welcoming and friendly. Remember, all applicants are nervous even though some may not reveal it, and a relaxed applicant is going to be a better conversationalist than an intimidated one.

Next, briefly tell the applicant what the job entails, such as specific duties, hours, pay, and conditions, then ask the applicant to give an overview of experience, training, interest, and other background related to the job. If an interview is begun with a general and easy question, applicants are afforded the opportunity to talk about something they know a lot about—themselves. From there, you can move into progressively more specific and difficult questions with more relaxed applicants.

As memory does not serve most interviewers well, it is suggested that brief notes be taken during the interview. These notes can prove useful in reviewing all of the applicants interviewed in a single day or over a period of time, when a decision has to be made about who will be hired or considered at a later date. Such notes can also be immensely helpful for employers trying to defend themselves against a discrimination claim, provided the notes are written objectively. Other than brief moments to jot down positive or negative responses from applicants, the interviewer should maintain sincere and friendly eye contact and a relaxed but businesslike posture.

CHECKLIST: INTERVIEW PREPARATION AND SETUP[1]

Selecting Interview Day, Time, and Location

Job Type	Day	Times
Nonexempt, lower level	Tuesday–Thursday	40–50 minutes
Professional, technical, and administrative	Saturday preferred Monday, Wednesday, or Friday	1–1½ hours
Managerial and executive	Saturday preferred, or Wednesday, or Friday if travel is required	1–2 hours

---

[1]   Levesque, *The Complete Hiring Manual*, pp. 211–212.

Location Features

☐ Private and quiet room without noise or distractions
☐ Well-lit and nicely furnished room that represents the company's proper image
☐ Comfortable seating and desired seating arrangement
☐ Conference room or orderly office setting

Selecting Rating Factors, Form, and Basic Questions

☐ Review test element lists
☐ Review job description and/or job analysis documents
☐ Discuss important job requirements and working conditions with immediate supervisor
☐ Identify rating factors and write definitions
☐ Assign scoring weights or rating values to each rating factor
☐ Prepare rating form
☐ Prepare basic questions to be asked of all applicants

Selecting and Training Interviewers

Interviewers selected on their possession of such skills and traits as:

☐ Objectivity and neutrality
☐ Job knowledge
☐ Casual friendliness
☐ Professional poise
☐ Interpersonal assessment ability
☐ Observation and listening skills
☐ Natural curiosity and ability to pose probing questions

Interviewers trained on such legal issues as:

☐ Discriminatory inference questions
☐ Intrusive privacy rights questions
☐ Misrepresentation of the job or company

Interviewers trained on interviewing conduct and behavior issues:

☐ Applicant physiological awareness
☐ Interviewer behavior and conduct
☐ Interviewer evaluation errors

Preparation and Use of Advanced Interviewing Techniques

☐ Use of panel interview rather than individual interviewer considered; if used, panel interviewers scheduled

☐ Advanced question techniques developed and reviewed with interviewers:
    ☐ Accomplishment questions
    ☐ Situational questions
    ☐ Three-tiered questions
☐ Interviewer(s) instructed to take notes and use for descriptive evaluations of each applicant
☐ Rating of applicants based on use of quantitative and qualitative scoring
☐ Collaborative decision making used for selection of the prospective new hire

Materials Needed for the Interview Day

☐ Copy of applicable job description
☐ Sufficient number of rating forms plus a few extras
☐ Application materials for each interviewer
☐ Writing pad, pencil, and pen for each interviewer
☐ Water or other refreshment and glasses

What Interviewers Should Know About Legal Issues[2]

The two most formidable areas of employment laws with which interviewers should be familiar are discrimination and privacy rights legal issues. Presuming that your recruitment effort acquired a diverse group of applicants and your application screening advanced an equally representative group of applicants through your testing process, then it follows that your interviewers should be seeing a similar diversity of people during interviews. You should also be aware that preemployment interviews are one of the most common places where both overt and covert discrimination occurs, as well as unreasonable intrusion into legally protected privacy of applicants.

To train otherwise quality interviewers on legal issues, there are a couple of approaches you should consider. First, you or whoever is to provide training should be thoroughly familiar with state and federal laws, regulations, and significant court decisions that bear on discrimination and privacy right employment practices. Second, you will need to convey this information relative to conducting interviews to your interviewers. There are several ways in which to accomplish this, but the best approach is a combination of structured (classroom) instruction, briefly compiled written information, and a brief review of salient points just prior to the beginning of every interviewing day.

Structured instruction can easily be assembled and supplemented by state laws appropriate to your locale. Alternatively, you may wish to retain a consultant-trainer who is qualified to provide the instruction to a larger group of managers and supervisors as part of a professional development program, but with emphasis on legal aspects of interviewing. Required reading material can also be easily

---

[2]   Levesque, *The Complete Hiring Manual*, p. 202.

prepared in the way of written guidelines for interviewers such as the sample provided at the end of this chapter. Such a condensed document can be an effective way of reminding interviewers about what questions and evaluation errors should be avoided during interviews. Finally, each interviewer or panel of interviewers should receive a fifteen to thirty minute verbal orientation before beginning an interview day to set the stage and focus on such matters as legal issues, essential responsibilities and qualifications of the job under consideration, and special features of the work setting that interviewers should give special attention to.

What interviewers need to know most about legal issues is what types of questions are disallowed because of their discriminatory inference or privacy rights intrusiveness.

DISCRIMINATORY INFERENCE QUESTIONS

Discriminatory inference means that the question places particular focus on a personal characteristic of the applicant that is, or has the appearance of being, unrelated to the responsibilities or qualifications for the job. The inference, of course, is that the personal characteristic is being regarded as a potential disqualifier by the interviewer or person posing the question, such as contained in the question, "Do you have preschool-aged children?" As a general rule, if any part of an interview question is not *directly* job related, or verbally qualified to the applicant as such, then the question has discriminatory potential. At the end of this chapter you have been provided with a listing of illegal interview questions on the basis of their discriminatory inference. You may wish to copy the listing and use it during interviewer instruction and briefings.

INTRUSIVE PRIVACY RIGHTS QUESTIONS

There may be any number and type of questions that employers need to have answered about an applicant before making a hiring decision, but interviews are not the place or interviewers the people to make such inquiries. Privacy topics that tend to occur most frequently, and where legal rights to their protection exist under federal or most state laws, consist of the following:

- Applicant's use of drugs or alcohol
- Applicant's acts of dishonesty (lying, stealing, concealing, falsifying, and misappropriation of company property or assets)
- Applicant's arrest or conviction history
- Applicant's sexual behavior, life-style, or proclivities
- Applicant's activities during personal time
- Applicant's family member histories

Question areas such as these should quite simply be eliminated from the interview test method. If disclosure is *necessary* to the function of the job or legitimate interests of the employer's business, then such inquiries should be left to more suitable test methods as outlined in Chapter 12. By eliminating such sensitive and vulnerable inquiries from the interview, it will give your interviewers more time to delve into specific areas of job and employment conditions suitability of your applicants.

Illustration of Discriminatory Interview Questions[3]

As an Equal Employment Opportunity employer, the company wishes to avoid potential claims of discriminatory hiring practices by those who seek employment with the company. In an attempt to ensure that job applicants do not have reason to believe they have been discriminated against during employment selection processes, the following have been prepared for your reference. These samples of discriminatory, or potentially discriminatory, questions should be known by all supervisors and managers having hiring authority, interview involvement, or other types of participation in the company's hiring processes. Please read them carefully for complete familiarity. Should the company discover that you have posed such unlawful questions to job applicants, or employees, your involvement in the hiring process will be terminated and you may be subject to additional personnel action by the company.

Subject	Unacceptable Questions	Acceptable Questions
Age	Any question expressing or implying a preference for a specific age group, particularly those which identify applicants over 40 years of age.	Are you over 18 years of age? If hired, can you furnish proof of your age and date of birth?
Race/National origin	What is the origin of your surname? Asking certain applicants if they speak particular foreign languages based on their physical or surname appearances.	No reference to an applicant's color or race is acceptable. Asking all applicants about one particular foreign language skills required in the job. Are you a U.S. citizen or can you furnish proof of your legal right to be employed in the United States?
Arrests/ Convictions	Have you ever been arrested? Questions that do not relate to the job under consideration. Arrests do not necessarily mean guilt, and not all types of convictions are predictors of future job behavior.	None; this aspect of an applicant's qualifications are to be ascertained by other means.
Sex	Why do you think a man/woman is best for this job? Do you think you can supervise men/women? How well do you work with men/women who don't like to work with other men/women?	What do you think are the abilities required for successful job performance? What has your supervisory experience been? How well have you worked with both men and women?

---

[3] Levesque, *The Complete Hiring Manual*, pp. 213–214.

Subject	Unacceptable Questions	Acceptable Questions
Family/ Transportation	Marital status, family plans, ages of children, child care arrangements, or references to spouse. With whom do you reside? Do you live with your parents, husband/wife, children? Do any of your relatives work? Do you own a car? What make and year is your car?	Is there anything that would prevent you from meeting scheduled workdays/hours? Do you have relatives working at this company? Do you have a reliable means of transportation to ensure regular work attendance?
Education/ Experience	Do you have a high school diploma/college degree? Are you willing to take courses on your own time and at your own expense if you get this job? How many years have you been performing this work?	What educational coursework or special training have you had that provided you with the knowledge and skills to perform this job? What type of experience have you had performing the work related to this job?
Religious/ Political affiliation	Any question that solicits information about the applicant's religious or political beliefs or practices.	Is there anything known to you that would interfere with your performing this job, working overtime or weekends (if required by the job), or complying with company policies?
Physical condition	Do you have any physical disabilities? Have you ever had a job related injury? Have you ever filed a workers' compensation claim? Any questions about physical handicaps that the applicant may have or appears to have.	Do you have any physical conditions which may limit your ability to perform all of the physical demands of this job? Are you aware that employment may be contingent on passing a physical exam?
Financial/ Credit	Do you have any overdue bills? Have you ever had a wage garnishment? Do you own or rent? Have you ever filed for bankruptcy?	If appropriate to the job, this information can only be ascertained by other means. How long have you resided in this area?

Preparing Basic Interview Questions[4]

Interviewers usually like to create their own questions based on their knowledge (or perception) of the important aspects of either the job under consideration or what they regard as an ideal applicant. Here is where many of the problems start

---

[4]   Levesque, *The Complete Hiring Manual*, pp. 200–201.

with respect to the subjectivity and illegality of conducting interviews. If interviewers are not *highly* skilled and trained in this test evaluation method, they will instinctively use their personal perceptions, values, beliefs, and biases to determine the course of the interview, rather than using the more objective role of test evaluator based on preestablished standards. To provide interviewers with the needed touch of objectivity, you should prepare several initial questions that are directly related to each rating factor, probing for different types and levels of applicant response and legally appropriate to the job.

From your list of interviewing questions, interviewers can select the number and type of questions they will have time to ask each applicant as "basic" questions. Then, basic questions can be supplemented with more "applicant-specific" questions that allow the interviewer to probe into related areas of inquiry particular to the background of each different applicant. Also, you should keep in mind that interview time passes very quickly. Therefore, the time allotted for questioning should be regarded as extremely precious given the monumental goal of evaluating a normally diverse field of applicant characteristics. Because of this intense value that should be placed on the effective use of questioning time for evaluation purposes, the interview should move quickly from opening pleasantries to casual, friendly, but probing questions.

The following are a few basic questions often used to get the structured interview underway. Again, these are general examples for purposes of illustration. Your basic questions should be tied to rating factors specific to the job under consideration. Further, basic questions should follow any questions or clarifications asked about each applicant's uncertain work history, chronology of events portrayed on their application form, or other items you may have marked as curious (or suspicious) on their application material.

SAMPLES OF BASIC INTERVIEW QUESTIONS

1. What appeals to you most about this job?

2. What do you know about (Company name)?

3. What do you regard as the more important responsibilities and performance results of a (job title)?

4. In what ways do you feel your prior work experience, training, and education makes you particularly suitable for employment in this job?

5. What are your strongest skills and how were they developed?

6. What parts of this job do you feel the most knowledgeable about?

7. What skills, knowledge, and abilities do you feel you need to develop or improve to achieve full competence in this job?

8. Do you prefer working alone or with coworkers (small or large groups of coworkers)?

9. What part of this work gives you the most satisfaction and why? What is it you would tend to like least about this work?

10. Describe the characteristics of supervisors you liked least from your past experience, and what effect it had on you.

You will note from these few questions that they are all (1)job or employment related (legally valid); (2) aimed at evaluating the applicant's job skills, knowledge, abilities or traits (reliable); and (3) allow for a range of responses (measurable). Additionally, the questions are "open ended," thus allowing the applicant to give a personalized answer, and they are short phrases so that most of the interview time is dedicated to applicant answers, not interviewer questions. Unless you are merely verifying facts, you should never use interview time with true-false questions, nor should you use leading questions or those that seek an obvious response.

For example, a *leading* question for our Customer Service Representative job might ask, "Do you like to work with people?" What applicants in their right mind would answer "No"? Thus the question leads the applicant to the desired response. Similarly, an *obvious* question for this same job might ask, "If a mildly angry customer used profanity would you hit him/her or try to disregard the rude behavior?" Such a question may be so obvious as to appear ridiculous, but you might be shocked at how many untrained interviewers ask these types of wasteful questions. To ensure that each interview is conducted properly, *all* interviewers *must* be adequately selected and trained for the role as indicated in the following section.

Using Advanced Questioning Techniques to Draw Out Applicant Distinctions[5]

Since the emergence of the personal interview as the predominant testing method used to make hiring decisions in the 1970s, not much changed about the fundamental nature of how to get the best results out of interviews until the late 1980s. Preemployment selection interviews had been traditionally structured around the objective of acquiring job task information about the applicant. This was based on the theory that the applicant's job skill, knowledge, and abilities were the primary determinant of performance success. Interview questions and rating factors were therefore framed around the applicant's explanations of their past work experience, education and training, and responses to questions about their type and level of job abilities.

It was then recognized that these were task traits, and tasks measure only the "what" of job performance. What was missing was the "how" of job performance along with associated behavioral measures of how the applicant would be most inclined to adapt to environmental, operational, and organizational conditions that are unique to each employer.

Increasingly, employment interviews became the subject of numerous books, articles, academic research, and nationwide seminars where underlying theories

---

[5]   Levesque, *The Complete Hiring Manual*, pp. 206–208.

and objectives were being reexamined due to unreliable results from traditional design of interviews that tainted the reputability of this testing method. For interviews to become a more reliable testing method, the fundamental objective would have to be changed to reflect a more practical outcome of interviews. Given this broader view of job context, the redefined objective of interviews became "to acquire an accurate and complete understanding of each applicant's likelihood of performance success and employment fit."

Thus, emphasis shifted from task interviewing to behavioral interviewing. Behavioral interviewing incorporates tasks but assumes that the better qualified applicant is the one who demonstrates those ability and trait characteristics that define *how* the job is to be performed successfully. Measurement of applicant distinctions in likely success factors is based on questions aimed at doing (task), thinking (cognitive reasoning and attitudes), and interacting (behavioral orientation). For example, the applicant response of, "I know how to operate all types of office equipment" is traditional task-only information. However, this information is not measurable to any reasonable extent nor does it convey more important traits such as how the equipment is operated, what priorities or work methods are used before use of the equipment, nor how the applicant works with others using the same equipment.

To conduct this type of advanced interviewing, employers have to take a much closer look at each job to identify what specific task and trait characteristics are most important for job performance as well as employment success. Further, these factors have to be suitable for measurement in the interview setting. Once task and trait factors are identified, the next step is to frame questions that replicate actual job situations in a sufficiently probing, revealing, and distinguishing manner. To accomplish advanced interview results that lead to more accurate and reliable selection decisions, you should incorporate one or more of the following questioning techniques into the interview process.

ACCOMPLISHMENT QUESTIONS

The past accomplishments of applicants related directly or even indirectly to the job under consideration are good indicators of applicant-job *matching*. Accomplishments represent a preexisting demonstration of what the applicant has done, how and why he or she did it, and what the performance outcome was. What should be clarified when asking accomplishment questions is whether the applicant initiated and handled them, or merely had partial or indirect involvement in them. By not making such clarifying inquiries, you can easily be deceived by an applicant who makes such inference remarks as, "I reduced the company's staffing budget by $458,000 in 1991 through a study of job realignments." It is not clear from this statement as to exactly what the applicant did in relation to the study or its resultant savings to the company.

In posing questions to applicants about their accomplishments in areas related to the job under consideration, applicants can additionally be led into associated questioning about work-related attitudes and reactions to situations that arose in the course of past accomplishments. These responses then become measures of the applicant's prospective employment *fit*. It should be understood that fit does not mean cloning; rather, it means that the applicant:

- Can lead and follow in the right situations.
- Will work well in the type and variety of circumstances associated with the job and operational conditions.
- Has a desirable, compatible orientation toward work, relationships, problem solving, creative expression, and the nature of the organization's business.
- Is aligned with the organization's philosophy, culture, policies, and ways of conducting business.

When interviews focus on job matching and employment conditions fit characteristics, applicant (scoring) distinctions become much more apparent and selection decisions more vivid.

SITUATIONAL QUESTIONS

The use of situational questions are another advanced interviewing technique because, if used properly, they can be effective measures of both task abilities and trait characteristics of differing applicants. Too, situational questions are more reliable and valid indicators of performance success than speculative task-only questions if they are properly framed to replicate actual job responsibilities and conditions. To be effective at bringing out distinctive applicant abilities and traits, questions should be selected on the basis of either actual or reasonable hypothetical situations; they should be moderately difficult in their situational complexity; and they should involve both task and trait elements. The following are a few general examples of situational questions where both task and trait elements are present.

1. "What would you do if you were reconciling monthly customer records and discovered that another employee was making consistent errors?"
2. "If you were out on a job site working with a group of three other employees and two of them were 'horseplaying' by dueling with shovels, what steps would you take if one of them was seriously injured?"
3. "One of the five employees you supervise is regularly late to work, immaturely defiant toward your directions, and makes excuses to cover up their work errors. Describe the actions you feel should be taken with this employee."

As you can see, the questions are drawn from real job conditions with task and trait elements. Moreover, they are worded such that the range of desirable answers are not obvious; therefore, the applicant is more likely to answer the question from his or her own perspective rather than speculation as to what the interviewer wants to hear. Situational questions of this type have the advantage of allowing you to evaluate the applicant's job knowledge, possible types of skills applied to differing situations, and reasoning, methods, values, and belief traits—all of which are more accurate measures of how well differing applicants are likely to perform since questions reflect actual job and employment conditions.

THREE-TIERED QUESTIONS

Three-tiered questions are like a "rolling scenario" in that the question is framed in three progressively more difficult parts to measure distinctions of skill, knowledge, and/or trait characteristics among applicants. This technique is the most advanced and telltale about applicants because it allows interviewers to evaluate each applicant's *depth* of job and employment suitability. You can use either job knowledge, past accomplishments, or situational questions as the basis of framing three-tiered questions by merely breaking the type of question into three distinguishing levels of difficulty.

If the applicant is vague, inaccurate, or has difficulty with the first tier, you need not create an embarrassing interview situation by posing the second or third level of difficulty of the same question. Rather, you should evaluate the applicant according to their level of question performance. Consider, for example, the following two illustrations of three-tiered questions.

1. *Job Knowledge Question*

    First Tier (easy): "What are the five basic functions of management?"

    Second Tier (moderate): "What does 'controlling' mean with respect to a company's operating policies?"

    Third Tier (difficult): "What is the relationship between personnel policies and a company's need to control productivity of its employees?"

2. *Situational Question*

    First Tier (easy): "What would you do if your supervisor was absent for the day and you were uncertain about the priority of work given to you by three different people?"

    Second Tier (moderate): "Suppose that the last person to assign work to you was the company President. Would your decisions or actions change? If so, why?"

    Third Tier (difficult): "How would you be inclined to handle this work situation if one of them was the aggressive Sales Manager, another was your supervisor's boss—the compassionate Administrative Director—and the third was the company President known to be suspicious of the Administrative Director's productivity?"

In addition to evaluating the applicant's *level* of abilities and traits in handling three-tiered questions, you should also evaluate such related factors as their decisiveness, justified changes in decisions or actions, methods and approaches, and similar characteristics that are by-products of their responses to increasingly more difficult job conditions.

Conducting and Controlling the Interview[6]

If you have selected interviewers who possess the traits and skills needed for conducting interviews, training them about interview conduct and rating applicants should be easy. Doing so will also put an important final touch to the professionalism and quality of results you can expect from interviews. Instruction materials and discussions should focus on these three topics for interviewers to gain a deeper appreciation of the behavioral dynamics involved in preemployment interviews.

APPLICANT PHYSIOLOGY AWARENESS

Interviews are highly interactive in nature, and the character of these interactions are often valid measures of an applicant's predisposition toward such possible job factors as the right type and level of confidence, sensitivity toward others, eagerness, pride of accomplishment, and several other traits that stem from one's inner self. Often these thought patterns, feelings, attitudes, and personality features will manifest themselves into observable physiological functions and mannerisms of the applicant during questioning. While interviewers should not go beyond the "layperson" realm of evaluating applicant traits that are observable and reasonably measurable, there are some fairly reliable physiological conditions of applicants that can be useful sources of evaluation.

First, interviewers should be aware, and expect, that applicants are likely to display signs of nervousness, anxiety, and perhaps even fear during the first several minutes of an interview. Physiological response to such *subdued* thoughts and feelings is often displayed in the way of excessive perspiration, shaky hands, quick arm or leg movements, tight or quivering voice, and flushness of skin. At the other end of the physiological spectrum are the applicant's reactions to *assertive* or *dominant* thoughts and feelings that can be stimulated during interview questioning. These types of reactions take the form of bodily rigidity, defensive or sarcastic answers, voice intonation, becoming argumentative, and observable signs of controlled anger.

Applicant physiology that results from subdued thoughts and feelings should be accommodated by casual, friendly, and informally light conversation to give the applicant a chance to settle down and become comfortable. Only until this occurs is the applicant likely to feel confident enough to talk freely which is the primary objective of interviewing—to listen and evaluate. Conversely, physiology that results from assertive or dominant thoughts and feelings should be allowed only to the extent of evaluating the applicant's suitability to job or employment conditions, and either controlled or cut off by the interviewer thereafter.

Second, interviewers should be trained to observe and evaluate the mannerisms and body "language" of applicants throughout the interview process. In particular, interviewers should make note of:

- "Nonconjunctive" expressions (e.g., saying "I like to work with people" in a disinterested or annoyed tone of voice, or facial expressions that are contrary to what is being said);

---

[6]   Levesque, *The Complete Hiring Manual*, pp. 203–205.

- Evasive, vague, or distracting (changing the subject) answers accompanied by a notable change in eye contact with interviewers; and

- Other physical mannerisms that appear peculiar to "normal" behavior such as fidgeting, staring out a window for prolonged periods, taking an unusual amount of time to respond to questions, sitting slumped in their chair, rambling conversation, continuous handling of a pencil (or other object), and similar applicant activities.

Interviewers should not, however, make presumptive conclusions about mannerisms that are either within the normal and expected range of behavior considering dynamics inherent in interview situations, nor those associated with possible cultural differences. For example, many nervous mannerisms fade once rapport with the interviewer is established, and there are some cultures in which it is impolite to maintain eye contact or sit too close to another person.

INTERVIEWER BEHAVIOR AND CONTROL

Professional interviewers must also be aware of their own behavior, manner, and appearance since the interviewer is one of the more important "environmental" features that will influence the course and results of interview dynamics. Just as the physical environment of the interview location should evoke a pleasant and professional image of the company, so too should the attire and manner of the interviewer instill comfort and confidence in the applicant.

Behaviorally, the interviewer should approach the interview process and each applicant subject to it in a positive, enthusiastic fashion. The interviewer should be well prepared for each applicant through familiarity with his or her application materials and make this familiarity known to the applicant by framing at least some questions around specific background information. All interviews should start as if they are the first one of the day, meaning the interviewer should be fresh, attentive, friendly, casual, interested, and sincere. Further, they should remain this way throughout the interview, which is one of the reasons interviewing is hard work and requires especially talented people to conduct them.

Caution: Interviewers must also stay in control of the interview. This includes both themselves and the applicant, as well as how the interview proceeds during the course of questions and answers. Interviewers must be cautious of posing questions that are likely to arouse unintentional antagonism, insult, or defensiveness among applicants. Therefore, the interviewer needs to be trained in framing questions properly, use of voice tone and intonation, facial expressions that communicate what is intended, and similar mannerisms aimed at conveying particular messages or soliciting particular responses—except "poker faces" which are usually construed by applicants as boredom or callousness.

Interviewers must be prepared to control rather unexpected reactions and behaviors of applicants. These can range from mild forms of obvious discomfort such as anxiety, to uncontrolled perspiration or even vomiting (nervous stomach after consumption of a meal—a good reason not to conduct lunch interviews), to an occasional applicant that turns hostile or obnoxious. Likewise, the timing of interviews must be observed carefully so that they start and end on schedule, do not get distracted with elaborate, uninformative answers, and at least all basic questions get a chance for response and evaluation.

INTERVIEWER EVALUATION ERRORS

Finally, interviewers should be trained on frequently encountered types of evaluative errors that stem from the interviewer's own set of biases and other predispositions that have the effect of "polluting" the rating of applicants during interviews. You will also recall that the absence of personal bias and similar predispositions is one of the selection traits of professional interviewers, but the fact remains that human nature predisposes everyone to some type of perceptive screening device.

One such perception screen that interviewers should be aware of, and therefore guard against, is the temptation to make a premature evaluation on the basis of an applicant's first impression. Research in this area has indicated that many interviewers tend to rely on the impression created by an applicant during the first two to six minutes of an interview. To counter such a fundamental predisposition of an applicant's first impression, interviewers need to be reminded to keep an open mind so that changes in applicant characteristics can be more objectively evaluated as a result of the entire interview as it unfolds. Likewise, the interviewer's general perception of applicants who display certain types of attire, grooming, speech, and mannerisms should be controlled within the context of the job and employment setting and evaluated accordingly after the conclusion of the interview to allow a more complete view of the individual.

Two other influential types of evaluation errors result from either singular statements by applicants in the course of an interview, or from an interviewer's lack of ability to make critical distinction judgments about other people. Singular statements of applicants that trigger a highly positive or negative response by interviewers to the extent that all other applicant statements become secondary are referred to as either halo effect or oppositional effect. Conversely, when an interviewer's own nature is to avoid making a distinctive range of judgments about other people, this poses a problem with compressed scoring of applicants referred to as leniency (scoring all applicants higher than they should be for purposes of making critical distinctions), or central tendency (scoring all applicants in a closely clustered range of average to high-average scores).

The time to set up interviews and prepare for them to be conducted professionally and the selection and training of professional interviewers are abundantly worth the effort. The payback can be measured quickly and concisely in the quality of new hires, higher morale and productivity from more satisfied coworkers, and reduced turnover—assuming all other employment practices of the company are handled with equal integrity.

CLOSING AND EVALUATING THE INTERVIEW

Employers have the power to select or reject prospective employees, but it's always prudent for the interviewer to leave the applicant with a favorable impression of the business organization. Applicants should be asked, in conclusion, if *they* would like to add any comments about their qualifications not brought out during questioning, and if *they* have any questions about the job, working conditions, or the organization.

Once an applicant has left, after you have shown appreciation of his or her interest and time, you should dress up your notes and evaluate or score the applicant on an Interview Rating Form for your records. Such a sample form is provided here, following the Checklist/Glossary of Interview Rating Factors and Definitions.

Rating the applicant is sometimes difficult because of personal differences between the applicant and interviewer. An effort should be made to avoid judging the applicant on the basis of personal compatibility with the rater's thinking (the *similar-to-me* approach), for it is the applicant, not the rater, who is being evaluated. The effectiveness and implications of an applicant's answers should be considered rather than whether the answer was the one the rater felt was correct. (Frequently, more than one right answer is possible, depending on one's perspective or experience.)

It is best to maintain an open mind until the interview is over and all the evidence is in. Then rate the applicant on relative merits, using a full range of scoring. To make effective decisions, do not hesitate to use both ends of the rating scale. Only by assigning higher scores to better qualified applicants and lower scores to those less qualified will you ensure that the oral interview has its proper weight. Nor should you be afraid to rate an applicant unacceptable if the person clearly lacks important job qualifications.

CHECKLIST/GLOSSARY: INTERVIEW RATING FACTORS AND DEFINITIONS (Supervisory and Management Positions)

☐ **Written Communication Skills**: Makes effective written communications in an understandable, clear, and concise manner. Is able to condense desired message into grammatically correct and succinct written passages. Makes smooth transitions between thoughts. Is able to read and comprehend written materials. Uses reading materials as resources for problem-solving or decision-making purposes.

☐ **Oral Communication Skills**: Speaks in a clear and understandable manner so listener grasps message. Is able to persuade verbally, summarize, and justify effectively. Elicits feedback and is able to draw others into conversation. Listens attentively to others.

☐ **Decision-Making Skills**: Is able to identify and choose appropriate solutions from a variety of alternate choices. Makes judgments on all possible decisions and realizes ramifications or possible impact of each decision. Recognizes when a decision is necessary and exhibits readiness to make decision.

☐ **Ability to Analyze and Solve Problems**: Integrates and categorizes information, and recalls relevant data, perceives similarities and differences, separates important from superfluous information, and distills essence of idea or problem. Is able to identify problem and its causes. Breaks complex problems into components that are amendable to analysis. Is able to recognize when more information is necessary and to research and obtain necessary information through a variety of methods, that is, reading materials, staff personnel, verbal or written communication with others, independent thinking. Exhibits innovation in problem-solving skills.

☐ **Planning and Organization**: Sets priorities and coordinates and schedules tasks or events in a logical manner to maximize staff and material resources, increase efficiency, and anticipate problems. Is able to meet a predefined goal with a prescribed timetable. Anticipates problems and is proactive rather than reactive to problems. Takes steps to alleviate problems.

☐ **Budget Analysis Skills**: Is able to make cost estimates and financial projections for upcoming budget, progress, or work needs. Is able to make simple mathematical computations, interpret charts and graphs, analyze financial data, and make costwise judgments.

☐ **Management Control Skills**: Coordinates and delegates work within office. Is able to assess capabilities and skills of staff to optimize utilization of staff personnel. Is able to train and develop staff members, keep staff members informed of new developments, and handle or prevent personnel problems.

☐ **Leadership Skills**: Guides and motivates individuals to achieve tasks. Is able to control and influence individuals to focus on a particular issue or arrive at a solution to a problem. Is properly assertive. Does not shy away from action because of feared risk of outcome. Shows initiative and extends beyond what is normally required.

☐ **Interpersonal Sensitivity Skills**: Interacts with individuals without eliciting negative or hurt feelings. Is aware of the needs and feelings of other individuals. Is able to make appropriate statements or actions to pacify hostile persons or situations. Answers questions diplomatically and avoids excessive argumentation. Maintains open and approachable manner.

☐ **Flexibility**: Adapts to changing circumstances. Changes behavior or attitudinal responses to fit situation to obtain desired goal. Is open-minded and is able to separate personal feelings from issues at hand. Exhibits willingness to see other points of view. Listens to suggestions and takes criticisms. Remains impartial and is willing to compromise own objectives for those more beneficial to the organization.

☐ **Control**: Maintains positive attitude despite circumstances. Remains calm in stressful or frustrating situations. Sticks to solutions and perseveres under adverse conditions. Maintains high energy level and motivations. Is able to think clearly under pressure.

☐ **Completion**: Is able to complete a task or set of tasks within given *time* constraints, and in sufficient detail as to fulfill *content* requirements. Ties all ends together and includes key issues. Submits all required information on time.

☐ **Professional Development/Demeanor**: Demonstrates possession of thorough and current knowledge of significant issues affecting the profession. Displays a sincere interest, desire, or willingness to keep abreast of professional developments. Shows positive attitude toward the duties and responsibilities of the position. Presents self in the attire and manner that is appropriate to the position, and demonstrates a desired level of self-assurance.

Applicant's Name _____ Date _____

SAMPLE INTERVIEW RATING FORM

Rating Element/Definition	Point Value	Score
1. Oral Communication Skills Speaks in a clear and understandable manner so listener grasps message. Is able to persuade verbally, summarize, and justify effectively. Elicits feedback and is able to draw others into conversation. Listens attentively to others.	10	
2. Decision-Making Skills Is able to identify and choose appropriate solutions from a variety of alternate choices. Makes judgments on all possible decisions and realizes ramifications or possible impact of each decision. Recognizes when a decision is necessary and exhibits readiness to make decision.	15	
3. Ability to Analyze and Solve Problem Skills Integrates and categorizes information and recalls relevant data, perceives similarities and differences, separates important from superfluous information, and distills essence of idea or problem. Is able to identify problem and its causes.	10	
4. Budget Analysis Skills Is able to make cost estimates and financial projections for upcoming budget, progress, or work needs. Is able to make simple mathematical computations, interpret charts and graphs, analyze financial data, and make costwise judgments.	15	
5. Leadership Skills Guides and motivates individuals to achieve tasks. Is able to control and influence individuals to focus on a particular issue or arrive at a solution to a problem. Is assertive. Does not shy away from action because of feared risk of outcome. Shows initiative and extends beyond what is normally required.	15	
6. Interpersonal Sensitivity Skills Interacts with individuals without eliciting negative or hurt feelings. Is aware of the needs and feelings of other individuals. Is able to make appropriate statements or actions to pacify hostile persons or situations. Answers questions diplomatically and avoids excessive argumentation. Maintains open and approachable manner.	10	
7. Flexibility Adapts to changing circumstances. Changes behavior or attitudinal responses to fit situation to obtain desired goal. Is open-minded and is able to separate personal feelings from issues at hand. Exhibits	10	

SAMPLE INTERVIEW RATING FORM—*continued*

willingness to see other point of view. Listens to suggestions and takes criticisms. Remains impartial when performing duties of manager and is willing to compromise own objectives for those more beneficial to the organization.	
8. Professional Development/Demeanor Demonstrates possession of thorough and current knowledge of significant issues affecting the profession. Displays a sincere interest, desire, or willingness to keep abreast of professional developments. Shows positive attitude toward the duties and responsibilities of the position. Presents self in the attire and manner that is appropriate to the position, and demonstrates a desired level of self-assurance.	15
	100

Comments _____

_____

_____

_____

- ☐ Could perform *full range* of duties/responsibilities with a minimum of supervision and/or training.

- ☐ Could perform *significant range* of duties/responsibilities but should receive instructive supervision, supplemental training, and/or further career experience.

- ☐ Could perform *many* of the duties/responsibilities but thorough adaptation would depend on and require substantial supervision, training, and/or experience.

- ☐ Could perform *some* of the duties/responsibilities but successful adaptation would require an inefficient amount of supervision, consequence of errors, cost and time of development, possibly detrimental to career development.

_____
Interviewer's Signature/Title

NOTIFYING APPLICANTS OF INTERVIEW RESULTS

Now that these interested applicants have taken the time and effort to have an employer consider their potential as employees, the employer must advise them that a hiring decision has been made. Consider the public relations implication of interviewing, say, ten people for one job, and then never communicating the outcome to nine of them who are no doubt anxious to learn about their future. Such a poor business practice leaves a sour taste in the mouths of applicants who may know potential customers, clients, or others, and may express an uncomplimentary opinion of the business. Do your organization a favor—treat others as *you* would want to be treated.

Chapter 26

CONDUCTING PAY SURVEYS, ESTABLISHING RATES, AND DEVELOPING A PAY PLAN

All employers will find it helpful to develop a meaningful pay plan based on certain equity factors such as prevailing rates of pay and contributory worth. Many employers avoid this part of their personnel management program for any number of reasons; one reason is that they are fearful of what they may find about their own pay rates. If an employer's pay rates are low, the employer usually knows it; employees will complain, or they will leave after gaining more competitive skills. This high level of turnover costs the employer more in the long run than does paying better wages.

Another frequent mistake is the fragmented approach to wage setting. Here, the employer may adjust the basic wage rate of a person or particular job (perhaps after a justified complaint from an employee or supervisor) without considering the impact such a rate increase may have on other jobs, thus sending other employees a message about how one goes about getting a pay increase.

From the legal perspective, probably the three most serious errors businesses make in paying employees are (1) paying them below minimum wages (e.g., commission or only for revenue-generating work), (2) incorrectly classifying jobs as exempt to avoid overtime premiums, and (3) assigning employees who perform essentially the same work to different pay grades (not to be confused with merit raises within a pay grade), which violates the Equal Pay Act. A quick review of some of the laws and court decisions in Part Three gives ample testimony as to why employers should avoid these kinds of pay practices.

Whether an employer has established pay rates and schedules or is just beginning to examine this issue due to a start-up or growth, there are some important factors and methods that should be accounted for to develop a well-conceived pay system that serves the business and its employees equally. It is also advisable for employers to keep in mind three fundamental principles about personnel operations that are particularly valid to wage matters:

1. Once anything is established, change does not come easily and usually carries with it a price to be paid.

2. It is almost impossible to change one thing without its affecting someone or something else (domino effect).

3. Left unattended, an inequity will worsen.

Collectively, these principles of workplace management represent some of the greatest dilemmas of business managers: How do I know I'll get the desired effect if I do this? What will happen to those if I do this to these? What might occur if I don't do this? These and many more questions can plague business managers trying to cope with pay and other personnel decisions unless a systematic approach is taken in these matters. With regard to pay, perhaps the best starting point is to consider what pay accomplishes, job factors that influence pay, gathering and comparing pay information, and a few different approaches to designing pay schedules.

The following discussion is intended as a practical guide to setting, adjusting, and scheduling pay in a meaningful and legal manner, rather than dealing with the complexities of compensation analysis.

SOME BASICS ABOUT PAY

There are a variety of terms used, and confused, concerning pay. A brief definition of each may help.

Pay	The total dollar value received in wages or salary for work performed
Wage	The amount of pay received for work performed, usually expressed in hourly, weekly, *and* monthly amounts
Salary	The fixed monthly or annual amount of pay received for work performed regardless of hours worked
Rate	The specific dollar amount under differing work conditions (e.g., basic rate, overtime rate, premium rate)
Compensation	The total dollar value of pay and employment benefits that represents a *direct* cost to the employer to sustain an employee

Although these terms are often used interchangeably, they do mean different things. For example, a *salary* survey refers to exempt positions, while a *prevailing wage* survey refers to nonexempt positions. *Hourly* employees are nonexempt wage earners, meaning they get paid only for hours worked and are eligible for overtime pay at rates of time and one-half or double their base hourly rate.

Pay represents the fair value reward for work performed by employees. Pay and pay systems tend to vary in complexity depending on such factors as the number of employees and variety of jobs in the organization and the emphasis placed on individual equity during the last twenty-year evolution of our now highly divergent work force.

Pay is also the primary reason people work, and for many, it is the reason for seeking promotions, other employers, and new careers. Our culture and our economy teach us to seek more—more pay, more status, more leisure, and more possessions. One would think, therefore, that pay would be a source of power, which the employer could use to achieve greater productivity. However well such a concept may have worked twenty to forty years ago, pay provides motivation in only two circumstances today.

First, the prospect of more pay will motivate the employee dedicated to the work ethic only if it is connected to some form of job enrichment like new responsibilities, more challenging work, or a promotion to higher status. Pay alone does not work as a motivator with this employee. This person wants to get ahead in both status and monetary reward, but if the challenge is not proportional to the pay, this person will probably decline the promotion and seek a better opportunity. This is one reason employers are now finding it difficult to get good supervisors—the pay is often disproportionately low compared to the grief of the job (pay is low compared to challenge and pay of subordinate employees).

Second, pay becomes a negative motivator when it is known to be well below what employees get paid by other employers for the same work. Under these low-pay conditions, employees may be motivated to unionize, quit, work overtime grudgingly, or add an outside job to make ends meet. Employers who do try to correct this condition by giving competitive wage increases are usually stunned by the seeming lack of motivational influence over employees. They expect certain returns on their dollar; productivity, loyalty, and gratitude—perhaps valid expectations, but a bit medieval. (When was the last time you actually witnessed a measurable increase in productivity following a pay raise?) Employees, on the other hand, will view the pay increase as due them in the first place, and second, be annoyed that it took so long.

Employers should also watch for signs of a common pay-versus-productivity condition in the workplace called *equity theory*. Simply stated, this theory postulates that if employees *perceive* a discrepancy between their pay and the amount or value of their work, they will create compensating forms of equity (within their control) to make up for low pay (beyond their control). Examples of employee-initiated equity adjustments to work include taking long coffee breaks, visiting with other employees, arriving late or leaving early, conducting personal business on the telephone, and eventually working more slowly. Most employers see these activities as a potential disciplinary problem, but they should first seek answers to why changes in employee behavior are occurring before applying corrective measures—lest they be the wrong measures.

While our employees need pay to sustain a particular life-style, they have an equal need to view their pay as equitable, with future opportunities for higher pay (or at least maintenance of their buying power) and job growth. Without these ingredients, employers are likely to find that pay is not, in itself, a motivator, and their work force may be transient in nature and of lower caliber than is desired. To evaluate systematically the integrity of their pay practices, employers should gather and examine comparative information from external sources (surveys) as well as study the internal relationship of job content to pay. Both must be considered to gain the most useful results. Armed with these results, the employer will be in a much more reliable position to set the pay rates of existing and new jobs, and to design an effective pay schedule. The balance of this chapter will explain how to go about doing just that.

ESTABLISHING PAY RATES

Assuming that it is the employer's intent to pay above minimum wage for a given job, the questions that usually arise are, "How much is enough?" and "What's fair (competitive) and reasonable (to employer and employee)?" There are no simple or uniform answers to such questions. There are, however, a variety of different influences that go into each business's pay-setting decisions. The major influences consist of the following.

1. Size and type of business — (*ability* to pay certain rates, based on profits)

2. Organizational philosophy — (*willingness* to pay certain rates and *attitudes* about ranking among competitors)

3. Nature and diversity of work — (degree of *specialization*, work variety, and technology)

4. Regional economics — (*prevailing rates* and rates of inflation)

5. Availability of labor supply — (*competition* for particular jobs)

6. Value of work contribution — (*worth* of a particular job to the business)

7. Unionism — (forced *inflation* of certain pay rates)

8. Pay supplements — (*incentives* and *benefits*)

9. Reputation of organization — (*competitiveness* of pay and social *recognition* as high- or low-paying)

Factors 1–3, 6, and 8 are predominantly internal considerations for pay setting, while the others are principally influenced by external sources. Because these factors influence the setting of pay rates in different ways, each factor should be given some thought. A simplified illustration may help to clarify your deliberation.

Let us say that you have developed a job description for the new position of Accounting Specialist and you want to determine what pay rate to establish for this position. After gathering pay data from other employers (prevailing wage survey), you find that the average of comparable positions is $8.80 per hour. You now know that you can probably get a qualified person if you pay that rate or higher. Next, you should examine some of the internal considerations. You may wish to ask yourself these questions about the $8.80-per-hour rate.

- Can the business afford to pay this rate? If not, can the business scale the job and pay down? Is there a lesser cost alternative to this job function (e.g., part-time employee or contracting for the service)?

- Is the business willing to pay this rate, given what other jobs are paid? Does the business care about what other employers are paying for similar jobs?
- To what degree does the specialized nature of work, skill, responsibility, consequence of error, and difficulty of this job compare with other jobs in the business (where does it fit in)?
- If the business pays a lower rate, will it experience difficulty in getting a sufficiently qualified employee?
- How does the business view the worth or value of the work to be produced by this position?

Once these internal considerations are factored in, the employer will have a clearer picture of precisely what rate of pay should be established for a new position or one that has been reclassified because of changes in duties and responsibilities.

REASONS FOR, AND TYPES OF, PAY SURVEYS

There are a number of reasons businesses conduct pay surveys. Here are a few of the more common reasons.

1. As part of a particular job analysis when a new job is created or a job is being reclassified.
2. To gather more information about minimum and/or maximum rates of pay for certain jobs.
3. To see what types of pay plans (schedules) other employers are using.
4. To evaluate annually or periodically pay inflation among other employers to keep pace with market pricing of jobs, and determine the amount of internal adjustments to pay or the pay schedule.
5. To examine pay differentials, incentives, and benefits other employers provide.

The first question to be answered by the employer is, "What do we want to accomplish from a survey? If the object is any of the first four reasons, then the employer will be conducting what is referred to as a Base Pay Survey, as only pay rates and pay-related information are needed. If, on the other hand, the employer wishes to examine or compare pay rates, incentives, the cost of benefits, and any other form of employer expense directly related to sustaining jobs (overtime, uniform allowances, and the like), then the employer will want to conduct a Total Compensation Survey. These surveys are now becoming more common among larger employers, or where the workplace is unionized, because of the trend of these employers toward diversifying pay and benefits, and because of greater competition and employment conditions among workers. Unless a small-business employer has developed liberal pay and benefit provisions for its employees, the Base Pay Survey should serve the small-business employer well for most purposes.

COMPARABILITY OF SURVEY INFORMATION

To achieve the greatest validity of pay surveys, the employer conducting the survey should have some assurance that the information collected is comparable—comparing apples to apples, so to speak. Therefore, before beginning the survey, decisions must be made with regard to which jobs the employer wishes to compare and what other business organizations should be selected. It is recommended that the employer select about 25 percent more businesses to survey than are needed because it is common to eliminate about that many during the survey, and because it is found that either the business or the job is not in fact comparable. The following are a few of the more critical comparability factors employers should consider in selecting other businesses to use in the survey:

Job Comparability

1. Ninety percent (90%) or better *identical* in types of duties, levels of responsibilities, and employment requirements
2. Substantially the *same* level of difficulty, importance, and complexity of tasks (e.g., equivalent number of employees supervised, strong similarities in the complexity of the same tasks)
3. Length of service of job incumbents (unless there is a fixed pay range)

Business Comparability

1. Kind of business (manufacturing, services, distribution, etc.)
2. Type of business (retail, wholesale, public, private, nonprofit)
3. Number of employees (of total company and of type being surveyed)
4. Annual revenue/budget (financial abilities, business growth)
5. Unionism (influence of collective bargaining)

Once the employer has devised the survey form upon which to enter data or to mail out, and selected the survey businesses, a decision might have to be made concerning jobs to include in the survey. The employer may have already decided this earlier by virtue of a predetermined special purpose of the survey. If, however, the employer is conducting an annual review for purposes of considering an across-the-board adjustment to pay (cost-of-living raise) or a modification of the business's pay plan, then the employer may want to identify a limited number of "benchmark" jobs—particularly if the business has several different types of jobs. Benchmark positions have substantial commonality in work scope, tasks, responsibilities, and employment standards within or among certain industries. In terms of job pricing or making pay-related decisions, usually only very minor differences will occur among well-selected benchmark positions used for prevailing wage surveys. Examples of benchmark positions might include Teller, Secretary, Operations Vice President, and Marketing Director. Any pay decisions on benchmark jobs then become the basis of pay determinations among other internal jobs in terms of their

alignment or relationship to benchmark jobs, given such factors as skills required, physical/environmental demands, complexity of tasks, and similar influences.

Critical to making pay decisions between benchmark and nonbenchmark jobs is adopting a clear and reasonable pay-relationship philosophy. To illustrate this point, let us say you have the following jobs involved in a pay consideration.

Benchmark (Survey)	**Nonbenchmark**
General Office Clerk	Receptionist
Secretary	Steno Clerk

After concluding the external pay survey and identifying internal pay influences, you set the rate of the General Office Clerk at $4.90 per hour and the Secretary at $6.75 per hour. Now, given the similarities and differences in job factors mentioned earlier, the employer can establish a pay rate of nonbenchmark positions based on the "philosophical" weighting of the job factor relationships between benchmark and nonbenchmark positions by either a certain monetary amount or a percentage difference in pay. Since both nonbenchmark jobs in this example are typically less diversified in duties and less responsible for independent decisions, and require fewer skills than their benchmark counterparts, their pay rates should reflect a corresponding relationship by a certain amount or percentage difference. In order of least pay to most pay, they would be arranged thus:

Receptionist

General Office Clerk

Steno Clerk

Secretary

Finally, once pay rates for these jobs are tentatively established, they should be compared to dissimilar jobs to assure overall internal pay equity.

COMPILING AND EVALUATING SURVEY DATA

The most common methods of collecting pay survey information are by mailed questionnaire, telephone or personal interviews, using survey data compiled by others, or some combination of these methods. The major disadvantages of mailed questionnaires is the time required to prepare a form the employer would be proud to mail to others, the time lost waiting for return of forms, and the exceedingly low number of returns—other employers have their own business priorities! Telephone interviews work well if handled properly, preferably by getting to know the appropriate contact person and arranging a convenient time in advance for you to talk to that person. Personal interviews generally take too much time and travel and are not sufficiently flexible. Use of other surveys can be a valuable *supplement* if they are current, reflect pay rates in your region, and cover comparable jobs and businesses, but they are not recommended as the only source of pay information.

Employers who wish to use available survey information as a supplement to their own surveys should refer to the listing of survey sources at the end of this chapter. Perhaps the best method of gathering pay survey data is a combination (internal use) survey form and telephone interview. The telephone interview can yield the kind of information that can be entered onto the form during the telephone discussion, and the caller can obtain much more accurate comparisons between jobs than would be produced by other methods. In designing the (internal use) form, the employer can think through and customize the categories of information desired, and modify them when the results of telephone conversations with differing employers make it necessary.

When all the data have been compiled on the survey summary form, the next step is to make some sense of the information by evaluating results in different ways. For example, the survey pay rates can be averaged by adding all pay rates and dividing by the number of employers (mean), the middle pay rate can be identified by eliminating an equal number of the highest and lowest pay rates (median), or the standard deviation can be calculated to reveal the degree to which any pay rate deviates from the average (mean) by using the formula:

$$S = \sqrt{\frac{E\,(x - \bar{x})^2}{n - 1}}$$

where

E = the sum of
$(x - \bar{x})^2$ = the variance squared, the raw number total minus the mean;
squared difference
x = raw number total
$\bar{x}$ = mean number
n = number of samples
$n - 1$ = use this if sample less than 30

Going back to our benchmark jobs to illustrate the differences in calculating survey pay data, we might get results like the following:

	General Office Clerk	Secretary
Company A	$3.95/hr	$5.80/hr
Company B	$4.60/hr	—
Company C	$5.70/hr	$7.35/hr
Company D	$3.80/hr	—
Company E	$5.55/hr	$7.70/hr
Company F	—	$6.40/hr
Company G	$5.80/hr	$6.50/hr
Average (mean)	$4.90/hr	$6.75/hr
Middle (median)	$5.08/hr*	$6.50/hr
Standard deviation	$ .90/hr	$ .76/hr

*Average of two middle pay rates.

As can be clearly seen from this example, we get very different results depending on the method used to calculate the rates gathered. Comparing the mean and median of pay rates, we can see that the General Office Clerk job goes up 18 cents per hour while the Secretary job goes down 25 cents per hour. The mean percentage difference between the jobs turns out to be about 38 percent, and the gap closes to 28 percent if we calculate the median difference.

Other modified methods can, and in some cases should, be utilized. Some employers prefer to stay with one method, say, averages of survey data, for consistency from year to year using the same companies and benchmark positions. They may elect to eliminate the one highest and lowest survey pay rate under the assumption that there will always be employers who pay pathetically low and unjustifiably high, and this method excludes such extremes. For this reason, an employer should examine the variation or spread of survey rates once compiled, and eliminate those that are too extreme before tabulating results. Extremes in pay rates can also reflect noncomparability—in the job or business—that has been overlooked.

DEVELOPING A PAY PLAN/SCHEDULE

After establishing particular pay rates for different jobs through the evaluation of external and internal information, the employer may now want to design a pay plan (schedule of pay rates to which all jobs in the business are assigned). Pay plans can be very useful for making a number of pay-related personnel decisions, such as:

- The pay relationship between all jobs in the business.
- Length of service or performance opportunities for pay increase.
- Pay rates for promotional jobs.
- Minimum, midpoint, maximum, or all-rate steps in a range of pay for jobs.

Undeniably, there is an almost limitless number of pay plans that have been devised over the years. However, the one common feature to all plans is that they guide the business toward a systematic means of paying jobs what they're worth, allowing for differentiation of worth among dissimilar jobs, and providing an opportunity for pay advancement based on the merit of one's performance. To these ends, it is recommended that employers develop their own pay plans, after studying examples provided at the end of this chapter. Failure to adopt pay plans has consistently resulted in confusion about the organization's pay policies, has caused trouble for many employers with compliance agencies and has led to internal morale problems.

A special word of caution is appropriate here. Employers should *never* assign two different pay rates (or pay grades) to employees working under the same job description or performing substantially the same work, unless the differing pay rates are attributable to merit (performance) increases available to anyone working the same job. Assigning different pay rates will almost always be construed as a violation of the Equal Pay Act, which requires *all* employers to provide equal pay for equal work, effort, and responsibility.

Another frequent practice among employers of all sizes is to hire employees at an arbitrary starting pay rate based primarily on their previous employment pay rate. Employers can save themselves and the business's profit-and-loss statement some grief by abandoning such a practice, as recent trends in the courts have taken a harsh view of employers' using this method. If it is wiser—and safer—to adopt a pay plan, assign separate jobs to the pay plan, and pay employees based on corresponding amounts in the pay plan. If it is found that the pay plan devised is too narrow, too broad, inflexible, or in other respects insufficient, revise it! The idea is to start somewhere, and it may well serve the business manager's interests to solicit the opinions of other managers, supervisors, employees, or outside advisors before adopting a plan in an effort to maximize the plan's workability under varying pay conditions.

The two most prevalent types of pay plans among smaller businesses are the flat-rate plan, wherein each job is assigned a singular hourly, weekly, or monthly pay rate, with perhaps annual across-the-board adjustments, and the pay-grade plan, wherein each job is assigned to a grade number, each having a predetermined number of pay steps within the grade as shown here.

Pay Grade	Step 1	Step 2	Step 3	Step 4	Step 5
1	$3.45	$3.50	$3.55	$3.60	$3.65
2	3.60	3.65	3.70	3.75	3.80
3	3.75	3.80	3.90	3.95	4.00

In this example of hourly pay rates, the pay plan provides for overlapping rates from one grade level to the next higher level. The manner in which the rates in one grade relate to the next grade or the amounts between steps, is a matter of individual design. What is more important is that there is some rational consistency. In the example given, the consistency lies in equal amounts between pay steps and equal amounts between grade levels. Some employers use equal percentage (5 percent is common) between pay steps.

As shown in the sample pay plan at the end of this chapter, rates can be expressed in hourly, weekly, and monthly amounts. If the jobs assigned to these rates are nonexempt positions, the pay plan should *always* include hourly rates with weekly and/or monthly equivalents optional. Exempt positions should be expressed in monthly rates *only*. If the business's accountant has some pressing reason to break exempt salaries down into hourly rates (perhaps for severance pay or vacation accrual payoff), keep the hourly equivalent record with the accountant and not among the business's official personnel documents, where it can possibly be mistaken for a pay plan.

Because exempt positions are paid a flat monthly salary, and the amount of pay is typically greater than that for nonexempt hourly workers, some businesses find it useful to adopt a separate pay plan for salaried employees. This pay plan can be with or without merit step increases. When it is without merit steps, salary increases are usually granted in varying amounts and on a "when deserved" (irregular intervals) period of time performing the job.

In Example 1, advancement to one or more higher pay steps is at a predetermined salary rate (increments of 5 percent between steps in this case). Example 2 is a more flexible variation of the same plan concept. In such pay plans, employees are often hired at either the entry rate (step A) or the midpoint (step C) rate depending on experience, special skills, and like considerations. Thereafter, the employee may be reduced or increased in salary rate in any amount between the minimum and maximum rate assigned to the grade.

Given an employer's attention to the few details concerning the establishing of pay rates and pay plan discussed in this chapter, it is considerably less likely that the business will experience the many problems associated with the inconsistent and inequitable decisions that result in illegal practices. Also, once the pay system has been devised, it needs to be revised only periodically—to update it, or to enhance its usefulness.

Example 1. Merit Pay Plan for Salaried Employees

Salary Grade	Step A	Step B	Step C	Step D	Step E
1	$1,200	$1,260	$1,323	$1,389	$1,459
2	1,300	1,365	1,433	1,505	1,580
3	1,400	1,470	1,544	1,621	1,702
			Midpoint		

Example 2. Merit Pay Plan for Salaried Employees

Salary Grade	Step A	Step B	Step C	Step D	Step E
1	$1,200	—	$1,350	—	$1,500
2	1,300	—	1,450	—	1,600
3	1,400	—	1,550	—	1,700
			Midpoint		

Pay Schedule: Sample A

Grade/ Step	Hourly	Weekly	Monthly	Grade/ Step	Hourly	Weekly	Monthly
1 A	$4.038	$161.538	$ 700	10 A	$ 7.993	$317.308	$1,375
B	4.327	173.077	750	B	8.221	328.846	1,425
C	4.615	184.615	800	C	8.510	340.385	1,475
2 A	4.471	178.846	775	11 A	8.365	334.615	1,450
B	4.759	190.384	825	B	8.654	346.154	1,500
C	5.048	201.923	875	C	8.942	357.692	1,550
3 A	4.904	196.154	850	12 A	8.798	351.923	1,525
B	5.192	207.692	900	B	9.086	363.461	1,575
C	5.481	219.231	950	C	9.375	375.000	1,625
4 A	5.336	213.461	925	13 A	9.231	369.231	1,600
B	5.625	225.000	975	B	9.519	380.769	1,650
C	5.913	236.538	1,025	C	9.808	392.308	1,700
5 A	5.769	230.769	1,000	14 A	9.663	386.538	1,675
B	6.058	242.308	1,050	B	9.952	398.077	1,725
C	6.346	253.846	1,100	C	10.240	409.615	1,775
6 A	6.202	248.077	1,075	15 A	10.096	403.846	1,750
B	6.490	259.615	1,125	B	10.385	415.385	1,800
C	6.779	271.154	1,175	C	10.673	426.923	1,850
7 A	6.634	265.385	1,150	16 A	10.529	421.154	1,825
B	6.923	276.923	1,200	B	10.817	432.692	1,875
C	7.211	288.461	1,250	C	11.106	444.231	1,925
8 A	7.067	282.692	1,225	17 A	10.961	438.461	1,900
B	7.356	294.231	1,275	B	11.250	450.000	1,950
C	7.644	305.769	1,325	C	11.538	461.538	2,000
9 A	7.500	300.000	1,300	18 A	11.394	455.769	1,975
B	7.788	311.538	1,350	B	11.683	467.308	2,025
C	8.077	323.077	1,400	C	11.971	478.846	2,075

Step A—Hire rate.
Steps B and C—Annual eligibility from hire date.

PAY RATE STRUCTURE CHART: SAMPLE A

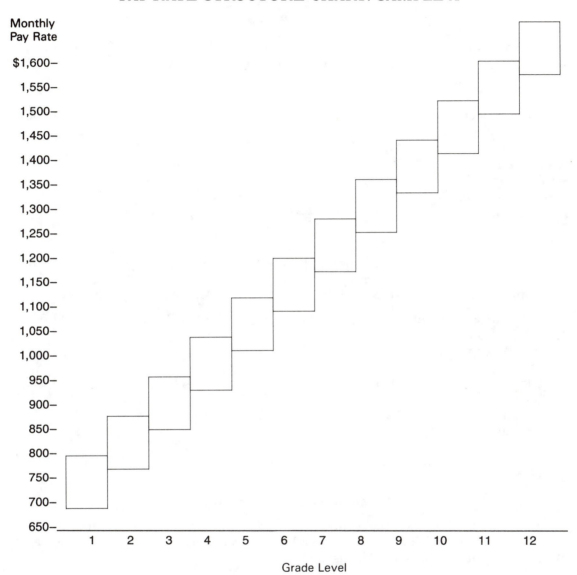

Pay Schedule: Sample B

Nonexempt Pay Ranges

Job Title	Grade	Minimum	****	Midrange	****	Maximum
Receptionist	N-5	$725	—	$ 850	—	$ 975
Check Filer						
Clerk I						
Senior Clerk Typist	N-6	850	—	975	—	1,100
Proof Operator						
Teller						
Secretary I	N-7	975	—	1,100	—	1,225
Bookkeeper I						
Customer Service						
Representative	N-8					

N = Nonexempt.

Exempt Pay Ranges

Job Title	Grade	Minimum	****	Midrange	****	Maximum
Administrative Assistant	E-10	$1,150	—	$1,325	—	$1,500
Note Supervisor						
Operations Supervisor						
Assistant Operations						
Officer	E-11	1,275	—	1,450	—	1,625
Investment Officer						
Operations Officer I	E-12	1,400	—		—	
Real Estate Loan						
Officer I	E-13					

E = Exempt.

Merit Increase Standards

Pay increases are based on the achievement of specific levels of performance as determined by regularly scheduled evaluations. In recommending or initiating pay increases, the following guidelines should be used.

	Percentage Increase		
Performance Level	**90-Day**	**180-Day**	**Annual**
Operates below job standards	0	0	0
Meets job standards (satisfactory)	2–3%	3–4%	4–5%
Exceeds job standards (good)	3–4	4–6	6–10
Excels at job standards (excellent)	5–7	7–10	10–15

SOURCES OF COMPENSATION INFORMATION

Business and Professional Journals and Magazines

The following lists identify business and professional journals and magazines and organizations that perform or provide some form of compensation survey. The item in parentheses describes the particular type of survey the identified unit performs or reports.

Administrative Management (reports AMS surveys)

Business Automation (EDP personnel salaries)

Business Management (boards of directors)

Business Week (annual survey of executive compensation)

Chemical and Engineering News (chemists)

Chemical Engineering (chemical engineers)

Chemical Week (computer systems specialists)

Datamation (data processing positions)

Dun's (executive compensation)

Engineer (engineers)

Financial Executive (financial and accounting management)

Forbes (senior management)

Fortune (senior management of *Fortune* 500 organizations)

Hospital Administration (nurses)

Industrial Engineering (industrial engineers)

Industrial Research Development (scientists, engineers working in R&D, quality control)

Industry Week (executive compensation)

Infosystems (data processing personnel)

Medical World News (reports on survey by American Academy of General Practice)

Modern Office Procedures (white-collar workers' pay and benefits)

Monthly Labor Review (reports on BLS surveys)

Nation's Business (AMS white-collar surveys)

Professional Pilot (professional pilots)

Profit Sharing (profit-sharing distributions)

Public Relations Journal (public relations personnel)

Sales Management (sales and marketing executives)

U.S. News & World Report (employee benefits, management compensation)

U.S. Government Sources of Compensation Information

Civil Service Commission, Bureau of Intergovernmental Personnel Programs (one hundred state government job classes)

Department of Labor, Bureau of Labor Statistics (described in text)

Department of Commerce, Bureau of the Census (study of income)

Organizations Providing Major Pay Surveys

Administrative Management Society (AMS), Maryland Road, Willow Grove, PA 19090 (as described in text)

American Association of Engineering Societies, 345 E. 47th Street, New York, NY 10017 (engineers' salaries)

American Association of University Professors (AAUP), Suite 500, One DuPont Circle, NW, Washington, D.C. 20036 (college and university faculty)

American Chemical Society, 1155 16th Street, NW, Washington, D.C. 20036 (professionals in chemistry)

American Compensation Association (ACA), P.O. Box 1176, Scottsdale, AZ 85252 (compensation management positions, payroll budgets for salaried employees)

American Federation of Information Processing Societies, 2100 L Street, NW, Suite 420, Washington, D.C. 20037 (information processing personnel)

American Hotel and Motel Association, 888 7th Avenue, New York, NY 10019 (seventeen hotel and motel unionized job classifications; management jobs)

American Management Association (AMA), 135 W. 50th Street, New York, NY 10020 (as described in text)

American Society of Association Executives, 1 Las Olas Circle, Apt. 20, Fort Lauderdale, FL 33316 (association executives)

American Society of Corporate Secretaries, One Rockefeller Plaza, New York, NY 10020 (corporate directors' fees and other reimbursements)

Association of Consulting Management Engineers (ACME), 347 Madison Avenue, New York, NY 10017 (consultants)

Bank Administration Institute, P.O. Box 500, Park Ridge, IL 60068 (bank officers)

Battelle Institute, 505 King Avenue, Columbus, OH 43201 (R&D scientists and engineers)

Business International Corp., One Dag Hammarskjold Plaza, New York, NY 10017 (expatriate allowances and fringe benefits)

Chamber of Commerce of the United States, 1615 H Street, NW, Washington, D.C. 20062 (employee benefits and workers' compensation by stock)

Child Welfare League of America, Inc., 1346 Connecticut Avenue, NW, Washington, D.C. 20036 (thirteen administrative and professional child welfare staff jobs)

College and University Personnel Association, 11 Dupont Circle, Suite 120, Washington, D.C. 20036 (administrative positions in higher education)

The College Placement Council, Inc., 65 East Elizabeth Avenue, Bethlehem, PA 18018 (job offers for college graduates)

Committee on Corporate Law Department of the Association of the Bar of the City of New York, 42 West 44th Street, New York, NY 10036 (law department attorneys)

The Conference Board, Inc., 845 Third Avenue, New York, NY 10022 (total top executives compensation package)

The Dartnell Corp., 4660 Ravenswood Avenue, Chicago, IL 60640 (executive compensation, sales personnel)

Educational Research Services, Inc., 1815 N. Fort Myer Drive, Arlington, VA 22209 (salaries paid professional personnel in public schools)

The Endicott Report, Northwestern University, Evanston, IL 60201 (job offers for college graduates)

Engineers Joint Council, 345 E. 47th Street, New York, NY 10017 (engineers)

Financial Executives Institute, 633 Third Avenue, New York, NY 10017 (financial and accounting managers)

Health Insurance Institute, 1850 K Street, NW, Washington, D.C. 20006 (health insurance plans)

International Foundation of Employee Benefits Plans, P.O. Box 69, Brookfield, WI 53005 (employee benefits)

International Information/Wood Processing Association, 1015 North York Road, Willow Grove, PA 19090 (fourteen job titles in information/word processing)

International Personnel Management Association, 1313 E. 60th Street, Chicago, IL 60637 (Sixty-two job classes in governmental jurisdictions)

Life Office Management Association, 100 Colony Square, Atlanta, GA 30361 (midmanagement, top seven officers, actuarial personnel, and area differentials for life insurance industry)

Midwest Industrial Management Association, 9845 W. Roosevelt Road, Westchester, IL 60153 (managers of manufacturing, distribution, and warehousing firms)

Mortgage Bankers Association of America, 1125 15th Street, NW, Washington, D.C. 20005 (mortgage bankers compensation)

National Association of Mutual Insurance Companies, 7931 Castleway Drive, Indianapolis, IN 46250 (executives in the insurance industry)

National Education Association, 1601 16th Street, NW, Washington, D.C. 20036 (classroom teachers)

National Society of Professional Engineers, 2924 Stuart Drive, Falls Church, VA 22042 (all branches of engineering)

National Telephone Cooperative Association, 2626 Pennsylvania Avenue, NW, Washington, D.C. 20037 (thirty-one job classifications in the telephone industry)

New York Chamber of Commerce and Industry, 200 Madison Avenue, New York, NY 10016 (six different surveys on office salaries, personnel practices, and benefits)

New York Port Authority: 1 World Trade Center, New York, NY 10011 (wage and salary survey)

Scientific Manpower Commission; 1776 Massachusetts Avenue, NW, Washington, D.C. 20036 (biennial survey of engineers)

Society for Human Resource Management (SHRM), 606 North Washington Street, Alexandria, VA 22314 (human resource managers)

Tool and Die Institute; 77 Busse Highway, Park Ridge, IL 60068 (tool and die industry)

Chapter 27

ACQUIRING GROUP MEDICAL INSURANCE, CAFETERIA BENEFIT PROGRAMS, AND COBRA COMPLIANCE

GROUP MEDICAL INSURANCE

Group insurance is a significant economic, social, and political issue. As health care costs have been rising faster than both the inflation rate and the average individual's disposable income, the issues related to acquiring health care and containing premium rate increases has become more complex. Also, the cost of medical insurance has increased at a greater rate than almost any other goods or services desired by the employee. For example, the growth in premium income received by all private insurers between 1961 and 1971 was approximately 154 percent. Between 1964 and 1974, the daily cost of hospital care rose from an average of $38 to an average of $118, and over the same ten-year period, doctors raised their fees by more than 75 percent. Employers have seen their health-related benefit costs per employee quadruple since 1974.

Group medical insurance, whether it is mandated by law, negotiated through collective bargaining, or voluntarily made available by the employer, is the cornerstone of the employee's benefit plan. Employers offer benefit plans for many reasons, one of which is that they believe in the long run it will be beneficial to the organization in greater productivity, or in attracting or keeping qualified personnel.

There are a number of unique characteristics of group insurance as compared with individual insurance. With few exceptions, group insurance is issued without medical examination or other evidence of insurability, the individual is not responsible for the paperwork involved, and the premiums are considerably lower and are usually subject to an experience rating. There are several types of organizations eligible for group insurance. By far, most contracts are written with individual employer groups. Others include multiple-employer groups such as trade associations; labor union groups; creditor-debtor groups associated with lending institutions; associations of teachers, lawyers, and physicians; fraternal societies; religious groups; and other people with a common bond who are considered a group.

From the viewpoint of the insurance carrier, insurance is provided to individuals in a group without any inquiry as to the quality of the individual's risk to file a claim. The employee census information provided by the employer enables the carrier to evaluate the risk involved in a particular group. Objectives of the carrier would be (1) to obtain a proper balance of risk to allow predictability of future results, (2) to establish standards to permit acceptance of a large majority of groups at standard premium rates, and (3) to secure the largest possible proportion of the average and better than average risks.

Carriers adopt underwriting rules and develop standard schedules to cover the needs of the employer, an employee's ability to pay if the plan is contributory, and the overall cost of the plan to the organization.

The trend today is for the employer and the employee to share in the cost of the medical insurance premium. Each employer needs to evaluate its own particular situation before presenting the medical insurance package to its employees.

The advantages claimed by proponents of the *noncontributory* basis for premium payment include the following:

1. Simplicity of administration; savings in accounting, as there are no payroll deductions.
2. All employees are insured, maximizing participation and narrowing the risk in the experience rating.
3. Tax advantages to the employer.
4. More control of the plan by the employer regarding changes of coverage and benefits offered.

The advantages claimed for the *contributory* basis are as follows:

1. Additional coverage or higher amounts of current coverage could become available if there is an increase of premium money.
2. Greater employee interest, participation, appreciation, and abuse.
3. Employer's funds not used for medical insurance could be channeled into other benefit areas.
4. Employees have more control in that the employer will be more likely to listen to their opinions.

CHECKLIST: GROUP MEDICAL PLAN COST-CONTAINMENT FEATURES

In evaluating the benefit provisions of group medical plans, employers should give particular attention to the following:

Inpatient and Outpatient Services

All plans should include:

- ☐ Provisions that require an evaluation of the need for hospitalization and the appropriateness of the length of stay
- ☐ Provisions that require preadmission testing when feasible and medically appropriate
- ☐ Coverage of second opinion regarding the need for selected surgeries—particularly major surgery
- ☐ Coverage of outpatient surgery in freestanding ambulatory surgicenters meeting licensing and/or accreditation standards
- ☐ Coverage of hospice, skilled nursing, and home health care services when they may represent an alternative to hospitalization
- ☐ Provisions requiring that anesthesia benefits be related to surgical benefits but with dollar maximums that may not necessarily relate to surgery maximums
- ☐ Coverage of outpatient diagnostic services
- ☐ Coverage of emergency transport (ambulance) when necessary

Consideration should be given to adding:

- ☐ Deductibles and/or coinsurance for each hospital admission
- ☐ Per-confinement deductibles of one day board and room charge, a daily board and room allowance scheduled where more than one cost is involved, or a fixed daily copayment
- ☐ Emergency room deductibles or coinsurance per visit
- ☐ Coverage of comprehensive rehabilitation services
- ☐ First-dollar coverage of preadmission testing with a schedule of test benefit allowances
- ☐ Incentives for second opinion on selected surgeries (i.e., 100 percent coverage of second opinion and higher copayment for surgery recommended through second opinion)
- ☐ First-dollar coverage for outpatient surgery (including anesthesia and diagnostic services)
- ☐ A schedule of fixed surgical, anesthesia, and diagnostic benefits or coverage based on a percentage of "usual, reasonable, and customary" charges
- ☐ First-dollar coverage of skilled nursing services without copayment if hospital stay can be reduced and/or eliminated
- ☐ Coverage of licensed adult day health care services

Consideration should be given to eliminating:

- ☐ Coverage based solely on hospital's average semiprivate charges
- ☐ Unlimited coverage of "miscellaneous charges"
- ☐ Coverage of emergency room services on a first-dollar basis
- ☐ Coverage of a second series of diagnostic tests when results of first tests are still valid
- ☐ Deductibles or copayments for preadmission testing
- ☐ Payments for surgical, anesthesia, and diagnostic services made on the basis of 100 percent of usual, reasonable, and customary (substitute with 80 percent or 90 percent or a schedule)
- ☐ Coverage of anesthesia services included in (and therefore, unidentifiable) hospital miscellaneous charges
- ☐ Requirements for prior hospital confinement for coverage of skilled nursing and home health services

CAFETERIA BENEFITS: WHAT ARE THEY AND ARE THEY RIGHT FOR YOUR COMPANY?

The majority of the work force now, and for the foreseeable future, is a conglomeration of young singles, single parents of which most are women, and partners in two-paycheck relationships. For many of them, group benefit plans provide coverage that is often too much, too little, or not the right kind. This "new breed" of work force has a much keener interest in having a wider realm of income loss-protection plans (e.g., major medical, disability, life insurance) and tax-deferred income plans available to them than were the majority of workers in the 1960s.

Employers have begun to realize that employee satisfaction and morale may rise when employees are allowed to select benefits most appropriate to their individual needs. Flexible benefit plans permit this kind of choice. These plans are also called "cafeteria plans" because they provide a "menu," or choice, of benefits, from which employees select those benefits they want or need.

The pioneers of flexible benefit plans recognized a growing diversity in the work force; therefore, they sought to expand benefits in a way that would allow employees to become more involved in determining the shape and scope of their packages. Most of these first-generation plans did little more than offer employees a choice between the additional insurance and cash. The growth of these plans stalled, however, when a small section of the Employee Retirement Income Security Act of 1974 put a hold on them until Congress could study the tax implication. The tax difficulties were apparently resolved with the passage of the Revenue Act of 1978, which has been construed to permit employees to take the unused portion of a benefits allotment as either cash (taxable) or deferred compensation (nontaxable until distribution). A second generation of flexible-benefit plans was thus ushered in, and they became known as cafeteria plans. These plans were more responsive to employee needs than the old group plans, but they often worked to meet the employer's need for benefits cost containment as well.

In a conventional program, employer alternatives for cost control include placing a freeze on new benefits, taking away or cutting back existing coverages, and asking for larger employee contributions. These approaches have met with employee or union resistance, so companies have been reluctant to push them. Exit conventional programs; enter flexible programs, allowing the employer better control over the amount of money dedicated to pay and benefits, so compensation expenditures can rise more slowly than in a conventional system. Employees find themselves better off because their options are in areas deemed important to them.

There are numerous approaches to flexible compensation, one of which is to set basic levels of pay and benefits for all employees and give them a supplemental allowance in one form or another that they can allocate as they choose. The benefit reimbursement account, for example, is a credit reserve under which the individual can allocate flexible credits to pay for certain medical, dental, or legal needs; dependent care; or other expenses not covered under the group program.

Under a flexible system, each optional form of pay or benefits has a specific price to be paid by those selecting it. An increase in its cost increases the price employees pay for it but does not necessarily increase the employer's cost commitment. The employee pays for it through payroll deduction. Conversely, an employee who elects not to use all the employer contribution can flow excess amounts into a capital-accumulation plan or take the difference in cash. Any cash election, however, constitutes taxable income. The next year, the cost of the medical plan options rises and the employer decides that an additional benefit option—say, dental coverage—would make the flexible program more attractive. The third year, the cost of certain coverages rises and a new option, say, dependent care assistance, is added. This time, however, the employer decides to enrich the pool of flexible dollars by adding $100 per year, for example, to each employee's flexible account. In reality, the dollars probably would be expressed as a percentage of pay. What does all this mean? Throughout the program's operation, the employer's commitment to support it was independent of the prices charged employers. New options could be added but not necessarily at the employer's expense. The employer added money when conditions warranted it.

An additional advantage of the flexible approach is that it offers employees a choice among taxable and nontaxable options. Employees at all earning levels are tax conscious; tax-effective benefits and savings are well received. If Congress expands the list of nontaxable items, more employers may offer such options rather than expand their compensation costs in the current environment.

Another plan is called a reimbursement account—sometimes called a "benefits bank" or a "flexible-spending account"—and it operates like a checking account. Employees draw against an individual annual benefits allotment that is set aside by the employer for reimbursement of certain eligible expenses that are not covered elsewhere in the benefits package. The basic free-of-charge core package consists of life insurance, short-term disability coverage, educational assistance eligibility, and the usual time off for vacations, holidays, and illnesses. That's where the similarities end. In our example, we allot each employee, say, $250 per year to buy such things as supplemental life insurance and/or long-term disability coverage. The one requirement is that those who cannot claim medical coverage elsewhere must purchase the company policy.

Any money left over when the shopping is finished goes into the reimbursement account. These so-called flex dollars can be used to reimburse expenses for dental work, child care, vision or hearing treatment, and miscellaneous medical expenses, including the deductibles on the aforementioned insurance policies. Those who still find themselves with unspent money at the end of the year can roll it into the following year's reimbursement account or dedicate it to a deferred compensation—401(k)—plan. The sum can also be taken as cash, but those who elect to do so must pay tax on it. On the other hand, those who find that their needs exceed their benefits allotment can boost their buying power by selling back some vacation time or by entering into a salary reduction program whereby payroll deductions serve to reduce an employee's taxable income as they increase the size of the employee's reimbursement account.

The arrival of the reimbursement account represents the third generation of a flexible-benefits evolution that began ten years ago. Not only does this structure provide more categories of benefits than were available under group plans, but it actually provides more benefits to the employer than do other cafeteria-style plans. When employees present receipts for reimbursement of benefits-related expenses instead of filing insurance claims, they get dollar-for-dollar coverage, not the typical 80/20 or 50/50 split that insurance companies offer. Those companies that choose the reimbursement account over the cafeteria structure effectively circumvent technical problems that make cafeteria plans more difficult to design.

While there are numerous policy, procedural, and legal issues to be dealt with when installing a cafeteria benefits plan, the significant impact is in the human resource information system (HRIS) of the organization. The benefits processes incorporated in the HRIS will necessarily be affected by this type of plan. Without appropriate planning and consultation with the HRIS coordinator, initiation of a cafeteria plan may be extremely costly, or worse, may never be successfully implemented. Few, if any, information systems were designed with cafeteria plans in mind, so they will require modification in order to accommodate such a plan. The extent and feasibility of these modifications can be substantially improved by considering the HRIS when designing the cafeteria plan.

To truly maximize a company's investment in the employees, the employer might wish to begin thinking in terms of a totally flexible human resources system. Such a system should consist of three basic elements:

1. Benefits and compensation—covering base pay, incentive/bonus plans, capital accumulation/thrift plans, benefits, and prerequisites.
2. Work environment—including flexible hours, special summer hours, reduced workweek, job sharing, work at home, and phased retirement.

3. Career development—providing access to dual career paths, interdisciplinary changes (that is, permitting and even encouraging employees to make career shifts from one field to another), management development programs that are clearly communicated and consistently applied, and second-career development programs.

The spread of the flexible human resources concept will, of course, be slow. The critics will again point out the problems and the reasons it can't work—that tax laws limit plan design, the administration of the plan will be too difficult and costly, management will never accept such a program, and so on. Twenty years from now, however, most companies will probably be offering some form of flexible human resources or a flexible compensation program. The ultimate pay-off—improved productivity and morale, better control of benefit costs, and an enhanced ability to attract and retain top performers—is well worth the initial investment in time, human resources, communications, and legalities. However, critical to a well-designed and time/cost-effective cafeteria benefits program is the size of the business in terms of the number of employees, which determines the employer's buying power with insurance companies. Some cafeteria plans have failed because the employer tried to offer too many options among too few employees.

By now, it should be obvious that choosing group medical insurance and cafeteria benefit plans requires complex and confusing decisions. For that reason, it is best to seek professional and independent advice on such matters prior to making choices or changes. Additionally, employers would be well advised to acquaint themselves with at least the fundamentals of the Employee Retirement Income and Security Act (ERISA), Internal Revenue Service laws applicable to employee benefit programs, and labor laws where relevant to collective bargaining of employee benefits. A reprint of basic ERISA compliance issues has been provided to give you a little more insight into this rather complex realm of administrating employee benefit plans; however, there are expert consultant-advisors who can assist employers with both ERISA and IRS laws. For labor relations matters, employers should contact competent labor attorneys or professional labor consultants.

REGULATORY ENVIRONMENT OF EMPLOYEE BENEFIT PLANS[1]

The regulatory environment of employee benefit plans has changed dramatically over the past thirty-five years. Major legislation was passed in 1942, 1958, and 1974, with a continuous flow of regulations and rulings from then until the recent passage of the Economic Recovery Tax Act of 1981 (ERTA) and the Tax Equity and Fiscal Responsibility Act of 1982 (TEFRA). The combined effect of these laws and rules has been to make the administration of employee benefit plans increasingly complex.

---

[1]   Reprinted by permission of Dallas L. Salisbury as it appeared in *The Handbook of Employee Benefits: Design, Funding, and Administration,* ed. by Jerry S. Rosenbloom © Dow Jones, Homewood, Ill., 1984.

This chapter briefly reviews the regulatory environment for private pension and welfare plans; insurance programs; federal, state, and local government pension plans; and disability programs. It is intended to heighten awareness of the complexity of the regulatory environment.

The chapter is not intended to provide legal guidance or to be a guide to compliance. There are several loose-leaf services available that should be consulted to keep abreast of the constant changes taking place.

PRIVATE PENSION AND WELFARE PLANS

Pre-ERISA

Before the enactment of the Employee Retirement Income Security Act (ERISA) on Labor Day 1974, only three principal statutes governed private pension plans: the Internal Revenue Code (IRC), the Federal Welfare and Pension Plans Disclosure Act of 1958 (WPPDA), and the Taft-Hartley Act, more formally known as the Labor Management Relations Act of 1947. The latter regulated collectively bargained multiemployer pension plans.

Amendments to the Internal Revenue Code enacted in 1942 established standards for the design and operation of pension plans. The principal purposes were to prevent plans from discriminating or disproportionately benefiting one group of employees over another and to prevent plans from taking excessive or unjustified tax deductions. Until 1974, the Internal Revenue Service was not concerned with the actuarial soundness of plans.

The Federal Welfare and Pension Plans Disclosure Act of 1958 was enacted to protect plan assets against fraudulent behavior by the plan administrator. The act mandated that, upon request, participants concerned with plan malpractice would be provided with information concerning the plan. If misuse or fraud was suspected, it was up to the participant to bring charges against the administrator. A significant amendment to the WPPDA was enacted in 1962. That amendment authorized the Department of Justice to bring appropriate legal action to protect plan participants' interests, and authorized the Department of Labor to interpret and enforce the Act. For the first time, the burden of plan asset protection was placed on the government rather than on the individual participants.

Employee Retirement Income Security Act of 1974

The shift to government protection of participant's rights enacted in 1962 would carry through to ERISA. It reflected a concern for workers, which was confirmed by President Kennedy in 1962 with appointment of a Committee on Corporate Pension Funds and Other Retirement and Welfare Programs. That committee issued its report in 1965, concluding that private pension plans should continue as a major element in the nation's total retirement security program. The report advocated many changes in the breadth of private plan regulation.

The report received widespread attention and led to the introduction of a number of legislative proposals. Congress concluded that most plans were operated for the benefit of participants on a sound basis, but some were not. To solve this problem, Congress enacted ERISA. ERISA governs every aspect of private pension and welfare plans and requires employers who sponsor plans to operate them in compliance with ERISA standards.

TITLE I: PROTECTION OF EMPLOYEE BENEFIT RIGHTS

Title I of ERISA places primary jurisdiction over reporting, disclosure, and fiduciary matters in the Department of Labor. The Department of the Treasury is given primary jurisdiction over participation, vesting, and funding. This "dual jurisdiction" led to a number of problems for plans during the first years of ERISA, which were addressed in 1979 by Reorganization Plan Number 4, discussed in a later part of this chapter. As a result of reorganizations and administrative experience under ERISA, many requirements have been adjusted, resulting in a reduction of regulatory burdens.

Reporting and Disclosure

Plan sponsors are required to provide plan participants with summary plan descriptions and benefit statements. They also are provided access to plan financial information. Documents provided to participants are to be written in "plain English" so they can be easily understood.

Plan sponsors file an annual financial report (Form 5500 series) with the IRS, which is made available to other agencies. In addition, plan sponsors must file amendments when modifications to the plan are made. Taken together, these provisions seek to assure that the government has accurate information on employer-sponsored plans.

Fiduciary Requirements

Plan sponsors are subject to an ERISA fiduciary standard mandating that the plan be operated solely for the benefit of plan participants. The fiduciary standard, or "prudent man standard," requires that the plan fiduciary perform duties solely in the interest of plan participants with the care a prudent man acting under like circumstances would use. This means any person who exercises discretion in the management and maintenance of the plan or in the investment of the plan assets must do so in the interest of the plan participants and beneficiaries, in accordance with the plan documents, and in a manner that minimizes the risk of loss to the participant. The standard applies to plan sponsors, trustees, and cofiduciaries, and to investment advisors with discretionary authority over the purchase and sale of plan securities. Underlying the standard are prohibitions against business or investment transactions between the plan and fiduciaries or interested parties. Upon violation of the prohibitions, the fiduciary may be held personally liable to the plan for any misuse, fraud, or mismanagement. Exemptions can be applied for when parties feel that actions are not to the detriment of the plan and its participants and should be allowed. Both the IRS and the Department of Labor are responsible for enforcing the fiduciary standards. The Department of Labor may file charges on behalf of the participants if the fiduciary has breached or violated the standards imposed by ERISA. The IRS may fine the employer and revoke the plan's favorable tax treatment. Both civil and criminal actions may arise for violations.

TITLE II: MINIMUM STANDARDS

Title II of ERISA contains minimum standards for participation, vesting, and funding of benefits, which must be satisfied for qualification of a plan. It also contains amendments to the IRC that increase the scope of federal regulation over certain pension plans, whether tax qualified or not.

Participation

Although ERISA does not require every employer to set up an employer pension or welfare benefit plan, it does impose requirements on those who do. For those employers sponsoring plans, the age of employee eligibility cannot be higher than 25. A maximum of one year of service and 1,000 hours of work also may be required for eligibility.

Vesting

Upon satisfying the participation requirements, further conditions must be met for the participant to become entitled to receive a benefit—that is, to have a vested right to the benefits. There are three alternative vesting requirements contained in ERISA:

- Full vesting after 10 years of service, with no vesting before the 10-year requirement is met.
- Graduated vesting from the time the participant completes 5 years of service (full vesting after 15 years).
- Graduated vesting, which requires that vesting begins when the participant has completed at least 5 years of service and when the age plus years of service totals at least 45, or after 10 years of service, irrespective of the participant's age, full vesting occurs when the participant has at least 15 years of service or age plus years of service equal at least 55. (This is called the "rule of 45.") In addition, the IRS has specified a 4–40 graded vesting schedule which can be used by plans. This schedule has been adopted by many small plans.

Benefits

Under ERISA, benefits generally must be earned in a uniform manner while the participant is employed. This does not affect the levels of benefits provided by the plan, only the rate at which the benefits are earned.

Funding

The minimum funding standards attempt to ensure that plans will have sufficient assets to pay benefits. Those employers with plans subject to the standards must establish and maintain a funding standard account. The sponsor must annually contribute the normal cost—the annual cost of future pension benefits and administrative expenses—plus amounts necessary to amortize in equal installments unfunded past service liabilities and any experience losses less experience gains. The amortization period in the former case generally is 30 years, and in the latter case, 15 years. The presence of these standards has changed the environment for pension plans, creating greater need for long-range planning.

Tax-Qualified Plans

Requirements for tax qualification of plans have not changed materially since 1942. Meeting these requirements allows the employer to deduct contributions from income and makes investment earnings on plan assets exempt from current taxation.

The structure of tax-qualified plans is determined by ERISA requirements. The terms of the plan must be set forth in a written document. Copies of the plan and related documents must be made available to participants. In addition, a summary of the plan must be made available. The plan sponsor must have created the plan with the intent of permanency.

The provisions of the pension plan are also dictated by the requirements of the IRC.

- As referred to above, the plan must meet minimum participation, vesting, and funding standards, and plan assets must be legally segregated from other assets of the sponsor.

- The plan must not benefit only a limited number of favored employees but must benefit employees in general in such a way as to be deemed nondiscriminatory by the IRS. This status must extend to contributions and benefits such that officers, shareholders, or highly compensated employees are not favored when the plan is viewed in its entirety.

- The pension plan must provide definitely determinable benefits.

Overall, the IRC implementing regulations and rulings have had the goal of fostering accrual and preservation of benefits for present and potential plan participants and beneficiaries.

The requirements for a tax-qualified profit-sharing plan are somewhat different in that the plan must cover all employees and the benefit is not determinable. In addition, the profit-sharing plan is not always a retirement income vehicle.

Fulfillment of all tax qualification requirements entitles the employer to a current deduction from gross income for contributions to the plan. The participating employee recognizes no taxable income until the funds are made available in the form of benefits or are distributed as a lump-sum distribution. When the distribution is made upon termination of service (an amount received as an annuity from a qualified plan) there are two applicable rules. If the employee's investment can be recouped from annuity payments within three years, all payments are tax free until the employee's investment has been recouped, at which time all future payments become fully taxable. If the investment cannot be recovered within three years, an exclusion ratio is used.

Employees may be allowed, or in some cases required, to make contributions to qualified plans. The employee's required contributions are limited to the maximum amount provided in the plan and no tax deduction is allowed; in other words, the contribution is made with after-tax dollars. For voluntary contributions, up to $2,000 may be contributed on a tax-deductible basis.

Nonqualified Plans

Nonqualified employee benefit plans have not been designed to satisfy the IRC requirements and may either be funded or nonfunded. Under the funded plan, the employer agrees to make contributions to the plan for the benefit of the employee. Under an unfunded plan, the employer promises to provide a benefit to the participant at some future time. Most funded plans must satisfy ERISA, while unfunded plans must only meet ERISA's reporting and disclosure provisions.

TITLE IV: PLAN TERMINATION INSURANCE

Title IV of ERISA established the Pension Benefit Guaranty Corporation (PBGC), a governmental body that insures payment of plan benefits under certain circumstances.

Most defined benefit pension plans (those that provide a fixed monthly benefit at retirement) are required to participate in the program and pay premiums to the PBGC.

There are certain restrictions and limitations on the amount of benefits insured, which is adjusted annually to reflect the increasing average wages of the American work force. The limit applies to all plans under which a participant is covered so that it is not possible to spread coverage under several plans to increase the guaranteed benefit. To be fully insured, the benefit must have been vested before the plan terminated and the benefit level must have been in effect for 60 months, or else benefits are proportionately reduced. Further, the guarantee applies only to benefits earned while the plan is eligible for favorable tax treatment.

In an effort to protect against employers' establishing plans without intending to continue them, ERISA introduced the concept of contingent employer liability in the event of plan termination for single-employer plans and for multiemployer plans in the event of employer withdrawal or insolvency. Additional complex requirements that apply to multiemployer plans also were established by Congress in 1980. Such changes may soon be adopted for single-employer plans.

The PBGC has served to change substantially the environment in which plans operate. For present sponsors, and for those thinking of establishing new defined benefit plans, Title IV should be carefully reviewed to assure that its implications are fully understood.

ADDITIONAL REGULATORY AGENCIES

Labor Laws

A number of other laws, from both statutory and case law, give the Department of Labor authority to monitor and regulate employee benefit plans.

Among them is the National Labor Relations Act, which promotes collective bargaining between employers and employees' representatives. The Taft-Hartley Act contains specific provisions similar to ERISA and the IRC relating to plan structure and content. The landmark case of *Inland Steel Company* v. *the National Labor Relations Board* prohibits an employer from refusing to bargain with employees upon a properly presented demand to bargain regarding employee benefit plans.

Equal Employment Opportunity Commission

The EEOC's interest in employee benefit plans stems from various acts that prohibit discriminatory plan practices. The Civil Rights Act of 1964, Title VII, is interpreted by the EEOC as defining discrimination between men and women with regard to fringe benefits as an unlawful employment practice. The Equal Pay Act of 1963 makes employer discrimination between the sexes in the payment of wages for equal work unlawful. Benefits under employee benefit plans are a form of wages and must be free from discrimination, held one EEOC decision. The Age Discrimination in Employment Act of 1967 and its 1975 and 1979 amendments clearly prohibit discrimination on the basis of age and moved toward elimination of mandatory retirement ages.

Securities and Exchange Commission

Under the Securities Act of 1933, information concerning securities publicly offered and sold in interstate commerce or through the mails is required to be disclosed to the SEC. At first blush, the act does not seem to apply to employee benefit plans. However, a security is defined by the act as including participation in any profit-sharing agreement. The Securities Exchange Act of 1934 affects the administration of plans by imposing disclosure and registration requirements and antifraud provisions. The SEC has not actively enforced requirements, but the scope of legal SEC jurisdiction has been debated and litigated.

The Investment Company Act of 1940 regulates reporting and disclosure, structure, content, and administration of investment companies. A pension benefit plan could be subject to this act if it fits the definition of an investment company. An investment company, as defined by the act, is one engaged in the business of holding, trading, investing, or owning securities.

Other Acts and Agencies

The Small Business Administration (SBA) receives complaints from small businesses regarding the relationship of small business to agencies of the federal government.

Banking laws also apply. The National Bank Act permits national banks to act as trustees in a fiduciary capacity in which state banks or trust companies are permitted to act under the laws of the state where the national bank is located. This affects private employee benefit plans because banks act as fiduciaries. The Federal Reserve Act and the Federal Reserve System can affect pension and welfare plans, since plans may either be borrowers or lenders. Because there is regulation of interest payable on deposits in banks that are members of the Federal Reserve System, IRA and Keogh plans are affected in terms of possible rates of return. The Federal Deposit Insurance Act also affects these plans that are not covered by the PBGC since funds held by an insured bank, in its capacity as fiduciary, will be insured up to $100,000.

The Commerce Department is concerned with ERISA's impact on the health of the economy. The Department of Health and Human Services (HHS) tries to keep track of individuals with deferred vested benefit plans as well as administering Social Security and other public programs that have a substantial impact on private plan design.

EVALUATION OF ERISA ADMINISTRATION UNDER REORGANIZATION PLAN NUMBER 4

In 1978, President Carter mandated that the administration of ERISA be evaluated. Reorganization Plan Number 4 was developed to provide an immediate solution to some of the existing and potential problems caused by shared agency responsibilities under ERISA. The plan provides that the Department of Labor has rulemaking responsibility concerning employee benefit plan fiduciary matters and the Department of Treasury responsibility for participation, vesting, and funding standards.

An evaluation of Reorganization Plan Number 4 was released in 1980. It indicated improvements in the agencies' administration of ERISA. The plan was credited with leading to:

1. Speedier processing of requests for exemptions from prohibited transaction provisions.
2. Expediting the issuance of regulations by both the Labor and Treasury Departments.
3. Reduction of the paperwork associated with ERISA.

As a result of a recommendation coming from the evaluation of Reorganization Plan Number 4, President Carter signed a January 7, 1981, Executive Order which created an Interagency Employee Benefit Council. The council is composed of the secretaries of Treasury, Commerce, Labor, Health and Human Services; the attorney general; the director of the Office of Management and Budget; the administrator of the Small Business Administration; the chairman of the Equal Employment Opportunities Commission; plus representatives from the Federal Trade Commission, the Securities and Exchange Commission, and the National Labor Relations Board. Besides assisting in interagency coordination of proposals affecting employee benefits under ERISA, the council will seek to develop comprehensive long- and short-term policies applicable to plans covered by ERISA.

COMPLYING WITH THE CONSOLIDATED OMNIBUS BUDGET RECONCILIATION ACT (COBRA) OF 1985

This federal law was enacted in response to a national concern for the large and ever-increasing number of workers, and their dependents, who become ineligible for health care benefits at the time the worker's employment ceases (referred to as "qualifying events"). COBRA thus requires employers to provide written notices to employees of their rights and obligations to keep the employer informed about qualifying events affecting the worker's eligible dependents, and to establish appropriate personnel policies and practices that will ensure compliance with COBRA regulations.

Employers with more than 20 employees are required to comply with COBRA regulations, including maintenance of COBRA qualified and existing group health plans. Those employers not having group health plans are not required to comply with COBRA requirements until such time as a group health plan is adopted by the employer and offered to employees. As a technical revision to the original act, Section 11702 of the Revenue Reconciliation Act (part of the 1990 Omnibus Budget Reconciliation Act) amended Section 4980 (B.d.l.) of the IRS code. This amendment had the effect of relieving smaller employers of the excise tax imposed when their group health plan failed to meet COBRA continuation requirements as a result of the number of employees falling below 20 on a typical business day. The excise tax "forgiveness" would, under these circumstances, take effect in the calendar year *following* the calendar year in which the lowered employee count occurred.

Qualifying Events—Eligibility and Duration

Qualifying Event	Duration
1. Employees who would otherwise lose coverage due to termination from employment for any reason other than gross misconduct.	Eighteen months from the date coverage would have stopped
2. Employees whose work hours are reduced having the effect of making them ineligible for coverage under the employer's health plan.	Eighteen months from the date coverage would have stopped
3. Spouses and dependent children of the covered employee where plan coverage would be lost due to: a. The employee's death. b. The employee's termination from employment excluding for reason gross misconduct. c. Becoming eligible for Medicare. d. Divorce or legal separation from the employee. e. Ceasing to satisfy the plan's coverage requirements (e.g., age for dependent children).	Three years from the date coverage would have stopped

Benefits Entitlement

Eligible individuals must receive a continuation of the same benefit coverages under COBRA as they enjoyed under normal participation in the employer's group health plan. Depending on benefits provided under the employer's group plan, such coverage may include medical, dental, vision, and prescription drug benefits, but not life insurance or disability benefit plans.

Benefits and coverage under the plan may be discontinued by the employer if:

1. The employer terminates (not merely changes) the qualifying plan.
2. The covered individual fails to pay the premium, which may be up to 102 percent of the actual premium cost.
3. The covered individual becomes covered under another health care plan.[2]
4. The covered individual becomes eligible for Medicare.

Employers are required to notify their plan administrator within sixty days of the employee's divorce, legal separation, or loss of dependent child status. Similarly, employees must accept or reject continuation of COBRA coverage within sixty days after notice from the employer and pay the premium within forty-five days after acceptance of continuation.

COBRA Amendments

The Omnibus Budget Reconciliation Act (OBRA) of 1989 contained five noteworthy changes affecting COBRA compliance and administrative conditions, namely:

1. For qualified employees who become totally disabled from performance of their job, within the meaning of the Social Security Act, such an employee is entitled to receive up to twenty-nine months of COBRA continued participation in the employer's group health plan, unless terminated for misconduct. However, due to the likely added impact such an employee might have on the employer's premium rates, the employer may charge the disabled employee up to 150 percent of the normal premium cost after the eighteenth month at 102 percent of the premium. COBRA entitlement may also be terminated by the employer thirty days after Social Security makes a determination of nondisability, eligibility for Medicare coverage, or coverage under another group health plan, whichever occurs first.
2. After 1989, an employer may not discontinue COBRA entitlement when a qualified individual obtains coverage under another plan, if the other plan contains a preexisting condition clause.

---

[2] However, in *Oakley* v. *City of Longmont* (1989), the U.S. Court of Appeals for the Tenth Circuit held that a disabled firefighter who was covered by his spouse's health plan must be offered COBRA continuation under his employer's plan because the spouse's plan offered lesser benefits (did not cover rehabilitation).

3. An employee covered by COBRA, but who becomes eligible for Medicare, must have COBRA coverage extended to eligible dependents for thirty-six months starting from the date the employee became eligible for Medicare.

4. No COBRA payment is required to be paid to the employer by the employee until *at least* forty-five days after the date the employee elected COBRA coverage.

5. An employer is permitted, not required, to consider the loss of coverage—rather than the event itself causing loss—as a "qualifying event" as a matter of policy in extending COBRA coverage to employees.

A more recent COBRA amendment occurred in 1990 with regard to IRS policy pertaining to an employer's treatment of activated reservists. Pursuant to IRS Notice 90-58, employers have two options:

1. Continue normal coverage and payment for the reservist's health plan, including normal dependent coverage, on a *voluntary* basis; or

2. Comply with the COBRA continuance requirements in Section 4980(B) of the IRS Code and thus allow the reservist to continue normal participation in the employer's group health plan, at the reservist's full expense, including normal dependent coverage. Here, the IRS has indicated that the reservist's automatic coverage under the military health plan does *not* qualify for discontinuation of Cobra entitlement.

Chapter 28

CONDUCTING EMPLOYEE PERFORMANCE AND DEVELOPMENT EVALUATIONS

Sooner or later the question arises whether employees should be rated on the basis of their job performance. Actually, supervisors and administrative officials are continually rating their subordinates. No supervisor, for example, directs the work of subordinates without frequently making judgments as to their cooperation, the quality and quantity of their work, their dependability, and so forth. Such judgments are informal ratings. When the question is viewed in this light, the problem is not whether to rate employees, but how shall employees be rated, and how should they be used?

Employee rating systems were first used around the time of World War I and the word "efficiency" was often used in their titles. Supervisors were required to follow a systematic procedure of recording their impressions of all employees under their direct supervision, and the ratings were used as a basis for administrative actions such as pay increases, promotions, demotions, and transfers. These and similar rating systems have not proved too satisfactory, as they tend to hamper the development of good relations between employees and their supervisors. Experience indicates that supervisors generally are unwilling to record adverse ratings for an employee, the ability of the supervisors to rate employees varies considerably, and raters often tend to evaluate employees in terms of their own job outlook. There is evidence that the factors or traits in the older rating systems are not subject to fine distinctions among employees.

In recent years there has been a shift away from the traditional employee rating system—which places emphasis on the use of such ratings for administrative actions—to *service and results expectation ratings*, which serve as a basis for counseling employees regarding the improvement of their performance on the job. For example, many personnel authorities believe that disciplinary matters should be treated in terms of the specific causes rather than in terms of a general service rating program. The "new look" in employee ratings emphasizes the use of performance evaluation as an opportunity for the supervisor to give the employee a better understanding of the job and what is expected of the employee.

While this new type of performance review is simple in concept, it is still necessary to use a prescribed procedure not only to formalize the periodic review but also to provide a record of the employee's performance review.

Some employees will try to take undue privileges or will become careless in work habits. Consequently, a degree of disciplinary control, ranging from the regulation of attendance to dismissal, is necessary. The absence of attendance regulations and records may result in a loss of output representing large sums of money. Supervisors who permit employees to work regularly less than the standard working hours or to report unwarranted leaves of absence with pay as sick leave are spending funds for services that have not been received. Records providing frequent checks on absences, sick leaves, tardiness, and time reports are also a necessary part of each employee's performance history. The main check, however, should be on employee performance, for too rigid control over incidental matters may be at the sacrifice of the real objective—a high standard of output.

HOW PERFORMANCE APPRAISALS SHOULD BE USED

Employee evaluation requires one person to make an official judgment about another person. Few supervisors like this role of judge and few employees like to be rated, yet over the years more and more objectives have been sought by performance ratings. If ratings had accomplished all these objectives, most of the problems of human resource administration would have been solved! Here is a list of the varied uses made of performance ratings:

1. To keep employees informed of what is expected of them and how well they are performing.
2. To recognize and reward good work.
3. To help supervisors recognize and remedy weaknesses in employee performance.
4. To identify employees who should be given specific types of training.
5. To provide a continuing record of an employee's performance history.
6. To serve as a guide to promotions, layoffs, transfers, and other human resource actions.
7. To help determine whether an employee will be given a pay increase, and in what amount if deserved.
8. To check on the reasonableness of established performance standards.
9. To check on the accuracy of job descriptions and classification.
10. To check on the effectiveness of recruitment and examination procedures.
11. To provide productivity measurement.

All these objectives are vitally important to both management and employees. It might be expected therefore that performance rating plans would be generally accepted and approved. This is far from the case. No aspect of human resource administration has had a stormier history than that of performance ratings. No rating plan has yet received complete acceptance, and most have suffered criticism and frequent modification.

PROBLEMS THAT PLAGUE THE EFFECTIVENESS OF PERFORMANCE SYSTEMS

Many of the problems associated with performance appraisal systems lie in three areas:

1. They are designed and used (mostly by rating supervisors) improperly.
2. They suffer from legal vulnerabilities brought on by wrongful discharge litigation.
3. They remain highly subjective tools due to human factors influencing diverse perceptions of performance standards rather than prescribed norms.

To understand better, and therefore control operationally these types of problems, review the following with an eye toward how these conditions can be more suitably managed. Further advice is provided later in this section.

The Fourteen Elements of a Poor Appraisal System

Evaluate these in light of your existing performance appraisal program, and consider what you can do to remedy them when you devise/revise a new approach.

1. Rating factors are so vague or ambiguous that they're meaningless.
2. Rating factors do not apply to particular employees.
3. Rating scales are too restrictive, expansive, or ill defined.
4. Appraisals are done inconsistently or not at all after top salary.
5. Appraisals are rarely done on time.
6. Appraisals are sometimes used as a cumulative disciplinary tool.
7. The rate is not objective for all employees.
8. The employee can score poorly because of insufficient training.
9. Supervisors are not sufficiently trained in necessary fundamentals of effective supervision.
10. The rater uses a "halo effect" or "central tendency" in all appraisals.
11. The employee is not previously told about a particular performance deficiency.
12. The rater fails to discuss rating results with the employee.

13. The employee is not given an opportunity to comment on the appraisal.

14. Appraisals are isolated from other work considerations—they stand alone. There is no consequence of marginal or excellent performance and appraisals are not linked to policies, goals, objectives, or productivity measures.

The Legal Vulnerabilities and Causes of Action Created by Performance Appraisals

Every human resource manager, or other person responsible for personnel operations, needs to consider the question, "How well would we do in court if we had to defend a claim of wrongful discharge (or other adverse action) where our action was based on poor performance—and the claimant's appraisals were subpoenaed by his or her attorney?" Based precisely on these kinds of cases where employers lost in court, the following illustrate the kinds of shortcomings several courts found in the design or use of performance appraisals as a management decision-making tool.

1. Performance (measurement) criteria were far too subjective, ill-defined, and vague when applied to a *particular* position.

2. Documented performance events were insufficient to justify specific ratings and, in particular, there was a lack of detail/honesty concerning specific deficiencies.

3. There was no system for communicating the standards, expectations, and rating factors *in advance* to employees, and providing them reasonable time and guidance to improve in specified weaknesses.

4. There was evidence of negligence/Duty to Use Reasonable Care—pertinent information was knowingly omitted; management was not honest about deficiencies and did not inform the employee of problems and their consequences.

5. Management failed to prepare written instructions and training for raters on the use and conduct of appraisals.

When any of these elements exists in a performance appraisal system, and the employer takes adverse action against an employee under the auspices of unsatisfactory performance of some kind, it can trigger litigation based on such causes of action as:

Discrimination	Wrongful discharge
Defamation	Constructive discharge
Fraud	Retaliatory discharge
Negligence	Emotional distress
Harassment	Deprivation of privacy rights

The Human Factor in Rating Performance

As supervisors play such a key role in rating, any organization that seeks to administer an employee evaluation program with some success must remember that supervisors are human. They will therefore tend to react favorably toward some employees, unfavorably toward others. The most common causes of rating errors are:

1. *Halo Effect*

   Many times supervisors evaluate the employee in terms of a general mental attitude rather than by *systematic attention to particular traits* to be rated. For example, if an employee puts out a large volume of work, a supervisor may also rate the accuracy of work, dependability, and cooperation higher than these traits actually deserve. Conversely, the employer may downgrade another employee on all counts because the employee sometimes makes mistakes. The basic question a supervisor must ask to minimize the halo effect is: "Am I rating this trait on performance or on my general perception of this employee as 'good' or 'bad'?"

2. *Prejudice and Partiality*

   It is unfortunately true that some supervisors will be influenced by matters like race, sex, religion, or nationality, and some may have a tendency to favor friends, or people with interests and activities similar to their own. The basic question a supervisor must ask to minimize the possibility of prejudice or partiality is: "Am I making this judgment on the basis of the real individual or on the grounds that the employee is a protestant—a black—a man—a fellow member of the Elks Club?"

3. *Leniency*

   Leniency occurs when the supervisor rates higher than the realities of employee performance warrant. The effects are (a) to force ratings so drastically toward the top of the rating scale that they are valueless and (b) to create unrealistic employee confidence when improvement in performance is really needed and quite possible. Leniency is by far the most common rating error. There are a number of pressures on supervisors that tempt them to be lenient: the wish to avoid unpleasant scenes, the feeling that low ratings reflect poor supervision, the desire to retain the friendship of their employees, and often the belief that other supervisors do not rate fairly and they do not want to penalize their own employees.

4. *Central Tendency*

   In any normal distribution, more people will of course be rated closer to the mean than to any other point on the scale. A rating near the norm becomes a central tendency error only when it does not reflect a true evaluation of performance. It is most likely to occur when the supervisor does not know a worker very well or when there is difficulty in collecting sufficient data or observations of the employee's varied work activities. One of the most frequent errors made by raters that blatantly reflects central tendency is to give an employee the same rating level of performance in each rating category—a condition that is nearly impossible to achieve given basic human differences.

5. *Contrast Error*

   This type of rating error arises from the tendency of some supervisors to rate employees in terms of their own expectations and aspirations. In other words, employees who satisfy the personal needs of the supervisor will generally be rated higher and vice versa. Questions like: "Do I make this rating because I expect others to be like me?" can help to overcome contrast error.

6. *Association Error*

   This kind of rating error is caused by several types of "associations." Some supervisors find it difficult to differentiate between traits because they overlap semantically for them. For example, they may tend to equate dependability and cooperation and rate one trait higher or lower than is proper. This error is similar to the halo type of error. The positions of traits on a scale and the time at which the supervisor encounters them also constitute associations that may produce errors. For example, it has been found that the ratings on traits adjacent to each other on a scale are apt to be more consistent than those some distance away on the form. The association of error with fatigue is also common, and so is the error that can occur because of the time at which the supervisor comes to the rating of a given individual. For example, an employee may be rated higher if the supervisor has just rated John than if the supervisor had just rated Paul.

Proponents of employee evaluation cannot, and do not, deny that problems of error will plague any formal rating system. They contend, however, that a great many decisions and actions in the course of human relationships depend on opinion. Instead of lamenting this fact, attention should be given to finding a means of putting such opinion on a more systematic and factual basis.

WHAT PERFORMANCE DIMENSIONS SHOULD BE USED FOR VALID RESULTS?

Regrettably, in many instances it has been the courts who have forced human resource practitioners to be more precise and analytical about administering various personnel functions. Such has been the case with analyzing jobs for compliance with a host of fair employment laws, and it now applies to being more thoughtful, and thorough, with regard to designing and using appraisal systems that result in greater reliability/validity of ensuing employment decision making.

Consequently, the emphasis that must be placed on new or revised performance appraisal instruments is twofold:

1. Performance dimensions to be evaluated must be defined, and applicable, for *each* distinct and separate job to ensure true validity.
2. Each dimension must be assigned a relative weighting factor (percentage of frequency, importance, and difficulty of the total job is suggested) to give ratings proper perspective.

One of the first steps to be taken is to convert weak and/or legally vulnerable performance dimensions into more meaningful dimensions that better measure realistic productivity and contribution to the organization. Here are a few illustrative examples:

Weak Dimension	Job-Related Dimension
Loyalty	Adaptation to work conditions
Dependability	Reliability for thorough/timely work
Health	Appearance and demeanor
Attendance	Attendance to duties
Intelligence	Job knowledge and skills
Promotability	Job progress
Attitude	Behavior
Risk taking	Judgment and decision making
Results	Achievement of established goals

In terms of the "what" and "how" being evaluated within each job, you may wish to incorporate the following into your appraisal instrument. After all, the most important features of each employee's performance to the organization is *what they do* and *how they do it* (methods, procedures, approaches, skills, etc.). See how some of these rating categories are used in the sample Employee Performance Evaluation Report in Chapter 8.

What	How
Job function characteristics	
Routine tasks	Methods and techniques
Projects	Processes and procedures
Special assignments	Behavior and conduct
Traits and skills	Adaptations
Performance measurement dimensions	
Results	Efficiency and economy
Quantity	Timeliness, accuracy, and amount
Diversity	Quality
Proficiency	Work habits

DEVELOPING A RATING PLAN

While no one rating plan can be recommended for all employers, a few general guidelines can be suggested that will help you adapt various rating approaches to meet your own needs.

The size and character of the organization should be considered first. In a small- or medium-sized organization it would be unwise to adopt an elaborate system requiring highly technical research in the development and administration of the plan. Although relatively simple rating plans are generally preferred, it should not be inferred that simplicity of the rating form itself is necessarily a virtue or that a rating form that can be quickly filled out is necessarily simple to administer. If ratings are to be used to guide decisions on personnel matters, they must cover all pertinent job factors, and supervisors must make their decisions with care and deliberation. A "simple" rating system is one that supervisors and employees understand and find acceptable.

The supervisor is the crucial factor in employee evaluation, and it takes time to train supervisors to rate accurately and fairly. For this reason, it is generally wise to proceed from a simple plan to a more refined plan as the need for improvement is recognized and as supervisors and employees demonstrate their ability and willingness to refine evaluation procedures.

Regardless of the type of rating plan selected, it is desirable to analyze the positions to be rated to select the personal traits or qualities of employee behavior that are to be measured, to key rating factors to the type of job tasks being performed, and to determine the job performance standards to be applied in developing a rating form.

GATHERING PERFORMANCE DATA AND CONDUCTING EMPLOYEE REVIEWS

It is absolutely essential that supervisors keep regular records of commendable or deficient work of individual employees. If supervisors rely on their memory, there is great hazard that when the time comes to rate, the most recent positive performance will predominate over the longer-standing weaknesses for some employees, and the weaknesses over the positive for others. These records are made when performance situations arise and become a part of the supervisor's desk notes. (See Chapter 29 for a more detailed discussion of supervisory desk notes.)

It is essential that supervisors discuss with each employee the ratings given, openly and in as much detail as is needed for common understanding, if not full agreement. It is only through such discussions that supervisors can put service ratings to their most important use—pointing out strengths and weaknesses to every subordinate and suggesting ways in which the employee can improve performance.

The employee should be required to sign his or her name to the rating form to indicate that it has been received. The signature is not an endorsement of the rating, but merely attests to the fact that the rating has been disclosed through discussion, and an unaltered copy given to the employee.

A counseling interview to improve employee performance must be based on factual information, but the success of the interview will depend on how facts are presented and discussed.

Planning and Preparation for the Review Meeting

1. Review the employee's job and what it takes to do it as well as the employee's record, experience, and training allow. Review your evaluation of the employee's performance.
   a. Consider why you evaluated the employee's work as you did.
   b. Have available specific facts or illustrations to substantiate your position.
2. Determine what you want to accomplish in the interview and plan your discussion accordingly. You might want to accomplish some of the following:
   a. Leave the employee with more *will to work*.
   b. Give as much information of *specific strengths and weaknesses* as the situation warrants.
   c. Give a *specific or general statement of the employee's overall effectiveness*.
   d. Work out with the employee a few specific steps that both of you are to undertake for betterment. This might include a special assignment in a field where there is weakness, thereby providing additional training.
3. Plan to meet in private. If this is the employee's first evaluation interview, anticipate some curiosity, tension, or anxiety—and prepare to reduce it.

Manner for the Review Meeting

The most effective evaluation interviews are those in which the stage has been set properly. Here are some things to think about:

1. Create the impression that *you* have time for the interview and you consider it highly important.
2. Throughout the interview, place primary emphasis on development and growth of the individual. Make the employee feel that the interview is a constructive, cooperative one. Avoid implications that the meeting is or could be used for disciplinary purposes.
3. Be open-minded to the opinions and facts presented by the employee. Be willing to learn more about the employee, and be prepared to change your estimation in the light of additional, or persuasive evidence.
4. Don't dominate or cross-examine, avoid argument, listen attentively as well as politely, and give confirming feedback.
5. Remember that the employee must do most of the talking at some points of the interview:

   a. Try to bring opinions and feelings to the surface and to your attention.

   b. Give the employee an opportunity to better understand his or her own expectations in light of the organization's expectations and perceptions.

The Review—Beginning

Pick the right time, day, and place. Don't conduct the interview too soon after a disciplinary action or a disagreement. Pick a time when you're in a good mood and when you have reason to believe the employee feels the same.

1. Put the employee at ease. If necessary, talk first about informal interests or the general purpose of the Performance and Development Program. Be friendly!
2. Get the employee talking.
3. Explain the objectives of the evaluation interview; point out that everyone is involved; invite the employee to raise questions and introduce problems; give a feeling of security. Express an interest in helping the employee with his or her job and future.

The Review—Techniques

Talk about good points first, then cover each point in detail. This starts the heart of the interview off on the right foot, as any criticism is prefaced by comment on the more favorable aspects of the employee's performance.

    Remember that the aim is to encourage improved performance, not to chastise the employee. Here are a few more techniques:

1. You may want the employee to start with a self-evaluation.
2. Show appreciation of past successes.
3. Be direct, factual, and tactful in dealing with deficiencies. Move the discussion into prevention of future deficiencies. Build upon strengths.
4. In almost every case allow for face-saving. Explain that you yourself may share some of the blame for work failures.
5. Guide the interview. Don't let it get out of hand. Pull the employee back from detours, escapes, or fruitless conversation.
6. Don't talk about the *employee;* instead, talk about the employee's work relative to the organization's standards.

Closing the Review Meeting

1. Review the points made in the interview and encourage the employee to summarize those points.
2. Always reassure the employee of your interest in his or her progress, and indicate your willingness to continue the discussion at any time.

3. Close when you have made clear the points you intended to cover; when the employee has had a chance to review problems and release any emotional tensions that may exist; when plans of action have been cooperatively developed; and when you and the employee are at a natural stopping point.

EVALUATING THE PERFORMANCE OF NEW EMPLOYEES[1]

This issue is somewhat of a judgment call depending on such conditions as the new employee's existing abilities and learning rate, the complexity of the job and/or company operations, the duration of the initial employment (integration) period, and the time required for the new employee to be exposed to a representative range of job responsibilities. However, as a general rule, effective performance evaluation programs for new employees typically require that they be formally evaluated at least three times during their initial employment period. If, for example, the job is such that initial employment is as brief as ninety days, then written appraisals would be conducted at the end of each thirty-day period. Should the job require an initial employment period of more than six months, formal appraisals should be conducted at the end of every second or third month.

Informal appraisals should be a matter of daily and weekly occurrence. Informal appraisals consist of verbal evaluations made by the supervisor to the new employee in a casual manner as notable performance events occur. They range from complimentary comments to corrective meetings. Complimentary comments should be made on those occasions when the employee demonstrates his or her use of skills or information learned—positive performance feedback—which serves to reinforce and motivate the employee toward desired performance. Corrective meetings, at the other end of the performance feedback spectrum, should be conducted in private by the supervisor with the new employee. These meetings should be conducted for the purpose of discussing progress or problems regarding *specific* performance areas or to agree on a corrective plan of action concerning a serious performance deficiency.

It is extremely important for these types of performance comments and discussions to be communicated at the time notable events take place, or otherwise materialize, rather than deferring them until the formal appraisal is prepared. Quite simply, people will be more responsive to the learning aspect of performance feedback, whether verbal or written, when it is communicated at the time of a notable event or pattern of performance, when it is done honestly and fairly, and when it is done with genuine interest.

Observing and Documenting Performance Events

To evaluate the performance of new employees properly, the supervisor must ensure that five preexisting conditions are met. These conditions are:

---

[1]   Levesque, *The Complete Hiring Manual*, pp. 276–277.

1. The supervisor should be confident that the employee is receiving adequate training and guidance on employment matters.

2. The supervisor should have provided the new employee with thorough details about the performance expectations, standards, and rating levels at the time of orientation, or soon thereafter.

3. The supervisor should be deliberate about assigning the new employee progressively more responsible, diverse, and representative tasks of the job to evaluate a sufficient cross section of the employee's abilities and adaptations.

4. The supervisor should take the time and opportunity to interact frequently with new employees so that they have a solid basis of observation of the employee's performance results.

5. The supervisor should have adequate documentation of notable performance events that support performance ratings and commentary.

Since the first three conditions should have been met by recommendations made earlier in this book, it is the last two conditions that should be the focus of attention at this stage in the new employee's relationship with the company.

What Is Reasonable Performance Observation?

Reasonable performance observation means that the evaluating supervisor has regular, frequent, and direct contact with the new employee concerning their work activities. This interaction between the supervisor and new employee should be such that the nature of contact provides the supervisor with sufficient opportunity to fully observe performance activities, behaviors, and results. To do so, the supervisor should be located in a place where routine visual observation can be made such as from the supervisor's office or by normal activities performed in the vicinity of the employee.

Supervisors also need to develop a trained eye concerning what aspects of a new employee's performance should be observed for purposes of evaluation. Most supervisors tend to watch for only performance ability characteristics in new employees such as the nature of skills applied to the job, quality and amount of work produced, the extent of the employee's job knowledge, and other aspects of the job itself. While these are important observations to make, they are too narrow since they concentrate only on the job and omit other employment relevant characteristics of the employee's adaptation to conditions. In this regard, the supervisor should make a point of additionally observing such performance related concerns as:

1. Is the nature of the employee's interaction with co-workers pleasant, cooperative, supportive, caring, and in other respects team oriented?

2. Is the employee responsive to supervision and management?

3. Does the employee comply with policies, procedures, and established practices?

4. Does the employee demonstrate a sincere interest in the company, operating objectives, their work, and the people involved?

5. Is the employee self-motivated about seeking more work, given greater responsibility, getting questions answered, and obtaining guidance?

6. Does the employee bring enthusiasm and contributory ideas to his or her work?

These are just a few thought-provoking questions that supervisors should be asking themselves when conducting performance appraisals that consider both performance results and employment adaptations of new employees. However, to evaluate these joint performance characteristics, supervisors must condition themselves to be observant, and then document them properly for future reference when conducting meetings or formal appraisals with the employee.

Other Sources of Performance Information[2]

Companies would do well to establish an operational culture of everyone in the work unit, and related work units, having a stake in the success of new employees. When such cultures operate, there is a greater likelihood of a new employee's integration success because there is more uniform support for the employee's achievement. The additional benefit is that it provides the new employee's supervisor with more direct linkage to other sources of performance evaluation information.

It is also interesting to note the existence of a rather peculiar set of contradictory practices relating to the acquisition and use of performance information on employees. On the one hand, employers customarily try very hard to obtain performance-related information from former employers (virtually unknown sources of reliable information) about prospective new hires to evaluate the applicant's suitability for employment. Yet, once we hire someone, we overlook using internal, and presumably more reliable, sources of information about the new employee's actual performance. This contradiction suggests that employers are not taking advantage of available and firsthand reliable sources of additional performance information concerning the abilities and adaptive characteristics of new employees. In those organizations that establish a culture of "shared ownership" in the success of a new employee, the supervisor can broaden the base of performance information to the new employee's coworkers, other supervisors, and departmental managers having work exposure to the new employee, and even customers or clients having contact with the new employee.

To be as impartial as possible, and to obtain sufficient information for the purposes of rendering thorough evaluations, it is imperative that the supervisor use these types of additional sources of constructive performance information. Experience has shown that when employees are evaluated from more than one source of perceptual judgment, they tend to give the results of the evaluation more

---

[2]   Levesque, *The Complete Hiring Manual*, pp. 278–280.

credibility. This added credibility reinforces the concept that performance evaluations are intended to serve as a positive method to guide the employee's growth and success in the job. Consequently, the employee becomes more responsive to its findings rather than feeling pitted against the singular judgment of his or her supervisor. It also suggests to the employee that suitable performance must be displayed toward everyone, not merely when the supervisor is present.

Progress Conferences: Keeping the New Employee Informed and Building Confidence

New employees are more than casually interested in how they are doing in their new job and fitting into the organization, assuming of course you have hired quality people. This interest in obtaining performance feedback is much more intense with new employees because they usually need affirmation from those they are responsible to, and work with, that they fit in, do good work, are liked, demonstrate progressive adjustment and learning, and in other respects are recognized for their contributory worth. New employees also want others to see them in the same light as they see themselves. They obviously sold you on their abilities and worth, so it becomes natural for them to want external feedback that you and others agree with their assessment—that they belong.

Again, using the parallel of a new born's development, when humans are placed in unfamiliar and uncertain situations, they need more frequent, thorough, and consistent reinforcement of desired behavior than when self-confidence is obtained. To create a positive and accepting self-image in youngsters, we know that we should give them frequent recognition and reward for demonstrating positive actions and behavior. We have also been misled to believe that continuing this supportive form of human reinforcement is unnecessary once people achieve adulthood. Nothing could be further from the truth since human nature, rather than the age or stage of development of humans, dictates that all people experience varying levels of self-confidence and will thus periodically need supportive reinforcement to maintain a positive self-image—a requisite condition to feeling good about oneself and toward others.

Given the vulnerability of a person's self-confidence produced by new employment conditions, it is important for supervisors to be aware of each new employee's need for positive reinforcement of their performance abilities and adaptations. Positive reinforcement means complimentary comments as well as constructively worded criticisms. Both should be supportive in nature and convey the intent to provide guidance to the new employee. Because new employees will be inherently sensitive to any form of criticism, the manner in which they are posed should always be done in a positive fashion, followed by seeking opportunities to compliment the employee for their corrected action or behavior.

Reinforcing interaction with new employees should be a consciously planned part of the integration, training, and evaluation process—the period in which confidence can be created or broken. The key opportunities to build a new employee's confidence are at the time positive performance is observed by making brief comments that acknowledge and reinforce the performance, and during progress conferences with the new employee. These conferences should be conducted in conjunction with formal evaluations where the totality of the new employee's performance and adaptive progress is discussed openly and thoroughly. They should be conducted by either the employee's supervisor and department manager or the employee's supervisor and another closely associated supervisor (or perhaps even a senior-level employee familiar with the employee's work).

During the progress conference, emphasis should be placed on what has occurred since the employee's hire—or last appraisal—performance achievements, complimentary examples of performance events, and mention of the value such performance has on the operational unit. This discussion should be followed by any areas of performance or adaptation needing further development, concentration, or correction. Again, examples should be used to clarify the employee's understanding of these issues and reinforce further learning about where the company places value. The discussion should also encourage the new employee to participate in the conversation and conclude with mutually agreed plans for work activities and further performance development during the next evaluation period. Keep in mind that progress conferences should *always* end on a positive note. Remember, your objective is to build confidence, self-esteem, and successful employees who will want to share their success with others in the organization. If you can achieve this result, you have made the right hiring choice.

TRAINING SUPERVISORS TO RATE EMPLOYEES

The key to improved employee evaluation is development of the rating abilities of supervisors. All experience indicates that it is impossible to devise a rating form or system that is self-operating and foolproof. Any training undertaken to improve supervisory abilities is a step toward better rating results, but there is need for training supervisory personnel in the principles and procedures of rating as such. Higher-level managers who have influence on the evaluation of line employees are no exception. They, too, must understand and use the same objective principles of judging performance and attendant decisions as those initiating the ratings.

CHECKLIST: DEVELOPING AN EFFECTIVE PERFORMANCE APPRAISAL SYSTEM

- ☐ Design appraisals with weighted dimensions that are job related and measurable and account for all aspects of performance, not just job tasks.
- ☐ Develop clear and concise policy statements on the purpose, application, occurrences, and consequences of appraisal results.
- ☐ Link organizational, departmental, and/or work unit goals and objectives to the appraisal system in terms of measurable productivity standards.
- ☐ Prepare written guidelines on the use of the appraisal system for rating supervisors and managers.
- ☐ Require by policy that all formal appraisals are to be discussed with applicable employees, they are to be given a copy of the appraisal, and correction of deficiencies are to be followed up and documented.
- ☐ Establish a review mechanism whereby employees can request review of the appraisal by a higher authority—without reprisal.
- ☐ Centrally review all appraisals before deposit into employee personnel files.

CHECKLIST: PERFORMANCE APPRAISAL SYSTEM SUPPORT COMPONENTS

- ☐ Merit pay increases
- ☐ Performance recognition awards
- ☐ Distinguished performance pay
- ☐ Performance bonuses
- ☐ Suggestion incentive awards
- ☐ Employee training and development program
- ☐ Consequences of marginal performance
- ☐ Evaluation of initial and promotional performance
- ☐ Consequences of unacceptable performance
- ☐ Causes of discipline and other corrective actions

Chapter 29

DISCIPLINE AND DISCHARGE: CONTROLLING PERFORMANCE AND CONDUCT IN THE WORKPLACE

THE CHANGING NATURE OF WORKPLACE DISCIPLINE

There is little doubt that discipline presents one of the most, if not *the* most, difficult and vulnerable tasks of managers and supervisors. By the time a particular problem employee is in a position necessitating disciplinary measures, the attending supervisor is usually frustrated, annoyed, and often angry—and may show a corresponding change in attitude toward the employee. The situation can frequently become adversarial where personalities and differing perceptions take over, resulting in the creation of a new problem between supervisor and employee instead of a solution to the work problem. This capsulization of the disciplinary process points to one fact that business managers have been avoiding for years—if not handled correctly, discipline rarely works as a modifier of employee behavior—particularly when the more serious forms of discipline (demotion, pay reduction, and suspension) are imposed. In many instances, some forms of discipline will transform a difficult situation into an impossible one.

True, these are very generalized statements, and they can be dangerous considering the vast array of conditions leading up to a particular disciplinary matter. However, some generalizations may prove helpful in gaining better insight into some of the critical considerations of specific disciplinary circumstances.

Discipline rarely works to effectively resolve some problem employee situations for three reasons. First, our disciplinary methods do not have the same behavior modification effect on our present work force, with its new values, ideals, and perceptions, as these same methods did two or more decades ago. Second, discipline tends to be used as a remedy for the *effect* of an employee's action rather than to ascertain and attempt to deal with the *cause*. Third, the actual handling or imposition of discipline is often poor because of a lack of the analytical and human skills necessary to proper fact finding, counseling, documentation, and objective decision making. For the skeptic who doubts these contentions, one needs only to examine the increasing number (and cost) of discipline and discharge cases disfavoring the actions of employers through judgments of the courts, compliance agencies, and arbitrators to be thoroughly convinced that 1960s practices are no longer effective in the contemporary work setting.

The point has been made that today's work force is substantially different from that of earlier decades. To illustrate this issue briefly and correlate it to working conditions that employers will have to deal with, consider the following features of today's work force:

- The work force is equally represented by men and by women.
- Over three-fourths of the work force consists of two wage earners (not economically influenced if suspended for a few days).
- A significant and growing number of the work force are single parents (stress, tardiness, absenteeism, sick leave use).
- The work force is better educated and exposed to more media information (willingness to confront unreasonable/unfair situations).
- Personal values emphasize self, individuality, short-term goals, identifying with inequities, and following "causes."

The list is nearly endless. Each distinguishing characteristic of this new work force will manifest itself in some equally distinguishing behavior, or perception of what is fair and reasonable, in the workplace. It may be in demands for more equitable pay, a desire for more time off, or a disregard for the employer's standards of performance or conduct. Today's employees will clearly present the employer with some of the most unusual and challenging situations ever imagined—and some never imagined!

Managers and supervisors must learn to avoid using discipline as a means of dealing with the effect of a problem, rather than treating the cause. For example, an employee begins to show up from ten to twenty minutes late once or twice a week. The employee is regarded as a good worker, the amount of time lost is not serious and was apologized for, so no action is taken but observation continues. Sure enough, the pattern of tardiness persists (or reappears perhaps after a verbal warning), and the supervisor must act. At this juncture, there are two courses for the supervisor: (1) The supervisor can give the employee a verbal or written reprimand and hope it warns the employee that the company will not tolerate tardiness (effect), and the employee may be fired if it continues (punishment). (2) The supervisor can identify the cause of the tardiness, advise the employee of how the tardiness affects work and others (consequence), and work with the employee to eliminate the real problem—which may well be a car problem, a babysitter problem, or any number of other problems that may be within the employer's power to help resolve or accommodate, rather than disciplining a good employee. Good employees don't stop being good employees without reason. There is usually a physical, emotional, or personal event that precedes a decline in performance or a marked change in an employee's behavior. The skilled supervisor will deal with such causes before they evolve into disciplinary problems and will then truly be "managing human resources."

ELEMENTS OF AN EFFECTIVE PROGRAM

Generally, there are three conditions leading to the need for discipline, and they are:

1. The employee is performing below job standards in terms of work quantity, quality, method, timeliness, or cost. These are the performance measures upon which all employees are evaluated for overall effectiveness, and they should be measurable in very precise terms when they become a disciplinary matter. A word of caution here. Performance deficiencies that are disciplinary in nature should be dealt with apart from the employee's scheduled performance evaluation. The only thing that *may* be appropriate to show on the performance evaluation is the *effect* the deficiency had on a particular performance rating—not the crime itself.

2. The employee disobeys prescribed rules of conduct, behavior, or general performance (reporting to work on time), presuming of course the employee knows about such rules.

3. The employee interferes with the performance of others, or does something damaging to the reputation or welfare of the employer, other employees, or to the employee's own credibility.

The need for discipline is usually caused by performance-related conditions on the job or conduct on—and sometimes off—the job. The most essential point to remember is that the cause of discipline must be directly (or reasonably) related to the employee's job, the effect upon other employees, or the reputation and welfare of the employer.

CHECKLIST: ELEMENTS OF AN EFFECTIVE DISCIPLINE PROGRAM

- ☐ A written discipline policy that expresses the organization's intent and philosophy concerning discipline.
- ☐ Clear, concise, and reasonable written rules of conduct and performance standards.
- ☐ Written and well-thought-out job descriptions and job-related performance appraisal standards.
- ☐ Thorough written and verbal communications with employees.
  - ☐ Provide and explain above documents
  - ☐ Communicate deviations rapidly, and explain reasons
  - ☐ Keep a supervisor's "desk log"
- ☐ Organizational continuity.
  - ☐ Leadership style
  - ☐ Consistency of enforcement decisions
  - ☐ Objectivity and flexibility
- ☐ Use of "progressive discipline" wherever appropriate.
- ☐ Supervisors and management trained to avoid the Seven Sins of Discipline
  - ☐ Not gathering sufficient facts
  - ☐ Losing one's temper or showing inappropriate emotions
  - ☐ Not being precise or expedient with the problem
  - ☐ Not allowing the employee to tell his or her story
  - ☐ Not taking accurate notes/preparing documents
  - ☐ Not taking some decisive action
  - ☐ Holding a grudge or stigmatizing the employee
- ☐ A well-publicized and impartial dispute resolution/grievance procedure through which employees can obtain higher-level review of complaints of unfair treatment.

DEALING WITH COMMON DISCIPLINE PROBLEMS

To help guide business managers and supervisors in the analysis and handling of some of the more frequently encountered workplace problems, the following pages contain an outlined overview of several situations. There are many similarities in the causes of these problems and many crucial differences. The similarities should draw out a certain pattern of disciplinary action that can be established, while the differences may allow a degree of flexibility where sound judgment and discretion become essential.

Tardiness

Tardiness is perhaps not a blatant abuse, but it is disruptive and expensive for any organization. It can be more difficult to remedy. For example, arriving late for work, leaving early, or taking excessively long lunch breaks may be regarded by employees as customary and within the informal tolerance levels of the organization. This view may even be reinforced by the behavior of a supervisor, who also is inclined to disregard the formal timekeeping policy.

Efforts to deal with such a problem require a twofold approach. First, the organization must communicate to all employees precise details of any new or previously disregarded rules. Second, supervisors must communicate their expectations of employees according to the rules and provide a proper example themselves when the rules apply to them equally. Standards for dealing with offenders must be applied consistently and equitably.

Arbitrarily singling out one individual employee for disciplinary action when the incidence of the offense is widespread is inadvisable. However, supervisors should not refrain altogether from taking corrective action on an individual basis. Maintaining accurate records of punctuality enables supervisors to determine which employees are repeated offenders. For these repeated offenders, each violation should be called to their attention. The supervisor should try to determine why the employee was not punctual and if there was any justification for the tardiness. In such a case, supervisors are essentially performing as counselors. They should fully acquaint the employee with the reasons for the policy, emphasizing the importance of employee cooperation.

Absenteeism

The most prevalent disciplinary problem in most organizations is absenteeism. It is a difficult violation to deal with because of the problems in establishing that absence was in fact an abuse. A supervisor considering discipline should reflect on the following questions before imposing discipline:

- Is the employee's absenteeism well beyond the average for other employees?
- Was there a pattern (absence before and after days off)?

- Was there a thorough investigation and documentation?
- Is it reasonable to conclude that the absence was not due to a continuing medical condition?
- Were there prior efforts to counsel and assist the employee in improving attendance?
- Is there likelihood of improvement in the future?
- Was the attendance policy clear and communicated to the employee?

Insubordination

There are certain essential ingredients that must be present before an employee can be disciplined for failure to obey a direction of a supervisor. For insubordination to exist:

1. There must be an order or a clearly directed expectation expressed to the employee.
2. The order must be reasonable.
3. The order must be communicated clearly to the employee.
4. The order must be communicated by someone with the proper authority.
5. The employee must have understood the order.
6. The employee must actually refuse to comply verbally or by failure to act.

Actions of an employee toward a supervisor are classed as insubordination where those actions involve a resistance to, or a defiance of, the supervisor's authority. Two of the most common types of insubordination are insolent or obscene language used to challenge a supervisor's authority and the refusal to obey an order of a supervisor.

In determining whether the language used by an employee should be classed as insubordination, a supervisor must take cognizance of the normal language used in the workplace. An employee cannot be held insubordinate for swearing at a supervisor if the words used by the employee are commonly used by other employees and the supervisor. The key element that *must* be considered is whether the words and actions of the employee are such that they challenge the supervisor's authority.

The "work now, grieve later" rule is well established. However, there are instances where an employee may be justified in disobeying an order. Employees may in some instances refuse to comply with a supervisor's order when it involves the following circumstances:

- A danger to personal health and safety.
- The involvement in an illegal act.

- An invasion of an employee's privacy.
- A reasonable personal excuse.

Once it has been determined that an employee's refusal to obey a supervisor's order properly constitutes insubordination, the following factors should be considered in assessing discipline:

1. To what degree was the refusal to obey a specific order intended as an obvious undermining of managerial authority (the employee's attitude)?
2. Was the employee provoked into the disobedience?
3. Was the act an instant reaction and did the employee apologize (was the employee remorseful)?
4. Was the act an isolated one or another example of continuing difficulties with the supervisor-employee relationship; was the act another example of the employee's persistent defiance of authority?
5. Was the order given in conflict with orders given earlier or with generally accepted organization rules?
6. What is the employee's seniority and work record—good or poor?

If termination is indicated, it must be shown that termination of employment is the only reasonable course of action, especially in cases where the insubordination might result more from a personality conflict between the supervisor and the subordinate, or where the supervisor's managerial style could be found wanting (for example, biased or authoritative). Consideration must also be given to the severity of discipline in terms of management's past efforts to rehabilitate the employee and the mitigating circumstances surrounding the insubordination (workers who are under severe emotional strain because of family problems; spontaneous as opposed to premeditated insubordination).

Violation of Policies and Rules

Employers have the right to issue a wide variety of work and conduct rules as long as they are not inconsistent in their application. To be enforceable, such rules must be reasonable and easily understood. They must have been made known to employees and administered fairly and consistently.

Incompetence/Inefficiency

Employees face performance problems in doing their work in a satisfactory manner. It is important to distinguish between carelessness—which borders on misconduct—and incompetence or the inability of an otherwise well-intentioned employee to perform satisfactorily.

Incompetence is one of the most difficult bases on which to justify discipline, particularly termination. Arbitrators are generally reluctant to terminate the employment of an employee found inefficient/incompetent at performing specific job responsibilities. They want to be convinced that the employer has given the employee every assistance to succeed, has considered every employment option, and has reasonably concluded that termination is the only course of action.

An organization considering discipline for incompetency should ask the following questions prior to taking such discipline:

- Were standards of performance set that were not met by the employee?
- Were standards of performance realistic and made known to the employee?
- Did the employee receive proper instruction as to the nature of the duties and responsibilities?
- Was the employee given a "reasonable opportunity" to demonstrate performance?
- Was the employee advised of shortcomings and given a reasonable opportunity to improve?
- Was the employee offered counseling and retraining?
- Was the performance assessed objectively, fairly, and properly without discrimination against standards that could be reasonably considered attainable by the average worker?
- Was consideration given to the assignment of other duties?

Theft

Where theft is proven, substantial discipline is upheld for even a minor theft. While termination is the usual penalty, the following factors must be considered in possibly lessening the penalty:

- What is the value of the property stolen (is it substantial or nominal)?
- Had the employee really stolen the article or sincerely been under the impression that the item was merely being borrowed (tools, equipment)?
- Had the employer consistently applied its rules regarding thefts?
- Was the employee's act of theft impulsive or premeditated?
- Was the particular incident an isolated incident or part of a continuing scheme of theft?
- What kind of service record does the employee have? How many years' seniority?
- Is the employee in a position of trust?
- Is this the first case of theft for this employee?
- Are these extenuating circumstances to the theft, circumstances that might call for compassion?

Falsification of Records

In falsification involving time cards, production records, overtime sheets, or any other official records, discipline is normally justified except where falsification might have arisen from provocation, strong momentary impulse, or other extenuating circumstances. The following mitigating circumstances are normally considered:

- The previous record of the employee.
- The service of the employee.
- Whether the offense was an isolated incident in the employment history of the employee.
- Provocation.
- Whether the offense was committed on the spur of the moment or premeditated.
- Whether the penalty imposed had created a special economic hardship for the employee in the light of his or her particular circumstances.
- Evidence that the organization's rules regarding falsification have not been uniformly enforced, thus constituting a form of discrimination.
- The seriousness of the offense in terms of organization policy and obligations.

Assaulting a Supervisor

It is a general rule that assaulting a supervisor calls for bypassing the steps of progressive discipline. On the premise that an employee's fight with a supervisor essentially destroys the supervisor-subordinate relationship, termination may be supported for a first offense. Some compassion has been shown, however, where the personalities of the individuals were obviously in direct conflict; where the outburst could be due to extenuating personal circumstances (marital or financial problems), where the employee has an unblemished record, where the act was obviously a temporary outburst for which the employee is in deep remorse, or where the employee was provoked by inappropriate action of the supervisor.

Employee Fighting

Altercations between two employees at the work site normally warrant some type of discipline. Termination may be supported in cases where the employer's property has been damaged, where serious injury has resulted, where a dangerous weapon was used in the altercation, where the fight was vicious or one sided, or where the altercation can be readily seen as a culminating incident in the poor record of a particular employee. Lesser discipline is usually appropriate where the altercation was a momentary flare-up, where it did not result in any major injury, where it is due to extenuating circumstances, and where there is remorse after the altercation.

An organization considering discipline for fighting should weigh the following factors:

- The identity of the person attacked.
- Whether the assault was a momentary flare-up or a premeditated attack.
- The seriousness of the attack.
- The presence or absence of provocation.
- The disciplinary record of the employee.
- The presence or absence of an apology, and correction of the cause of th altercation.

Horseplay/Pranks

Discharge is seldom imposed for employees being involved in horseplay at the work site. In most cases, much lesser degrees of discipline are sufficient, especially in relation to minor pranks. However, more severe discipline, including termination, may be applied where the horseplay or prank is a breach of safety rules, where someone is, or could have been seriously injured, or where the perpetrator has been unduly harassing another employee.

Off-Duty Conduct

The general rule is that an employee's life outside work hours is that employee's personal business. The possibility of an employer's having to discipline an employee for off-duty conduct depends on a variety of factors, including the type of conduct, the on-the-job duties of the employee, the nature of the employer's operations, and the effect of the conduct on the employee-employer or employee-supervisor relationships at the workplace.

An organization contemplating disciplinary action for off-the-job activities should ask the following questions:

- Was the employee's conduct sufficiently injurious to the interests of the employer or co-workers?
- Did the employee act in a manner incompatible with the due and faithful discharge of duties and responsibilities?
- Did the employee do anything prejudicial or likely to be prejudicial to the reputation of the employer?

If disciplinary action is to be sustained on the basis of a justifiable reason arising out of conduct away from the workplace, the organization must show the following:

- The conduct of the employee harms the organization's reputation.
- The employee's behavior renders the employee unable to perform duties satisfactorily or in a credible manner.
- The employee's behavior leads to refusal, reluctance, or inability of the other employees to work with the employee.
- The employee has been guilty of criminal conduct, rendering the conduct injurious to the general reputation of the organization and its employees.
- The offense for which the employee has been found guilty makes it difficult for the organization to carry out its function of managing its work force efficiently.

Criminal Offenses

It is generally accepted that an employee who is convicted of a criminal offense committed during the course of employment, which jeopardizes the employer's property and security, its public reputation, or the interests of the other employees, may be terminated. Similarly, an employee who is convicted of a criminal offense during off-duty hours, if it prejudices any one of those interests, may also be terminated by the employer. Conversely, however, it has also been held that where an employee is convicted of a criminal offense that is unrelated to the employment relationship, and that does not affect the employer's legitimate interest, the employee cannot be disciplined or terminated for that misconduct alone. The employee's lack of availability to work because of incarceration is another matter. The ultimate disposition of the case will necessarily depend upon the nature of the offense and the duties of the employee. Professional counsel can be invaluable in these cases.

An organization considering discipline for criminal conduct should remember the following factors:

- Whether the criminal conduct involved acts constituting a felony or moral turpitude.
- Whether the presence of the employee can be considered a reasonably serious and immediate risk to the organization.
- Whether the conduct is particularly harmful, or detrimental, or adverse in effect to the organization's mission.
- Whether the conduct will have a harmful effect on other employees.
- Whether reasonable steps have been taken to ascertain if the risk of continued employment might be mitigated through such techniques as closer supervision or transfer to another position.
- Whether any new facts or circumstances have come to the attention of the employer.

CHECKLIST: ANALYZING DISCIPLINE PROBLEMS

☐ *Seriousness of the Problem:* How severe is the issue or infraction?

☐ *Time Span:* Have there been other, similar, discipline problems in the past by this employee and, if so, over how long of a time span?

☐ *Frequency and Nature of Problems:* Is the current problem part of an emerging or continuing pattern of problematic behavior or disciplinary infractions?

☐ *Policy/Rule Violated:* If a policy or rule was violated, was the rule (or supervisor's order) reasonably related to the employee's job and performance? Was every effort made to ensure that the employee did, in fact, violate the rule or management order?

☐ *Employee's Work History:* How long has the employee worked for the organization without problems, and what has been the overall quality of job performance?

☐ *Malice/Intent:* Did the employee commit the offense spontaneously as a matter of strong personal impulses, or is there evidence of premeditation?

☐ *Extenuating Factors/Provocation:* Are there reasonable extenuating circumstances related to the problem such as provocation by another person?

☐ *Degree of Orientation:* To what extent has management made an earlier effort to educate the problem employee about existing discipline rules or performance expectations, and the consequences for violations?

☐ *Investigation:* Was the employer's investigation conducted fairly and objectively? Was the investigation completed fully before disciplinary action was taken and was there substantial evidence or proof of the employee's guilt?

☐ *History of Organization's Discipline Practices:* How have similar infractions been dealt with in the past—has there been consistency in the application of discipline procedures or are there unique conditions that would set this particular situation apart from others?

☐ *Implications on Other Employees:* What impact will this decision have on other employees in the work unit and/or organization—will it be seen as fair, reasonable, and just or discriminatory treatment?

☐ *Progressive Discipline:* Is the nature and severity of the problem appropriate to use progressive disciplinary measures as a means of trying to correct the problem? Do personnel policies *require* progressive discipline on *all* infractions (should be avoided)?

☐ *Justification:* If the employee decides to take his or her case to higher management (or the courts), is there reasonable evidence (documentation) to justify the disciplinary/termination decision?

DOCUMENTING DISCIPLINARY EVENTS

The survival of a business may rely on thorough documentation of just one termination. If supervisors object to this kind of administrative detail, they should probably be reminded that it is precisely those details that define the need for their job.

Another point that comes up frequently is, "How does one know when a seemingly innocent act by an employee will turn into sufficient cause for disciplinary action?" One doesn't, and therein lies the need for anyone who oversees the work activities of others to keep a record of noteworthy events. Under the auspices of the annual performance evaluation, supervisors should be keeping a running record—referred to as supervisory desk notes—in a locked or private desk drawer (or file cabinet). The notes should be highly relevant to the employee's performance or job conduct, and typically consist of the date and a brief statement of what occurred with whom. One of the best justifications (if one is needed) for requiring supervisors to maintain desk notes on *all* their employees is that studies have shown the active memory for recalling an employee's performance profile to be about three weeks—yet a supervisor is judging an entire year's performance. No wonder some employees start behaving differently a few weeks prior to evaluation time, particularly if a pay decision is attached to the annual evaluation! The other conclusion of similar studies is that supervisors tend to remember negative events longer than positive ones. The point here is that supervisory desk notes serve as a more reliable means of capturing positive, negative, and other events related to the employee's job throughout the year, and therefore provide a more realistic performance profile. Many supervisors also find it helpful to be able to cite specific events to back up their performance ratings when employees ask (and they will), "Why did I get a lower rating this year in the category of Attention to Detail?"

A second reason supervisory desk notes are important is that the supervisor must be able to cite specific dates and details of an occurrence such as tardiness if counseling hasn't worked and formal discipline is now being contemplated. In the absence of precise dates, amount of times tardy and reasons, what was said and done, and what agreements were made, the supervisor technically has no grounds for initiating discipline, particularly in the prevailing legal environment on these matters.

Here are a few examples of the kinds of entries that might appear in a supervisor's desk notes:

Mary Smith, Order Clerk

1/23 I overheard Mary speaking impatiently to a customer on the phone; she told him, "Perhaps you would get better service at XYZ Company," then hung up. When I talked to Mary about the incident later in the day, she said that customer calls every few days and screams at her, but she admitted she could have been more tolerant.

2/16 Mary 20 minutes late to work; ran out of gas; apologized, no discussion.

2/20   Mary left work 45 minutes early to take husband to pick up his car; approved, no discussion.

2/27   An angry customer was at the counter complaining about persistent errors in his orders and Mary handled the situation calmly, objectively, and with diplomacy. She immediately processed the order corrections and was able to save the account. I commended her for it after the customer left.

3/6   Mary called in *after* being 1½ hours late because of a flat tire she tried to change before getting help. She arrived at work at 10:15 A.M. At 2:00 P.M., I called Mary into my office to discuss her last three occasions of tardiness and early departure to explain the reasoning behind the company's policy. She acknowledged the policy and said she'd be more diligent about observing working hours in the future.

The supervisor should remember that notations should be factual statements of when, what, and why events occurred rather than judgmental statements. The facts will speak for themselves when it comes to performance and discipline, and these situations *should not* be colored by subjective judgments that may imply supervisor bias. It is surely unnecessary to point out that under no circumstances should the supervisor walk around carrying a little black book or ledger and be seen writing in it by employees every time something happens. The most common reaction of employees is to begin taking notes on the supervisor as a means of potential self-defense. Take the notes discreetly, and store them in a safe place to assure the employee's privacy, even though the records are unofficial.

CHECKLIST: DISCIPLINARY DOCUMENTATION

Documentation of disciplinary events, or those that may lead to discipline, is vitally important if the disciplinary action is to be supported by upper management and sustained by outside authorities. Remember that informal documentation such as supervisory desk notes should not be placed in the employee's personnel file. Rather, such notes provide the basis for *specific* and *detailed* examples cited in the formal disciplinary notice to the employee—and these examples should all relate to the same (or a similar) theme of wrongdoing (unsafe acts, discrimination, insubordination, absenteeism, etc.). It will be helpful to review the following points to ensure completeness of the disciplinary document.

- ☐ Do you have notes indicating the date, specific details of the infraction, witnesses or others involved, and your action at the time?
- ☐ Have the time, location, and other pertinent details of the incident(s) been recorded?
- ☐ Have you stated in clear terms what the employee did or failed to do that caused the infraction?
- ☐ Have you stated the company's policy, rule, practice, or performance standard that has been violated? Are you prepared to show that the employee knew, or should have known, about the policy, standard, and so on?

☐   Have you compiled all records, reports, or other written documents related to the incident, and are there witnesses who can testify to the incident if necessary?

☐   Have you explained the sequence of events in an orderly, chronological manner that illustrates the progressiveness of the infraction?

☐   Is the notice written in an objective style and tone, recording observations rather than personal judgments? Is your information based on your own observations or investigation rather than on hearsay?

☐   Has the employee been given previous warnings or instructions? Have you indicated the employee's response or reactions to previous warnings?

☐   Is the type of discipline being recommended consistent with company policy and precedence of similar incidents? Is it appropriate to the offense? Have you discussed this incident with upper management and/or personnel staff to determine conformance with company procedures and practices?

☐   If your company has a grievance procedure allowing employees to appeal disciplinary decisions, have you noted this right on the disciplinary notice to the employee?

DISCIPLINARY NOTICES

Verbal warnings and reprimands are not considered official or formal discipline, and therefore should be noted only in the supervisor's desk notes. *No record should be placed in the employee's official personnel file.* When a reprimand is written, it is placed in the official file and considered formal discipline. To avoid filing a written reprimand, some businesses use a Warning Notice (see Chapter 8 for sample). Such forms are used by supervisors when those situations arise that may not be appropriate for a formal reprimand, yet they want to put the employee on notice to correct a situation before it becomes disciplinary. Examples of these kinds of incidents may include unintentional neglect of equipment, an unorthodox use of sick leave, or antagonizing another employee. In these cases, the supervisor writes up the incident; discusses it with the employee, including consequences of continuance; gives the employee a copy of the form; and places the original in an unofficial file. After a reasonable amount of time has lapsed without evidence of recurrence of the same type of incident, the supervisor should remove that form from the file and destroy it.

More formal notices—consisting of written reprimands and written notices of suspension, pay reduction, demotion, and discharge that are placed in the official personnel file—require a particular type and sequence of information. The following is an outline of the content and order of such disciplinary letters, memos, or notices. (See Sample Letters, Chapter 11.)

1. Date of notice, full name of employee, and employee's position title (and department or work location, or mailing address).

2. The specific disciplinary action being initiated (or recommended to a higher authority), date the action will take effect (except on written reprimands, which are immediate), and a detailed description of the offense or violation.

3. A citation and quotation of the policy, rule, or directive that was violated.

4. A statement of the consequence of a repeat or continuation of the same, or substantially similar, violation (demotion, pay reduction, termination).

5. If applicable, a statement advising the employee of the right to have the matter reviewed by a higher authority within a specified number of days of the notice by virtue of the organization's grievance procedure.

In many states, employees have a right to inspect their official personnel files at convenient times and locations for the employer, as well as to have a representative of the employee's choice present during disciplinary discussions with company officers. In such cases, it may be prudent for the employer to give the employee a copy of any other document (excluding supervisory desk notes) upon which a disciplinary action is being used as evidence by the employer. *In any case, no adverse document of any kind, including performance evaluations, should be placed in the employee's official file unless the employee is given an exact duplicate copy.* Additionally, if a reasonable amount of time has elapsed without any sign of further violations of the same incident, consideration should be given to destroying the written disciplinary notice. The best way to keep track of such considerations is to pencil a recall date on the notice when it's placed in the official file and note the recall date on a calendar or in a "tickler" file. Perhaps the best way to destroy the notice, once it is removed from the file is to send it (confidentially) to the affected employee with a notice of its removal.

CHECKLIST: SOME DO'S AND DON'TS IN HANDLING DISCIPLINARY SITUATIONS

- ☐ Employees should *never* be reprimanded in front of other people.
- ☐ Managers should *never* overlook or avoid taking proper action against an employee for disciplinary conduct merely because the employee is under the jurisdiction of another manager.
- ☐ Disciplinary actions and conduct should *always* be documented thoroughly by the person observing the event like any other performance related event, then acted on.
- ☐ Formal disciplinary letters should be:
    - ☐ Specific in detail (who, what, when, where, how).
    - ☐ Cite effect of action/conduct and what standards were violated.
    - ☐ State what remedial action is to be taken.
    - ☐ Warn against further occurrence.
    - ☐ State what, if any, appeal procedures are available to the employee.
    - ☐ Discuss with the employee and give him/her a copy of letter.
- ☐ When sending the personnel file copy, recommend a date the document is to be reviewed for possible removal from the file.
- ☐ Don't use the personnel file as a repository for disciplinary "notes."
- ☐ Don't mail disciplinary or termination letters to employees unless sent by "registered receipt" mail, and don't use intercompany mail unless it's sealed and marked "confidential."
- ☐ *Always* follow up on disciplinary actions by monitoring and documenting the employee's subsequent performance reactions.

CONDUCTING THE DISCIPLINARY INTERVIEW

Disciplinary interviews are unlike interviews for any other purpose. They require more thought, more emphasis on factual details, and more mental preparation to assure the right frame of mind (objective and unemotional). The person handling any disciplinary matter should consider the following items before an interview or counseling session:

1. Gather all the facts available on the situation.
2. Allow the employee to tell his or her side of the situation.
3. Be precise in dealing with the problem.
4. Take accurate and factual notes of the incident.
5. Remain uninvolved emotionally.
6. Take clear, decisive action.
7. Be objective before, during, and after the situation.

A checklist for conducting the disciplinary interview has been provided at the end of this chapter. Every person in the organization who supervises others should keep a copy of it, and review it periodically until the detail becomes second nature.

CHECKLIST: CONDUCTING THE DISCIPLINARY COUNSELING INTERVIEW

Prepare for the Interview

- ☐ Avoid a significant time lapse from date of incident.
- ☐ Select a time and place that is private and free from interruption to avoid embarrassing the employee. Ensure confidentiality.
- ☐ Review all the facts.
- ☐ Have the personnel record and other information on hand at the time of the interview; prepare an outline.
- ☐ Consider what you know about the employee: personality, personnel record, and the particular job requirements.
- ☐ Consider exactly what you want to accomplish by the interview.

Conduct the Interview in a Constructive Manner

- ☐ Start on a cooperative, positive note.
- ☐ Be ready to help the employee overcome any resentment.
- ☐ Avoid blaming or punishing the employee.
- ☐ Stick to the facts; don't become involved in personalities.
- ☐ Listen to what the employee has to say; practice "constructive silence."
- ☐ Encourage the employee to express feelings; don't show disapproval.
- ☐ Openly focus questions; avoid yes-or-no alternatives.
- ☐ Reiterate and paraphrase statements made by employee.

Elicit Cooperation

- ☐ Cooperation exists when one party shares the likes and dislikes of the other.
- ☐ Common association includes cooperative feelings.
- ☐ Acknowledge any help or information of value that is received from the other party.
- ☐ Be descriptive, not judgmental.
- ☐ Be specific rather than general.
- ☐ Deal with things that can be changed.
- ☐ Consider motives of the employee for giving you certain feedback.
- ☐ Give feedback when it is desired.

Make Sure the Employee Understands

☐ Discuss the requirements of the job. Point out the facts that show how the employee is not meeting these requirements and what the effects are on the work group.

☐ Help the employee decide how to correct the problem and avoid repetition of the offense.

☐ Help the employee uncover the real cause of the problem—not only what is being done wrong, but why the employee is doing it.

☐ Explain fully the purpose of any action as a corrective measure rather than a punishment.

☐ Make sure the employee completely understands that behavior must change. Indicate the consequences if behavior doesn't improve.

Use Constructive Criticism

☐ Focus on behavior, not on the person.

☐ Make observations, not inferences.

☐ Describe behavior in terms of more or less rather than good or bad.

☐ Focus on behavior related to specific and recent situations rather than on the abstract.

☐ Share ideas and information instead of giving advice.

☐ Explore alternatives.

☐ Stress the need for mutual cooperation.

☐ Limit the amount of different information.

☐ Concentrate on what is said, rather than why it is said.

Provide for Follow-up

☐ Set up a plan for improvement with the employee.

☐ Include in the plan commitments both by the employee and by you to the steps you will take to bring about the desired improvement.

☐ Include specific time limits for accomplishing the desired goals and for formal reevaluation of the employee's behavior.

Make a Written Record of the Interview

☐ Note in your calendar or diary the time, date, and content of the disciplinary interview.

☐ Ensure that you have your boss's support.

☐ If the disciplinary action is to be formalized, draft the formal documentation, give a copy to the employee, and place the original in the employee's personnel file.

CHECKLIST: OVERCOMING DISCIPLINARY ACTION CONFRONTATION BARRIERS

Place Emphasis on

☐ Staying in one's organizational role as a manager.

☐ Remaining objective, including what to do when you can't.

☐ Keeping performance and organizational interests as a prominent focus.

☐ Maintaining a sense of responsibility to control the outcome of each event.

Action Guidelines

☐ Conduct your discussion with the other person in private, never in front of others or in a public place.

☐ Determine the proper time and location of your meeting.

☐ Gather and write down all the facts and issues you wish to discuss; determine if each is objectively stated and relates to performance, job-related behavior, or organizational interests.

☐ Present the issues in emotional moderation, and be sensitive enough to employees to allow them to tell their story.

☐ Talk calmly and slowly, covering point by point; then be a good listener.

☐ Be precise about disposing of an employee's excuses, faulty reasoning, vague responses, or other diversions; remember, you're there to confront and resolve a problem, not merely get through the experience.

☐ If a discussion begins to get hostile, control it or break off the discussion and take it up again in a day or two when your superior can sit in.

☐ Be alert to differences in perception and clarify them. Try to sway inaccurate perceptions using explanations and examples.

☐ Determine how you want to conclude your discussion in terms of each issue, what has been concluded, where agreement is or is not, and what happens from here.

☐ Document the discussion thoroughly.

DISCHARGE: WHEN ALL ELSE FAILS

In a well-managed business, an employee is almost never surprised at being fired. The supervisor has already provided a number of counseling sessions with the employee to help redefine goals and clarify any failure to meet standards of performance or the employee has been subject to some lesser level of disciplinary action.

Transfer to another department or position is rarely an effective substitute for work force problems. If an employee does not meet the standards set for the job and does not respond to a supervisor's help, then termination may be the only appropriate answer.

The person having the authority to discharge an employee should be clearly convinced that this is the only course of action that will alter a completely unacceptable situation. If not, or if all the facts haven't been gathered, or if other remedies haven't been tried, don't start the process—it's irreversible. If additional facts are needed, get them. If there's one more thing to try, try it. Manage human resources before disposing of them.

If discharge is the only reasonable course of action left, follow these suggestions:

1. If circumstances permit, take care of the administrative details beforehand in order to minimize the amount of after-termination time required on the premises.

2. Come directly to the point and don't be vague.

3. Give your reasons, but spare the agonizing details. Briefly and clearly state your perception of the person's work or the circumstances that have brought you to your conclusions.

4. Mention the qualities that have been appreciated—why the person was selected in the first place and what was liked about the work performance observed, but don't encourage the person to think the discharge decision will be changed.

5. Don't try to argue with the person's feelings. Usually, the maintenance of self-image demands a defense. This is understood and should be accepted. Just do a lot of listening. Expect to be the brunt of the person's feelings and understand these for what they are.

6. Do what can be done to help the ex-employee begin the process of thinking through what should be done in facing the new situation.

7. All associates of the terminated employee should be informed by their supervisor after the employee has been terminated with a very brief explanation of why, if circumstances permit (if it would not be a breach of private or confidential information).

8. Write up the exit interview document for the file while the information is fresh. Secure written comments from others who may have been involved in the assessment.

REFERENCES AND RESOURCES

BOOKS AND PERIODICALS

Personnel Policy Manuals, Handbooks, Forms, and Letters

Anson, Edward, *How to Prepare and Write Your Employee Handbook.* New York: American Management Association, 1983.

B.B.P. Personnel Policy Manual. Stamford, Conn.: Bureau of Business Practice, 1981.

Bland-Acosta, Barbara A., "Developing an HRIS Privacy Policy," *Personnel Administrator,* July 1988.

BNA Policy and Practice Series. Washington, D.C.: Bureau of National Affairs. A supplemented collection of bulletins, reports, study findings, and sample policies on various personnel topical areas.

Carlson, Robert D. and James F. McHugh, *Handbook of Personnel Administration Forms and Formats.* Englewood Cliffs, N.J.: Prentice Hall, 1978.

Cobb, Normal B., *How to Prepare a Personnel Policy Manual.* Mich.: Angus Downs, 1982.

College and University Personnel Policy Models. Washington, D.C.: College and University Personnel Association, 1974.

Cook, Mary F., *Personnel Manager's Portfolio of Model Letters.* Englewood Cliffs, N.J.: Prentice Hall, 1985.

Dictionary of Occupational Titles. Washington, D.C.: U.S. Department of Labor, 1977.

Ellman, Edgar S., *Put It in Writing: A Complete Guide for Preparing Employee Policy Handbooks.* New York: Van Nostrand Reinhold, 1983.

Famularo, Joseph, *Handbook of Personnel Forms, Records and Reports.* New York: McGraw-Hill, 1982.

Human Resources Management. Chicago: Commerce Clearing House. A five-unit collection with supplements on various personnel topical areas, including practices and policies.

Johns, Horace E. and H. Ronald Moser, "Where Has EEO Taken Personnel Policies?" *Personnel,* September 1989.

Lawson, J. W. and B. Smith, *How to Develop a Personnel Policy Manual.* Chicago: Dartnell, 1978.

Ramey, Ardella and Ronald Mrozek, *A Company Policy and Personnel Workbook.* Successful Business Library Series, 1983.

Rosen, Benson and Schwoerer, "Balanced Protection Policies," *HR Magazine,* February 1990.

Roxe, Linda A., *Personnel Management for the Smaller Company: A Hands-on Manual.* New York: American Management Association, 1979.

Scheer, Wilbert E., *Personnel Administration Handbook.* Chicago: Dartnell, 1983.

Simmons, Richard J., *Employee Handbook and Personnel Policies Manual.* Calif.: Castle Publications, 1983.

The Encyclopedia of Personnel Policies. Stamford, Conn.: Bureau of Law and Business, 1984.

The Personnel Manager's Policy and Practice Update. Washington, D.C.: Bureau of National Affairs. A monthly news bulletin of current events shaping personnel policy.

Ulery, John D., *Job Descriptions in Manufacturing Industries.* New York: American Management Association, 1981.

Salary and Benefits

Alden, Philip M., *Controlling the Costs of Retirement Income and Medical Care Plans.* New York: AMACOM, 1980.

Burgess, Leonard R., *Wage and Salary Administration.* Columbus, Oh.: Merrill, 1984.

Geisel, Jerry, "Administration Favors Cafeteria Plan Limits," *Business Insurance,* February 20, 1984.

Greenberry, Karen and Mary Zippo, "Flexible Compensation Cuts Costs and Meets Employee Needs," *Personnel,* March/April 1983.

Griffes, Ernest J. E., *Employee Benefits Programs.* Homewood, Ill.: Dow Jones-Irwin, 1983.

Harker, Carlton, *Self-funding of Welfare Benefits.* Brookfield, Wisc.: International Foundation of Employee Benefit Plans, 1981.

Henderson, Richard I., *Compensation Management: Rewarding Performance,* 3rd ed. Reston, Va.: Reston, 1982.

Hoff, Roger, "The Impact of Cafeteria Benefits on the Human Resource Information System," *Personnel Journal,* April 1983.

Howard, Jan and Anselm Strauss, *Humanizing Health Care.* New York: John Wiley & Sons, 1975.

Latham, W. Bryan, *Health Care Costs: There Are Solutions.* New York: American Management Association, 1983.

Noyes, Margaret C., *An Analysis of Proposals to Mandate Cafeteria Style Health Benefit Plans for Health Care Cost Containment.* Brookfield, Wisc.: International Foundation of Employee Benefit Plans, 1981.

Rosenbloom, Jerry S. and G. Victor Hallman, *Employee Benefit Planning.* Englewood Cliffs, N.J.: Prentice Hall, 1981.

Rosenbloom, Jerry S., *The Handbook of Employee Benefits.* Homewood, Ill.: Dow Jones-Irwin, 1984.

Rutstein, David D., M.D., *Blueprint for Medical Care.* Cambridge, Mass.: The MIT Press, 1974.

Seltz, C. and D. L. Gifford, *Flexible Compensation: A Look Forward.* New York: AMACOM, 1982.

Treiman, D. J. and H. I. Hartmann, eds., *Women, Work, and Wages: Equal Pay for Jobs of Equal Value.* Washington, D.C.: National Academy Press, 1981.

Wojohn, Ellen, "Beyond the Fringes," *Inc. Magazine,* March 1984.

Zippo, Mary, "Flexible Benefits: Just the Beginning," *Personnel,* July/August 1983.

Employee Behavior

Davis, Keith, *Human Behavior at Work.* New York: McGraw-Hill, 1977.

Mindell, M. G. and W. I. Gorden, *Employee Values in a Changing Society.* New York: American Management Association, 1981.

Mitchell, T. R., *People in Organizations: Understanding Their Behavior.* New York: McGraw-Hill, 1978.

General Personnel Management

Allen, Jeffrey G., *The Complete Q & A Job Interview Book.* New York: John Wiley & Sons, 1988.

Amante, Liz, "Help Wanted: Creative Recruitment Tactics," *Personnel,* October 1989.

Arthur, Diane, *Recruiting, Interviewing, Selecting & Orienting New Employees.* New York: AMACOM Books, 1986.

Atwood, Caleb S. and James M. Neel, "New Lawsuits Expand Employer Liability," *HR Magazine,* October 1990.

Bachler, Christopher J., "Walking the Privacy Tightrope," *Human Resource Executive,* July 1990.

Bahls, Jane Easter, "Getting Full-Time Work from Part-Time Employees," *Management Review,* February 1990.

Bakaly, Charles G. and Joel M. Grossman, "How to Avoid Wrongful Discharge Suits," *Management Review,* August 1984, pp. 41–46.

Beach, Dale S., *Personnel: The Management of People at Work,* 4th ed. New York: Macmillan, 1980.

Beatty, R. W. and C. E. Schneier, *Personnel Administration: An Experiential/Skills Building Approach,* 2nd ed. San Francisco, Calif.: Addison-Wesley, 1981.

Brady, Robert L., *Employment at Will.* Stamford, Conn.: Bureau of Law and Business, 1983.

Branch, James A., Jr., *Negligent Hiring Practice Manual.* New York: John Wiley & Sons, 1988.

Cascio, Wayne F. (ed.), *Human Resource Planning Employment & Placement.* Washington, D.C.: The Bureau of National Affairs, 1989.

Casey, Thomas F., "Making the Most of a Selection Interview," *Personnel,* September 1990.

Cherrington, David J., *Personnel Management: The Management of Human Resources.* Ia.: Wm. C. Brown, 1983.

Chruden, H. J. and A. W. Sherman, *Personnel Management: The Utilization of Human Resources,* 6th ed. San Francisco, Calif.: South-Western Publishing Co., 1980.

Coates, Joseph F. and others, "Workplace Management 2000," *Personnel Administrator,* December 1989.

Compton, Jo Ann L., "Interview to Determine Potential Success, Fit," *Personnel Administrator*, April 1988.

Cook, Mary F., *Human Resources Director's Handbook*. Englewood Cliffs, N.J.: Prentice Hall, 1984.

Cook, Suzanne H., "Playing It Safe: How to Avoid Liability for Negligent Hiring," *Personnel*, November 1988.

Crane, Donald P., *Personnel: The Management of Human Resources*, 3rd ed. Boston: PWS-Kent, 1982.

Decker, Kurt H., *A Manager's Guide to Employee Privacy*. New York: John Wiley & Sons, 1989.

Douglas, James A. and others, *Employment Testing Manual*. Boston: Warren, Gorham & Lamont, 1989.

Dube, Lawrence E., Jr., "Employment References and the Law," *Personnel Journal*, February 1986.

Evans, Karen M. and Randall Brown, "Reducing Recruitment Risk Through Preemployment Testing," *Personnel*, September 1988.

Feldman, Diane, "Employing Physically and Mentally Impaired Employees," *Personnel*, January 1988.

Fitz-enz, Jac, "Getting—and Keeping—Good Employees," *Personnel*, August 1990.

Frierson, James G., "Religion in the Workplace: Dealing in Good Faith?" *Personnel Journal*, July 1988.

Goddard, Robert W., "Work Force 2000," *Personnel Journal*, February 1989.

Grant, Philip C., "What Use Is a Job Description?" *Personnel Journal*, February 1988.

The Guide to Background Investigations. Tulsa, OK: National Employment Screening Services, Source Publications, 1989.

Holly, W. H. and K. M. Jennings, *Personnel Management: Functions and Issues*. New York: The Dryden Press, 1983.

How to Write an Affirmative Action Plan. Madison, Conn.: Bureau of Law & Business, 1989.

Ivancevich, J. M. and W. F. Glueck, *Foundations of Personnel/Human Resource Management*, rev. ed. Plano, Tex.: Business Publications, 1983.

Joiner, Emily A., "Erosion of the Employment-at-Will Doctrine," *Personnel*, September/October 1984, pp. 12–18.

Kahn, Steven C. and others, *Personnel Director's Legal Guide*, 2nd ed. New York: Warren, Gorham & Lamont, 1990.

Koral, Alan M., *Employee Privacy Rights*. New York: Executive Enterprises, 1988.

Levesque, Joseph D., *The Complete Hiring Manual: Policies, Procedures and Practices*. Englewood Cliffs, N.J.: Prentice Hall, 1991.

Levesque, Joseph D., *The Human Resource Problem-Solver's Handbook*. New York: McGraw-Hill, 1992.

Levesque, Joseph D., "Controlling the Preservation of Employee Privacy Rights," *Proceedings from the 41st ASPA Conference*, Boston, June 1989.

Levy, Martin, "Almost-Perfect Performance Appraisals," *Personnel Journal*, April 1989.

Libbin, A. E. and J. C. Stevens, "The Right to Privacy at the Workplace, Part 4: Employee Personal Relationships," *Personnel*, October 1988.

McGee, Lynne F., "Innovative Labor Shortage Solutions," *Personnel Administrator*, December 1989.

Mendelson, S. R. and K. K. Morrison, "The Right to Privacy at the Workplace, Part 2: Testing Applicants for Alcohol and Drug Abuse," *Personnel*, August 1988.

Munchus, George, "An Update on Smoking: Employee Rights and Employer's Responsibilities," *Personnel*, August 1987.

Nobile, Robert J., "The Drug-Free Workplace: Act on It!" *Personnel*, February 1990.

Odiorne, George and Patrick Henry, "Hiring Ex-Offenders," *Personnel Administrator*, September 1988.

Panaro, Gerald P., "Minimizing the Danger of Giving References," *Personnel Journal*, August 1988.

"Personnel Records May Not Be as Confidential as You Think," *Personnel Practice Ideas*, September 1988.

Peters, James E., "How to Bridge the Hiring Gap: Linking people with disabilities with employers who need qualified workers," *Personnel Administrator*, October 1989.

Phillips, Kenneth R., "Red Flags in Performance Appraisal," *Training & Development Journal*, March 1987.

Plachy, Roger J., "Writing Job Descriptions That Get Results," *Personnel*, October 1987.

"Psychometric Testing: Facts and Fallacies," *Human Resource Executive*, July 1990.

Schmidt, Frank L. and others, "Impact of Job Experience and Ability on Job Knowledge, Work Sample Performance, and Supervisory Ratings of Job Performance," *Journal of Applied Psychology*, Vol. 71, No. 3 (1986).

Sloane, Arthur A., *Personnel: Managing Human Resources*. Englewood Cliffs, N.J.: Prentice Hall, 1983.

Soveriegn, Kenneth L., "Pitfalls of Withholding Reference Information," *Personnel Journal*, March 1990.

Stanton, Diane, "Negligent Hiring—The Big New Legal Trap," *Boardroom Reports*, 1989.

Stevens, George E., "Exploding the Myths About Hiring the Handicapped," *Personnel*, December 1986.

Terpstra, David E., "Who Gets Sexually Harassed?: Knowing how to educate and control your work environment," *Personnel Administrator*, March 1989.

Tobias, Lester L., "Selecting for Excellence: How to Hire the Best," *Nonprofit World*, March/April 1990.

Turner, Isiah, "Training and Retraining: Preparing for the Year 2000 and Beyond," *Proceedings from the 41st ASPA Conference, Boston*, June 1989.

Wallace, M. J. and others, *Administering Human Resources*. New York: Random House, 1982.

Watts, L. R. and H. C. White, "Assessing Employee Turnover," *Personnel Administrator*, April 1988.

Weston, David J. and Dennis L. Warmke, "Dispelling the Myths About Panel Interviews," *Personnel Administrator*, May 1988.

Human Resources Information Systems

Kirrane, D. E. and P. R. Kirrane, "Managing by Experts Systems," *HR Magazine*, March 1990.

Lederer, Albert L., "Information Technology: Planning and Developing a Human Resources Information System," *Personnel*, May/June 1984, pp. 14–27.

Mamis, Robert, "A Manager's Guide to Integrated Software," *Inc. Magazine*, February 1985, pp. 64–76.

Magnus, Margaret and David J. Thomsen, "Microcomputer Software Guide," *Personnel Journal*, February 1990.

Simon, Sidney H., "The HRIS: What Capabilities Must It Have?" *Personnel*, September/October 1983, pp. 36–49.

PUBLISHERS OF PERIODICALS

Business Week. Weekly. Newsmagazine covering business outlook, new developments in business. Includes articles on compensation, personnel matters, business education. McGraw-Hill, Inc., 1221 Avenue of the Americas, New York, NY 10036.

Compensation Review. Quarterly. Analyzes employee pay practices and systems; also includes book reviews and digests of articles. American Management Association, 135 West 50th Street, New York, NY 10020.

Harvard Business Review. Bimonthly. Offers in-depth articles on the handling of decisions and plans in many areas of management, including personnel topics. P.O. Box 291, Uxbridge, MA 01569.

HR Magazine. Monthly. An informative, nontechnical journal for personnel managers. Society for Human Resource Management, 606 North Washington Street, Alexandria, VA 22314.

Human Resource Management. Quarterly. Contains articles on personnel problems within the organization. Graduate School of Business Administration, University of Michigan, Ann Arbor, MI 48104.

Journal of Small Business Management. Quarterly. Articles in this magazine deal with both the practical and the theoretical aspects of small-business management development. National Council for Small Business Management Development, 600 West Kilborn Avenue, Milwaukee, WI 52303.

Manage. Monthly. Offers articles on supervision and problems of people at work. National Management Association, 2210 Arbor Avenue, Dayton, OH 45439.

Management World. Has articles on management, including personnel matters. Administrative Management Society, Willow Grove, PA 19090.

Occupational Hazards. Monthly. Covers safety practices and regulations, on-the-job factors relating to health, and workers' compensation matters. P.O. Box 5746 U, Cleveland, OH 44113.

Personnel. Bimonthly. Provides articles on practices, new approaches, surveys, and research relating to human resources. American Management Association, 135 West 50th Street, New York, NY 10020.

Personnel Journal. Monthly. Provides articles on many aspects of personnel management and labor relations. Also has book reviews. ACC Communications, Inc., 245 Fischer Ave., B-2, Costa Mesa, CA 92626.

SAM Advanced Management Journal. Quarterly. Explores management topics, including personnel matters, for the operating managers. Society for Advancement of Management, 135 West 50th Street, New York, NY 10020.

Training. Monthly. Describes aspects of training and presents new ideas in the field of training. Lakewood Publications, Inc., 731 Hennepin Avenue, Minneapolis, MN 55403.

Training and Development Journal. Monthly. Features news, developments, and instructional techniques of interest to those engaged in training. American Society for Training and Development, Inc., P.O. Box 5307, Madison, WI 53705.

ASSOCIATIONS

Administrative Management Society. 1927 Old York Road, Willow Grove, PA 19090. A chapter-type organization whose membership includes administrative services executives, systems personnel, management engineers, supervisors.

American Management Association. 135 West 50th Street, New York, NY 10020. A membership organization which conducts management training seminars and publishes books, research reports, magazines, and salary surveys of use to personnel and other executives.

American Society for Training and Development. P.O. Box 5307, Madison, WI 53705. A membership organization which encourages research and disseminates information on all phases of training, including instruction in private and public institutions.

International Foundation of Employee Benefit Plans. 18700 West Bluemound Road, Brookfield, WI 53005. An organization offering comprehensive materials, reference sources, and excellent books dealing with various aspects of developing, designing, and administering a wide range of employment benefit plans.

National Safety Council. 425 Michigan Avenue, Chicago, IL 60611. Publishes reports and presents conferences on various aspects of safety and industrial hygiene.

National Small Business Association. 1225 19th Street, NW, Washington, DC 20036. Compiles and publishes information for owners and managers of small businesses.

Society for the Advancement of Management. 135 West 50th Street, New York, NY 10020. A chapter-type professional organization of executives in industry, commerce, government, and education.

Society for Human Resource Management. 606 North Washington Street, Alexandria, VA 22314. A national organization of professionals working toward the advocacy and development of human resource polices, laws, programs, and management of organizations, with local chapter affiliates throughout the United States and abroad.

INDEX